THE WAY THINGS WORK BOOK OF NATURE

THE WAY THINGS WORK

BOOK OF **NATURE**

An Illustrated
Encyclopedia
of Man & Nature

SIMON AND SCHUSTER   NEW YORK

Original German language edition entitled

WIE FUNKTIONIERT DAS? DER BEGRIFF © 1975

by Bibliographisches Institut Mannheim

Translation in this edition by John Cuthbert Brown

Copyright © 1980 by George Allen & Unwin, Ltd.

Published by Simon and Schuster

A Division of Gulf & Western Corporation

Simon & Schuster Building

Rockefeller Center

1230 Avenue of the Americas

New York, New York 10020

SIMON AND SCHUSTER and colophon are trademarks of Simon & Schuster

Designed by Helen Barrow

Manufactured in the United States of America

1 2 3 4 5 6 7 8 9 10

Library of Congress Cataloging in Publication Data

Brown, John Cuthbert.

The way things work book of nature.

Translation and adaptation of Die Umwelt des Menschen,
compiled and edited by the Fachredaktion für Naturwissenschaft und Medizin,
Bibliographisches Institut A.G., Mannheim.

Includes index.

1. Ecology.   2. Human ecology.   I. Bibliographisches Institut A.G., Mannheim.
Fachredaktion für Naturwissenschaft und Medizin. Umwelt des Menschen.

II. Title.

QH541.B75   1980   304.2   80-17219

ISBN 0-671-22455-7

FOREWORD

Everyone speaks of the "environment" and of "environmental pollution," but very few feel themselves to be affected personally. Serious involvement in the matter is left to the technical specialists, the ecologists, and comfort is taken from the fact that various action groups have been formed in the community to come to grips with the problems.

One of the main reasons for this fatal lack of interest stems from an insufficient appreciation of the many ramifications and side effects of the cycles and reaction mechanisms that play a part in nature and in the technical and civilizing processes of the world.

We thus need, in the first place, to have the basic facts regarding the concept of the environment itself and the conditions under which the environment operates—or fails to operate, as the case may be. Only then will we be competent to think, talk and act responsibly in collaboration with one another on environmental questions. This is the objective of this book. We do not try to present any particular segment of the spectrum of the environment but embrace the subject in its entire complexity: the functional developments in nature and the ecological effects of human activities designed to deal with them. Manifest in this are many interwoven human sectors, both beneficial and progressive on the one hand and threatening and destructive on the other, and the technologies connected with them.

The cardinal feature of the book is the concern with the functioning of nature: living organisms and their ecological relationships. Human civilization and technology constitute the main ingredient in chapters dealing with the various forms of energy, including nuclear energy. Further topics extend from the processes and cycles in the atmosphere, hydrosphere, pedosphere, and lithosphere, past the hazards resulting from pollution of the living space in soil, air, and water, including the numerous noxious substances working all the time on ourselves and our environment, and the disposal or recycling of the waste products of civilization, as far as the menacing problems of growth in the technological field of civilization, and in particular those of population growth.

The practice adopted in previous volumes of **The Way Things**

Work *series of illustrating the information given in the text wherever possible and appropriate with facing diagrams in two colors proves to be of particular value in this case.*

We are convinced that this book, which in its complexity must be the only one of its kind so far produced, will provide the practical prerequisites for meaningful discussion of the environment.

THE PUBLISHERS

CONTENTS

Part Three: The Inhabited Environment

Part Four: Organisms Living Together in Harmony or Hostility

Part Five: Fundamental Phenomena of Life

Part Ten: Land Settlement and Configuration of the Landscape

Part Eleven: Transport and the Environment

Part Twelve: Atmospheric Pollution and Its Prevention

Part Sixteen: Waste Disposal and Utilization

Part Seventeen: Energy and the Environment

Part Eighteen: Growth and the General Economic Aspects of Growth

THE WAY THINGS WORK BOOK OF **NATURE**

Part One—Technical Environment: The Situation and the Goal

THE EARTH A SPACESHIP SET ON A COLLISION COURSE?

Since its beginning, the human race has exerted an influence on the environment and has changed it, though not always in the best interests of either. In practice, however, this has never been a cause for particular concern. Deliberate planning of the environment as it is understood today is something quite new. Only in recent years, with the inauguration of flights to the moon, have humans come to regard the earth as a planet and to see it in the guise of a spaceship, with all the attendant limitations and dangers.

Increasing activities in a limited space must one day be reflected in limits on growth. Attainment of thresholds or temporarily overstepping them may result in the exhaustion of expensive, irreplaceable raw materials and having to live without them thereafter. This applies today to our most important source of mineral energy, petroleum, and to a lesser extent, fortunately, to coal. It is also true of a range of important metals such as aluminum, zinc, copper, mercury and silver. Disregarding the thresholds also leads to disturbances in important recovery cycles. Thus overloading a waste-water system can deprive water of its self-purification properties, or agricultural production may be impeded by overuse of the soil and by erosion.

Hazards of this sort are a challenge. By pursuing a reasonable and responsible course of action—that is to say, by active protection of the environment—we have an opportunity of passing on to our descendants a satisfying quality of life.

But why all the fuss? What is new about the situation? In the course of history, the human race has always utilized and often overutilized the possibilities afforded by the environment at the expense of succeeding generations. In some cases this has given rise to sharp reverses, either in the shape of supply crises and famine or in the form of war or of immigration to areas not yet affected. The destruction of woodlands in the Mediterranean basin for the purpose of shipbuilding, followed by a decline in agricultural production and erosion of the soil, heralded the destruction of the Roman Empire —one example of many. A new feature of the situation today is that we are not touching on the threshold at just individual, isolated points, but rather that the world is now functioning as an integrated economic unit and is overloaded in its entirety. And we have come to be conscious of this fact as it affects the entire world in a remarkably short space of time.

The Conference on the Human Environment held in Stockholm in 1972 was an outward manifestation of this economic unity and at the same time of the differences still operating. Today the world is contained in an all-embracing network composing a single information unit. The communication satellites in outer space are an outward and visible sign of this. In this way the essential requirement is fulfilled that the world can function politically as a coherent system, although distinguished by sharp internal differentiations and by considerable fields of friction. Another new feature, however, is that we now recognize the critical nature of our position and can thus adopt plans for the future worked out on a global basis.

With breathtaking rapidity we arrive at the conclusion that the preservation of the environment calls for instantaneous remedies. At the Stockholm Conference, most of the countries in the world submitted comprehensive reports on the environment and immediate programs. Then came the discussions. The developing countries feared that the environmental crisis would be used and exploited by the industrial powers to freeze growth throughout the world and to perpetuate the existing differences between rich and poor nations. The enthusiasm of the first few hours gave way to reservations, half-measures and doubts.

Does this provide grounds for pessimism? On the contrary! We have seen how quickly the fundamental problem of worldwide environmental protection was grasped. It should not surprise us that the realization yet to be achieved in detail requires a totally different time span. In the first place, the conflicts of interest have to be settled and compromises arrived at. What then has to be changed in detail? How can it be achieved without catastrophically distorting the operation of our now highly complicated life? Consideration is required, and a measure of prudence in the process.

The spaceship earth is undoubtedly in need of course correction. The new course is clear enough in broad outline, but in detail the necessary measures must be carefully checked and selected; and this is by no means exclusively a task for experts. Many fundamental decisions need to be made which concern everyone. We can all make our contributions as individual citizens, in the family circle and our circles of friends, in our professions, and within the organizations of our different communities. Our democracy offers the optimum prior requirements for cooperation among individuals and for the coordination of groups, for a general consolidation of opinions, for party enterprise, for civic initiative, and for criticism. Democracy flourishes by reason of the fact that a sufficient number of citizens avail themselves of these basic rights. It thrives on critical debate.

This assumes, however, that each and every person is acquainted with the situation and is eager to acquire firm information regarding it. We must be sure how the environment functions and at what points its functions are hampered or destroyed. Objectivity must be combined with responsibility and personal engagement if reliable solutions are to be achieved. This can entail a severe struggle. The vitality and stability of our democracy emerge precisely at the point where tolerant contemplation can be combined with the severest criticism, without in any way restricting the free play of personal expressions of opinion. Therein lies our best chance of mastering the environmental crisis.

The aim of this book is to acquaint the reader with the way in which our environment works, and in particular with the dangers and disturbances to which it is subject. It does not confine itself to the description of intact issues, but deliberately highlights the darker sides, the disturbed areas, as these are in the greatest need of attention and remedial aid. The immediately ensuing chapters give a synopsis of our situation and of the global tasks we must undertake if we are to secure an environment fit to live in. After that, a survey is provided of the essential basic functions relevant to the environmental conditions to be found on the earth's surface—notably of the inorganic elements of air, water, and the earth's crust. Then come some aspects of life—biochemistry, evolution and ecology. The emphasis falls mainly on the interaction between people in this technical age and the environment as modified by us. Mainly, established and threatened disturbances are discussed in conjunction with the solutions adopted or proposed for dealing with critical situations. Principal factors in this context are consumption and waste, energy, industry, water consumption, traffic and agriculture. All the topics are presented in such a way that they can be read separately according to the taste, motivation and requirements of the reader.

PRODUCTION AND CONSUMPTION

The environment we live in today is primarily the world of highly rationalized industrial and technical production, which sets our life-style. This by no means applies exclusively to actual industry itself, for many other areas also bear the imprint of industrial mass production: our domestic culture, and all the service sectors such as trade, transport, health care, administration, education, and scientific research, as well as the organized leisure sector. And too little consideration is given to the fact that the same standards apply to agricultural production.

If we ignore all the details and do our best to assemble the most important processes that are relevant to the environment, our technical world seems to impose itself on the "natural" environment in the following way:

Present-day humankind wants a diversified and abundant selection of raw materials, foodstuffs, beverages and consumer goods to be made available to it, together with a wide range of equipment, living space, services and entertainment. This is known as "demand." It reflects requirements that, owing to various influences, assume a multitude of forms. The influences include the inherited nature of humans, their education, social status, prevailing fashions, and advertising. Advertising can exercise an effect through the interaction of supply and demand to the point of requirement suggestion.

Requirement satisfaction assumes that productive work is being performed. Whereas in primitive communities small units (families, clans and villages) produced pretty well all their own requirements (subsistence communities), the high performance of present-day industrial production is based on a high-level division of labor. The individual applies himself to the production of whatever it may be and receives wages in return, out of which he buys in the market whatever it is he requires. The whole process is kept going by means of complicated economic systems: a free market economy, a publicly assisted market economy (which is the most easily adaptable), or a planned economy.

Now, how do production and consumption fit into the picture? Two sectors of production are to be distinguished: industry and agriculture. Whereas the former is concentrated mainly in urban settlement areas, the latter extends over a wide surface and is closely associated with the "natural" environment, in fact is practically identical with it, if by "nature" we understand the open landscape occupied by vegetation and animal life. Both sectors of production provide for consumer requirements, and both produce waste. Industry draws raw materials and water from the environment and generates waste but also provides means of production for agriculture (machinery, fertilizers and biocides).

This outline indicates in a particularly simple way the part to be played by protection of the environment in the system. The environmental crisis has two main aspects—namely, raw-material depletion and pollution—and devices must be inserted somewhere to reduce the movement in both directions. For industry and consumption this entails the recycling of waste prod-

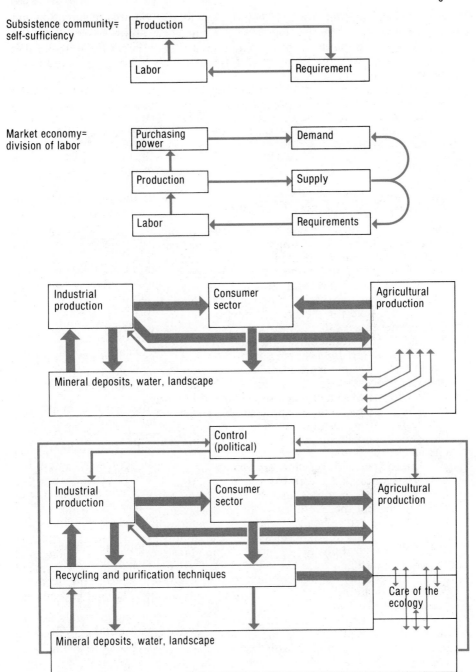

Subsistence community≠
self-sufficiency

Production — Requirement
Labor — Requirement

Market economy=
division of labor

Purchasing power — Demand
Production — Supply
Labor — Requirements

Industrial production — Consumer sector — Agricultural production
Mineral deposits, water, landscape

Control (political)
Industrial production — Consumer sector — Agricultural production
Recycling and purification techniques
Care of the ecology
Mineral deposits, water, landscape

ucts as far as possible for reutilization, partly as raw material (metal, glass, slag), partly as energy (burning of waste), and also as refuse-sludge compost which serves a useful purpose in agriculture, etc. As far as agriculture is concerned, this represents a quest for ecologically sparing cultivation processes.

These tasks will naturally not solve themselves. Their solution will be achieved rather by public control, which must accordingly be reintroduced in the proper place in the economic mechanism. The publicly assisted market economy affords all the starting points that may be required for the purpose.

EVOLUTION OF THE ENVIRONMENT

The present state of the environment is the result of a long history of development, in the course of which the world has constantly changed. Nothing in the environment is constant, and no element in it is automatically worth preserving. The protection of the environment is not aimed, therefore, at preventing any change and so at obstructing any development. We have consequently to consider in broad outline which stages of development have been responsible for the present environment to enable us to identify the decisive new stages that confront us. We must ask ourselves what tomorrow can and should produce from the modern environment.

We will start by assuming a period at which no life yet existed on the planet (stage 1), one marked rather by a succession of purely chemical and physical processes. It was in this epoch that the preconditions must have developed for the emergence of organized life, such as somewhat complicated organic molecules (amino acids, porphyrin, etc.). A special atmosphere free from oxygen but rich in carbon dioxide, methane, hydrogen, nitrogen, ammonia and water was the starting point for this—the period of chemical evolution.

Life began with the first emergence of cell-like formations capable of self-propagation and the transmission of heritable characteristics, and it is of relatively minor importance how they may have appeared. Now began the long road of the evolution of organisms. During this period the face of the earth changed radically. A layer of vegetation began to spread from the water's edge over the land mass, and the atmosphere acquired a different chemical composition: the reducing compounds were on the way out, and oxygen and nitrogen were assuming sway. Only now could the new forms of animal life and the majority of plant organisms develop. From the decaying remains of dead organisms there formed huge deposits of coal and oil, our present-day fossil sources of energy (stage 2).

A new era opened with the emergence of humans as toolmakers. Of course, the human was only one member among many in the field of living organisms. Owing to their still low level of technical resources, the low population level, and the many enemies they had to contend with, humans exercised no more influence in the world than many other animal species. The hard struggle to assert themselves over hostile forms of animal life and to overcome the obstacles of nature must often have dominated the early life of the human species.

Certain qualities peculiar to humans gave them more and more advantages in their struggle for existence, and these were reflected in the increase

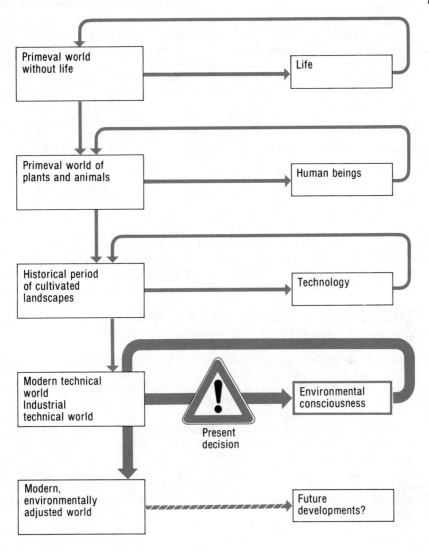

Primeval world without life	→	Life
Primeval world of plants and animals	→	Human beings
Historical period of cultivated landscapes	→	Technology
Modern technical world Industrial technical world	! Present decision →	Environmental consciousness
Modern, environmentally adjusted world	- - - →	Future developments?

in numbers of the population. A vital factor was that in contrast to other animals, humans were capable not only of inventing and producing tools, but also of passing on the acquired experience to others. In this way experience was built up and an increasingly promising position was developed, comparable to an accumulation of capital, for new inventions. Quite independently of genetic transmission, which is prominent throughout the animal kingdom, human development is characterized primarily by transmitted experience. In this way human beings increased their capacity exponentially to assert themselves over the rest of the animal world. Ultimately it did not take long, as historical times were reached, for large stretches of land to be converted by humankind into cultivated areas (stage 3).

The development of sciences, especially of the natural sciences, and the discovery of their value for technical purposes in the military and economic fields, led finally to the unfolding of our specifically Western industrial and technical culture. This led, in the form of the scientific and technical revolution, which is still in full bloom today in the East and West alike—irrespective of the different concepts underlying particular sectors of the economy—to the transformation of our environment, throwing everything existing previously into the shadows. It gave rise to modern industrial areas, road networks, and concentrations of population. Undreamed-of expansions in all economic and technical processes became possible. Furthermore, the economic system came to be so organized that it presupposed a permanent growth in economic volume. In this way we rapidly approached the limits on expansion imposed by the environment. We were now at stage 4 of the modern world.

What lies before us? We are obviously on the brink of a further stage, in which the accent will no longer be on "growth" but on "equilibrium" in a stabilized system in a deliberately created and cared-for environment. We still do not know how this "new model" will be regarded in detail. Nevertheless we are all called on to cooperate creatively in its formation and determine its limiting features.

THE ENTICEMENT OF SCIENCE: NATURAL SCIENCE IN ITS RATIONALIST CAPACITY

Our modern industrial-technical world, which is seen simply as a result of the Industrial Revolution and described as such, and which in terms of duration covers a mere hundred years or so, in fact developed slowly and formed as a history of the mind during the preceding cultures of antiquity, of the Western countries of the Middle Ages, and finally of the Renaissance.

The basis is provided by specific scientific rationality as a trained manner of thinking. We are so accustomed to it that we find it difficult to stand back and recognize this manner of thinking as a highly one-sided one among many that are possible. Let us try to segregate certain tendencies in the historical development of this style of thinking in order to better understand the role of our natural scientific rationality as the pathfinder of industrial techniques.

The first step, one that was accomplished by the Greeks, lies in the breakdown of the complete reality presented to us into a so-called rational —that is to say, logically soluble and penetrable—element, and into an irrational element embracing all that is emotional, open to the senses, but also ethical and religious. The next step presents a delicate aspect: the fact that the rational is positively communicable (or, as it can also be put, objectifiable), whereas the irrational lies in the hardly communicable zone of subjective perception, leads to the rational being identified as the only true and real, while the irrational, nonobjectifiable sector is stigmatized as unreal and immaterial.

The theocratically slanted medieval high culture had originally left little room for natural scientific thought. The concept of reality was at that time heavily oriented toward the other world. The ethical and religious sector's sense and value concepts had a first reality. During the Renaissance, resistance set in to this predominance of the religious sector. The leaning toward natural-scientific research, initially tolerated by the church as something unattractively worldly, made it possible to create a spiritual free zone. In

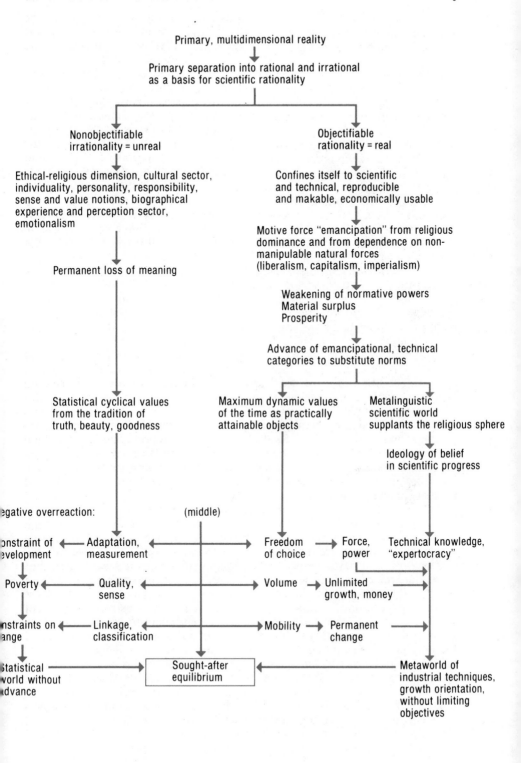

Primary, multidimensional reality

Primary separation into rational and irrational
as a basis for scientific rationality

Nonobjectifiable
irrationality = unreal

Objectifiable
rationality = real

Ethical-religious dimension, cultural sector,
individuality, personality, responsibility,
sense and value notions, biographical
experience and perception sector,
emotionalism

Confines itself to scientific
and technical, reproducible
and makable, economically usable

Motive force "emancipation" from religious
dominance and from dependence on non-
manipulable natural forces
(liberalism, capitalism, imperialism)

Permanent loss of meaning

Weakening of normative powers
Material surplus
Prosperity

Advance of emancipational, technical
categories to substitute norms

Statistical cyclical values
from the tradition of
truth, beauty, goodness

Maximum dynamic values
of the time as practically
attainable objects

Metalinguistic
scientific world
supplants the religious sphere

Ideology of belief
in scientific progress

Negative overreaction:

(middle)

Constraint of
development

Adaptation,
measurement

Freedom
of choice

Force,
power

Technical knowledge,
"expertocracy"

Poverty

Quality,
sense

Volume

Unlimited
growth, money

Constraints on
change

Linkage,
classification

Mobility

Permanent
change

Statistical
world without
advance

Sought-after
equilibrium

Metaworld of
industrial techniques,
growth orientation,
without limiting
objectives

this way, however, in contrast to the religious concept of reality, a worldly oriented concept of reality associated with the Greek way of thinking was set up. The motive force for this was emancipation from theocratic predominance.

Apart from various complications in detail, the general outcome was not a final reconciliation of the two concepts of reality so much as a realignment whereby each shared the full reality: the church the hereafter, and science the life in this world. Natural science, for its part, however, enjoyed the advantage of technical application. This led in the first place to arms production, and so to the possibility of the exercise of military power and finally to the development of industrial production. This development was characterized by liberalism, capitalism and imperialism. The influence and power of nonobjective reality became ever weaker, and the notions of value and sense lost their influence on technical development. The old value concepts of truth, beauty and goodness, the ideals of measure, sense and order, paled into insignificance. Their place was taken by dynamic objects of technical development which may be set out as strivings toward preferences, the greatest possible volume and freedom of movement.

If scientific development had first restricted our perceptions of reality to the rational, as technical development advanced there would be further limitations. In fact, not everything is still rational, only what is scientifically and technically reproducible and feasible; ultimately a character of practical reality is still displayed only by what is economically interesting and viable. The scientific approach to reality is characterized by the segregation of individual problems and factors and by the causal-analytical investigation of mechanical functions. Everything that cannot be investigated in this context falls outside the scope of the exercise. Technical and economic science brings to people an increasing sense of power. Science, which has made this fullness of power possible, assumes more and more the role of a kind of substitute for religion, from which by means of technical developments we promise ourselves a solution to all the evils of the world. This development is described by people as a belief in science and progress. The ultimate result is a world of science marked to an ever-increasing extent by specialized knowledge in which the layman has less and less say and the specialist gets increasingly involved.

If the old static value notions of standards, sense and order had led in their unilateral effects to lack of freedom, poverty and inflexibility as their negative counterparts, the dynamic maximum values of the technical period would lead, if they were realized unilaterally, to a striving for power, unlimited growth, and permanent change. This development has been described as an "abandonment of the middle course," but this completely overlooks the fact that the present one-sidedness is basically a consequence of the preceding static one-sidedness. This means that what was really necessary was not a return to the static notions, but a well-balanced equilibrium of the static and complementary dynamic ideas. In such an equilibrium, dynamic technical self-development had to be adjusted to people's ideas of sense and values again and related to the ecological limits of our possibilities. In our complicated scientific world, however, this was not possible without the help of a new science, reflecting fundamental aspects. Science was the seductive force making for the present industrial technology, and it must now lend its support to overcoming the difficulties that have arisen.

SCIENCE IN A SUPPORTING ROLE: ENVIRONMENTAL RESEARCH, ECOLOGY, HUMAN ECOLOGY

The development of natural sciences in the Western world was the historical prerequisite for the modern technical industrial world. This has enriched us enormously—but it has also left us with the overall crisis of the environment. How is this to be overcome? We are coming to recognize ever more clearly that it is precisely those sciences which led us into the crisis that must help to get us out of it. The use of scientific knowledge enjoys a high measure of choice of action. The objects at which scientific results are aimed can be set from "outside," possibly from the political angle. Accordingly, research will tend to be concentrated upon those questions and will primarily develop those subjects that serve to advance the objects set. The primary purpose so far has been to promote technical industrial development. This takes in, among others, economics, educational sciences, medicine and biology (especially biochemistry) but gives top priority to physics, chemistry and the fields of applied technology.

Now the prodigious problems of maintaining the basis of our existence —and the protection of the environment means just this—have to be dealt with. Important aspects of the task are:

Reduction in the consumption of raw materials facing exhaustion; the recycling of waste products and recourse to substitute products

Reduction of pollution of the environment to a level corresponding to the natural regenerative capacity of the polluted media; thus corresponding purification of waste gases and sewage; disposal of waste by composting; and reduction of noise (as "acoustic effluent")

Preservation of open landscape areas under natural verdure; and a ban on extensions of built-up areas and roadways

Restrictions on contamination of land, water and foodstuffs with noxious substances; restrictions on damage to land by erosion of the landscape; and consequent development of ecologically beneficial methods for the destruction of insect pests and for agriculture

Solutions can be arrived at only by the application of scientific knowledge. The main aims of environmental policy are formulated rapidly, but their practical realization requires time and considerable effort in detail. Science is thus faced with a new task. In many fields the task has already been embarked on, and disciplines bearing on the environment have been further developed. In Western Germany, for instance, numerous research programs based on environmental reports have been launched by the government and regional authorities and have been partly financed by them. This applies in particular to obviating pollution of air and water, assessing pollution of the environment, and developing waste-disposal technologies for conservation of the environment. These national and regional programs are flanked by international programs under the aegis of UN organizations, such as the program entitled "Man and the Biosphere" by UNESCO.

Originally the sciences provided the incentive for furnishing the venture with unlimited technical developments, but they now serve as "aids" to smoothing the path toward overcoming the environmental crisis and achieving an ecological future. With this reorientation, three stages of scientific approach are distinguishable, which for practical purposes can be equally significant:

1. General analytical environmental research
2. Special investigation of living conditions by means of ecology and system theory
3. Interdisciplinary investigation of the classification of people in ecological categories by means of human ecology

General analytical environmental research is comparable in its methods, though new in its aims, with the traditional tasks. Physics, chemistry, geology, some aspects of geography, biology and medicine, together with the technical disciplines employed, all seek to shed light on the raw-material supplies in the world, on the various possibilities for energy extraction, the existence and the reduction of noxious substances, the effects of noxious substances on human beings and on animals and plants, methods for measuring concentrations of noxious substances, and the resources available for technologies favorable to the environment. It is a question here of the solution of clearly definable individual problems and of limited though often comprehensive tasks. The results of this work are needed in political and public life to assist the making of decisions.

To the layman it is highly confusing to have to find a way through the multiplicity of disciplines, for with the advance of knowledge and of techniques the traditional subjects are split up into ever more complicated overlapping individual disciplines. Thus the field of geology breaks down into the specialized sectors of meteorology, hydrology, pedology, oceanography and geochemistry; chemistry breaks down into trace chemistry and radiochemistry; and the biosciences into environmental medicine, social medicine, cancer research, radiation treatment, toxicology, sewage biology, genetics, limnology and agricultural biology.

Today all these sectors are called upon to repair the damage that in recent times has been caused indirectly by themselves. They will be assisted in their efforts by previously neglected sciences, the object of whose researches is the analysis of highly complicated structures in the interplay of many individual factors: ecology and systems theory (or systems analysis). The outcome is that these subjects lead ultimately to an overlapping attempt at a human ecology.

The central problem of the environmental crisis thus lies not so much in the fact that this or that particular problem remains unsolved as in the fact that altogether the interplay of the individual factors no longer leads to a meaningful whole or results in an object that can be represented in relation to and is possible in the existing biosphere. The range of problems presented falls in the research fields of ecology and systems research. These disciplines are designed to embrace and grasp how the complicated coordination of all the interwoven processes operates and which development tendencies can be recognized therein. They are also aimed at an understanding of how such "systems" can be geared to specified objects or of how their "course" at least can be corrected, without giving rise to undesirable side reactions.

Ecology, which has evolved out of biology, is concerned with the background of organisms living with one another and their interrelations with their environment; it examines their formation in time, the crises in their development, and mechanisms for the recovery of equilibrium. Systems research, evolved from economic business analysis, deals with all possible systems on a formal mathematical basis, irrespective of whether living creatures are integrated into them or not; and it plays a primary role in advising undertakings regarding market analysis. Systems research can provide ecology with a mathematical basis for its special "ecosystems." Ecology avails itself, in addition, of the findings of any special ground research by linking the individual data obtained in an overall understanding, and so demonstrates the conditions and the possibilities for stable or critical developments in the future.

Ecology can thus provide information regarding the load capacity of ecosystems—rivers, lakes, woods, agricultural cultivation areas and such. It can clarify for us the consequences of specific operations (such as chemical pest control). In relation to the special sciences aimed at the implementation of particular claims, ecology also offers a philosophical contribution that is not to be underestimated: it provides training toward cooperative thought and reflection. This suggests a moral core for the crisis of the environment.

In applying itself—with or without the utilization of formal system theoretical aids—to the complex interactions among human beings, their technical world and the ecosystem sustaining it (ultimately the entire biosphere), ecology depends on the cooperation of many other branches, the social sciences and the humanities included. At this point the wide range of individual disciplines is basically ignored; only more problem-oriented, interdisciplinary and branch-overlapping group operations are possible. Ecology extended in this way becomes the field of human ecology, which must no longer be understood as a new discipline but as the counterpart of each specialization, as an attempt to solve the problem of the environment by incorporating every possible aspect.

To this extent the introductory chapters in this book are concerned with human ecology. The study entitled "Limits on Growth" (see Part Eighteen), carried out at the instigation of the Club of Rome, was the most comprehensive attempt at that time to write about human ecology on a formal basis—that is to say, on the basis of a mathematical system. Human ecology teaches us that it is not the growth in part of a system (say of human technique) but only a dynamic equilibrium between all parts of a system that provides a basis for long-term stability. To draw the right political consequences from this thesis is our biggest problem.

THE ARTIFICIAL ENVIRONMENTAL SYSTEM OF MAN

Environmental research as just outlined is primarily concerned with natural scientific data. The ecological, and ultimately the human ecological, approach leaves the frontiers of what the environment really is somewhat vague. Is the world we live in really definable in natural-scientific terms? Are our surroundings not composed rather of culture, tradition, fashion and knowledge, of works of art, pictures, buildings, people and personal associations? Are we not hemmed in by a legal system and the state?

Now as before the natural-scientific ecological concept of the environment furnishes the guidelines for everything we are able to perform in conjunction with nature as a basis for existence. But how we can convert this knowledge into action, what in it is feasible and desirable for humankind, what compromises we can adopt in relation to conflicts of purpose will be recognized only when we consider and assess the complex diversity of the human environment.

Actually, a person does not grow up in childhood in open natural surroundings, but from the moment one is given one's first meal develops personal relationships and connections. The first "play area" consists of the house, the neighbors and the street. After that children face a varied educational system (school, youth groups, religion, etc.), a complicated world of information, cultural traditions, rules of conduct, etc. One source of confusion for the aspiring child is the intricate traffic system confronted in the street. It may be that a city dweller sees no open landscape for many years on end, but only an industrial landscape based on purely technical considerations.

We see therefore that people live in a complicated "system" of their own creation, which is integrated more or less completely into the natural ecosystem. This system permits one to operate in a community in the stress area between one's inborn nature and the conditions of external nature. In this complicated environmental system we can now segregate subsystems from one another, characterized as they are by a certain independence and individual dynamic:

1. The *cultural subsystem*—that is to say, tradition, speech, manners and customs, and education. Without this independent field, which is sometimes described by critics as "repressive," and which sees that we move in a historical dimension, human existence would be unthinkable. On this basis we are bound together in fact by powerful forces; it is on this basis that we form our objectives in life and our standards of morality. The cultural subsystem finds reflection today in powerful, far-reaching restructuring, by which its guiding influence on our community is severely weakened and undermined.

2. The *social subsystem* concerns the method, which varies from country to country, of building up communities, groups and organizations, the method and means of living together, the rules for making contact, and the forms of mutual coordination and subordination. Human life cannot function without the traditions for an orderly community structure.

3. An especially heavily restructured sector of the social sphere is the *political subsystem,* on which we depend for the maintenance of order in the country and the regulation of interstate relations. It is to the disadvantage of all when this subsystem is too weak. On the other hand, it is of the greatest danger when the subsystem gets too powerful and dominant. Democracy is considered by us to be the best possibility for preserving the balance between the two extremes. Its objective is a manageable system that maintains a responsible course under control and under constraint.

4. The task of the *economic subsystem* is to promote the production of goods and the fair distribution of commodities and other goods in our highly specialized community based on the division of labor. The economic system is an instrument, not an end in itself. The principles on which this subsystem is based can in themselves be selected freely; our political constitution prescribes no particular system under this heading. This freedom will naturally be decisively curtailed by the historical background and by our compulsive desire for continuity and the avoidance of critical upheavals. At the moment we should certainly try to avail ourselves of the flexibility incorporated in the concept of a social market economy in order to cope with our problems.

5. The *scientific-technical subsystem* should really be known more precisely as the natural science–technical subsystem, for what emerges as a "unit" in this subsystem is the close connections between natural science and the technical application of the information it provides. The modern world is in fact the scientific-technical world, in which the "scientificization" often assumes ludicrous coercive forms, especially as a result of the ever more intensive schooling and theorizing of vocational training. Notwithstanding its innate

15

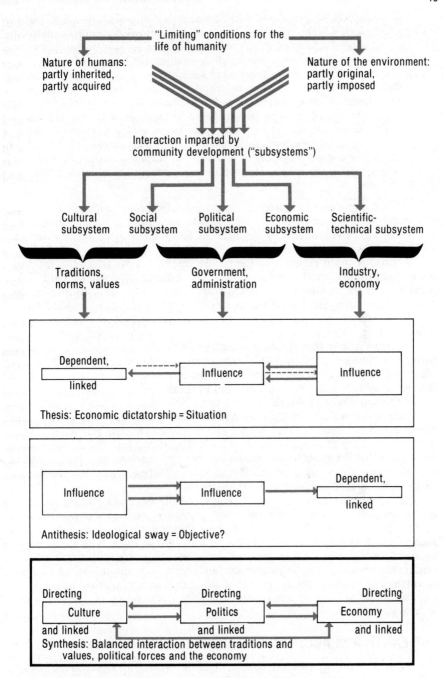

"Limiting" conditions for the life of humanity

Nature of humans: partly inherited, partly acquired

Nature of the environment: partly original, partly imposed

Interaction imparted by community development ("subsystems")

Cultural subsystem · Social subsystem · Political subsystem · Economic subsystem · Scientific-technical subsystem

Traditions, norms, values

Government, administration

Industry, economy

Dependent, linked — Influence — Influence

Thesis: Economic dictatorship = Situation

Influence — Influence — Dependent, linked

Antithesis: Ideological sway = Objective?

Directing Culture and linked — Directing Politics and linked — Directing Economy and linked

Synthesis: Balanced interaction between traditions and values, political forces and the economy

DISTURBANCE IN THE RELATIONSHIP OF COMMUNITY COMPONENT FORCES TO ONE ANOTHER AS A CAUSE OF THE ENVIRONMENTAL CRISIS

independence, the scientific and technical field is closely linked to the economic sector. This is so true that from outside, one is hardly aware of the
"dual nature" of any particular industrial enterprise, in which the aims of the
technical specialist are often in sharp conflict with those of the industrial
economist. Compared with the other subsystems, therefore, the last two can
also be regarded as a uniform, independent sector, so that the strong penetration power of our economy depends specifically on its industrial production
basis. On the penetration power, however, also depends the approach to
growth limits and so to the environmental crisis, which manifests itself in the
same way in all (Western and Eastern) industrial countries. The special economic system is ecologically of secondary importance. Social criticism that is
aimed only at the economic system thus overlooks the problem of the environment.

If we compare our pictures of the social subsystems with our knowledge
of the crisis of the environment on the one hand, and with our insight into
the historical development of the present technical world on the other, the
following thesis appears justified:

Thesis: A main element of the environmental crisis takes the form of a
deep disharmony in the subsystems. The cultural-normative field is too
weakly, and the economic-technical-scientific field too sharply, delineated.
The political subsystem is consequently all too heavily demarcated from the
industrial sector and too lightly from normative, and so from overriding
objectives.

To set against this thesis, an *antithesis* could consequently be raised:
through a change in the system these accents could be reversed. Overriding
ideas and objectives in the normative-cultural sector must take the lead, and
the other sectors must be subordinated to them.

Criticism: Where would such a turnabout get us? If we assume that
precisely those objectives that seem ideal to us at any time will get the upper
hand and direct society, that seems absolutely excellent. But what if ideologies that we reject should take over? We then move into the dictatorship of
ideologies that do more to obstruct a flexible approach to new problems than
our present system. And for this it makes no difference whether theocracies
or socialist or fascist ideologies are involved.

This suggests that we should seek a middle course between our thesis
and antithesis in favor of the following *synthesis:* neither one nor the other
system but a compromise between the subsystems offers an assurance of
vital, free development. We must certainly allow ourselves to be guided
again more directly than in the past by overriding objectives and must re-
strain the economic sector within certain limits. We should be well advised
nevertheless to allow the economic sector a dynamic of its own again. Crises
regarding the setting of aims need not then necessarily result in crises in
industry.

THE EARTH A SPACESHIP—OR A DIVIDED WORLD?

Our efforts to protect the environment often meet with objections from the
left to the effect that the crisis of the environment is only an overplayed
fabrication by capitalists in their own defense aimed at disguising and con-
solidating the inequalities in the world: all the talk of a nil rate of growth is
only an attempt at some new form of colonialism. To this it might be replied
that the Eastern bloc faces even greater difficulties than confront us. The
argument might well be returned, in fact, by pointing out that critics on the

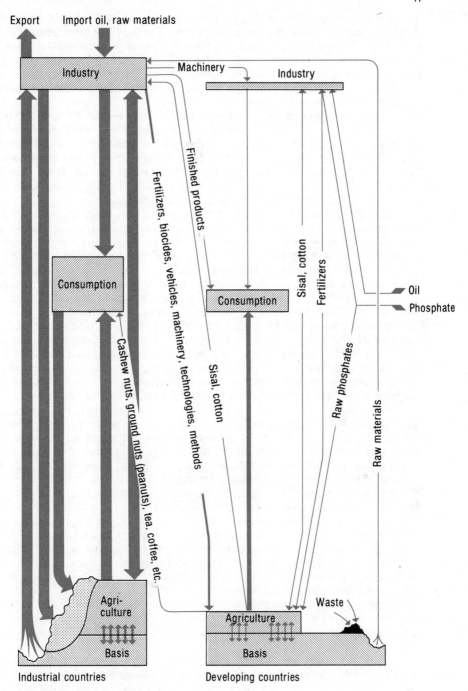

**ECONOMIC INTERRELATIONSHIPS BETWEEN
INDUSTRIAL AND DEVELOPING COUNTRIES**

left resort to sympathy with the developing countries only to soften the impact of our criticism of enormous growth. Yet they are programmed up to the hilt for scientific and technical progress by way of solution, far more so in fact than the Western economies themselves. Furthermore, it is precisely the socialist states in the East that provide the least development aid.

However slanted the motives for the argument may be, the reproach is actually giving rise to serious concern, to which expression was given by the developing countries at the Stockholm Conference on the Human Environment. There it was stated that problems connected with overloading of the environment relate to a particular sector of the industrialized nations: for the developing countries growth and development have for a long time now been a top priority set above protection of the environment. It was not put forward at the conference, however, that even in the developing countries problems of the environment are seriously increasing.

This draws attention to two points: in the first place, these countries participated in a conference on the environment and were convinced by it that the whole biosphere is to be regarded as a unit and serious dangers confront us all—our earth is a spaceship! In the second place, it is realized that this spaceship has very different "decks," from which the problems are assessed very differently. A series of regions, or rather, different groups of countries, can be lumped together—e.g., industrialized capitalist countries such as the United States, the western European countries, South Africa and Japan; industrialized socialist countries such as the USSR, the German Democratic Republic and the other countries of eastern Europe; the various, now immensely rich oil states; the two giants, both special cases, of China and India; and finally, a large number of poor, often overpopulated developing countries, mainly dependent on agricultural production, occupying a large part of the surfaces of Africa, South America and southern Asia.

The oil states could—though we do not know whether they are yet in a position to do so from a political angle—call on us to provide effective development aid indirectly by passing on the increases in revenue they obtain from higher oil prices in the form of credits to the developing countries, which for their part could use the money to buy goods from us. So far, however, the "poor" developing countries have felt little benefit from this. They suffered more severely from the increased prices than we ourselves. The advances in agriculture were based in those countries on modern energy-intensive and raw-material–intensive methods of the so-called Green Revolution. A two- or three-fold increase in energy costs has priced fertilizers, pesticides and mechanical aids out of the market in many regions. Production threatens to collapse. This can bring poor countries to the verge of bankruptcy—and means death for millions from starvation. Help would come only from an immediate switch to biological cultivation methods that save energy and raw material. But for development on these lines no development aid has so far been forthcoming. Our scientists—in particular those concerned with agrarian ecology—are thus once again called on to serve new objectives.

Here we come up against a difficulty. Cultivation methods that save energy and raw materials belong to the so-called applied technologies. These are processes that do not necessarily correspond to the latest technical advances but are geared rather to suitable economic, social and ecological measures applied to the sector concerned in each case. For the most part they are labor-intensive processes with a relatively low capital and machine element. Many politicians in the developing countries turn down such adaptations for prestige reasons. They fear that we want to feed them with second-grade technologies. In this situation both sides require a high level of good feeling, a sense of realism and insight into the inevitable, in order to come to a compromise.

China has successfully taken the uncompromising path of labor-intensive adaptation, setting its sights finally on modern technology. Whether it is merely following the path taken by the industrial nations with all their mistakes or will stop at some modest intermediate stage remains to be seen. A series of rigorous checks on growth in the field of urban development and population policy provide grounds for hope; other things leave room for thought.

Let us juxtapose the extremes in a human ecological system in all their stark simplicity in order to be clear about the alternatives: in the industrial countries, on top of high import and export rates we have a powerful industry and a highly developed agricultural system together providing a well-equipped consumer sector. For this purpose the ecological basis is drawn upon to the utmost and is in part jeopardized. The exhaustion of material, demands made on the land and the disposal of waste that defiles the environment are all excessive. It is quite otherwise in the developing countries: here there is reciprocal interaction between an obviously undercharged consumer sector on the one hand and an underdeveloped agriculture and an only emergent industry on the other. Many manufactured goods, technologies, machines, information, etc., have to be imported to sustain the economy. But how are they to be paid for? There is only a trifling production surplus available. This consists mainly of certain agricultural raw products. But these are subject to severe competitive pressure in world markets; and the price ratio between these goods and manufactured products is likely in the course of time to be even less favorable. Consequently it will hardly be possible for these economic regions to become stabilized and cease to depend on our assistance. Yet in all these territories there are plenty of ecological reserves available. But whereas in our case the ecological limits are being strained by the overdevelopment of the industrial production space, the environmental problem in the developing countries assumes another aspect: all measures for stabilization and economic development are threatened there by excessive growth in the population. An almost insoluble vicious circle is building up in those countries. We are well aware that effective control of the population is possible only when social and economic stability are achieved. On the other hand, it is precisely this population problem that is responsible for the collapse of many development projects. No one has yet found a practical solution for this problem.

LEGISLATION TO PROTECT THE ENVIRONMENT

New problems of environmental deterioration have triggered a new and complex collection of laws. For example, prior to 1965 there was relatively little pollution control law in the United States; today it is a legal specialty in itself. Not only has the amount of legislation increased, but its perspective has changed. The federal government, rather than the states, has assumed more responsibility, and the laws have shifted to attempt to prevent environmental destruction rather than simply to punish those responsible after the fact.

This period of rapid development in legislation is characterized by what some observers call diversity and others call inconsistency. Air pollution regulations are quite different from water pollution laws; and federal, state and local laws can vary in both approach and content. There are differences in definitions of pollution or other environmental threats and also in the types of protection offered. Some parts of a law are designed with costs in mind, while others intend to protect the environment, regardless of expense.

A landmark in environmental law is the National Environmental Policy Act (generally called NEPA), which went into effect in 1970. This law says that the federal government has a responsibility to restore and maintain environmental quality. NEPA has had a major impact on programs ranging from housing and highway construction to leasing of oil drilling sites.

The most important provision of NEPA requires all federal government agencies to prepare statements on the predicted impact of any major programs that may significantly affect the environment. Although the law does not prohibit activities expected to have adverse effects, it does provide a legal lever for public intervention. It requires officials to consider and publicly discuss environmental consequences of planned activities.

More than 800 suits have been filed demanding that projects be postponed until adequate environmental impact statements are prepared. In the Trans-Alaska Pipeline case, for example, court actions brought by conservation groups delayed the start of the pipeline for four years, and the environmental analysis required by law led to several changes of the pipeline design which are expected to minimize adverse impacts. In other cases, environmental assessments have convinced agencies to give up plans for bridges, airports and pesticide uses.

The general approach of NEPA has been adopted by both state and foreign governments. More than 25 states have passed "little NEPAs," and 16 other nations now require environmental impact statements from government agencies. California has one of the most impressive laws, requiring environmental impact reports on both private and governmental projects. In the 1970s, approximately 6000 reports were filed there annually.

The first comprehensive program attacking air pollution was the Clean Air Act, as amended in 1970. It instructed the Environmental Protection Agency to set national air quality standards to protect, first, human health and subsequently crops, livestock, buildings and other factors that contribute to public welfare. The EPA set standards for automobile emissions, but delays and extensions several times postponed their going into effect. Standards are also being set for fixed installations, such as power plants, that are major air polluters. In addition the EPA is developing regulations to clean up areas where the air is already too polluted and to prevent significant deterioration in areas where the air quality is currently high. Generally the states have been left responsible for the enforcement of the air quality standards.

Water is another aspect of the environment in need of protection. In 1972 a complex law for the first time refuted the assumption that wastes could be freely dumped in rivers, lakes and streams. The tactic chosen in the Federal Water Pollution Control Act is uniform regulation, through a system of permits, of discharges into waterways. The EPA sets limits based on the technology available and the related costs. In addition, the agency must make regulations to control plant site runoff, leaks, waste disposal, spillage and drainage of pollutants associated with industrial manufacturing or water treatment processes.

Protection of wildlife includes hunting restrictions and endangered species regulations (see Part Eight). In addition, animals are affected by the Federal Insecticide, Fungicide and Rodenticide Act, which is intended to protect ecological systems by requiring registration and testing of pesticides before they are released throughout the environment and are allowed to enter the food chain (see Part Eight).

Another chemical-regulating law, which should guard the environment as well as human health, is the Toxic Substances Control Act. More than 1000 new chemicals are introduced into the environment each year. The toxic substances law requires manufacturers to notify EPA before beginning production of new chemicals and requires the producer to carry out, pay for and report tests to show that the chemical will not pose an unreasonable risk to people or the environment.

Finally, newer laws increase the role of the federal government in protection against solid and hazardous wastes. The Resource Conservation and Recovery Act of 1976 sets two goals: (1) management of solid and hazardous wastes in a manner that will protect health and the environment and (2) conservation of natural resources through recovery and reuse of materials in solid waste. The EPA is charged with setting standards for hazardous waste management from its generation to its disposal, a policy sometimes called "cradle-to-grave." Another goal of the law is the elimination of all open dumps. This is the first federal law to recognize that land is just as important to the environment, and just as limited, as air and water and thus needs to be protected by law.

All these laws are in a state of flux in their administration, interpretation and enforcement because their approaches and their contents are new. The laws have left far behind the more limited legal sources from which they arose—the more traditional concepts of nuisance and of trespass. Some groups, particularly in industry, feel that too many laws are being passed too fast for even the federal agencies to handle, let alone manufacturers, the public and the courts. On the other hand, environmentalists' expectations are not being realized as rapidly or as fully as hoped. Many steps forward in environmental protection have been made only after lengthy court action brought by individual citizens and public interest groups. Each short-term oil shortage, and the specter of an eventual energy shortage, encourage people to forego those measures to protect the environment that require energy. There remains a great need for further establishment and implementation of national programs to curtail the destruction by this technologically advanced society of the environment that supports it.

WHAT CAN THE INDIVIDUAL DO? TIPS REGARDING THE ENVIRONMENT

The problem of environmental pollution is closely linked with economic growth and with the consumption and industrial processing of raw materials. Every single member of the community in his capacity as a consumer can exercise an influence on the extent of pollution of the environment.

A. ENERGY

1. Be sparing in your use of every form of energy. Switch off all electrical appliances (lights, ovens, radio, etc.) as soon as they are no longer required.
2. Save fuel by better insulation of your home.
3. Choose light colors for the walls and ceilings of your living rooms, as this saves artificial lighting.
4. Take a stand against unnecessary illuminated advertisements.
5. As far as possible, avoid buying anything in aluminum containers (such as fruit juices and beer). With each empty nonreturnable container you throw away a lot of energy, since aluminum production consumes considerable electric power.

B. WATER

1. Do not waste drinking water; repair leaking taps and water mains immediately.
2. Take showers instead of baths; you will use only one-fifth as much water that way.
3. Use your washing machine only for full loads; let dirty linen accumulate until there is enough to fill the machine.
4. Do not wash your car too often; use a bucket and sponge to wash it rather than a hose.
5. Be careful not to spill any oil; one quart of oil can make one million quarts of drinking water undrinkable. Have your fuel oil tank tested regularly.
6. Do not buy colored paper products, including those "decorator" paper towels and toilet tissues; buy plain white whenever possible. The toxic chemical wastes generated in manufacturing the dyes for these products are major contaminants of our waterways—and one of the more senseless causes of pollution.

C. PACKING MATERIAL

1. Refuse to buy products that are offered in unnecessary disposable wrappings.
2. For your shopping, use an "old-fashioned" shopping bag; that way you also save money on the plastic carrier-bag.
3. Reject all aluminum foil; do not buy prepared foods offered in aluminum containers meant to be thrown away.
4. Buy your drinks in returnable bottles; disposable bottles are more expensive and raise problems of refuse removal.
5. Collect your scrap (newspapers, rags, paper) for delivery to welfare organizations for recycling in bulk.
6. When you go on a hike or a picnic, take a carrier-bag to put rubbish in, which can later be emptied into a garbage pail.
7. Choose paper packing, which is kinder to the environment, rather than plastic wrappings.
8. Do not use disposable cups, plates, tablecloths, table napkins, etc., as the cost of these articles bears no relation to their use.

D. ATMOSPHERE

1. Before you buy a car, consider whether you really need one, and think of the cost (purchase price, gasoline, tax, insurance, repair bills, accident costs, etc.). In case of doubt, go for the smaller car; it consumes less energy.
2. For longer journeys, use the railway. The train causes far less pollution and, in relation to space and energy, carries far more passengers than an automobile. Furthermore, rail travel is more relaxing.
3. For shorter distances, go on foot or use a bicycle.
4. Never leave the car engine idling unnecessarily.
5. Make sure that the setting of the oil burner in your heating system is adjusted regularly.
6. Do not burn grass or weeds. Greenery and leaves can be used for compost.
7. Do not smoke, or at least show consideration for nonsmokers.

E. FOOD

1. Buy vegetables and fruits that are produced by biological-dynamic processes, that is, without recourse to toxic insecticides and artificial mineral fertilizers. Support the undertakings that produce such foods.
2. If you have a garden of your own, find out about biological methods of cultivation and plant protection.

F. NATURE AND RECREATION

1. Take a stand with your local council on the creation of green plots and parks. The greenbelts on housing lands should not only be sown with grass but also be planted with shrubbery and trees, and enhanced with small lakes and ponds. A medium-sized deciduous tree regenerates the atmosphere more than 1 hectare (2.47 acres) of greenery.
2. Suggest that building sites standing vacant for a long time should not be used as dumps but should be sown with grass and if possible made available to the public.
3. Support the creation of big landscape and nature-preserve areas.
4. Do not disfigure the landscape by the careless discarding of refuse.
5. If it is possible, hang nesting boxes in the trees of your garden. Also make provision, in agricultural regions and in the garden, for natural nesting places such as bushes and hedgerows.
6. Support measures for the preservation of animals threatened with extinction by refusing, for instance, to wear garments manufactured from the skins of these animals.
7. Give your children the opportunity to enjoy the beauties of nature, and awaken in them an understanding of ecological requirements.

Part Two—Scientific Classification of the Environment

The earth is generally thought of as consisting of three elements: land, sea and air. Scientific considerations call for a somewhat different breakdown, however, into the lithosphere, which consists of rock formations; the pedosphere, composed of disintegrating compounds of earth and stone; the hydrosphere, which is a layer of water penetrating the lithosphere and the pedosphere; and the atmosphere, which is a layer of air embracing all the preceding categories. This breakdown is broadly covered by the branches of scientific research designated as geology (study of the earth, especially rocks), pedology (study of soil), hydrology (study of water), and meteorology (study of weather). Biology, the study of life in all its forms, is concerned with the biosphere (living space), which pervades all the inorganic spheres.

All the sectors just mentioned are interdependent and all interact on one another. The atmosphere contains water which it has absorbed from the evaporation of open waters and from exhalations by living creatures. On attaining a certain saturation point, the atmosphere emits the water it has absorbed and restores it to the other components of the earth in the form of rain, snow, etc. Solid particles are suspended in the earth's atmosphere in the form of dust emanating from earth, stone and microorganisms. In the hydrosphere, gases such as life-giving oxygen are dissolved, rocks are decomposed, their eroded particles are carried away, and they are deposited in new formations. This is the original breeding-ground for all organisms. The lithosphere is impregnated with water and gases. It also contains organic compounds, such as coal and oil, and special forms of life which have adapted to this sector. In pores in the pedosphere, the loose erosion products of rock and dead organic substances, there is a constant interchange of water and air. In the soil are the mineral deposits of many forms of life, which are released from the lithosphere with frequently changing intensity. The biosphere, which embraces plants, animals and microorganisms, is contained in the cushion of air nearest to the earth, probably penetrates the entire hydrosphere, and is present in the upper layer of the earth's mantle.

As has already been indicated, the close spatial integration of the various spheres of the environment is reflected in an intense reciprocal interaction between the various sectors. Account must be taken of this fact whenever a change is made by humans in a particular sphere. Take the case of a change in the course of a river, an intervention in the water sector. The consequences have to be investigated not only in this sector, in the form of a reduction in the oxygen absorption as a result of the restriction of surface areas and the related loss of self-purification potential, but also concerning the effects it will have on other sectors. As regards the pedosphere, one result will be a drop in the groundwater level, giving rise to changes in the flora and fauna. The release of water into the atmosphere will be reduced, resulting in further changes in the vegetation and consequently in the animal world. The faster flow of water will increase its eroding effect, which will cause a more rapid dispersal of rock material and produce substantial changes in the relief pattern. These few examples give some idea, on a most superficial level of assessment, of the enormous side effects of decisions affecting the environment for all the sectors involved.

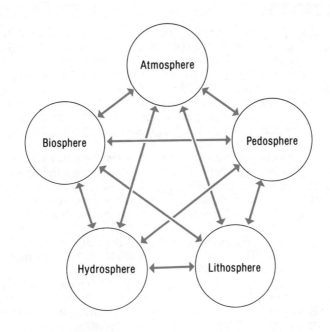

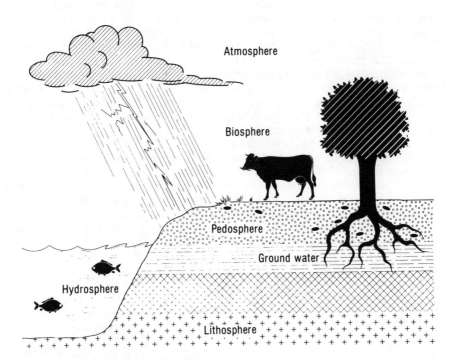

DIAGRAMMATIC REPRESENTATION OF THE FUNDAMENTAL REGIONS OF THE ENVIRONMENT

THE ATMOSPHERE

The presence of a gaseous atmosphere around the earth may be due to a balance existing between the forces of gravity, which hold gases (in the same way as other masses) to the earth's surface, and the characteristic motion of molecules, which left to themselves would let the gases evaporate rapidly into outer space by diffusion. The molecular motion is greater the smaller the molecular and atomic masses and the higher the temperature. If the gases have low molecular masses, at constant temperatures they will attain higher velocities and so have a greater chance of escaping into outer space against the pull of gravity.

The atmosphere presumably owes its existence to exhalations (in the form of gases) from rocks. This thesis is supported by the remarkably high content in the atmosphere of the inert gas argon, which is derived in turn from the radioactive disintegration of the potassium isotope ^{40}K. This isotope is present, though only in small quantities, in almost all rock on the earth's crust. The quantity of argon present in the earth's atmosphere corresponds roughly to the amount that may possibly be released from the potassium content of the crustal rock. As argon has a high molecular density, it is not emitted into outer space.

Except as regards its water vapor content, which is subject to sharp variations, the atmosphere consists of a gaseous mixture that changes very little in its composition. Only in the layer of atmosphere within 10 to 50 meters (33 to 165 feet) of the earth's surface do minor variations appear, as a result mainly of the influence of organic life. The principal constituents of the atmosphere are the gases nitrogen and oxygen. The only other component present in significant proportions is the inert gas argon. Apart from these there are a large number of so-called trace gases, which are present in such small quantities that they are measured not in the ordinary way by volume percentage but in ppm (parts per million). At a level of 1% to 4%, water vapor in the atmosphere ranks ahead of the inert gas argon. Despite the comparatively low water element in the atmosphere, water vapor is still very important from the meteorological point of view since it is present as steam, liquid water, and ice.

Up to a height of about 100 kilometers (60 miles) the composition of atmospheric air is unchanged, apart from the rapid reduction in the water vapor content. Above 100 kilometers the atmosphere changes completely under the influence of ultraviolet radiation. The gases present in the lower atmosphere as polyatomic molecules break down at higher levels into their component parts.

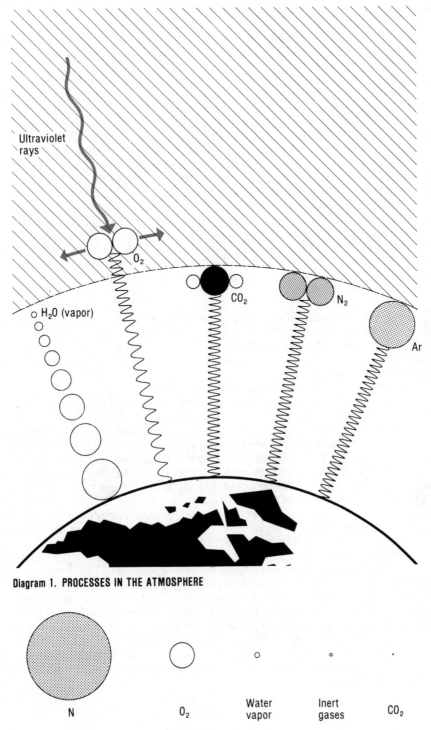

Diagram 1. PROCESSES IN THE ATMOSPHERE

Diagram 2. COMPOSITION OF THE ATMOSPHERE

THE RADIATION BALANCE OF THE EARTH

The energy needed to sustain life on the earth is provided by solar radiation. This consists of electromagnetic rays of different wavelengths, from shortwave roentgen rays (x-rays), which are absorbed in the upper atmosphere, to longwave radio waves. The earth would get constantly hotter if an energy flow were not directed from it to the universe, whereby the energy absorbed from the sun is emitted again into outer space. There is thus an exchange of energy between the universe and our planet, as a result of which the solar inflow and the thermal outflow tend to balance one another.

In order to make an assessment of radiation conservation for the hemisphere concerned, the intensity of the incoming solar radiation at the outer boundaries of the atmosphere is put at 100 units, and the intensity of all other radiation flows is related to this figure.

Before the solar radiation reaches the earth's surface, it is diverted by air molecules (in an atmosphere assumed for the time being to be cloudless), with the result that part of the incoming solar radiation is reflected back immediately into outer space. The earth's surface also reflects back part of the radiation; and in a cloudy sky there is also the reflection from the cloud layer. As a result of these occurrences—which are referred to collectively as *albedo*—the earth loses altogether about 34% of the inflow of energy. About 20% of the energy produced by solar radiation is absorbed by the molecules of the gases (water vapor, carbon dioxide, ozone, etc.) present in the atmosphere, and this results in a rise in the temperature. Directly or by diffusion in the earth's atmosphere 46% of the solar radiation accordingly arrives at the surface of the earth and is absorbed by it after deduction for reflection attenuation.

Every body emits radiations, the wavelengths of which are determined essentially by the surface temperature of the body. And the wavelengths of the rays emitted get shorter as the temperature rises. As the sun's surface is considerably hotter than that of the earth, the maximum length of the rays on the earth compared with those on the sun goes from the lower end of the scale to the upper end. The earth thus emits longwave heat rays, which (in view of the higher temperature prevailing on the earth's surface in relation to the atmosphere) amount to about 112 units. These are not radiated into outer space, however, but are retained for the most part by the atmospheric gases and the clouds, as water vapor and carbon dioxide are not highly permeable to longwave heat radiation. Thus 98 of the 112 units take the form of atmospheric radiation from the earth's atmosphere.

Altogether the earth's surface receives 32 more units than it emits (46 units received from shortwave solar radiation, 14 units lost by longwave thermal radiation), so that a positive radiation balance results. This is counterbalanced by the fact that the atmosphere loses 66 units by longwave radiation of gases and clouds into outer space. The accretion to the atmosphere of 132 units from shortwave scattered radiation and longwave radiation from the earth is more than counterbalanced by the loss of 164 units from atmospheric radiation and longwave radiation into outer space; that is to say, there is a loss of 32 units. The overall radiation position of the earth is thus balanced.

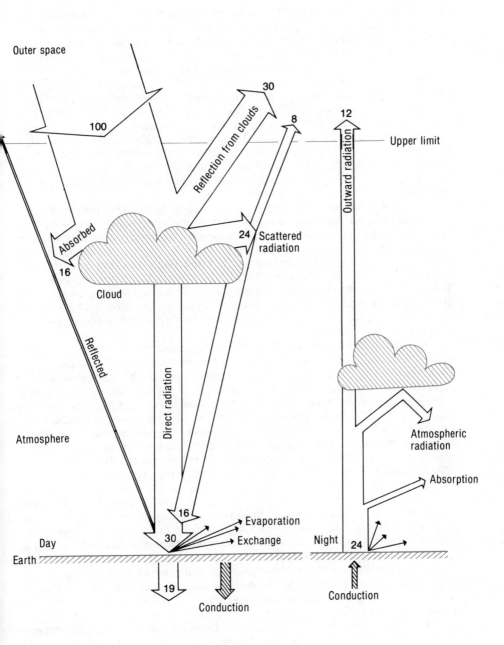

RADIATION BALANCE

CARBON DIOXIDE—ITS ROLE IN THE ATMOSPHERE

Carbon dioxide (CO_2), a gas produced by the combustion of carboniferous substances such as coal, petroleum products and wood in industry, automobiles and households, is not directly toxic for human beings and animals, as it also is formed in every living creature by respiration and is emitted. It is harmful only in very high concentrations (asphyxiation).

Part of the carbon dioxide generated by combustion is assimilated by plants while they are bathed in light, and oxygen is given off in its place (this ratio is estimated at about 50%), or it is dissolved physically in waters. The rest of the carbon dioxide is dispersed in the atmosphere.

The oxygen-based atmosphere of the earth probably began forming two to three billion years ago by the assimilation of carbon dioxide by plant life. The carbon remaining in the plants as a result of the assimilation was deposited upon fossilization in the earth's crust and remained there in the form of petroleum, coal, natural gas, and peat.

For many decades now, the human race has been exploiting these carbon deposits to an ever increasing extent as a source of energy, and has thus been combining the carbon with oxygen again. This results in the production of carbon dioxide and the consumption of oxygen. Since industrialization began, the carbon dioxide content of the atmosphere has increased in consequence by 15%. By the year 2000 it is estimated that the increase will amount to 30%. In industrial regions the carbon dioxide contained in the atmosphere is particularly high, because not only is more of it produced there but the stock of plant life, which absorbs carbon dioxide and gives off oxygen, declines steadily.

By reason of its structure, the carbon dioxide molecule has the property of absorbing infrared rays and converting them into heat. Consequently, a slight increase in the carbon dioxide content of the earth's atmosphere considerably increases the heat-retaining capacity of the air. Normally the earth's surface disseminates into the universe again a large part of the entering sunlight, in the form of infrared heat rays. This prevents the temperature on the earth from constantly rising under the influence of solar radiation. But if the carbon dioxide content of the atmosphere increases, a larger part of this reflected infrared radiation will be absorbed into the atmosphere, and so will remain on the earth and thereby raise the temperature.

An increase in the temperature can change the climate of the earth considerably in the long run. A rise in average temperature throughout the world by 2°–3°C (35.6°–37.4°F) would very probably result in the melting of large quantities of polar ice, and so lead to a rise in the sea level and to the loss of large tracts of land. That this development has not yet occurred, despite the rising carbon dioxide content of the atmosphere, is due, surprisingly, to the pollution of the atmosphere by particles of dust. Alongside the growth in the carbon dioxide content the dust content has risen simultaneously in the higher layers of the atmosphere, and solar radiation has been reduced considerably by dispersion.

The first assessments of the carbon dioxide content of the atmosphere at the beginning of the Industrial Revolution show a concentration of 280 parts per million (0.028%). By today the level has risen to 330 ppm, showing an annual growth rate of 0.07 ppm. By the year 2000 the figure is likely to rise to 379 ppm. According to present information, the overall average temperature rises by 0.5°C (0.9°F) for each increase in the carbon dioxide content by 18%. By the year 2000 an increase is consequently to be expected of 1°C (33.8°F).

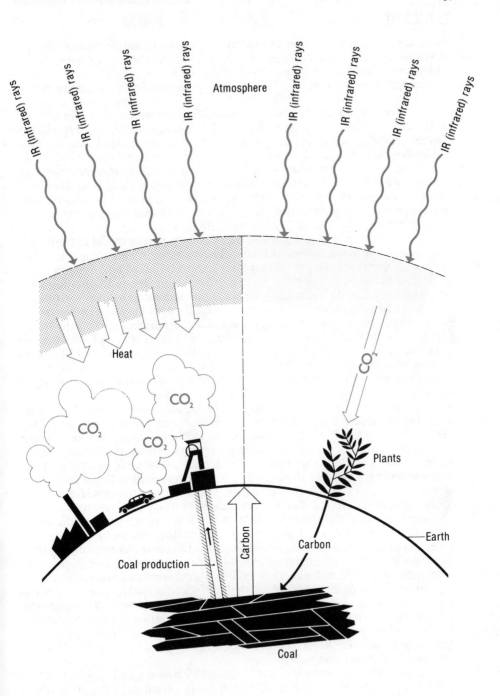

THE ROLE OF CARBON DIOXIDE IN THE ATMOSPHERE

THE WIND

Wind can be defined in the conventional sense as "air in motion." This definition applies, however, only to large movements of air in general (trade winds, monsoons). In the strictly scientific sense, some further characteristics (conditions) are required for an exact definition of the phenomenon of "wind": the airflow must be directed, and in addition it must have a specific speed of flow over a considerable distance. Thus under strong solar radiation on the earth's surface, owing to the decline in temperature, fine interchange currents can develop in the movement of the air into the atmosphere, without their being described as wind. Such air currents become wind in the proper sense only when they combine to form so-called anabatic (upward-moving) wind flows. In vertical currents in storms, anabatic wind speeds of up to 30 meters (98 feet) per second have been recorded. Usually, only air movements in a horizontal direction are described as wind, but vertical air movements are by no means without significance.

Wind arises as a result of differences in air pressure in the atmosphere, from which the air acquires velocity. The particles of air then follow the decline in air pressure from high-pressure areas to low. The direction of the decline in pressure follows the pattern of the air pressure distribution. It is either recorded in the form of isohypse (assumed contour lines of constant height demarcating areas of equal air pressure) on air density charts, insofar as the air pressure field in the open atmosphere is concerned, or it will be given in the form of isobars (assumed lines between regions of the same air pressure at 0°C related to sea level and the force of gravity at 45° latitude) on ground-weather charts. The smaller the distances between the individual isohypsen and isobars, the greater will be the isobaric slope shown vertically on these lines.

Apart from acceleration due to the drop in air pressure, the air particles also acquire acceleration (in the case of wide-ranging movements over long distances) from the divergent effect of the earth's rotation (Coriolis force). The Coriolis acceleration plays an important part in the movements in the atmosphere, knowledge of which is essential to an understanding of the motion system. The Coriolis force directly affects the directional movement of the air particles and increases as the speed of the particles rises. In the southern hemisphere it deflects the air particles to the left, and in the northern hemisphere to the right; on the equator it deflects them downward (in the case of movements toward the west, in the direction of the sinking sun) or upward (in the case of movements toward the east). As regards the wind direction in the northern hemisphere, this means that with a drop in pressure from south to north, not a south wind but a west wind will arise.

In the layer of air near the earth's surface, the direction and speed of the wind will also be determined, as well as by the factors just described, largely by the friction of the air particles on the earth's surface and deflection caused by the features of the terrain. So the speed of the wind is less on land than over open water. The direction of the wind can also be deflected by mountain chains and valleys.

In the upper air above the level affected by friction, up to a few hundred meters (or yards) above the earth's surface, the conditions are so different that the Coriolis force and pressure gradients have effect only if they are in equilibrium with one another. What is known as geostrophic wind, which arises here, blows parallel to the isobars. This high-level wind is of practical interest in the assessment of wind and pressure conditions in the atmosphere and of diffusion movements in cloud banks.

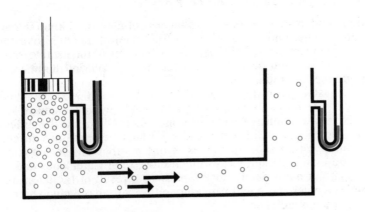

Diagram 1. AIR PARTICLES FOLLOW THE PRESSURE GRADIENT
FROM HIGH TO LOW PRESSURE

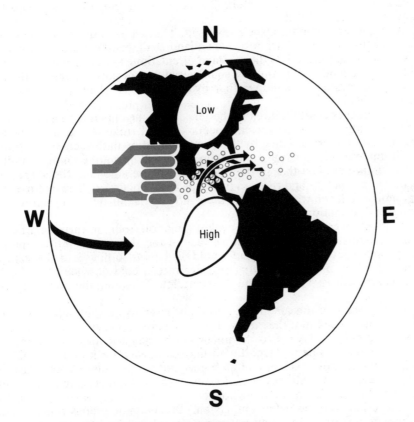

Diagram 2. DEFLECTION OF THE WIND BY THE CORIOLIS FORCE

WIND SYSTEMS OVER LIMITED AREAS

Limited wind systems extend over an area of about 100 km (60 miles) in the horizontal plane and less than 1 km (0.6 mile) in height above the earth's surface. They are strongly influenced by features of the local terrain, by heat capacity, by ground or water surface, and by day and night variations in solar and thermal radiation.

In coastal areas in fine-weather conditions, a land-sea wind system develops, which in bad weather is not much in evidence and is often dominated by more extensive weather conditions. Owing to the different heat-conduction properties of water and solid land, temperature differences are to be found within short distances of one another on the coast. Solid land warms up under the sun's rays much more than water does and also cools down again at night much more rapidly as a result of radiation loss. Water maintains a much more uniform temperature, as it has a much higher thermal capacity than mineral soil.

By day, air temperatures rise more sharply on land than over the cooler area. Higher air temperatures over the land surface lead there to a rise in the heated air masses, with the result that pressure differences develop between land and sea. The cooler sea air flows into the lower-pressure zone over the land, so that a sea-land movement sets in in the layer of air close to the earth's surface; this is counterbalanced by a movement in the opposite direction at a higher level.

At night these conditions are reversed. The sea is warmer and the land cooler, so that near the earth's surface a land-sea movement sets in. This is not so sharply delineated as the sea-land circulation, as the cooling down at night over the land occurs only in shallow patches of air over the earth, so that the wind system is shallower than by day and the surface friction exerts more of a check.

In consequence of features in the terrain, upcurrents due to slopes and mountain and valley wind systems occur on land. Like the land-sea wind system, these too are affected by the diurnal variation in the sun's radiation. The air immediately flanking a mountain slope will be warmed more rapidly by the sun's rays than that in the open atmosphere adjoining the slope. In this way it gets lighter and rises up the slope as an upcurrent. The upcurrents carry moisture-laden warm air from the valley up the hillside and so contribute to cloud formation.

At night, because of the high level of radiation from the earth's surface, the air immediately enveloping the surface of the slope cools more rapidly than at higher levels, and the heavy cold air begins to flow into the valley under the force of gravity, giving rise again to a cold downcurrent. Both currents flow across the direction of the valley, following the down line of the slope.

During the day the air masses flow out laterally to the valley, and at night they flow back into the valley. From this flow process develops a hill-valley wind system. Owing to the upcurrent by day, air masses are drawn out of the valley, to be replaced by air masses flowing back into the valley. At night cold air flows as a mountain breeze out of the valley. In contrast to the upcurrents, by which only a shallow layer of air is affected, the mountain and valley breezes permeate the whole cross-section of the valley. Owing to the connection with the upcurrent system, the mountain-valley breezes are no simple circulation, but they possess a complicated spatial structure, as air masses also flow over the lateral ridges of the valleys.

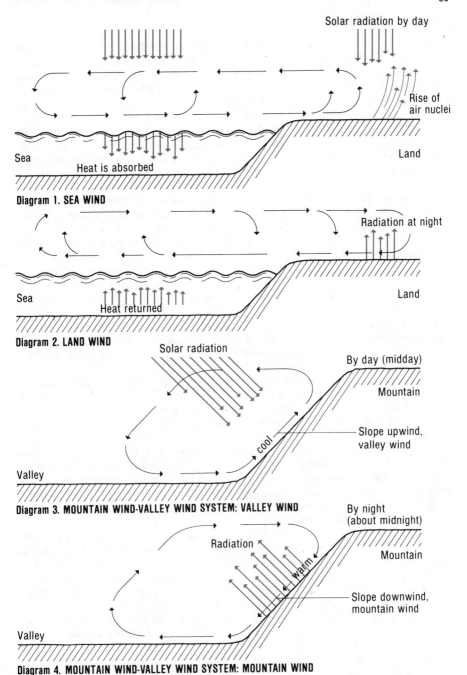

Solar radiation by day

Rise of
air nuclei

Sea

Heat is absorbed

Land

Diagram 1. SEA WIND

Radiation at night

Sea

Heat returned

Land

Diagram 2. LAND WIND

Solar radiation

By day (midday)

Mountain

Slope upwind,
valley wind

cool

Valley

Diagram 3. MOUNTAIN WIND-VALLEY WIND SYSTEM: VALLEY WIND

By night
(about midnight)

Mountain

Radiation

warm

Slope downwind,
mountain wind

Valley

Diagram 4. MOUNTAIN WIND-VALLEY WIND SYSTEM: MOUNTAIN WIND

A similar system to that for the downcurrents occurs also in the case of glacier breezes. As the air in the valley warms up, the cold upper surface of the glaciers produces a downcurrent along the glacier, which in the daytime (with its sharper temperature difference) blows more strongly than at night.

CLOUD FORMATION

Owing to solar radiation, the atmosphere is warmer in its layers close to the earth than in its higher reaches. As molecules possess more kinetic energy in warmer air than in colder, they are in a position to pick up more water molecules from the liquid zone and to transmit them in the form of vapor. Warm air can accordingly absorb more water vapor than cold air. Warm air moreover is lighter than cold, so that warm air rises in the atmosphere while cold air sinks. As they rise, the warm air masses gradually cool down, with the result that the water molecules lose energy again and combine again into bigger units. If a position is reached in which no more water molecules pass from the liquid to the vaporous state, this is known as water-vapor saturation.

If the vapor saturation limit is achieved by cooling down, it still cannot be assumed that the water molecules will consolidate into water droplets. Experiments have established that the condensation into an air-and-water-vapor mixture free from any dust particles can be delayed well beyond the saturation point. This is due to the fact that upon the intrusion of water molecules in minute particles, the vapor pressure must overcome the cohesive pressure of the particles. In order to form even a minute initial droplet, a powerful oversaturation is necessary, which is not present. For the formation of such a droplet an initial impulse must accordingly be provided. This can be done by an electrical charge produced by ionizing (cosmic) radiation. In the atmosphere this is of little moment, however, as condensation occurs in this way only under very high oversaturation, which is not present there.

Condensation nuclei, small particles of matter, form an initial droplet, to which further water molecules can adhere. The effect of such nuclei (their material composition plays no part as long as they are not water-repellent) depends on their absorbing surplus kinetic energy from the water molecules at the moment of adhesion. This can be deduced from the fact that only when the saturation vapor pressure is exceeded will the big nuclei, which can absorb much energy, first become effective. Additional effect is achieved when the nuclei consist of salts soluble in water; in that case, when the humidity of the atmosphere is below the saturation point, an adhesion of water occurs, as salts soluble in water are hygroscopic—that is, they strongly take up and retain water.

With less than 100% relative moisture in the air, vapor develops, and it is assumed that such nuclei are present in the air. The predominant proportion of the nuclei probably consists, however, of nuclei not soluble in water or of mixed nuclei which are composed of soluble and nonsoluble parts.

The formation of condensation nuclei stems essentially from combustion processes, volcanic eruptions, and wind effects. The combustion processes release sulfates and nitrogen compounds into the atmosphere, and these combine with ammonium sulfate and act as condensation nuclei. Nuclei of salts, primarily sodium chloride, which pass into the atmosphere in the form of spray, are of less importance than was originally assumed.

The drop formation from the condensation nuclei arises from the adhesion of water vapor to the nucleus, whereby cloud drops up to a diameter of 10 micrometers (μm) can be formed. The substantially larger raindrops are formed by other processes.

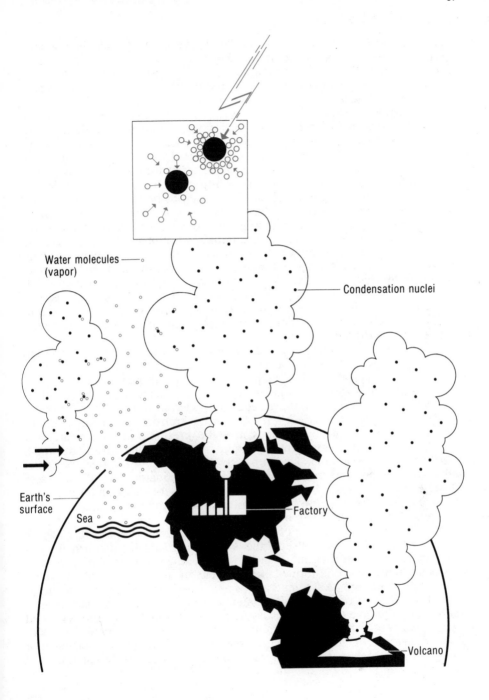

Water molecules
(vapor)

Condensation nuclei

Earth's
surface

Sea

Factory

Volcano

FORMATION OF CLOUD DROPLETS ON CONDENSATION NUCLEI

HOW RAIN IS FORMED

The water droplets (mist) present in clouds are so small that they cannot leave the clouds without evaporating. For raindrops to be formed that will reach the earth before they evaporate, up to a million cloud droplets must coagulate. For the aggregation of the cloud droplets, adhesion and condensation are not sufficient in themselves to explain the phenomenon.

There are two different hypotheses regarding the mechanics of raindrop formation, each of which is valid under different climatic conditions. The first of these presupposes that not all the cloud droplets present in a cloud are the same size. The larger droplets fall faster than smaller ones, so that a bigger drop will overtake and absorb all the smaller ones lying in its downward path, unless an air current forms around the falling drop that causes part of the smaller droplets suspended in the air to be bypassed, so that the actual agglomeration is smaller than it might be. Nevertheless, a big cloud whose droplets have a long way to fall and are sufficient in number will still produce raindrops in this way. In addition, in a rising cloud there will be considerable upcurrents by which big drops will be held in suspension while smaller ones are caught up and merge with the big ones. If the individual drop gets too big it will lose its stability and burst, and the fragments will again be caught up and merged until they eventually fall from the cloud in big drops. This kind of raindrop formation, which is sometimes referred to as the Langmuir chain reaction, is most likely to occur in the hot, humid atmosphere of the tropics.

The second hypothesis is based on the observation that in the temperate zone all the clouds from which rain falls in big drops consist, at the higher levels, of ice crystals. In the temperate zone the ice phase is obviously a precondition for formation of rain in big drops. Just as in the case of condensation—the transition from the gaseous to the liquid stage—a condensation nucleus (dust particle) is necessary, so for the transition from the liquid to the solid phase a freezing nucleus must be present. The temperature at which the transition occurs from the liquid to the solid phase depends on the size and structure of the molecular lattice of the nucleus. The freezing nuclei effective in temperate zones generally allow a supercooling of the water droplets to $-15°C$ (5°F) before the ice formation sets in. Upon formation of the ice crystals they go on growing rapidly and in consequence fall faster and absorb additional supercooled droplets on their way down, which contribute in turn to the growth of the crystals. The more droplets that adhere to it, the faster a crystal falls and the less time remains for the formation of the crystal form, so that out of the original hexagonal crystal a shapeless, unwieldy lump of ice is formed, which melts at less than the atmospheric 0°C (32°F) limit (and so at temperatures above 0°C) and becomes a raindrop.

The adhesion of supercooled water droplets to ice crystals is considerably more effective than the process described by Langmuir. Hail is formed when as a result of strong upcurrents the grains of sleet are held in suspension longer and the ice particles become so large, owing to the adhesion of supercooled droplets, that they remain in the form of ice at temperatures of over 0°C.

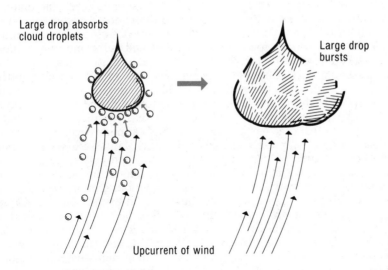

Large drop absorbs
cloud droplets

Large drop
bursts

Upcurrent of wind

Diagram 1. RAIN FORMATION, FIRST HYPOTHESIS

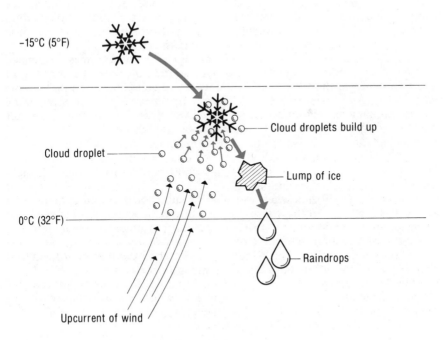

−15°C (5°F)

Cloud droplets build up

Cloud droplet

Lump of ice

0°C (32°F)

Raindrops

Upcurrent of wind

Diagram 2. RAIN FORMATION, SECOND HYPOTHESIS

FOG

Fog forms in the atmosphere close to the earth's surface when the relative moisture content reaches 100%, that is, when the vapor pressure equals or exceeds saturation point. As the physical processes of cloud formation and fog formation are identical, fog can also be described as "clouds close to the ground." The approach to saturation point and the formation of small visible drops of water can have different explanations, however, according to the different types of fog that can be distinguished:

Ground fog is the characteristic form. It forms in the evening and at night when the radiation balance of the earth is negative, that is, when outward radiation from the earth exceeds inward radiation from the sun. By day the atmosphere near the earth's surface is charged with water vapor, which because of the sharp drop in temperature at night condenses. Fog formation is intensified when, owing to a flow of cold air in the valleys, cold air accumulates or when the water content of the ground (in marshland, wet meadows, etc.) is very high. As ground fog occurs in "radiation nights" and is always associated with temperature inversion in the atmosphere near ground level, it is often referred to as "radiation fog."

Mainly in the autumn an inflow of cold air spreads across warm water or warm moist earth and gives rise to *dank fog*. As in such areas the temperature differences between cold air and warm water may amount to 10°C (50°F) or more, the surface water evaporates quickly and the water vapor condenses again immediately in the cold air. The fog so formed breaks rapidly, owing to the unstable temperature layers (warm below cold), and takes on the appearance of smoke. A similar pattern is observed in the summer over woods and roads when the sun comes out again. The water evaporates, owing to the powerful energy input on the woodland and road surfaces, and condenses again immediately in the rising air.

We speak of *mixing fog* (warm-front fog) when warm air is suspended above a layer of cold air close to the ground so that, owing to the interchange and turbulence of the water vapor, the warm air can penetrate into the cold air below it. As a result of the drop in the temperature of the mixture caused by intermingling in relation to the saturated warm air, the saturated moisture pressure will be reduced and the water vapor condensed.

Owing to thermal radiation in the atmosphere under low-lying inversions, *high-level fog* is formed. Often it extends downward and so becomes ground fog. Although other factors may contribute to its formation, high-level fog is primarily a radiation fog.

Advection fog forms when warm air of subtropical origin extends over a colder layer of air in the warm-air zone of a depression. In this case, the warm air is cooled down by a turbulent exchange from ground level upward, so that upon reaching the point of condensation, fog is formed. Such fog formation occurs only in the winter months, when the temperature differences between the subtropical and the temperate zone are substantial. In the summer the differences are too small to promote any noteworthy cooling off. Fog formation of this order also occurs when warm moist air passes over cold water surfaces. This phenomenon is common to all cold marine currents and occurs mainly in the summer.

41

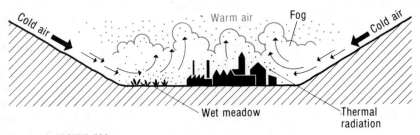

Diagram 1. GROUND FOG

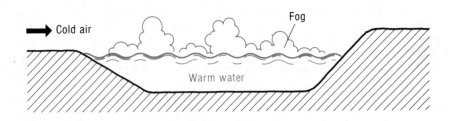

Diagram 2. DANK FOG

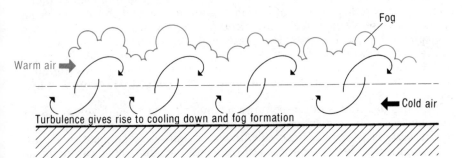

Turbulence gives rise to cooling down and fog formation

Diagram 3. MIXING FOG

EVAPORATION AND TRANSPIRATION

A large part of the water vapor present in the atmosphere is formed by the evaporation of water in areas of surface water or uncultivated ground. Under similar climatic conditions there can be considerable differences in evaporation in the two areas, insofar as the earth's surface is not well supplied with water. Evaporation from open surface water is the maximum possible and is consequently also referred to as potential evaporation, whereas actual or positive evaporation from the earth's surface over wide areas is as a rule considerably less, as the ground surface dries out rapidly and replacement of the water from deeper down is that much more difficult.

In temperate climates the rate of evaporation clearly depends on the temperature. Viewed over a complete year, the rates in winter are extremely low, rising rapidly in the spring, reaching their peak in July and August, the hot months, and falling off again in the autumn.

Evaporation also rises sharply with increases in wind velocity. This does not apply, of course, without qualification, as the temperature of the prevailing wind is also important. If the wind brings cold air, evaporation will be reduced, but if it provides heavily overheated air masses (as in the case of upcurrents), very high rates of evaporation will be achieved.

Radiation from the sun also influences the rate of evaporation. In the shade of a woodland area, for instance, evaporation will be very much less than in open meadowland.

On the mainland the evaporation from plants (transpiration) plays a special role, especially in areas of dense vegetation. Plants are able to absorb carbon dioxide because they transpire. Heavy transpiration thus points to high production; lower transpiration to restricted photosynthesic activity (see also photosynthesis discussion in Part Six).

Transpiration also depends heavily on climatic factors. But since in transpiration a living system exercises regulatory functions, not only physical laws are operative. The effect of atmospheric influences (chemical and physical elements active in the atmosphere) on transpiration cannot therefore be compared with their effect on evaporation. Wind, for example, increases transpiration in the short term; but as the wind velocity rises, a transpiration value is very quickly attained that cannot be increased any farther. Owing to the closing of the plants' stomas (openings) as they begin to fade (under the influence of increased transpiration), the transpiration rate can even fall, when exposed to long-term wind effects, below the normal level in stillness.

Under the effects of temperature a similar pattern can develop. As the temperature rises, transpiration is at first increased. But as a sharp rise in temperature is as a rule connected with water shortages, the plants will close their stomas and lower their rates of transpiration; thus their water conservation is not strained too severely.

Evaporation from the ground and the transpiration of plant life can often not be determined separately by measurement on open ground. Consequently, in order to assess the water consumption of a particular growth these two phenomena are generally treated in conjunction with one another (evapotranspiration).

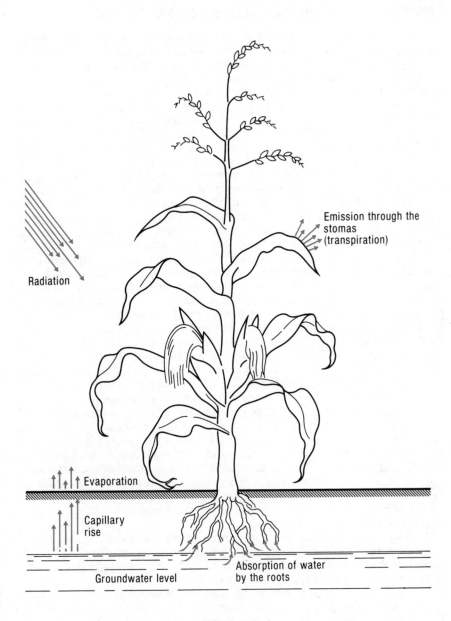

Emission through the stomas (transpiration)

Radiation

Evaporation

Capillary rise

Groundwater level

Absorption of water by the roots

EVAPOTRANSPIRATION IN THE WATER BALANCE OF PLANTS

TEMPERATURE OF THE AIR LAYER NEAR THE GROUND

A factor of far-reaching importance for the life processes in the biosphere is the temperature. The temperature, as measured by changes in the volume of mercury in a thermometer, is a reflection of the average kinetic energy in a molecule of air, which is derived essentially from the impact of solar radiation on the earth's surface. The temperature of the layer of air nearest the ground is thus determined by the extent of the solar energy radiated. This in turn is influenced by the composition of the atmosphere, the geographical latitude, the nature of the soil or rock surface, the features of the terrain, etc. The inflow of cold or hot air masses from extensive currents can change the temperature of the layer of air near the ground very substantially.

By day part of the sun's rays penetrate the atmosphere to reach the earth's surface, where some are converted into thermal radiation (infrared rays) and returned to the atmosphere. This thermal radiation is absorbed by the atmosphere, which thus becomes richer in energy, i.e., warmer. As most of the energy is imparted to the molecules nearest to the source of energy, that is, the earth, the air immediately above the ground is warmed most. In the temperate zone on a fine summer's day with no wind, temperatures of over 21°C (70°F) are recorded in the atmosphere close to the ground. The warm air close to the earth's surface is lighter in specific gravity than the cold air above it, and consequently it tends to rise. During the upward flow, the energy-rich molecules impart energy to the surrounding atmosphere, until an energy balance is achieved. Owing to the radiation of solar energy by day, a temperature gradient forms in the layer of air close to the ground. The air temperature falls as the height above the earth's surface increases. This process always occurs during radiation, but is naturally more marked when air movements are slight. Strong air movements change the temperature conditions in the layer of air near the ground considerably.

At night the thermal radiation from the soil or rock surface of the earth is no longer replenished by solar radiation. As the energy source is lacking, radiation during the night weakens progressively. Consequently the cold air descending toward the ground is not warmed up again and remains as a layer of cold air on the earth's surface. According to the nature of the terrain, the cold air will flow under the pull of gravity into depressions such as valleys, ravines and sink holes to form cold air pockets. Temperature differences of 10°C (50°F) and more between cold air pockets and the warmer zones at higher levels are by no means rare.

Clouds reduce the radiation of thermal energy considerably, by deflecting it from their underside. Sudden temperature increases of 5°C (41°F) and more are observed in the vicinity of a cloud bank. Strong winds also obstruct the formation of a temperature gradient at night.

The temperature gradient in the layer of air near the ground is consequently subject to constant reversal between day and night. The conditions that lead to the formation of these gradients can be affected by wind, by the character and structure of the terrain, and by cloud formation and other atmospheric influences.

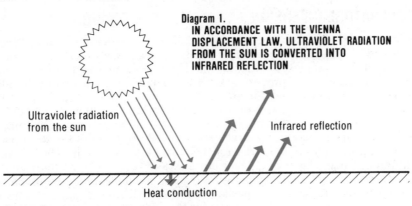

Diagram 1.
IN ACCORDANCE WITH THE VIENNA DISPLACEMENT LAW, ULTRAVIOLET RADIATION FROM THE SUN IS CONVERTED INTO INFRARED REFLECTION

Ultraviolet radiation from the sun

Infrared reflection

Heat conduction

Diagram 2.
AIR MOLECULES ARE EXPOSED TO INFRARED RADIATION AND SET IN SHARPER OSCILLATION

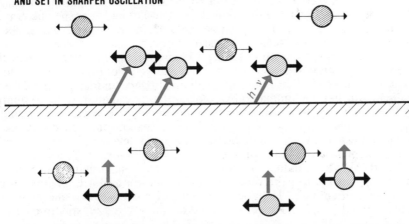

Diagram 3.
STRONG OSCILLATION OF THE AIR MOLECULES DENOTES A RISE IN TEMPERATURE. HEATED AIR RISES, WHILE COLD AIR DESCENDS, AS, OWING TO LOWER OSCILLATION ENERGY, THE AIR MOLECULES COME CLOSER TOGETHER

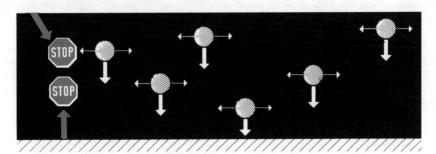

Diagram 4.
AT NIGHT TEMPERATURES IN THE ATMOSPHERE DECLINE BECAUSE THERMAL RADIATION FROM THE GROUND CEASES

TEMPERATURE INVERSION

As just stated, in the air layer on the earth's surface a temperature gradient is formed in which the temperature falls by day as the height above the earth's surface increases, whereas at night the temperature rises as the altitude increases. This process is known as temperature inversion. If in the course of the following day the ground warms up again, the night's inversion will be canceled out by the supply of energy from the ground to the cold air above it, and the normal temperature gradient will be restored. The form of such inversions depends to a large extent on the structure of the terrain and the climatic conditions and is not for the most part very stable. The situation is different when a layer of cold air flows away over a warm air mass so that an extensive inversion of temperature occurs. Such weather conditions can be very persistent, lasting for perhaps days or weeks.

The significance of the inversion for the exchange of gas in the air layer near the ground lies in the difference in specific gravity of colder and warmer gases in the same combination. Cold air heated up by the ground rises and cools. If it reaches the layer of warm air, because of its lower specific gravity any further rise of the cold air as it warms up is now checked. Thus, above the boundary layer no exchange of gas can occur.

Such thresholds create special problems for the layer of air near the ground in industrial agglomerations. The low-lying cold air is consumed in combustion processes in households, transport and industry, and the end product is further contaminated by combustion gases and dust. If no boundary layer existed, these noxious elements would be carried away into the upper atmosphere by normal dispersal processes and thereby dispersed to such an extent that there would be no immediate danger of injury to people, animals or plants. If an inversion occurs at a lower level (30–100 meters or 98–328 ft) above an industrial and housing area, the combustion products emitted are unable to penetrate the boundary layer and are retained in the lower layer of cold air. The concentrations of noxious gases and dust then increase rapidly and cause considerable damage to the biosphere (see Part Three).

In unfavorable valley regions and hollows the nightly inversion can also make itself felt in this way. That the inversion situation in valley basins is very stable is clear from the often immobile fog banks. Columns of smoke from chimneys stop at the boundary layers as if cut off; the smoke itself gathers below the boundary layer and forms great billows. If the chimney rises above the boundary layer the smoke can disperse freely. If the smoke is held down by high atmospheric moisture it will spread right across the boundary layer without penetrating it.

The frequency of such inversion situations depends on the season of the year. In summer, because of sustained and powerful solar radiation, there is very little inclination to inversion. As the days shorten, the excess of solar radiation over thermal radiation from the earth does not necessarily coincide with sunrise or sunset; and the thermal radiation may exceed solar radiation for several hours before sunset and several hours after sunrise. Solar radiation on the short winter days, thus, hardly has any effect even in fine weather, so that the frequency and duration of the inversion situation are greater in winter.

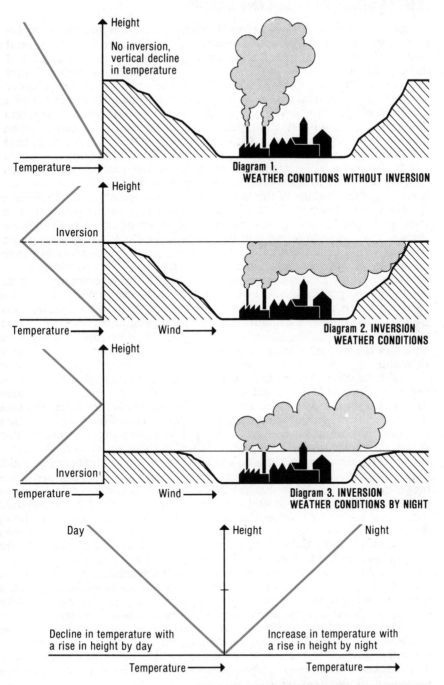

Height

No inversion,
vertical decline
in temperature

Temperature

Diagram 1.
WEATHER CONDITIONS WITHOUT INVERSION

Height

Inversion

Temperature

Wind

Diagram 2. INVERSION
WEATHER CONDITIONS

Height

Inversion

Temperature

Wind

Diagram 3. INVERSION
WEATHER CONDITIONS BY NIGHT

Day

Height

Night

Decline in temperature with
a rise in height by day

Increase in temperature with
a rise in height by night

Temperature

Temperature

Diagram 4. DIAGRAMMATIC TEMPERATURE MOVEMENT
IN THE ATMOSPHERE BY DAY AND BY NIGHT

TEMPERATURE IN THE PLANT CANOPY

Temperature conditions similar to those for bare earth also apply to open plant communities (e.g., young plantations). In extreme cases (southern slopes), when the wind is still and solar radiation on the earth's surface is at its peak, temperatures of 70°C may be attained within the canopy of leaves; that is, 20°–30°C (68°F–86°F) above the temperature of the air. Temperatures of this order damage the young seedlings at the base of the stalks, as these will not yet have developed any final heat-insulating tissue. Sometimes this results in the withering and death of the plants. Most seriously affected by this are the shoots of trees. Cultivated plants that come out mainly in the spring and autumn are rarely exposed to such extremes of temperature.

If there is a close plant canopy covering the ground, the maximum temperature likely to be reached is reduced considerably. The active surface is no longer the surface of the topsoil but the tops of the plants exposed to the sun's rays. The temperature will now be reduced by the heavy transpiration of the plants. In open communities this is not possible, as evaporation stops at once as soon as the thin layer of soil dries out, whereas on ground covered with foliage the whole of the area occupied by the roots of vegetation gives off water to the atmosphere through the plants. In a comparison between a grass plot and bare sand, under the same temperate climatic conditions the grass plot will give off nearly twice the quantity of moisture on the average for the year. Owing to the fact that in an area of plant growth, for instance, a meadow, the radiation penetrating to the soil from the upper surface of the plants drops very rapidly, the temperature distribution in the planted zone is quite different from that on surfaces with no vegetation.

Like radiation, the temperature achieves its maximum at the topmost vegetation level, and owing to the poor heat-conducting capacity of the plant parts is not imparted to the rootstock. As the height of the vegetation level increases, the maximum temperature changes. The leaf position in the vegetation is also an important factor for the level and the determination of maximum temperature. In a meadow in which the main mass of the leaves stands vertically, the rise in temperature (owing to the greater penetration range of the radiation) does not occur at one particular level but permeates the entire foliage space, so that extreme values are not attained. If the leaves in the vegetation are horizontal, the active surface of the foliage will draw together at the upper level so that the maximum temperature will be clearly determined at that point.

On clear nights the external layer of the foliage will be the radiating level (as in the case of bare ground), so that the minimum temperature will be established here, while the temperature in the vegetation will tend to rise near the ground. As a result, the temperature variations between day and night will be less marked in vegetation than in the case of bare ground. Consequently the average temperatures will be somewhat lower.

The temperature distribution in wooded areas will be determined on windless days by the distinction between an extreme crown-level climate on the active surface of the forest and a moderate trunk-level climate that is very balanced. The temperature conditions in woodland areas will also be influenced by the density of the forest. In light foliage, in which the sun's rays penetrate to the ground, there will be a second temperature maximum at that point. In dense foliage the ground temperature will correspond to that at the trunk level.

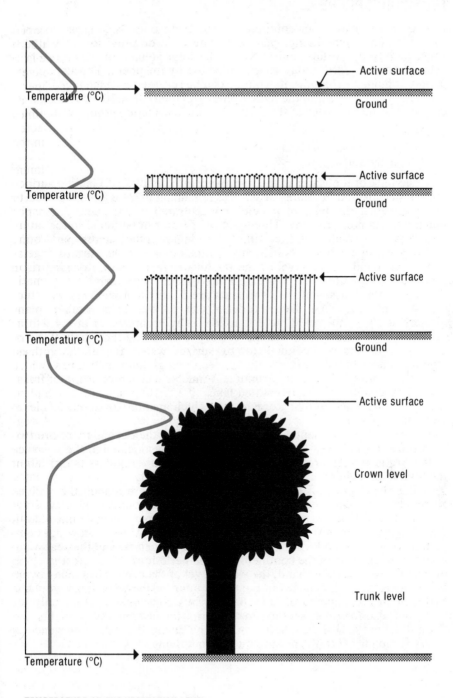

TEMPERATURE AT THE VEGETATION LEVEL

THE HYDROSPHERE

Biological processes can continue on the earth only as long as water is available. For every living system the presence or provision of water is consequently of cardinal importance. The total volume of water reserves available on the earth today is known as the hydrosphere. Throughout the period of human evolution, its volume can be regarded as unchanged.

The water present in the hydrosphere (totaling 1.4×10^{18} cubic meters) can be classified in order of size in three main distribution groups as follows:

1. The oceans
2. Water in the continental land masses
3. Water in the atmosphere

The bulk of the water in the hydrosphere (about 97.3%) is contained in the big oceans and adjoining seas. The remaining 2.7% is distributed over the continents, the bulk of it being concentrated in the giant glaciers of mountain and polar regions. The quantity of water to be found in the atmosphere is very small, not exceeding a one-hundred-thousandth part of the hydrosphere as a whole. Its influence on the climate in the various regions of the earth and on the level of the freshwater reserves on dry land is, in relation to its quantity, of the greatest importance, however.

The water masses of the continents are distributed unevenly over various storage areas. First place in order of size of the reserves is taken by the glaciers at 2.9×10^3 cubic meters, followed by groundwater at 8.4×10^{15} cubic meters. Of the total volume of groundwater reserves, only 0.066×10^{15} cubic meters is accounted for by surface water. By far the greatest amount is distributed fairly evenly between two groundwater zones, which sink to a depth of 800 meters or more. A much smaller proportion of freshwater is accounted for by rivers and lakes (0.2×10^{15} cubic meters) and by the water contained in living organisms, which amounts to about 0.0006×10^{15} cubic meters.

Besides the continental freshwater tables, in the oceans there are two big freshwater reserves—namely, the water masses located in the polar ice of the Arctic and Antarctic, which together account for no less than 1.8% of the total hydrosphere, and so are relatively important.

This distribution of the water in the hydrosphere among the various sectors has not remained unchanged throughout the course of history. Over the past two million years the ice caps of the polar regions have thawed out periodically and then frozen again. If these ice caps were to thaw out completely today, the sea level would rise by over 60 meters, and the sea would inundate large parts of the continents. In the periods of the greatest icing-up of the seas, on the other hand, the water level of the oceans has fallen by up to 140 meters. Such changes in the distribution of the water masses of the hydrosphere over the earth have had serious consequences, not only for these but also for other sectors, in the form, for instance, of droughts and flood disasters. The lithosphere can also be changed by the emergence of heavy ice loads exerting pressure on the underlying rock.

Distribution of water in the hydrosphere

Hydrosphere as a whole	1.4×10^9 cu km	
Oceans	1.3×10^9 cu km	(97.3%)
Glaciers and polar ice	2.9×10^3 cu km	
Groundwater	8.4×10^6 cu km	
Lakes and rivers	0.2×10^6 cu km	(2.7%)
Atmosphere	1.3×10^4 cu km	
Biosphere	0.6×10^3 cu km	

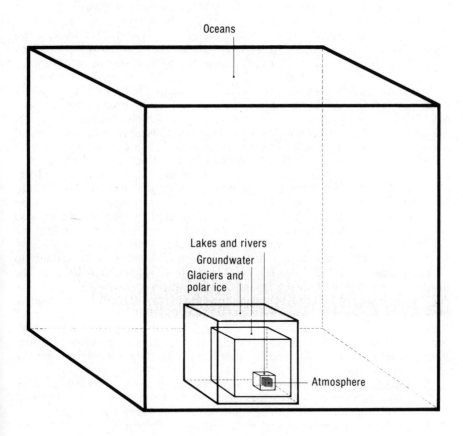

Oceans

Lakes and rivers
Groundwater
Glaciers and
polar ice

Atmosphere

WATER CIRCULATION

The three great water reservoirs of the earth—the seas, the continents and the atmosphere—are not in any sense self-contained units but are in constant communication with one another. The relationships take the form of a circulation. Under the influence of solar radiation, water is constantly vaporized and emitted into the atmosphere in the form of water vapor. This process can occur in a great variety of ways. On the one hand, water evaporates directly from the surface of seas, lakes and rivers, from glaciers and snowfields, or straight out of the ground. On the other hand, in the process of breathing, all living organisms, animals and plants alike, emit both carbon dioxide and water vapor into the atmosphere. A third process is the emission of water vapor by the combustion of organic materials such as wood, coal and oil, which are to be found all over the earth. Easily the highest proportion of vaporized water emanates directly from the oceans, however.

The water suspended in the atmosphere in the form of water vapor is of the greatest importance to the climatic conditions on earth. It conditions the composition of the air masses, exerts an influence on the energy conditions of the atmosphere, and substantially governs and sustains the water circulation.

The water content in the atmosphere is measured in terms of the relative humidity of the air. Whereas some portions of the vaporized water masses remain permanently suspended in the atmosphere in the form of moisture, others are condensed back by the cooling down of ascending airstreams and emerge in the form of clouds, fog, rain or dew. If the water cools still further, snow or hailstones may build up in the clouds. When the clouds get too heavy, precipitation begins and the moisture returns to the earth in the form of rain, snow or hail. If the precipitation goes straight into the sea or into lakes having no outlet, the water circulation will be complete. If it falls on land, some of it will accumulate by surface drainage in brooks, streams and rivers and so return to the ocean. Other forms of precipitation seep into the earth and replenish the groundwater, or if retained at an upper ground level as trap water will evaporate from there. The trap water is also available to sustain plant life, which absorbs it through its roots and returns it to the atmosphere as water vapor by respiration and transpiration.

This circulation, like all others on the earth, cannot occur in the absence of some motive force. The entire cycle is maintained by the regular inflow of solar energy. Of the total amount of energy absorbed by the earth, about one-third is utilized in maintaining the water circulation. The temperature, humidity and movement (wind) in the atmosphere together determine the level of evaporation.

Although the total volume of atmospheric moisture is very small in comparison with the total hydrosphere, owing to the circulation of the atmosphere an enormous amount of water movement takes place in the course of a year. To produce the annual precipitation on the earth of about 470,000 cubic kilometers, the water in the atmosphere (about 12,300 cubic kilometers) must be replaced 35 to 40 times a year.

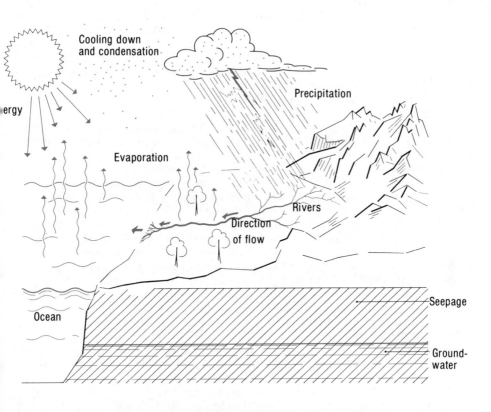

DIAGRAMMATIC PRESENTATION OF WATER CIRCULATION IN NATURE

THE SEA AND THE SEABED

The oceans cover nearly 71% of the earth's surface, or about 361 million square kilometers. This enormous volume of water is not spread evenly over the earth's surface, but varies sharply in area and depth. Three extensive oceans separate the main land masses of the American, Eurasian and African continents from one another. With an area of 180 million square kilometers the Pacific Ocean accounts for nearly half the total sea surface of the world. It is followed in size by the Atlantic Ocean with a surface area of 106 million square kilometers, and the Indian Ocean with 75 square kilometers. The other seas (Mediterranean, Black Sea, North Sea, Baltic Sea, etc.) are included in the Atlantic area.

There are also substantial differences in the matter of sea depths. The greatest known sea depths are in the Pacific Ocean, where they extend at some points to over 10,000 meters (6.2 miles), whereas the average sea depth is no greater than some 3700 meters (2.3 miles).

Near the coast the sea is generally quite shallow, and the seabed declines gently to an average depth of 200 meters (656 feet). The shallow coastal ledge surrounds almost all the coasts of the continents like a girdle. This girdle of shallow seabeds is known as the *continental shelf*. The sediment that is carried down into the sea by the rivers all the year round is deposited primarily in this area. The continental shelf is bordered by the continental margin, from which the continental slope drops away. From this point the seabed falls sharply to greater depths. This often provides gradients of 1:15 and angles of gradient of over 45°. Occasionally a vertical face is found in this region. At about 3000 to 6000 meters (1.8 to 3.7 miles) from shore the continental slopes give way gradually to the deep-sea bed. The decline to the deep-sea bed seldom occurs in the continental slope in a uniform manner, however; it is often punctuated by hollows and ravines. The deep-sea bed proper is uniform and even over wide areas. But in certain sectors the seabed is intersected by still deeper troughs, the deep-sea trenches. At these points it may drop to a depth of 7000 meters (4.3 miles) or more. Most of these deep-sea trenches are to be found on the fringe of the Pacific adjoining Asia.

In other sea regions, on the other hand, the seabed rises to form big plateaus, which cover wide areas of the oceans. These plateaus, or submarine ridges, can be likened to the mountains on the continents, though they are much more sharply delineated. The biggest known sea obstacle is the Mid-Atlantic Ridge, which stretches in the shape of an S from north to south midway across the Atlantic Ocean and roughly follows the coastline of the American continent. Such submarine ridges and plateaus play a very important part in setting the pattern of ocean currents and the exchange of waters between the individual regions of the sea.

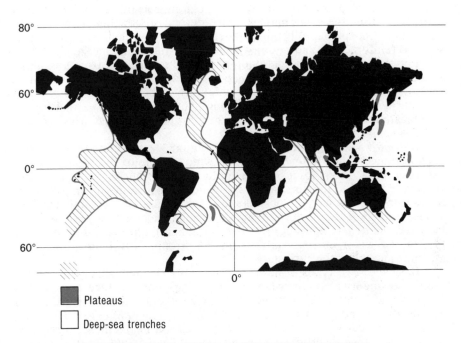

80°

60°

0°

60°

0°

■ Plateaus

□ Deep-sea trenches

Diagram 1. THE PRINCIPAL OCEANS, DEEP-SEA TRENCHES AND OCEAN PLATEAUS

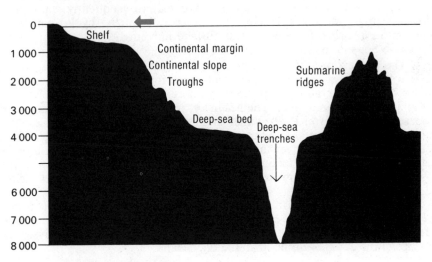

0

1 000

2 000

3 000

4 000

6 000

7 000

8 000

Shelf

Continental margin

Continental slope

Troughs

Deep-sea bed

Deep-sea trenches

Submarine ridges

Diagram 2. PROFILE OF THE SEABED

SEA CURRENTS

The water masses in the oceans are not dormant bodies but are in constant motion. If the movements of the water are on established lines they are referred to as *marine currents*. The causes of these currents are very different. The most important factors affecting marine currents are wind, density variations within the water masses, and differences in the heat flow between water and atmosphere. When these factors occur in combination they may serve to reinforce one another as well as to neutralize one another.

For the most part the direction of individual ocean currents is determined by the earth's rotation, the shape of the continents, submarine ridges, and tidal currents. Owing to the multiplicity of determining factors, any estimate of the direction of the resulting marine current is extraordinarily complicated. The velocity of the ocean currents compared with those in rivers is substantially lower.

If the wind sets the surface water in motion, the direction of the current does not necessarily follow that of the wind. Owing to the rotation of the earth and the Coriolis forces generated thereby, the currents in a particular sector are linked to the direction of the wind. In the northern hemisphere all the currents are deflected clockwise to the right, and in the southern hemisphere to the left. Since at the same time the prevailing winds are deflected likewise, the deflecting forces receive additional reinforcement. The deflection of the water currents is thus all the stronger the deeper the water columns are below the surface.

Basically, two types of marine currents are distinguished: surface currents and underwater currents. The most important surface currents are found in the equator belt between the northern and southern tropic zones. The northeast and southeast trade winds provide the motive force for these big equatorial currents. Between the individual continents these currents are diverted in their directions and deflected to the north and south. Since the Coriolis forces are intensified as the geographical latitude increases, the original current direction is gradually reversed. Consequently a powerful flow of surface currents develops. In the middle of the cycle, zones are encountered with relatively modest surface movements (for example, the Sargasso Sea in the North Atlantic).

The pattern of surface currents is roughly the same in all the oceans. The water masses that flow north and south from the equator toward the poles cool down gradually on the way, more and more rapidly as the geographical latitude increases. Their density rises in the process, so that water masses sink to a lower level as they go and eventually return to the equator as cold seabed currents. In all cases in which the wind carries off big masses of water, these must be replaced by a return flow. This happens as a result of either an influx of surface water or an influx of water from a lower level. Water masses flowing toward the poles and so becoming cooler set off the deep-water currents.

Regions in which surface currents combine to produce deep-water currents are known as convergence areas. Under the influence of surface, deep-water and seabed currents, a constant exchange of water masses develops in the course of time in all the big oceans.

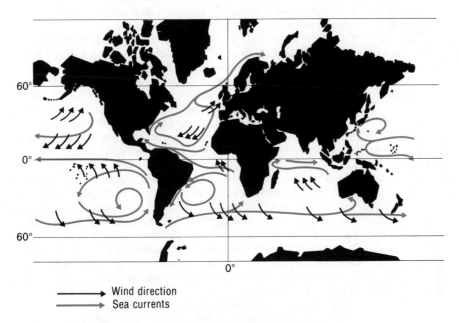

Wind direction
Sea currents

Diagram 1. THE PRINCIPAL SEA CURRENTS AND DIRECTION OF WINDS

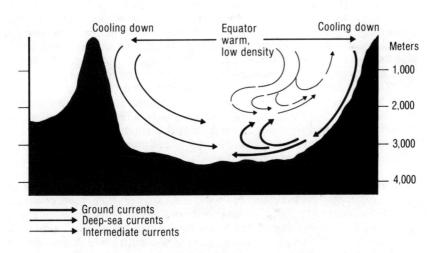

Ground currents
Deep-sea currents
Intermediate currents

Diagram 2. PRINCIPAL CURRENTS BELOW THE SURFACE (the Atlantic is taken as an example)

TIDES

The periodic alternation of ebb and flow on the seacoast is caused by forces that, in addition to wind and the earth's rotation, are exerted by the influence of sun and moon on the water masses of the oceans.

The flow of the tides is highly complicated, and varies from place to place. Since the days of Isaac Newton the attraction forces of the sun and moon have been recognized as the cause of the movement of the tides. Their influence is vastly different in strength, however, and the stronger effect must be attributed to the moon.

Two separate lunar forces have to be distinguished: the attraction power of the moon and the centrifugal force arising from the rotation of the moon and the earth (at the same point of concentration). Whereas the centrifugal force remains constant at each point of the earth's surface, the attraction force of the moon changes in inverse ratio to the square of its distance from the earth. This means that the attraction force of the moon on the side of the earth facing away from the moon is less than that on the side of the earth facing it. The result of this is a horizontal force that tends to concentrate the water masses of the earth at two specific points, of which one is directly facing the moon and the other is on the precisely opposite side of the earth. At these two points (A and B in the diagram) tidal crests are thus produced. In consequence of the earth's rotation and of lunation (the approximately 29-day period between two successive new moons) in an ideal situation, these would travel round the earth in a period exactly corresponding to the length of a lunar day (24 hours 50 minutes).

The sun too exerts tidal forces on the earth. The sun's mass is, of course, substantially greater than that of the moon, but it is also at a very much greater distance from the earth. Because of this, the tidal forces of the sun amount to only 46% of those of the moon.

The change of tidal forces in the course of a month emerges from the interplay of the forces of the sun and moon. Thus the pull from the sun and the moon reach their peak at times of full and new moon and combine to produce spring tides. In the first and last quarters of the moon the orthogonal directions of their forces are directly opposed to one another, and so lead to a reduction of the tidal forces and result in the occurrence of neap tides. Spring tides and neap tides occur twice in the course of a lunar month.

The position of the continents prevents the tides from registering ideal periodic changes and so produces many irregularities. As the vast water masses, once they are in motion, record a natural period of oscillation, the periodic changes in the tides and the natural motion of the water can overlap and so produce very complicated tidal phenomena. On occasion this can result in resonances, which will produce a maximum expansion of the tidal range (up to 14 meters), as can sometimes happen on the coast of Brittany. In tidal power plants an attempt is made to use this energy for human needs.

Apart from the tidal forces, wind and air pressure have considerable influence on the extent of the tidal variations. Thus constant wind pressures are capable of producing independent tidal ranges of about 1 meter. Storm conditions sometimes give rise to extreme anomalies which manifest themselves as storm tides.

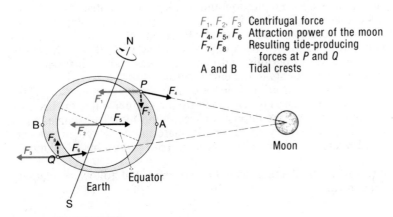

F_1, F_2, F_3 Centrifugal force
F_4, F_5, F_6 Attraction power of the moon
F_7, F_8 Resulting tide-producing
             forces at P and Q
A and B   Tidal crests

Diagram 1. TIDE FORMATION

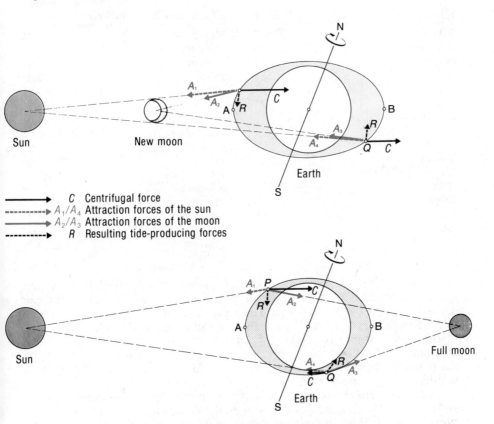

C Centrifugal force
A_1/A_4 Attraction forces of the sun
A_2/A_3 Attraction forces of the moon
R Resulting tide-producing forces

Diagram 2. CAUSATION OF SPRING TIDES BY THE INFLUENCE OF THE SUN AND MOON

COMPOSITION OF SEAWATER

Seawater is a complex solution of various salts, trace elements and gases. There is a measure of equilibrium between the input of soluble matter by the rivers, elutriation (or removal of suspended particles) from the atmosphere by rain, and the loss by precipitation and absorption of nutrients. The bulk of the soluble matter is washed into the sea through the weathering and erosion of rocks from the solid crust of the earth. Much of this matter is soon precipitated to form new rock deposits on the seabed, which become stratified over geological periods and can form new mountains again as a result of pressure movements in the earth's crust.

In shorter periods, variations can be caused in the composition of seawater by biological processes (occasioned by the temperature, for instance) and today in particular by the deposit of waste and toxic substances in the sea. In general, the quantity of inorganic material dissolved in seawater amounts to 35 grams per kilogram of water. This represents a solution of 3.5%.

To come down to details, seawater contains the following elements (average concentration):

SUBSTANCE	Concentration (milligrams per liter)	SUBSTANCE	Concentration (milligrams per liter)
sodium	10,600	aluminum	0.01
chlorine	18,990	lithium	0.18
magnesium	1,350	barium	0.05
sulfur	885	iodine	0.05
calcium	400	phosphorus	0.0001–0.1
potassium	390	arsenic	0.003
carbon (as carbonates and carbon		iron	0.002–0.02
dioxide)	23–28	manganese	0.001–0.01
strontium	8.1	copper	0.001–0.01
bromine	65	zinc	0.005–0.01
boron	4.6	lead	0.00003
silicon	0.02–4	selenium	0.00009
fluorine	1.5	cesium	0.0004
nitrogen	0.02–0.8	uranium	0.003
rubidium	0.12	silver	0.0003
		thorium	0.00005

Most of these elements are present in seawater in the form of salts, and a smaller portion in the form of dissolved gases. The most important of these are oxygen and carbon dioxide. The oxygen content fluctuates between 0 and 8.5 milliliters per liter. The high concentrations occur near the surface of the water, where the oxygen is in equilibrium with the oxygen in the atmosphere. A second source of the oxygen dissolved in the sea comes from the photosynthesis of phytoplankton, the drifting oceanic plant life. At great depths it may happen that (owing to the intense activity of bacteria and animals that absorb oxygen) the oxygen content of the seawater falls to zero. In many places, however, owing to the downward trend of the convection currents, a large quantity of dissolved oxygen from the surface water is carried to considerable depths in the sea.

An important part is played by carbon dioxide gas, which is present in considerable quantities in seawater. Since the basic ions of sodium, potassium and calcium are also present in large quantities in seawater, this facilitates the solution of a relatively high percentage of carbon dioxide. Carbon dioxide is one of the basic substances for photosynthesis (see Part Six). The plants living in the sea (especially plankton) take the carbon dioxide they need for photosynthesis directly out of the surrounding water. The second important effect of carbon dioxide in seawater is its function as a buffer (dissolved matter which keeps the pH value of the solution practically constant over wide areas). Normally the pH value of seawater lies between 7.5 and 8.4. As carbon dioxide and its associated marine chemicals are in equilibrium, the pH value of seawater is approximately constant as regards the input of both acids and bases.

The other gases from the atmosphere are dissolved in seawater in much lower concentrations than oxygen and carbon dioxide. The concentrations are as follows:

SUBSTANCE	Concentration (milligrams per liter)	SUBSTANCE	Concentration (milligrams per liter)
nitrogen	between 8.4 and 15	argon	0.6
helium	0.000005	krypton	0.0003
neon	0.0001	xenon	0.00005

A particular phenomenon is the enrichment of seawater by trace elements that occur in considerable concentrations in living organisms. An example is provided by the ascidian (a tunicate), a small, mostly clinging animal that increases the element vanadium in seawater up to 50,000 times its normal concentration. It is known today that many other trace elements such as iodine, arsenic, nickel, zinc, titanium, chromium and strontium are also very much increased in the water by decaying organisms. Certain fish are known to contribute chromium, nickel, silver, tin and zinc. Similarly, some of the substances produced by humans get into the sea as waste substances. As such a buildup of substances in the food web takes some time, the damage caused by them is often not noted until too late. The increase of chlorinated hydrocarbons, for instance (especially pesticides such as DDT), reaches its maximum concentration in fish only after a period of 11 years from its production.

Also of great importance in its effects on life in the sea is the content of ammonium compounds, nitrates and phosphates. As these are absorbed by plants to build up their bodies, their content in seawater varies considerably according to the presence of plant life. The following concentrations in seawater have been established:

SUBSTANCE	Concentration (milligrams per liter)	SUBSTANCE	Concentration (milligrams per liter)
ammonia	0.4–50	organically combined nitrogen	30–200
nitrate	1–600	phosphates	1–100
nitrous oxide (particularly NO_2)	0–15	organically combined phosphorus	1–30

THE SEA AND ITS TEMPERATURE

Like the mainland and inland waters, the oceans of the world are also subject to seasonal temperature variations. In the sea, however, these changes
are more limited. This is due to the water circulation that takes place constantly within the oceans, coupled with the extremely high specific heat of
salt water and the capacity that goes with it for storing energy. Except in
the shallow shelf that surrounds the continents, the temperatures in the seas
are consequently very uniform. In low geographical latitudes on each side
of the equator, temperatures of up to 30°C (86°F) are recorded in the surface
waters, while in shallow and enclosed waters they may rise in coastal regions to as high as 50°C (122°F). Except in extreme cases the temperature
variations between the coldest and warmest areas are in the 30°–35°C (54°–
63°F) range. In polar regions and in equatorial waters the temperatures over
the year remain remarkably uniform. As for deep-sea water, a constant
water temperature can be assumed in all the oceans. The lowest temperatures are to be found in polar sea regions, where they can come close to the
freezing point of seawater (−1.9°C, or 28°F).

Whereas in the lower latitudes seawater absorbs warmth from the atmosphere, at higher latitudes it emits warmth into it. The cooling of the
water surface caused in this way leads to the formation of convection currents, which results in the intermingling of the water masses and the equali-
zation of temperature between surface and deep water. This phenomenon
arises from the fact that seawater (salt content 35‰) attains its maximum
density at −3.5°C, or 25.7°F (compared with 4°C, or 39°F, for pure water).
In this respect seawater behaves quite differently from freshwater. It freezes
on cooling before it reaches its maximum density. From this it follows that
no stable temperature stratification takes place in winter or in arctic regions,
as in the case of freshwater, but that the intermingling in the sea is not
interrupted. The heat accumulated in seawater is emitted into the atmosphere as the water cools, not as in freshwater where below a shallow
surface layer the water maintains a constant temperature of 4°C (39°F). It is
from this property that the sea acquires its importance in moderating the
climate.

Because of its lower specific gravity, at lower latitudes the warm surface water cannot promote convection currents. This gives rise to considerable drops in temperature between the surface and deep-water levels and to
the development of so-called boundary surfaces between the two layers,
which occur at depths of 100–500 meters (328–1640 feet). In temperate
latitudes a seasonal change takes place in the formation of convection currents and boundary surfaces. During the summer months, when the surface
water is warmed by increased solar radiation, the boundary surfaces form at
a depth of 15–40 meters (49–131 feet). In the autumn, when the water is
gradually cooling off, the boundary surfaces disappear and convection currents build up.

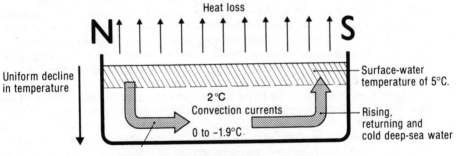

Heat loss

N ↑↑↑↑↑↑↑↑↑↑ S

Uniform decline in temperature

Surface-water temperature of 5°C.

2°C
Convection currents
0 to −1.9°C

Rising, returning and cold deep-sea water

Sinking, cooling heavier water

Diagram 1. CIRCULATION PATTERN IN THE HIGHER LATITUDES

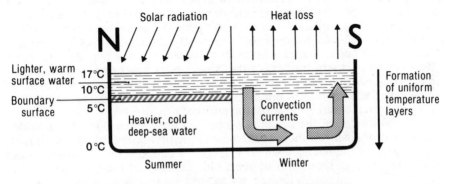

Solar radiation   Heat loss

N ///// ↑↑↑↑↑ S

Lighter, warm surface water — 17°C
10°C
Boundary surface — 5°C

Heavier, cold deep-sea water

Convection currents

Formation of uniform temperature layers

0°C

Summer   Winter

Diagram 2. CIRCULATION CONDITIONS IN THE TEMPERATE ZONES

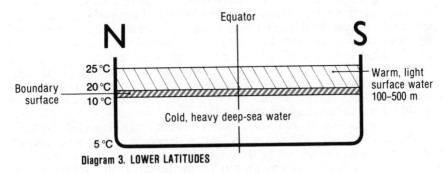

Equator

N   S

25°C
Boundary surface — 20°C
10°C

Warm, light surface water 100–500 m

Cold, heavy deep-sea water

5°C

Diagram 3. LOWER LATITUDES

Diagrams 1—3. FORMATION OF CONVECTION CURRENTS AND BOUNDARY SURFACES

INLAND WATERS

Inland waters owe their origin to precipitation and thus form part of the water circulation of the hydrosphere. Distinctions are drawn between underground and surface waters, and between flowing and static waters. In contrast to flowing waters, static waters (lakes, pools, etc.) accumulate large quantities of precipitated moisture; also, in static waters the volume of water is renewed, often not noticeably, by inflow and outflow of water over extended periods.

Lakes are big, enduring expanses of water without direct links with the sea. They are dotted about in all the continents in a quite arbitrary fashion. In terms of the world's historical span they are still very recent developments. According to their origin, four principal types are distinguished. *Tectonic lakes* were formed by subsidence and settlement and had their origin in the Tertiary period. To this type of lake belong Lake Tanganyika and Lake Baikal in the USSR. Typical of the tectonic lake is its great depth and, because of its age, the unhindered further development of the Tertiary animals that inhabit it. The formation of *dammed lakes* is often due to the action of glaciers or volcanoes; landslides too may lead to their creation. To them belong some of the lakes of North America and the lakes in northern Germany. *Glacier clearance lakes* are mostly the result of glacial erosion. They include corrie (cirque) lakes in mountain regions and the big valley lakes on the northern borders of the Alps. *Crater lakes* and *lunar lakes* are volcanic in origin. Crater lakes occupy the craters of extinct volcanoes, and lunar lakes accumulate in craters caused by subterranean gas explosions. They are often circular in shape and mostly fairly deep.

A knowledge of the origin of lakes is of great importance to an understanding of their form, their heat balance, the organisms that breed in them and in general the life they support. Lakes of glacial origin are hardly more than a few tens of thousands of years old, and most of them are much more recent. Their existence is limited in time, as they tend to fill with organic and inorganic sediment. From the stratification of the sediment, conclusions can be drawn regarding their age and the biological processes of earlier periods.

Running waters are in general considerably more difficult to classify than lakes. Here we are concerned with gullies and the surface water they carry away. Rivers have their origin in springs, groundwater outlets, and lakes. The water movement always follows the line of the underlying terrain and, except in closely confined regions, is very turbulent on the riverbed. The velocity of flow depends on the gradient, on the volume of water carried, and on the average width of the outlet channel. As all these factors change constantly from the source of a river to its mouth, the character of the river is subject to constant variation.

In the upper reaches of rivers, rock is constantly eroded, and this leads to regressive weathering of valley declivities, deepening of the watercourse, and the removal of solid matter. In the middle and lower reaches there is a sedimentation zone in which the eroded matter gradually settles and in course of time fills the riverbed. There the coarse rubble which is carried, sliding and rolling down, tends to accumulate. As the pulling force of water declines, its volume increases and its turbulence diminishes. The finer and finest particles it carries float about in the water and are carried farthest by the current. Much of it does not settle before reaching the river mouth or being carried out to sea. Owing to the heavy precipitation, the valley fills and the flow of water is arrested.

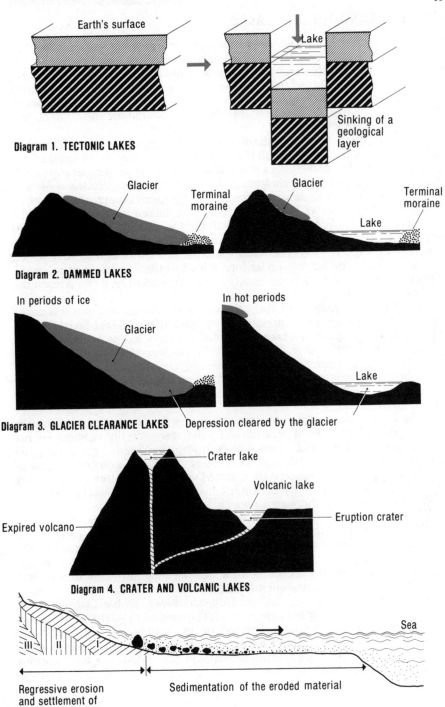

Diagram 1. TECTONIC LAKES

Earth's surface

Lake

Sinking of a geological layer

Glacier

Terminal moraine

Glacier

Terminal moraine

Lake

Diagram 2. DAMMED LAKES

In periods of ice

Glacier

In hot periods

Lake

Diagram 3. GLACIER CLEARANCE LAKES   Depression cleared by the glacier

Crater lake

Volcanic lake

Eruption crater

Expired volcano

Diagram 4. CRATER AND VOLCANIC LAKES

Sea

Regressive erosion and settlement of the ground (I/II/III)

Sedimentation of the eroded material

Diagram 5. STRUCTURE OF A WATERCOURSE

PHYSICAL CONDITIONS IN LAKES

Certain characteristics of water are responsible for the physical conditions prevailing in lakes. The most important of these is the density phenomenon. The density of the water depends on temperature, pressure, and the concentration of matter dissolved in it. As the quantity of dissolved matter (which in inland waters other than salt lakes is normally less than 1 gram per liter of water) rises, the density increases. Minor differences in the salt content give rise in static waters to the formation of stable layers.

Of great importance are the density variations caused by changes in temperature, as they in turn lead to changes in the specific volume of the water. In normal circumstances water achieves its maximum density at 4°C (39.2°F). Above and below that value its density declines. Between 24° and 25°C (75° and 77°F) the density difference is 30 times greater than between 4° and 5°C (39.2° and 41°F). This feature is explained by the asymmetrical structure of the water molecule, in which the two positively charged hydrogen atoms do not form a straight angle with the doubly charged oxygen atom, but an angle of 109°. The water molecule is consequently a very strong electrical dipole. Its strong dipole forces lead to the formation of molecule clusters, which then require unusually large amounts of heat to increase the molecular motion in the water.

For the living things in a lake, the density phenomenon in the water— that is to say, the density maximum above freezing point—is of basic importance. The deep layers in a lake cannot fall in cold seasons below 4°C. This means that a lake can freeze only from the surface downward. A sheet of ice on the surface hinders freezing at lower levels, since, like ice, water has very low heat conductivity. Lakes of sufficient depth can thus never freeze completely, and this provides a safeguard for the survival of the plant and animal life in them.

The heat balance of a lake is conditioned by the absorption, distribution and emission of heat. Heat is acquired by the absorption of radiated energy (particularly longwave radiation). The heat absorbed can be given off again into the environment by thermal radiation, evaporation and the outflow of surface water. Heat can also be transmitted to the lower water levels. Owing to the low heat conductivity of water, this occurs almost exclusively as a result of movement of the warmer water.

The motive force for this movement is provided by the wind. Wind produces a surface current that is deflected downward at the bank of the lake, so that the penetration of the surface current in depth depends on the speed and direction of the wind and on the temperature of the surface water: the higher the temperature, the less the effect of the surface current. Periodic seasonal changes consequently occur in the heat distribution of a lake. In the summer with its high temperature conditions, stable thermal layers develop. The same thing happens in winter, owing to the density phenomenon. In the spring and autumn, because of the cooling and warming of the water, the total water mass of a lake goes into circulation. Consequently references are often made to winter and summer stagnation and to spring and autumn circulation.

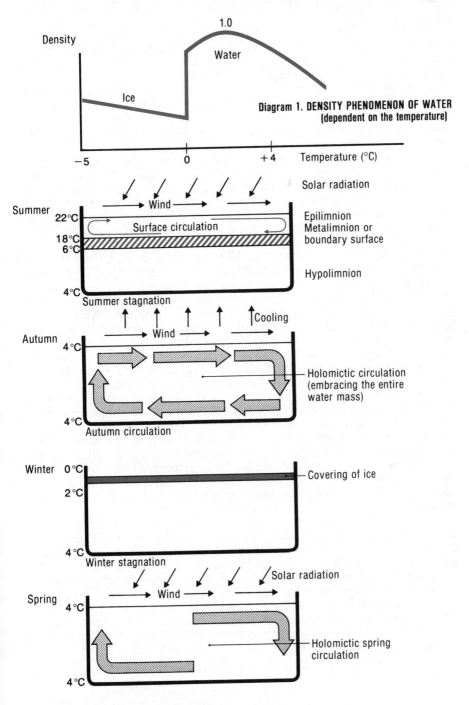

Diagram 1. DENSITY PHENOMENON OF WATER
(dependent on the temperature)

Diagram 2. HEAT BALANCE OF A DIMICTIC SEA TYPE
(northern Europe and Asia and North America)

TEMPERATURE CONDITIONS AND GAS CONTENT IN FLOWING AND STATIC WATERS

In contrast to lake water, in which alternating periods of stagnation and full circulation occur, river water is in continuous movement. In rivers, as in lakes, the heat balance depends on solar radiation and its emission again from the earth, on evaporation, and on the exchange of heat with the substratum and with the atmosphere. For rivers, however, the exchange of heat with the air is of even greater importance. According to their water volume, running waters display a rhythmic change between maximum and minimum temperatures that is connected with the daily rhythm of radiation from the sun. This change is most pronounced in the summer. The production of the maximum temperatures is determined by the intensity of the sun's rays. During the day the water is warmed by solar radiation, and at night the river emits heat and cools. The cooling and warming seem, because of the movement (flow), to be differentiated in space. The daily variation in the temperature at any particular point on a river is thus influenced by a point farther up. From the spring onward the rivers carry warmth downstream from the source, so their average temperature rises gradually until well into the summer. This increase is of course subject to the daily variations in temperature.

Of the gases dissolved in the water, only oxygen and carbon dioxide play an important role. Other gases, such as nitrogen and hydrogen sulfide, have only a local effect in the metabolism of particular microorganisms. The spatial distribution of the gases dissolved in the waters results largely from an interplay of thermal and wind influences on the water, and to a lesser extent from current movements and disturbances in the water flow. The molecular diffusion of dissolved substances proceeds much too slowly in water to be of any importance to the distribution of substances.

The solubility of the gases depends on pressure and temperature. Oxygen, the concentration of which in water declines as the temperature rises, comes partly from absorption from the atmosphere and partly as a result of photosynthesis by vegetation in the waters. Owing to the respiration of aquatic animals, the decomposition of organic substances, and losses into the atmosphere as a result of heating, it is extensively or completely removed. In lakes with full circulation the total volume of water has an approximately uniform concentration of oxygen. In stagnant water, however, there can be sharp vertical concentration differences.

Carbon dioxide is highly soluble, as it can combine with water to form carbonic acid gas and with cations to form carbonates. It comes partly from the atmosphere, from rainfall and from groundwater; in addition, substantial quantities are produced by the metabolic activities of animals and of reducing bacteria. The reduction in the carbon dioxide content of water occurs above all else as a result of heating and of photosynthesis, which take place primarily in the upper water layer in which water plants live. At lower levels, on the other hand, the carbon dioxide is increased by the activity of the reducing bacteria. The highest concentration of carbon dioxide is found mostly on the bed of the lake or river.

Diagram 1. REGIONAL AND TEMPORAL SHIFTS IN THE TEMPERATURE OF A RIVER (related to a particular volume) IN SUMMER

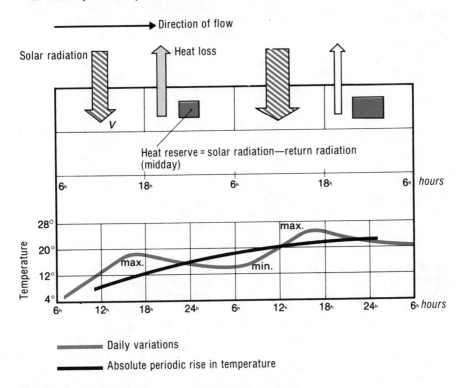

Daily variations

Absolute periodic rise in temperature

Diagram 2. DIURNAL VARIATION IN O_2 IN A STRETCH OF THE RIVER

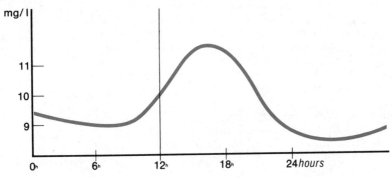

CO_2-lime equilibrium:

$$Ca(HCO_3)_2 \underset{\text{with a } CO_2 \text{ surplus}}{\overset{\text{with a } CO_2 \text{ deficiency}}{\rightleftarrows}} CaCO_3 + \boxed{CO_2}\uparrow + H_2O$$

CHEMICAL CONDITIONS IN INLAND WATERS

In contrast to seawater, freshwater contains mainly carbonates, among which calcium carbonate occupies a leading position. Nitrates and silicates are also found in inland waters in considerable quantities. Iron, manganese and ammonium compounds are present, together with trace elements in lower concentrations.

Contrary to the case with gases, the solubility of solid substances increases as the temperature rises and quite independently of the pressure prevailing. Most of the substances found in water are dissolved as molecules or are in the form of ions. But there are also some important inorganic and organic substances that are present in water only in colloidal form—that is, in a state of extremely fine suspension. These include, for example, humic acid, silicic acid, and hydrate aggregates of ferric oxide.

Chloride and nitrate are particularly soluble. Carbonates of the principal alkaline-earth metals (magnesium and calcium) and hydrate aggregates of some of the heavy metals are soluble to only a limited extent. Compounds of nitrogen are present as nitrates, nitrites, and ammonium and in organic form as intermediate stages of proteolysis (the breakdown of proteins to simpler substances), and in free compounds (amino acids). Nitrates and ammonium compounds are thus the most important sources of nitrogen for green plants.

Phosphorus normally appears, in the form of organic phosphorus compounds, only as traces. Phosphorus can be supplied to lakes and rivers by the erosion of phosphoric rocks (apatite) and soil. Dissolved phosphates do not pass into the water from natural, untreated soil, as they are firmly combined with this. As a rule three phosphate fractions are present in inland waters alongside one another: as dissolved material of inorganic origin, as dissolved material of organic origin, and as organically combined phosphate (organisms and metabolism products). The phosphate fraction in inland waters is subject to a diverse biological metabolism. Phosphates derived from organic remains are normally deposited as iron phosphate in sediments, as this is not soluble in the presence of oxygen. In the complete absence of oxygen the trivalent iron is reduced again to bivalent, and iron phosphate is dissolved. In fully circulating waters, therefore, the phosphate is not evenly distributed, but is retained in considerable quantities in the sediment and so is largely withdrawn from the circulation of matter. Only when sulfides are still present in the sediment can phosphate also be dissolved under the influence of oxygen, as the iron phosphate is reduced by sulfide.

Sulfur occurs in inorganic compounds in water mainly in the form of sulfate. It can thus be absorbed directly from the green plants. Hydrogen sulfide, which is produced by albumin replacement, is oxidized to sulfur by molecular oxygen. A further chemical process, in which bacteria are involved, is the formation of sulfides, primarily from iron sulfide in the sediment.

Owing to its low solubility, iron is to be found in the water in comparatively small quantities. Compounds of trivalent iron are almost completely insoluble. It is mostly bivalent iron that is present in solution. The presence of humic acid hinders the precipitation of iron from the hydrous solution. Necessary prerequisites for the dissolution of iron are an oxygen saturation of less than 50%, the presence of abundant free dissolved carbon dioxide and of decomposable organic substances, together with a pH value below

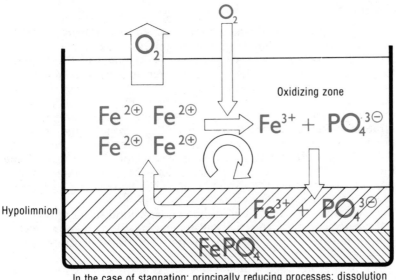

In the case of stagnation: principally reducing processes; dissolution of the iron and phosphates out of the sediment

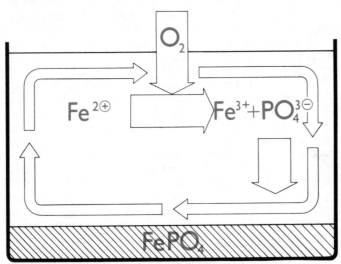

In the case of full circulation: mainly oxidation reactions, precipitation of the iron and phosphate in the sediment

IRON-PHOSPHATE REACTION IN A LAKE WITH A CHANGE OF STAGNATION AND CIRCULATION PERIODS

7.5. These conditions are satisfied in stagnant water. During full circulation, iron first combines with oxygen and eventually is precipitated in the form of iron hydroxide.

GROUNDWATER

A large part of the precipitated water (rain, snow, dew, etc.) sinks into the ground and supplements the underground water reserves. To be specific, two forms of subterranean water supplies can be distinguished: water that percolates through from the surface, and groundwater proper. Where the rainfall is light, the precipitation penetrates by seepage only into the upper strata and remains suspended in the highest levels. This is particularly evident when the ground consists of peat or other very clayey material. The highest stratum is then described as a water-retentive zone. If the precipitation is greater or the subsoil is very sandy or gritty, the seepage water penetrates the upper strata and joins the groundwater. In the lower-lying underground strata the seepage water spreads mostly over an impenetrable rock layer and so provides the groundwater. The water-carrying ground layers are described as groundwater layers.

Particularly rich in groundwater are the underground strata of sand and grit, which mostly emanate from the Pleistocene epoch, as many small fissures open up between the individual soil particles; these fissures can be filled with water.

Connecting lines between groundwater levels of the same size are commonly described as groundwater equivalents. From these it is seen that the groundwater is in constant interchange with the rivers. As a general rule the groundwater level is higher than the neighboring riverbed. The groundwater layer follows the line of the riverbed, though considerably more slowly, as the river flows downstream, and forms a reservoir for the river; when the river water level is low it is replenished from the groundwater, and when the water level is high it releases surplus water to the groundwater reserves.

In dry regions the groundwater lies considerably deeper than in wet regions. The seepage-water zone contains only ground moisture and as occasion offers also groundwater, which overcomes the force of gravity to rise by capillary attraction. As a result of the evaporation of the capillary waters on the surface, the minerals dissolved in the water are precipitated as salt and gypsum at or in the highest level.

In the bedrock a distinction can be made between quarry water and groundwater. Quarry water seeps through small hollow "reamers," or holes, in the bedrock, and serves gradually to enlarge them by physical and chemical processes. The chemical processes are particularly marked with a salt and gypsum subsoil or a limestone rock, owing to the high carbon dioxide content of the seepage water. Ground-stratum water is found primarily in sedimentary rock such as sandstone and loess. If impermeable strata are above or below, big subterranean water systems can be formed that can be tapped by artesian wells.

As a rule, groundwater is very rich in soluble matter. The concentration depends on the duration of the subterranean flow of water, the temperature, the solubility and composition of the rocks. Owing to the usually low oxygen content, oxidation processes occur in these layers only to a limited extent, so that the solubility of many compounds is retained. If such waters come again to the surface to be combined with oxygen, the dissolved compounds will be precipitated as oxides.

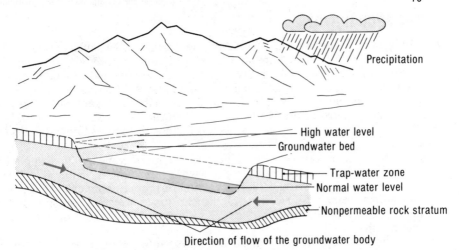

Precipitation

High water level
Groundwater bed
Trap-water zone
Normal water level
Nonpermeable rock stratum

Direction of flow of the groundwater body

Diagram 1. GROUNDWATER AND RIVERS

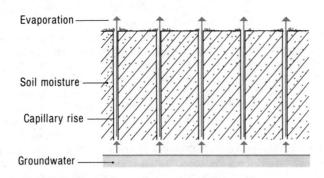

Evaporation

Soil moisture

Capillary rise

Groundwater

Diagram 2. GROUNDWATER IN DRY REGIONS

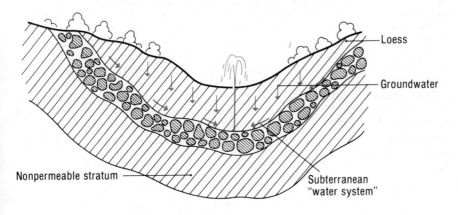

Loess

Groundwater

Nonpermeable stratum

Subterranean
"water system"

Diagram 3. FORMATION OF ARTESIAN WELLS

THE PEDOSPHERE

The ground covering the surface of the earth consists of loose and solid stone and rock and of humus. Changes of temperature, the freezing and thawing of water in rock fissures, and the dissolving and crystallization of salts reduce the rock to such an extent that loose weathering products result. Under the influence of weathering elements such as oxygen, carbon dioxide and water, many minerals on the upper surface so created are subject to chemical erosion, as a result of which further decomposition products are formed.

The layer of weather-worn material so created comes to be occupied by lower- and higher-order organisms, by whose exudations and intake of mineral nutrients the decomposition is carried further. Excrement, dead plants, and animal remains form the organic substance which is decomposed by microorganisms and other soil-dwellers into carbon dioxide or transmuted into humus.

The outcropping geological seams are thus reconverted into soil by weathering and new clay formation, the decomposition of organic matter and humus formation, and the transposition of soil components (by wind or water). The soil is thus a very complicated dynamic system in which physical, chemical and biological processes are interwoven.

The pedosphere is no precisely demarcated zone, but it passes gradually into the other zones and is in turn infiltrated by them. The pedosphere is a meeting ground for air from the atmosphere, water from the hydrosphere, minerals from the lithosphere, and, with the settling of the products of weathering, the organisms of the biosphere. All the soil-formation processes are governed directly by the spheres designated and so do not represent systems that are alien to the land but pertain directly to the pedosphere.

In contrast to chemically defined substances, the ground components constitute a three-phase system consisting of a solid element (mineral), a fluid element (water) and a gaseous element (ground air), which are in a state of constant flux. The parent rock with its different grain sizes, newly formed clay minerals, and salts belongs to the inorganic component of the ground. Living organisms such as bacteria, fungi, worms and mites belong, like the roots of plants and dead organic matter (which consists of plant remains and dead microorganisms and other ground life), to the organic components of the ground. A distinction is drawn between mineral soils, which are formed from rocks and stone, and organic soils (peat) which come exclusively from dead organic substances.

The soil is the breeding ground for plants and offers living space to a number of ground animals, as we will see. The plants draw from it their needed nutrients, water and oxygen. In return, from the roots of the plants the earth draws carbon dioxide and absorbs their waste substances. These properties are combined in the term *soil fertility*. This finds different expressions in the variety of the soil-forming processes and it can be influenced by human activities.

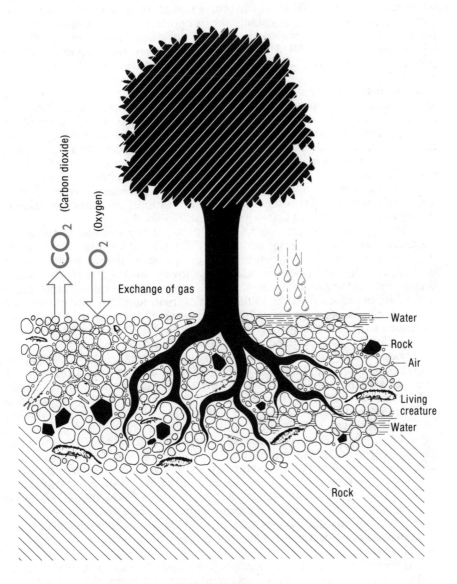

THE PEDOSPHERE

AIR IN THE GROUND

The ground volume is made up of the three components of mineral elements, water and ground air. Whereas the proportion of the mineral elements to the total volume is broadly constant, the proportions of air and water vary inversely in relation to one another. When the ground is dry, practically the whole void volume is filled with air, whereas when the ground is wet the proportion of air varies, according to the nature of the ground, between 0% and 40%.

Air in the soil consists roughly of the same components as air in the atmosphere. The proportions the components bear to one another, however, often differ considerably from those in the atmosphere. This is particularly true of carbon dioxide and oxygen. Whereas the proportions of oxygen and carbon dioxide in the atmosphere are practically constant, in air in the soil they vary at ground level considerably, the variations in the oxygen content exceeding those in the carbon dioxide content. The respiration of animals in the soil and of plant roots consumes oxygen and produces carbon dioxide. The respiration of roots accounts for about a third of the carbon dioxide in the ground, and bacterial activity for about two-thirds.

Owing to the different composition of air in the soil and in the atmosphere, an exchange of gases occurs by diffusion between the two sectors. The partial pressure of oxygen in the atmosphere is always higher than in the soil, and that of carbon dioxide always lower, so that a diffusion current sets in toward the ground in the case of oxygen and toward the atmosphere in the case of carbon dioxide. In the event of frost, humidity or condensation on the earth's surface, there will be restrictions on the exchange of gas and increase of the carbon dioxide within the ground. When that happens, the carbon dioxide content of the ground air may rise to as high as 5%.

The humidity of air in the ground is usually greater than in the atmosphere. The moisture fluctuations in the ground are not so sharply marked; as a result of the rapid drying out of surface air that is sometimes possible, differences can arise in the humidity above and below the surface. The moisture content below the surface will hardly ever fall below 95% relative humidity, however.

The generation of carbon dioxide in the soil and the resulting consumption of oxygen are strongly influenced by temperature and humidity, so that daily and seasonal variations occur. At warm seasons of the year humidity is the decisive factor determining the generation of carbon dioxide, while in cold weather it is the temperature. At temperatures below 0°C (32°F) and in conditions of severe dryness, the generation of carbon dioxide comes practically to a standstill. Excess moisture, on the other hand, supplants the oxygen need of plant roots and microorganisms and so checks the generation of carbon dioxide.

Between ground air and atmosphere a high rate of exchange of gases and consequently good ventilation are necessary if living things are to survive. Ventilation is determined largely by the proportion of large-pore (macropore) volume to the total pore volume; the low frictional resistance to airflow offered by macropores makes a major contribution to the ventilation of the ground. Heavy soils (clay soils) with excessively fine pores thus suffer poor ventilation, while light ones (sandy soils) with predominantly large pores are well ventilated. As the depth below the surface increases, the exchange of gas is slowed by the frictional resistance, so that the carbon dioxide content of the ground air increases.

Poor ventilation has an unfavorable effect on plants and soil. If there is

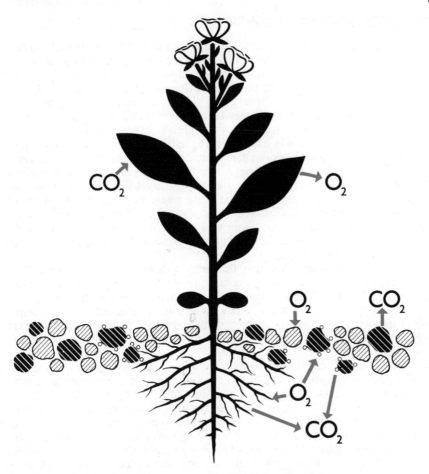

Diagram 1. EXCHANGE OF GASES BETWEEN ATMOSPHERE AND GROUND

Diagram 2. EXPULSION OF GROUND AIR BY WATER

a shortage of oxygen, the root growth of plants will be hindered, the nutritional and water intake reduced thereby, and the entire growth reduced. The anaerobic microorganisms (those that live predominantly in the absence of free oxygen) then drive out their aerobic counterparts. Putrefaction processes set in, the effects of which extend to the plant roots. Products from the putrefaction processes such as methane, organic acids and hydrogen sulfide are poisonous to the taller plants.

THE IMPORTANCE OF GROUNDWATER

The main sources of groundwater are precipitation and underground (phreatic) water. The water delivered by precipitation penetrates the ground or, when more water falls than the earth can absorb or pass on, flows off as surface water. In ground that consists of coarse particles and thus has big pores, the water penetrates rapidly and sinks into a porous stratum. In this way salts are dissolved in the upper layer of earth and build up in the lower layer. Those particularly involved are sulfates, chlorides and carbonates, some of which are valuable as fertilizers. Salts that do not dissolve easily, such as calcium and magnesium carbonate, can nevertheless be dissolved in seepage water and washed away. According to the quantity of the rainfall and the strength and nature of the ground, the salts dissolved will sink into the underground water and leave the solid phase or form so-called enrichment layers lower down. Displacements of clay and humus particles by the seepage water are found inter alia in acid soil. This leads to the formation of clay and humus enrichment layers below ground and corresponding impoverishment of the upper layers.

When water evaporates from the earth's surface, groundwater will rise to the upper layers and also evaporate. Its salts are deposited and, as the concentration rises, salt and calcium crusts are formed on the earth's surface. In the temperate climatic zones these phenomena are of minor importance, however, as water movements in the ground in zones under oceanic influences are determined by the heavy rainfall and are mostly from above downward.

Strata that are highly impervious to water, such as clay soils and rubble, impede the downward movement of the seepage water, so that water tends to accumulate. If the concentration continues for any length of time it is described as groundwater, but if the phenomenon is transient it is known as tail water. Underground static or tail water forces the ground air out of the pores. Oxygen is consequently removed from the iron and manganese compounds in this region; it is chemically reduced and so becomes easily soluble in water. Because of their molecular motion, dissolved compounds are distributed over the entire space occupied by the solvent. This diffusion results in the removal of the iron and manganese compounds. If the groundwater level declines or the tail water dries up, the oxygen concentration will build up again and iron or manganese will be deposited as oxide or hydroxide.

The microbial decomposition and restructuring of organic substance from the remains of plants or animals in the ground is effected mainly by bacteria, the activity of which is determined ultimately by the water supply. If there is an accumulation of moisture, the production of oxygen will be meager and the anaerobic bacteria will take over the decomposition. But because the oxygen required for the complete mineralization of the organic substance is lacking, the decomposition will not be complete and will result only in intermediate products. Under these conditions, organic matter will build up in the ground. If the organic substance consists of plant particles that do not decompose easily, this will result in the formation of substantial rough humus layers or moorlands.

If the ground dries out, the micropopulation will give way to the lower fungi, whose decomposition performance does not equal that of the bacteria. If the absence of water is more severe, all the microbes will ultimately assume their spore forms or will die off. The mineralization of the organic substance will then likewise come to an end. The optimum decomposition conditions are present when the water occupies about half the storage capacity available in the ground.

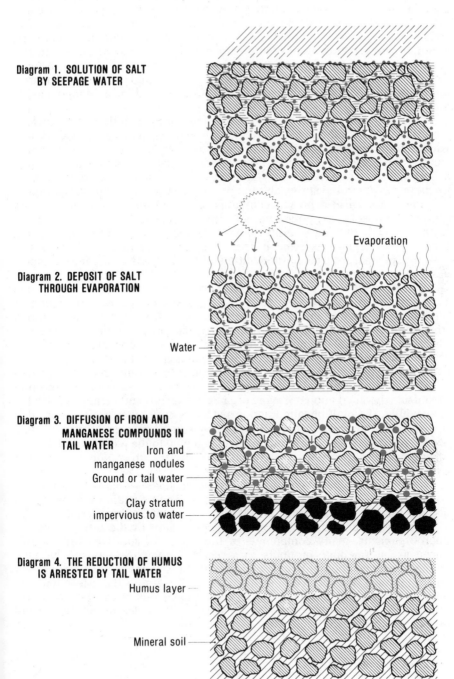

Diagram 1. SOLUTION OF SALT BY SEEPAGE WATER

Evaporation

Diagram 2. DEPOSIT OF SALT THROUGH EVAPORATION

Water

Diagram 3. DIFFUSION OF IRON AND MANGANESE COMPOUNDS IN TAIL WATER

Iron and manganese nodules

Ground or tail water

Clay stratum impervious to water

Diagram 4. THE REDUCTION OF HUMUS IS ARRESTED BY TAIL WATER

Humus layer

Mineral soil

THE SIGNIFICANCE OF ORGANIC MATTER IN THE SOIL

The essential properties of soil are determined by the quantity, form and composition of its organic matter, which includes decomposed plant remains, animal excrement and carcasses, fungi and bacteria. Loam and clay soils are inclined to an insufficient exchange of air and humidity because of their fine pores. Ventilation is therefore assisted by the coarse-pored organic matter from root remains and parts of dead plants on the earth's surface. The coarse-grained structure of the organic matter allows rain to penetrate more rapidly, so that the siltation of level stretches and the erosion of slopes are prevented.

In sandy soil, which is pervious to water and which dries out quickly, more favorable conditions are provided for plant growth by organic matter, which can retain three to five times its own weight of water. Dark areas, such as those produced by the brown humus substances above the surface, absorb the sun's rays better than light ones. Consequently the ground warms up more rapidly in the spring and the period of vegetation is prolonged.

In natural soils the provision by the organic substance of plant nutrients (nitrogen, phosphorus, potassium and trace elements) is important for the further growth of plants. Nutritional substances incorporated in organic form (amino acids) are found in the body substance of animal life in the soil and in microorganisms and ultimately converted again into a plant-absorbable mineral form.

The production of plant nutritional substances is thus dependent on the biological activity of the soil. In woodland areas, where decomposition of the fallen foliage does not occur or goes on very slowly for climatic reasons (the ground being too cold or too dry), arrested growth of the trees is often observed. Organic substance is also capable of assisting plant growth by retaining mineral nutritional substances such as sodium nitrate, which, owing to its good solubility in water, is subject to erosion in the upper soil.

Fallen foliage provides the basis of existence for saprophytes (ground organisms that feed upon decaying organic matter). If sufficient nourishment is available, the multiplication and growth of saprophytes are assisted, and parasites are suppressed. In addition, many soil microorganisms are able to absorb nitrogen from the air and make it available to the plants. If the supply of organic matter to the soil is eliminated—by the utilization of litter, for example (in some areas the leaves and cones from the woods were used up to twenty or thirty years ago as litter in horse stalls)—this will lead to the collapse of the saprophytic organisms. In order to sustain their biological activity there is thus a constant need for a supply of organic matter.

During the decomposition of the organic matter by the activities of soil microorganisms, many compounds of the nature of additives will be produced as intermediate products as a result of their metabolism. Notable among these are the antibiotics and growth substances formed from fungi. Vitamins have also been found in the soil. Regarding the effect and the persistence of such substances, little is yet known because of the difficulties in investigating them. Growth materials artificially added to the soil rapidly decompose there.

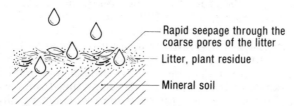

Rapid seepage through the coarse pores of the litter

Litter, plant residue

Mineral soil

Diagram 1. LOAM AND CLAY SOILS ARE BROKEN UP BY THE ORGANIC MATTER

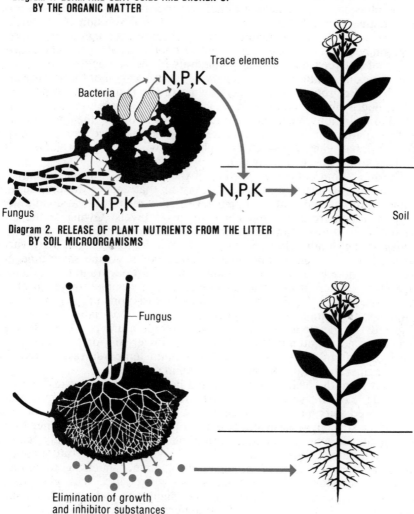

Trace elements

N,P,K

Bacteria

Fungus

N,P,K

N,P,K

Soil

Diagram 2. RELEASE OF PLANT NUTRIENTS FROM THE LITTER BY SOIL MICROORGANISMS

Fungus

Elimination of growth and inhibitor substances

Diagram 3. AS INTERMEDIATE PRODUCTS OF MICROBIAL METABOLISM COMPOUNDS ARE FORMED WITH THE CHARACTER OF ADDITIVES

GROUND TEMPERATURE

In relation to biological, chemical and physical occurrences in the pedosphere, the temperature of the ground is of the utmost importance. Germination and the root and shoot growths of the taller plants improve as the temperature rises. The activity of ground animals and of the decomposing soil bacteria and fungi also rises with the temperature. The organisms react unfavorably, however, to excessively high temperatures such as occur on exposed or only thinly cultivated ground on days of high solar radiation on the earth's surface. Whereas the mobile animals seek refuge from the excessive heat in deeper and cooler zones, for plant life this is not possible and injury or death of the plants results, particularly in the case of seedlings.

The physical and chemical weathering processes are also dependent on ground temperature. If the temperature of the soil solution rises, further salts can be dissolved if enough moisture is present. At high temperatures, the margin between the hot external and the cool internal layer will increase, as will that between dark and light minerals in the soil aggregates, and so lead to their dissociation. The air and water conservation of the soil are also affected by the ground temperature, owing to the increase in evaporation.

The energy for the increase in the ground temperature comes essentially from solar radiation. When daytime radiation is stronger, the counterradiation (from gathering clouds, from trees and other earth coverings) can furnish additional energy on clear nights. Dew and fog formation also contribute to the energy supply at the upper level.

The most comprehensive portion of the energy loss from the earth is accounted for by outward radiation. It is this that causes the pronounced day and night variations at the upper level. As a result of heat conduction, energy is drawn from the upper soil to lower levels. Owing to the heat capacity of the soil solution and to the mineral components, the energy flow declines as the depth below the earth's surface increases. The daily variations are less pronounced, and their range narrows. At the same time, because of the time lag in the heat conduction, a shift occurs in the maximum temperature, which at lower levels can lead to a complete reversal of the temperature range. Besides the day and night variations in the ground temperature, in the temperate and cooler zones seasonal variations can be distinguished. In the upper soil a maximum temperature is recorded in the summer and a minimum in the winter. In the lower soil, on the other hand, there is a shift in the maximum and minimum temperatures, so that the ground temperature is higher in winter than in summer.

Apart from the heat conductivity and heat capacity, color and the conditions on the earth's surface also help to determine the ground temperature. Light-colored soils, poor in humus, do not warm up in the spring—because they reflect strongly—as much as dark-colored humus soils. Other things being equal, the generation and growth of plant life are accordingly better in soils rich in humus. In moorland and marshy soil, the temperature conductivity is very low because of the high pore volume. Under nighttime radiation the energy stored in a thin layer is rapidly expended. This gives rise to extreme temperature variations between night and day, which on clear nights may lead to frosts even in the summer.

A similar effect results from loosening of the soil. The air found in the coarse pores delays the heat conduction, so that the upper soil warms up sharply in the day but at night cools off just as rapidly. By energy absorption ground cover reduces the energy input from radiation and likewise the heat

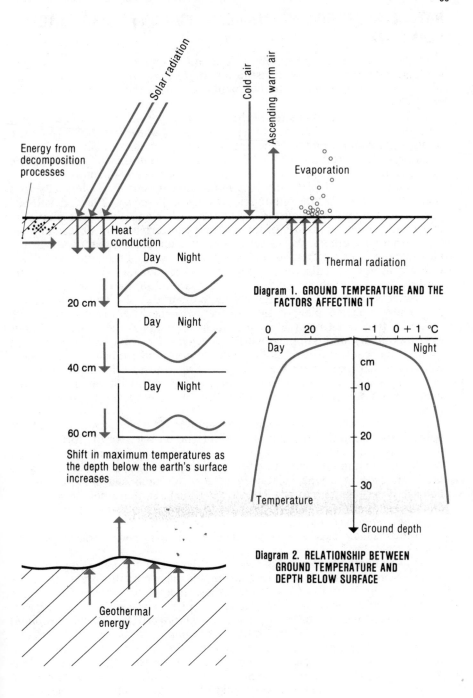

Diagram 1. GROUND TEMPERATURE AND THE FACTORS AFFECTING IT

Shift in maximum temperatures as the depth below the earth's surface increases

Diagram 2. RELATIONSHIP BETWEEN GROUND TEMPERATURE AND DEPTH BELOW SURFACE

level. The variations in the ground temperature of the upper soil from night to day are thereby more evenly balanced.

NATURE OF THE SOIL AND ITS IDENTIFICATION ACCORDING TO PLANT LIFE

Next to the climate, the nature of the soil is one of the most important ecological factors for the constitution of plant growth, since particular plants have very different requirements regarding the composition of the soil.

The factors that characterize the different types of soil are of a chemical (nutrient and trace element content, and pH value) and physical nature (grain size, water content, temperature, osmotic pressure, aeration in conjunction with the stability of the friable structure, and the soil colloids). The type of microbial population is also a pointer to the type of soil.

Many plants adapt themselves metabolically and physiologically to a region of a particular type (among the various soil types) and have developed special adjustment mechanisms. While there are plants that make no particular demands on the nature of the soil and can thrive more or less in most types, there are others, the so-called soil-constant plants, that need particular soil conditions for their sustenance. With the help of the latter, which are referred to as soil indicators or pilot plants, conclusions can be drawn regarding the composition and nature of the ground in the region concerned.

Some varieties of plants require large quantities of nitrogen, for example. These "nitrate plants" thus thrive particularly on refuse sites with waste containing nitrogen. They include such plants as the goosefoot genus (*Chenopodium*) and stinging nettles (*Urtica*). The nettles also indicate ground that contains iron, as they come up around rubbish dumps where iron scrap has been deposited. In meadows treated with liquid manure, nitrate-loving cow parsnips (*Heracleum*) thrive well. Cultivated plants that need a good soil treated with potash salts include beetroot, potatoes and tobacco.

Many dry soils that have no connections with the groundwater have lichen growths, in the north in particular, where they take the form of reindeer moss. The sandy soils of the sand dunes, which are also dry but are warm and contain nitrogen, support xerophytic halophytes which tolerate a high salt content in the soil, need little water, and can survive without damage if they happen to be smothered by sand. To these belong sea wheat (*Agropyron junceum*), seabeach sandwort (*Arenaria peploides*), lyme grass (*Elymus arenarius*), and shore orache (*Atriplex litoralis*).

Moist sandy clay soil is preferred by field horsetail (*Equisetum arvense*).

In soil containing salt in proximity to the sea and in salty steppe land a special flora has developed. In spite of the high osmotic pressure of the ground (a result of its salt content), these halophytes are able to absorb nutrients and water against the gradient. Typical representatives of the salt-loving plants are the marsh samphire, or glasswort (*Salicornia europaea*) and the sea aster, or sea starwort (*Aster tripolium*).

Especially pronounced are the differences that exist in the soil indicators for a particular calcium content of soils. Coupled with this as a rule is also the pH value of the soil, which in the case of soil lacking in calcium tends to be acid, and in the case of soil rich in calcium tends to be neutral or

Diagram 1. NITROGEN INDICATORS

| Stinging nettle | Pigweed | Cow parsnip |

Diagram 2. POTASSIUM-LOVING PLANTS (cultivated plants)

| Potato | Tobacco |

Diagram 3. XEROPHYTIC PLANTS

Lime grass

Shore orache

Seabeach sandwort

slightly alkaline. In plants that avoid calcium the roots are able to absorb nutrients only if there is a certain degree of acidity in the soil, whereas the calcium-loving plants need neutral or slightly alkaline soil. Typical calcium-avoiding plants are, for instance, corn chamomile, or field chamomile (*Anthemis arvensis*), field trefoil (*Trifolium arvense*), common broom (*Sarothamnus scroparius*), wild radish (*Raphanus raphanistrum*), corn spurry (*Spergula arvensis*), common whortleberry (*Vaccinium myrtillus*), lesser sorrel dock, or lesser garden sorrel (*Rumex acetosella*), and red sandwort spurry (*Spergularia rubra*). Among calcium-loving plants the following are to be noted: field mustard (*Sinapis arvensis*), speedwell (*Veronica officinalis*), goose-grass potentil (*Potentilla anserina*), common senecio (*Senecio vulgaris*), small stinging nettle (*Urtica urens*), nodding thistle, or musk thistle (*Carduus nutans*), red dead-nettle, or red archangel (*Lamium purpureum*), and sun spurge (*Euphorbia helioscopia*).

Acid soils, which are mostly very moist, tend to produce fungi and particular varieties of moss, such as tongue weeds (*Dicranum*), plume moss (*Hypnum cristacastrensis*) and haircap mosses (*Polytrichum*). On the other hand, neutral soils provide optimum living conditions for bacteria.

Special plant communities are to be found on high moorlands. The soils in this region are very wet and thus rank among the infertile soils. They are very deficient in nutrients, especially trace elements, which are partly conditioned by humic acids. Characteristic plants are varieties of peat moss (*Sphagnum*), common hair moss (*Polytrichum commune*), slender hair moss (*Polytrichum gracile*), starred moss (*Mnium undulatum*), sundew (*Drosera*), common ling (*Calluna vulgaris*), hoary heath (*Erica tetralix*), bog bilberry (*Vaccinium uliginosum alpinum*), small whortleberry (*Vaccinium oxycoccus*), red whortleberry (*Vaccinium vitisidaea*) and cranberry (*Betula pubescens*).

On soil with a high zinc content are found the calamine plants, the ashes of which can contain up to 20% zinc. To these belong the calamine pansy (*Viola lutea* var. *calaminaria*) and the vernal sandwort (*Minuartia verna*).

With the help of soil-indicator plants it is thus possible to make an assessment of the soil without resorting to intensive examination of it. It is most important, however, not to draw conclusions from the presence of any particular type of plant even if it is present in large quantities. Only when several varieties of plant indicating a particular type of soil are growing in a biotope can any final conclusions be drawn regarding the character of the soil.

Diagram 1. SALT-LOVING PLANTS

Shore aster

Glasswort

Diagram 2. CALCIUM-LOVING PLANTS

Sun spurge

Red dead-nettle

Diagram 3. CALCIUM-AVOIDING PLANTS

Field trefoil

Corn spurry

Field horsetail

Diagram 4. HIGH MOORLAND PLANTS

Bog bilberry

Red whortleberry

Sundew

DETERIORATION OF THE LAND

The area of land surface that is potentially available for agricultural use declines from year to year. Vast cultivation areas have already become practically unusable by erosion. In the tropical and subtropical zones in particular, agricultural production has been jeopardized by erosion and impoverishment of the soil. One of the main causes of deterioration of the land is deforestation by fire clearance. The burning of forests removes practically the entire nitrogen supply for vegetation. The other nutrients (calcium, potassium, phosphorus, etc.) are still available in soluble form within the resulting ash and so can still be used by the plants. In the early years following clearance by fire, the land can therefore still be used for agricultural purposes. But as absorptive clay minerals will be missing from the soil, the nutrients cannot be retained. Since they are soluble, on the other hand, they will be removed to lower levels where they are no longer accessible to growing plants. There will thus be a rapid loss of quality of the soil and a consequent decline in the vegetation.

Apart from the loss of nutrients there will also be a drop in the water supply and a change in the microclimate. The absorptive effect of the forest land, which previously served to even out the fluctuations between the dry season and periods of rainfall, will no longer be available. Consequently, in periods of rainfall there will be flooding and in the dry season, drought. With heavy rain the ground surface will become sodden and congested with fine particles caught up in the rainwater, so that on drying out a hard crust will form. In this way the oxygen supply required to promote the root activities of plants will be cut off. For most plants this will cause a sharp drop in growth, but will give a competitive advantage to resistant grasses. In this way a prairie is formed, which cannot be used for agricultural purposes.

The second main cause of deterioration of the land is wind erosion. This, in the form it mostly assumes in dry regions with strong winds, is normally held in check by the fact that the land is protected by a thick covering of plants and is consolidated by the root growths. In this way the removal by wind (and water) of the valuable upper humus layer is prevented. When the land is used for agriculture this covering of plants is removed and replaced by cultivated plants. As these are regularly harvested and replanted, the ground is exposed periodically (as after plowing and while the newly planted cultivated plants are still small) to the unfavorable effects of wind and water. The wind erosion can be kept within narrow limits when the cultivated plants are sown in mixed cultivations or when the fields are small and the ground is also covered with organic material. On the other hand, the weathering process can be accelerated by alternating effects once the wind erosion has already begun; the more sharply the ground is eroded, the less fruitful will it be and the less thickly and the less rapidly will the plants grow on it. With a lower rate of growth the wind erosion is intensified.

Similar to the causes of wind erosion are those of water erosion. This arises especially in areas of high precipitation. Water erosion develops in particular when the protective plant covering on the ground is destroyed on steep slopes (as by the clearance of woodland or by road-building), so that the water running away in the rainy season can wash the ground surface. Often all that is left is a bare cliff, on which vegetation is hardly possible.

By 1968, 28 million hectares of prairie had already been formed by deforestation in Indonesia, 17 million in India and 7 million in Pakistan. During the 1930s in the midwestern United States, out of a total useful area of about 3 million square kilometers, 2.35 million were severely damaged by wind erosion. A quarter of this eroded area is still not serviceable even now and has assumed a desertlike appearance. In the south of Russia almost 60% of the land is severely eroded. By erosion the productive capacity of the land can be reduced by between a half and two-thirds. As a result of soil erosion the production of arable land in South Africa has fallen since 1870 by about 30%. An eroded agricultural zone extends right across Africa from Guinea to the south. The countries most severely affected in East Africa are Ethiopia, Kenya, Zambia, Uganda and Burundi.

What can be done to prevent erosion of the soil? Wind erosion can be checked, in the first place, by planning agricultural cultivation in an ecologically sensible manner. This means mixed cultivation instead of monocultivation; the abandonment of artificial fertilization with easily soluble mineral fertilizers in favor of organic fertilization, and the planting of copses, thickets and trees in the agricultural area to provide wind protection and at the same time to establish an ecological equilibrium.

The same applies to the prevention of water erosion. Soil erosion from the clearance of woodland areas should be countered, firstly, by abandoning deforestation for the creation of new arable land and by regenerating the areas that have been turned into prairies by erosion of the soil. This can begin with reconversion of the prairies by laying out agricultural pioneer plants (for example, selected deep-rooted plants of the pea family, Fabaceae), which live in symbiosis with nitrogen-fixing bacteria and so can supply their nitrogen fertilization out of the air themselves. With their deep root systems they can also absorb the water from the deeper water layers, so that even in months of drought they can still remain green. In many cases such regenerated soils can be planted within two years with other useful plants such as oil palms, soybeans, corn and cotton. In addition to this restoration of eroded areas to agricultural use, part of the recovered areas should be reforested. The woodland can then make a contribution to protection against erosion and to the stabilization of water conservation and of climate.

WATER EROSION

Everywhere on earth except in extreme desert areas and in polar regions the ground is exposed to water erosion, unless it has some covering to protect it from rainfall. Water erosion takes two main forms: geological and accelerated erosion. In the broadest sense, geological (or biological) erosion is a normal process representing the removal of the land surface in its natural surroundings without human intervention. The erosion is accelerated by cultivation and the construction of houses, streets, railways, etc.

Water erosion embraces the three aspects of sheet and rill erosion, gulley erosion, and sedimentation.

In sheet erosion, a more or less extensive layer of soil is removed from a region that is poor in vegetation. This is a relatively inconspicuous form of erosion, as each time precipitation occurs in the ordinary way only a very thin layer of earth is removed. Over a fairly long period, however, it can achieve considerable proportions. Sheet erosion can, in fact, occur on slopes with a gradient of as little as 1°. Its presence is characterized by a light-colored surface on the upper slope that is revealed when the darker surface containing organic substance is removed. Two basic processes are responsible for sheet erosion. First, the soil particles are separated from the body of the soil by raindrops, and then the soil particles are carried away from their original location. Raindrops that fall on wet ground form a crater. Under the impact, water and earth are thrown up into the air and scattered around the crater. In this way particles of earth can be thrown up to a height of 50–60 centimeters (20–24 inches) and come down over a radius of up to 1.5 meters (5 feet).

If the volume of rainfall exceeds by much the rate at which the water infiltrates the ground, the water will flow away over the earth's surface. It will pick up the soil particles detached by the raindrops and carry them away. If the gradient is gentle and regular, the water will flow away in a thin sheet. If the land surface undulates irregularly, as is usually the case in agricultural areas, for instance, the water will collect in depressions and from there follow the line of least resistance. In this manner the surface water will run away, carrying its content of earth particles into rills and microchannels. The detachment and transport of earth particles are greater in rill erosion than in sheet erosion, as the speed of flow in the rills is greater than that of the sheets. The volume of earth carried away by running water is in proportion to the square of its speed; that is, if the speed is doubled, the amount of the erosion is quadrupled. The transportation capacity of the water increases by the fifth power of its speed; that is, if the speed of flow is doubled, the transportation capacity rises 32 times.

If the water volume and the flow speed continue to increase, the rills often turn into sizable gulleys. They may attain a width of 30 meters (100 feet) or more and a depth of from 1 to 15 meters (3 to 50 feet) and more. Soil that is eroded from its original situation will, of course, always be deposited elsewhere. It may settle near its point of origin or be carried away to the sea, or finish up at an intermediate point between the two extremes.

The bulk of the material eroded from the slopes is deposited at the foot of the slope, where it covers the original ground and can cause damage to any crops that have been planted there. Other soil masses are deposited in canals, rivers and reservoirs, from which their removal may entail considerable expense.

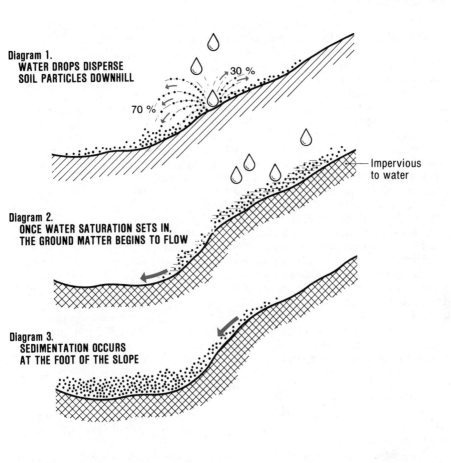

Diagram 1.
  **WATER DROPS DISPERSE
  SOIL PARTICLES DOWNHILL**

30 %

70 %

Impervious
to water

Diagram 2.
  **ONCE WATER SATURATION SETS IN,
  THE GROUND MATTER BEGINS TO FLOW**

Diagram 3.
  **SEDIMENTATION OCCURS
  AT THE FOOT OF THE SLOPE**

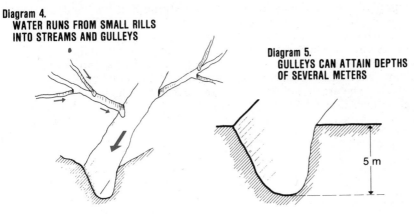

Diagram 4.
  **WATER RUNS FROM SMALL RILLS
  INTO STREAMS AND GULLEYS**

Diagram 5.
  **GULLEYS CAN ATTAIN DEPTHS
  OF SEVERAL METERS**

5 m

WIND EROSION

In contrast to water erosion, the displacement of earth particles by wind movements plays only a subordinate part in most temperate areas. The areas most seriously affected are the semiarid (Mediterranean) and arid desert regions, which during long periods of drought bear no vegetation at all or only sparse vegetation and so offer the wind good opportunities for attack. If the air is in motion over the earth's surface, a wind scale will develop above the earth: the closer the approach to the earth's surface the lower will be the wind speed because of the frictional effects. Ordinarily, the speed of the wind at a distance of 0.03 to 2.5 millimeters from the ground is nil. Above that there is a narrow zone with a laminar (steady) flow. Adjoining that is a turbulent zone, and the turbulent currents produce erosive forces. Very small earth particles do not reach the turbulent zone and so are not affected. Earth particles that do get caught up in the turbulent zone are subject to the wind forces. Insofar as they do not combine firmly with others, they will be displaced from their original location.

If the earth particles are diverted by turbulence, three forms of movement are possible, with *springing* being the most usual form. The particles are raised, remain for a short time in the turbulent zone, and then fall to the ground again a few centimeters or millimeters farther on. This form of movement is normal for particles in the 0.05–0.5 millimeter range. *Rolling* occurs mainly in the case of particles that are too heavy to be raised by the turbulence forces. Rolling is often touched off by the action of springing particles. Particles that are removed by rolling are of the order of 0.5–2 millimeters in size. The third form, *suspension,* is the movement of fine particles of earth that are caught up in the airstream. Their separation from the ground is also touched off by the action of springing particles. If they get caught up in the turbulent air layer they are often carried along at some height and may be deposited up to several kilometers away. This usually happens in the lee of natural or artificial wind barriers. It also helps to explain the shifting of sand dunes: the sand grains that are eroded on the windward side are always deposited downwind.

The factors determining the extent of the wind erosion are the number and volume of the erodible particles and the strength of the wind. Furthermore, the erosion effects are increased with the extent of the surface affected by wind erosion, as more and more detached ground particles are freed by its impact. On the windward side of the erosion area the soil movement is consequently limited. It rises steadily to windward until it reaches a maximum that is determined by the velocity of the wind and the factors given above. The erosion incidence of the soil can be affected sharply by the cultivation measures adopted by humans.

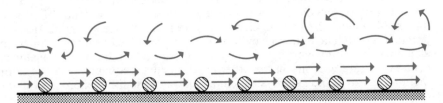

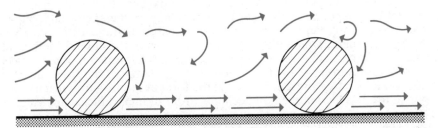

Diagram 1.
PARTICLES OF SOIL IN THE REGION
OF LAMINAR FLOW ARE NOT MOVED

Diagram 2.
PARTICLES OF SOIL IN THE REGION OF TURBULENT
AIR FLOW: HERE MOVEMENT CAN SET IN

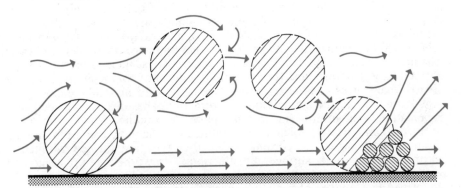

Diagram 3.
SMALL SOIL PARTICLES CLUSTERED TOGETHER ARE THROWN UP INTO THE TURBULENT
AIRSTREAM UNDER THE IMPACT OF SPRINGING PARTICLES

THE LITHOSPHERE

The external rock crust of the earth, the lithosphere, extends from the earth's surface, which is partly covered with water, to a depth of 70 kilometers (45 miles). Its geochemical structure is of intense scientific and economic interest. The minerals and rocks that form the earth's crust consist of elements of widely varying abundance. Gold and platinum, for instance, occur very rarely. Iron, on the other hand, occurs frequently. Precise information regarding the geophysical composition of the lithosphere is available at present for only the outer surface down to a depth of 16 kilometers (10 miles).

At about 46% abundance, oxygen (in the form of its various compounds) is the most common element in the lithosphere. It is followed in second place by silicon, with about 28%. Silicon does not occur in the lithosphere in its pure form any more than oxygen does. Silicon is often present in compounds with oxygen, particularly in the chemically inactive and consequently very durable compound quartz. Third place is taken with 8% by aluminum, which plays an important part in the composition of silicates and in particular is a basic component in the formation of alumina. In fourth place is iron (5%), which is found everywhere—if only in small quantities—and is often present in rock in the form of red iron ore, magnetite or brown ore. Following them in declining order of importance come calcium, sodium, potassium and magnesium.

The solid substances present in the earth's crust exist mainly as numerous forms of crystals. The crystalline state is the principal form of solid matter. The crystal forms that occur as inorganic natural substances in the earth's crust are described as *minerals*. Of the large number of known crystals, only comparatively few are present in rocks. Rocks generally represent mixtures of different types of minerals. Small parts of the earth's crust certainly consist also of an individual type of mineral (for instance, gypsum). The rocks are distinguished from one another by their mineral content, their chemical composition, their physical characteristics, their properties as determined by structure, and their texture (the form of composition generated by external causes and the spatial arrangement of the mineral composition).

According to their conditions of formation, the rocks are graded into magmatite, sedimentite, and metamorphite. Magmatite, which is also described as an igneous, volcanic, unstratified or magmatic rock, is solidified from molten magma. According to whether they are formed within the earth's crust or on its surface, a distinction is drawn between plutonic and extrusive rocks. Sedimentite, also known as stratified or sedimentary rock, is formed by deposits of rock substance destroyed or separated by weathering, especially in the sea. A distinction is made, according to the nature of the weathering to which the rock substance was subject, between clastic (due mainly to physical weathering), chemical (mainly chemical weathering), and organogenic sedimentary rock (such as coal, peat and amber formed from organic substances). Metamorphite (metamorphic rock) comes from the transformation of other rock. The reactions leading to the formation of metamorphic minerals occur because of the retention of the crystalline condition in the presence of water vapor in temperatures above 300°C (616°F) and under high pressures; that is, mostly at considerable depths below the earth's surface.

Magmatite and metamorphite occupy about 95% of the upper part of the earth's crust, so far known to a depth of about 16 kilometers (10 miles),

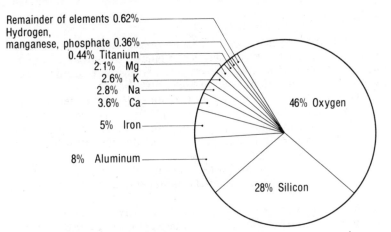

Remainder of elements 0.62%
Hydrogen,
manganese, phosphate 0.36%
0.44% Titanium
2.1% Mg
2.6% K
2.8% Na
3.6% Ca

5% Iron

8% Aluminum

46% Oxygen

28% Silicon

Diagram 1. PROPORTION OF ELEMENTS IN THE EARTH'S CRUST

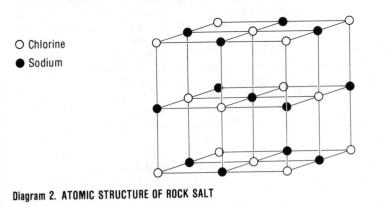

○ Chlorine
● Sodium

Diagram 2. ATOMIC STRUCTURE OF ROCK SALT

95% Magmatite
and metamorphite

Sedimentite

75% Sedimentite

25% Magmatite
and metamorphite

Diagram 3. FREQUENCY OF MAGMATITE, METAMORPHITE AND SEDIMENTITE WITHIN THE 16-KM(10-MI) ZONE OF THE KNOWN LITHOSPHERE (RIGHT) AND ON THE EARTH'S SURFACE (LEFT)

whereas the sedimentary rocks account for only about 5%. But if the surface rather than the volume of the earth's crust is considered, 75% of it is covered by sedimentary rocks and only 25% by magmatite and metamorphite.

ORE DEPOSITS

In a mining context, *ore* is understood to mean minerals and mixtures of minerals from which metals and metal alloys can be obtained in an economically feasible manner. These metals are extracted from the plutonic rocks and magmatic substances in which they are finely distributed.

Even in the magma flux, separation into fractions of various densities is possible. Chromite, magnetite, titanite, platinum and diamonds, for instance, are all linked with the heavy, basic constituents and sink in combination with them. The concentrations can enrich themselves until the time comes to exploit them.

Lead, zinc, uranium, beryllium, boron, lithium, and others are associated with the silicic rocks (granite), which crystallize out as the temperature and pressure fall.

Hydrothermal seams of ores containing gold, silver, copper, lead, nickel and antimony come from the residual aqueous fission products of the magma, which are combined with slightly fluid substances.

The economic value of these seams is constantly declining as time advances because of the exploitation that has been going on for thousands of years. On the other hand, the importance of seams in which the ores have been mechanically or chemically enriched by the physical or chemical weathering of other rocks is increasing. After the rocks have been weathered or destroyed by chemical processes, the decomposition products are carried away by water for the most part, are separated according to their density and grain size, and are aggregated again. By this sorting process many useful deposits are produced, which in the case of ore deposits are known as alluvial ores. In the extraction of gold, diamonds, platinum, tungsten and other heavy metals, this plays an important part.

The economic value of these seams is constantly declining as time advances because of the exploitation that has been going on for thousands of years. On the other hand, the importance of seams in which the ores have been mechanically or chemically enriched by the physical or chemical weathering of other rocks is increasing. After the rocks have been weathered or destroyed by chemical processes, the decomposition products are carried away by water for the most part, are separated according to their density and grain size, and are aggregated again. By this sorting process many useful deposits are produced, which in the case of ore deposits are known as alluvial ores. In the extraction of gold, diamonds, platinum, tungsten and other heavy metals, this plays an important part.

Owing to the action of surf in shallow seas and on beaches for extensive geological periods, detrital deposits have arisen on a considerable scale. In shallow coastal areas, iron ore deposits in shore areas are sometimes swamped. An example of this is provided by the iron ore seams at Salzgitter in Lower Saxony.

Metal enrichment often depends on solution and precipitation processes. In particular the elements iron, copper, aluminum, chromium, lead and manganese enter into a number of soluble compounds as a result of weathering processes. The solubility of the minerals depends for this on the pressure, temperature, redox (mutual reduction and oxidation) potential and pH value. The activities of organisms, particularly the metabolic processes of microbes, also affect the precipitation of metals and other elements.

Bog iron ore is formed by an oxidative process. In the groundwater layer, which is very poor in oxygen, bivalent iron is easily soluble. Free carbonic acid from the underground water can operate as acid for the solu-

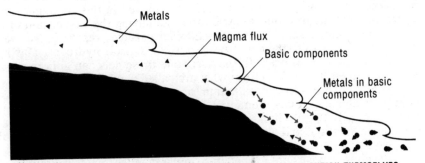

Diagram 1. HIGHER-DENSITY METALS SINK IN THE MAGMA FLUX AND ENRICH THEMSELVES

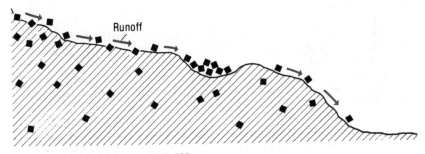

Diagram 2. EMERGENCE OF ALLUVIAL ORE

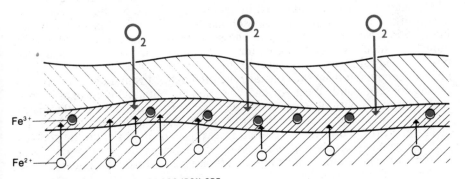

Diagram 3. FORMATION OF BOG IRON ORE

tion of iron. In dissolved form the bivalent iron rises by a capillary process out of the reducing groundwater zone into the oxidizing zones that are richer in oxygen and is there oxidized into insoluble trivalent iron by taking on oxygen. In the case of manganese, the process is very similar.

ORE DEPOSITS (continued)

In a region rich in oxygen, iron (like manganese) can be transported in water in colloidal form only. An important part is played in this by humic acids, which convert the iron into a ferric form, stabilizing the suspension of colloids in the humic acid. When the colloidal particles reach the seawater, which is rich in salt, they will be deposited as iron hydrogels and after dehydration will form ores. In the surf zone these gels can adhere to sand grains and their minerals to form what are called banded iron ores.

The main providers of aluminum are dissolved feldspars. Whereas in cold, wet climatic zones aluminum is deposited in the form of aluminum silicate, in a hot, dry climate under mildly alkaline conditions silicic acid remains in solution, and aluminum hydrates (such as bauxite) form valuable deposits.

Uranium deposits are formed in a similar manner to petroleum deposits. In sulfate form uranium is highly soluble, but occurs only in subterranean waters, in limited quantities. If the solution seeps into porous rocks in an area of organic sediments (bitumen or coal, for instance), these will act as reducing agents and will bring about the precipitation of the uranium. For this purpose porous reservoir rock and declivities (such as petroleum declivities) must be available.

In the form of sulfate, copper too is easily soluble and can be carried far when plenty of oxygen is present. In stagnant water under oxygen-free conditions and in the presence of hydrogen sulfide, copper is deposited as sulfide (copper shale).

In the near future the steadily rising need for raw materials will have to be covered more and more from ocean sources, about the extent and importance of which nothing is precisely known at present. On the ocean bed so far concretions (nodulelike conglomerations of mineral substances) have been recovered the size of potatoes, containing 25%–40% manganese, up to 0.2% cobalt, and copper, nickel, titanium, iron and rare metals. The formation of such concretions may well proceed more rapidly as the world consumption of these metals rises.

Phosphorite nodules with a content of 31%–32% phosphorus pentoxide (P_2O_5), and which are adulterated by metals, are found on the shelves. The extent of these for the phosphorus supplies needed for food production and industry is estimated at 10^{10} tons. The supplies of manganese nodules with numerous ancillary metals are estimated to amount to some 10^{12} tons. Deposits in coastal regions have been utilized for some time already. Iron ores are thus recovered from the coastal zone off Tokyo. From diamond deposits off the coast of South-West Africa five carats are obtained per ton of barren rock, compared with no more than one carat per ton obtained on the mainland. Titanium deposits are to be found off the coast of Florida, and off the coasts of Brazil and India there are rare earths. The deposits on the shelves and the seabeds are being increasingly investigated by oceanological research, for which more and more funds are being made available by the leading industrial countries.

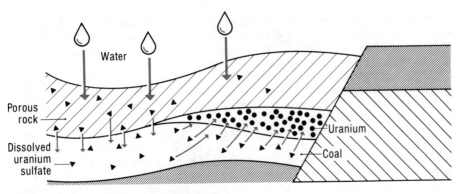

Diagram 1. FORMATION OF URANIUM DEPOSITS

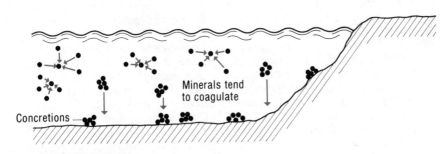

Diagram 2. OCEANIC DEPOSITS

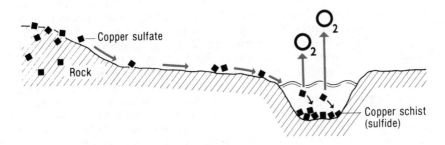

Diagram 3. FORMATION OF COPPER SCHISTS

COAL BEDS

As the energy requirements of the human race increase, the demand for coal as a source of energy along with petroleum and natural gas is further intensified. In addition to energy, coal also provides important raw materials for the chemical industry.

The prerequisites for the formation of coal beds, which result from an immense accumulation of carbonized plant substances, are favorable climatic conditions, which promote high plant growth, together with the deposit of the plant substance in coal seams to which only a little eroded rock is introduced from the mainland. The plants must remain in the water or sink into it rapidly if eventual decomposition by aerobic microorganisms into carbon dioxide and water is to be avoided. From the observation that in many coal beds substantial deposits are available, or several are superimposed on one another, it can be concluded that the reserves have sunk slowly and by stages, so that during the standstill period a new plant covering was formed, which then sank into the water in its turn. So-called stump layers in the coal seams displaying upright stems, and root stumps of trees at the base of bituminous coal seams, show that the coal has formed on the site of plant growth. Very rarely do the deposits consist of material that has been washed together.

First, the material deposited in the water from which air is largely excluded turns to peat. Thus highly polymerized cellulose, the principal constituent of the plant mass, is formed from simple sugars that are readily polymerized. Albumin and aromatic cell components such as lignin are also converted chemically and microbially by the separation of carbon dioxide and water into brown humus substances. According to the degree of decomposition, the original plant structures may still be discernible in the peat.

In the further process of carbonization, the proportion of carbon will rise with further loss of hydroxyl (OH) groups, water and methane. In the lignite so produced the plant structures are now hardly recognizable. This process is activated primarily by the rise in temperature as the peat layer subsides. The compression of the lignite material leads at this point to a loss of pore water, so that at a high pressure lignite can assume the appearance of bituminous coal.

According to the degree of carbonization, lignite is classified as earthy brown coal (lignite), soft brown coal (bituminous), and hard brown coal (anthracite). For the utilization of lignite an important factor is its suitability for use in briquettes. In the case of coal produced under alkaline nutrient conditions (low moorland), the plant substance is very much decomposed, so that highly polymerized humic acid is formed. Such forms of coal are unsuitable for briquette production. If the brown coal comes from high moorland of an acid nature and deficient in nutrients, in which the plant substance has been worked on by only bacteria and fungi to a limited extent and so is still well preserved, it will be well suited to briquette production.

During the transition from the lignite to the bituminous coal stage, the humic acids that have formed will be largely destroyed. In their place methane will be produced and the bituminous coal, which was originally rich in gas, will progressively lose its gas to finish up as hard coal or anthracite.

Bituminous coal formation is known to be pre-Cambrian in origin. In Scandinavia, coal is extracted that emanates from the Devonian system. The most valuable coal deposits in the world come from Carboniferous formations and peat. The most important lignite beds were formed in the Tertiary period.

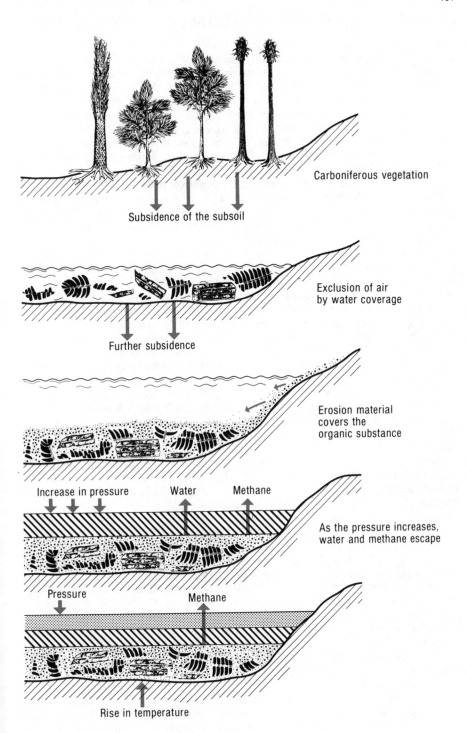

Carboniferous vegetation

Subsidence of the subsoil

Exclusion of air
by water coverage

Further subsidence

Erosion material
covers the
organic substance

Increase in pressure   Water   Methane

As the pressure increases,
water and methane escape

Pressure   Methane

Rise in temperature

COAL FORMATION.

PETROLEUM AND NATURAL GAS—THEIR ORIGIN AND FORMATION

Petroleum and natural gas are the most important sources of energy and are the raw materials most in demand by the chemical industry today.

For the most part, petroleum comprises a mixture of several hundred or even thousand hydrocarbon constituents. In many cases these are the only constituents, while in others a large number of other organic compounds are present, such as oleic acid, asphaltene, gums and a variety of sulfur and nitrogen compounds. The vast proliferation of hydrocarbons stems from the tetravalence of carbon and its many possible compounds—in the form of chains of different lengths with single, double and triple bonds, of rings of different bond types and sizes and of the most varied bonding with one another; and it also allows the formation of side chains. Gums and asphaltenes are high-molecular-weight organic compounds, which give to the oils their dark color and increase their viscosity. The sulfur and nitrogen compounds are in the form of chains or rings, in which carbon atoms are replaced by sulfur or nitrogen atoms.

The explanation of how petroleum is formed is one of the most difficult problems encountered in geological research. Almost all the facts point to its organic development from decomposition products of plant and animal organisms that were deposited in the mud beds of waterways, were preserved there from immediate putrefaction by the lack of oxygen, and then formed rock bitumen. One problem regarding this explanation of the origin is that organisms are composed to a large extent of oxidized compounds, whereas petroleum consists of reduced (oxygen-free) compounds. Reduction is conceivable, however, only as a result of energy input. In the first phase of transformation at least, the necessary energy could not have been derived from the heat of the earth, as the petroleum would then still contain elements from the chlorophyll and blood pigment, which will not sustain a higher temperature than 200°C (424°F) and will persist only in an oxygen-free environment. One possible reaction, which also occurs in lower temperatures and is anaerobic (without free oxygen) is biological reduction by bacteria. In the sediment in water and in oil a whole series of anaerobic bacteria can be recognized that are able to reduce organic substances and to transform them into fatty acids, methane, and ethane, and also into other hydrocarbons. The hydrocarbons in question do not form petroleum, however.

The further transformation of the long-chain compounds (fatty acids) into petroleum with its light paraffins (5–7 carbon atoms) can occur only at lower temperatures and in the absence of active clays as catalyzers or at great depths under high pressures by thermal decomposition. Under this thermal decomposition or fission, long-chain hydrocarbons will be split up into methane and other light gaseous hydrocarbons.

Natural gas is produced in the same way, but contains carbon dioxide, nitrogen, hydrogen sulfide, and mixtures of rare gases in addition to hydrocarbons. A distinction is made here between dry gases, which consist almost exclusively of methane, wet gases (ethane, propane, butane, etc.), and acid gases with mixtures of hydrogen sulfide.

The formation of petroleum and natural gas thus possibly represents a process that embraces some very different reactions (bacterial and thermal decomposition or fission) and extends over long periods. The formation of the most recent petroleum fields dates back roughly one million years.

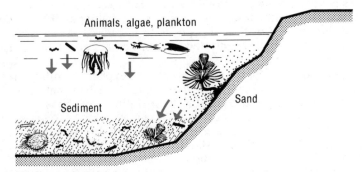

Animals, algae, plankton

Sediment

Sand

Diagram 1. SEDIMENTATION

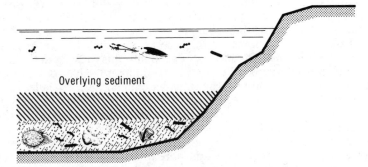

Overlying sediment

Diagram 2. ANAEROBIC BACTERIA DECOMPOSE THE ORGANISMS DEPOSITED

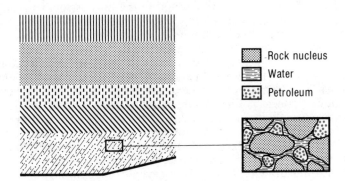

Rock nucleus
Water
Petroleum

Diagram 3. DIFFERENT DEPOSITS INTENSIFY THE PRESSURE

OIL FIELDS

The petroleum source rocks are mainly close-grained mud deposits in which oil is finely distributed. At 6%–7%, the content of these sediments in organic substances is not very high. Of this portion, however, only fractional parts are converted into hydrocarbons, so that it is not really possible to speak of oil fields at this stage. For the oil deposits to form fields in the strict sense of the term they must be concentrated, and this comes about by diffusion of the oil in the rock pores.

Various hypotheses have been presented to explain the diffusion movement of the oil in the rocks. One of these is to the effect that at depths of 1500 meters (4900 feet) and over, the temperature and pressure rise to a point at which the oil assumes a gaseous form in which it becomes diffusible in the rock. In a liquid phase, the oil can diffuse only in permeable rock when the rock pores are filled with oil over a long period, so that what is known as a continuous zone is formed.

Another explanation of oil diffusion is based on the assumption that at an early stage of its formation oil forms a colloidal suspension with water. Since marine sediment contains a great deal of water, there exists in it a continuous watery phase with which the oil can travel. If the oil source rocks come into contact with porous, permeable rocks (such as sandstone), water and oil will be compressed into the porous rock by the pressure of new overlying sediments. Oil and water seep into this rock up to the point at which diffusion is interrupted by contact with impermeable rock (for example, argillaceous rock). Oil and gas then accumulate in a so-called trap. In the deeper parts of the sediment basins the pressure of the overlying rocks is greater, so that the solutions seep shoreward. This has the result that oil reserves are concentrated heavily in the shore areas.

The assumption that oil diffusion tends to occur in aqueous suspension is supported by the fact that many oils were never deposited at great depths. Other important indications of the validity of this hypothesis are the distribution of oil molecules and the presence of emulsifiers in the waters of the oil reserves.

Oil traps are mainly to be found in the porous rocks in the peak zones of the anticlines (saddle ridges), also in rocks which abut on dislocations (faults) with sealing properties and on the flanks of salt beds and similar zones which prevent the oil from spreading farther. As such traps can also be impervious to water, edge water can build up that for the most part displays a high salt content. In addition there are so-called lithological traps, or zones in which the rocks have greater porosity and bigger pores than neighboring zones. Oil has a substantially lower surface tension than water and consequently it spreads readily. If the oil has collected in the big pores, it will remain there, as it cannot penetrate the small pores and capillary tubes against the capillary pressure of the water. Traps of this type include sand lenses and old buried watercourses filled with rough material.

The oil is drawn off from the reservoir rocks through probes in which it rises under the pressure of the head of gas or pressure of water on the oil deposit, or by the expansion of the gases dissolved in the oil when the pressure is released.

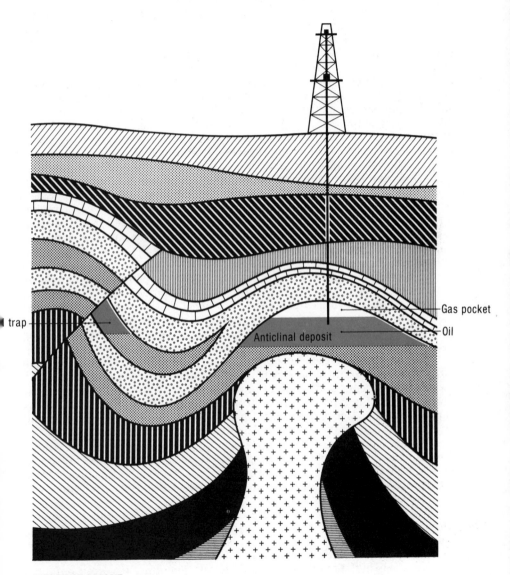

trap

Gas pocket

Oil

Anticlinal deposit

PETROLEUM DEPOSIT

SALT DEPOSITS

In the weathering of volcanic rocks, the compounds dissolved are mainly those of the alkaline-earth metals calcium and magnesium, together with those of the alkali metals sodium and potassium, whereas the oxides of silicon are in effect insoluble. Part of the potassium is removed from the weathering solution by clay minerals, in which the potassium is incorporated. The potassium, calcium and sodium, along with magnesium, dissolved carbon dioxide, and sulfur compounds, are carried down the rivers into the oceans, where they eventually form salts.

In open seawater the salt concentration is too low for the salts to be deposited. Owing to evaporation of the water, however, the concentration can be raised to the limit, which results in the deposit of the precipitated salt. This presupposes the delimitation of sea basins, in which certain conditions must be present. The loss by evaporation must exceed the inflow of water. And the shores of the inland lake or of the sea bay must be so flat that no more material is fed into the basin from the land.

The first substances to settle are the least soluble carbonates and sulfates. This can also occur in very small concentrations biogenetically in the case of marine organisms which by their metabolism absorb the lime as a stroma (supporting tissue) substance in their scales. Some 40% of the seabed is covered with what is known as foraminiferal ooze, formed from the shells of dead protozoa and from clay substances. In the further process of deposit and sedimentation, rock salt is produced, and finally the most easily soluble potash salt.

The sinking of the bed of the basin, a rise in its shoreline and an inflow of new water masses will mean that the water formation process is repeated. The salt formation thus occurs only during a static phase in part of the earth's crust. In many regions several such cycles can occur in succession. The clays washed into the basin at times of increased erosion of the surrounding land surfaces protect the salt deposits from being washed away.

Salt formation is possible both in inland waters and in the sea. The salts differ from one another, however, in their chemical composition, which is the more astonishing in that not only the inland waters but also the seas receive their mineral constituents from the land surface. This involves the supposition that the oceans have an original supply of salt which is only slightly modified by the fresh supplies washed in from the land.

As the various salts are deposited one after the other, they tend to remain in layers one upon another. Clay and carboniferous rocks are deposited first from the shore of the basin into the middle; sulfates and chlorides are deposited in the basin's interior. In this way salt basins are formed with their typical salt distributions.

From salt deposits, which are overlaid by sediment, salt masses can form. This depends on the fact that salt begins to flow even when there is very little difference in tension in the sediment. Differences in tension are produced, for instance, by movements in the earth's crust or differences in erosion levels in the overlying rocks. The salt then flows into zones of lower pressure, and accumulates to form salt cushions. At this point the overlying rocks are raised; and at the point at which the salt is carried away they subside. Through the further excavation of the arching rock, which accumulates in the adjoining depression, the downward pressure is increased and the difference in pressure is accordingly accentuated. In consequence, further salt flows into the salt mass. This process can continue until such time as the salt has penetrated to the earth's surface.

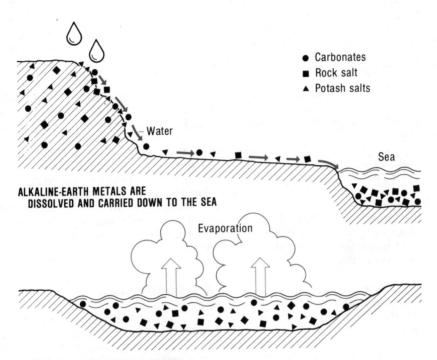

Carbonates
Rock salt
Potash salts

Water

Sea

**ALKALINE-EARTH METALS ARE
DISSOLVED AND CARRIED DOWN TO THE SEA**

Evaporation

**A HIGH EVAPORATION RATE PRODUCES
CONCENTRATION OF SALT IN WATERS WITH LIMITED INFLOW**

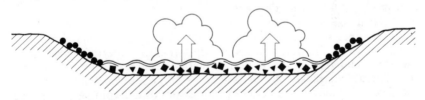

**SEDIMENTATION OF CARBONATES THAT ARE
DIFFICULT TO DISSOLVE ON THE BANKS OF THE WATERS**

**COMPLETE SEDIMENTATIONS IN ZONES
OF DIFFERENT SOLUBILITY**

PHYSICAL EROSION

By physical erosion is understood the mechanical disintegration of rocks without any change in their chemical composition, caused by a drop in pressure, change of temperature, frost in the fissures, and salt blasting. If compact rock masses are leveled, the pressure is reduced on the underlying layers and these are thus able to expand. During the expansion process, cracks, fissures and crevices will appear in the expanding layer. The rock that has sustained these fractures will now be exposed to other erosive forces.

Temperature erosion depends on two physical properties of the rock:

1. Differences exist in the expansion coefficients of the rock-forming minerals; that is, different minerals expand and contract on heating and cooling to different extents, so that at the contact surfaces tensions arise that result in fissures.

2. By reason of the low heat conductivity of the material, a temperature gradient occurs inside the rock mass—that is to say, the temperature of the external layer (several millimeters to centimeters thick) varies considerably from the internal temperature—so that at temperature-boundary surfaces, tensions arise which cause the rock to crack. The effect of the temperature disruption is particularly great when the temperature and the speed of changes in temperature reach extreme levels (for example, in deserts, where the difference between day and night can be as great as 50°–60°C, and on high mountains).

The damage caused by frost in the fissures arises from the fact that, on freezing, water increases in volume by about 10%. If water infiltrates the fissures in rocks, a layer of ice forms on its upper surface when it freezes and acts as an "ice-block" by cutting off the water below it. On continued freezing it is prevented from expanding further and so develops forces that operate on the surrounding rock. The highest pressure that can be generated by ice fission is put at 2200 kilograms per square centimeter. In high mountain regions, frost damage through frequent alternations between freezing and thawing under heavy snowfalls is mostly more severe than damage caused by temperature changes.

A further possibility of mechanical fragmentation arises from salt fission. Soluble substances are not washed away in dry regions but, owing to evaporation of the water, are concentrated in the external rock layers. If salt crystals seal up the cavities filled with the supersaturated salt solutions, considerable explosive forces will come into operation when the supersaturated solution crystallizes out, since the sum of the volumes of the saturated solution and of the crystals deposited is greater than the volume of the supersaturated solution. Salt fission also depends on the volume increase of the salt crystals in the hydrate formation. Counterpressures of several hundred kilograms per square centimeter can be overcome. The volume increase upon hydration results from the fact that water molecules accumulate on the upper surface of the crystals, and crystal-forming ions detach themselves from the crystal lattice and are surrounded by water molecules. Frequent alternations from drying out to penetration of moisture increase the effects of this process.

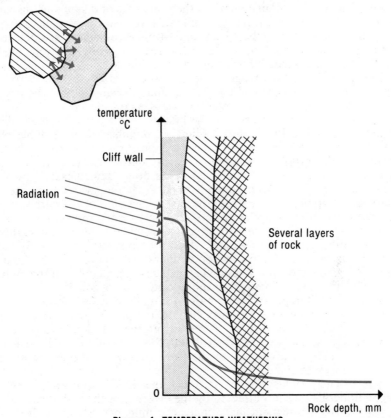

temperature
°C

Cliff wall —

Radiation

Several layers
of rock

0

Rock depth, mm

Diagram 1. TEMPERATURE WEATHERING

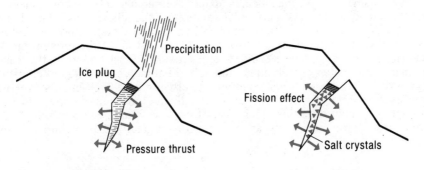

Precipitation

Ice plug

Pressure thrust

Diagram 2. FROST WEATHERING

Fission effect

Salt crystals

Diagram 3. SALT FISSION

CHEMICAL AND BIOLOGICAL EROSION

An important preliminary for chemical and biological erosion is provided by fragmentation of the outer surfaces of the rock under the effects of physical erosion. Chemical erosion comprises the processes of dissolving, disintegration and hydration (the property of minerals to absorb water or to accumulate it on their surface), the extent and strength of which are determined inter alia by the surface structure of the rock. Fragmented rock surfaces offer the chemical agents better working conditions.

The most important reagent for the processes of chemical erosion is water. Its effect is reinforced by organic and inorganic acids; the temperature factor too influences the erosion processes considerably.

Solution erosion concerns, in the first place, the easily soluble alkaline and alkaline-earth salts. In humid climatic regions, highly soluble potash salts in particular are never present on the earth's surface. In semiarid and arid regions (deserts) less soluble rock salt, saltpeter, etc., are sometimes found. Solution erosion is intensified by carbonic acid dissolved in water. This is obtained from carbon dioxide that passes into water from the air or by erosion of organic matter from the earth. The bulk of the carbon dioxide is retained in the water in the form of gas; only a small portion is converted into carbonic acid. This primarily affects calcium and magnesium carbonate, which are difficult to dissolve and which are converted into easily soluble hydrogen carbonate. At low water temperatures more carbon dioxide is dissolved in the water; the solution balance changes in favor of the hydrogen carbonate, which is maintained in solution by free carbon dioxide.

At a higher temperature the carbon dioxide escapes and calcium carbonate (lime) is deposited. In warm climatic regions the dissolved carbonate is deposited again only a short distance from the solution area (lime sinter basin). As limestone is widely distributed, this type of solution erosion is of great importance. It gives rise to the formation of sinkholes (depressions) and of big crevices and caves.

The silicates (feldspar, quartz, etc.), the most important of the rock-forming minerals, are not affected by the erosion mechanisms just outlined. They are broken down, in fact, under the influence of the hydrogen and oxygen ions in the dissociated waters. This process is known as hydrolysis. The hydrogen ions split the silicates up into their acid and basic components, and the silicic acid forms a colloidal solution. If the silicic acid is largely or completely carried away, aluminum and iron hydroxide are deposited in the residue. The latter gives rise to intense red coloration of the erosion products (for example, bauxite). This type of erosion occurs mainly in the transitional region between subhumid and subarid climates. In a humid climatic region the solubility of silicic acid and its erosion by a high humus content are severely limited. In this way new silicon-aluminum compounds are formed—the clay minerals. This kind of erosion results in the production, from rock with a high feldspar content, for instance, of porcelain clay or kaolin.

Diagram 1. SOLUTION EROSION

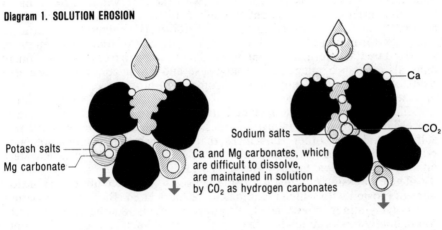

Potash salts
Mg carbonate

Sodium salts

Ca and Mg carbonates, which
are difficult to dissolve,
are maintained in solution
by CO_2 as hydrogen carbonates

Ca

CO_2

Diagram 2. CARBONATE SOLUTION

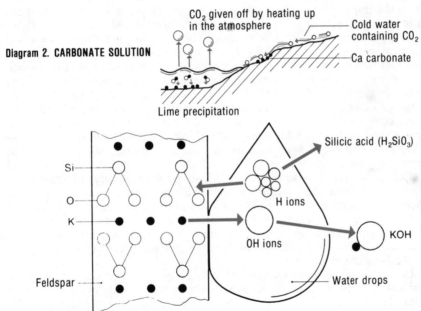

CO_2 given off by heating up
in the atmosphere

Cold water
containing CO_2

Ca carbonate

Lime precipitation

Silicic acid (H_2SiO_3)

Si

O

K

H ions

OH ions

KOH

Feldspar

Water drops

Diagram 3. HYDROLYSIS

CHEMICAL AND BIOLOGICAL EROSION (continued)

The redox potential (oxidation-reduction potential), which is determined firstly by the oxygen partial pressure and the pH value of the ground solution, gives rise—primarily in the upper ground layers—to erosion by oxidation. When oxygen is in equilibrium with the air, water of pH 7 has a redox potential that is sufficient to convert bivalent iron to trivalent. Iron (III) carbonate, iron (II) silicate and other iron (II) minerals disintegrate under the formation of iron (II) oxides. The erosion of rocks is often characterized by the emergence of intense red or rusty brown colors, since many minerals contain bivalent iron. Manganese and sulfur compounds are also oxidized. Sulfides turn into sulfates, from which brown ore, for instance, is obtained.

Flue gas erosion is also included in chemical erosion. In the combustion process in big towns and industrial areas, large quantities of carbon dioxide, sulfur dioxide and other substances that form acids in combination with rainwater are given off. In the rainwater they fall on brickwork, and work on it by carbonic acid erosion and salt fission.

The expression *biological erosion* is used to embrace all the manifestations of erosion with which plant life can be associated. Biological erosion is of relatively minor importance in its physical effects. As the burrowing and rooting activities of animals living on the earth's surface are limited in the main to the upper part of the loose sediment on the earth's surface, only the disintegrating effects of plant roots need to be considered.

The predominant effect of plants is of a chemical nature. The outer surface of rocks is colonized by lower plants such as seaweed, mosses, lichen and fungi, which infiltrate the crevices. There they gradually decompose the rock by absorbing nutritional substances and to some extent silicic acid (as in the form of diatoms) from the ground soil, and so promote the silicate disintegration. The separation of complex-forming organic compounds such as salicylic acid, tartaric acid, citric acid, pyrocatechol, ketogluconic acid and salicylaldehyde leads to the release of metallic ions from the silicates and their incorporation in complex compounds which can be carried away by rainwater.

The higher plants also add to the erosion, especially by the removal of plant nutrients from the ground and the separation of complex-forming substances. Hydrogen ions are released by the plant roots and exchanged with the cations (e.g., potassium, magnesium and calcium) from the clay minerals and the organic exchangers in the ground. The hydrogen ions thus introduced into the mineral constituent have an increased effect in turn on the hydrolysis of the silicate.

In addition, the dead parts of plants falling to the ground increase the microbial activity. Organic acids are also released by the decomposition of detrital deposits, and this too contributes to the erosion of minerals.

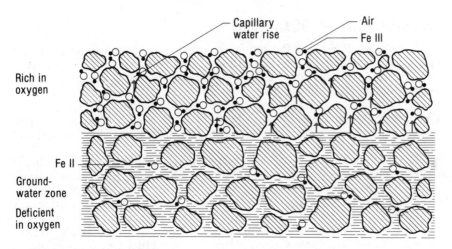

Capillary water rise

Air

Fe III

Rich in oxygen

Fe II

Groundwater zone

Deficient in oxygen

Diagram 1. EROSION BY OXIDATION

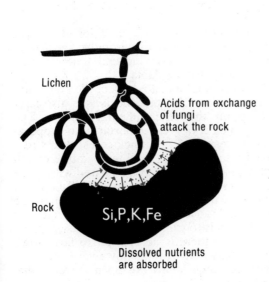

Lichen

Acids from exchange of fungi attack the rock

Rock

Si,P,K,Fe

Dissolved nutrients are absorbed

Diagram 2. BIOLOGICAL EROSION

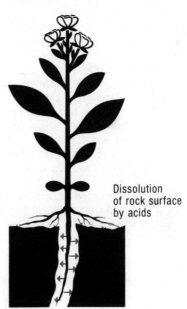

Dissolution of rock surface by acids

Fission effect of thickening of the plant roots

Part Three—The Inhabited Environment

THE BIOSPHERE—ECOSYSTEMS

The biosphere, defined as the entire area of the earth that is inhabited by organisms, extends from the ground sector (the pedosphere) over the water zone (the hydrosphere) into the layer of atmosphere that envelops the earth. The functional units of the biosphere are the ecosystems in the form of forests, savannas, lakes, seas, etc., which are in a constant phase of development and are consequently capable, to a certain extent, of self-regulation. Ecosystems are operating complexes for life communities (biocenoses) and nonbiological environmental factors.

The composition and classification of life communities in ecosystems are determined, inter alia, by climatic factors such as the precipitation level, solar radiation, and the temperature and movement of the atmosphere. Thus the spread of holly (*Ilex aquifolium*) is due to climatic factors. The boundary of its distribution coincides with a hypothetical line through the points at which a maximum temperature of over 0°C (32°F) is achieved on 345 days in the year. In the Kerguelen Archipelago in the Indian Ocean, a group of islands constantly wracked by severe storms, flying insects have become extinct from constant exposure to winds carrying them into the sea. The earlier types of flying insects have been supplanted by wingless varieties and insects with a restricted flight range.

Within the climatic limits to a plant's growth, the qualities of the soil naturally determine the emergence and frequency of particular species. A distinction thus has to be made between lime-loving and lime-resistant plants, and between salt-loving and salt-resistant plants.

It is not true today to say that only abiotic factors affect life communities and their distribution; it is truer to say that biocenosis (see also later discussion) exercises an influence on the environmental factors. The strength of the wind, for example, which is of great importance to evaporation, is much reduced in woodland areas, and in a thick forest drops to a value of practically nil. Forest land also influences local temperature conditions: in a wooded region the extremes of temperature compared with those occurring on open land are much more moderate. Heat from the sun's rays is almost wholly consumed at the crowns of trees. On the other hand, the cold air that arises as a result of thermal radiation from the outer surfaces of the leaves on the crowns of trees descends to trunk level and mixes with the warmer air present there. Consequently there is no cold air to flow down wooded slopes, which is a vegetation advantage on the downward side.

As regards their energy balance, ecosystems are open systems that absorb energy from the sun unilaterally. The natural matter cycles in an ecosystem are balanced, so that a dynamic equilibrium, a so-called balanced flow, sets in. The organisms are traversed by a constant flow of exchange material and energy in the form of nutrients. The balanced flow produces a quasi-stationary condition in relation to the chemical compounds involved in the exchange processes. This emerges from the fact that the concentration of both the gases, carbon dioxide and oxygen, involved in the photosynthesis of plants (see Part Six) shows no change over a long period.

The ecological balance is characterized by the fact that every change in the ecosystem automatically promotes a counterchange through an automatic control system, and this to a large extent reestablishes the previous

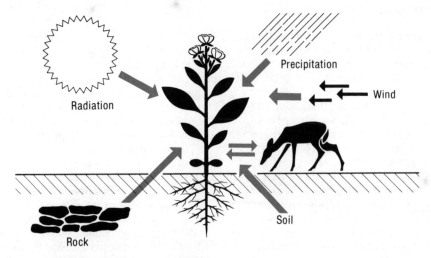

Diagram 1. FACTORS AFFECTING THE BIOSPHERE

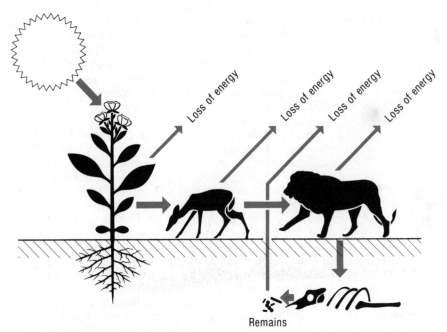

Diagram 2. ENERGY FLOW IN AN ECOSYSTEM

situation. Thus in the case of voles and hares, pronounced population waves are distinguishable which are explained by the fact that as the population expands either the nutrient base becomes scarce or the vermin and parasites also increase. The system fluctuates as a rule between specific boundary values.

BIOTOPES

Biotopes are life zones which, by reason of the environmental conditions that exist in them, are relatively clearly demarcated from neighboring areas. Examples of typical biotopes are marshes, springs, caves, water meadows, and pools. These furnish plant and animal life with the basic living conditions answering their requirements. This applies in particular to the so-called character types peculiar to a biotope. Thus the common petasite weed (*Petasites hybridus*), which thrives in low-lying deciduous forest areas and on the banks of streams, is a character type for biotopes with a high groundwater level: deprived of water the petasite withers away rapidly.

Besides character types, other species are found in a biotope that also occur in other biotopes or that can, in general, be widely distributed. Such species are designated ubiquists (ubiquitous types). Examples of these among plants are ubiquitous funguses and among animals rats.

Finally, there are species in a biotope that flourish best in some other biotope and so can hold out only temporarily in this alien zone. These types are designated visitors, or alien to the biotope. Migrant birds are one example of this type.

All the organisms of a biotope—character types, ubiquists and visitors—together form a life community (biocenosis).

As a biotope—a beech wood, e.g.—may extend over a considerable area (surface), it is not to be expected that all the organisms living in the biotope are present in all cases in the same proportions. There are many regions in which a specific organism, such as the enchytraeid in the layer of fallen leaves in a beech wood, is present in large quantities, as that is where it finds its optimum conditions for feeding, protection, moisture and temperature. Such areas characterized by special environmental conditions in a particular biotope are known as *biochorions*.

If, owing to a reduction in or the disappearance of the feeding base, a change occurs in the living conditions for the inhabitants of a biochorion—as happens, for instance, in the layer of fallen leaves in a beech wood before the foliage falls again in the following year, as a result of the feeding activities of the organisms living in it—this will give rise (if only temporarily) to a change in the composition of the life community concerned. A case such as this, in which various life communities take over from one another in a particular area of a biotope, is known as ecological succession.

If in the course of the succession the environmental situation does not always return to the situation prevailing at the outset—as happens in the case of the layer of fallen leaves owing to the periodic fall of foliage—then the succession gradually moves toward a stable final position (climax stage), in which the production of an organic substance by the green plants stands in a balanced relationship to the decline produced by consumption and destruction (see also Part Six).

Only fully mobile animals are in a position to select and locate their biotopes, such as birds of passage, who change their biotopes according to the season of the year, or insects (necrophagous and coprophagous) that live on carcasses and dung and whose nutrients are also available elsewhere. For many other animals, on the other hand, their biochorions are identical with their birthplace.

Visitor

Character types

Ubiquist

Detrital deposit (as biochorions)

Destructive elements

CO_2

CO_2

Deposits of organic matter that
do not decompose easily

THE VARIOUS ELEMENTS IN A BIOTOPE AND THE ECOLOGICAL SUCCESSION

BIOCENOSIS—THE BEECH WOOD

All natural communities of plants consist of a varied mixture of different types of plants that have come together because they make identical or similar claims on the soil and climatic conditions and because they harmonize with and supplement one another. They are described as a natural life community, a biocenosis, in which the animals living in it are also included. As regards their individual contribution to the maintenance of biological equilibrium in the biocenosis, a distinction is made regarding the individual organisms in the biocenosis among producers, reducers and consumers.

The green plants are the real *producers* in a biocenosis. With the help of photosynthesis, they build up organic compounds out of simple inorganic material (carbon dioxide, oxygen, water, and mineral salts).

The reconstitution of organic material from dead organisms into simple inorganic compounds is effected by the activity of numerous living creatures known as *reducers*. These consist primarily of bacteria and fungi. A good woodland soil contains per cubic decimeter about 1 billion algae and protozoa, 30,000 threadworms, 500 rotifers, 1000 springtails, 1500 mites, 100 insects (mainly larvae), small spiders and millipedes, 50 bristleworms, and 2 earthworms.

The *consumers* are living creatures that depend for their nourishment on plants, either directly (as herbivores) or indirectly by consuming herbivores or animals that live on herbivores. Creatures of this sort that live in beech woods include mice (in the ground layer); insects, snails, amphibia, wild boars, deer, etc. (in the vegetable and partly in the shrub layer); squirrels and birds (mainly in treetops).

A typical example of a biocenosis is a natural beech wood. This is a plant community consisting of many species built up in layers, one on top of the other. The upper layer consists of the tops of grown trees. Next comes the shrub level (to which the young plants of the trees also belong), which is not very prominent in the case of a beech wood. After the shrub layer comes the vegetation layer and right on the ground the moss layer. In the upper soil below the moss layer is the fungal layer, which is pierced by the roots of the plants growing overhead and which consists mainly of fungal hyphae.

According to how the upper levels are shaped, the supply of light in a beech wood can vary considerably. In the spring, as long as the leaves of the shrub and tree layers have not yet opened and in view of the good light distribution, the vegetation layer with its spring blossoms is able to develop an active life. Examples of such early blossoming plants in a beech wood are the wood anemone and the pilewort. When the leaves of the beech are fully formed, the tops of the grown trees receive the most sunlight. The remaining light which penetrates to a lower depth serves the needs of the other plants. These are consequently mostly adapted, at the vegetation and moss level, to a shadowy existence. Plants such as the wood sorrel that have a particular need for shade, when exposed to clear sunlight, even go underground. Least light of all penetrates to the moss layer, which in a fully grown beech wood in summertime probably receives no more than one-hundredth part of the full daylight. Mosses are thus not at all demanding. They grow very slowly, are in the ordinary course highly resistant to drought, as they can suspend their life activity to a great extent, and are very sparing in the formation of minute, single-cell spores. In beech woods they settle primarily in rock and stumps of trees.

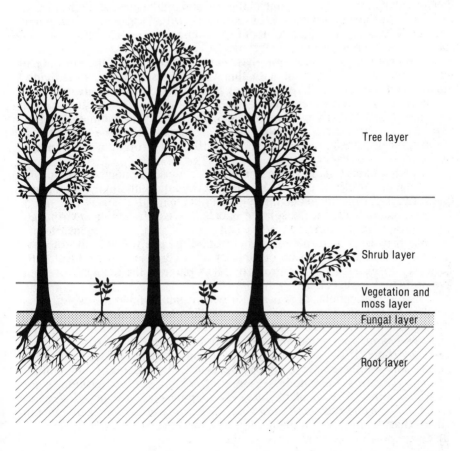

Tree layer

Shrub layer

Vegetation and
moss layer

Fungal layer

Root layer

STRUCTURE OF A HIGH BEECH WOOD

LIFE IN THE SOIL: GROUND FAUNA

Many forms of animal life, from the most primitive monocells to highly developed mammals, are at home in the soil and on the ground. Some remain there only during certain periods of their lives, while others pass their whole lives underground. For most of them the transformation of matter and soil formation are of the greatest importance.

Soil protozoa, whose active phases are connected with the presence of water, subsist in the ground with thin water films to which organic and mineral soil particles adhere. They are smaller for the most part than their counterparts in open water. The varieties that can be distinguished include amebae, flagellates and ciliates, which with the help of rudimentary feet, flagella and cilia, can move about freely in the water. Some species feed autotrophically on inorganic matter, absorbing chloroplasts, while others live on dead or living organic matter.

To what extent many ground monocells reduce the numbers of decomposing agents of organic matter by the extermination of soil bacteria, fungi (yeast fungi, for instance) and algae is still not clear.

Like many bacteria, the soil protozoa survive unfavorable environmental conditions in the form of *cysts:* when various organelles degenerate, the plasma shrivels up and the animals surround themselves with a protective capsule in which they remain capable of life over a long period (often for decades). Propagation of the protozoa takes place in the main on a vegetative basis by simple cell division.

Of the multicellular organisms, of which innumerable forms are domiciled in the soil, the lower earthworms may first be mentioned. As these are not capable of independent burrowing activities, they creep through gaps and crevices in the ground and are found mainly in the layer of soil penetrated by roots. If the living conditions are unfavorable, they retreat into a capsule and are there able to survive drought and extremes of temperature.

Threadworms (nematodes), some of which act as harmful plant-parasites, either live on plant juices by tapping plant tissues, or feed on bacteria, algae and protozoa, or devour other nematodes. As regards threadworms that do not prey on plants, it is assumed that they also play a part in the decomposition of plant remains.

The molluscs, or snails, also play a part in the decomposition of fallen foliage in woodland areas when sufficiently large moist openings such as earthworm casts are available. Otherwise their biological importance for the soil is modest, apart from the fact that by consuming lichen fungi covering bare rock they hinder the contribution of the lichens to soil formation.

Of great biological interest as regards the soil are the representatives of two families of annelids: enchytraeids and earthworms. *Enchytraeids* are whitish worms 2–40 mm long living mainly in fallen foliage or in the upper layer of soil. They are more often found in loose than in firm soil, as they are able to dig through earth to only a limited extent. Their diet consists mainly of decaying leaves and pines. They also seize on nematodes, which live on plants, thereby aiding plant growth. The enchytraeids are very vulnerable to frost and drought. Only their egg cocoons can withstand wide temperature variations and drought. Consequently their population density is greatest in moist ground in the summer, falling significantly in dry ground in the cold seasons of the year.

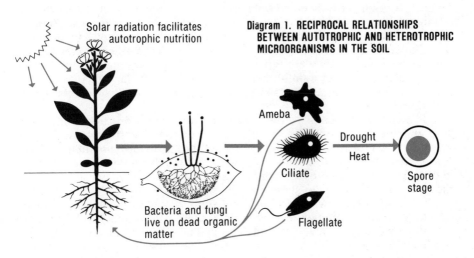

Solar radiation facilitates autotrophic nutrition

Diagram 1. RECIPROCAL RELATIONSHIPS BETWEEN AUTOTROPHIC AND HETEROTROPHIC MICROORGANISMS IN THE SOIL

Ameba

Ciliate

Drought

Heat

Spore stage

Bacteria and fungi live on dead organic matter

Flagellate

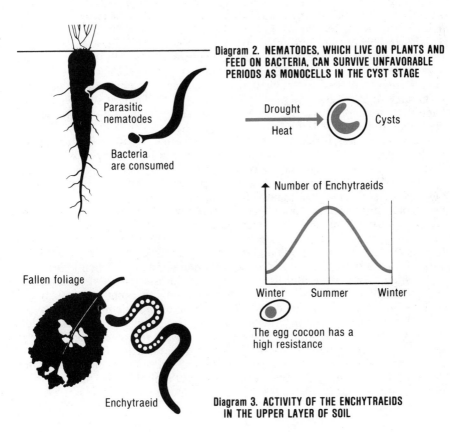

Parasitic nematodes

Bacteria are consumed

Diagram 2. NEMATODES, WHICH LIVE ON PLANTS AND FEED ON BACTERIA, CAN SURVIVE UNFAVORABLE PERIODS AS MONOCELLS IN THE CYST STAGE

Drought

Heat

Cysts

Number of Enchytraeids

Winter   Summer   Winter

The egg cocoon has a high resistance

Fallen foliage

Enchytraeid

Diagram 3. ACTIVITY OF THE ENCHYTRAEIDS IN THE UPPER LAYER OF SOIL

LIFE IN THE SOIL: GROUND FAUNA (continued)

The best-known earth-dwelling creatures are the *earthworms,* which are also of far-reaching importance to land used for agricultural purposes. Various types and layers of soil are inhabited by different species of earthworms. Some varieties live in the upper organic soil layer, while others prefer deeper mineral soils, and as they are sensitive to light they only come to the surface at night or when heavy rainfall has swamped their tubular casts so that air for respiration is scarce. Earthworms live on the remains of plants which they take into their casts.

The composition and volume of the organic matter present in or on the ground influence the types and density of population of earthworms. The pH value and the moisture of the soil also affect the earthworm population. Acid soil is largely avoided, and in dry conditions the earthworms move down into deeper, moister subsoils where, as in the colder seasons of the year, they encase themselves in slime and hibernate.

Because of the low level of nutrient supplies and frequent disturbances caused by tillage activities, earthworms are less well represented on arable land than in forests or meadowland. This can be remedied to some extent by fertilization of the soil with organic substances which serve as a nutrient base. The most favorable temperature and moisture conditions for earthworms occur in the spring and autumn. Temperatures of over 28°C (82°F) can be fatal to earthworms.

Earthworms bore actively into the ground, which they eat their way through; they may leave particles on one side as they go. In the process they leave holes in the ground, the walls of which are reinforced with a coating of slime. The abandoned worm casts make it easier for plant roots to penetrate to greater depths, and the plant roots also get the benefit of chemical nutrients such as phosphorus, nitrogen, potassium and calcium compounds contained in the slime left behind.

Like the enchytraeids, earthworms are hermaphrodites. After reciprocal crossbreeding they deposit their egg cocoons in the upper soil. Young earthworms germinate in the cocoons.

Among the Arthropoda, *mites* are of particular biological importance as regards the soil. They live mainly at the litter level and in the upper soil. The predatory mites among them feed on threadworms, springtails and other small creatures. They are not evenly distributed in the soil but tend to bunch together. Horn mites, which are found particularly in moist ground in pine forests and deciduous woods and in meadowland, feed on plant remains as well as on bacteria. As the nutritional elements that are difficult to decompose (such as cellulose and lignin) pass through the mite's gut unchanged, the importance of their feeding activities from the point of view of soil biology lies chiefly in the mechanical reduction of organic matter.

Also of interest among the insects are the *springtails* (order Collembola). Owing to their limited sensitivity to lower temperatures, these are among the most widely distributed earth dwellers. They feed on plant remains, animal carcasses, microorganisms and many of them also on undecomposed cellulose. Like the horn mites, collembolans participate in the preparation of plant substances for further decomposition by bacteria and fungi.

Diagram 1. EARTHWORMS ACTIVELY BORE WORMHOLES IN THE GROUND

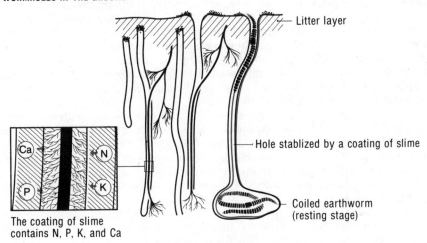

Litter layer

Hole stablized by a coating of slime

Coiled earthworm (resting stage)

The coating of slime contains N, P, K, and Ca

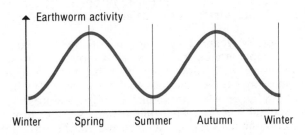

Earthworm activity

Winter   Spring   Summer   Autumn   Winter

Diagram 2. SEASONAL ACTIVITY OF EARTHWORMS

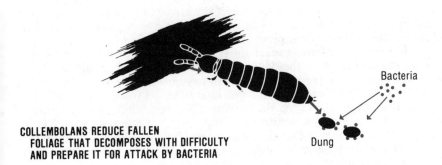

Bacteria

Dung

COLLEMBOLANS REDUCE FALLEN FOLIAGE THAT DECOMPOSES WITH DIFFICULTY AND PREPARE IT FOR ATTACK BY BACTERIA

GROUND FLORA

In the decomposition of the organic remains of the higher plants and dead animals, *ground flora,* among which ground bacteria, actinomycetes (ray fungi), fungi, algae and lichens are numbered, play an important role.

Among the most important organisms regarding the decomposition of matter are ground bacteria. In terms of numbers they outweigh all other forms of life in the soil. Often they are covered by a coating of slime, which gives rise to the life digestion of the inorganic soil particles and the coherence of bacteria in so-called microcolonies. The coating of slime has further importance in the solution and assimilation of mineral nutrients that are hard to come by, such as iron and phosphorus.

In the face of unfavorable environmental conditions, such as desiccation and heat, which often occur on the surface in hot seasons of the year, the bacteria protect themselves by the formation of resistant spores with a very strong cell wall. Each bacterium develops a spore from time to time, which in favorable environmental conditions germinates a bacterium in its turn. Further continuous forms, known as cysts, are found in certain nitrogen-fixing bacteria.

The bacteria obtain the energy needed for sustaining life and forming new cells either by a chemical autotrophic process (the oxidation of inorganic compounds and, by using the energy so released, the assimilation of the carbon dioxide), or they live heterotrophically (they need organic carbon sources—carbohydrates, proteins and fats—to satisfy their energy requirements).

The actinomycetes (ray fungi), which are associated with the bacteria, make their appearance during the decomposition of animal and plant remains (when the easily decomposable substances have largely decomposed); they grow more slowly than the other bacteria and the fungi. Compared with the bacteria they prefer drier soils; and furthermore they are more sensitive to acid ground reaction. Their main sources of nutrition are high molecular organic compounds such as cellulose and chitin. Actinomycetes also play an important part in the formation of humic substances.

A further group of earth-dwelling microorganisms are the slime bacteria (Myxobacterales), which are found mainly as cellulose-decomposing agents in decaying plant material.

Of the vegetable microorganisms, next to bacteria the fungi are the most extensive group of earth dwellers. In dry or acid soils they sometimes outweigh the bacteria in cellular substance. They always live heterotrophically, that is, on organic matter, and in contrast to bacteria they possess a genuine nucleus. Some of them cause plant diseases. For the most part they decompose carbohydrates. Many, especially stem fungi, demolish especially the lignified parts of plants by the decomposition of lignin and cellulose. Many varieties of stem fungi live with tree roots in symbiosis (see also Part Four), which plays an important part in the nutrition of forest trees.

Like the higher plants, earth-dwelling algae and blue-green algae contain chlorophyll and so are autotrophic. But some varieties can also live on organic matter at lower soil levels without light for some time. Owing to the capacity of certain blue-green algae to absorb atmospheric nitrogen, they constitute an important element in the nitrogen cycle.

With regard to lichens, it is really a question of a life community of fungi and algae. As earth dwellers they are only of secondary importance.

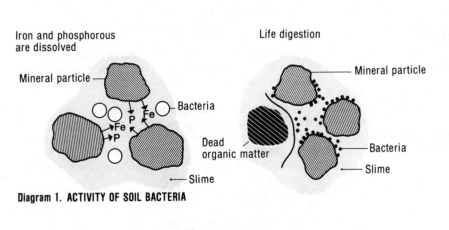

Iron and phosphorous
are dissolved

Mineral particle

Fe

P

Fe

P

Bacteria

Slime

Diagram 1. ACTIVITY OF SOIL BACTERIA

Life digestion

Mineral particle

Dead
organic matter

Bacteria

Slime

Bacteria with
slime coating

Dryness

Spore

Diagram 2. SPORE FORMATION

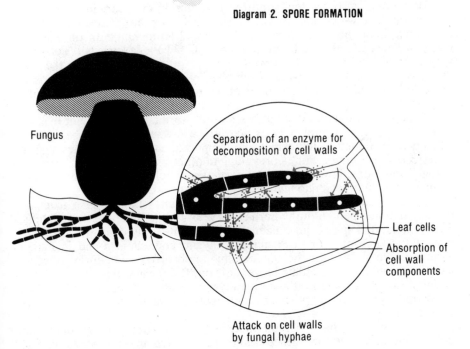

Fungus

Separation of an enzyme for
decomposition of cell walls

Leaf cells

Absorption of
cell wall
components

Attack on cell walls
by fungal hyphae

**Diagram 3. STEM FUNGI DECOMPOSE LIGNIN AND CELLULOSE
IN LIGNIFIED PLANT PARTS**

SPRINGS AND LIFE IN SPRINGS

When a flow of groundwater emerges on the earth's surface, a spring is formed. This happens when an impervious layer of earth such as clay, loam or rock, which arrests the downward progress of the water, crops out on the earth's surface. According to the way in which the water emerges from the ground, three types of spring are to be distinguished:

The *running spring* appears mainly on mountain slopes. In this case the water spurts out of the ground often with great force and runs straight down the slope toward the valley. As the water flows at great speed, the watercourse is clear of water plants.

In the case of the *basin spring,* the mouth of the spring is on the bed of a pool of greater or less depth. The water emerging from the spring first fills the basin which overflows into a watercourse (rill). As the water only flows slowly in this case, water plants gather on the banks of the basin. If the rate of flow from the spring is not great, sludge can accumulate on the bed of the basin and promote a vigorous growth of plant life.

In open undulating country *swamp* or *marsh springs* are the rule. In this case the entire area surrounding the spring is a swamp in which groundwater flows in only at a few points. These marsh springs can extend over considerable areas. As the water flows slowly in them, they will be overgrown with marsh plants.

Springs possess special ecological properties which give rise to specific spring fauna and flora. An important factor determining the presence of aquatic animal life is the temperature range during the year. In contrast to stream and lake water, spring water maintains a roughly constant temperature throughout the year. Whereas the annual temperature in the surface water of lakes can change by more than 20°C (37°F), in springs it does not vary by more than a few degrees. This narrow variation is due to the fact that the daily outflow of water from the spring is groundwater, which is protected from seasonal fluctuations of temperature by the overlying layers of earth.

In comparison with other surface waters, spring water is cooler in summer and warmer in winter. Consequently, springs are a suitable habitat for animals accustomed to uniformly low temperatures and for species that in winter the lower temperatures prevailing in other waters may harm. Springs in high mountains, however, can be particularly cold, even in summer, and temperatures may reach no higher than 2°–3°C (35°–37°F).

Spring water has a very low oxygen content, often ranging from no more than a few percent up to perhaps 50% of the possible oxygen content. In any individual spring the concentration remains fairly constant, irrespective of the time of year. The highest oxygen content is found in marsh springs, since in this case the water is able to absorb oxygen during its slow passage through well-ventilated layers of soil. If the water flows off from the spring into a little stream, it absorbs oxygen rapidly, as the water will then be stirred up by the many rocks and pebbles and will come into closer contact with the air.

As springs are the transition point between the unlighted groundwater of the inner earth and the surface waters, animals from groundwater are also found in springs, examples being the blind cave amphipod and various similarly eyeless eddy worms. These remain hidden for days at a time, mostly under rocks and plants.

Most springs are very poorly provided with vegetable nutriment. The

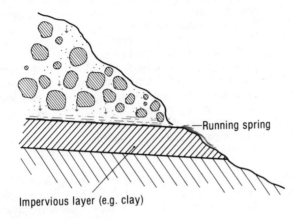

Diagram 1. **RUNNING SPRING**

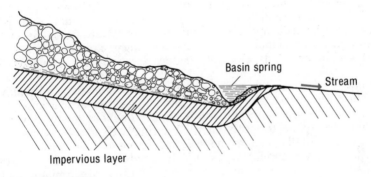

Diagram 2. **BASIN SPRING**

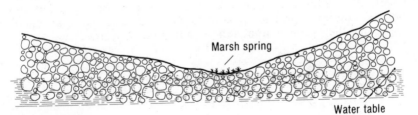

Diagram 3. **MARSH SPRING**

plant-eating animals that live in them have to depend in consequence on the remains of decaying water plants, on parts of plants that fall into the springs, and often even on minute particles of organic matter carried in with the groundwater (detritus). The typical spring animals are very small. They are adapted to life in clean, uniformly cool water comparatively poor in oxygen and in nutriment. They consist mainly of eddy worms, minute spring snails of the genus *Bythinella*, water mites, quiver fly larvae, and beetles. The stream amphipod (*Gammarus pulex*) has developed a smaller form that lives in springs. Most spring animals are herbivorous and are hardly ever predators. A special characteristic of insects that live in springs at the larva stage is their early flying period at the beginning of spring, sometimes as early as February. This is because, owing to the relative warmth of spring water in winter, the larvae are able to develop in the cold months and fully formed insects emerge in the early spring. Examples of this are sugar midges and stone flies.

A completely different biotope from the normal cold spring is the *thermal spring*. The thermal spring is fed with groundwater that comes from deep down where higher temperatures prevail. For this reason the water maintains a temperature throughout the year that is consistently above the seasonal temperature in the neighborhood. Thermal springs occur primarily in tectonic fragmentation zones in the vicinity of extinct or active volcanoes. Thermal springs are inhabited by specific hot-water forms of animals, which are mostly distributed over the entire earth. In thermal springs with temperatures of up to about 40°C (104°F) normal life communities are still found, resembling those elsewhere. In springs of over 40°C (104°F) and up to about 45°C (113°F) these normal life communities tend to drop out, their place being taken by animals adapted to conditions in hot water. The highest water temperature in which plants such as blue-green algae can flourish is around 83°C (181°F). Other plants can only endure temperatures of up to 40°C (104°F).

The maximum tolerable water temperature for animals is around 55°C (131°F). The animals best able to face high temperatures are various monocells or the microscopic rotifers. But a variety of more highly developed animals are also to be found in thermal springs. Examples of these are certain species of snails (such as the *Bithynia thermalis*, which lives in up to 53°C, or 127°F) and of threadworms, which can also live in temperatures of over 50°C (122°F). Just as in normal springs, in thermal springs particular hot-water forms of larvae of various species are to be found, including sugar midges, Stratiomyiidae, salt midges and other Diptera, also diving, water and whirligig beetles, and water bugs. Today over 180 species of animals are known which are able to live in thermal springs. Of these the beetle, with 45 species, is the biggest group. As these animals can be studied at only a few points in thermal springs, many questions regarding their particular habits, especially their propagation, still remain to be answered.

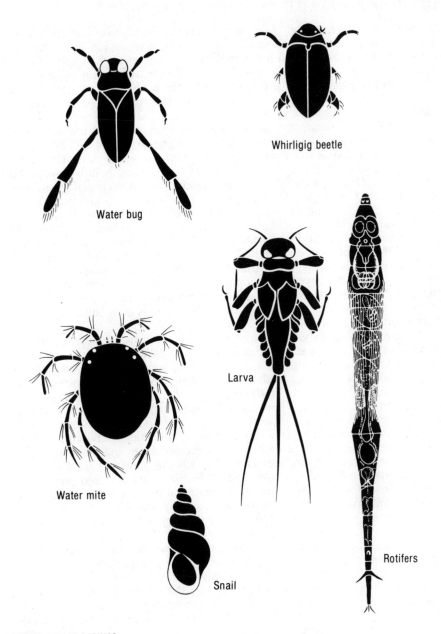

Whirligig beetle

Water bug

Larva

Water mite

Snail

Rotifers

ANIMAL LIFE IN SPRINGS

LIFE IN GROUNDWATER

Groundwater fills the gaps in the layers of rubble and gravel and the fissures in rocks, collects in the rock stratum in many hollows and in some places in big underground basins and flows in streams often more than half a mile in width deep below the surface of the ground. The accumulation and direction of flow of the groundwater are governed by the positioning of strata impervious to water, which collect the rainwater seeping through and carry it away.

Although in contrast to surface waters underground waters are always in total darkness, various life forms have adapted to life in this biotope. It is, of course, possible to examine this habitat only at points at which groundwater comes to the surface—that is to say, in springs, hollows, wells and mine shafts. Owing to the absence of sunlight there is no green plant life in groundwater. Consequently all the organisms that live in groundwater depend on the provision of organic matter from outside, that is, from the earth's surface. Mosses and ferns are certainly often to be found in surprising abundance in hollows to which only traces of daylight can penetrate. Beyond these points only bacteria, fungi and animal organisms are present. These live mainly on the fine particles of decayed plant remains which pass into the groundwater with the seepage water. But as the water has filtered through the layer of topsoil, the input of nutriment is in most cases insignificant, so that the population density of the animals dependent on it is severely limited.

Animals living in groundwater (Stygobiontes) are confined mainly to worms, crayfish and snails. The real groundwater animals consist primarily of pond flatworms of the genus *Dendrocoelum,* webbed-foot crabs (subclass Copepoda), water lice and freshwater shrimps. Also present in limited numbers are certain varieties of bristle worms, water mites and mussel-shrimps. A common feature of these species is vestigial or missing eyes and a whitish, more or less translucent body covering. To make up for the absence of sight, in most cases their taste and sense of smell are highly developed, which often manifests itself in the shape of enlarged antennae and bristles.

As the water temperature remains practically constant throughout the year at between 8° and 10°C (46° and 50°F), there are no fixed propagation periods for groundwater animals. Consequently, gestating females and young animals of different ages are always to be found at the same time. It is an interesting fact that the females lay few eggs. To make up for this the average life-span of individual animals is greater.

As far as can be judged at present, underwater animal life derived from species above ground that immigrated to the groundwater zone at some time in the past. Presumably they were mainly light-shy (photophobic) varieties which live even today under stones and in the sludge of shady woodland streams. It is also conceivable that the "migration" occurred under the influence of the Ice Age: as the Ice Age set in, the surface water got steadily colder and living conditions for water life got progressively worse. It is thus highly probable that groundwater, with a constant temperature level of between 8° and 10°C (46° and 50°F), became a refuge for animals from above ground, who were driven from the surface by the icy conditions and in the course of their evolution have adapted to the subterranean conditions in groundwater. Conversely, the groundwater may have offered a refuge to

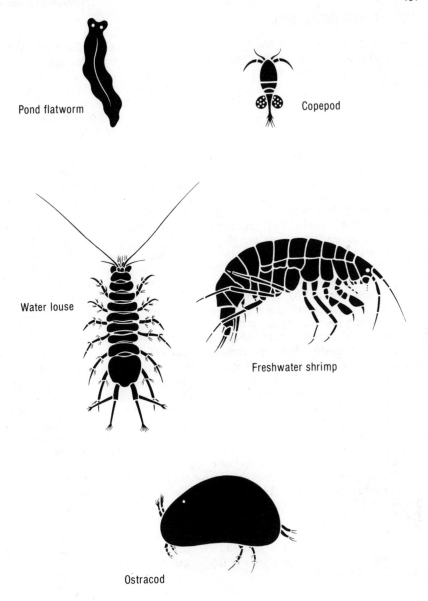

Pond flatworm

Copepod

Water louse

Freshwater shrimp

Ostracod

LIFE IN GROUNDWATER

those animals that had become accustomed to lower temperatures during the Ice Age and were attracted to the cooler waters below ground when temperatures began to rise again as the Ice Age ended.

LIFE IN THE DEEP SEA

Sunlight penetrates the sea to a depth of about 1000 m (3000 ft). Animals living in this twilight zone consequently have very big eyes and exceptionally wide pupils. Like many nocturnal animals on dry land, deep-sea animals have all the sensory cells of their retinas protruding on rods. These rods, which serve to pick up what little light there is and convert it into nerve impulses, are unusually long and large. A nerve cell from the optic nerve is linked simultaneously to several rods. Under this arrangement an extremely high sensitivity to light is achieved.

At a depth of below 1000 m (3000 ft) or so, at which almost total darkness prevails, the fish have either no eyes at all or only very small eyes of limited capacity. It is now known that such deep-sea fish find their way in the dark with the aid of sensory organs with which they are able to detect vibrations in the water. Many deep-sea fish have very long organs of touch of a most remarkable kind: tentacles of great length with feeler-type floating ends and extensive tail ends. Many fish have long feelers furnished with claws and sharp points, which also serve to locate and trap their prey.

Certain sea organisms are able to illumine their paths of their own accord or to radiate more or less intensive light (bioluminescence). In many cases a glow is cast by certain cells which are surrounded by reflecting cell groups. Other animals can emit luminous substances into the surrounding water which provide light away from the animal concerned for some time and probably serve to camouflage its activities. In particular cases a symbiosis is established between luminous bacteria and fish whereby the luminous bacteria are in effect kept in a tissue culture by the larger animal. Some varieties emit projectorlike light beams that probably help to locate the prey. Other deep-sea fish have luminous bait at the end of long extensions, which take various forms and colors. In some varieties the luminous bait even hangs from an enormous jaw. In other cases light organs may help the male and female of a particular species to locate one another on the seabed for mating purposes. Many sea organisms can switch their light beams on and off, as it were, so as to confuse their opponents.

Many deep-sea fish have enormous teeth and jaws. And their maws are often extremely flexible. This points to the fact that their nutriment may be found only at rare intervals, and it may then be very bulky and have to quell the animal's hunger for long periods.

A number of aspects regarding deep-sea fish still remain to be clarified, however. We often have to depend on chance discoveries, and animals that are brought to the surface are apt to die quickly, so that intensive investigations are not possible.

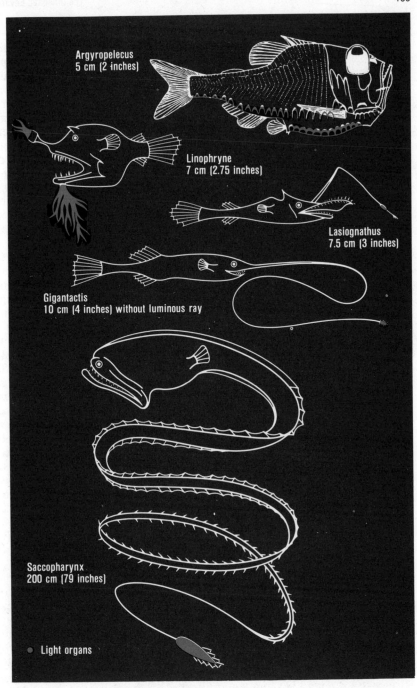

Argyropelecus
5 cm (2 inches)

Linophryne
7 cm (2.75 inches)

Lasiognathus
7.5 cm (3 inches)

Gigantactis
10 cm (4 inches) without luminous ray

Saccopharynx
200 cm (79 inches)

● Light organs

MORPHOLOGICAL FEATURES OF DEEP-SEA FISH

WATER PLANTS

The higher water plants (hydrophytes), which have probably developed from moisture-loving shade plants (hygrophytes) and have adapted to total life in the water, are distinguished from land plants by a number of characteristic features.

Whereas land plants in most cases absorb mineral nutrients from the soil only through their roots, water plants can absorb salts dissolved in the water over their entire surface, especially through their leaves. The leaf surfaces of water plants are usually bigger than those of the related species on land; and furthermore their epidermis (outer surface) is thinner and more sensitive. This allows an active exchange of substances over the entire surface of the plant.

Water plants have two possible ways of absorbing carbon dioxide: direct absorption of carbon dioxide gas dissolved in the water through the epidermis of the split leaves, and reduction of calcium bicarbonate, which is often present in the water in large quantities. The carbon dioxide so produced is absorbed by the plants, and the residue left behind is often deposited in the form of a white calcium crust.

While carbon dioxide dissolves fairly freely in water, the solubility of oxygen in water is considerably less. Many water plants consequently have intercellular vents formed from star-shaped cells, in which the oxygen produced by photosynthesis throughout the day can build up as a respiration reserve to be drawn on at night. These air chambers also impart a measure of buoyancy to the plants, which keeps them upright in the water. Thanks to the buoyancy so imparted, the plant stems need far less strengthening tissue to support them in water than on the land. Consequently no lignification takes place for most of the plants. Similarly, there is no secondary thickness growth. The only serious stress to which water plants are subject occurs in flowing water, and to resist this the plant stems must possess considerable tensile strength. In most cases such strength is not provided by a peripheral sustaining tissue but by a stable central core. Insofar as roots are present, these serve only marginally, if at all, for the absorption of nutrients and primarily for anchoring the plants.

According to the varying ecological conditions between the shore and the deep-water region, the water plants display a marked diversity of form. In the case of marsh plants (helophytes), only the root organs and possibly the lowest shoot parts are covered by water. They can thus be regarded as a transition from genuine land plants to water plants. When a marsh dries out in summer, most marsh plants can survive this dry period.

In the next adaptation phase, amphibious plants and plants with floating leaves are encountered. In the case of the former, a considerable portion of the plant lives permanently inundated in water, while the bloom-bearing shoot parts, often in company with part of the green leaves, project far out of the water. Examples of this are the pond rush and arrow grass. In the case of floating-leaf plants, all or part of the leaves float flat on the water surface, so that the upper side is exposed to the air and the under side to the water. In these forms, too, the blooms project in most cases well above the surface (e.g., pond lilies and water lilies). As these still have their upper leaf surfaces exposed to the air, the gas exchange of carbon dioxide and oxygen takes place on the upper side of the leaves.

From these forms the true submerged water plants are derived. Many of them no longer develop blooms, but propagate exclusively on vegetable lines (e.g., offshoots, dismemberment of shoot parts).

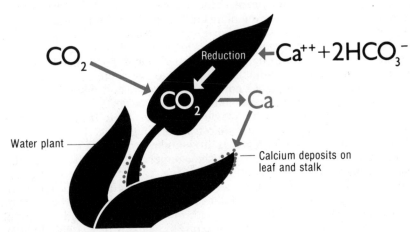

$$CO_2 \quad \text{Reduction} \quad \leftarrow Ca^{++} + 2HCO_3^-$$

$$CO_2 \rightarrow Ca$$

Water plant

Calcium deposits on leaf and stalk

Diagram 1. ABSORPTION OF CARBON DIOXIDE AND CALCIUM DEPOSITS IN WATER PLANTS (HYDROPHYTES)

1. Sedge
2. Rushes
3. Water plantain
4. Pond rush
5. Arrow grass
6. American Frog's-bit
7. Flowering rush
8. Reed grass
9. Cat's tail
10. Water Smartweed
11. Water lily
12. Hornwort
13. Water milfoil
14. Stoneworts

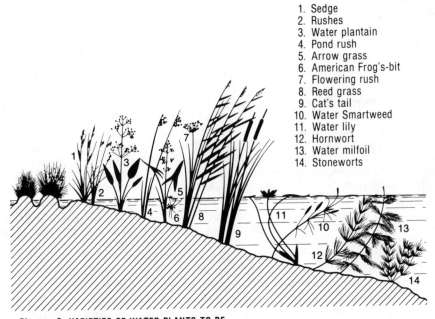

Diagram 2. VARIETIES OF WATER PLANTS TO BE FOUND ON THE BANKS OF PONDS

INSECTIVOROUS PLANTS

In their feeding habits, insectivorous plants occupy an intermediate position between autotrophic and heterotrophic regimens of life. There are altogether about 500 varieties of flowering plants in the world that trap animals for their sustenance. They live mostly on barren ground that is very poor in nitrogen, and they absorb the nitrogen they need mainly by the assimilation of animal protein. This is done through enzymes that decompose the flesh of their victims (mostly insects). Sometimes decomposing bacteria also take part in this process. All these plants contain chlorophyll and have roots, so that they can also consume nutrients autotrophically.

According to the way in which they seize their prey, insectivorous plants are classified as lime-twig, flap-trap, and pitfall catchers.

A typical *lime-twig catcher* is the sundew (genus *Drosera*), which is found mainly on upland moors. On their upper side the leaves bear numerous glandular hairs which secrete at their tips a vesicular viscous slime, and in the sunlight this shines like a dewdrop. Insects that crawl across these leaves get caught up in the glandular hairs, stick fast, and in their efforts to free themselves come into contact with more and more heads of the glandular hairs. This touches off a curvature movement of the glandular hairs around the prey. If the leaf is stimulated especially strongly by a bigger animal the leaf surfaces will also curve inward, so that the victim will be completely enclosed. The glandular heads of the hairs will now secrete a digestive liquid which, in the course of a few days, will decompose the protein substance of the insect until only the chitin remains are left.

Another lime-twig catcher is the butterwort (genus *Pinguicula*), which occurs in moist peaty soil, especially in low-lying bogland. The upper side of its thick pulpy leaves is thickly covered with minute glandular hairs which secrete a viscous slime. When an insect is caught in this slime, an enzyme-containing secretion is released by the chemical stimulation of the animal protein. At the same time the edges of the leaves curl inward. In a short time the protein substance of the insect decomposes and is absorbed in the same way as in the case of sundew.

One of the *flap-trap catchers* is the bladderwort (genus *Utricularia*), a floating water plant with small vesicles on its stalks, which constitute an interesting trapping arrangement. The walls of these water-containing traps, which are sealed above by a flap furnished with stiff bristles, are bent inward elastically, so that a lower pressure exists in the vesicles. When a water insect (e.g., a water flea) touches one of the bristles, which operate like a lever on the flap, this opens inward and the vesicle walls spring open. The water flowing into the vesicle carries the victim in with it.

The Venus's-flytrap (genus *Dionaea*), a native of North America, catches insects by suddenly closing its leaf span. The end of each trap leaf consists of two parts, which are furnished on the outside with two little teeth and have on the inside three sensory bristles each. When an insect touches these, the leaf surfaces snap almost instantaneously together so that the insect is trapped between the leaves. Thereupon a digestive liquid is discharged onto the leaf surfaces from small glands, whereby the insect is assimilated.

The *pitfall catcher* is exemplified by the pitcher plant (genus *Nepenthes*), which climbs high up into trees in the humid primitive forests of Asia. The trapping organism consists of a pitcher-shaped structure that spar-

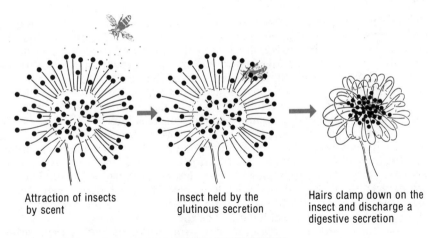

| Attraction of insects by scent | Insect held by the glutinous secretion | Hairs clamp down on the insect and discharge a digestive secretion |

Diagram 1. OPERATION OF THE TRAP MECHANISM OF THE SUNDEW

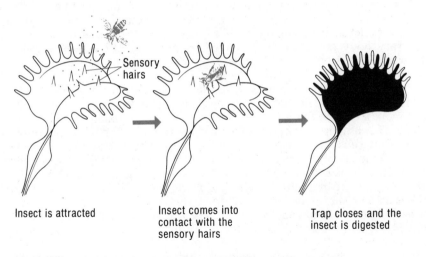

| Insect is attracted | Insect comes into contact with the sensory hairs | Trap closes and the insect is digested |

Diagram 2. OPERATION OF THE TRAP MECHANISM OF THE VENUS'S-FLYTRAP

kles on the outside in variegated colors. Inside is secreted nectar which attracts insects. The inner wall of the pitcher is so smooth, however, that the insects cannot secure a foothold and drop into the pitcher where they drown in a digestive liquid.

INSECTS

Of over one million animal species known today, approximately three quarters are insects. The total number of insect species is probably considerably greater than this when it is considered that numerous species have not yet been discovered. Insects display an enormous variety in size, appearance, habits and distribution. In the hot months of the year, in particular, hardly any living space is free from insect life of some sort.

In the light of current scientific knowledge insects have been on the earth for about 300 million years. The earliest insect fossils date back to the Carboniferous period, the age of the coal forests. Insect development was then in its heyday. About 60 million years ago, at the beginning of the Tertiary period, a new extensive evolution of insect life set in (see diagram). These insects were very similar in appearance to those of today. The best preserved animals have come down to us embedded in amber. Particulars of their formation can still be established with the aid of a microscope. Many of them have changed hardly at all since the Tertiary period.

Insects are in no sense a primitive form of life. Judged by their organization level, adaptability to the environment and way of life, they match up in many respects to vertebrate animals.

All the insects have essential characteristics in common. In contrast to the vertebrates, which have an internal bone structure, insects depend on an outer skeleton enclosing their bodies, mainly as a hard chitin cuticle. The necessary body movement is provided by division into various segments which are linked by a thin, flexible chitin and are adjustable in relation to one another.

The insect's body comprises the head, the thorax (made up of three segments: front, middle and rear breast) and the abdomen, consisting of up to 11 members. The thorax carries three pairs of legs and up to two pairs of wings. The principal material of which an insect's body is composed is *chitin*. This substance possesses peculiar properties in many respects from both a chemical and a physical point of view. Chitin combines great hardness with low weight. It constitutes the thick casing of the beetle and the delicate wings of the butterfly, the hair covering of the bumblebee and the proboscis and sucker of the mosquito. Every insect's legs and feelers are formed of and strengthened by chitin. The trachea system in every insect's body is lined with chitin as far as the chitin-free spiracles, which supply the individual cells with oxygen.

As insects have an outer skeleton, their muscle system is inside. The rigid chitin cuticle permits no growth, so that the growing insect, i.e., the larva, must shed its skin from time to time, and each time this happens a new and bigger chitin skeleton is formed.

Insects have adapted themselves to different ecological conditions in a variety of ways. This is evident, for instance, from changes in the mouth parts. The basic type is represented by the biting-chewing appendages of the grasshopper and the butterfly caterpillar. Many beetles, ants and bees have chewing-licking appendages, by means of which they absorb pollen and sap from plants. Licking-sucking appendages serve only to absorb liquid nutrients, so that the mandibles have become functionless or have dropped out altogether, as in the case of the hovering fly. This type is to be found primarily in flies and butterflies in the form of a proboscis. A further evolutionary advance was the formation of piercing-sucking mouth parts, as a tissue often has to be pierced first before the nutrient in the form of sap or

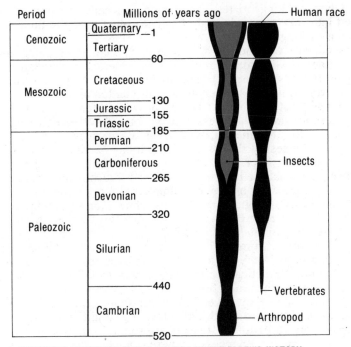

Period	Millions of years ago		Human race
Cenozoic	Quaternary —1		
	Tertiary		
	—60—		
Mesozoic	Cretaceous		
	—130		
	Jurassic —155		
	Triassic —185—		Insects
Paleozoic	Permian —210		
	Carboniferous —265		
	Devonian —320		
	Silurian		
	—440		Vertebrates
	Cambrian		Arthropod
	—520—		

Diagram 1. EVOLUTION OF INSECTS IN THE COURSE OF THE EARTH'S HISTORY

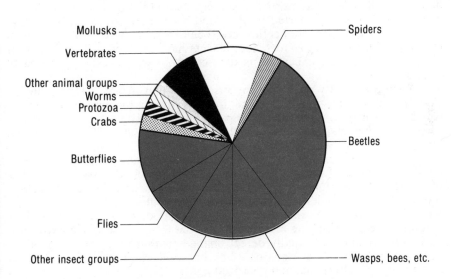

Mollusks — Spiders
Vertebrates
Other animal groups
Worms
Protozoa
Crabs
Butterflies — Beetles
Flies
Other insect groups — Wasps, bees, etc.

Diagram 2. NUMBER OF INSECT SPECIES ON THE EARTH COMPARED WITH THE NUMBER OF SPECIES OF OTHER ANIMALS

blood can be reached. These different piercing appendages are all formed on the same basic pattern: the lower lip (labium) has become an external guide tube in which the upper and lower mandibles (mandibles and maxillae), formed into pricking bristles, are located. A saliva to prevent clotting is injected into the wound through a salivary duct, and the fluid is extracted through a sucking tube.

Insects vary enormously in size. Among the biggest are certain beetles. The hercules beetle from tropical South America, for instance, attains a length of 16 cm (6.3 inches). The male of the species has two powerful forward-projecting horns which are a continuation of the neck carapace (the upper, longer protuberance) and of the brow. The female, on the other hand, is considerably smaller and less conspicuous. Another extreme case is the owl moth of South America, which has a wingspan of over 32 cm (12.6 inches). The longest of the insects living today is the South American giant stick grasshopper, over 30 cm (11.8 inches) in length. At the other end of the scale, the smallest insects of the earth are not much larger than the single-cell paramecium or slipper animalcule. Among these smallest insects belong the dwarf springtail and various ichneumon flies, which attain sizes of from 0.1 to 0.3 mm. It is astonishing how tiny all the vital insect organs are in these small organisms.

Like the other arthropods, insects are easily the most successful of all the animal groups in the settlement of the living space in the world. They have understood practically everywhere how to utilize the sources of nutrient available to them and how to adapt to various environmental conditions. In the tropics they have evolved an impressive range of species. But even in areas of the earth with difficult living conditions, hardly any insect-free regions are to be found. Insects are found in the steppes and in torrid deserts, in sludge in deep recesses where sunlight never penetrates, on small islets and on mountain glaciers. There are tiny glacier fleas inhabiting snowfields in high Alpine passes and polar regions and living on organic matter contained in dust transported by the wind. In the Himalayas ants, wasps, bees, butterflies, bugs and beetles have been found at heights of up to 5000 m (16,000 ft). In inland waters, too, insects have evolved in a proliferation of species. The only exception is the sea, from which insects are nearly absent.

A special faculty developed by insects of many kinds is that of flight. This has been "discovered" in nature four times: by birds, bats, flying lizards and insects. Dragonflies, in particular, have raised it to a fine art. They attain flying speeds of up to 50 kilometers per hour (30 mph), change direction in the air with lightning rapidity, and can fly backward.

A further special characteristic of insects is their complex eyes. In contrast to those of other animals, the eyes of insects consist of a number of hexagonal individual eyes, which together form a complete eye. Each of the facets of a complex eye is aimed in a particular direction, whereby a mosaic-type composite image of the neighborhood is obtained. With their complex eyes, swift-flying insects such as the dragonfly can see extraordinarily clearly and can rapidly detect changes within range of their vision. Particularly wide vision is possessed by bees, which in contrast to humans can distinguish ultraviolet and polarized light.

In the field of natural events, insects also fill an important role. Butterflies, bees and bumblebees are the most important pollinators of flowering plants, and so assist their propagation. Beetles such as the burying beetle, the carrion beetle and the silpha see to the removal of animal remains. Particular members of the insect population in dead tree-trunks and tree-stumps ensure their complete demolition and their reincorporation in the cycle of nature. (See also Part Four.)

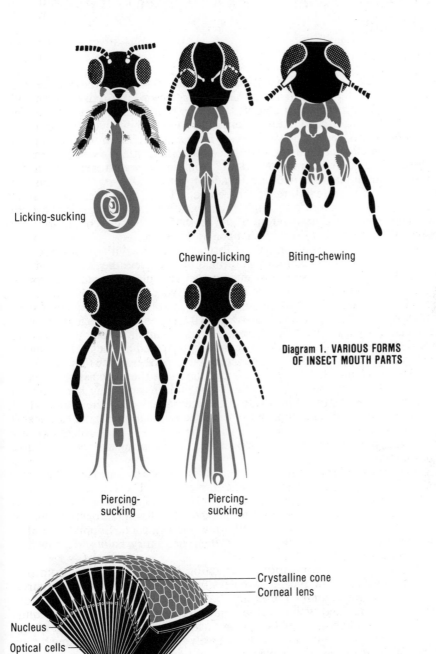

Licking-sucking

Chewing-licking

Biting-chewing

Piercing-
sucking

Piercing-
sucking

Diagram 1. VARIOUS FORMS
OF INSECT MOUTH PARTS

Crystalline cone
Corneal lens

Nucleus

Optical cells

Diagram 2. THE FACETED EYE OF INSECTS

Part Four—Organisms Living Together in Harmony or Hostility

COLONIES OF INSECTS

Apart from the species of insects that live alone—and this applies to the great majority of them—there are certain species whose individuals band together to form permanent colonies. The gradual formation of substantial colonies is best seen among the order Hymenoptera (bees, wasps and ants). The *Anthophora* (potter flower bees), for example, lay out their tubular structures on clay and mortar walls, close together, often in large numbers. In these big colonies common action is sometimes undertaken, when, for instance, the animals set upon an invader together. They will even do this when their own interests are not threatened. These skin bees continue to live together, however, only until their eggs are laid and provided with nutriment. Continued association of the mothers with their young or of the young with one another does not happen at this stage.

The next highest stage in colony formation occurs with bumblebees. In the spring the bumblebee colony is formed by the queen bee, a hibernating female. The queen bee develops, in some suitable place (a small earth-hole or the like), a number of oval cells with beeswax kneaded with pollen or resin. The cells are filled with pollen or honey and lined by the queen with a number of eggs. The nest is also provided with a spherical storage bin, which the queen fills with honey. The maggotlike larvae are first fed by the queen. They develop into female working bees with atrophied ovaries. They collect honey and pollen, feed the young larvae, build further combs and tend the nest. The more female workers grow up, the more the queen is relieved of her burdens, so that she is then able to concentrate on laying her eggs. As summer approaches this will result in the emergence of fertile females and of males. Toward the autumn the bumblebee population begins to die off. By then several hundred bees will have developed. The fertilized young queens hibernate throughout the winter and in the spring are ready to form new colonies.

A colony similar to that of bumblebees is formed by wasps and hornets, though these colonies are more prolific in members. The substance used for building the nests is a paperlike pulp of finely masticated wood mixed with a glutinous saliva. The rounded-to-hexagonal cells stay together in the honeycomb. They are furnished with only one egg each. Supplies are provided by the wasps and hornets with their predatory habits. The nest is protected in concert.

A particularly high form of organization is displayed by ant colonies. Here we have very big queens, wingless barren female workers, and small males. In big ant colonies there may be several queens. Female workers with large bodies and well-developed jaws that have been specially nourished are earmarked as soldiers. The ant nests consist of a system of chambers and passages and are used primarily to nurture the young. It is interesting that the South American leaf-cutting ants grow fungal cultures. The bigger female workers carry pieces of leaves into their earth nests. These are masticated by the smaller female workers into a leaf pulp, injected with fungi and constantly fertilized with saliva and excreta. The resultant lush fungal culture constitutes their main food supply.

Diagram 1. NEST STRUCTURE OF A
SOLITARY SOIL-LIVING BEE

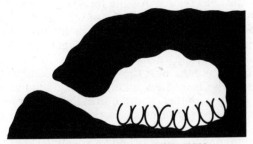

Diagram 2. NEST STRUCTURE OF BUMBLEBEES

Diagram 3. NEST STRUCTURE OF THE GERMAN WASP

BEE COLONY

The colony of honeybees consists of a single queen bee and from 40,000 to 70,000 female workers, to which in springtime several hundred males (drones) are added. In the usual case only the queen can lay eggs, and all the other occupants of the beehive come from her. She has a life-span of from four to five years.

The workers are barren females who, other than laying eggs, perform all the duties for the colony and only live for a few weeks in the spring and summer. The working duties are strictly regulated. From the first to about the tenth day of their lives the workers perform labors inside the hive. For the first three days they keep the hive clean and sweet. From the fourth day they feed the young brood, for which purpose they emit a special secretion, so-called pap. Thereafter, according to the age of the grub (larva), honey and pollen are added to the pap. From the tenth to the twentieth days the working bee turns its efforts to building the honeycomb. For this purpose, it has glands (between the rings on its hindquarters) that secrete beeswax in the form of small scales. These scales are removed with its legs, transferred to the mandibles and there kneaded thoroughly. Then the so-called working bees set these globules one upon another until a hexagonal honeycomb cell is formed. It is still not known to this day precisely how the extraordinary regularity of the cells (as regards the thickness of their walls in particular) is achieved. On about the twentieth day of their lives the workers start to keep watch on the entrance to the hive. With their sense of smell they are able to detect the presence of any bees not belonging to the swarm and of other animals, all of whom they debar from entry. To help returning members of the swarm in locating the nest they secrete a scent; and for this purpose, at the entrance to the hive, they extend their hindquarters vertically into the air. In association with their guard duties the workers spend the rest of their lives (as members of a swarm) collecting pollen and nectar. In so doing, in company with other pollen-seeking insects, they fill an important role in nature by pollinating the flowers and so assisting the seed and fruit formation of flowering plants.

If the bees performing a particular task drop out, other bees can take over their tasks. In that case organs that had ceased to function (such as the sex organs or the wax glands of female workers) are rejuvenated, or particular organs can come into operation earlier than usual. The bee community can thus be regarded as an organism of a higher order.

The drones take no part in the work of the community, but they feed on the stores collected by the workers. Their task is to mate with the queen. Once this has happened they are driven out of the hive or killed (''slaughter of the drones'').

In the hive of honeybees there are found several vertically aligned honeycombs with hexagonal prismatic wax cells stacked close together. The cells are situated with the brood at a particular point in the middle of the nest. In the neighborhood of the brood, pollen is stored. The honeycombs filled with honey hang in front of and behind the brood nest.

The internal temperature of the hive remains constant (except in winter) at between 34.5° and 35.5°C (94° and 96°F). Bees have a very acute sense of temperature, which enables them to register temperature differences of no more than one-fifth of a degree centigrade. Any change of temperature inside

Diagram 1. EVOLUTION OF HONEYBEES

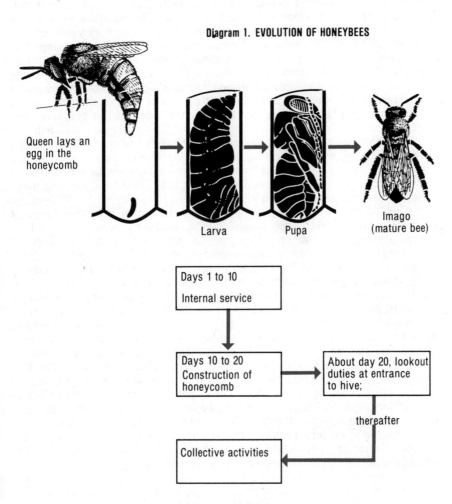

Queen lays an egg in the honeycomb

Larva

Pupa

Imago (mature bee)

Days 1 to 10
Internal service

Days 10 to 20
Construction of honeycomb

About day 20, lookout duties at entrance to hive;

thereafter

Collective activities

Diagram 2. CHANGE IN ACTIVITIES OF HONEYBEES

the hive is adjusted immediately: if the temperature is too high, the bees bring water into the empty cells and so use the cooling effect of evaporation to lower the temperature; in addition, by vibrating their wings, they accelerate the evaporation process. If the temperature drops below normal, on the other hand, the bees boost their metabolism by taking honey out of store and raise their body temperatures by muscular vibration and vibrating their wings. This is all done to protect the brood, in particular the brood honeycombs, where the bees congregate close together. In winter, when breeding activity is at an end, the bees combine to form a tight cluster, in which the temperature barely drops below 20°C (68°F). From time to time the colder bees on the periphery change places with the bees in the center of the cluster.

Except in the case of bumblebees, the reestablishment of the bee colony is not effected by the queen bee alone. When the bee community has grown to a certain size, the old queen leaves the hive with some of the bees as a swarm. This provides the nucleus for a new colony. In the old hive the place of the old queen is taken by a new one.

Of particular importance for the social behavior of honeybees is their ability to communicate ("bee language"). Community bees that have discovered a store of nectar or pollen pass the information on in the hive by performing distinctive dances. Experimental research in this field has been carried out by Karl von Frisch. According to his findings the community bees perform simple round dances on the honeycomb when the food store is located near the hive. If the food supply, possibly a blooming fruit tree, is more than 80 to 100 m (262 to 328 ft) from the hive, the round dance gives way to a sort of shimmy or waggle: a figure 8 is described, in the course of which the dancer rapidly wags her hindquarters up and down. The course followed by the dancer indicates the direction in which the food lies in relation to the position of the sun. If, for instance, the food store lies precisely in the direction of the sun, the shimmy will be performed vertically. If the food store is situated at a particular angle to the sun, the bee indicates this by changing the direction of the dance to precisely the same angle from the vertical on the side concerned. The more remote is the food store, the slower are the gyrations, but the more intensive will be the shimmy. By the number of gyrations per unit of time, the bee thus indicates precisely to her companions the flight performance that is required in order to reach the food store. For this purpose the land structure and wind influences are all taken into account. Thanks to the bees' capacity to perceive polarized light, a glimpse of blue sky is all they need to size up the position of the sun.

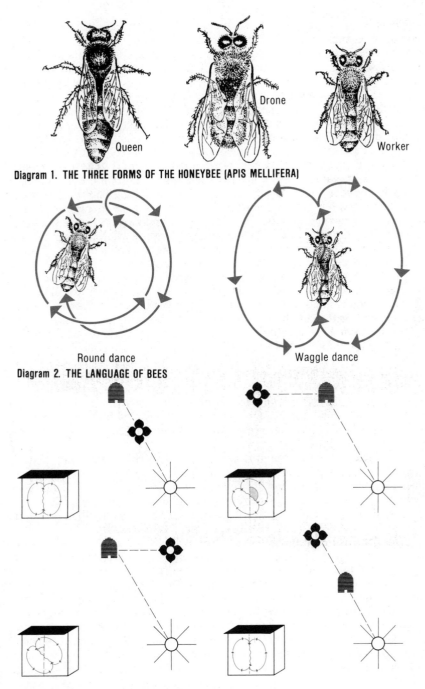

Diagram 1. THE THREE FORMS OF THE HONEYBEE (APIS MELLIFERA)

Queen

Drone

Worker

Round dance

Waggle dance

Diagram 2. THE LANGUAGE OF BEES

Diagram 3. DIRECTION INDICATORS BY BEES IN A WAGGLE DANCE
ACCORDING TO THE POSITION OF THE SUN

SYMBIOSIS

Symbiosis is an association of two or more organisms of different kinds in which each partner, unlike the case of parasites, benefits by the relationship. Autotrophic and heterotrophic organisms are often associated by symbiosis. Autotrophic organisms may be green plants that are capable of living on inorganic matter, from which with the help of the sun's rays they build up the organic matter they need for growth. Heterotrophic organisms, on the other hand, need organic, energy-bearing compounds for their sustenance.

In a symbiosis between an autotrophic and a heterotrophic partner, the heterotroph offers the autotroph protection and sustenance, while the autotroph delivers in return a part of the organic matter it has built up.

An interesting example of this is provided by *lichens*. These are treated as a systematic plant category in their own right, although they represent a symbiosis between algae or blue-green algae and fungi. The morphological connection between the two partners is so close that in practice a new "organism" is developed having specific form and constant, systematically determinable characteristics. By examining a cross section through a lichen its symbiotic character instantly emerges. Its main tissue consists of fungal fiber, which gives the lichen its characteristic form. Among these fungal tissues, especially in the case of thallophytes, there are green algae and blue-green algae, which have a capacity for photosynthesis. A symbiont category is determined for each particular type of lichen. In particular there are single-cell or thread-shaped multicellular representatives of green algae (Chlorophyta) or blue-green algae (Cyanophyta); in the case of fungi they are mainly tube fungi (Ascomycetes) but often stem fungi (Basidiomycetes). Symbionts living in association with a lichen can surprisingly also remain separated from one another on an artificial feeding ground. Nevertheless they flourish in symbiosis considerably better. In symbiosis the fungus first receives part of the assimilation products of the partner, and attends to the supply of water and salts to the lichen itself. In this way it makes it possible for the algae and blue-green algae, which normally flourish only in moist areas, to live in relatively dry places.

It is interesting to note that algae or blue-green algae have lost the capacity to propagate independently in lichen. The propagation of lichen comes about by the formation of fruit organs on the part of the lichen fungus, in which small young lichens develop, which already possess certain algae or blue-green algae, so that when they are scattered by the wind and settle on suitable terrain, they are able to develop in symbiosis from the outset.

Another form of vegetable symbiosis is the association between a fungus and a higher plant in the form of *mycorrhiza*. In many forest trees, such as the Scotch pine and the beech, the swollen root-ends are surrounded by a thick layer of fungus fiber (mycelium). These fungal threads replace the root hairs missing from the host plant and so take over the supply of water and minerals to the tree. For this they receive assimilation products from the host plant, which they absorb from the cortex tissue of the roots. Both the fungi and the host plants can often have several symbiotic partners. There are quite specific symbioses, however, such as those between the larch and the elegant boletus and between the birch tree and the birch fungus.

Of considerable importance, too, is the symbiosis of nitrogen-fixing nodule bacteria and some members of the legume family. The nodule bacteria of the *Rhizobium* genus, living freely in the ground, penetrate the cell

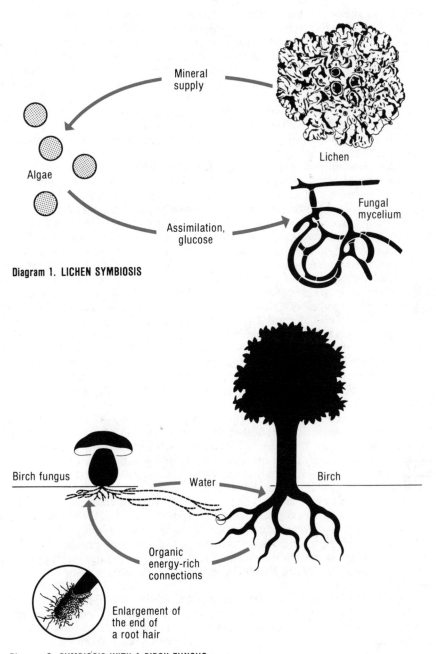

Mineral supply

Lichen

Algae

Assimilation, glucose

Fungal mycelium

Diagram 1. **LICHEN SYMBIOSIS**

Birch fungus

Water

Birch

Organic energy-rich connections

Enlargement of the end of a root hair

Diagram 2. **SYMBIOSIS WITH A BIRCH FUNGUS**

walls of the plant's root fibers and cause these to develop (rather like gall formation by the gallfly) an exuberant growth of tissue, the so-called root nodules. In these nodules a sharp increase of bacteria takes place. These have the capacity to form nitrogen compounds from the elementary nitrogen in the air. When the increase in the bacteria exceeds a certain level, the host plant will begin to assimilate part of them. In this way the plants not only recover part of the carbon compounds previously removed from them by the bacteria, but come into possession of the nitrogen absorbed by the bacteria. As nitrogen is of cardinal importance to plant life, the Leguminosae infected with nodule bacteria can also flourish in soil very poor in nitrogen. As only part of the bacteria is ever assimilated, upon the death of the plants and decomposition of the nodules far more bacteria will be returned to the soil than ever infiltrated the plants.

Many examples of symbiosis are found in the animal kingdom as well. Various animal monocells, such as the slipper animalcule (*Paramaecium bursaria*), contain in their cells single-cell green algae which, owing to their capacity for photosynthesis, can emit assimilation products and oxygen. The host, in turn, provides protection for the green algae, transports them on the basis of its capacity for progression into favorable light conditions and imparts to them carbon dioxide from its respiratory metabolism, which again helps the green algae with the synthesis of its assimilation products. In general the symbionts are resistant to the assimilation enzymes of the host. It can happen, however, that a surplus of algae, which are constantly increasing through cell division, are reabsorbed or assimilated from the host.

A frequent type of symbiosis is found in animals that live on an unbalanced diet which is hard to assimilate. Cellulose, for instance, can be assimilated immediately by only a few herbivorous insects. Many herbivores, such as hoofed animals and certain insects (particularly wood-eating termites), can assimilate cellulose only by virtue of the fact that they live in symbiosis with bacteria or other monocells so that they decompose the cellulose in their alimentary canals. As regards ruminants, their huge rumen and reticulum represent a big "fermenting room" in which, owing to the bacterial metabolism, the cellulose is degraded. This results in a massive increase in the bacteria. In the succeeding alimentary sectors a large number of the bacteria, which have formed body-building substances from the cellulose, are again assimilated by the host. Unassimilable cellulose has become an assimilable bacterial substance.

One example of symbiosis between two highly developed forms of insect life is the association of particular types of ants with aphids or plant lice. The ants carry the aphids onto certain host plants, which then serve the aphids as a source of nutriment. At the same time the ants protect the aphids from their natural enemies, so that the aphids can propagate rapidly. In return the ants are able to "milk" the leaf lice and obtain a sap containing sugar as a nutrient.

Many symbioses occur between sea anemones and hermit crabs. The hermit crab (which lives in empty snail and mussel shells), on moving into a new shell, takes the sea anemone that was sitting on its old shell with it. The nettle pods of the sea anemone serve to protect the crab from enemies, and on the other hand, the sea anemone partakes of the remains of the crab's nutrients.

Diagram 1. PARAMECIUM BURSARIA
(SLIPPER ANIMALCULE) WITH
GREEN ALGAE

Diagram 2. HERMIT CRAB WITH SEA ANEMONES

PARASITISM

Parasites are organisms that live at the expense of other organisms, called the hosts, and that are temporarily or permanently attached to or living in the hosts. The boundaries between parasites and predatory organisms, which devour or suck nutrients from other organisms, are not sharp. A distinction is made between facultative parasites (casual parasites), which normally live on a substance that is decomposing by a natural process but can also penetrate from the alimentary tract or from an incision into a living organism, and obligate parasites, which have so adapted to a host that without it they are no longer capable of independent life. There are harmless parasites, which inflict only minor damage on their hosts, and others that injure them severely and sometimes even kill them.

According to their location, a distinction is made among organ parasites, which live in particular organs or in cavities they have made themselves (e.g., tapeworms, mawworms and liver flukes); abdominal cavity parasites, which live in the abdominal cavity between organs (e.g., ichneumon flies, whose larvae are parasitic in or on other insects); blood parasites, which get into the bloodstream or blood corpuscles and propagate there (e.g., the protozoan malaria which is transmitted by a blood-sucking mosquito); and muscle parasites (trichina and the bladder worm, which is an intermediate stage of the tapeworm).

In the majority of cases, a parasite is associated quite specifically with a particular host. The infestation of a host by a parasite is often a complicated interplay. When a parasite has invaded the host, the host may turn out to be the stronger and overpower the parasite by its defensive reaction. When the host is weaker than the parasite, mass reproduction by the parasite may result sooner or later in the death of the host. When the balance of power between the two is more or less even, the parasite may remain a long time in a host that can sustain the burden without serious damage. A working arrangement between parasite and host of this order holds out the best prospects for the parasite of constant propagation and dissemination of its species.

Most parasites tend to adjust to their living conditions, such as by deterioration of mobility and sense organs which are no longer needed; increase in numbers of eggs (which in the case of the mawworm may be as high as 50 million), since owing to the often very complicated development process heavy losses can occur; self-fertilization of the parasites by parthenogenesis, since a change of location for intercourse between male and female is often not possible; loss of pigmentation, as in the case of cave dwellers; and deterioration of the mandibles and digestive organs insofar as the nutrient is already chemically decomposed or in liquid form, as in the case of parasites in the alimentary canal or blood ducts.

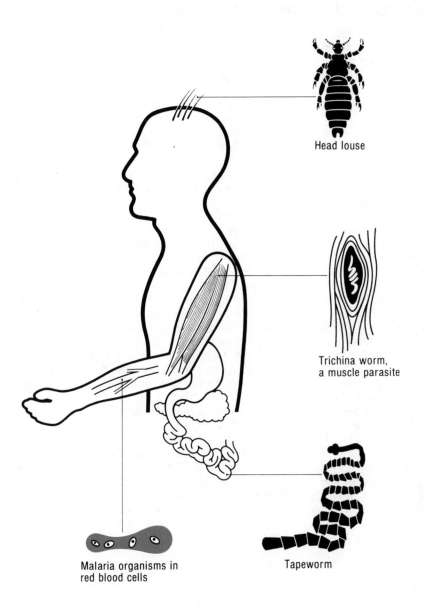

Head louse

Trichina worm,
a muscle parasite

Malaria organisms in
red blood cells

Tapeworm

DIFFERENT MANIFESTATIONS OF PARASITISM

CHANGE OF HOSTS BY PARASITES—THE TAPEWORM

A parasite may spend various stages of its development on or in different hosts. By a change of host, prolific propagation and diffusion from host to host is ensured.

An example of a change of host is provided by the tapeworm. There are a number of tapeworm species that dwell at a reproductive stage in the alimentary systems of vertebrates, on whose food intake they live. With the aid of up to four suction cups and a hook ring, the tapeworm attaches itself firmly by its head to the wall of the alimentary canal. Behind the head is the start of an often long body which is split up into segments. In each of these segments are male and female sex organs. In some species of tapeworm the segments are occupied by first male and then female reproductive organs. By this means the front segments of the worm can mate with its hind segments, but it is also possible for a segment to fertilize itself. In each case the rear segments containing numerous fertilized eggs are then released and passed out with the excreta. In conjunction with the fertilization, each egg forms a tough skin. In consequence the egg of the tapeworm can last a long time. If it gets into the alimentary tract of a suitable intermediate host, it emits a small larva, which owing to its hook is known as a hook larva. With the hook it bores its way through the wall of the alimentary tract of the intermediate host, gets into its bloodstream and is carried into its muscular system or one of its organs, such as the liver or brain. There it settles down and forms a second larval stage, the so-called bladder worm. This is a hollow bladder inside which the structure for a new tapeworm head is formed from an indentation in the lining. If the intermediate host is devoured by another animal, or in the case of cattle, pig or fish tapeworms, if a human consumes raw meat, this bladder may finish up in the devouring animal's alimentary tract. There the head structure will be turned outward like the finger of a glove, the body of the bladder worm will be divided, and a new little tapeworm is produced. This again attaches itself firmly with its suction cup to the wall of the alimentary tract, and the process starts all over again.

In the case of the small dog tapeworm, the bladder worm propagates in addition on a vegetative basis, in that it forms many heads. In this way the bladder worm gets bigger, which can result in the formation of large tumors in the liver or lungs of domestic animals and even of people. Thousands of small tapeworms can be formed from one hook larva. As a major portion of the individual propagation occurs at the bladder-worm stage, the dog tapeworm possesses only a few segments.

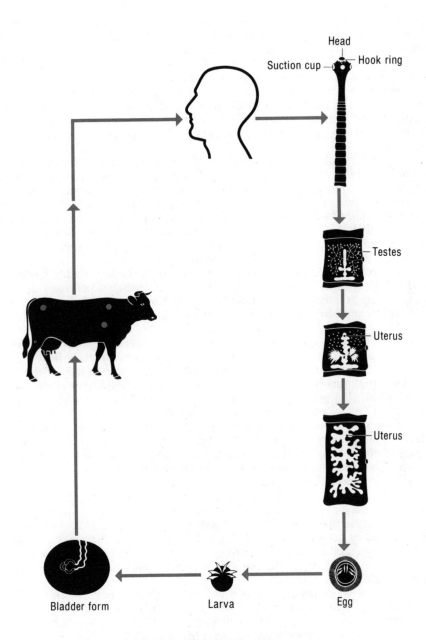

Head

Suction cup — Hook ring

Testes

Uterus

Uterus

Egg

Larva

Bladder form

DEVELOPMENT CYCLE OF A TAPEWORM

Part Five—Fundamental Phenomena of Life

The complexities of life manifest themselves in an impressive variety of forms. Even a single-cell organism displays all the essential features of existence. Life is based fundamentally on a biological constituent element, the cell. The cell is the foundation stone of all life. The sum of all the cells of an organism in turn forms a unit and represents a corporate whole. Each cell comes from a parent cell by segmentation; in the process the heritable information stored in the nucleus of the parent cell in the form of genes is transmitted to the daughter cells. All cells are distinguished by irritability. In the higher animals we also find special organs for the perception of stimuli and response.

A further fundamental principle of life is metabolism (a process unknown in the inorganic sector), which subjects the material basis of an organism to constant change. Almost all the structural elements of the cells and of the body are constantly being decomposed and reformed. The entire albumin content of the human body, for instance, is decomposed to half every 80 days or so and reconstituted. This constant change in the body of an organism is characterized primarily by the fact that its specific organic structure is not changed thereby in any respect.

Although all organisms have a typical form peculiar to their species, this still varies within certain limits. The human species is precisely defined; yet no man exactly resembles another except in the case of identical twins. The difference is rooted in variations in heredity and in environmental influences.

Another basic quality of organisms is their regenerative capacity. Parts of the body that are lost or damaged are replaced completely in form and function to an astonishing extent. Examples of this are the legs of the salamander, the arms of starfish and a missing half of the body of earthworms. In addition, all organisms are capable of healing small wounds and of replacing defective tissues by systematic cell growth.

To maintain the regular processes of life, energy is needed. Green plants derive their energy from sunlight, while nongreen plants (e.g., fungi) and animals cover their energy requirements by recourse to energy-bearing organic nutrients, which owe their origin ultimately to metabolic processes within the green plants. These nutrients are decomposed by stages in the metabolism of the organism, and the energy is stored in specific metabolic molecules such as adenosine triphosphate (ATP).

A process that is similarly inherent in all organisms is that of growth. The period of growth is limited. Monocells grow until they reach a size at which they segment. The growth of plants is limited through aging processes that end in the death of the plants. In humans growth takes place mainly until the end of adolescence.

Every kind of organism has a characteristic life-span. While many insects live only for a few days or weeks once they are fully grown, certain big reptiles, such as the giant tortoise, may live for several hundred years. Among the mammals elephants have a life-span of 70 to 100 years, horses 20–30 years, cows 20 to 25, dogs 12 to 15, and rats about 3 years. Many birds attain a good age; falcons, owls and parrots live to be from 50 to over 100 years old. Queen ants are known to live for 12 to 15 years. The life-span of most other segmented animals is considerably less, however.

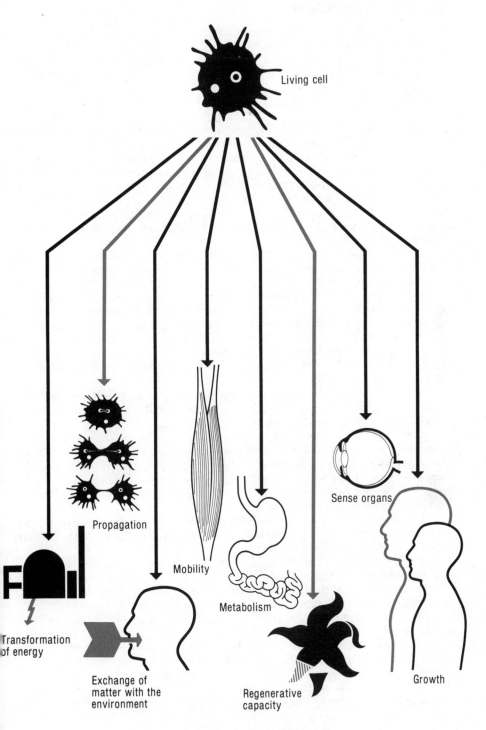

Living cell

Propagation

Transformation
of energy

Mobility

Exchange of
matter with the
environment

Metabolism

Sense organs

Regenerative
capacity

Growth

CHARACTERISTICS OF LIFE

IRRITABILITY IN PLANTS

Reactions to irritation are not nearly so pronounced in plants as they are in animals with their freedom of movement, since in the ordinary course plants have little mobility. Plants are capable of reacting to variations in light, temperature and humidity, to the forces of gravity and to chemical and mechanical stimuli. As regards the reaction to these stimuli a distinction is made between growth and turgor pressures, and plasma movements inside the cells.

In the case of green plants, reaction to light stimuli is vital to their existence, since they need light for photosynthesis (see Part Six). Light that impinges from one side causes a change in growth known as phototropism. A young shoot turns toward the light, and this is called positive phototropism. Roots, on the other hand, and this applies in particular to aerial roots, are negatively phototropic—that is, they turn away from the light toward the ground. In the case of Kenilworth ivy, before pollination the flower stems are positively phototropic, but after pollination they turn negatively phototropic.

Another reaction to light stimuli is found in certain plants, such as wood sorrel and the robinia, which in a poor light open their plumules out flat but in strong sunlight close them up to protect them from intense radiation. It is a question here of turgor pressures, for which various pressure conditions inside the cells on both sides of the relative parts of the organism are responsible. The direction of movement is thus predetermined by the organism, in this case by the formation of a "joint." Such movements that are not caused by the direction of the stimuli in question are called *nastic movements,* or in the special case of light stimuli under consideration here, *photonastic movements.*

Similar considerations apply when flowers open and close under the influence of changing light intensity. A certain influence is often exercised also by humidity in the atmosphere.

What are known as *sleep movements (nyctinastic movements)* occur primarily as a result of autonomous internal stimuli corresponding to the day-night rhythm. These are observed, inter alia, in the leaves of the scarlet runner; when night comes the leafstalk is raised and the plumules are lowered. The leaves of the wood sorrel also display nyctinastic movements in addition to photonastic movements.

The sensitivity of plants to light can be great. High-intensity flashes lasting no more than one-thousandth to two-thousandths of a second are often enough to produce a reaction.

Hand in hand with light reactions go growth movements in plants that are touched off by heat stimuli (*thermotropism*). If the movements occur toward the source of the heat they are described as positively thermotropic, and in the reverse situation as negatively thermotropic.

A determining factor for the direction of growth of a plant and its parts apart from the influence of light and heat is the force of gravity. The movement reaction in response to gravity is known as *geotropism*. Thus the main root of a plant displays positive geotropic growth while the offshoots display negative geotropic growth. This is also the reason why a broken cornstalk, for instance, will go on growing upward, and a tree on a steep slope grows vertically in relation to the earth's surface and not at right angles to the

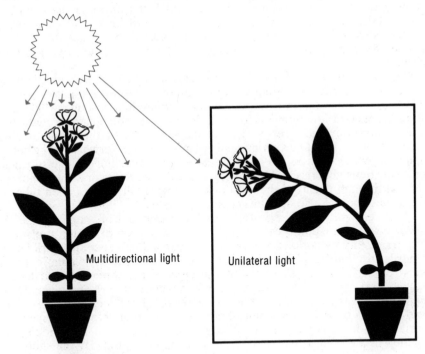

Multidirectional light

Unilateral light

Diagram 1. PHOTOTROPISM

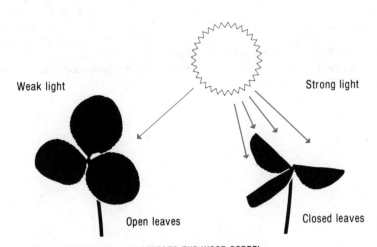

Weak light

Strong light

Open leaves

Closed leaves

Diagram 2. PHOTOTROPISM AS IT AFFECTS THE WOOD SORREL

slope. In contrast to the offshoots and the main root, the lateral branches show a transverse geotropic growth, in which the angle to the main axis (monopodium) or to the force of gravity is set out in the site plan for the plants. Nevertheless, in the spruce, for instance, if the leader shoot is lost, a side shoot may spring up to replace it on a basis of negative geotropic growth.

In *chemotropism,* chemical substances in different concentrations are determining factors regarding the direction of growth of a plant or parts of it. Upon the diffusion of a substance in a medium in a gaseous or dissolved state, a concentration grade is formed. Positive chemotropism (growth along a concentration grade) results in the fungal hyphae or the food-absorbing organs (haustoria) of certain parasitic plants pressing forward to the source material, which may be, for example, a self-decomposing organic substance or a nutritious host tissue. Other substances can have the opposite influence, that is, through negative chemotropism. The growth of the pollen tubes on the seed structure also operates chemotropically.

The growth trend in accordance with the amount of water present (*hydrotropism*) corresponds essentially to the mechanism of chemotropism.

Irritability by contact occurs as a mechanical influence, primarily in the tendrils of climbing plants (Virginia creeper, sweet peas, clematis, pumpkins, etc.). In search for support, the ends of the thread-shaped tendrils make rotary movements until they come into contact with an object. Thereupon they work their way about as a result of increased growth of the surface cells opposite the point of contact, and so envelop the object. For certain tendril creepers the contact is even directed to the middle, free portion of the tendril, whereupon this rolls up in a spiral. By the shortening produced in the tendril, the plant is drawn closer to the support. The growth so promoted by contact stimulation is known as *haptotropism* or *thigmotropism*.

The mimosa is a well-known example of *haptotropism* that occurs very rapidly and is caused by turgor variations in its double-striated leaves. Normally the striae are extended on the leaves or leaf axes. If a striated leaf is touched, then the striae will rapidly close in pairs, the stalks of the striated leaves will come together, and finally the leafstalk will drop back, for all the striated leaf parts possess "joints." After a time the leaf recovers and slowly resumes its former position.

Force of gravity

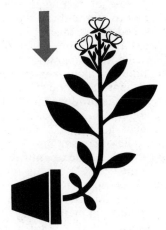

Diagram 1. GEOTROPISM

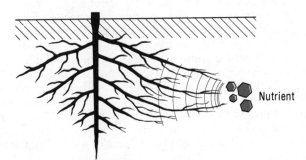

Nutrient

Diagram 2. CHEMOTROPISM

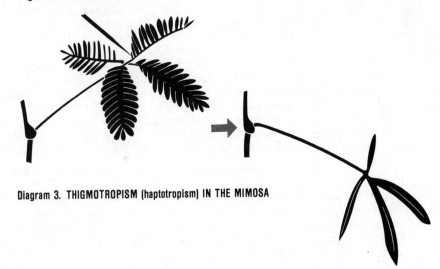

Diagram 3. THIGMOTROPISM (haptotropism) IN THE MIMOSA

IRRITABILITY IN ANIMALS

One of the most interesting phenomena in life is the capacity of living organisms to react to stimuli from the environment. For a stimulus to have effect it must exceed a certain size, known as the threshold. A distinction is made between external stimuli, which operate on the organism from the environment (e.g., light, temperature, and mechanical and chemical stimuli), and internal stimuli, which operate from inside the body (e.g., stimuli that promote movement, hormone stimuli and growth stimuli).

A reaction is produced in the cells receiving the stimulus (often specific sense cells), creating a specific change in the protoplasm, the exact physical and chemical nature of which is not yet known. The reaction extends throughout the organism, mostly by way of a nerve fiber, very rapidly, either directly through a reflex pathway to the organs responding to the stimulus, or through the central nervous system (the brain or, in lower animals, nerve nodules), whereupon, mostly unconsciously, an "order" is given for a response to the stimulus. This response reaction may take the form of a movement or a change in metabolism.

Manifestations of stimuli in monocellular organisms such as amebae, paramecia animalcules, and flagellates are particularly interesting. As these organisms consist of only a single cell, that cell must perform all the functions necessary to life that are performed in the higher animals by numbers of specific cells or by organs. In a monocellular organism each particle of the fluid cell plasma is equally sensitive and capable of reaction. This can be observed easily under a microscope when an ameba is found on one side of a strong luminous stimulus, a chemical stimulus, a heat stimulus or a contact stimulus. It first reacts on the side exposed to the stimulus, and in most cases it tends to withdraw from the point at which the stimulus is received. If, however, the stimulus is caused by a food nodule, the ameba will react by extending a pseudopodium and reaching out toward the food. On each occasion the excitation spreads in a short time throughout the body of the cell and embraces the entire organism, which thereupon moves away from or toward the center of irritation.

A further interesting case is that of certain colored flagellates (such as *Euglena viridis*). These occupy a middle position between animals and plants. Like most plants they contain the green leaf pigment chlorophyll, from which with the aid of sunlight they build up their strength. They are related to animals in that they possess a flagellum by means of which they can propel themselves. Many of these green flagellates also possess a red eye-spot with which they are able to detect the intensity and direction of light. If a number of these animals are kept in a glass jar which is exposed on one side to a strong ray of light, in the course of time they will congregate on the side facing the light, since they need the light for photosynthesis.

There are various forms of stimulus to which organisms react in different ways. The following can be distinguished:

Chemotaxis: behavior in relation to the concentration gradient of a particular chemical substance

Thermotaxis: the search for a particular optimum heat zone in a temperature gradient

Phototaxis: the search for a place enjoying a particular, optimal light intensity

Galvanotaxis: behavior within an electrical field, such as orientation according to the direction of the current or toward a particular pole

Geotaxis: reaction to the force of gravity in the earth

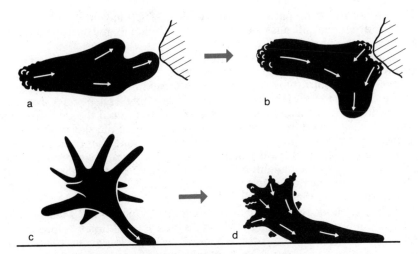

Diagram 1. REACTION OF AN AMEBA TO STIMULI:
(a AND b) NEGATIVE REACTION TO A CHEMICAL STIMULUS;
(c AND d) POSITIVE REACTION TO CONTACT WITH A SUPPORT
(→ DIRECTION OF MOVEMENT OF THE CYTOPLASM)

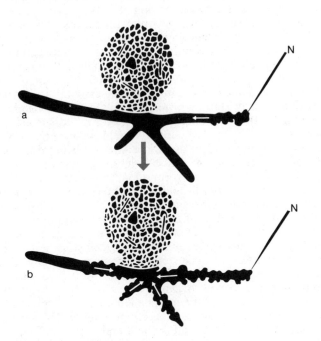

Diagram 2. RESULT OF STIMULATION
AND DIRECTION OF EXCITATION IN THE CASE OF THE ENCASED AMEBA DIFFLUGIA.
(a) WEAK AND (b) STRONG STIMULATION OF A PSEUDOPOD WITH A
NEEDLE, N. (REVISED VERSION OF VERWORN)

PROPAGATION

Life is represented by particular individuals, which have only a limited life-span. In order that life may continue, the individuals must propagate. This can be done by an asexual or sexual process.

The simplest asexual propagation by a single-cell organism is by division, which occurs upon the parent cell attaining a certain size. First the cell nucleus divides into two, the heritable information being contained in the nucleus in the form of chromosomes. The whole cell begins at once to narrow down from the cell wall toward the middle, until the two halves are completely separated from one another. According to the size of the cell and the type of living conditions, cell division may take from ten minutes to several hours. Many of the organelles in the parent cell are reproduced after division in each of the daughter cells. In the ameba each daughter cell forms a new pulsating vacuole. And in the case of flagellates a new flagellum is formed for each of them after division.

In many monocellular organisms, especially parasites, which multiply profusely and rapidly, the cell nucleus divides several times before the separation of the protoplasm. Then when the cell division occurs, the body of the cell cleaves into several daughter cells.

In the propagation of unicellular organisms, in ordinary circumstances no substance from the parent is lost. A natural death—that is, the death of the individual body by formation of a "carcass"—does not therefore occur. Except in cases in which monocellular organisms succumb from external causes, they can therefore be regarded as potentially imperishable.

In addition to this asexual method of propagation, unicellular organisms also have various sexual reproduction processes. The main effect of the union of cell nuclei in sexual propagation consists in the new combination of heritable material. When copulation takes place between two monocellular organisms, two cells (gametes) fuse into a single cell (the zygote). A distinction is drawn here between *isogamy,* in which the gametes are of the same size and form, and *anisogamy,* in which the gametes are classified as macrogametes (big, mostly stationary female cells) and microgametes (small, mobile male cells). In the mating process, two individuals are involved simply in a passing superficial transfusion over a plasma bridge, which involves for them an exchange of nuclear material. After division of the nucleus for each partner, a nucleus combines as a migratory nucleus with the stationary nucleus of the other cell. This form of pairing occurs in particular in ciliates.

A principle of sexual propagation is fertilization, in which two nuclei fuse with one another. Whereas in monocellular organisms sexual propagation by cell division and fertilization are effected quite independently of one another, in the higher animals the two processes are connected. The multicellular organisms also go through a single-cell stage in the course of propagation. In the male and female sex organs, single-cell gametes (sex cells) are formed by cell division. Upon fertilization these fuse into a single-cell zygote, out of which a new organism develops by a process of many cell divisions. The sex cells of the multicelled animals display, on the outside, a sexual differentiation. Whereas the ovum is mostly bigger and incapable of movement, the male sperm cell is small and capable of movement and consists almost exclusively of genetic material.

As regards propagation in plants, an alternation of generation occurs between sexual and asexual generation. The conspicuous, predominant

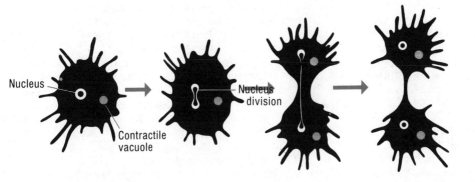

**Diagram 1. DIVISION OF AN AMEBA
(MODIFIED VERSION OF F. E. SCHULZE)**

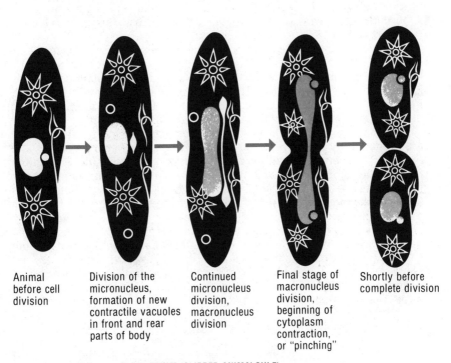

| Animal before cell division | Division of the micronucleus, formation of new contractile vacuoles in front and rear parts of body | Continued micronucleus division, macronucleus division | Final stage of macronucleus division, beginning of cytoplasm contraction, or "pinching" | Shortly before complete division |

Diagram 2. DIVISION OF A PARAMECIUM (SLIPPER ANIMALCULE)

plant form may be represented by asexual generation, as in the case of ferns, or by sexual generation, as in the case of flowering plants. Ferns are a good example of this alternation of generations: when a fern spore falls on a suitable moist patch in the woods, a tiny inconspicuous plant will form from it, the young shoot being known as a prothallium. On this usually heart-shaped young shoot there form, at the maturity stage, male (antheridia) and female (archegonia) sex organs, in which the female (static) egg cells or male (motile spermatozoa) sex cells develop. One drop of water then enables the ripe male gametes to fan out and float up to an archegonium, penetrate it and unite with an egg cell to form a zygote. Having performed this fertilization procedure, the young shoot has completed its task and withers away. Over the months and years a fern plant will grow from the zygote, and in the summer small brown globules known as spore cases (sporangia) will develop on the underside of the frond. In these, by vegetative (asexual) reproduction there form many minute cells, the spores, which contain the heritable material of the fern. On the outside they are covered by a strong skin, which enables them to survive for some time under rough environmental conditions. The spores work free when the sporecases (sporangia) ripen and burst, so that the spores are catapulted out. The spore formation, or asexual propagation, is the reproductive procedure now proper to the fern. Carried by the wind to a suitable patch of woodland, the spore germinates again, and the cycle begins afresh. In this way a sexual generation (young shoot) alternates with an asexual generation (the true fern plant which forms the spores).

In many mosses, sexual and asexual generation have become almost equally clearly recognizable. In the maidenhair moss, for example, a well-known variety in European woodlands, the small green plant denotes sexual generation. After the fertilization process, a new plant grows on the old moss plant and forms a spore capsule on top. This is the asexual generation of the maidenhair moss, which contains no more chlorophyll.

Propagation of the higher plants takes place by means of seeds. These are produced by fusion between a female and a male sperm cell. In addition to the cell nucleus the seed possesses a more or less considerable amount of food tissue, mostly fats, which serve the seedling as nutriment. According to how the seeds of a particular species of plant are distributed, they are likely to develop differently. If they are scattered by the wind, they either will be very small and light (as in orchids) or will have a cilium or "parachute" as a sort of fringe (as in the dandelion). Other seeds possess stiff hairs or bristles with a barbed hook which get caught in the coats of animals and are distributed in that way. Again others have a fruit covering which is consumed by animals and, while still undigested and capable of germination, is deposited in excrement in a variety of places (on berries snapped up by birds, for example).

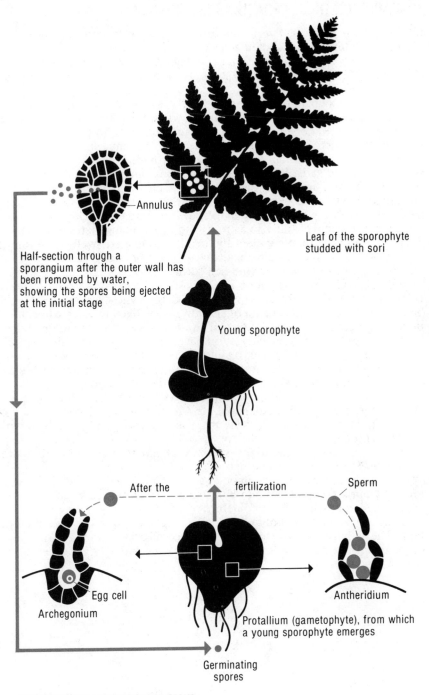

Annulus

Leaf of the sporophyte
studded with sori

Half-section through a
sporangium after the outer wall has
been removed by water,
showing the spores being ejected
at the initial stage

Young sporophyte

After the   fertilization   Sperm

Egg cell

Archegonium

Antheridium

Protallium (gametophyte), from which
a young sporophyte emerges

Germinating
spores

ALTERNATION OF GENERATIONS IN FERNS

ALTERNATION OF GENERATIONS IN ANIMALS

In the case of animals, two forms of alternation of generations are distinguishable: heterogony and metagenesis.

In *heterogony* the alternation is between generations with bisexual and unisexual (parthenogenic) fertilization. Heterogony occurs mainly in parasites.

A typical example of alternation of generations of this order is provided by the vine louse, a pest affecting vine growths, for which five to six unisexual generations and one bisexual generation occur each year. In the spring, greenflies (gall lice) hatch out of fertilized eggs that have survived the winter and suck the leaves of the vulnerable vine or hybrid plants and so produce small pot-shaped galls. Without exception these are wingless females which represent the first unisexual (parthenogenic) self-fertilizing generation. They are called maybugs (cockchafers). Out of the remaining 200 to 500 unfertilized eggs that these females lay in each leaf gall, females again hatch out in the form of greenflies and also as root vine-lice which penetrate the soil and attack the roots of the vine plant by forming nodulated swellings. From the greenflies also come certain unisexual generations of greenflies and root vine-lice, and from the root vine-lice further unisexual generations of root vine-lice carrying over (by hibernation) into the following year. In the late summer, however, there also develop from root vine-lice (by the development of a nymph stage) a further generation of winged females which attend outside the soil to the distribution of the parasite on other vine plants and lay their eggs, which differ in size, on parts of the vine plants aboveground. These eggs form the bisexual, again wingless generation of vine lice, and from the smaller eggs males are bred. The animals of this generation possess only rudimentary mandibles. Consequently they can devote themselves in practice only to propagation. Upon the laying of the now fertilized eggs, winter eggs, the complicated annual life-cycle of the vine louse is now complete. The real damage to the vine plant is caused by root vine-lice, which are also able to propagate in the soil.

In *metagenesis*, generations with sexual and asexual (vegetative) propagation alternate with one another.

Metagenesis also occurs among various Cnidaria, in which jellyfish are formed from a polyp generation by asexual fertilization. The clinging polyp develops shoots which become detached and form free-floating jellyfish; or by cross-division of the polyp, a jellyfish is formed from the separated portion. The jellyfish are the animals with sexual organs which form the sex cells. In this way polyps are again formed from the jellyfish generation by sexual propagation.

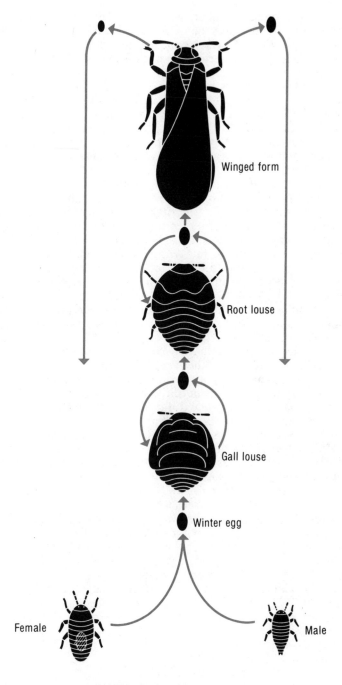

Winged form

Root louse

Gall louse

Winter egg

Female

Male

GENERATION CYCLE OF THE VINE LOUSE

DIFFERENTIATION

One of the most interesting and absorbing phenomena of life is its capacity for differentiation. In the inanimate world a natural tendency prevails to move toward a position of ever increasing disorder. The principle formulated in the second law of thermodynamics is that in a closed system the probability of any particular state existing is greater, the greater the disorder it displays. A measure of its disorder is what is known as *entropy*. Any self-contained system left to itself experiences, with time, a state of ever increasing entropy. The layout in a box in which black and white balls are arranged in a particular pattern is not improved by shaking but spoiled. The molecules of a gaseous substance that are present in a higher concentration at a particular point in space seek to distribute themselves by diffusion and so assume a state of higher entropy.

Life possesses an astonishing capacity for achieving a high measure of order in the face of the forces of disorder. This is produced by a process of differentiation. Each body cell of an organism possesses in its nucleus the complete genetic information of the entire organism. Every organism develops from an individual cell (the fertilized egg cell in the case of multicellular organisms and the parent cell in the case of unicellular organisms). The fertilized egg cell is still not differentiated. Besides the cell nucleus it contains a smaller or larger quantity of food tissue. As a result of repeated cell and nuclear division, from the individual egg cells there arises in course of time a multicellular stage which is converted by embryonic development into a young organism. In this organism, which is capable of living alone, many types of quite different cells appear, all of which have developed from the same egg cell: epithelial cells, muscle cells, nerve cells, fat cells, liver cells, blood cells, etc. In each of these cells the complete genetic information of the egg cell is present, but only part of this information is actually used.

In the embryonic development of the various organisms a distinction is made between the early-determined differentiation and the long-sustained regenerative capacity. In the case of tunicates (sea squirts and ascidians adhering to the seabed), the individual cells are differentiated very early in the embryonic stage. If one takes individual cells at the segmentation stage of the cell division (the earliest stage after fertilization), there develop from them only the cell types, organs or body parts of the larvae, which would also have developed from them in the normal embryonic formation. Thus one cell of the two-cell stage provides a right-hand or left-hand half embryo. If at the four-cell stage the two forward are separated from the two rear segmentation cells, only the two forward or the two rear halves of the embryo will develop. Such cells, in which the later significance of the individual cells is already firmly determined, are called mosaic cells. In most other species, however, the embryos possess a more or less considerable regenerative capacity. In consequence, disturbances in the development, such as the removal of pieces of the embryo can be repaired by the neighboring cells. From parts of the embryo, complete intact organisms, though reduced correspondingly in size, can still be produced. If the two first sedimentation cells of an amphibious embryo are separated, for instance, a complete larva will come from each half, followed later on by a complete young frog or newt. Complete organisms can also be produced at a later stage in the operation. As far as man is concerned, an early division of the embryo leads to the formation of identical twins.

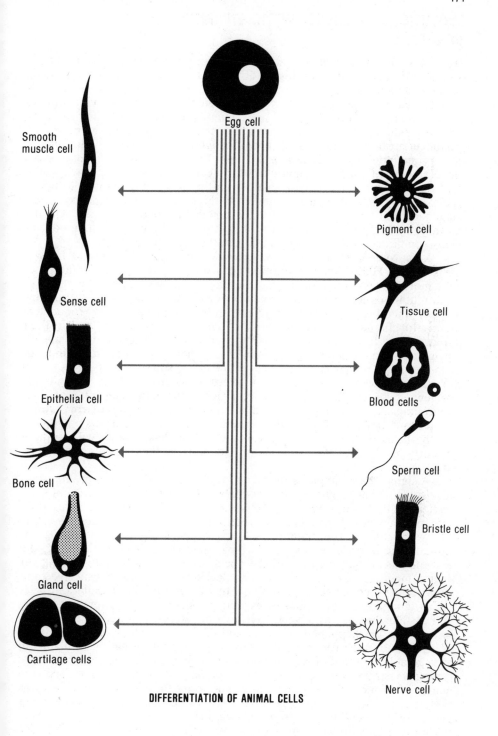

Egg cell

Smooth
muscle cell

Sense cell

Epithelial cell

Bone cell

Gland cell

Cartilage cells

Pigment cell

Tissue cell

Blood cells

Sperm cell

Bristle cell

Nerve cell

DIFFERENTIATION OF ANIMAL CELLS

EVOLUTION—INFLUENCE OF THE ENVIRONMENT ON THE GENOTYPE

By *evolution* is meant the genealogical development of organisms from their simple, primitive forms into highly developed species. Up to the beginning of the nineteenth century, the study of biology was based on the hypothesis that the various species were created by an act of divine providence and were immutable. This belief was undermined increasingly by the discovery of fossil remains of primitive plants and animals that were for the most part no longer around. In the light of these discoveries, a theory of evolution was first propounded by J. B. Lamarck (1744–1829) to explain the progressive development of species. Lamarck put the causes of evolution down to the fact that, apart from an innate instinct on the part of the animals to better themselves, changed environmental conditions and the use or disuse of particular organs would lead to heritable changes in body structure and the evolution of new species (Lamarckism). It is now known that the modifications conditioned by the environment generally are not heritable.

A plausible explanation of evolution was arrived at by Charles Darwin (1809–1882). His theory of evolution consists of two parts: (1) In each species more or less frequent random heritable changes occur. The cause of such mutations may be radioactive rays or chemical influences. Mutations are not geared to any particular objective; that is, the variation produced is purely fortuitous. The vast majority of mutations are detrimental in their effects. Very few (well under 0.1%) are of advantage to the organism. (2) Owing to the natural increase in population, there are always more individuals in any particular species than the means of subsistence permit; therefore a struggle for survival must necessarily ensue. This struggle for existence takes the form of a selection process: the better they adapt to their environment, and the greater the advantages they receive from minor chance mutations, the faster will even slightly superior organisms propagate. On the basis of the selection advantages, their descendants will multiply proportionately, and after a number of generations the original form will be largely superseded.

A significant example of the selection process today is the proliferation of pests resistant to chemical insecticides. As described in the chapter on pesticides (Part Nine), many of the pests previously controlled successfully with poisons have since become resistant to them. This came about as follows: first a random mutation resulted in one of the pests becoming immune to the insecticide concerned. Next time the poison was applied, the descendants of that member of the species had a decided advantage over their competitors for survival. Thus a selection of the parasites survived and after a short time formed a predominantly poison-resistant population.

Although many questions on evolution remain to be answered, it is now known that the species alive today have developed from common original forms. This has happened over a period of 1 to 1.5 billion years. Evidence of it is found in the rock strata of various geological formations in the form of vegetable or animal fossil remains of organisms in existence when these geological strata were formed. The discovery of such fossils is largely a matter of chance. Furthermore, as a rule, only the hard portions, such as skeletons or shells, are preserved, and the soft portions survive only under particularly favorable conditions in the form of rock impressions. From these fossil remains the history of the organisms can now be deduced. The oldest of the fossils date back to the Precambrian era of about 1.5 billion years ago. They consist of water algae, monocelled animals, and bacteria.

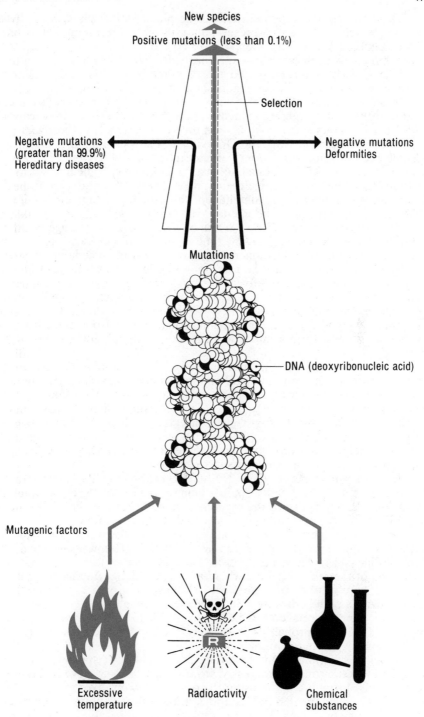

New species

Positive mutations (less than 0.1%)

Selection

Negative mutations
(greater than 99.9%)
Hereditary diseases

Negative mutations
Deformities

Mutations

DNA (deoxyribonucleic acid)

Mutagenic factors

Excessive
temperature

Radioactivity

Chemical
substances

MUTAGENIC FACTORS INFLUENCE THE HEREDITARY SUBSTANCE

The first geological period that can be pinpointed fairly specifically in time and which contains well-preserved fossils is the Cambrian, dating back 500–600 million years. It is interesting to note that all the forms of invertebrate animals (protozoa, molluscs, arthropods, etc.) already existed at that time. Particularly well represented was the three-lobed crab (Trilobita). The plants were represented, inter alia, by blue, green and red algae.

In the animal kingdom, the Silurian period (440–500 million years ago) produced the first vertebrate animals. These were crustaceous, jawless fish with a cartilaginous spinal column. The only plants were still the algae.

The succeeding period, the Ordovician (400–440 million years back), was the peak development period for invertebrates. There were crustaceous animals over 2 m (6.6 feet) long known as Gigantostraca. The first scorpions and millipedes began to ravage the country. They were protected from dehydration by chitin scales. Simultaneously with these first land animals, naked ferns were the first land plants to develop on the banks of waterways.

The Devonian period (350–400 million years ago) was the age of fishes. Bony fish were developing at that time from the earlier cartilage fish and included lungfish and fringe-finned fish (Crossopterygii). The latter, fish with fins fringed with rays, were the forerunners of land vertebrates. Originally they were known only from fossil remains, until some living examples of them were found in secluded ocean areas. Toward the end of the Devonian period, some amphibians began to evolve from these or similar forms, some of them living in water and some on land. Land plants also evolved from the naked fern a stage further into true ferns, horsetail and club moss or stag's horn.

In the following Carboniferous period (270–350 million years ago) the club moss or stag's horn, horsetail and ferns developed into extensive forests. These are known as carboniferous forests, as the present-day coal seams stem from these forest growths. From the amphibians the first reptiles developed, as did also the first winged insects, of which the dragonfly grew to a size of 80 cm (31.5 inches). Toward the end of the Carboniferous period, the first seedlings evolved from ferns and club moss. These were the forerunners of the present-day gymnosperms.

In the Permian period (255–270 million years ago) the Palaeozoic era came to an end. The humid tropical climate turned to desert and steppe conditions. Reptiles formed the predominant animal group. The first precursors of the modern birds and mammals made their appearance.

The Jurassic period (135–180 million years ago) witnessed a major development and expansion in the reptile population. This was the age of the lizards (dinosaurs). They took over all the living space in the world with the exception of the arctic regions, where as heat-exchange animals they could not live. There were flying lizards with a wingspan of over 8 m (26 feet) and ground lizards with bodies over 30 m (98 feet) in length.

In the Upper Cretaceous (Chalk) period (70–135 million years back) the big lizards died out, probably as a result of climatic changes. Then began the multifarious development of mammals.

From this outline of the historical development of species, it is clear that the evolution of life progressed from simple to ever more highly organized forms. From life in the water the organisms went over increasingly to life on land, accompanied by variations in their organization in conformity with changing conditions in the environment.

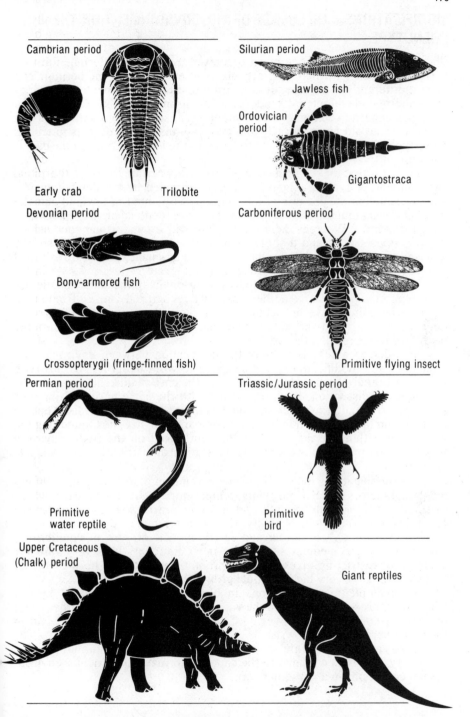

EARLY PERIODS OF THE EARTH'S HISTORY WITH TYPICAL REPRESENTATIVES

MODIFICATIONS—INFLUENCE OF THE ENVIRONMENT ON THE PHENOTYPE

The physical characteristics of an organism are broadly determined by inheritance. How is it, then, that organisms of exactly the same heritage can have a different appearance? It is entirely due to environmental influences that inherited development tendencies are promoted or suppressed. If a particular inherited characteristic is suppressed, some other characteristic is likely to come out more strongly and may eventually take over its functions altogether. This is the more likely to happen, the less pronounced the differentiation of the organism.

Thus it is that the organism can adapt, within certain limits, to the actual environment. A typical example of this is provided by the dandelion. If a young dandelion is split in half and one half is planted in lowland and the other half in a mountain region, the two plants of identical origin will develop quite differently. Whereas the lowland plant will show a straight and strong growth, open leaves and a short root, its mountain counterpart, which is exposed to strong ultraviolet radiation, will be of small, stumpy growth, will be hairy, and will have a deep strong root.

Such different formations in individual growths of the same species are known as *modifications*. Another generally recognized cause of modifications is the influence of nutrients. The production or size of useful plants depends primarily on the nutrient content of the soil, irrespective of the quality of the seeds and the weather.

In order to assess accurately the connection between environmental influences and modifications, it is essential to work as far as possible with growths of precisely the same family, as in the case of unicellular organisms produced by dissection. Such organisms with the same heritage, obtained from an individual growth, are known as clones. If clones are raised from a paramecium in sufficient numbers and compared for size, it is found that the sizes vary within certain limits. A diagram based on the frequency with which the various sizes occur shows the statistical distribution on each side of the mean.

The modifications in the size of the paramecium are the result of many individual factors (such as nutrients, temperature, light and oxygen), which in some cases promote growth and in others restrict it. In this respect, according to the laws of probability, the most frequent chance combinations are those in which promoting and restricting factors are in equilibrium. Consequently the medium size is the most frequent. It is very rare for exclusively restricting or exclusively promoting factors to be present, so that very small or very big individual growths arise.

An example of modifications in blossom color is provided by the Chinese primrose. According to the variety, these plants may be either white or red. In temperatures of over 30°C (86°F) the flowers are white, and in lower temperatures red.

In no case are any of the modifications passed on, nor can they be. The hereditary quality is confined to the capacity to react to particular environmental conditions in a particular way.

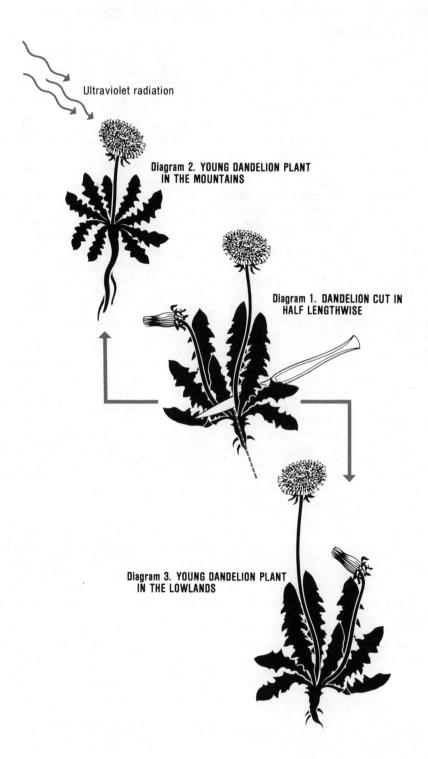

Ultraviolet radiation

Diagram 2. YOUNG DANDELION PLANT
IN THE MOUNTAINS

Diagram 1. DANDELION CUT IN
HALF LENGTHWISE

Diagram 3. YOUNG DANDELION PLANT
IN THE LOWLANDS

HEREDITARY INFORMATION—ENVIRONMENTAL POISONS AND HERITABLE DAMAGE

The hereditary information that determines the structure and function of every organism is stored in a macromolecule, the deoxyribonucleic acid (DNA), of the chromosomes. The DNA is contained in each cell nucleus and, upon cell division, is duplicated and a complete reproduction is transmitted to each daughter cell.

The capacity of the DNA to transmit information depends on the specific structural characteristics and the order of particular structural elements in the molecule. Each feature of an organism has its origin in the hereditary substance. Genes are the basic units of heredity. A gene is a segment or group of segments of DNA located in a specific part of a chromosome.

The specific hereditary information contained in a gene is encoded in its sequence of nucleotides. Nucleotides are the building blocks of nucleic acids and are composed of sugar–phosphate backbones linked to one of four nitrogenous bases (adenine, guanine, cytosine and thymine). It is the base sequence that determines the nature of the protein to be synthesized, and control of protein synthesis is the mode of transmission of heredity.

Protein synthesis is a complex process which occurs in the cell cytoplasm on specific organelles known as ribosomes. The DNA specifies the order of amino acids in a protein via a code of nucleotide triplets. Thus, the sequence AAA (3 adenine bases in succession) represents the amino acid phenylalanine. In the nucleus of the cell, a complementary copy of a gene is made; this is known as the messenger RNA (mRNA). On the ribosome, the genetic information contained in the mRNA is translated into a specific sequence of amino acids (via the transfer RNA) and the protein is assembled. Any variation or mutation in the DNA, therefore, may result in the synthesis of a structurally altered protein with an altered function. This is the basis of mutagenesis.

These complicated transformation and synthesis mechanisms can very easily be upset as they progress, so that hereditary variations (mutations) occur. It only requires an exchange or the elimination of one base in a crucial place to upset the enzyme synthesis and consequently the metabolism. The hereditary variation arising from the change in the base sequence in the DNA is known as a point mutation.

Another type of variation in the hereditary substance is chromosome mutation. In this case part of the DNA molecule is broken off or another portion is attached to the end of a DNA molecule. The gene sequence that is changed thereby gives rise to a change in the characteristic product, since the characteristic product determined in a gene is also influenced by the neighboring genes. If a genome (the complete genetic information of a cell) contains too many or too few chromosomes, this is known as genome mutation.

The two last-named mutations (chromosome and genome) are often microscopically detectable, and have been recognized in recent years as the cause of hereditary diseases of man that have been known about for a long time (e.g., mongolism and Klinefelter's syndrome). In mongolism, three copies of chromosome 21 are present instead of two. In Klinefelter's syndrome, it is a question of having three sex chromosomes (XXY) instead of two (XY).

In normal circumstances, mutations occur independently of the milieu and nondirectionally. Only an extremely low number of mutations is dis-

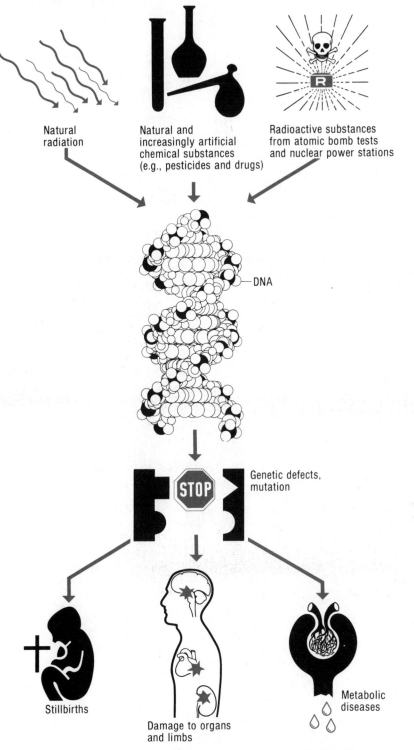

Natural radiation

Natural and increasingly artificial chemical substances (e.g., pesticides and drugs)

Radioactive substances from atomic bomb tests and nuclear power stations

DNA

STOP Genetic defects, mutation

Stillbirths

Damage to organs and limbs

Metabolic diseases

HEREDITARY DAMAGE BY TOXIC SUBSTANCES IN THE ENVIRONMENT

played in the variation of the characteristics. These mutations are known as natural mutations, in contrast to the mutations induced by ultraviolet light, radioactivity, heat and chemicals.

The operating mechanisms of mutagenic substances depend on specific groups within a molecule. Substances for instance that contain base analogues thus operate mutagenically in such a way that the analogues are incorporated into DNA instead of the correct nucleotide, creating false hereditary information. Other agents such as nitrite, hydroxylamine and alkylating compounds (e.g., ethyl methane sulfonate, dimethyl sulfate and nitrous acid) change the bases in their chemical properties, so that false hereditary information is transmitted in this case too. Acridine dyes change the spatial arrangement of the bases on the helical DNA molecule, which will result in a loss of a nucleotide or the insertion of an additional base. In this case, the altered base sequence will be present in the mRNA, and faulty protein synthesis will occur. The operating mechanism of the x-ray, ultraviolet and other radiation has not yet been finally clarified; but it looks as if the mechanism acts mainly on the nucleic acid.

In the course of their long evolution, organisms have adapted to the environment to the best advantage, although over 99.9% of all the hereditary variations represent no advance for the organism as regards the aim of "natural selection." Hereditary variations that put an organism at a disadvantage are generally described as hereditary damage. The most important and most thoroughly investigated forms of hereditary damage for human beings and domestic animals are stillbirths, anatomical defects (faults or disfigurements in parts of the body), metabolic weaknesses (causing mental retardation, allergies, and the failure of particular bodily functions), and psychological disturbances.

As a result of advances in science and technology in the highly civilized world today, more and more synthetic materials are manufactured and put to use. These products can contain substances of a mutation-promoting character. So far hundreds of chemical compounds are recognized as being potentially mutagenic.

Every year thousands of new chemical substances come onto the market that did not previously exist in nature or in the environment of man. The examination of these new substances from the mutagenic point of view is being carried out in industry, at the universities and in other research centers; but owing to the multiplicity of the substances concerned and their potentially additive effects, these efforts are not sufficient. A considerable portion of the research and testing is the responsibility of industry. The government confines itself to a supervisory role but has powers to prevent misuse of mutagenic substances under specific laws (pharmaceuticals and food protection laws; worker protection laws; laws against air and water pollution, etc.).

A problem arises today in connection with the utilization of insecticides, for instance, which have now been on the market for some time but have not yet been examined in accordance with the latest scientific findings from a mutagenic point of view (although many people are suspicious of their mutagenic potential).

In the various processes for the examination of substances from a mutagenic point of view, consideration is given to the level of exposure from which damage may result, the nature of the damage and how the operative mechanism works. Bacteria, fungi, fruit flies (*Drosophila*), mice and Syrian hamsters (golden hamsters) are used as test organisms, as well as cell cultures of human lymphocytes and of fibroblasts from connective tissue. Among these tests, the most useful are those in which the organisms reproduce rapidly and in which the results are clearly applicable to humans. Of particular value as routine tests are trials with bacteria, since bacteria have a particularly high propagation rate.

Certain substances, though not mutagens themselves, can be converted into active mutagens after being metabolized in the body. Several test systems have been developed to take this phenomenon into account. For example, a group of enzymes called the microsomal enzymes can be obtained from the liver of animals such as rats or mice. These enzymes can change, or activate, many molecules that would otherwise be inert in bacterial tests. Presumably, the microsomal enzymes serve to duplicate what would happen within the more complex mammal, such as the mouse or rat or even man. A large variety of other short-term tests also are in wide use. Some of these tests involve looking for changes in cellular growth characteristics that, for example, a typical cancer-causing chemical might produce among human cells that are growing in vitro. Although the reliability of such tests is still debated, they provide a rapid and relatively inexpensive means of screening many chemicals for their potential hazards.

Substances that have been named as genetically active in at least one mutagenic test include the following: dieldrin, a chemical used in agriculture to combat insects, mites and spider mites, and the insecticides dimethyl and methyl parathion. In bacteria tests the herbicides MCPB and MCPA and in tests with fungi the herbicide pentachlorphenol and the fungicide captan proved to be mutagenic. Mutagenic action was also displayed by DDT, which has since been prohibited and can now be used only in exceptional cases approved by the authorities, and by its chemical derivative DDA, by which chromosome mutations are produced in human lymphocytes.

The problem of hereditary damage by mutagenic influences from the environment is a timely subject. In the history of humans, the mutations that have arisen from natural causes and are harmful to the organism have been eliminated by a very severe selection pressure (people afflicted by a hereditary disease do not, for the most part, reproduce), so that a "deterioration" of inheritance has been averted. This selection pressure has been sharply reduced, however, by the advance of civilization, by modern medicine, and by social welfare work. This has the result that the "negative" mutations now present have a much greater chance of being transmitted and so of varying the inheritance of humans in a negative sense. For this reason the number of substances present in the environment of humans that can damage their inheritance must be kept as low as possible.

Part Six—Metabolic Processes in the Organism

ENERGY CONSERVATION OF THE CELL

Living organisms consist of a great number of diverse organic compounds. In each of these organic compounds there is an enormous but specific quantity of energy differentiated according to the type of molecule that is released upon decomposition and conversely is supplied for the synthetic process of the molecules concerned. When an organism can obtain the energy it needs for the synthesis of its own organic material and the maintenance of its biological processes only by the decomposition and conversion of organic matter received from outside, it is known as *heterotrophic;* but when, on the other hand, it does not depend unconditionally on the absorption of organic matter from outside but can acquire its energy by other processes (e.g., by photosynthesis), it is known as *autotrophic.* Heterotrophy embraces all animals and the human race, but also many plants, fungi and the majority of bacteria. Autotrophy occurs only in the plant kingdom. It involves, for the most part, solar radiation from which autotrophic plants absorb their energy. In addition there are certain lower organisms (such as purple and sulfur bacteria) that obtain energy for the development of organic matter (chemosynthesis) from the oxidation of inorganic material (such as ammonia, hydrogen sulfide, nitrite and hydrogen).

Cells need energy for all biological processes. For the operation of muscle cells mechanical energy is required; for the operation of nerve cells electrical energy; for building up tissue chemical energy; and for the maintenance of body heat thermal energy. As in the inanimate world, the principle of energy conservation applies also to cells. In the energy balance of living cells, in principle, there are thus two kinds of energy processes in operation: the release of energy and the utilization of energy for living processes. The organism obtains the energy by the reduction (respiration or fermentation) of nutrients (carbohydrates, fats, etc.).

The reduction processes are not linked directly with energy-consuming processes, however, but through a refined indirect cycle. In this indirect cycle a standard compound full of energy known as an adenosine triphosphate (ATP) is developed, which supplies energy to the cell for practically all energy-consuming processes. The ATP is derived from various reduction processes (discussed later).

The ATP molecules, which are composed of adenine, a ribose molecule and three molecules of anhydrous phosphoric acid, are stored for a longer or shorter time in the cells, until they are again hydrolized in energy-consuming processes. The phosphate residue is now combined at a high-energy level with another molecule. When a phosphate residue is given off by the ATP (by the action of an enzyme), some 7 kcal of energy is produced per molecule of ATP. In this process, from the ATP comes adenosine diphosphate (ADP), which now contains only two phosphate residues. After this reaction the ADP returns to the cycle and again goes into the energy store of the ATP. The formation of ATP takes place primarily in the mitochondria, and its reduction occurs at any point at which energy is consumed (muscle, nerve and gland cells, for example).

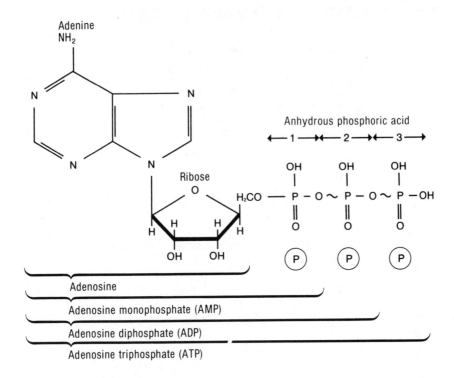

Diagram 1. CHEMICAL COMPOSITION OF ATP

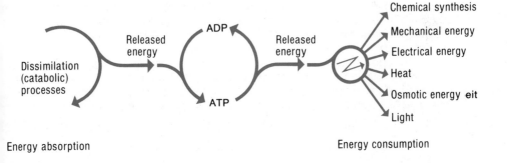

Diagram 2. PLAN OF ENERGY BALANCE IN THE CELL

ENERGY BALANCE AND EXTERNAL INFLUENCES

According to its living conditions, every organism has a specific overall energy expenditure, which is also influenced by external factors. Of practical and clinical importance is what is known as *basal metabolism*. In the case of humans, this is strictly defined as energy expenditure in a state of complete inactivity at a neutral temperature (28°–30°C, or 82.4°–86°F, outside temperature, unclothed) after 12 hours fasting and two days without protein. This normally amounts to between 40% and 60% of the energy consumption in a state of full activity and varies with sex, age and body weight.

The following average values apply for human basal metabolism:

AGE (in years)	MALE	FEMALE
	(kcal per sq m body surface in 24 hours)	
5	1180	1160
10	1050	1020
15	1000	910
20	930	850
30	880	840
40	870	835
50	860	815
60	840	785
70	810	760

The basal metabolism depends on a number of internal and external factors. In cases of fever, for instance, the basal metabolism rises by up to 40% above the normal figure. In the case of overactivity of the thyroid glands it may rise to 75% above the normal level, and in cases of underactivity of the thyroid glands it may be 50% below the normal level. External factors that influence the basal metabolism include the nature and thickness of the skin and the outside temperature.

An interesting feature is the connection between basal metabolism and body size. In comparison with its volume a small animal has a relatively greater surface area than a large animal, and a greater surface area signifies a greater radiation of heat to the atmosphere. The basal metabolism of the shrew mouse, for instance, is 65 times greater per unit of weight than that of a human, and some 200 times greater than that of the elephant.

As blood circulation has the important function of energy conduction (glucose, oxygen and heat), the rate of heartbeat is an important measure of the level of basal metabolism. The following table illustrates the differences between large and small animals with the same body temperature.

SPECIES	BODY WEIGHT (kg)	HEARTBEATS (per minute)
Elephant	3000	46
Horse	390	55
Human	65	75
Sheep	50	70–80
Dog	6.5	120
Cat	1.3	240
Greenfinch	0.022	690
Goldfinch	0.0127	750
Blue titmouse	0.01	960

Since the basal metabolism depends on the external temperature, it is also influenced by the geographical distribution of a living organism. The smaller the animal is, the greater the relative amount of energy it must expend in order to maintain its body temperature in the face of a cold environment. Small mammals therefore restrict their emission of heat by their particular habits, such as hibernation or the construction of underground nests. Two rules emerge regarding the connection between the energy metabolism of an organism and its geographical distribution: (1) The proportional rule lays down that mammals in colder regions have more compact bodies and shorter limbs, ears and tails than the related species in the temperate zones. Animals are often found in warmer regions with slender, long body features—such as the giraffe with its long neck and the antelope with its long, thin legs—that could not survive in a cold climate because the ratio between the outer surface and the volume of the long body parts is unfavorable. (2) The Bergmann rule lays down that the size of mammals of the same species or family increases as the North and South Poles are approached. Thus the Siberian deer, for instance, is bigger than a deer in central Europe, and this in turn is bigger than a Spanish or Italian deer.

Many animals bridge the cold season with a rest in winter or by hibernating. At this period the energy requirements and metabolism are severely limited. By a winter rest is understood a long restful sleep, whereby the body temperature is not reduced. Examples are the bear, the badger and the squirrel. The energy metabolism thus remains at the level of the basal metabolism. These animals often wake up several times during the winter and either go hunting for food or draw on accumulated reserves. Other species hibernate throughout the winter. Examples are the bat, the hamster, the hedgehog and the marmot. At this stage, all living processes are reduced to a minimum. The body temperature falls to a few degrees above 0°C (32°F).

The table provides a comparison between heat production by hibernating animals during their growth stage in the summer and during hibernation:

SPECIES	SUMMER		WINTER	
	Body weight (kg)	kcal per kg body weight per hour	Body weight (kg)	kcal per kg body weight per hour
Marmot	1.87	2.1	2.15	0.086
Hedgehog	0.68	3.5	0.9	0.075
Ground squirrel	0.23	4.5	0.275	0.085
Dormouse	0.13	5.0	0.13	0.07
Common dormouse	0.019	13.0	0.023	0.17

During the cold season, heat-exchange animals (amphibians, insects, reptiles, etc.) lapse into a sort of winter trance, from which, as a result of their own production of heat, they do not emerge until the ambient temperature (in spring) reaches a certain level. During the winter trance, heat-exchange animals can go hungry for many months. Their body temperature is not entirely dependent on the external temperature, however. In the growing stage certain animals are able to raise their temperature, by their own heat production, above the temperature of their surroundings, as in the case of flying insects, incubating reptiles and hibernating bees, which keep the temperature in the beehive constant by vibrating their wings.

PHOTOSYNTHESIS

The most important biological process for life in the soil is the photosynthesis of green plants. This is the process by which practically the whole of the organic matter in the soil is produced and the supply of energy for almost all living organisms is assured. At the same time, by photosynthesis the carbon dioxide exhaled by living organisms is converted into oxygen, which is essential to life for animals.

The processes that play a part in photosynthesis can be set out very simply as follows: together with the water absorbed through the roots, the carbon dioxide, absorbed from the atmosphere through pores called stomates in leaves, is converted, with the assistance of sunlight and chlorophyll, into glucose. As a result of this reaction, oxygen is produced and given off into the atmosphere. By photosynthesis energy it is absorbed from the sun's rays and transformed into a chemical compound rich in energy. In this way, by the release of oxygen, hydrogen is given off from the water and incorporated into a metastable carbon compound. The carbon dioxide thus has the role of a receiver for the hydrogen (hydrogen acceptor) that comes from the water taken up. By the separation of hydrogen and oxygen, more energy is consumed than the amount which is released by water formation from hydrogen and oxygen (the so-called oxyhydrogen gas reaction). This excess energy is obtained by the plant from its absorption of sunlight. The general formula for photosynthesis is as follows:

$$6 \ CO_2 + 6 \ H_2O \rightarrow C_6H_{12}O_6 + 6 \ O_2$$

Under this formula, photosynthesis seems to be a relatively simple process. Extensive research in biochemistry in the past twenty or thirty years has shown, however, that numerous individual reactions occur in photosynthesis which interact on one another in a most complicated manner. Some reactions only occur in light (light reactions), but others can also take place in the dark (dark reactions).

The absorption of the light radiation that is necessary for photosynthesis is effected by *chlorophyll,* the green leaf-coloring pigment in plants, which is stored in the chloroplast contained in the plant cell. This occurs primarily in the plant cells that are directly exposed to light. The accompanying diagram shows the absorption of light rays by one of the two types of chlorophyll, *a* and *b,* depending on the length of the light rays. The illustration below the diagram shows a green alga thread which is incorporated in a light spectrum extended by a prism. It can be seen that the assimilation effect is strongest in the wave range of 400–500 nanometers (blue light) and 600–700 nm (red light). This emerged, in the course of the research, from the fact that to these green algae were attached oxygen-loving bacteria capable of movement which, after a short time, found their way to the points of maximum production of oxygen by the green algae. The more bacteria present at any given point, the greater the oxygen production and the greater in consequence the rate of photosynthesis. The most important coloring pigment in photosynthesis is chlorophyll *a*, which occurs in all photoautotrophic organisms, and its absorption maximum is 660 nm.

The light reactions operate as follows: when a chlorophyll *a* molecule absorbs a light quantum, the molecule goes over to an energy-rich (stimulated) state. This condition lasts for no more than some 10^{-9} seconds. If the

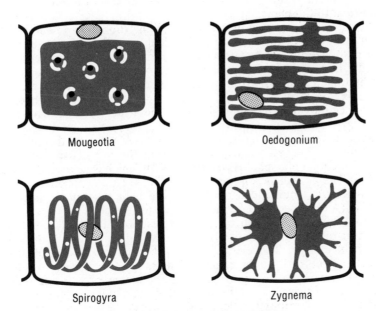

Mougeotia

Oedogonium

Spirogyra

Zygnema

Diagram 1. DIFFERENT TYPES OF CHLOROPLASTS FORMED IN ALGAE

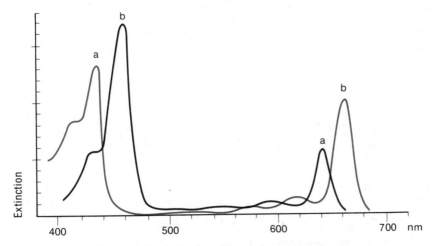

Diagram 2. ABSORPTION SPECTRUMS OF CHLOROPHYLLS A AND B IN ETHER

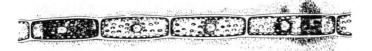

Diagram 3. ENGLEMANN'S BACTERIAL RESEARCH: A SPECTRUM IS PROJECTED
ON THE CHLOROPLAST THREADS OF A GREEN ALGA (OEDOGONIUM). A STRONGER
AGGREGATION OF AEROPHIL BACTERIA INDICATES OXYGEN PRODUCTION

energy released is not utilized, it is emitted in the form of a red fluorescent light and is lost to the plant.

So that the energy stored in the activated chlorophyll can be utilized, it must be transmitted in the form of a chemical potential, that is, of an energy-bearing molecule. The energy stored in the chlorophyll molecule will therefore be used for the following chemical reactions: (1) Water is split into two hydrogen atoms (two protons and two electrons) and one oxygen atom. The oxygen is given off into the atmosphere. (2) The two hydrogen atoms produced by the decomposition of the water will be transmitted by an energy-consuming reaction to an acceptor molecule, known as a nicotinamide-adenine dinucleotide phosphate ($NADP^+$). In this way it is converted into an energy-bearing compound of the reduced nicotinamide-adenine dinucleotide phosphate ($NADPH + H^+$), which is needed in the dark reaction. (3) The adenosine diphosphate molecule (ADP) consumed during the dark reaction is built up again during the light reaction to adenosine triphosphate (ATP), the standard energy store for the cells.

The formation of ATP during the light reaction takes place within the framework of the photosynthetic cycle, an electronic cycle which is motivated by light energy. The electrons are activated by the stimulation of chlorophyll molecules by light quanta; that is, they are raised to a higher energy level and converted into the iron-containing protein, ferredoxin. From here the electrons return through a chain of catalysts (plastoquinone, cytochrome f) to chlorophyll, whereby they supply the energy for the phosphorous alloy ADP. In this way energy-bearing ATP is formed from ADP and inorganic phosphate. In addition to this cyclical transfer of electrons, there is also a noncyclical transfer. This occurs by the formation of the energy-bearing compound NADPH. In this way the electrons from the ferredoxin are transferred back, not to the chlorophyll, but to the $NADP^+$. This is thus carried over in the energy-bearing form of NADPH while at the same time absorbing two hydrogen ions. In this process the hydrogen ions emanate from the splitting of the water.

Alongside these light reactions, dark reactions are also taking place. From the carbon dioxide molecules come the sugar molecules of glucose consisting of six carbon atoms. For a long time it had been assumed that one glucose molecule came directly from each six molecules of carbon dioxide, but experimental investigations, carried out mainly by Calvin and his colleagues, have now shown that the formation of glucose from carbon dioxide occurs in a very different way—namely, by a cyclical process (the Calvin cycle). The original substance is a sugar consisting of five carbon atoms with two phosphate residues: ribulose-1,5-diphosphate. To the ribulose molecule a carbon dioxide molecule is added. In this way a C_6 substance is formed which is immediately split by an enzyme reaction into two C_3 substances—namely, phosphoglyceric acid (see diagram). The phosphoglyceric acid is then converted by an energy-consuming process into two molecules of triose-3-phosphate. From each molecule of ATP and $NADP^+$ come the molecules ADP and $NADP^+$, which have a lower energy content. In the Calvin cycle at this point (see diagram), there are twelve of these C_3 molecules which are capable of reacting with a high-energy content. In each case two of these twelve C_3 substances combine to form a glucose molecule (C_6). The remaining ten C_3 bodies are converted back by a complicated cycle taking

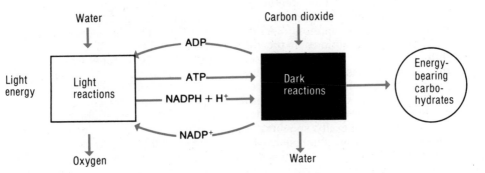

Diagram 1. MUCH SIMPLIFIED DIAGRAM OF THE TOTAL PROCESS OF PHOTOSYNTHESIS

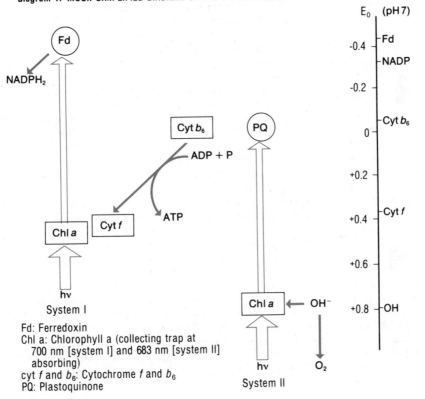

Fd: Ferredoxin
Chl a: Chlorophyll a (collecting trap at
    700 nm [system I] and 683 nm [system II]
    absorbing)
cyt f and b_6: Cytochrome f and b_6
PQ: Plastoquinone

Diagram 2. SIMPLIFIED DIAGRAM OF LIGHT REACTIONS IN PHOTOSYNTHESIS
    (modified version of G. Grimmer)

C_3, C_4, C_5 and C_7 bodies into the original substance, ribulose-1,5-diphosphate, whereupon the cycle starts all over again.

The process of photosynthesis thus occurs through light quanta which stimulate chlorophyll molecules. These pass on the energy for the separation of water and the formation of ATP and NADPH + H^+. The energy obtained from the light reactions in the form of energy-bearing molecules is then utilized to build up the glucose consisting of six carbon atoms from carbon dioxide molecules by stages in a complicated cycle (the Calvin cycle) in the dark reaction.

Photosynthesis in green plants depends on certain external factors, such as light, the carbon dioxide content of the air, atmospheric humidity and temperature. Generally speaking, it can be said that the rate of photosynthesis rises with an increase in the strength of radiation. Above a certain saturation value, however, it will not continue to rise with any further increase in the light intensity. The saturation values vary for the different species of plants. They are lower, for instance, for plants that grow in the shade than for plants that are conditioned to strong sunlight. A limiting factor for the level of the photosynthesis rate in the plant's natural location is frequently the carbon dioxide content of the atmosphere, which generally remains constant at 0.03%. In greenhouses the carbon dioxide content of the air can be raised, and under favorable radiation conditions the photosynthesis will thereby be increased. The humidity in the atmosphere affects the aperture of the stomates in the leaves and with it the absorption of carbon dioxide. While the photochemical reactions of photosynthesis are broadly independent of temperature levels, the dark reactions vary in amount with a temperature increase of 10°C by the factor 2. The extent to which the rate of photosynthesis depends on temperature can be illustrated diagrammatically by means of a typical optimum curve. For plants in our latitudes the optimum temperature lies between 20° and 30°C (68° and 86°F); and the minimum is around freezing point (32°F). Plants in extreme locations (such as lichens), however, have minimum temperatures well below zero (32°F), while the maximum temperatures for plants in desert areas range from 35° to 50°C (95° to 122°F).

The photosynthetic performance of green plants is impressive. On an hourly basis 1 square meter of leaf surface produces about 1 gram of sugar. On this basis the annual assimilation performance of the total vegetation coverage in the world amounts to about 100 billion tons of carbon. This is about 100 times the amount of the total coal output of the entire world. The effective rate of energy conversion in photosynthesis works out at about 30%. It thus stands far above the effective rates so far achieved in the conversion of light into chemical or electrical energy. The highest effective rate is attained in tropical forests, in which the plant growths are disposed in various stages and are thus able to utilize the incident sunlight to the best advantage.

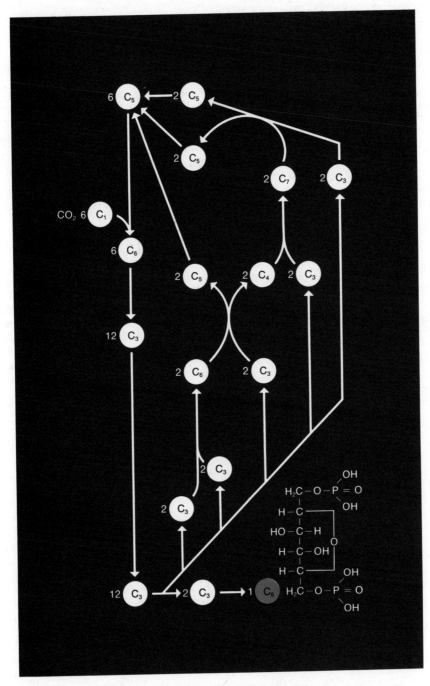

DARK REACTIONS WITHIN THE FRAMEWORK OF PHOTOSYNTHESIS (CALVIN CYCLE)

CHEMICAL SYNTHESIS

Photosynthesis by green plants (as just discussed) is certainly the most important but not the only way in which autotrophic organisms can build up organic matter. There are, additionally, similar processes in which either the nature of the energy supplied or the original substances are different.

The purple bacteria also photosynthesize, but as original substances they utilize carbon dioxide and hydrogen sulfide (instead of carbon dioxide and water). Their chlorophyll is distinguished, both by its chemical composition and by the position of its principal absorption range, from the chlorophyll in green plants. The principal absorption range of the bacterial chlorophyll lies between 800 and 900 manometers (in the infrared range), which cannot be utilized further by the green plants. As a source of hydrogen the purple bacteria use no water molecules but inorganic sulfur compounds, in particular hydrogen sulfide (H_2S). The full formula for the photosynthesis of purple bacteria reads:

$$6 CO_2 + 12 H_2S \xrightarrow{\ radiation\ } C_6H_{12}O_6 + 12 S + 6 H_2O$$

The sulfur is stored in the cells in the form of polysulfide particles, which are visible under a light microscope.

Besides these photoautotrophic bacteria we have chemical autotrophic bacteria, which obtain their energy for the assimilation process not from light rays but from chemical reactions, that is, from the oxidation of various inorganic substances. Oxidation occurs here not only for combination with oxygen but also for the emission of hydrogen or the absorption of electrons. One interesting example is provided by nitrite and nitrate bacteria, which occur in conjunction with one another. The nitrite bacteria of the nitrosamine variety obtain their energy from the oxidation of ammonia:

$$2 NH_3 + 3 O_2 \rightarrow 2 HNO_2 + 2 H_2O + 158 \text{ kcal}$$

The nitrous acid or its salts, the nitrites, produced by this process are then utilized (by the nitrate bacteria) for a further energy-producing chemical reaction in accordance with the formula:

$$2 HNO_2 + O_2 \rightarrow 2 HNO_3 + 36 \text{ kcal}$$

In the nature cycle these nitrite and nitrate bacteria fill an important role. They serve to ensure that the ammonia produced by the decomposition of protein is not released into the atmosphere (as a result of which it would be lost to the plants), but is converted by compounding with nitrite and nitrate into a form in which it is available to plants. The acids produced by the chemical synthesis of these bacteria are thus neutralized in the ground, so that nitrite and nitrate form as salts which can be absorbed by the plant roots and used to build up the plant organism. In the vicinity of stalls and cesspools, the masonry is often adorned with "flowering wall saltpeter," white salt plants that hang like rime from the brickwork. These stem from the bacterial oxidation of the ammonia that is present there.

The iron bacteria assimilate bivalent iron ions, which are dissolved in the water as ferrous hydrogen carbonate, and oxidize them into trivalent indissoluble ferrous oxide. This can often be seen on the beds of streams and pools in the form of brown flakes. The formula for this process runs:

$2H_2S + O_2 \longrightarrow$ Sulfur-oxidizing bacteria $\longrightarrow 2H_2O +$ energy

Sulfur-oxidizing bacteria $2H_2O$ + energy

$4Fe^{++} + 4H^+ + O_2 \longrightarrow$ Iron-oxidizing bacteria $\longrightarrow 4Fe^{+++} + 2H_2O +$ energy

Precipitation
$Fe(OH)_3$

$2NH_3 + 3O_2 \longrightarrow$ Nitrite bacteria $\longrightarrow 2HNO_2 + H_2O +$ energy

$2HNO_2 + O_2 \longrightarrow$ Nitrate bacteria $\longrightarrow 2HNO_3 +$ energy

Vegetable nutrient

$2H_2 + O_2 \longrightarrow$ Oxyhydrogen-gas bacteria $\longrightarrow 2H_2O +$ energy

DIFFERENT FORMS OF CHEMICAL SYNTHESIS

$$4\ Fe(HCO_3)_2 + 2\ H_2O + O_2 \rightarrow 4\ Fe\ (OH)_3 + 8\ CO_2 + 64\ kcal$$

Other bacteria obtain the energy for the constitution of organic material from the oxidation of hydrogen, hydrogen sulfide, sulfur and other inorganic substances.

GLYCOLYSIS

By glycolysis is understood the anaerobic oxidation of carbohydrates in the organism and the biological production of energy connected therewith. The starting point for glycolysis is provided mainly by polysaccharides—that is, hexoses combined with one another (a sugar with six carbon atoms to the molecule) such as glucose—which are split into their component parts by a process of phosphorolysis prior to glycolysis. The molecules of the polysaccharides are broken down, molecule for molecule, under the influence of an enzyme, whereupon the individual glucose molecules that are released combine immediately with a phosphate residue. In this way glucose-1-phosphate is formed. This is converted by a further enzyme into glucose-6-phosphate, which is the initial substance for the process of glycolysis. Sugars such as maltose and galactose are first converted into glucose by the action of certain enzymes.

The precise sequence of glycolysis is as follows (see diagram): glucose-6-phosphate is converted enzymatically into fructose-6-phosphate. By the consumption of energy (adenosine triphosphate, ATP, is converted into adenosine diphosphate, ADP) a second phosphate residue is attached to this molecule, so that fructose-1,6-diphosphate is produced. This molecule is split by the enzyme aldolase into two C_3 bodies. In this way two different isomeric C_3 bodies are produced, which stand, however, in chemical equilibrium to one another and can be converted into one another. For the further development of glycolysis only one of the two C_3 bodies can be utilized; when this has been decomposed, the second one is similarly utilized.

The energy released is utilized for the production of one molecule each of adenosine triphosphate (ATP) and reduced nicotinamide-adenine dinucleotide phosphate (NADH + H$^+$). The C_3 bodies produced by this reaction are then converted by an intermolecular process, and water is released. This gives rise to phosphoenol pyruvic acid, which is converted by the formation of an ATP molecule into enol pyruvic acid. The latter is an important by-product which passes by decarboxylation into the citric acid cycle and is further decomposed there.

An important question regarding biological energy conversion processes is one relating to energy balance. Let us consider the development and utilization of ATP molecules in glycolysis as they occur: in the first place the glucose molecule in conjunction with two molecules of ATP was charged with two residues of phosphoric acid as a reaction primer. This investment yields a profit: for by this means four molecules of ATP (two in each case for a C_3 body) are obtained in return. The net profit thus amounts to 2 moles of ATP (corresponding to 14 kcal) per mole of glucose. This return seems small at first, but the provisional end product, the pyruvic acid, represents a relatively energy-rich compound, which by further metabolism provides further energy. Furthermore the two (NADH + H$^+$) molecules represent a potential source of energy, since later in the respiration chain they also are oxidized and so provide energy.

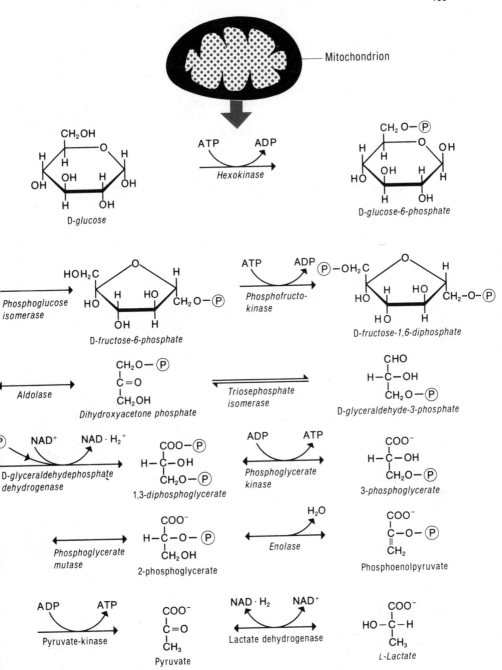

Mitochondrion

ATP → ADP
Hexokinase

D-glucose → D-glucose-6-phosphate

Phosphoglucose isomerase

D-fructose-6-phosphate

ATP → ADP
Phosphofructo-kinase

D-fructose-1,6-diphosphate

Aldolase

Dihydroxyacetone phosphate

Triosephosphate isomerase

D-glyceraldehyde-3-phosphate

NAD⁺ → NAD · H₂⁺
D-glyceraldehydephosphate dehydrogenase

1,3-diphosphoglycerate

ADP → ATP
Phosphoglycerate kinase

3-phosphoglycerate

Phosphoglycerate mutase

2-phosphoglycerate

H₂O
Enolase

Phosphoenolpyruvate

ADP → ATP
Pyruvate-kinase

Pyruvate

NAD · H₂ → NAD⁺
Lactate dehydrogenase

L-Lactate

THE INDIVIDUAL STAGES OF GLYCOLYSIS

CITRIC ACID CYCLE

The citric acid cycle, which is localized in the mitochondria, occurs for the most part in plants and animals, where it assumes an essential role in the metabolism of nutrients by oxidation. It is connected with (nonoxidational) glycolysis and stems from pyruvic acid.

In the citric acid cycle, the pyruvic acid must first be activated. This happens by virtue of the fact that carbon dioxide and hydrogen are released by the C_3 bodies of the pyruvic acid, whereby acetic acid is produced and at once forms an energy-bearing compound with the substance known as coenzyme A. From this arises the substance acetyl coenzyme A, which plays an important part in the metabolism of organisms and is also known as "activated acetic acid." This acetyl coenzyme A enters into the citric acid cycle as the inaugural substance. In addition it is an important precursor in many biosyntheses (e.g., the biosynthesis of fatty acids, carotenoids, terpenes and steroids). The acetyl coenzyme A does not occur in the process of glycolysis, but it does occur in the decomposition of fatty acids and in various metabolic reactions of amino acids.

In the citric acid cycle the acetyl residue, which is combined with coenzyme A, represents the real driving force. The citric acid cycle is a cycle of C_4 and C_6 bodies, in each cycle of which a C_2 body (acetyl coenzyme A) supervenes and from time to time two C_1 bodies (carbon dioxide) are released. As the accompanying diagram shows, at the commencement of the cycle the acetyl coenzyme A is combined with the oxalacetic acid (oxalacetate) consisting of four C atoms. In this way citric acid is formed. This is transformed intermolecularly into isocitric acid, whereby in a subsequent reaction stage-1 carbon dioxide is released. At the same time, in an energy-liberating process, two hydrogen atoms are released, whereby one molecule of nicotinamide-adenine dinucleotide (NAD) is converted into reduced nicotinamide-adenine dinucleotide (NADH + H^+). This generates ketoglutaric acid, from which a second molecule of carbon dioxide is released. At the same time, a further molecule of NADH + H^+ is formed from a molecule of NAD. By a reaction promoted by the coenzyme A, succinic acid is now produced, and the energy-liberating character of this reaction is utilized for the formation of a molecule of guanosine triphosphate (GTP) from guanosine diphosphate (GDP).

By the formation of reduced flavine-adenine dinucleotide ($FADH_2$), a similarly heat-retaining molecule, from the succinic acid now comes fumaric acid. By absorption of water this is transformed into hydroxysuccinic acid, which by the further formation of NADH + H^+ is transformed into the original product, oxalacetic acid. The cycle now begins all over again, as a new acetyl coenzyme A is combined with this oxalacetic acid.

Of importance again is the overall equilibrium of the citric acid cycle. The energy output per cycle amounts to no more than one GTP molecule, which is the equivalent of ATP. At the same time, however, three molecules of NADH + H^+ are formed and one molecule of $FADH_2$. From this it is clear that the main contribution of the citric acid cycle consists, above all, in the provision of hydrogen in a reactive state. This hydrogen is combined with coenzymes (NAD and FAD) which introduce it into the respiration chain, where it is then oxidized upon the formation of ATP molecules. At the same time the hydrogenous NAD and FAD molecules are important reaction partners for other metabolic reactions in which hydrogen is required.

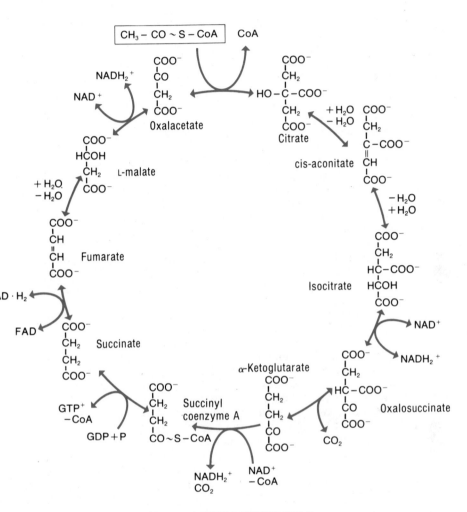

THE INDIVIDUAL STAGES IN THE CITRIC ACID CYCLE (CITRATE CYCLE)

THE RESPIRATORY CHAIN

To enable it to maintain the functions essential to life and to sustain its substance, the living organism requires energy, and this it obtains mainly from the decomposition of energy-bearing compounds. The main input of chemical energy from the decomposition of nutriment is obtained through the respiratory chain. When carbohydrates are extensively broken down by glycolysis and the citric acid cycle, hydrogen is left, which is combined with coenzymes. This hydrogen is present primarily in the form of reduced nicotinamide-adenine dinucleotide (NADH + H^+), and to a lesser extent in reduced flavine-adenine dinucleotide ($FADH_2$). The hydrogen represents a substantial energy potential, which can be released by the combination of the hydrogen with oxygen (oxidation).

The inorganic reaction of hydrogen and oxygen (reaction of oxyhydrogen gas) is known to be accompanied by a considerable release of energy. The organisms that breathe oxygen are now in a position to control the oxygen reaction of hydrogen by stages, so that the energy is not released suddenly in the form of heat but can be gradually allocated by stages to ATP molecules over several reactions (respiratory chain). This process, by which energy-bearing adenosine triphosphate (ATP) is produced from adenosine diphosphate (ADP) and free phosphate residue, is also known as oxidative phosphorylation.

The potential difference between hydrogen and oxygen amounts to 1.23 volts. This corresponds to an energy amount of 57 kcal, which was released in the formation of one mole of water. As the hydrogen is not present here in molecular form, but is combined with a coenzyme, the potential difference is in fact somewhat lower. In the case of the NADH + H^+ it amounts to 1.12 volts, corresponding to a free energy of 52 kcal per mole. This large amount of energy is released in the course of several successive reactions. As the accompanying diagram shows, the hydrogen atoms, or electrons, are transmitted in a chain of redox systems (respiratory chain). The successive redox systems have a progressively higher positive redox potential. In each electron promotion from one system to another, a part of the energy is consequently released. For every two hydrogen atoms (corresponding to one NADH + H^+), three ATP molecules are thus formed.

The oxygen required for this reaction is absorbed from the environment. In the case of unicellular and other small creatures that live in water, this is done by direct absorption, as the oxygen dissolved in the water is diffused in the bodies of the animals. The higher animals distribute the oxygen from their respiratory organs through their blood circulation into their individual cells.

Also of importance is the overall balance of the reaction: two molecules of ATP come from glycolysis, in which one glucose molecule is split into two molecules of pyruvic acid. As a result of oxidation in the respiration chain, the two molecules of NADH + H^+ produced by glycolysis acquire a further six molecules of ATP. The two molecules of pyruvic acid (C_3 bodies) are converted by the release of carbon dioxide into acetyl coenzyme A, whereby two more molecules of NADH + H^+ are produced. Upon oxidation in the respiration chain these give rise to six molecules of ATP. In the passage of the two molecules of acetyl coenzyme A through the citric acid cycle, a further 24 molecules of ATP are produced by the respiratory chain. In this way the aerobic decomposition of a glucose molecule results in the production overall of 38 molecules of ATP. These are at the disposal of the organism, as energy available at any time. The efficiency coefficient of

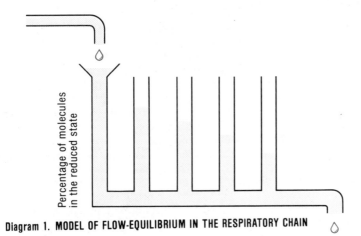

Diagram 1. MODEL OF FLOW-EQUILIBRIUM IN THE RESPIRATORY CHAIN

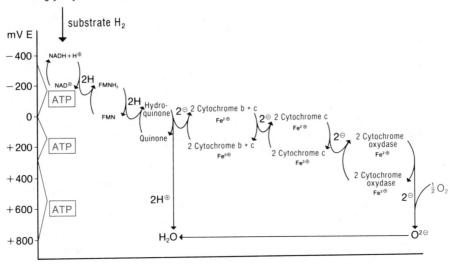

Diagram 2. PROGRESSIVE OXIDATION OF HYDROGEN IN THE RESPIRATORY CHAIN

the total decomposition works out at some 40%. As a comparison of these values with the anaerobic decomposition of carbohydrates in the different forms of fermentation shows, nutrients are best utilized by aerobic decomposition (respiration).

FERMENTATION

Many microorganisms, and also higher forms of plant and animal life (including human beings), are able to decompose organic matter in the absence of oxygen as a source of energy. A distinction is made between *essentially anaerobic* organisms or tissues, which can live only in an atmosphere free from oxygen, and *optionally anaerobic* organisms or tissues, which in the absence of oxygen can switch the decomposition of nutrient to a fermentation basis. An example of the latter is lactic fermentation in human muscles. This occurs when heavily stressed muscles are not receiving sufficient oxygen from the blood. The adenosine triphosphate (ATP) that is needed to sustain muscular functions is, in this case, derived from the anaerobic decomposition (fermentation) of glucose. The end product of the fermentation, lactic acid, builds up in the muscles to form what is known as "muscle binding."

The reduction mechanism in fermentation takes the form, as in the case of glycolysis, of "oxidation" of carbohydrates, with the difference, however, that instead of oxygen other simple compounds serve as hydrogen acceptors. The glucose molecule (C_6) is split up into two parts (C_3), of which one is oxidized by the other. The fermentation products differ according to the hydrogen acceptor concerned in each case, so that a distinction can be made between alcoholic fermentation, lactic fermentation, formic acid fermentation, propionic acid fermentation and butyric acid fermentation.

Alcoholic fermentation occurs with yeast, such as brewers' yeast. The original substance is glucose, which is reduced by the glycolytic reactions to pyruvic acid (C_3). This is not now reduced in the citric acid cycle but is converted by the separation of carbon dioxide into acetaldehyde. The latter is then converted by a further reaction into the end substance, ethyl alcohol. The energy gain from alcoholic fermentation amounts to no more than two moles of ATP per mole of glucose—very little in relation to the oxidation-reduction, in which 38 moles of ATP are produced per mole of glucose. The yeasts must consequently convert very large quantities of sugar to alcohol in order to cover their energy requirements.

Lactic fermentation follows a basically similar course. This is effected by numerous forms of bacteria. In the reduction of glucose the transition to the pyruvic acid level corresponds exactly to that for glycolysis. Here, however, the pyruvic acid is not converted into acetaldehyde, as in alcoholic fermentation, but serves rather as a hydrogen acceptor. In the process lactic acid is produced. In this case, too, the energy output amounts to only two moles of ATP per mole of glucose.

The reduction processes described here and in the chapters on glycolysis, the citric acid cycle and the respiratory chain take the same or a similar form for all organisms. The anaerobic form of energy production (fermentation) is probably the oldest in the history of life. This supports the view that in the early phases of life the earth's atmosphere was free from oxygen. Only as specialization increased were organisms able to draw on oxygen for the decomposition of their nutriment and the production of energy.

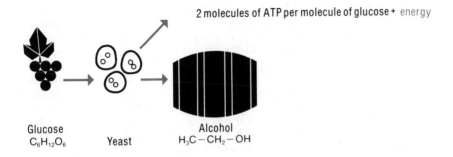

2 molecules of ATP per molecule of glucose + energy

| Glucose | | Alcohol |
| $C_6H_{12}O_6$ | Yeast | H_3C-CH_2-OH |

Diagram 1a. ALCOHOLIC FERMENTATION

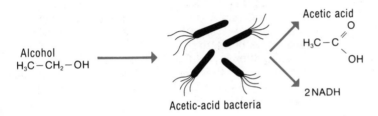

Alcohol
H_3C-CH_2-OH

Acetic-acid bacteria

Acetic acid

$$H_3C-C{\overset{\displaystyle O}{\underset{OH}{}}}$$

2 NADH

Diagram 1b. ACETIC-ACID FERMENTATION

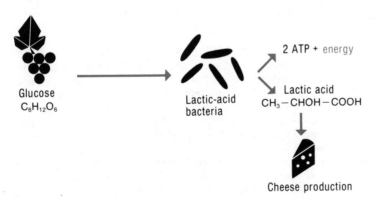

Glucose
$C_6H_{12}O_6$

Lactic-acid
bacteria

2 ATP + energy

Lactic acid
$CH_3-CHOH-COOH$

Cheese production

Diagram 2. LACTIC FERMENTATION

WATER BALANCE IN PLANTS

Whereas water plants (see Part Three) dry up rapidly when exposed to the atmosphere, ground plants have adapted themselves to the conditions prevailing in the atmosphere. During the vegetative period, a constant interchange of water and dissolved matter takes place in them.

The plants have two types of conduction paths: long "water systems" composed of dead cells, and filter channels which consist of living cells to distribute the protein and carbohydrates produced in the leaves throughout the plant. An important feature for the water conservation of plants is the xylem, which runs through the entire plant as a conduction cavity.

As the surface covering (cuticle) of plants is not quite impervious to moisture, and furthermore as water seeps out through the stomates in the form of moisture, the plants are constantly losing water by evaporation. When short of water, the plant can severely restrict its output by closing the stomates. This defensive measure cannot be maintained indefinitely, however, since permanent closure also inhibits photosynthesis (see earlier discussion). The water lost by evaporation is regularly replaced from the soil through the roots.

The result is a regular flow of water, which provides motive power for the transport of matter within the plant, by means of which the mineral substances absorbed from the soil are carried to the leaves. As the water evaporates, the mineral substances build up in the leaves. This can be demonstrated very simply by burning the leaves: the ash content in the leaves is always higher than in other parts of the plant. In this way the mineral substances absorbed from the soil are carried to the point in the plant at which the synthesis of protein and other substances essential to life takes place (with the assistance of minerals).

The evaporation of water from plants can assume substantial proportions. A big sunflower gives off up to 1 liter (0.9 quart) of water a day. On a hot dry summer's day, a fully grown free-standing birch tree loses 300–400 liters (270–360 quarts) by evaporation. In 1 hectare of fully grown beech trees, an average of some 20,000 liters (18,000 quarts) of moisture is lost by evaporation every day. The trees draw the water from the soil and emit it into the atmosphere, whence it can return to the soil in the form of rain. This gives rise to a water cycle and provides the prerequisites for a favorable climate.

The plant world has adapted itself most successfully to the various factors determining the availability of water in different localities (volume of precipitation, level of humidity in the atmosphere, seasonal distribution of precipitation, etc.). There are many bacteria, algae, fungi and mosses that sustain their existence in a dry atmosphere for an astonishingly long period of time. Many seeds are known to remain capable of germination for up to 50 years, and the seed of the lotus can germinate even after 250 years. Certain lichens survive in a dehydrated state for up to 5 years.

The plants acclimatized to arid regions (*xerophytes*) have adapted themselves in many ways to temporary or permanent dryness of the soil or the atmosphere. Their root system is extremely finely ramified and, in comparison with the parts of the plants aboveground, is very widely developed. The roots penetrate to depths of several meters—in the case of certain prairie plants up to 30 m (98 ft) below the surface. Evaporation from the leaves is

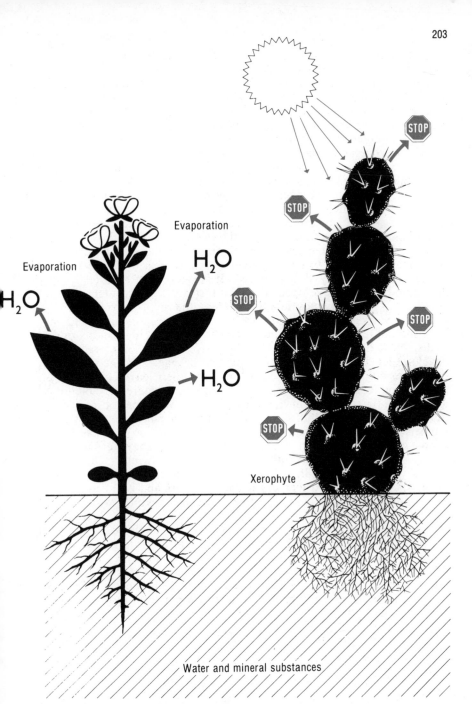

Evaporation

Evaporation

H_2O

H_2O

H_2O

STOP

STOP

STOP

STOP

STOP

Xerophyte

Water and mineral substances

EXCHANGE OF WATER BETWEEN PLANTS AND THE ENVIRONMENT IN HUMID AND DRY LOCALITIES

severely curtailed by restriction of their size. The outer covering of the leaves is often very thick and leathery (e.g., the sclerophyllous plants of the Mediterranean basin). A similar effect is produced by wax coverings or hair felts. The stomates are often deeply recessed and are frequently protected from the drying effect of the wind by folds and rolls in the leaves. When water is short, evaporation can thus be arrested almost completely.

A particular type of xerophyte consists of fatty plants (*succulents*). These absorb a large quantity of water in short periods of rain in prairie and desert areas, store it up internally, and are thus able to survive long periods of drought. The water is stored either in the leaves (leaf succulents, examples of which are the stonecrop and the houseleek), or in the stem, which will thereby be much thickened (as in cacti). In these stem succulents, the leaves are almost completely replaced (thorns, for example), so that the assimilation activity is transferred to the swollen stem. As the stomates open very rarely to permit evaporation of moisture, the exchange of gas and consequently the rate of photosynthesis are also sharply reduced. The fatty plants thus grow very slowly indeed. It is interesting to note that various plant families have developed succulent forms. Stem succulents in America thus belong to the cactus family, whereas the stem succulents in Africa, which are very similar in appearance, belong to the spurge genus *Euphorbia*.

Another form of adaptation (to regular variations in humidity or climate) is displayed by *tropophytes*. These mostly ligneous or oleraceous plants develop their leaves, put forth blooms and propagate in the wet season. In the dry or cold season of the year they shed their leaves or die off aboveground and continue their existence with their more durable parts belowground. There they survive through the difficult period of the year as tubers, rootstocks or bulbs. In the hibernation phase, as a result of low temperatures, the root activities of the plants are so restricted that it is almost impossible for them to absorb more water. If they were to retain their leaves they would consequently be bound to wilt in winter. They thus adapt to this season of the year by shedding their leaves (e.g., deciduous trees). Other species with hard leathery leaves (conifers and ivy) can reduce their evaporation so sharply that they pass through the winter without shedding their leaves.

A special form of water absorption occurs in the case of *epiphytes* (aerophytes), which flourish mainly in tropical forest regions. They grow there on other plant forms, to which they adapt in a wide variety of ways. They absorb the water directly through their leaf surfaces and store it in bulbs or other organs; or they form aerial roots, as in the case of the epiphytic orchids, by means of which they absorb water from the atmosphere like a sponge.

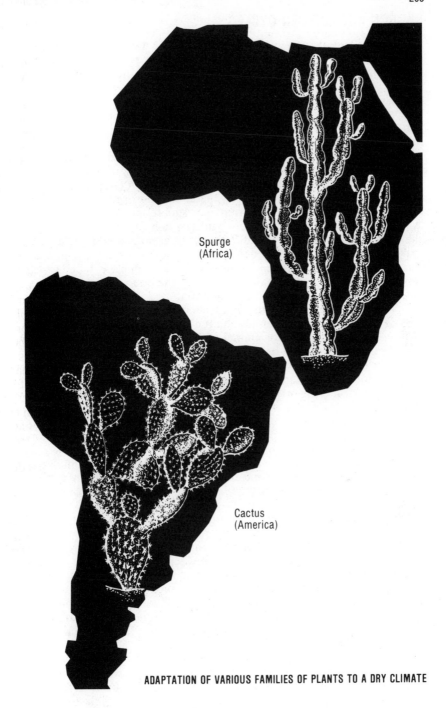

Spurge
(Africa)

Cactus
(America)

ADAPTATION OF VARIOUS FAMILIES OF PLANTS TO A DRY CLIMATE

CARBON AND OXYGEN CYCLES

The carbon and oxygen cycles in the biosphere are closely linked. The two cycles together form a system that comprises microbial decomposition processes, the photosynthesis of green plants, and the respiratory chain of animal organisms.

The reservoir for oxygen and carbon dioxide in the biosphere is the atmosphere. This contains, by volume, 0.03% carbon dioxide and 21% oxygen. The total volume of carbon dioxide in the atmosphere is estimated at about 2100 trillion kg.

At a rough estimate, the annual formation of carbon dioxide by the photosynthesis of land plants amounts to some 13–22 trillion kg. The carbon dioxide taken up by water plants should be well in excess of that for land plants. Under favorable conditions the annual absorption of carbon by sea algae is thus estimated at 360 grams per square meter of the sea's surface. As the carbon absorbed by photosynthesis comes almost exclusively from the atmosphere, on the face of it the carbon dioxide content of the atmosphere should be constantly declining. That this does not happen is due to the activities of microorganisms and the lower animals, which are regularly replenishing the carbon dioxide content of the atmosphere by the mineralization of organic matter and by respiration.

The oxygen present in the atmosphere derives almost exclusively from photosynthesis. This oxygen is required for the supply of energy needed to sustain life in the course of animal and vegetable respiration—namely, the decomposition of energy-bearing organic matter (sugar).

A large part of the carbon assimilated by plants serves to maintain their life functions and is immediately emitted again. The remainder is incorporated as a structural or reserve substance in the plant cells. By day the assimilation rate of plants is higher than the transpiration rate, so that an increase in the amount of organic matter is achieved. At night the photosynthesis comes to a halt, and by their transpiration the plants lose biomass— that is to say, they draw on reserve substances.

Animal organisms, which do not have the capacity to assimilate carbon, also contribute by their respiration to the return of carbon to the atmosphere. A grown man, for instance, breathes out about 1 kg of carbon dioxide every 24 hours.

But all the animals and human beings living on the earth today would not be able to mineralize again (by respiration) the whole of the organic matter built up by the plants and so maintain the necessary atmospheric supply of carbon dioxide. This function is performed for the most part by microorganisms (bacteria, fungi and actinomycetes). These have the capacity to mineralize organic matter, especially such as is not utilizable by other organisms—i.e., carcasses, excrement and fallen foliage—and so to produce enormous quantities of carbon dioxide. Thus the production of carbon dioxide per hectare of good-quality soil in which several billion bacteria are present in every cubic centimeter is estimated at 2–5 kg per hour. In woodland areas the respiration rate is even higher.

In earlier epochs of the earth's history carbon was absorbed by living organisms, so that it got into sediments and was withdrawn from the carbon cycle. Coal, natural gas and oil reserves all represent such established carbon deposits, from which carbon is similarly returned to the atmosphere in the form of carbon dioxide by means of heating appliances and heat engines.

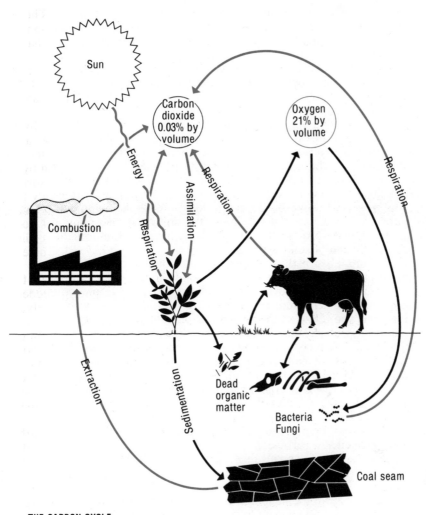

THE CARBON CYCLE

NITROGEN CYCLE

With a nitrogen content of 78%, the atmosphere is the most abundant nitrogen reserve on earth. Nitrogen is present there as N_2 (a nitrogen molecule containing two nitrogen atoms). In this form, nitrogen displays similar chemical properties to the inert gases. Under normal conditions prevailing on earth these hardly combine at all with other elements, being far from active. Consequently, with a few exceptions, the nitrogen in the atmosphere cannot be taken up and utilized by the organisms inhabiting the biosphere.

Nitrogen is one of the elements constituting the amino acids, which play a big part in all living organisms. The amino acids also represent the preliminary stage in proteins (albumins). The only organisms able to absorb nitrogen from the atmosphere are to be found among bacteria: nitrogen absorbers that live freely in the soil, and others that provide a symbiosis with plant roots. Both forms make the nitrogen available for autotrophic plants. When nitrogen absorbers die in the soil, the nitrogen present in the protein of these bacteria is broken down by other microorganisms into ammonia. For the optimum supply of nitrogen to plants, the soil must also contain nitrates, which are likewise produced from ammonia in several intermediate stages, partly with the aid of soil-dwelling bacteria.

The plants absorb the nitrogen through their roots and incorporate it into the protein in their own systems. If plants go to ground or if parts of the plant drop off (as in the annual fall of foliage), they are also decomposed by microorganisms in the soil, and the nitrogen is thus passed on to the succeeding generation. Part of the nitrogen deposited in the soil by the nitrogenous bacteria is absorbed by rainwater and washed into the groundwater layer, whence it can be carried away into streams and rivers. The extent to which nitrogen is washed away depends largely on the volume of precipitation and also largely on the structure of the soil. In ground that is poor in humus and has a low clay content, the nitrogen is not retained (in the humus and soil particles) and is easily washed away. On sloping ground, clayey soils are exposed to erosion, as in these conditions precipitated water penetrates only with difficulty, and this also leads to a loss of the nitrogen adhering to the eroded soil particles.

Gaseous ammonia can also be released from the soil by microbial activity. This process is known as *denitrification,* because faced with a lack of oxygen the bacteria release oxygen from the nitrate in the soil. If the ammonia resulting from the decomposition of the protein is not converted into nitrate, gaseous ammonia can also be produced in certain circumstances.

The nitrogen absorbed by animals in conjunction with plant nutrients is partly converted into bodily protein and partly discharged in the urine or excrement. The nitrogen so emitted is also utilized microbially and restored to the plants. In the same way the body protein incorporated in the animal organism passes into the soil when the carcass of the dead animal decomposes.

Apart from the biological nitrogenous compounds formed by bacteria, nitrogen also passes into the ground upon discharge of electricity into the atmosphere in thunderstorms. Owing to the high level of energy that is released by such discharges, nitric oxide forms from the nitrogen and oxygen present in the atmosphere, and this results in an increase in the nitrate content in the ground. This process is of importance, however, only in zones in which thunderstorms are frequent.

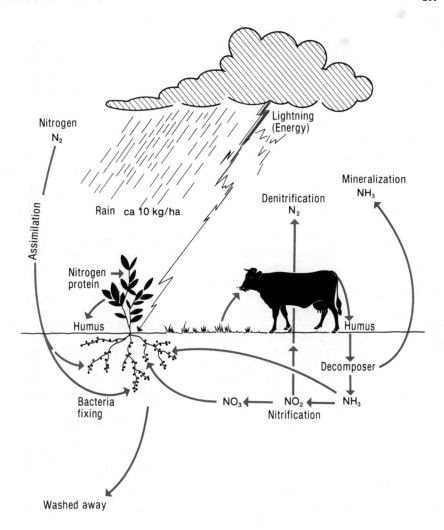

THE NITROGEN CYCLE

PHOSPHORUS CYCLE

Phosphorus is present in the biosphere almost exclusively in the form of phosphate. The elements calcium, iron and aluminum form phosphate salts, which are hardly soluble in water. The bulk of the phosphorus present on the earth is consequently integrated in rocks, soil or sediments and distributed fairly uniformly over the entire earth. In the course of the earth's history, deposits have formed at various points of the phosphorus-rich mineral apatite, and these have been used as natural reserves for the steadily rising phosphorus requirements of man.

Energy is required in connection with all the processes of life in the biosphere, and is converted by green plants from solar radiation into chemical energy. Of fundamental importance in the conversion process is adenosine triphosphate (ATP), a nucleotide consisting of one molecule of the base adenine, one molecule of the sugar ribose, and three molecules of phosphoric acid. As ATP is formed readily by the supply of energy from adenosine monophosphate (AMP) and adenosine diphosphate (ADP) and phosphoric acid, and decomposes again easily upon the release of the energy, it is a suitable compound for transferring energy for metabolic reactions or for storing energy released by decomposition reactions. In its combination with ATP, phosphorus is to be regarded as a key substance in life.

Phosphorus is obtained by plants out of the ground as a phosphate ion. Owing to the poor solubility of phosphorus in water, only a few phosphate ions are available in solution in the ground. The availability of phosphorus is heavily dependent on the soil acidity (pH value) and the form of phosphorus in the soil. In acid soils, iron and acid phosphates dissolve less easily as the decline in the pH value increases. If the ground is basic (alkaline), calcium phosphates are formed, the solubility of which declines as the pH value rises. Ground phosphates are available to plant life in large quantities when the soil reaction is neutral.

If the plants or parts of them die, the organic substance is returned to the soil and there decomposed by bacteria and fungi. In the process, part of the phosphorus incorporated in the plants will be absorbed by the microorganisms, and the rest will be released and pass into the ground. According to the soil acidity and the supply of iron, aluminum and calcium ions, the phosphorus will again be established in the form of iron, aluminum or calcium phosphate. If the plants are consumed by animals, the phosphorus contained in them will be ingested by the animal organism and ultimately be returned to the soil in excrement or with the carcass.

In the atmosphere, phosphorus is largely combined with aerosols. Its displacement in this form is of consequence only in dust- and sand-storms and volcanic eruptions. When the air turbulence subsides, the dust particles settle down again. Phosphorus normally gets into stream and river currents only through erosion of soil particles containing phosphorus. Phosphorus tends to dissolve in water, though to only a limited extent, and so is absorbed by water plants. By far the greatest part is deposited with the eroded soil particles.

In natural ecosystems the subsequent delivery of phosphorus into the biosphere results primarily from the weathering of phosphorus-bearing rocks. Under certain conditions, in water meadows for instance, the supply of phosphorus in sludge (which is deposited through the periodic flooding of these regions) may play an important part in the provision of phosphorus to

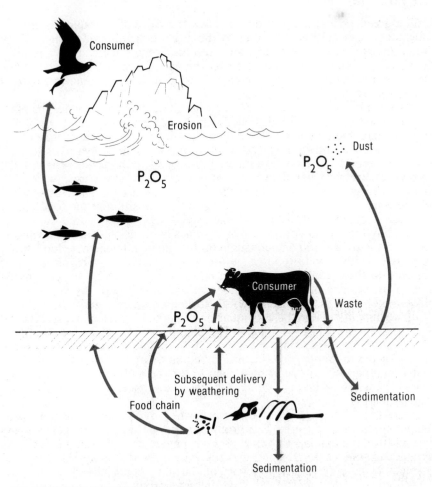

THE PHOSPHORUS CYCLE IN THE BIOSPHERE

the vegetation, while the removal of phosphorus is significant only in extremely dry regions with little plant growth and a high incidence of wind erosion.

THE FOOD CHAIN

Unlike green plants, animals do not have the capacity to build up organic substances out of inorganic matter by the direct utilization of sunlight. They rather have to cover their energy and structural requirements by recourse to the organic compounds synthesized by the green plants. Ultimately animal life, including human life, of course, is completely dependent on the vital activity of green plants.

Green plants thus form the first link in the food chain. In water the plant base is made up primarily of unicellular algae, whereas on land the higher plants predominate. The following members of the food chain represent the different animal consumers: first come the plant eaters (herbivores), followed in second place by flesh eaters (carnivores, predators). Whereas the herbivores are designated primary consumers, the carnivores, which for their part consume herbivores or other carnivores, are classified as secondary, tertiary, etc., consumers according to their position in the food chain. Between decided plant eaters and exclusively flesh eaters come those that will eat anything (omnivores), which are classifiable as consumers at various points in the food chain and consume both animal and vegetable foodstuffs. Organisms with a wide food range are also described as polyphagous, as opposed to those that specialize in a particular diet, which are designated monophagous. An intermediate position is occupied by oligophagous creatures, which vary in the selection of their diet within certain limits.

The human being, who consumes anything that is palatable, is a typical example of a polyphagous animal. The oligophagous species include many insects that live on a small selection of food plants not related to one another. To the monophagous organisms belong many parasites that are only found on a particular type of host plant or animal and often only on certain of its organs. Head and body lice, for instance, concentrate exclusively on human beings.

The final link in the food chain is formed by decomposing organisms (demolishers and reducers). This group consists of bacteria, fungi and many ground-dwelling animals that live (as saprophytes or saprozoa) on decaying organic substances (excrement, detritus, carrion)—that is, on anything that is rejected or left over by members of the food chain already described. They live in humus and in the final analysis produce inorganic matter as required in return by the plants for their sustenance.

As a large part of the food in the food chain is converted for energy production, and a further portion is rejected as unutilizable, the weight of an organism increases at a rough estimate by only one tenth of the weight of food absorbed. From this it follows that when a human being consumes 10 pounds of pike meat, for instance, he will increase in weight by no more than 1 pound. In order to produce this 10 pounds of meat, the pike will, in turn, have to devour 100 pounds of carp, while the carp will need 1000 pounds of algae to enable them to increase their body weight accordingly.

In the food chain, the organisms consumed are normally smaller than those that live on them. Grain, for instance, is smaller than the mouse that consumes it, and the mouse in turn is smaller than a cat. The successive increases in size need not be pronounced, however, as in the sequence plant sap–plant louse–ladybug–songbird–bird of prey. On the other hand, the prey can be disproportionately large, like the victims of snakes, or it can be diminutive in size, as in the case of the giant bearded whale, which lives entirely on plankton.

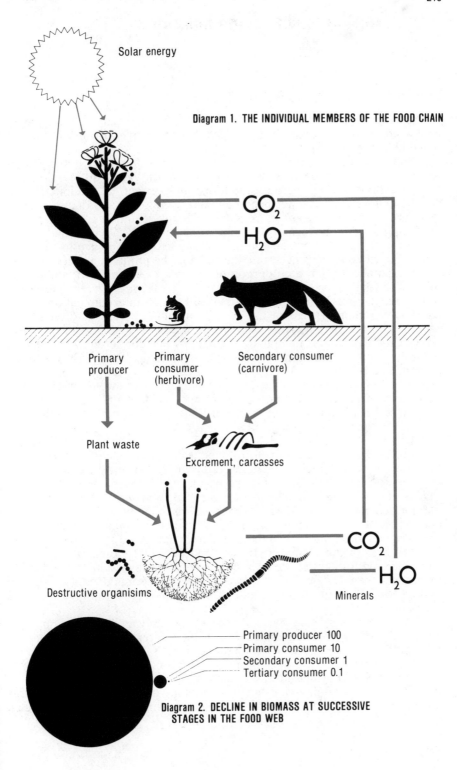

Solar energy

Diagram 1. THE INDIVIDUAL MEMBERS OF THE FOOD CHAIN

CO_2

H_2O

Primary producer

Primary consumer (herbivore)

Secondary consumer (carnivore)

Plant waste

Excrement, carcasses

CO_2

H_2O

Destructive organisims

Minerals

Primary producer 100
Primary consumer 10
Secondary consumer 1
Tertiary consumer 0.1

Diagram 2. DECLINE IN BIOMASS AT SUCCESSIVE STAGES IN THE FOOD WEB

Part Seven—Woodland and Moorland

WOODLAND AREAS IN JEOPARDY

In the balance of nature, forest land plays an important role. In highly populated areas, for instance, it influences air movement, water conservation and soil protection.

Forest land accounts for a regional increase of up to 20% in the precipitation volume over the year. Evaporation is much higher in forest regions than in cultivated areas because the forest limits runoff of precipitation. In deciduous forests, rainwater penetrates deeper into the soil than it does in open areas and it runs off more slowly. Water retention is aided by the prevailing shade, the canopy of vegetation and the layer of mulch and humus, which give woodland soil its crumbly texture. The depths to which roots of deciduous trees penetrate the soil and the proliferation of moss and weeds also allow a large proportion of the rain to be retained, stored and released in the form of springs and evaporation from the trees. Thanks to this "sponge effect" the danger is reduced both of an accumulation of surface water from heavy rainfall and of a drying-out in periods of drought.

In the case of pinewoods, however, the effects of forests on water conservation are not as favorable. The canopy in a coniferous wood shields the ground surface and soaks up the rainwater. Thus less water gets to the ground, and much of that runs off the surface and is not stored. In pinewoods, a layer of compressed earth partly impervious to water builds up not far below the surface, due to the effect of humic acid. Coniferous trees with their widespread root systems, therefore, facilitate the runoff of rainwater and reduce the forest's storage effect.

Thus, the makeup of much woodland is by no means optimal. In the United States today 58% of the forest land is deciduous and 42% coniferous. Pine forests yield a quicker and better return in timber, for the pine is almost fully grown after 80 years, while the beech or oak takes 150 to 200 years. The demand for coniferous lumber, also called *softwood,* is far greater than that for deciduous, or *hardwood,* timber. Consequently, softwood has been cut somewhat more rapidly than it grows, whereas since 1952 hardwoods have grown more rapidly than they have been harvested.

The area of the United States covered by forest increased after 1910, when clearing for agriculture ceased to exceed the reversion of farmland to forest. Between 1970 and 1978, however, the forest area decreased slightly —from 754 million acres to 740 million acres. About two-thirds of that land is commercial forest.

Reforestation by man does not necessarily imply an improvement in the quality of a forest. For economic reasons, the reforested areas are primarily monocultures (mainly pines), which do not match up to thick beech woods or mixed forest stands, either from an ecological standpoint or for recreational purposes. Furthermore, monocultures are highly susceptible to attacks by forest vermin, which can proliferate in vast swarms. Monocultures are also more exposed to damage from gusts of wind, since the trees are all

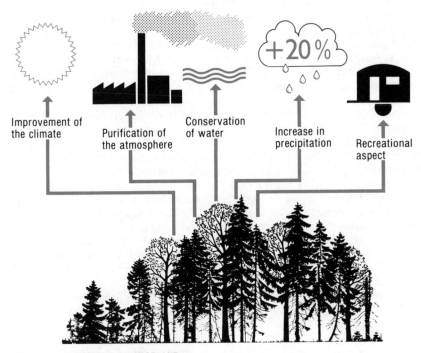

Improvement of
the climate

Purification of
the atmosphere

Conservation
of water

Increase in
precipitation

Recreational
aspect

ECOLOGICAL FUNCTIONS OF WOODLAND

about the same height. The seeds for reforestation, however, are produced by cross-pollination, so progeny have a varied genetic makeup. Even though the trees are all the same species, they thus retain some protection against destruction by insects and by disease.

The influence of woodland on water conservation, climate, atmospheric hygiene, and soil protection unfortunately confers no direct economic advantages. Most measures taken for woodland conservation are geared to maximizing the return on timber. That return is highlighted as the competition intensifies between the timber industry and other branches of the economy, such as the chemical industry with its plastics.

The recreational use of forest land has grown rapidly in recent years and has become important to forest planners. Participation in outdoor recreation increased about 56% between 1965 and 1980, and is expected to go up another 66% between 1980 and 2000. A growing number of people choose activities such as camping and hiking, in wilderness areas. The number of visitor-days spent in "unimproved" areas in National Forests was 139 million in 1978, compared with about 89 million in 1965. Visits to picnic sites and campgrounds also increased, but less dramatically. The National Park Service and Forest Service have the major portion of the difficult task of maintaining the physical character and wilderness feeling of the parks in the face of rapidly accelerating use.

The conflict between the timber industry and the wilderness preservationists is not always absolute. Much of the land protected as wilderness is steep and mountainous, so that it is of little value for timber production. In addition, some properties of the forest industries are being opened to the public for recreational use.

Environmental concern and the availability of imported wood have limited exploitation of U.S. forests. Loss of forest land is a far greater danger elsewhere on the globe, especially in developing countries in tropical regions. Each month the earth is losing an area of tropical forest approximately the size of Massachusetts, according to one estimate.

Each year the industrial nations import more and more tropical timber. Between 1950 and 1973, such imports increased by a factor of 12, and they are expected to almost double again by 2000. The major source of the timber is the Asia-Pacific region, especially southeast Asia.

Damage to forests extends beyond the loss of trees taken for timber. Loggers actually have use for only a few of the many types of trees found in a tropical forest, but the logging operation damages surrounding trees, making them susceptible to disease. In southeast Asia an estimated third of the trees remaining after logging are damaged beyond repair. Including such damages, timber exploitation eliminates more than 15,000 square kilometers (5800 square miles) of tropical forests each year.

An even greater area of forest is lost to people who, after the logging, move into a forest along the timber paths and settle down to cultivate the newly exposed land. Such "slash-and-burn" cultivators eliminate an estimated 200,000 square kilometers (77,000 square miles) annually. Finally, fuel wood collection and ranching operations (in Latin America) take further forest toll.

The demand for forest products, and the subsequent loss of forest land, is likely to continue rising above and beyond the population rate as standards of living, especially literacy, increase around the world. To meet that demand, wise intensive management techniques in the developed countries could increase wood provisions from the temperate area forests; this would ease the burden on tropical forests with their greater ecological diversity and valuable genetic variation.

Subsidies from the government to the forest industries might help maintain the benefits of woodland areas for the public. In addition, regulations might specify that the planting of new monocultures be reduced in favor of mixed forests, that the preservation of woodlands in the vicinity of urban centers be given preferential treatment, and finally that the various forms of forest use be adapted to meet sound ecological requirements.

WOODLAND CLEARINGS

In the original primitive forests, big woodland clearings were rare. Only the occasional severe storm or a calamitous forest fire would open up large areas and provide living space for particular plants and animals.

Owing to utilization of timber in recent centuries with consequent deforestation and replacement by coniferous stands poor in undergrowth, woodland clearings have increased in number and extent. This has led to a sharp increase in originally rare species of plants and animals in forest clearings. When forest land loses the protection of its crown cover, the sun can shine on the ground directly. The temperatures near ground level are then higher by day, and lower by night, especially in the absence of clouds. As a result of the change in temperature conditions the flora on forest land will alter in composition. Sun plants, quick-growing and luxuriant green plants, now flourish. Owing to the change in the surrounding climate, the decomposition of organic waste on the soil is stimulated by microorganisms. The plant nutrients (especially nitrogen) released thereby can be absorbed by the plants in the woodland soil as a natural manure. An unusually luxuriant range of vegetation is soon formed by plants such as the willowweed, woodstrawberry, foxglove, deadly nightshade, rushes, woodreeds, cudweed and groundsel.

If in a few years' time the rapidly converted nutrients in the soil are exhausted, longer-living plants, especially young trees and shrubs, will get a foothold. These are partly disseminated by birds, which eat the berries and disperse the seeds in their droppings. The luxuriant vegetable cover is thus supplanted more and more by shrubs and pioneer growths such as elders, birches, aspens, willows, and blackberries and raspberries. The plants grow rapidly and so form a dense stand, under the protection of which a genuine mixed forest gradually develops with its typical animal and plant world.

Apart from particular plants, some very specific kinds of animal are associated with forest clearings and open woodlands. Given the rich profusion of grasses, seeds, herbs, fruit and insects, mice are particularly prone to multiply hereabouts. These in turn attract animals that prey on mice such as foxes, screech owls and the common buzzard, which furthermore have better opportunities in forest clearings of hunting down their prey. In addition, some common buzzards, foxes and martens, have a preference for the berries and fruits in the clearings. For the same reason certain birds, such as the tree pipit and the fallow finch and among larger birds the moorhen and the hazel hen (the latter also because good possibilities of concealment exist in the clearings), are to be found here in increasing numbers. Forest clearings also play a large role in the lives of the bigger herbivores such as the deer and the roebuck. In forest clearings they find their favorite pasturage in the form of raspberries, blackberries, willows and aspens. In the normal timber forest the herbivores have to fall back on the much sparser vegetation present on the ground.

On top of these ecological factors for animals and plants, the clearings are also of considerable importance in the recreational value of the forest. The range of activities in the forest is much increased thereby. Woodland glades provide a center for leisure and relaxation. Unfortunately, however, owing to the withdrawal of agriculture into low-yield regions such as the highlands, meadows and clearings are getting ever rarer in valley areas. The terrain is expanding and in time becomes wooded. To avoid this, open stretches should be either regularly grazed or mown at least once a year.

HOW MOORS ARE FORMED

To qualify as moorland, the land must have a peat layer containing at least 30% organic matter, and in the undrained state the cover must be over 30 cm (12 in.) thick. According to its formation, a distinction is made between low-lying moorland in the rainwater zone above the groundwater level, and intermediate moorland areas situated between the other two moorland areas. Typical vegetation found in low moorland areas is cat's tail, sedges, reeds, alder and willow. At the intermediate level, pines and birches predominate. High-lying moorland is distinguished by the presence of bog moss, cotton grass, bell heather, broom heath and hair bulrush.

The primary requirement for the formation of moorland is an abundance of water, which favors the growth of moisture-loving plants. Furthermore, the surplus water produces anaerobic conditions, which arrest the reduction of dead plant remains by microbes and promote carbonization, leading to the formation of peat.

Following the last ice age, during the succeeding period of continuing cold, mud was formed from deposits of sludge in the lakes and backwaters built up from the melted ice and left between the moraines. As temperature levels rose, plant growth improved, and in the area between high and low water the plants on the verges of the moorland spread increasingly into the middle. This was the start of the low-lying moor formation. The reed banks became increasingly overgrown with sedges, which resulted in the formation of rush and sedge peat. Once the open water surfaces had dispersed, black alder stands and subboreal willow appeared. This soil horizon developed into subboreal peat.

Once the plant canopy on the intermediate moorland had been washed up over the groundwater with its high nutrient content, it was supplied thereafter only with rainwater, which was poor in nutrients. So it came about that the less demanding pines and birches gradually increased in number and came to determine the composition of the plant coverage. The residue from the subboreal pines and birches became intermediate moorland peat.

In the wetter climatic conditions of the Atlantic (Altithermal) period, peat mosses began to flourish as a result of increased precipitation, and the root growths of the trees at intermediate moorland level started to choke. These peat mosses have the capacity to soak up water like a sponge; their spore-filled dead cells can absorb twenty times their dry weight in water. They formed big sealed cushions which grew constantly bigger while the lower plant parts wilted away and turned into peat. The high moorland eventually curved up like a watch glass over the surrounding area.

Owing to splits occurring in the surface of peat moors, moorland lakes came to be formed.

The high moorlands, which are now between 3000 and 8000 years old, have formed peat beds from 3 to 5 m (10 to 16 ft) deep and sometimes very much more, representing an increase of some 1 mm of peat per annum. The more severely decomposed high moorland peat formed black peat, the less decomposed younger peat formed white peat, and the topmost layer of peat still permeated by living roots formed what is known as banking. Between black and white peat there is an intermediate horizon with a thick covering of cotton grass and heather remains.

The flower pollen blown year by year across high moorlands from the surrounding district provides a basis (by pollen analysis) for determining the

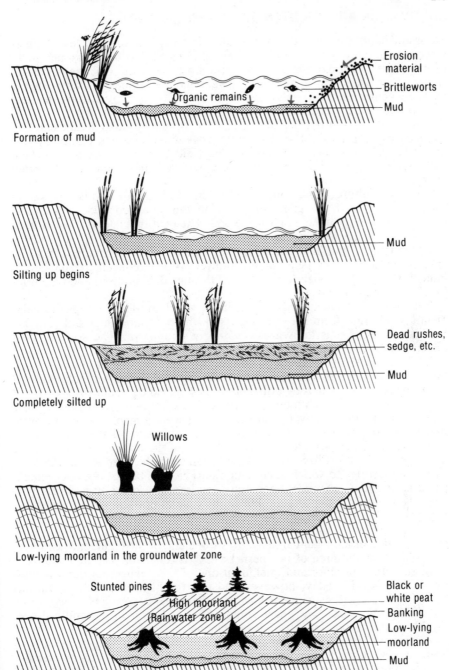

Formation of mud

- Erosion material
- Brittleworts
- Mud

Organic remains

Silting up begins

- Mud

Completely silted up

- Dead rushes, sedge, etc.
- Mud

Willows

Low-lying moorland in the groundwater zone

Stunted pines

High moorland (Rainwater zone)

- Black or white peat
- Banking
- Low-lying moorland
- Mud

STAGES OF MOORLAND FORMATION

composition of the vegetation of a forest stand, for example, during the period of the moor formation, and it also provides evidence of the climate prevailing at the time.

CULTIVATION AND MAINTENANCE OF MOORLAND

Moorland cannot be regarded as utilizable in an agricultural sense as long as it remains in its original primitive condition. Once it has been drained, however, and ventilation of the peat soil is possible, the water balance in the soil returns to normal and agricultural development becomes possible. In the past few centuries moorlands have mostly been utilized by cutting the peat as a source of fuel, fertilizers and litter.

As a means of procuring arable land, moorland has also been cleared in some cases simply by setting fire to the vegetation on it and planting seeds in the layer of peat ash left behind. The yield from this type of moorland cultivation, which is no longer in general use, was never impressive, however.

In peat culture, which originated in the Netherlands and is now rarely used, banked earth is again deposited on the depeated mineral soil and mixed with it to produce a cultivable soil. The peat that is extracted is used as fuel, for compost preparation or as litter.

Good water and heat conditions are secured in low-lying moorland by applying a sand layer (sand-layer culture), which reduces the danger of infertility (loss of reutilization of the turf through dehydration) and the harmful effects of late frosts.

In addition to such sand-layer culture, which produces a topsoil fundamentally different from the moorland soil, the pure moorland soil can also be utilized in what is known as *fenland black culture*. The soil obtained under this process is more suitable for grassland culture.

Instead of the very costly sand-layer culture, if the peat layers are not too deep they can also be mixed with the generally sandy mineral subsoil (sand-mix culture), whereby utilizable soils can also be obtained.

Drainage of the high moorland areas, an essential prerequisite for their utilization, is effected by the installation of a system of dikes and drain outlets. As the moors are drained of water, settlement of the land sets in, and this must be allowed for upon installation of the drainage system. After drainage, the first fertilizer to be applied must be in the form of lime. In most cases the best use to which such high moorland can be put is as permanent pasture, as the biochemical decomposition loss in use for agricultural purposes is about 1 cm per annum, but in the case of grassland is considerably lower.

The cultivation and industrial use of moorland have led and are leading to a reduction of moorland areas. Toward the end of the eighteenth century, almost 25% of the area of northern Lower Saxony, for instance, was still covered with high moorland, making it one of the richest moorland territories in the world. Today, however, most of the high moorland region has been dried out. Extensive areas have lost their peat covering by peat cutting for building purposes, by "peat consumption," by direct agricultural use, by cultivation and by industrial development.

For some time now nature conservation has been striving constantly to preserve for natural purposes the still unaffected remains of the former moorland regions. The small number of present-day moorland conservation areas are confined mainly to marshy lakes, which owing to their low borders are inadequately protected from drainage, however, so that their water level gradually sinks and silting up sets in.

In the high and dry land of the North German coastal region, numerous small, protected moorland areas are to be found in high-lying sandy soil. These were formed from gulleys underground, and they still provide an

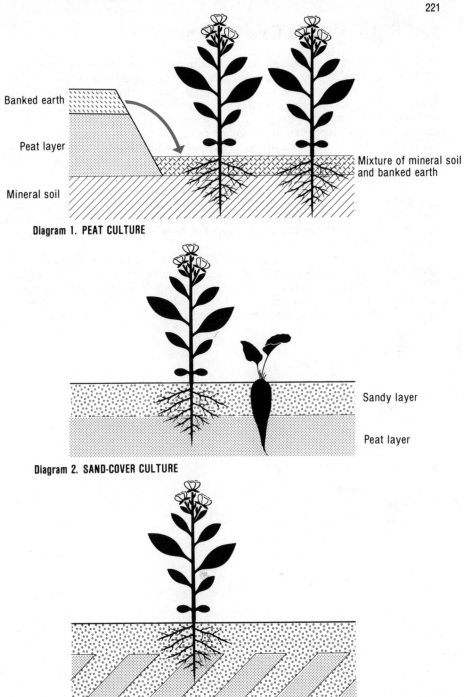

Banked earth

Peat layer

Mineral soil

Mixture of mineral soil and banked earth

Diagram 1. PEAT CULTURE

Sandy layer

Peat layer

Diagram 2. SAND-COVER CULTURE

Diagram 3. SAND-MIX CULTURE

opportunity for studying the various stages of moor formation, from the open water surface and the marshy swamp to the arching high moor.

Part Eight—Nature Conservation

With the growth of industry, the expansion of urban conglomerations and traffic networks, and increasing settlement in the countryside, the original natural landscapes are becoming increasingly rare. Efforts are consequently being made to protect particularly beautiful and characteristic areas and to preserve them for the benefit of future generations. The idea of preserving nature from the depredations of mankind goes back in origin to an early period of humanistic development. Today there are a variety of possibilities for the preservation of nature including: national parks and forests, state parks and forests, nature preserves and natural monuments.

National parks are extensive natural landscapes which, owing to their particular characteristics and impressive beauty, often have no parallel anywhere else in the world. They are subject to strict protective regulations as regards complete natural preservation, but they are also available to some extent for recreational purposes.

Nature conservation and preservation areas include regions that are protected because of their natural characteristics or in part on scientific or historical grounds, or because of local or national interest in their beauty or special features. They contribute to the enrichment of the scene and in the public interest deserve to be preserved and protected from damage.

PROTECTED ANIMAL SPECIES

Protection of wild animals in the United States—from hunting laws to the Endangered Species Act—stems from a nineteenth-century Supreme Court decision. It stated that wildlife is not the private property of an individual or a group, but rather the collective property of all the people. Before 1900, wildlife conservation was primarily the task of the individual states. More recently the federal government has taken an increasing role, first by prescribing remedies for specific, acute problems and then in the past decade by setting up more comprehensive programs to address broader wildlife conservation needs.

Four basic tools for federal wildlife legislation have been used. The first is restrictions on the "taking" of wild animals; in its broadest sense "taking" includes harassing, harming, pursuing, hunting, shooting, wounding, killing, trapping, capturing and collecting. The second is restrictions on interstate commerce involving animals, plants or products derived from them. The third is the acquisition of habitats to be used as wildlife reserves. Finally, regulations can specify that people take into consideration the impact of their enterprises on wild animal life.

The focus of animal conservation laws has broadened with time. At first federal legislation centered on game and furbearing animals. Then the protection was expanded, with laws reflecting a desire to preserve animals as symbols. The bald eagle and the wild free-roaming horses and burros were given federal protection long before concern for endangered species in general became widespread sentiment. Eventually, in the Endangered Species Act, "wildlife" is defined as any member of the animal kingdom.

The enforcement of some laws has shifted in emphasis. Laws protecting migratory birds, which limit the hunting seasons, originally were intended to preserve a food supply but now regulate a recreational activity. Similarly the Lacey Act, which prohibits importation of animals that could harm agriculture and horticulture, was amended in 1960 to prohibit importation of any animal injurious to native wildlife.

The current idea that a well-balanced ecology is the best wildlife protection was first presented forcefully in the Marine Mammal Protection Act. That 1972 law sets as its primary goal maintenance of health and stability of the marine ecosystem. To that end, the law initiated a moratorium of indefinite duration during which marine mammals could be neither killed, hunted, captured, harassed nor imported into the United States. Limited exceptions were made for science and museums, Eskimos and other Alaska natives and commercial fishing operations. The act attempted to establish an ambitious international program for marine mammal protection, and it authorized possible restrictions of imports from countries whose fishing practices or other actions threaten marine mammals.

Wildlife preservation is certainly not a matter that respects national boundaries. Marine animals and migrating birds are obvious examples where protection in one country is not sufficient to maintain species. The United States is a party to more than 70 international agreements protecting wildlife (especially fish) and the environment.

The 1973 agreement of the Convention on Trade in Endangered Species of Wild Fauna and Flora limits trade in animals, plants and their products. Not just mammals, birds and fishes, but also reptiles, amphibians, snails, clams and insects are included in that treaty. By assigning threatened species to one of three lists, the agreement for the first time distinguishes the varying degrees of vulnerability to extinction that species may face.

That international agreement spurred the United States to strengthen its own protection of endangered species. The Endangered Species Act of 1973 attempted to provide the means necessary for action early enough to save a vanishing species. The act prohibited the "taking" of endangered animals, where earlier wildlife laws had left such measures to the states. The act also strengthened the obligation of federal agencies to protect endangered species. Like the international agreement, the law distinguishes the degree of the threat; it provides the strictest regulations for "endangered" species, those in danger of extinction throughout a significant portion of their range. Species likely to become endangered are termed "threatened" and a different set of regulations may apply.

Indirect protection of wildlife (and plant) habitat is probably the most potent weapon of the act. The law instructs all federal departments to use their programs to protect endangered species and also to ensure that any actions they authorize, fund or carry out do not jeopardize such species or destroy or modify habitats "critical" to the species' survival. However, in 1978 an amendment to the Endangered Species Act undermined its strength by allowing exemptions for projects that jeopardize an endangered species if no reasonable alternatives exist and if the benefits projected for the activity clearly outweigh the benefits of preserving the species. A cabinet-level committee was established to resolve disputes between the Endangered Species Act and specific projects.

Cranes, pelicans, falcons, bats and kites have all come up against major highway and dam programs, but it is the case of the snail darter that best illustrates the strengths and limits of endangered species protection. The three-inch-long fish lived in the last 38 miles of clear, free-flowing water on the Little Tennessee River. Because the Tellico Dam, part of a $119 million regional development project of the Tennessee Valley Authority, would have replaced the stream with still water, conservationists in 1976 brought a lawsuit before the Supreme Court to halt work on the dam and won. Then Congress amended the Endangered Species Act to allow projects to be exempted, an action that was at least in part a response to the snail darter victory. The Tellico Dam was one of the first projects to be considered by the newly formed Endangered Species Committee, which voted unanimously not to exempt the dam, although it did exempt another dam from the regulations. The committee said that the Tellico Dam, irrespective of the snail darter, was economically unjustifiable. The dam, and not the snail darter, however, had the final word. A 1979 public works law provided the dam with complete exemption from federal laws, including the Endangered Species Act, occupational safety laws and workmen's compensation. Meanwhile snail darters transplanted to another Tennessee river appear to be thriving, although it is too early to tell for certain whether they will survive in the new habitat.

BISON

It is difficult to imagine bison (also called buffalo) being compatible with modern civilization. Herds of 60 million buffalo once wandered from Texas to Montana and back each year, in the days when a flock of a million passenger pigeons would settle on Ohio fields to feed. But unlike the passenger pigeon, some bison still survive; about 25,000 live in zoos and on reservations.

Before the arrival of the Europeans, bison provided most of the meat needed by the Plains Indians and prairie wolves. Each adult buffalo weighed over 1000 pounds and subsisted on the prairie grasses. Early Indians did wipe out one species of bison, but they apparently reached an ecological balance with the rest.

The buffalo became the victim, indirectly and directly, of the European colonists. These colonists provided horses and guns which allowed the Indians to stampede bison herds over cliffs, killing hundreds of animals to obtain the choice meat from only a few. The United States government chose to use bison killing as a means to subdue the Indians, who were dependent on the buffalo for food. The legendary Buffalo Bill gained fame by slaughtering bison; he shot over 4000 in one year. By 1887, no American bison could be found for a display at the Smithsonian Museum.

Luckily, on a private ranch in Montana, a small herd of bison had been maintained. The federal government purchased the animals and installed them in Yellowstone National Park. Explorers later discovered a few more animals that had taken refuge in a remote area of northwestern Canada, and the Canadian government established a reserve for those animals. When that herd later seemed in danger of dying out, animals from the U.S. herd were sent to revitalize the population. There are currently 10,000 bison in U.S. national parks and refuges and 14,000 in Canada. Animals in excess of the number that can be supported on the available land are shipped to zoos and parks in this and other countries. Although the bison are reproducing and prospering within protected reserves, it is unlikely that, with their nomadic habits and need of extensive space, they will ever again freely roam the plains. Even their image on the nickel was long ago replaced with a building, a product of civilization.

PROTECTED BIRDS

The whooping crane is the most widely known of American rare birds. White with a red crown, black moustache and black wing tips, it is a striking sight wading in shallow water or flying in the air. The five-foot-tall bird originally inhabited marshes in the prairie states and wintered on the Gulf Coast. The number of cranes was reduced by hunters, although the bird was not especially good to eat, and by loss of habitat when the marshes were drained for agricultural purposes. By 1938 only 14 whooping cranes were left in the country.

The effort to save the crane is probably the greatest ever made on behalf of an endangered bird. A reserve was established in Texas for the birds to spend the winter, and they breed in a national park in Canada in summer. 20 are in captivity where artificial breeding is being attempted. A novel approach, a "foster crane" program, is also under way: Eggs from nests of wild shooping cranes are being slipped into nests of sandhill cranes, a closely related but more abundant species. The resultant young whooping cranes are being reared, seemingly successfully, by sandhill crane parents, and zoologists hope the whooping cranes eventually will mate with each other.

Other bird species have been threatened, not by deliberate modification of the environment, but by efforts to protect it. A reduction in the number of destructive forest fires was significant in the dwindling of the numbers of California condors and Kirtland's warblers. The magnificent condor once inhabited the Atlantic shores, the Gulf states and the central plains into Canada. It ate abundant dead animals, such as rabbits; food that no longer litters these regions. The supply of rabbits and other small animals was lessened by (in addition to the effects of extensive ranching and farming) a reduction in the amounts of grass and other soft, edible plants because frequent fires no longer clear the sagebrush and woody plants. Without the clearing by fires, the condors also cannot spot carrion; it is now hidden by a dense foliage screen. Fires also created the open space needed by the condor, with its immense wingspread, to approach its food and to take off after eating. The remaining 60 condors are now confined to a coastal mountain area in California.

A much smaller bird was also a victim of fire prevention programs. Kirtland's warbler winters in the Bahamas and nests in northern Michigan among young stands of jack pine. The birds are so particular that the pine must be no less than 6 years old and no more than 20 years old. The jack pine cannot reproduce without experiencing a scorching fire. The heat opens its cones and releases the winged seeds. The seeds float down to the soil, just cleared of fire-sensitive vegetation, and they start a new pine grove. An experimental program of deliberate burning is now attempting to restore the specific habitat the warbler requires. Thus Kirtland's warbler has been called the "bird worth a forest fire."

Bird protection may be motivated by the ethical and cultural considerations of preserving species or by such material and commercial considerations as biological pest control. Birds play an important role in conservation of other species. By consuming seeds and berries they contribute to the dissemination of plants, and by consuming insects and hunting small animals

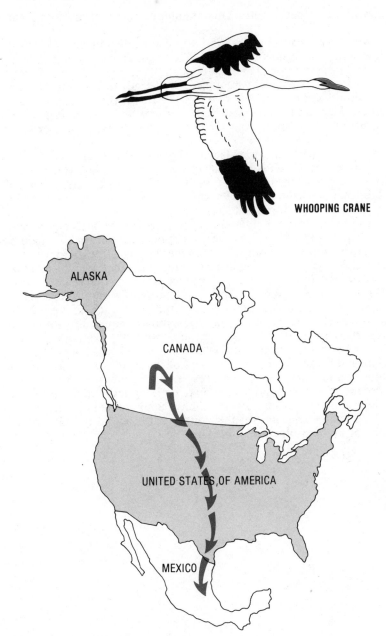

WHOOPING CRANE

MIGRATION PATTERN OF THE WHOOPING CRANE

they can contribute to pest control, maintaining the natural biological balance.

To many people, providing food and artificial nesting places to birds in winter seems sufficient protection of birdlife. Although such practical measures are important, attention also must be paid to the preservation of those bird species whose existence is threatened by the advance of civilization, with its agricultural and industrial economy. The threat is generally greatest to the varieties of larger birds, such as eagles, cranes, owls and herons. Only a few birds, such as the common pigeon and sparrow, thrive on modern city life.

Man can best protect wild animals when he understands their life habits. Extensive long-term research is necessary to acquire such knowledge. One form of bird protection is the identification of areas, with their natural animal and plant life, that are habitats of a variety of birds; then such areas could be protected as nature conservation sites.

Large regions, in which populations of rare species of birds can remain undisturbed, can be established only in exceptional cases. For the maintenance of a natural and multifarious bird community it is thus important to support ecological reserves on land in agricultural use. By the intensification and often misguided modernization of agriculture over the years, unprotected ecological habitats (such as hedges, borders of fields, free-standing large trees, strips of fallow land and small ponds and ditches) were often deliberately removed. The resulting enormous, monotonous cultivated areas cannot support many birds because they lack suitable nesting sites and refuge. Birds have been further eliminated by the toxic chemicals applied for pest control. The decline in the numbers of various birds of prey in the United States and in Europe is a direct result of pesticide use. A transition from the present chemical techniques employed in agriculture to more ecological, biological methods not only would have a favorable influence on the quality of food for people and on the countryside, but would also be an important factor in the protection of birdlife.

PRACTICAL MEASURES

The practical measures generally adopted for the protection of birdlife have consisted primarily of feeding the birds in winter and of providing nesting places. In a landscape untouched by civilization, such protective measures would not be necessary, but in our cultivated stretches of countryside, many birds have difficulty finding adequate food in the cold season. Providing food to birds, however, entails certain problems. Many animal lovers assume that what appeals to people must also be attractive to birds. But this is often not the case. It must be recognized that the winter feed people provide is only a supplement, which must be adapted to the bird's needs. The following points must be considered:

1. Some carnivorous birds, such as falcons and owls, subsist almost exclusively on living prey; others, like vultures and kites, also devour carrion. Since much prey, especially mice, appears above the ground in the winter as well as in the summer, providing winter feed for carnivorous birds is seldom necessary. During severe weather conditions, however, lumps of meat can be distributed, from which the animals can tear off strips as required. Under no circumstances should the meat be cut up into small pellets, as there is a danger that during cold spells frozen lumps of meat might be swallowed by the birds with serious or even fatal consequences.
2. The soft-food eaters, including titmice, nuthatches, thrushes, robins, wrens and woodpeckers, will eat such foods as rolled oats baked in fat, shredded nuts (including pine nuts), sliced plums and decaying fruit. Soft food can also be prepared according to the following recipe: Melt rendered, unsalted beef fat, then stir in an equal weight of wheat bran to form a thick paste. Pour this paste into flowerpots, coconut shells, tin cans or similar containers. When the food has cooled, the containers can be hung up or the mixture can be crumbled and spread on the ground. Soft foods also constitute the diet of most of the waterfowl which spend the winter on rivers and lakes. These can be fed on dry bread crusts, fresh vegetable and lettuce remains and, on frost-free days, cooked potatoes and mincemeat. Waterfowl are also partial to barley, oats, fodder-grain and corn, which can be scattered on the riverbanks.
3. The grain-eating varieties (finches, sparrows, pigeons, and to some extent titmice and nuthatches) can be fed in winter on sunflower seeds, oats, fodder-grain and lettuce. Once a feeding station has been established, it should be kept constantly supplied with food from late summer until the spring, because the birds will come to rely on finding food there. The feeding site should be protected from snow and rain and also from stray cats.

Another practical measure for the protection of birdlife is provision of nesting places. Natural nesting places are getting more and more scarce as hollow trees are felled, undergrowth and hedges are uprooted and modern buildings are erected in which it is rare to find corners and crevices in which a bird can install a nest. This shortage of sites is something that people can remedy. In a garden it is quite simple to plant thick hedges in which a number of birds can nest. Elderbushes, for instance, not only provide nesting places in abundance, but in late summer provide elderberries with high nutritive value.

For birds that nest in holes, such as the nuthatch and some species of flycatcher, one can install nesting boxes. They should be about 3 meters (10 feet) from the ground. When all the nesting boxes are occupied (in a small garden, three to five boxes is a reasonable starting number), more can be installed. It is best to erect the boxes in the autumn so that the birds can get used to them. If possible the box opening should be sheltered from the weather, perhaps facing south or east. In the autumn the nesting boxes should be emptied and cleaned out.

To provide nesting facilities for owls, sitting boxes can be installed in barns or sheds behind open hatches. For barn owls, for instance, these boxes should consist of a container about 50 centimeters (20 inches) high with a floor area of about a square meter (or square yard) and a large flight opening attached to the hatch. These boxes should be made to resemble old decaying trees by spreading peat dust on the floor. Boxes of this kind are sometimes occupied also by screech owls.

In districts in which water is scarce, another practical step for bird protection is to install a small birdbath in the garden or courtyard in summertime. The simplest method is to place a flat pan containing a couple of big flat stones under a slow-dripping tap. The lively way in which the birds disport themselves in the birdbath is always a joy to watch.

A frequent, sometimes fatal, trap for birds is a transparent glass panel, which is often not noticed by a bird in flight. Consequently a bird can fly into it and break its neck. This particular danger can be reduced by planting bushes or trees outside the pane or by hanging a Venetian blind. Alternative solutions are to cover the glass surfaces with curtains on the inside, to frost the glass or to adorn it with silhouettes to alert the birds to the danger.

On the question of assistance to young birds outside the nest, it must be realized that such birds generally have not been abandoned by their parents. Many young birds leave their nests before they are ready to fly and hop on the ground or in the branches. By specific calls they indicate to the parents where they are, so that the parents are always able to find and feed them. Such birds are therefore best left alone, unless they are on a road, in which case they can be picked up gently and placed in the nearest bush for safety. But the birds should not be moved far from the place where they are found or they will not be recovered by the parents. There are a few types of bird that will not again accept young birds that have fallen out of the nest and will not continue to feed them. All one can do in these cases is to restore the young bird to its nest, or rear it oneself (e.g., by giving it pea-sized pieces of fresh milk curd and meat). One can also consult a local nature refuge or the Audubon Society.

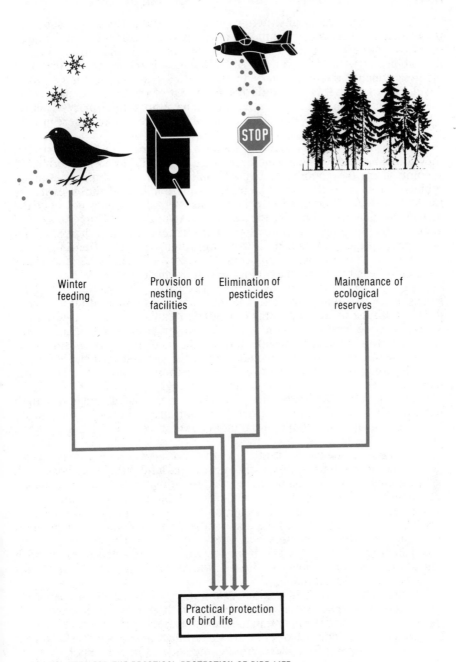

Winter feeding

Provision of nesting facilities

Elimination of pesticides

Maintenance of ecological reserves

Practical protection of bird life

POSSIBILITIES FOR THE PRACTICAL PROTECTION OF BIRD LIFE

NATURALIZATION OF NONINDIGENOUS ANIMAL SPECIES

Variations in the ecological structure of nature as radical as those caused by the extinction of particular animal species may result from the naturalization of species in new habitats. The best-known example is the introduction of the rabbit into Australia. As the Australian continent separated from the other continents relatively early in the earth's history, an animal world developed there that is very different from that of the other continents. In the Australian fauna, consequently, rabbits have no natural place. This realization came, however, only after some rabbits were let loose there in 1851 —a grave error.

Because rabbits had no natural enemies among the animals in Australia, they found agreeable living conditions there and by 1932 had proliferated to a point where they numbered over 20 million. By 1953 about one billion rabbits ranged over the area of a million square miles. At those levels the rabbits' presence amounted to a public disaster, threatening not only the ecological equilibrium but also the economy. Australia could have supported another 100 million sheep, according to one estimate, if the rabbits had not been grazing the land and, by burrowing, ruining rangeland and initiating soil erosion. Only through an epidemic caused by a virus, deliberately introduced into Australia, was the rabbit population finally reduced.

Another example is the mongoose, a beast of prey native to the East Indies and larger than a weasel. The mongoose was imported into Jamaica in 1872 with the object of hunting down the rats that had come ashore from ships and were wreaking havoc among the sugarcanes. The few specimens imported propagated rapidly and cut down the number of rats considerably. But as the number of rats, which are usually the mongoose's chief source of food, declined steadily, the mongoose turned to other animals for its sustenance: game, poultry, small birds and their eggs, lizards and snakes. The result was that these animals were practically exterminated, and in turn their natural prey, certain forms of insect pests, got increasingly out of hand. By 1890 the damage attributable to the mongoose far exceeded the good it had done.

From an ecological point of view, the naturalization of animal species that are not indigenous is thus likely to prove harmful rather than beneficial. If the animal does not disappear immediately, it may proliferate with amazing fecundity. Plans to naturalize animals suitable for hunting and fishing, therefore, must be treated with caution. The newcomer often competes directly with the natives for food and habitat, causing the native population to decline. Or the newcomers may prey directly and aggressively on the established residents. Bass and trout have thus eliminated Owens pupfish and Modoc sucker in many California waters, and the green sunfish has replaced the California roach.

Quite different is the situation regarding the scientifically prepared renaturalization of species that are threatened with extinction. In these cases the object is to restore or maintain the natural variety of the animal kingdom. Nevertheless, the number of effective reintroductions or successful regenerations of stock is still modest. Among the successful attempts have been the trumpeter swan, which was bred in a wildlife refuge in Montana after the population had fallen to just a few dozen birds. Eventually the swan was introduced into refuges in Oregon, Washington, Nevada, Wyoming and South Dakota, and by 1968 the trumpeter swan numbered more than 800 in the United States. Similarly members of the once-endangered southern

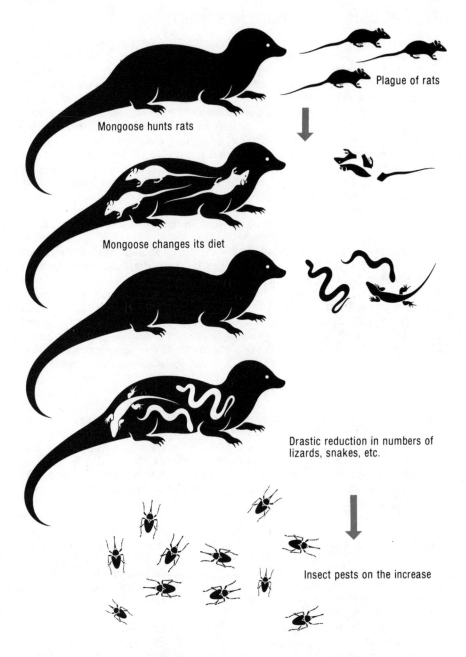

Plague of rats

Mongoose hunts rats

Mongoose changes its diet

Drastic reduction in numbers of
lizards, snakes, etc.

Insect pests on the increase

DISTURBANCE OF ECOLOGICAL EQUILIBRIUM BY NATURALIZATION OF THE MONGOOSE IN JAMAICA

square-lipped rhinoceros, protected for years on a Natal game preserve, have now been moved to restock regions where they once lived in abundance.

EXTERMINATION OF ANIMALS AND PLANTS

Owing to increasing exploitation and destruction of nature in recent times, there has been a reduction not only in the total number of wild animals and plants in the world, but also in the number of species. The latter represents a loss in the genetic resources of the earth. In the past 300 years more than 200 mammal and bird species have become extinct. Some 290 land mammal and bird species are currently approaching extinction, and a further 1000 are already rare. Water-dwelling animals face a similar fate. The French deep-sea explorer Jacques Cousteau has established in the course of his explorations that some 1000 varieties of animal (about 40% of those known in the sea) have disappeared from the seas in the past 50 years, in large part because of water pollution. The number of plant species also has fallen. Recultivation of moorland, removal of low-lying deciduous forest and marshland, and increasing replacement of natural areas by roads, airports, industrial installations and housing developments have deprived a wide range of plants of their last sanctuaries.

The disappearance of many forms of life, especially the smaller, inconspicuous varieties, goes unacknowledged because their existence had never been recorded. In 1939 about 1 million varieties of plant and animal were known to exist in the world. The current count is 1.6 million species and an estimate of the total number 5 to 10 million. To most people, the extinction of large animals clearly represents an impoverishment of nature and of life on earth. But without microorganisms the continuation of life in the long run is endangered. Those inconspicuous organisms are of far greater importance to the general balance of nature than, for instance, are the bison or the aurochs.

The unsuspected effects that interventions by man may create in nature are illustrated by the following example: In Borneo an assault with DDT was made on mosquitoes. To all appearances the onslaught was an immediate success; from then on hardly a mosquito was seen. Another species, however, the widely disseminated common cockroach, was not affected by the insecticide. Lizards, which eat the common cockroach, absorbed considerable quantities of the pesticide from the insects they preyed on. This built up in their bodies and left them victims of a serious nervous disorder. In consequence the lizards were now easily caught and eaten by cats. Owing to the buildup of poison in their prey, the cats died in turn after consuming several lizards. As a result of this, rats, now lacking predators, were free to multiply without hindrance. A second effect of the DDT was the extermination of a small insect that lived on caterpillars in the thatched roofs of natives' huts and had restricted their propagation. After DDT was in use, the roofs of the dwellings fell in under the incursions of caterpillars. An isolated application of pesticide thus had unfortunate effects in quite different and unpredictable areas.

Similarly in the United States DDT use had unexpected, detrimental consequences. When elms were sprayed with the chemical in 1947 to kill bark beetles and thus to slow the spread of Dutch elm disease, in some places birds, especially robins, began to die. The robin population at Michigan State University dropped from 370 to 4 over a four-year period, and the dead birds were found to contain high levels of DDT. The explanation was that sprayed DDT dripped from the trees to the soil, where it was ingested and concentrated by earthworms. The earthworms, in turn, were eaten by robins, who then died of DDT poisoning. The next step up the food chain

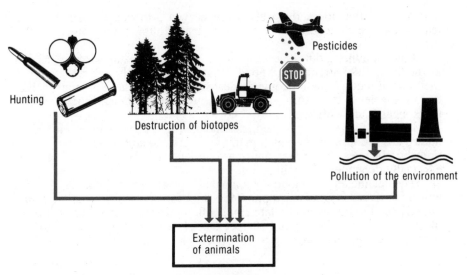

Hunting

Destruction of biotopes

Pesticides

STOP

Pollution of the environment

Extermination
of animals

VARIOUS CAUSES OF EXTERMINATION OF ANIMAL SPECIES

also suffered from DDT. Birds of prey, such as the peregrine falcon, bald eagle and osprey, underwent disastrous population losses, because they ate other birds and small animals that already had accumulated substantial amounts of DDT. In birds of prey, DDT interferes with calcium metabolism, so the birds produced eggs with only thin, weak shells—eggs that were easily broken or failed to hatch. In one Florida area the number of young bald eagles hatched fell from 150 in 1940 to 1 in 1958.

Another example of decimation of animal life is the killing of migrating songbirds in certain European countries. As a result of trapping and insecticide dissemination, in the past 70 years the number of insect-eating songbirds has fallen by 90%.

The biggest mammals on earth, the whales, have been almost exterminated by commercial interests, and the walruses, sea elephants, seals and sea lions all have suffered severe slaughter. There are today about 30,000 walruses in the Pacific. Every year some 7000 of them are shot for their ivory tusks, which are carved into ornaments. Because the natural rate of walrus reproduction does not exceed 5000 a year, the stock of walruses declines approximately 2000 per annum.

The same sort of extermination threatens other big mammals. Of five species of rhinoceros, only about 20,000 animals remain worldwide. The small Sumatran rhinoceros is in the worst position, because it has no protection and only about 100 remain. There are about 60 of the one-horned Javan rhinoceros left; most are on a reserve in Java. The northern square-lipped rhino is suffering from intense poaching and it now numbers between 500 and 1000, while its southern relative, which was seriously endangered 25 years ago, but has since been protected, now has a thriving population of 3000. The black rhino of Africa is currently the most common, but it is also being reduced by poachers. In the past 5 years, 90% of the black rhinos have been killed. The Indian rhinoceros, although severely threatened 20 years ago, now has a stable population of more than 1000. Rhinos are attractive to hunters because the horn substance commands a high price as an aid to potency and the horns themselves are carved into dagger handles. It is feared that the rhinoceros may be exterminated altogether in the course of the 1980s.

It is not hunting but the poisons used in agriculture and forestry, as well as the filling in of streams and ponds, that most seriously affect the animals that most directly benefit people by destroying pests. These animals include certain species that are rarely considered by conservationists, such as toads, frogs, lizards and ladybugs.

Not least affected by chemical and major technical interventions in nature are the insects on which many varieties of plant depend for pollination: bumblebees, butterflies and many others. Yields from fruit trees are especially dependent on pollination.

The decline and extinction of animal and plant species proceeds steadily and unobserved by most people. Measures for species protection consequently tend to be taken at a late stage, often too late. Estimates of the rate of extinction vary from 1 to 300 species per year, and projections for the next quarter century range up to 100 species lost a day.

PROTECTED PLANTS

Protection of plants historically has not had the same appeal to people as protection of wild animals. In U.S. legislation, the concept of wildlife seldom included plants, except occasionally those plants required to support wild animal life. Yet man's impact on the environment threatens the continued existence of many species of plant. A list of threatened plants prepared by the Smithsonian Institution includes almost 10% of the species in the United States. On the Hawaiian Islands, where many plants inhabit very limited areas having unusual conditions, more than 250 plants are already extinct and another 1270 are threatened.

Growing recognition of the value in protecting plant species from extinction—for esthetic and cultural, as well as practical reasons—brought a change in policy. An international meeting on endangered species considered plants on more nearly equal terms as animals. Consequently the Convention on Trade in Endangered Species of Wild Fauna and Flora, signed in 1973, restricted imports and exports of a wide variety of endangered forms of life. Plants, as well as mammals, birds, reptiles, amphibians, fishes, snails, clams and insects, are assigned to categories according to their vulnerability to extinction. Almost 50 plant species are listed in the category of the most likely to become extinct, and those species are thus made subject to the most stringent protection. The convention requires that for the most vulnerable species, export and import permits are to be granted only when specimens meet strict requirements. The specimens must be lawfully obtained, handled to minimize damage and not used primarily for commercial purposes. In addition, the transfer must not be detrimental to the species' survival.

Although two early versions of the U.S. Endangered Species Act had neglected plants, when the law was extended in 1973 just after the international agreement, plants were included. As of 1979, there were 58 plants protected by the act. Most of these grow only in limited areas. For instance, for one plant listed, a species of Hawaiian tree cotton, only a single tree remains growing in an arboretum. The list also includes a carnivorous green pitcher plant that grows in Alabama and a large number of cacti from the Southwest.

Through the Endangered Species Act, members of the plant kingdom were offered the protection of restrictions dealing with sales and shipment between states, as well as restrictions on international trade. The Secretary of the Interior was authorized to make further regulations necessary for conserving threatened plants and animals. Even in the Endangered Species Act, however, plants are not on completely equal footing with animals. The federal law does not prohibit destruction or "taking" of plants of endangered species, although it does forbid the taking of endangered wild animals. Some states have laws forbidding destruction of endangered plants, but their constitutionality is uncertain. Laws that tell a property owner he cannot destroy plants growing on his land may be in conflict with private property rights.

The most potent weapon of the Endangered Species Act, however, applies to plants as well as to animals. That is the section that charges the federal government with ensuring that federal activities do not jeopardize endangered or threatened species or destroy the habitats critical to those species' survival. The Furbish lousewort is an example of a plant that stalled construction of a major project. The species had been believed to be extinct, until it was spotted growing in the path of a proposed $700 million power project. The two massive dams originally planned would have eliminated about half the lousewort population. The Fish and Wildlife Service and the Army Corps of Engineers began negotiations to try to resolve the issue, while botanists attempted to transplant seedlings to establish a population of louseworts elsewhere.

Part Nine—Agriculture, Crop Cultivation and Animal Rearing

AGRICULTURE AND THE CONFIGURATION OF THE COUNTRYSIDE

The picture presented by the agricultural landscape is largely determined by the way in which the land is used (arable or pasture land), the configuration of the countryside (large or small plots), and the settlement structure. Whereas man was previously obliged to adapt his activities to a large extent to the natural conformation of the countryside, the advance of technology has made it increasingly possible to adapt the landscape to particular uses.

One of the most important elements in shaping the landscape is mechanization. The trend is clearly in the direction of ever more powerful machines. The machines can be employed on a rational and viable basis, however, only if the fields to be tilled are not too limited in size. Consequently, in arable areas which have been severely fragmented into small plots, the divisions must be removed and the fields aggregated again into workable areas. This means that in country regions fragmented by valleys and hillocks, the danger of erosion of cultivated fields situated on hillsides will increase. In addition, high-performance machines impose heavy axle loads, which in heavy soils causes compaction and intensifies the erosive effects. The damage caused by erosion itself, with its effects on water conservation, plant life and exploitation of the land, also changes the configuration of the landscape.

A further measure prompted by the desire to adapt the countryside would be the consolidation of farmland, possibly accompanied by evacuation of the inhabitants and the clearance of farm buildings. The consolidation of farmland entails a water plan whereby the ground is drained of stagnant water and open canals and streams are purified. In many cases, provided due caution is exercised, these measures can be highly successful. Sometimes, however, timber may be removed from the banks of streams and not replanted. This may be aggravated by a drop in the groundwater level and more rapid runoff of precipitation water. In periods of heavy precipitation this can lead to excessive concentrations of water, and in the dry season to severe desiccation of the soil in meadows and fields. The countryside is also deprived in these conditions of a variety of the stream vegetation. The landscape turns barren and loses its attraction.

Besides the water plan, a road plan may be introduced to provide access to the boundary zones. Old routes which had been developed fortuitously or to comply with legal requirements are eliminated and are often replaced by a regular road system based on the fact that rectilinear boundaries are advantageous from a practical point of view. Often, too, the trees and hedgerows flanking the routes are removed, so that the countryside is even further standardized.

Apart from the visual results of adaptation of land, the elimination of whole farms from closed village communities gives rise to social problems, since the association of people with one another, the exchange of experience and the cultural values of village communities are all impaired by dispersal of the inhabitants.

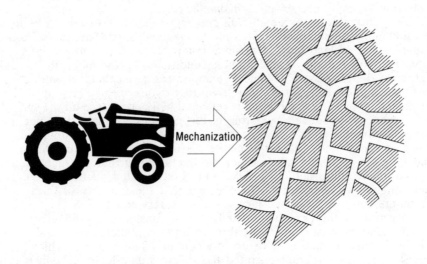

Diagram 1. BEFORE THE CONSOLIDATION OF FARMLAND GOT UNDER
WAY, MECHANIZATION COULD NOT BE ADOPTED TO ITS FULL EXTENT

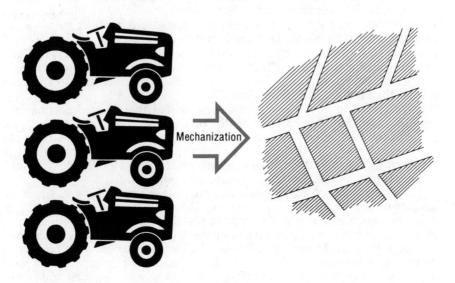

Diagram 2. WITH THE CONSOLIDATION OF FARMLAND, MECHANIZATION
CAME INTO ITS OWN

THE LEISURE ASPECT

Apart from the purely productive aspect of landscape adaptation, the question has come to the fore in recent years of the leisure value of the countryside from the point of view of town dwellers.

In many regions, especially hill country, as a result of relatively unfavorable climate and consequently shorter vegetation periods, the yield per square meter of land may be minimal compared with that in low-lying regions enjoying more favorable climatic conditions. Furthermore, the sloping nature of the land is an obstacle to manpower and mechanical production, and special machines (four-wheel drive tractors) have to be employed. The increased labor and capital input is reflected in a poor return on the agricultural products produced, and this is further aggravated by the fact that thanks to modern transport and refrigeration facilities, agricultural products from southern lands reach the market earlier and in better condition, so reducing the return on sales of local products still further. In such circumstances agricultural activities aimed purely at food production may prove unprofitable, as is borne out by the fact that the majority of farmers in certain regions now run their farms as a secondary occupation.

Eventually the persons affected give the business up altogether. The abandoned land passes gradually through an intermediate phase of desiccation and brush formation to revert to woodland. This process, which takes several decades to complete, often has deleterious effects on neighboring farmland, as weeds and vermin from the fallow land penetrate the cultivated areas. From the recreational point of view as well, untended, derelict regions of this nature are of little value.

Reforestation of this fallow land may not be good for the countryside in all respects. For commercial reasons it is often planted to pine monocultures, which not only seriously damage the soil, but by their monotonous appearance also impair the landscape. But as the reforestation of fallow land is still necessary to some extent in order to regulate water conservation and to safeguard the dust filter effects of woodland, more favored mixed forests should be planted, especially as the dust filter effects of deciduous trees are greater than those of coniferous trees.

One point to be observed, however, is that the wooded portion of a region should not exceed 60% of the area, as otherwise the recreational value of the landscape will decline; experience shows that the recreational value is enhanced by the presence of open areas. One example of this is provided by valley pastures which, when converted to woodland, lose much of their original attraction from a landscape point of view.

The provision of public funds can prove invaluable. They can provide an incentive for the farmer to preserve the landscape by the breeding of animals, which today is not very remunerative, and by the cultivation of meadow and pasture land to keep open particular portions of the landscape.

In any event, in any agricultural cost-benefit analysis with respect to so-called problem areas (such as hill districts), the recreational factor must certainly be considered. The provision of ecologically balanced and cared-for recreational areas also makes a valuable contribution to the maintenance of the quality of the air, the water and the soil.

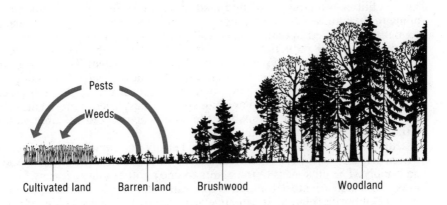

Pests

Weeds

Cultivated land   Barren land   Brushwood   Woodland

Diagram 1. DAMAGE TO CULTIVATED FARMLAND FROM NEGLECTED LAND

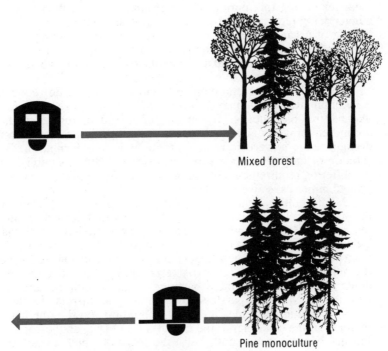

Mixed forest

Pine monoculture

**Diagram 2. REFORESTATION OF BARREN LAND: LIMITED RECREATIONAL
VALUE OF MONOCULTURES**

MONOCULTURES AND MIXED CULTURES

The conditions affecting cultivated land are quite different from those prevailing in the natural life communities (see Biocenosis in Part Three), which originally developed spontaneously and gave rise to humus formation by decomposition and reduction processes. Cultivated crops are produced in large quantities of selected plants for use by man as foodstuffs and for other practical purposes. To this end the practice has developed of sowing large areas to a single species of plant, such as wheat, strawberries, tomatoes, and cabbages, and in woodland areas to spruce trees, firs or pines. This style of cultivation (*monoculture*) enables the soil to be worked by labor-saving methods with big machine cultivators.

But just as a big field can be cultivated easily and rapidly by this means, so can diseases and pests be disseminated in monocultures equally easily and rapidly. The closeness of the plants to one another makes it easy for the parasites, which are mostly attached to a particular species of plant, to move on to neighboring plants. If effective pest control is to be achieved, vast quantities of plant protection compounds are consequently required (see later discussion).

In monocultures the ground is left unprotected for some time after the period of plant growth has ended, so that numerous wild plants spring up as weeds, and herbicides have to be applied to exterminate them. There is also a danger during this period of the ground being washed away by rain, of humus being blown away by wind, and of drought setting in and imperiling the life of organisms in the soil. A further factor affecting monocultures is that the heavy uniform demands on the soil will, over the course of time, exhaust its natural mineral ingredients so that intensive fertilization with mineral substances has to be undertaken.

These difficulties common to monocultures can be reduced or practically eliminated when *mixed cultures* are adopted, as these are much more like natural biocenoses. By means of mixed cultures an all-year-round ground coverage is achieved, whereby the soil is protected from flooding, drought and wind erosion. This promotes humus formation. By a prudent rotation of crops, weeds are prevented from getting established. Owing to the differing requirements of the individual kinds of crops, exhaustion of the ground minerals is also avoided.

Mixed cultures can be grouped in such a way that crops that exhaust the soil severely are planted alongside plants that draw less nutriment from the soil, and plants with deep roots alongside plants with shallow roots. Leguminous roots, for instance, promote the root growth of neighboring plants by their deep-penetrating root systems, which make for ventilation of the soil; thanks to their root bacteria, they do not depend on the nitrate content of the soil. Suitable partners in mixed cultures are cabbages and beans, tomatoes and parsley, and onions and carrots. In the case of the latter, aromatic pesticides are used to hold off, on the one hand, the onion fly and, on the other hand, the carrot fly. Other examples of plants suitable for mixed cultures are sunflowers, the seeds of which attract titmice, which in turn prey on both caterpillars and insects, and hemp, which by its aroma turns the cabbage butterfly away.

Owing to the many different ecological niches in a mixed culture compared with a monoculture, living opportunities for organisms beneficial to man in destroying pests are much improved, resulting in a further reduction

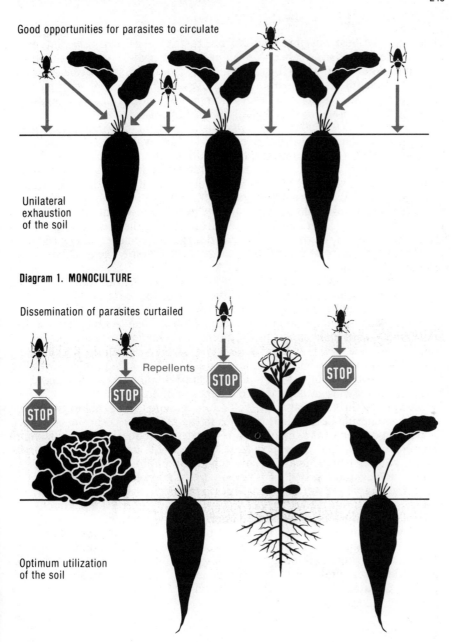

Good opportunities for parasites to circulate

Unilateral
exhaustion
of the soil

Diagram 1. MONOCULTURE

Dissemination of parasites curtailed

Repellents

STOP
STOP
STOP
STOP
STOP

Optimum utilization
of the soil

Diagram 2. MIXED CULTURE

in parasites. By using suitable combinations of plants, many positive effects can thus be achieved, although these have been closely examined to only a limited extent.

HORTICULTURE: MOUND CULTIVATION

To obtain the best possible results from restricted garden plots, intensive cultivation methods have been developed in the past 15 years (notably by Hermann Andrä and Hans Beba), which in contrast to the usual methods depend on the intensive use of organic material. This material is arranged in layers on mounds (hence the description *mound cultivation*). The mounds, which are about 180 cm (6 ft) wide, 80 cm (2.6 ft) high, and of a length to suit the particular situation, have the effect of expanding the surface area, which is important in view of the restricted space available. It is found from experience that a garden under mound cultivation measuring 100 to 200 sq m (120 to 240 sq yd) will satisfy the vegetable requirements of a family for which some 600 sq m (720 sq yd) would be required under normal circumstances. Extra labor is required for mound cultivation only at the outset, while the bed is still under construction. During the six years that the material in the mound takes to molder, apart from sowing the seeds and gathering the crops, no other major tasks are called for. Furthermore, raising the beds to a height of 50 to 80 cm (20 to 31.5 in.) considerably eases the work of attending to them.

For building up the mounds, all forms of organic waste from the kitchen and the garden can be used, either directly or in the form of compost. The base of the mound can consist of rough boughs and branches lopped from trees and shrubs, and of other ligneous residues of plants such as sunflower stalks and potato and tomato roots. For the next layer, the sods of turf cut from the surface of the existing bed can be used. Next comes a layer some 25 cm (10 in.) thick of wet autumn foliage, and then a layer of well-soaked rough compost. The mound is finally covered on all sides with sifted compost soil mixed with garden mold to a depth of about 20 cm (8 in.).

All plants thrive remarkably well on the mounds. This relates to the fact that the moldering of the plant residues in the mound has a hothouse effect. By decomposition of the organic matter, water, carbon dioxide and heat are generated. The carbon dioxide makes its way up the mound and is absorbed by the plants, which need the substance for photosynthesis and for the buildup of vegetable growth. The same effect is produced in hothouses by burning charcoal. Water and heat contribute substantially to the growth of plants, which thrive on the mounds as in a greenhouse. Tomato stocks, for example, which under normal cultivation have a maximum yield of 9 kg (20 lb) per stock, attain over 15 kg (33 lb) per plant under mound cultivation. The quality of the product is also improved by mound cultivation. Compared with hothouse products, the flavor and lasting qualities are both outstanding. This and their natural resistance to pests and diseases are also a result of the fact that the mound beds (except for particular crops such as asparagus) are planted in mixed cultures.

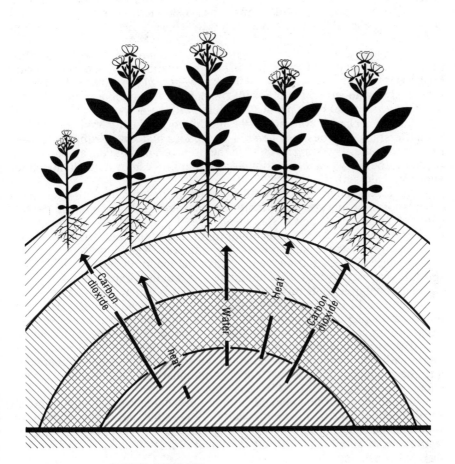

FORMATION OF AN ENRICHED MOUND BED

STOCK FARMING AND THE ENVIRONMENT—BATTERY METHODS

With the object of improving working conditions and increasing the return on the labor employed, stock farming has been modernized by a series of far-reaching changes which have important consequences for the environment.

In pig and poultry raising in particular, efforts have been made to reduce running costs per animal by increasing the population density of pigsties and henhouses. Against a ratio of 3 to 4 layer hens per square meter in henhouses previously equipped with a hen run, the density in big modern installations has risen to 10 to 20 birds per square meter with no hen run.

A further change consists in the introduction of labor-saving methods. In cattle stalls, pigsties and henhouses, fodder and water supplies can be fully automated. By doing away with the litter bed and having an opening in the floor, the daily task of clearing away droppings can be much lightened or eliminated altogether.

Since on modern stock farms the number of animals no longer bears any standard proportion to agricultural acreage, the dung and swill usually cannot be disposed of on the spot as manure. The farms are often situated in close proximity to big urban agglomerations and supply industries (feedstuff factories, for instance) and processing industries (slaughterhouses or sausage factories), so that arable land to take the manure is not available. The result is that waste water is contaminated with animal excrement.

The contamination ratio of waste water by cattle is estimated at the equivalent of 10 inhabitants per animal, i.e., each head of cattle causes as much contamination of waste water as 10 inhabitants of a big city; a pig causes as much contamination as 2 inhabitants, and a hen the equivalent of 0.1. If the total waste from a big layer-hen farm with a million birds—and farms with 2 to 4 million head of poultry are not uncommon—is channeled into the sewage system, for instance, contamination of the waste water will equal that of a city with 100,000 inhabitants.

Transport of surplus manure to thinly populated regions with sufficient agricultural acreage to absorb it is certainly possible, but is very expensive. Dehydration of the ordure in big drying kilns and its processing as organic fertilizer also entail very high costs, which ultimately have to be borne by the final consumer.

Apart from the sewage water problem, the problem of offensive odors, especially when there is a high animal population in the vicinity of dwelling houses, cannot be disregarded. The degree of air pollution by toxic gases such as ammonia and hydrogen sulfide as a result of stock farming is certainly very low, and is not to be compared with that produced on housing estates and in industrial zones. But organic gaseous compounds such as ethyl hydrosulfide emitted from the stalls do put a severe strain on the community. Owing to the high animal density, the discharge of air from the stalls is constantly rising, and it is not without its dangers to the animals too, so it is desirable that the spent air should be drawn off from the stalls through air vents and released into the atmosphere at some distance from the stalls after dilution with fresh air. The attempts occasionally made to reduce the smell nuisance by the admixture of deodorants with the spent air from the stalls can only be regarded as an emergency solution, as this process is very expensive.

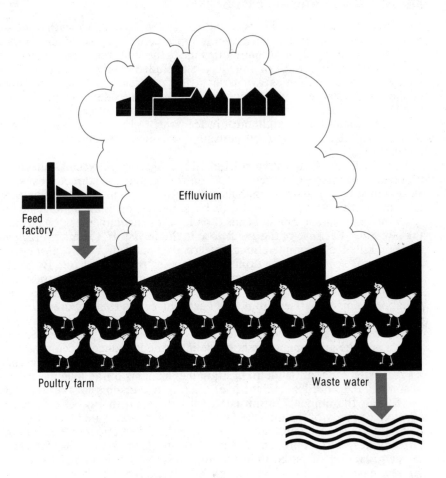

Feed
factory

Effluvium

Poultry farm

Waste water

ENVIRONMENTAL DAMAGE CAUSED BY LARGE-SCALE STOCK FARMING

ANTIBIOTICS IN ANIMAL FEEDSTUFF

The employment of antibiotics in the feeding of farm stock with a view to increasing production has been adopted in recent years especially in intensive stock farming. Not all antibiotics meet the requirements for feed purposes, and certain groups of animals are excluded from antibiotic feedstuff. Of the various antibiotics available in the market, only those should be applied to animal feeds which are hardly absorbed in the intestinal walls, if at all, so that they will get into the tissues only to a marginal extent.

Small quantities of antibiotics in feedstuff reduce the liability to infection in animals, increase food consumption, improve food utilization and accelerate growth.

According to exhaustive scientific investigations, it seems that the antibiotics consumed exert their effects on the animal by indirect means, that is, by influencing the intestinal bacteria. From experience with antibiotics in medicine, effects were therefore to be expected on both pathogenic (disease-causing) and nonpathogenic (nondisease-causing) microorganisms in the intestine. Because of the small dose in the feedstuff, the microorganisms are not killed off completely or selectively, but suffer only a change of metabolism, so that fewer noxious metabolic products arise. By way of example, the reduction of ammonia production in the intestinal tract under the influence of antibiotics in feedstuff can be cited: ammonia, a strong metabolic poison, arises from the bacterial separation of urea from the amino acid arginine in the intestines. By the addition of antibiotics the enzyme urease, which effects the separation of the urea, is restricted in its effects and the ammonia content of the intestine is reduced accordingly.

By introducing antibiotics in the feed, the production of toxic germs is also arrested, so that the detoxification mechanisms of the liver are relieved of some of their burden, and the liver is left free to discharge other functions.

Under the influence of ingested antibiotics, furthermore, a higher absorptive capacity of the intestinal tissue for the disintegrated feed could also be established, which probably depends on the direct effect of the antibiotics on enzymes. The improved utilization of the feed is thus due less to the direct reduction of pathogenic microorganisms in the animal than to the indirect easing of the load on the animal's defensive system.

Another aspect of the introduction of antibiotics into animal feedstuff emerges from the fact that after long use of antibiotics the bacteria become resistant (insensitive) to them. Resistant bacteria represent a danger to both man and animals. But the possibility that resistant bacteria will be transferred from animals to man and will unleash diseases that are hard to control is difficult to establish. In normal circumstances the independent bacteria are repelled by the intestinal bacteria present in the body, and a sort of self-purification takes place in the organism. However, the problem of contracting a disease from antibiotic-resistant germs should not be disregarded.

In the feeding of antibiotics, certain principles should therefore be observed: restriction of the use of antibiotics based on nonmedical indications; no antibiotics during final fattening; avoidance of antibiotics where serum is introduced into human or animal medicines; and avoidance of antibiotics that lead to the selection of resistant forms of intestinal bacteria.

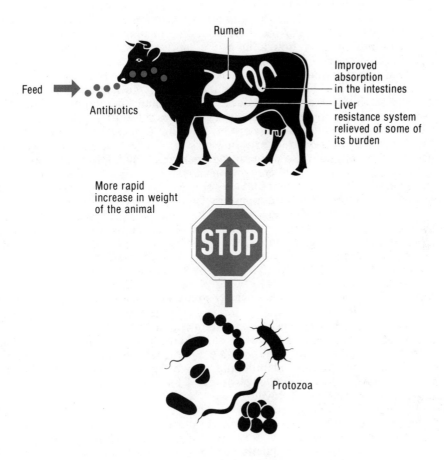

Feed

Antibiotics

Rumen

Improved
absorption
in the intestines

Liver
resistance system
relieved of some of
its burden

More rapid
increase in weight
of the animal

STOP

Protozoa

EFFECTS OF INCLUDING ANTIBIOTICS IN THE DIET

ECOLOGICAL EFFECTS OF PASTURE FARMING—THE HAY CROP

Before the Revolutionary War, when farm animals ranged in the field much of the year, little farmland was used for growing hay. The hay needed for fodder while the animals were kept in stalls in the winter was a by-product of existing meadows.

The increased demand of an expanding population for more and better meat and milk eventually led to modern, intensive production methods for livestock, with more year-round stall-feeding of animals. These methods required more intensive utilization of the soil, including two or more mowings of meadows each year purely for feeding housed cattle.

All the aboveground parts of meadow plants are affected by the mowing of the hay crop. In high-growth stands, most of the leaves of plants are abruptly removed at some height above the ground. Such an operation can be withstood only by plants that grow very rapidly after cutting or that before cutting accumulate sufficient reserves in their roots to ensure recovery. Climbing vegetables (everlasting peas and sweet peas, for example) meet both requirements. A wide range of perennials and upright grasses also survive this operation and present the flowery aspect of a hay meadow, especially if it is only cut twice a year. However, varieties of plants that are introduced into the meadow community from outside cannot survive.

The frequency of mowing and the time, quantity and manner of fertilization influence the composition and yield of a meadow. Once-a-year, and generally late, mowing can select plant species that flower and seed late and only build up their nutrient reserves slowly. As such meadows are, generally speaking, also poor in nutrients, slow-growing simple species of plants here may steal a march on faster-growing plants that require more nutrients. Purple moor-grass, for instance, thrives only in meadows cut once a year.

If cutting is repeated three or four times a year, the composition of the plant community will change because frequent cutting confers a competitive advantage on plants whose leaves lie close to the ground. This situation is in contrast to meadows cut once or twice a year, where such plants are suppressed by high-growing plants, like upright grasses and weeds, which overshadow them. Examples of plants lying close to the ground are dandelions, plantains and white clover.

By use of such farm-produced manures as stall manure and compost as fertilizers, the more demanding species of plants are promoted, especially in frequently mowed meadows. Full mineral fertilization favors the upright grasses, while excessive application of nitrogenous fertilizers (e.g., liquid manure) favors herbaceous plants, especially weeds such as bear's-foot and cow parsley. These plants develop sufficient leaves in a short time so they can even blossom and bear fruit between mowings.

According to the conditions present in the soil and the climate, the farmer can influence the composition, the nutrient value and the yield of hay by correctly selecting the cutting time, frequency of cutting, type and quantity of fertilizer and time of fertilization.

THE MEADOW

Over the years the form of pasture utilization has changed from the extensive woodland pasture to the standing meadow and finally, since the introduction of the electric fence, to its most intensive form, strip grazing with its very high animal trimming.

The effects of grazing are very different from those of hay cultivation. The various animals graze the plant growths in very different ways according to whether they find the individual plants more or less palatable. Thus not all plants are consumed to the same extent. Furthermore, the parts of plants that the animal cannot reach remain, of course, untouched. Since in meadowland the plants whose leaves lie close to the ground generally predominate, assimilation is never so sharply reduced as in hayfields.

In addition, the plants on meadowland are exposed to trampling underfoot by the animals, especially after heavy rain and on heavy ground. The trampling by animals in meadowland is much more serious than the damage done by tractor harvesters, as the hooves and claws of grazing animals are considerably sharper than the tires of tractors.

As compared with the mowing of meadowland, the provision of nutriment in pastureland is much better. Whereas in the case of hayfields the entire plant substance is removed with all its nutriment, which calls for particularly well-balanced manuring, grazing land receives back the plant feedstuffs in the form of animal excrement; and a little extra work is all that is needed to ensure that the excrement is evenly distributed.

The effects of grazing are determined essentially by the animal density. A mistake in the density will lead to undergrazing or overgrazing. In the case of undergrazing, the topsoil will provide more feed than the animals need. The animals will take only the most palatable feedstuff and will leave the less palatable practically untouched, with the result that the pasture gets overgrown with weeds.

If overgrazing occurs, the supply of feedstuff will be less than is needed. The animals then consume the whole of the more palatable feedstuff, and will also devour the less palatable elements or trample them into the ground.

These undesirable grazing effects (according to the taste and concentration of the plants and how they stand up to trampling), which lead to the development of meadowland of less value, can be countered by modifications of the grazing process: by measures in advance of or following the event, by providing a breathing space for the plants, by sprinkling in periods of drought and by changing the animal density in the grazing areas.

Various pasture forms have been developed: Common grazing rights, such as are to be found in highland and mountain regions, especially in the case of sheep rearing, mostly relate to common land administered under communal arrangements for daily grazing of large regions. As feedstuffs are available in sufficient quantities, the animals select palatable plants and avoid the less palatable. This procedure can easily result in undergrazing with all its undesirable consequences.

In rotation grazing the animals are grazed in turn in several fenced-in enclosures, whereby the shortage of common land is largely overcome.

In the case of strip (forage) grazing, many animals are put to graze in small areas for short periods (a half to two days). In this way, by a frequent change of area, the animals are provided with feedstuff of approximately equivalent quality all the time. Thus undergrazing is avoided by a high animal density, and overgrazing by a frequent change of grazing land.

The most intensive pasture form at present is the method of using pasture alternately for strip grazing and mowing, which combines the advantages of strip grazing (summer feed) and of the constantly mown meadow (winter feed), and results in a varied plant community and high soil fertility.

PLANT NUTRIENTS AND FERTILIZERS—NITROGEN

Nitrogen is one of the elements that are essential to the growth and normal development of plants and whose function in the plants cannot be performed by any other element. It is an essential element in the formation of protein material in the plants.

Among plant nutrients, nitrogen in the soil occupies a special position, as it can be absorbed only in the form of nitrates or ammonia compounds, and furthermore the initial nitrogen content of rocks is very low. The concentration of nitrogen in the soil derives from plants and animals. In the upper soil, nitrogen is mainly combined as organic nitrogen with animate and inanimate matter. It gets there from the almost inexhaustible nitrogen reserves in the atmosphere with the help of microorganisms, which absorb atmospheric nitrogen in the organic composition of their own body.

On a farm, nitrogen is as a rule introduced into the soil as mineral fertilizer in the form of nitrate or ammonia. Either form can be converted into the other in the soil by the metabolic activities of microorganisms. When there is a high oxygen content in the ground air, the nitrogen is mainly deposited as nitrate, and when the oxygen content is low it assumes the form of an ammonia compound.

The nitrogen is absorbed by plants from the soil by elutriation, by the erosion of surface material or by the release of gaseous ammonia. Both the nitrate form and the ammonia form can be taken up by the plants. The quantity of nitrogen received from the soil depends to a large extent on the nature of the cultivated plants. Thus potatoes, turnips, cabbage plants, beans and peas, to name a few examples, draw much nitrogen from the soil, while corn crops need very much less. If insufficient nitrogen is present in the soil, the plants will suffer from the shortage which will be reflected in stunted growth and in faded, pale yellow coloring of the leaves.

Overfertilization with nitrogen can also have unfortunate consequences for both plants and consumers. If too much nitrogen fertilizer is applied, leaf vegetables like spinach can accumulate nitrate, which in the cooking process is converted into nitrite, and this, if present in large quantities, has toxic effects on humans.

An important factor as regards the environment is the elutriation of nitrogen from the soil, particularly nitrate. As nitrate is highly soluble in water, it soon gets washed by rainwater into layers of soil well below the surface. This is particularly prone to happen in light soils, which precipitation water infiltrates rapidly. But loamy soil can also be affected in the same way. The effects of summertime precipitation are not so severe as in winter, as in summer the evaporation is heavy, and at times of high evaporation the penetrating seepage water rises by capillary action and carries the nitrate anions with it. In winter, on the other hand, especially when the snow begins to melt, the water movement in the ground is mostly vertically downward, so that the nitrate washed out of the upper soil gets carried away. In lakes and rivers in the neighborhood of intense agricultural activity (vegetable cultivation), heavy concentrations of nitrate and consequently of nutrients can thus be expected.

A similar result is also to be expected from the nitrogen of eroded ground matter passing into the outflow system. This nitrogen, too, is eutrophic in its effects; that is to say, it increases the nutrient material in the water, has a stimulating effect on the growth of algae, and disturbs the suspended biological equilibrium of flow.

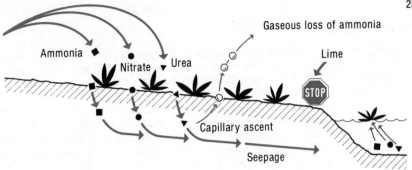

Diagram 1. NITROGEN IS FED INTO THE SOIL AS A MINERAL FERTILIZER

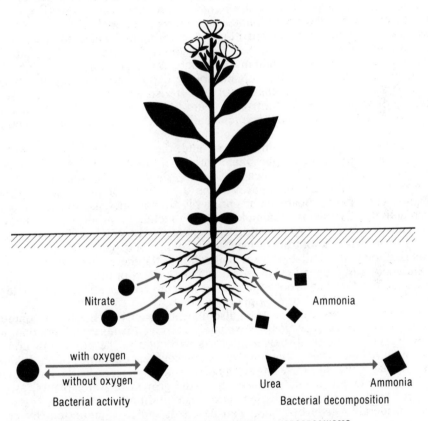

Diagram 2. TRANSFORMATION OF NITROGEN COMPOUNDS BY MICROORGANISMS IN THE SOIL

The losses of nitrogen occasioned by the gaseous release of ammonium nitride from the soil are of relatively minor importance in their effects on the environment.

PHOSPHORUS

Like nitrogen, phosphorus too belongs to the range of nutrients (macronutrients) that are essential to the normal development of plants and for which no substitute exists. But unlike nitrogen, whose content in the bedrock of the earth plays no role in the nitrogen nutrition of plants, the plants must meet their phosphorus requirements from the mineral phosphorus elements in the ground, which are made available to plants by the chemical weathering processes of rock (in particular apatite). In addition to the mineral form, phosphorus is also found in organic combination in plant remains, humus substances and ground organisms.

Phosphorus is a component of nucleic acid, of many enzymes, of phosphatides and of plasma membranes. Often, too, a phosphorus atom is combined, energized, with another atom (e.g., ATP) and so serves to transfer and store chemical energy in vegetable and animal organisms.

In agriculture phosphorus is used as a mineral fertilizer, especially in the form of Thomas meal (basic slag), a by-product of iron smelting, or in the form of superphosphate (phosphate incorporated with sulfuric acid), or as raw phosphate (ground apatite). The phosphate applied to the soil is rapidly transformed there: in soil with a low pH value, the phosphate is established as an iron-aluminum-phosphate aggregate, and in soil rich in lime as calcium phosphate. This phosphate deposit necessitates supplying phosphate fertilizers at regular intervals. It also explains why, after over-fertilization, no decline in growth occurs (as is the case with nitrogen or potassium), but rather that each application of phosphate exercises a positive effect.

Following intensive cultivation of land, the constant phosphorus fertilization leads to a gradual phosphate enrichment of the upper soil. This can be produced by what is known as *humate effect:* the accretion of organic substances in the ground improves the availability of phosphate for the plants. This effect probably stems primarily from an increase in microorganism activity. By means of complex-forming metabolic products, the microorganisms are able to combine large quantities of calcium ions, so that phosphate ions are not transformed into insoluble phosphates. The phosphorus thus remains available in the soil solution for the plants. Owing to the exudation of hydrogen ions in the immediate vicinity of plant roots, it is also possible for the plant roots themselves to convert the phosphates of low solubility into soluble form by pH reduction.

The processes just described also depend directly on the water content of the soil. In dry years less phosphate is removed from the plants than in wet ones. In intensively fertilized areas particularly, the erosion of upper soil material may lead to the removal of considerable quantities of phosphate by drainage into streams, rivers, etc. Here, too, phosphorus has a similar stimulating effect to that of nitrogen on the growth of water plants, especially algae, by which the biological balance of ditch and drainage systems is considerably disturbed. This can be countered to some extent by erosion-preventive measures such as reduction of fallow stretches or introduction of organic substances into the soil and measures to control water flow.

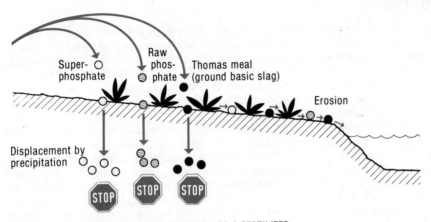

Diagram 1. PHOSPHORUS IS FED INTO THE SOIL AS A FERTILIZER

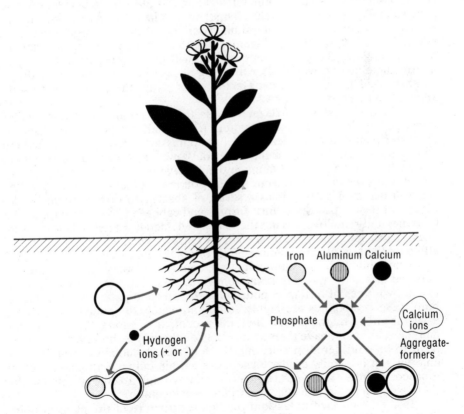

Diagram 2. COMPLEX FORMATION OF PHOSPHATE IN THE GROUND

POTASSIUM

Like nitrogen and phosphorus, potassium is one of the most important plant nutrients. The average potassium content of mineral soil is about 3%; but in organic (e.g., moorland) soil and in sandy soil poor in clay, the potassium content is considerably lower. Potassium is present in the soil solution as fixed potassium. It occurs between the layer packs of clay minerals, as building stone in the molecular lattice of various minerals and in natural organic and mineral ion exchangers.

Under natural conditions, potassium is transmitted by chemical erosion processes into the ground solution and converted into a form available to plants. From primary clay minerals (mica, feldspar), illite is formed, which after a further loss of potassium is transformed into vermiculite and montmorillonite. On drying out, the latter can again absorb the potassium ions and retain them between the layer packs. When they humidify again, the layer packs will again expand so that the potassium returns to the ground solution.

The process of potassium absorption by clay minerals is known as *potassium fixation*. In potassium fertilization this plays an important role, as potassium is fixed as a result of mineral fertilization. According to the particular circumstances, potassium fixation will have a promoting or a restrictive effect on the nourishment of the cultures. In ground rich in montmorillonite, the potassium fertilizer will pass by preference into the intermediate layers, where after a drying-out period it will be retained and so abstracted from the plants. On the other hand, the potassium fixation serves as a defense against erosion.

Eroded potassium (fertilizer) passes through ground or surface water into water outlets (streams, rivers, etc.), in which it acts as a fertilizer on the water plants. If heavy leaching of the potassium occurs, however, there will be a high salt loading in the water outflow, which eventually results in salt damage to the flora and fauna in the waterways.

Besides the loss by erosion, a reduction in the potassium content of the soil will occur in particular as a result of absorption of potassium by the plants. In this respect, potatoes, turnips and cabbages, together with alfalfa (lucerne) and red clover, make the heaviest demands on the potassium supplies in the soil. Garden crops such as carrots, cucumbers and cabbages attain extraction rates as high as 350 kg of potassium oxide per hectare.

Under intensive soil cultivation, this removal of potassium from the soil must be offset by applying potassium fertilizers. Here the choice lies between two types of fertilizer: potassium chloride and potassium sulfate. As both these compounds are highly soluble in water, the potassium ions are easily absorbed by the plants. Both the accompanying ions, the chloride ion and the sulfate ion, have their own effects on the plants, however, and these have to be considered in selecting the fertilizer. In humid conditions, the chloride ion is rapidly eroded. There are certain cultivated plants, such as tobacco, potatoes and vines, which react unfavorably to chloride, so that for these plants a potassium sulfate fertilizer is indicated.

In the absence of potassium the whole structure of the plants withers and fades. The reason for this is that potassium retains the water in the cell sap of the vacuole, as it has a swelling effect. Plants with an insufficient potassium reserve release the water easily, so that the cell pressure (turgor pressure) declines and the plant withers.

Maintenance of the tumefying effect of the plasma colloids, however, is

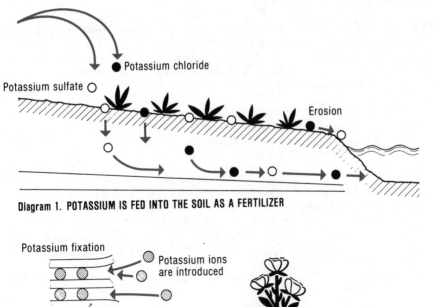

Diagram 1. POTASSIUM IS FED INTO THE SOIL AS A FERTILIZER

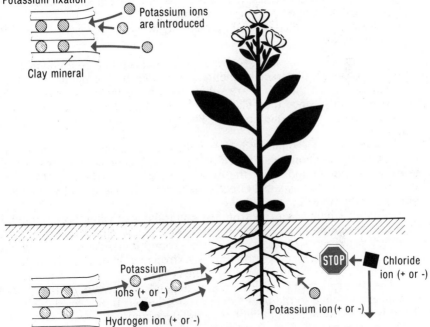

**Diagram 2. POTASSIUM FIXATION BY CLAY MINERALS AND POTASSIUM
ABSORPTION BY THE PLANTS**

not the only function of potassium in plants. It also plays an important role in photosynthesis and in the activation of certain enzymes in cellular variations.

TRACE ELEMENTS—COPPER

Plant nutrients are classified in the traditional manner into the principal ingredients such as nitrogen, phosphorus and potassium, and into the trace elements such as boron, zinc and manganese. This classification is graded into the quantitative requirements of plants for the individual elements. Thus the higher plants require some thousand times more potassium than boron, for example.

More practical is a subclassification from a chemical point of view, based on the effect the nutrients have on the plant organisms as worked out in recent years. On this basis the following groups of plant nutrients have been established:

1. The nonmetals comprise inter alia the basic elements of organic matter, including carbon, hydrogen, oxygen, phosphorus, sulfur, silicon and nitrogen.
2. In the alkali-alkaline earth group, which includes potassium, calcium, magnesium and manganese, the elements are present in the ground in the form of ions and are absorbed by the plants in that form. Their primary task is the neutralization of charges of organic ions which, because of their size, cannot migrate through the membrane system of the cells.
3. Among the heavy metals, special mention may be made of copper, molybdenum, zinc and iron.

The physiologically most active trace elements are to be found in groups 2 and 3. Although the trace elements are needed by the plants in only the very smallest quantities, they are still of great importance to the nutrition of cultivated plants, since they play a vital role as components of enzymes at essential stages of their metabolism. The case of copper can be taken as an example.

Copper in the ground is either concentrated in the clay fraction or is present in organic combination. Of all the trace elements, copper forms the most stable compounds with the organic substance in the soil. This in no way reduces its physiological effectiveness in relation to plant life, however, but rather improves it.

Copper, which is set free from the minerals by erosion, is combined out of the soil solution at the sorption points of the clay minerals. The bonding is a very firm one, so that copper in the ground is mobile to only a limited extent. The copper can be mobilized by strong acids or organic molecules which form complex compounds with the copper.

The absorption of copper by plants depends essentially on the quantity of copper available to the plants in the soil solution. In the vegetable organism it is probably present mainly in complex compounds.

The importance of copper (as also of most other heavy metals) lies in the fact that it is a constituent of enzymes, particularly of oxidases, which perform an important function in the metabolism of plants.

To improve the copper supply to cultivated plants, copper sulfate and metal meal flour containing copper are often added as fertilizers. How small is the consumption of copper is shown by the absorption value of an average corn crop, which amounts to no more than 20 to 30 grams of copper per hectare. To ensure adequate fertilization, however, many times this quantity must be distributed. In deficient areas, 5 to 10 kg (11 to 22 lb) of copper per hectare is recommended.

Barley, wheat and oats are the field crops most sensitive to a copper

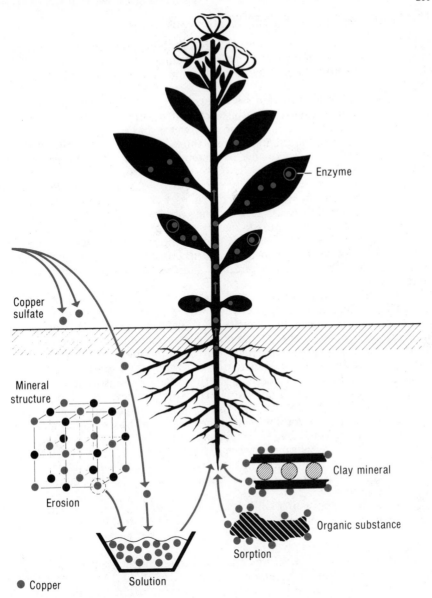

Enzyme

Copper
sulfate

Mineral
structure

Erosion

● Copper

Solution

Clay mineral

Organic substance

Sorption

COPPER-FEEDING OF PLANTS

deficiency. Any deficiency will be evident from the fact that the points of the leaves remain narrow and pale and curl in. If there is a severe shortage of copper, the ear or panicle formation is arrested, while in more favorable cases the ears remain at least partly sterile.

TEMPERATURE REQUIREMENTS OF PLANTS

In judging the quality of a region and its suitability for a particular range of plants, not only the temperatures of the region need to be considered, but also the temperature requirements of the individual plants and the factors that have a bearing on them.

The supply of heat to plants is determined first of all by solar radiation; and a certain (negligible) part is also played by the respiration of organic compounds in relation to carbon dioxide, water and energy. Solar radiation affects only parts of the plants, namely those aboveground, while the roots are not affected. It is reasonable to assume, therefore, that the same temperatures prevail at the roots as in the surrounding soil.

Leaves and stalks are directly exposed to solar radiation. Part of the radiation is reemitted, mainly the green part of the visible light and the thermal radiation (infrared). Leaves that are not too thick let through a further part, which again consists mainly of the green part of the visible rays and the thermal radiation. The remainder of the radiation is absorbed by the leaves. Part of the energy so absorbed is consumed in photosynthesis, a very much greater part in transpiration, and the remaining energy in heating up the leaves.

Exchange of heat with the surrounding atmosphere occurs on the surface of the leaves in exactly the same way as on the surface of the earth. This exchange increases in intensity as the air movement rises in the surrounding atmosphere. The air movement also encourages transpiration by the fact that water vapor is carried away from the immediate vicinity of the leaves, so that a greater difference arises in vapor pressure between the leaf and the surrounding atmosphere. Both these factors contribute to a cooling off of the leaf surfaces. Under solar radiation by day, the temperatures recorded on the leaf surfaces, like those on the surface of the ground, are mostly above the temperature level in the open air. The excess temperatures are largely conditioned by the thickness of the leaves, since thick, pulpy leaves absorb more energy, possess a smaller surface, transpire little, and provide a low heat exchange with the surrounding atmosphere. Thin leaves, on the other hand, are subject to sharper variations, as they can store less heat in their interior.

The water supply of plants is another factor determining the excess temperature. With a good water supply this can be kept at a low level by the increase in transpiration, but in unfavorable water conditions the leaves wilt and excess temperatures will be the rule.

Under excess temperatures the plants can suffer heat damage. Most vital processes occur in a temperature range of 0° to 40°C (32° to 104°F), which very few organisms can exceed. Under intensive radiation with little air movement, leaf temperatures of over 40°C (104°F) and up to 53°C (127°F) have been recorded, so it is easy to see that heat damage to forest and fruit cultures is occasioned more frequently by unfavorable conditions than is usually realized.

At night, outward radiation from the leaves causes a drop in temperatures, though these do not attain such extreme values as the excess temperatures by day. The lower temperatures on the leaf surfaces may be about 1°–2°C (1.8°–3.6°F) below those of the open air, whereas excess temperatures by day may be 10°–14°C (18°–25°F) above those in the open air.

EFFECTS OF LOWER TEMPERATURES ON PLANTS

During the cold season, the metabolic process in plant organisms is severely reduced, and the plants lapse into a state of repose. Even in this period of vegetation, however, the temperature in the vicinity of the plants has a certain influence on the plant organism, as the individual varieties of plants differ considerably in their sensitivity to cooler conditions. Plants are particularly vulnerable to low temperatures in the spring and late winter, when they have been "coddled" by occasional warm days or have already put out some young shoots that have not had time to harden.

As regards vulnerability to damage from low temperatures, three types of plants can be distinguished:

1. Many plants "catch cold" in temperatures of little over 0°C (32°F). Apart from tropical growths, these plants include cultivated plants such as tobacco, tomatoes and beans which, if they do not die off completely, are arrested in their growth at a later stage. It is possible that the damage done by the cold produces irreversible changes in the plasma structure of the cells, resulting in dislocation of the enzymatic equilibrium.
2. A large number of plants are only damaged by ice formation at temperatures of under 0°C. Particularly affected in this way are young shoots and parts of plants with a high water content. The hypothesis that the cell walls are fractured by the expansion of frozen water in the cells has not been substantiated. It is to be assumed, rather, that freezing to death is the result of the mechanical effects of ice crystals on the fine structures of the plasma, or that the cell plasma shrinks owing to the sudden withdrawal of water on freezing, or that damage is caused to the plasma by the sudden surplus of water on thawing.
3. Finally there are plants that can withstand severe temperatures of below 0°C with ice formation in the tissues without any damage at all. This type of plant includes various species of evergreen coniferous trees.

A special problem, among the effects of low temperatures on plant life, consists in the killing off of winter seed by frost, which mainly affects varieties of winter grain. Frequently this results from the growths being forced up by frost. This occurs when, owing to change of temperature, thaw water penetrates the ground, shortly afterward freezes there and, because of the expansion in volume that this causes, raises the ground level. The roots raised in this way either are physically damaged (ruptured) or are exposed on the surface and wither away.

After a luxuriant autumn growth of the winter seed, if the ground is too wet there is a danger of the plants getting choked by a shortage of oxygen and an accumulation of carbonic acid gas under a heavy and possibly still frozen blanket of snow. These conditions are usually accompanied by contamination of the stand by fungi and animal parasites (such as clover rot and psyllid larvae).

The frost resistance of the plants is subject to seasonal variations. It is always lower from the spring to the summer and increases steadily in the autumn, to reach a peak in the coldest season of the year. A close relationship exists at all times between the frost level and the sugar content of the plants, though it cannot be said with any certainty whether the sugar concentration is a concomitant of increased frost resistance or whether it is itself responsible for the higher level of frost resistance.

DEW AND HOARFROST—THEIR IMPORTANCE TO PLANT LIFE

Dew occurs when water vapor condenses on the earth's surface or on the outer surface of plants in temperatures of over 0°C (32°F); when the condensation occurs at below 0°C, hoarfrost is formed. The precise process of dew formation is as follows: the ground temperature declines at night owing to radiation of heat from the ground. If the ground temperature falls below the level at which the water vapor pressure of the surrounding air is sufficient to produce water vapor saturation (dew point), then the vapor sinks to the ground and condenses as water on the ground or plant surfaces.

In this process condensation heat is released. In addition, by the decline in the air particles out of the atmosphere, kinetic energy passes from the atmosphere to the earth's surface. The strength of these two energy currents is determined by the quantity of the ground heat radiated. On a clear night the heat radiation will be substantial, so that the fall of dew is also increased. After an overcast night, on the other hand, there will be little dew formation, as the radiated ground heat is reflected from the cloud cover.

At 0.5 mm of water the quantity of dew falling under favorable conditions is well below the theoretically adduced quantity of 0.8 mm. Dew-soaked meadows often give the impression that substantially more water is present. This impression stems from the fact that grasses in particular have the capacity to give off additional guttation water from water fissures, which is often wrongly thought to be dew.

Water vapor is deposited in the form of hoarfrost when, as noted, the ground temperature or the surface temperature of plants falls below 0°C. Thereupon the water passes directly from the vapor state into a solid form (ice crystals). In this process the air temperature plays no part; and in fact it may be well above freezing point. As in the case of dew formation, in the formation of hoarfrost the kinetic energy imparted to the ground by the ice formation process is removed again by the heat radiated from the ground.

In the temperate zones in particular, the effects of dew and hoarfrost deposits on the plants are of only secondary importance as regards water supplies to the plants. The groundwater content is not increased appreciably by dew (any more than by mist or fog). Nor does the direct absorption of dew by the leaf surfaces play a vital ecological role in the supply of water to the plants. But this does not apply, for instance, in the case of plants that grow on other plants but do not take advantage of the supply system of the host plant (epiphytes). By means of special organs such as air roots and suction scales these can absorb the dew-water deposits directly. The growth of lichens is also assisted by dew.

Greater interest attaches to the physiological significance of dew in the reduction of transpiration in plants (the emission of water vapor through the pore openings). With the onset of photosynthesis in the morning, the pores in plants open and transpiration increases. If there is dew on the leaves, transpiration is reduced or held up altogether. In this way the plants are able to survive short dry spells without sustaining any damage. Young plants in particular, which have not yet developed a positive root system, benefit from dew in this way.

Dew has an unfavorable effect especially in warm moist periods. It leads to saturation of plant growths with water moisture, promotes spore formation, and so encourages the growth of fungi that are harmful to the plants.

Diagram 1. DEW FORMATION

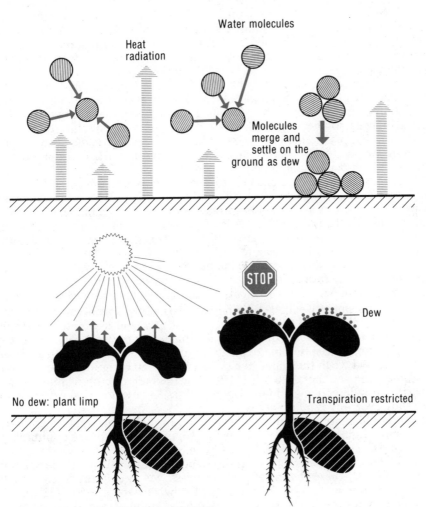

Diagram 2. THE EFFECT OF DEW ON SEEDLINGS

FROST PROTECTION

The great damage caused to sensitive cultures by radiation frosts and cold air penetration (advection frosts) at the start of the vegetation period in the spring and early summer calls for effective protection measures.

While very little can be done in preventing advection frosts, the formation of cold air fronts by radiation frosts can be prevented. This is done by the amelioration (ground improvement) of wet pastures and moorland (provided they are not subject to nature protection measures) and by the installation of heated tanks. Screening by the erection of living protective strips (hedges) can impede the inflow of cold air and the formation of cold air pockets. Accumulations of cold air can also be dispersed by demolishing the retaining barriers.

In addition to the preventive measures mentioned, direct protective measures are also of great importance. One form these may take is to reduce radiation from the ground by screening the radiation area above the plant stand. Owing to the very high labor cost, however, covering crops with mats, cloths, plastic material, glass windows, paper screens, straw, stable manure or potato vines is usually adopted only in market gardens. Large areas and tall plants cannot be protected in this way.

A more practical and cheaper frost protection measure is the formation of an air canopy, which can be effected by burning waste oil or vegetable waste (attended by thick smoke production); other possibilities are smoke cartridges and the release of chlorosulfonic acid. The air canopy method can be used only on level land surfaces and when the air is still (protective capacity effective down to about $-2°C$, or $28.4°F$).

Protection against frost can also be effected by conservation or generation of heat. The former is effected by previous sprinkling, by which heat is stored in the upper soil. An essential requirement for its success, however, is warm and sunny weather following the sprinkling. Furthermore, the process is suitable only in the case of low crops and mild frosts. Better results have been achieved with constant sprinkling during the frost. The protective effect of constant sprinkling depends on the fact that the solidification energy released when the water freezes keeps the temperature of the ice layer and the plants at about $-0.5°C$ ($31°F$). For the bulk of crop plants this mild degree of undercooling is in no way harmful. To obviate too severe an icing up, however, the rainfall intensity should be as low as possible, and sprinkling should continue until thawing sets in. Sprinkling for frost protection is widespread, in particular during the blossoming season for fruit cultures. In this way frosts of up to $-6°C$ ($21.2°F$) can be overcome.

The various methods of heating land developed to date are all very expensive. Of these the installation of oil stoves in cultures threatened by frost provides protection from frosts of down to about $-5°C$ ($23°F$). The technology for the supply of warm air to plant cultures from the open air, or of artificially heated air by means of a propellor, is not yet sufficiently developed. Very effective protection against frost should be attainable by selective plant-raising measures in the long run. However, the development of frost-resistant species requires time and patience.

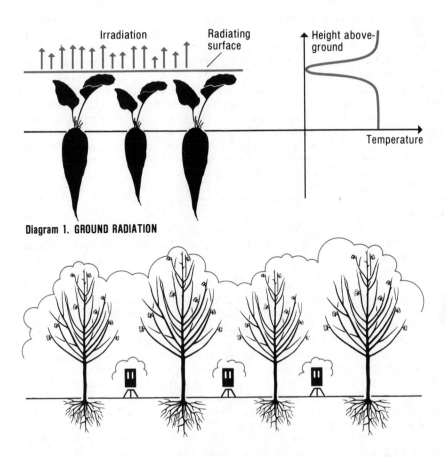

Diagram 1. GROUND RADIATION

Diagram 2. AIR TURBIDITY AS A FROST-PROTECTION MEASURE

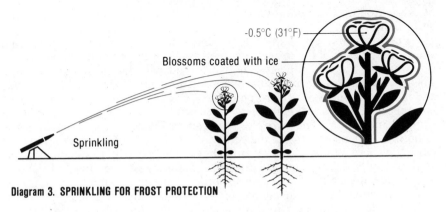

Diagram 3. SPRINKLING FOR FROST PROTECTION

WIND ACTION ON PLANTS

Climatic factors such as wind, solar radiation, cold, heat and precipitation exercise a great influence on the metabolism and formation of plant life in all its forms. Air movements of greater or less force are, on the one hand, physiological and, on the other hand, mechanical in their effects.

Air movements affect plants firstly by raising the transpiration rate. If the water supply is adequate, this is desirable in the interests of the metabolism. In dry climatic conditions, however, the water balance of plants is rapidly upset by wind effects. When wilting sets in, the pore openings of the leaves close up. Transpiration is, of course, reduced thereby, but at the same time the assimilation of carbon dioxide comes to an end. A slight air movement, however, promotes photosynthesis in plants by the activation of carbon dioxide out of the ground air.

The physical effects of wind on plants and parts of plants occur primarily in regions in which the wind frequently attains a high velocity. These include deserts and prairies where, in the absence of ground flora and stands of trees, the wind blows freely. Strong winds also occur on seacoasts and on isolated mountain peaks. Close to the ground the wind velocity is reduced by friction, so that low plant growths, such as grass, suffer little physical stress even in high winds.

Trees, on the other hand, especially if they are freestanding, are exposed to heavy physical pressures. Through striking and rubbing against one another the branches get broken and crushed and leaves are stripped. Broad leaves (on tobacco plants, for instance) can be lacerated and water may be squeezed out of the damaged tissues. Furthermore the to-and-fro movement of the leaves produces constant changes in volume in the intercellular spaces in the porous tissue of the leaves, so that even when the fissures are closed air is sucked in and expelled, which leads in turn to loss of water and drying out of the leaves. Particularly affected are the broad thin-skinned shaded leaves of trees, while the relatively small, thick-skinned leaves exposed to sunlight suffer far less from the wind effects.

The boughs of freestanding trees that face the wind (and also of trees on the edges of woods) are restricted in their growth by wind effects, while boughs sheltered from the wind display normal growth. This gives the impression that the tree is pointing in the direction opposite of the wind. In trees sheared by the wind, the branches on the windward side are removed altogether.

Fractures and uprooting are the most serious consequences of high winds. In the case of the former the treetop and/or large branches are broken off, while in the latter the tree is overturned with its entire root system. These wind effects are particularly conspicuous in old diseased tree stands and in monocultures. The pure pine forest provides a good example: Under natural conditions freestanding pine trees bear branches from the foot of the trunk to the crown. The sweep of the branches increases steadily from top to bottom of the tree, so that the center of gravity is well down the trunk. In closely packed stands the lower branches of the pine die from lack of light, so that only the treetop carries branches, the trunks being long and slender. The center of gravity of a tree of this order is therefore situated well up the trunk, which makes for instability in high winds. These trees are protected by better developed trees well provided with branches on the edge of the forest, which serve as a wind shield.

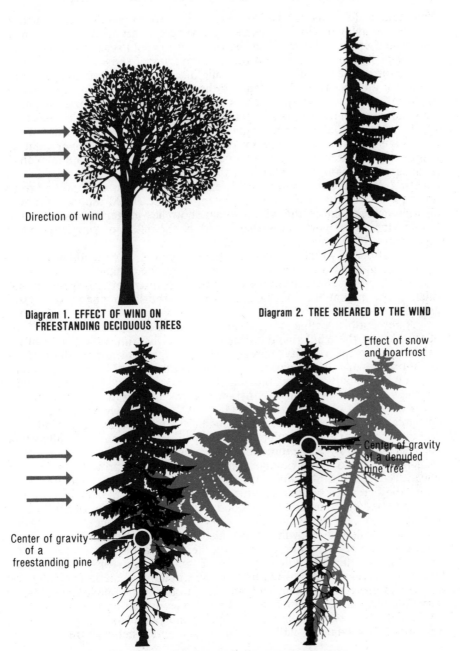

Direction of wind

Diagram 1. EFFECT OF WIND ON FREESTANDING DECIDUOUS TREES

Diagram 2. TREE SHEARED BY THE WIND

Effect of snow and hoarfrost

Center of gravity of a denuded pine tree

Center of gravity of a freestanding pine

Diagram 3. IMPACT OF WIND ON FREESTANDING AND DENUDED PINE TREES

WIND PROTECTION MEASURES FOR CULTIVATED STANDS

Wind damage to cultivated stands takes various forms: seeds may be uncovered, blown away or blown together, and wet cereal grain crops can be bent and broken under pressure from the wind. In the cold season the wind can do damage by blowing away a protective covering of snow. Seeds of weeds such as the dandelion, disease germs and insect pests such as the Colorado beetle are picked up by the wind and disseminated. Other damage is done by the effects of solid matter such as sand and snow which, carried along by the wind, land on the plants and cause physical damage to their tissues.

In order to reduce these wind effects, hedgerows and regular windbreaks are erected in many regions (e.g., in coastal zones and river valleys). A properly constructed wind protection screen in the form of a line of trees reduces soil erosion by the wind in the vicinity of light sandy soil, and by lowering the rate of evaporation this enables the moisture in the soil to be retained longer. Under cover of a protective wind shield the fall of dew is also intensified, and in the winter fallen snow lies longer in shaded areas. Finally, the air temperature is also raised, as the inflow of kinetic energy is not dispersed by convection currents.

The effect of windbreaks is nonetheless limited. It depends very much on the height and thickness of the screen and on the distance separating the individual screens. Screens of medium thickness offer better protection than thick ones, in that the blockage of wind by the latter encourages weed growth.

A perceptible decline in wind velocity is noticeable at a distance in front of the base of the wind shield corresponding to five times the height of the shield, though the velocity increases sharply again toward the foot of the windbreak, owing to retroactive effects of the blockage. The sharpest reduction in wind velocity occurs immediately behind the wind shield. From there on, the velocity rises again to a distance corresponding to some twenty-five times the height of the shield to 90% to 100% of the velocity in the open. Assuming the shield to be 15 meters high (50 feet high), another windbreak will thus need to be installed at a distance of 375 to 400 meters (1230 to 1300 feet) across the prevailing direction of the wind.

In addition to the advantages they confer for plant growths, in areas in which trees are not plentiful wind shields help to provide timber. Furthermore, they create a biotope in which animals and insects beneficial to man will find good breeding and living conditions. From the point of view of the landscape, too, natural wind shields offer positive advantages.

The installation of windbreaks also entails disadvantages, however, which have to be taken into account by the agriculturist: On modern mechanized farms difficulties will arise as regards cultivation; for instance, as the protective screens will always have to be circumnavigated. Their maintenance and protection will entail higher labor costs. The unavoidable loss of farmland also has to be considered. In wet regions, spring sowing will have to be deferred owing to the extension of the period of snow and water retention. Direct damage will result from competition between tree and plant

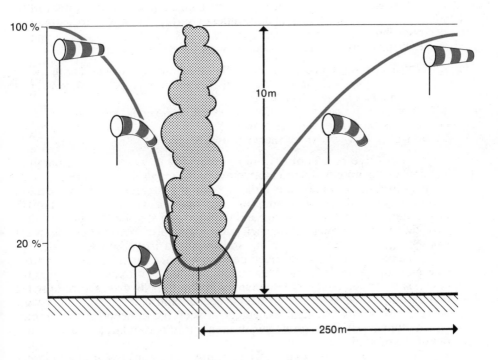

100 %

20 %

10m

250m

PROTECTIVE EFFECT OF A TALL HEDGEROW

roots for water (particularly in dry regions) and nutrients. In warm moist areas fungal growths may spring up immediately behind the protective shields.

By no means all the factors and effects of windbreaks have been thoroughly investigated; and as errors in the assessment of the stand and in the installation of the wind shield itself can have deleterious effects, prior examination and appraisal of each individual case is essential.

IRRIGATION

For plant life, water is one of the basic growth factors, and only gives the best return when it is available in optima quantities. Even in the wet regions of the world this is by no means always the case, however, so that measures have to be taken to supplement the supply.

By irrigation, water from regions of high rainfall can be conveyed to areas of low rainfall through underground or surface channels. Irrigation can also contribute to natural manuring.

Basically three irrigation processes are to be distinguished:

1. The dam or sewage process whereby delimited farmland is dammed or the water on a slope is channeled through ditches and culverts or over wide surfaces into meadows and arable lands.
2. Underground irrigation, by which the irrigation water is conveyed through a system of pipes into the ground.
3. Sprinkling, the system most commonly used today.

The positive results of irrigation, especially in years of low rainfall in which plants cannot make productive use of higher air temperatures because of the shortage of water, are striking. Toward the end of the vegetation period in particular, timely adoption of irrigation will extend the growth phase, delay premature ripening, and improve and stabilize the yield.

Like natural precipitation, irrigation water promotes the exchange of gas with ground air. In sprinkling and overhead irrigation, water absorbs oxygen as a result of its sustained contact with the air, penetrates into the soil, and supplants the ground air containing carbon dioxide. The dam process has a further effect. Overdamming in short spells drives vermin living underground such as mice, hamsters, beetles and caterpillars out of their nests or exterminates them altogether. Excessive concentrations of salt, which often arrest plant growth in dry regions in particular, also get washed out of the ground.

The possibility also exists of incorporating manuring and plant protection measures into an irrigation system at little labor cost by introducing fertilizer or insecticide into the irrigation water. Liquid manure and communal waste water can also be applied to irrigated fields in the same way. This has been severely criticized in recent years on hygienic grounds, however, as pathogenic organisms from sewage water can remain active in the soil for long periods, and there is always a danger that these germs could be passed back to consumers in the harvest crop.

Artificial irrigation does have certain disadvantages. The oversupply of water for short periods under the dam and sprinkling irrigation systems leads to the displacement of plant nutrients, clay minerals and organic colloids to lower ground levels. This impoverishes the upper soil, and in the lower soil concentrations occur which hinder root growth. The plant growths are also damaged by the fact that in consequence of short applications of dam water the roots do not receive sufficient oxygen from the air. Whatever the method of irrigation employed, attention must also be paid to ensuring that the system of drainage is adequate. Particularly at the start of the vegetation period, account must be taken of the fact that the irrigation water draws heat from the ground, so that germination and growth are delayed. For this reason especially, every care must be exercised regarding the way in which irrigation is carried out in the spring.

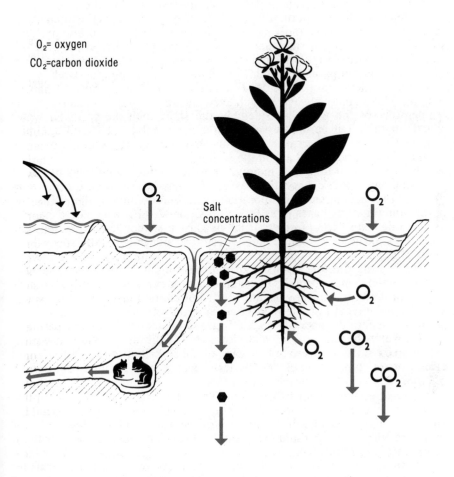

O$_2$= oxygen
CO$_2$=carbon dioxide

O$_2$

Salt
concentrations

O$_2$

O$_2$

O$_2$

CO$_2$

CO$_2$

VARIOUS EFFECTS OF IRRIGATION

IRRIGATION BY SPRINKLING

A sprinkler system consists essentially of a power unit, pump, hosepipes and sprinklers. The pump, which is operated by a stationary or mobile engine, propels the water through the hosepipes to the sprinklers, from which it is emitted through specially constructed nozzles. Only in exceptional cases, such as lawn sprinkling, are the pipelines installed in fixed positions. As a rule (as for field vegetable cultivation and frost protection) the lines are assembled from portable sections that clip together.

One of the most important factors affecting sprinkling is the intensity of application (mm per hectare). A distinction is made between low-pressure sprinklers (a number of small sprinklers are linked together in the system), medium-pressure sprinklers, and high-pressure sprinklers. The latter are installed mainly in parks and on lawns, in orchards and on grassland.

With artificial sprinklers, conditions should resemble those of natural rainfall. This cannot always be achieved, however, partly because of the temperature of the water provided. In the short time the sprinkler water spends in the air it certainly warms up considerably, but it still does not achieve the effect of warm air. It is thus an advantage if warmed water can be drawn from pools available in the vicinity.

As artificial sprinkling is mainly carried out under conditions of strong solar radiation, high evaporation losses are unavoidable. The drop in temperature that accompanies evaporation leads to a cooling of the plants and of the land (in many cases to as little as 3°C, or 37.4°F), which on occasion, as when delicate parts of plants (such as garden-lettuce leaves) suffer from the effects of the heat, can be highly desirable, but in general, especially at times of germination, can cause considerable delays in plant growth.

As regards the low intensity of natural rainfall, artificial sprinkling—even a low-pressure sprinkling system—cannot compare. Another point is that natural rain falls not by fits and starts but continuously. Artificial sprinkling of uncultivated arable land in general and of tilled arable land in the germination period, especially in heavy ground, encourages the formation of surface water, because of the very slow rate of infiltration, and consequent silting up or, on sloping ground, erosion of the soil. On pastureland, harmful effects of this type are substantially less because of the concurrent growth of crops.

Compared with other irrigation methods, for which surplus water must normally be used on account of the unavoidable losses by seepage, the sprinklers make considerably better use of the water, unless a low sprinkler output results in exaggerated evaporation. Losses by seepage are hardly to be expected, except in very light porous soil.

With sprinkling, the increase in productivity of cultivated plants depends more on the time selected than on the quantity of water applied. A good time to choose is just before the onset of water shortage, whereas leaving it until wilting has already set in will result in a lowering of productivity. Ill-timed sprinkling may even interfere with the pollination process and can lead to excessive leaf formation, and it also encourages weed growth.

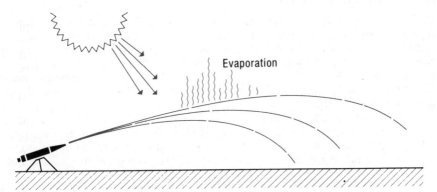

Evaporation

Diagram 1. STRONG SOLAR RADIATION CAUSES EXCESSIVE EVAPORATION

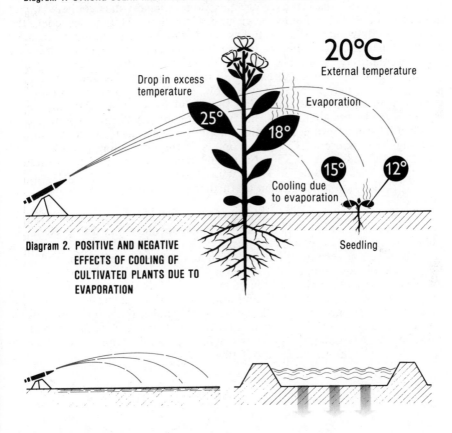

Drop in excess
temperature

20°C
External temperature

Evaporation

25°

18°

15°

12°

Cooling due
to evaporation

**Diagram 2. POSITIVE AND NEGATIVE
EFFECTS OF COOLING OF
CULTIVATED PLANTS DUE TO
EVAPORATION**

Seedling

**Diagram 3. LITTLE LOSS OF SEEPAGE WATER FROM SPRINKLING; HEAVY LOSS
FROM DAM IRRIGATION**

ARTIFICIAL PRECIPITATION

In the interests of agriculture, attempts have recently been made in areas of frequent hailstorms to avert them by getting the clouds in which hail is forming to precipitate the vapor early as rain. The procedure for achieving artificial precipitation by human intervention, which is known as *cloud seeding,* would also be of the greatest importance in dry regions. The presence of clouds is, of course, an essential prerequisite in all cases, for clouds cannot be formed by artificial means.

Most suitable for this purpose are source clouds in which the condensation droplets are already supercooled; and the cloud temperature must thus be below the limit of 0°C (32°F). Clouds that form in the airspace on the side of a mountain ridge facing the wind and rise to a great height also hold out good prospects of success for artificial precipitation measures.

Ascending water droplets are supercooled below the limit of 0°C and finally freeze at about −15°C (5°F) by natural crystallization nuclei. Further water adheres rapidly to the ice crystals, so that the crystals get heavier and heavier and eventually fall to the ground. If the limit of 0°C is exceeded, the ice crystals thaw out and again fall as raindrops. The production of artificial rainfall depends on the ability to bring the supercooled droplets to freezing point prematurely. For this, freezing nuclei are needed which come into operation at temperatures already well below 0°C. This is achieved by releasing dry ice, i.e., carbon dioxide snow, or silver iodide crystals onto the clouds from an airplane traversing the cloud tops, or by shooting silver iodide crystals into the clouds directly in small rockets. Silver iodide possesses a lattice structure and lattice energy very similar to those of ice, and so brings the supercooled water droplets to the congealing point at about −2° to −4°C (28.4° to 24.8°F). From that point on the raindrop formation follows the lines indicated in Part Two. Carbon dioxide snow operates less as a crystallization nucleus than by further supercooling of the water droplets.

To what extent hail formation can be avoided and artificial precipitation can be promoted in individual cases by cloud seeding is hard to predict. As only source clouds are suitable in practice for the production of artificial rainfall, it can never be established with any certainty beforehand whether the source clouds would not have precipitated rainfall in the next hour in any case or whether hail would have fallen at all. As the same clouds are no longer present under the same conditions, in judging the success of artificial measures for promoting rainfall one has to depend entirely on assumptions. After thorough examination of the question it seems reasonable to assume, however, that in damming positions before mountain ranges the precipitation rate can be improved by about 10%.

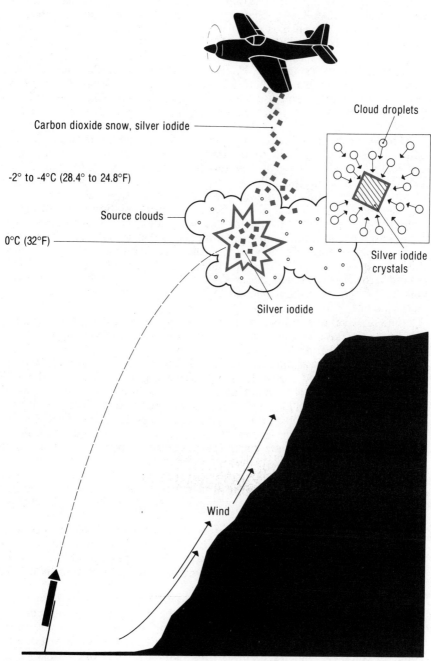

Cloud droplets

Carbon dioxide snow, silver iodide

-2° to -4°C (28.4° to 24.8°F)

Source clouds

0°C (32°F)

Silver iodide

Silver iodide crystals

Wind

ARTIFICIAL RAINFALL

WATER DRAINAGE

Surplus groundwater, which is harmful to plant growth, must be removed from the soil. For this purpose underground water systems consisting of suction pipes and collector channels are installed. The suction pipes are designed to draw the surplus water from the ground and convey it into the collector channels; and these carry the water into the receiving stream. The complete process of this type of water removal is known as drainage.

Until a few years ago the drains consisted of short clay pipes, at the junctions of which the water entered the suction pipes. Today the trend, on cost grounds, is increasingly toward producing collector channels and suction pipes from slotted PVC (polyvinyl chloride) tubes, which are also cheaper to install.

The best results are achieved in areas in which the groundwater level is high. Nevertheless, the effects of drainage operations are not confined to lowering the level of the groundwater, for they also benefit the water conservation of the soil, especially in heavy water-retaining soil which receives moisture from groundwater lying several meters below surface level.

The loosening of the soil produced by the installation of the drainage system is also a favorable influence. The drainage water percolates more freely into loose ground compared with packed soil, so that rainwater penetrates the heavy untilled ground area in the upper stratum toward the valley, and only seeps through a drain line deeper down. Finally, at times of deep ground frost, the loosened material in the drainage trench is easily compressed by the expanding packed soil and so contributes to the further loosening of the soil substance.

The removal of surplus groundwater by drainage leaves room for air to penetrate into the ground. In consequence the ground warms up more rapidly in the spring. Both processes (the improvement of the air content in the ground and earlier warming of the soil) promote the activity of microorganisms in the soil, and this in turn, by increasing the friability of the soil, contributes to the improvement of the soil structure and so to the water conservation of the soil (see also The Pedosphere, in Part Two).

If the main collector channel of the drainage system is connected to the outer air (normally at the outlet or, in the case of a ventilated drainage system, through a special air shaft), there is bound to be some air movement in pipes only partly filled with water, the direction of which will normally be outward by day and inward by night. Furthermore, wind movements set up intermittent air movements in the drainage system. These processes are referred to as "breathing" in the drainage system, and they also contribute to renewal of the ground air.

The effects of drainage are not equally good in all years and at all seasons of the year. They are at their best in wet periods in which groundwater has to be removed in large quantities. In dry periods and in light soil the results can be very poor, when urgently needed groundwater is carried away and denied to the plants.

Another aspect to be considered is that during periods of high humidity and in wet terrain the high water level for the discharge into the receiving stream is raised, especially in the case of light soils, by an increase in the outflow from the drainage system. To avoid this, cutoffs are inserted in the collector channels, which temporarily hold up the outflow of drainage water. Owing to the excess pressure built up in the collector channel, the water is expelled again and returns to the soil, which in periods of drought would be of great advantage.

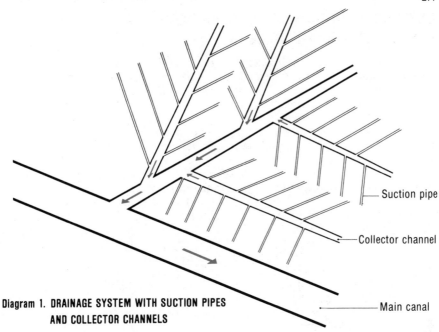

Diagram 1. DRAINAGE SYSTEM WITH SUCTION PIPES AND COLLECTOR CHANNELS

Suction pipe

Collector channel

Main canal

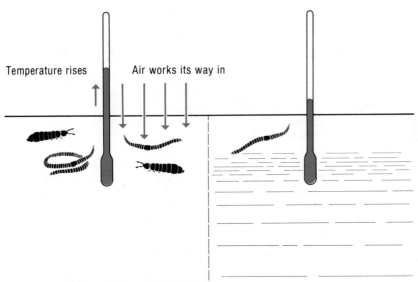

Temperature rises

Air works its way in

Diagram 2. EFFECTS OF DRAINAGE ON THE SOIL

DESTRUCTION OF INSECT PESTS AND CROP PROTECTION: PESTICIDES—HUMAN TOXICITY

Pesticides are chemical substances that are employed in agriculture, forestry and horticulture to combat animal and plant parasites. A distinction is made between *herbicides*, used in the struggle against weeds, *fungicides* against fungi, *insecticides* against insects, *acaricides* against mites, *nematicides* against nematodes, *rodenticides* against rodents, *molluscicides* against snails and slugs, and *seed dressings*. The application of pesticides in agriculture has risen sharply in the past, a development that is likely to continue as long as existing agricultural methods are retained.

As pesticides pass in most cases directly or indirectly into foodstuffs, for many pesticides legal limits (tolerance doses) are imposed regarding the residues that may be left in foodstuffs. By *tolerance dose* is meant the quantity of a substance that may be absorbed by one person from his daily diet in the course of a lifetime without coming to any harm as far as can be judged from present scientific knowledge. The principles according to which the legal limits for pesticides are laid down require that a sufficiently large population of at least two species of animal should be thoroughly examined for at least two years to establish the level (in milligrams per kilogram of body weight) at which a pesticide does no medical damage. In ordinary circumstances, one-hundredth part of this dose is then prescribed as the safe limit for a human being.

Whether this security factor for human beings serves its purpose is disputed for the following reasons:

1. The applicability of the results of experiments on animals to human beings is questionable, because men are more sensitive in many essential respects than animals (e.g., in the nervous system, and with regard to the more complicated metabolism). One example of this problem is provided by the Contergan (thalidomide) catastrophe. Individual species display marked differences in sensitivity to thalidomide. While in the experimental rat, a dose of 50 mg of thalidomide per kg body weight per day was needed to produce teratogenic damage (malformation), the corresponding teratogenic dose for man was no more than 0.5–1 mg per kg.

2. For the experiments on animals, only healthy animals were used. The effect of the pesticides on human beings afflicted by disease or other environmental influences has not been investigated.

3. Investigations into mutagenic (hereditable) effects is insufficient.

4. Only about 15% of the pesticides were examined for cancerous effects. And many of those investigated were not tested thoroughly, sometimes on only one species of animal and in limited doses.

5. Most of the substances harmful to the body are converted or decomposed in the body. But decomposition is not synonymous with detoxification. Conversion and decomposition products are in many cases more toxic than the initial product. The formation and effect of conversion products depend primarily on the specific metabolism of the individual organism: chemical substances can thus display different toxic effects in different organisms.

6. In each experiment on animals, only the effect of a particular poison is tested. The possible combined effects of several poisons is thus not examined. In the case of some poisons the effects increase in geometric progression. On top of this there are combination possibilities with other environmental poisons, medicines, foodstuff additives, beverages, etc.

DAMAGE TO HEALTH CAUSED BY PESTICIDE RESIDUES

Traces of pesticides are detectable in about half of the samples prepared from food bought in grocery stores around the United States. About 3% of these food samples have residues that exceed the legally prescribed limits or are considered excessive. The residues most frequently found include chlorine-containing compounds, such as dieldrin and DDE (a residue of DDT), in dairy products, meat, fish and poultry, and phosphorus-containing chemicals, such as malathion and parathion, in fruits and vegetables. How much damage to human health is caused by these toxic residues?

In the case of an acute toxic effect, it is normally easy to reconstruct the connection between the poison and the illness, as only a short period will elapse between the effects of the poison and the manifestation of the disease. Acute toxic effects occur for the most part as a result of high concentrations, which arise in the case of pesticides only from occupational exposure, incompetent handling, deliberate poisoning or accidents.

Much more problematic to the general population is any chronic toxic effect caused by a gradual buildup of one or more poisons over a long period. In these cases the causal connection is hard to establish because of the time lag, the possibility of the combined effects of several toxic substances, and, in the case of pesticide residues in foods, the lack of records on the type and quantity of poisons that may be involved.

One might assume that organic phosphorus compounds used as insecticides in agriculture and as insect sprays and insect strips in the home are poisonous only if taken into the body in large quantities, and that in smaller quantities they are rapidly broken down by the organism. Recent investigations show, however, that such compounds may cause long-term effects in the human body, such as cancer and hereditary damage.

The potential toxic effects of DDT, now forbidden for general use in the United States and other Western countries, have long been recognized. Patients dying from a wide variety of causes—brain tumors, brain hemorrhage, high blood pressure, cirrhosis of the liver, and various forms of cancer—have been found to have a high DDT content in their fatty tissues. Virtually all animals and people in the United States carry traces of DDT and other persistent pesticide residues.

Contaminants of pesticides themselves are also suspected of having serious consequences on human health. The herbicide known as Agent Orange, used by American forces to clear vegetation in Vietnam, contained 10 to 15 ppm (parts per million) of toxic compounds called dioxin. Thus through extremely heavy spraying and dumping of Agent Orange, an estimated 1000 pounds of dioxin entered the environment. The toxic compound has been measured subsequently in South Vietnamese river fish, shellfish and human milk; and increased rates of stillbirths and births of deformed babies have been reported by both the South Vietnamese and those American families whose husbands served in the area during the Vietnam War.

Pesticides also can be converted into chemicals potentially more dangerous than the original form. The insecticide heptachlor is converted by sunlight into a stable substance some 22 times as toxic as the original substance. Once it gets into the environment, this transformation product, which like DDT is decomposed again only with great difficulty, is considerably more toxic than DDT.

Many pesticides have the unfortunate quality of concentrating in the food chain. High concentrations of various pesticide residues have thus been found in mother's milk. One example is benzene hexachloride (lindane), an insecticide used in agriculture as seed dressing. Benzene hexachloride can be so concentrated in mother's milk that in some cases the milk is contaminated 10 times more severely than is permissible for cows' milk. DDT residues are also frequently found in human milk.

Recently it has been recognized that some pesticides in very low concentrations can produce neuropsychic variations in man, such as poor concentration, troubled sleep, nausea, increased aggressiveness, and impaired muscle control. So far only a few pesticides have been examined in this respect.

PESTICIDES—ECOLOGICAL PROBLEMS

As pesticides are destructive of life, on dissemination in the environment they can cause severe ecological changes. One of the most important changes relates to the powers of resistance built up in the pests affected: living organisms have the capacity to build up defense mechanisms and to develop strains that are resistant to particular poisons. By reason of mutations caused by natural or artificial substances, individual specimens constantly crop up in which a particular quality is changed in relation to the parents. Such a quality could be the capacity to resist a poison (e.g., a pesticide) that normally kills the species. These immunized specimens will survive a fresh application of the poison. They have the enormous biological advantage, furthermore, that as regards propagation in their own biological field they have no competitors. They will therefore multiply rapidly and a strain will be formed that can no longer be controlled by means of the original pesticide. The resistance buildup can thus usually be regarded as unavoidable, as it depends on generally valid biological principles. The stronger and more frequent the application of the poison, the faster the resistance develops to the poison.

Following the bulk application of chemical pesticides after the second World War, the number of pest species with powers of resistance increased dramatically. Most of the 600 and more species of pests known today are multiresistant (immune to a variety of pesticides). The increase in the powers of resistance means that ever higher concentrations of poison must be applied and that more and more poisons must be developed.

Another serious ecological consequence of the application of pesticides is the increase in pressure from parasites. On each form of animal life several limiting factors are imposed by nature in the form of diseases, natural enemies (insects and animals beneficial to man in destroying pests), and inert organisms. By the application of pesticides these limiting factors are modified or destroyed, so that the road is left open to a mass increase in species of pests. Various factors also result in the insects and animals that help to eliminate the pests being more seriously affected by the pesticides than the pests themselves. The natural enemies of plant lice such as ladybugs, lacewings and syrphus flies—which in one year may have no more than a few hundred young, whereas under favorable conditions plant lice can multiply several thousands of times in a couple of weeks—are so severely affected by pesticides that their normal low propagation rate is even further reduced. In addition, because of their predatory mobile habits, the insects given to exterminating vermin are far more likely to come into contact with spray

PROPAGATION OF DIELDRIN-RESISTANT GRAIN PESTS IN THE UNITED STATES

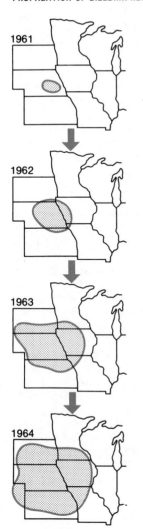

Pesticide	Multiple-resistance buildup in a pest strain of the red citrus mosquito in the United States: necessary increase in doses of poison in comparison with nonresistant pests
Trithion	15 000
Iso-Systox	8 570
Methyl Systox	8 000
Schradan	2 000
EPN	1 400
Parathion	883
Phosdrin	350
Pyrazoxon	300
Systox	266
Tetram	111
Delnav	100
Disyston	25
Diazinon	12
Malathion	8
Ethion	8

poison, even if they were not originally directly sprayed. Many pests, on the other hand, because of their static existence, are often not touched by the pesticide (as they cling to the underside of a leaf, for instance) and survive unscathed.

For these reasons a single application of pesticide may cause disturbance or destruction of the natural controlling factors for parasites. Unnoticed by most people, the numbers of many small and medium-sized creatures such as bumblebees, butterflies, beetles and lizards are reduced by the insidious operation of poisons in the environment.

POPULATION DYNAMICS—FINDINGS REGARDING THE DESTRUCTION OF INSECT PESTS

The density of a population (the total number of individuals of one species, race, etc., in a demarcated area) depends on four opposing processes: birth rate, death rate, immigration and emigration.

For all forms of animal and plant life, the number of offspring exceeds the number of individuals capable of propagating. This stems from the fact that a number of the individuals die prematurely from disease or attack. This is particularly true of insects. If the proliferation of insects were not reduced by outside factors, there would soon be an overpopulation of insects and consequent destruction of the fundamentals of life for the individual. As such a development could not be of advantage to any species, a number of limiting factors stand in the way of such overproduction.

An important limiting factor is the quantity of nutrients available in proportion to the density of population. If the density of population is too high, competitors will contend for the elements of life essential to survival, such as nutrients, breeding grounds and mating partners. The competitive struggle between members of a species is particularly severe, because these all have the same requirements. But competitive struggles also arise between members of different species. A further important limiting factor is the natural enemies (viruses, predators and parasites) of a species. A great influence on population density is also exerted by external physical factors such as temperature, air humidity, light intensity and strength of winds. Temperature, for instance, can affect the number and development of eggs, but indirectly it can also have an effect on parasites.

In relation to the efficiency of the individual environmental factors, for each form of animal and plant life there is a specific optimum. Thus an apple tree grows best and bears most fruit when the ideal conditions for its species or kind as regards temperature, air humidity and sunshine are present. The same applies to the parasites that prey on the apple tree.

A precise knowledge of the individual factors that play a role in population dynamics is essential for the effective biological destruction of insect pests. Especially, if one were to know the curves for the respective ecological optimums of the various useful plants and parasites, which unfortunately is the case today for only particular species, one would then be able to handle the destruction of insect pests more effectively by a favorable choice of location.

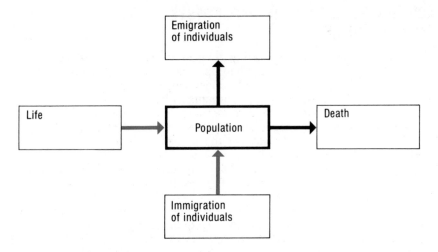

Diagram 1. VARIOUS FACTORS THAT SERVE TO MAINTAIN THE ECOLOGICAL EQUILIBRIUM IN A POPULATION

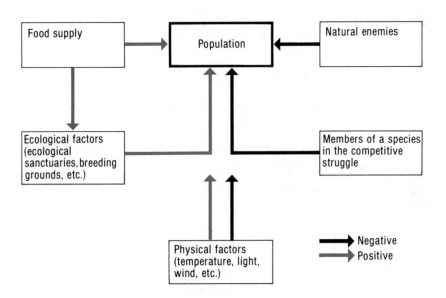

Diagram 2. FACTORS AFFECTING POPULATION DENSITY

ECOLOGICAL CONTROL OF INSECT PESTS— CULTIVATION MEASURES

Cultural methods can be adopted or revised to exercise an influence, in the landscape and environment, on the population density of parasites in agriculture and forestry. The principle underlying such measures is to render the living conditions of the harmful organisms less favorable, with a view to restricting their propagation and so keeping their population density below the danger threshold. In the long run these preventive measures, by means of which a solitary intervention in the landscape can produce long-term results, may provide the most elegant and at the same time a considerable labor- and energy-saving solution. Their application, however, presupposes a precise knowledge of the ecology of the useful plants concerned and of the harmful organisms affecting them.

The viruses of yellow fever and malaria, for example, are transmitted by mosquitoes. These insects can propagate on a large scale only when they possess sufficient marshland in which the larvae can germinate. By draining their breeding grounds in many countries, yellow fever and malaria outbreaks have thus been reduced drastically. Many insect pests, especially smaller ones, avoid the wind, as they are easily carried away by it. By planting carrots and cabbages in fields exposed to the wind, it has been possible to reduce the infestation of these cultivated plants by carrot flies and cabbage flies considerably.

Especially vulnerable to insect pests are monocultures of a particular species of plant, in which the insects can propagate and multiply unhindered. On the other hand, mixed cultures, in which two or more kinds of plants are grown together, offer reasonable possibilities for preventing the spread of insect pests from a fallen plant to a neighboring one, as the distance between the individual plants of the same kind is increased. An additional safeguard is to place two plants in a mixed culture which protect one another against insect pests. The planting of carrots and onions together in a mixed culture would thus provide effective protection against the carrot fly and the onion fly, since the onion fly avoids the essential oils of the carrot and the carrot fly avoids the odor of the onion.

Another very effective method of protecting plants is the cultivation and use of resistant kinds of culture plants. It was thus possible to arrest the severe damage to vineyards in Europe caused by the incursion of the vine louse (*Phylloxera*) in the second half of the nineteenth century by grafting the European vine onto American stock, which was not vulnerable to the vine louse. Today there are numerous plants that are not susceptible to damage from insect pests, such as potatoes that are resistant to viral diseases, and cereal crops that are invulnerable to rust fungi. Nevertheless, efforts in this area in future must be intensified considerably.

Another measure for the cultural destruction of insect pests is the planting of shrubs and hedges, which provide birds that prey on insects with cover and a breeding ground. Generally speaking, living communities and landscapes are the more stable against mass propagation of insect pests the more diversified and variegated they are. The general procedure for cultural defense against insect pests consists, therefore, in increasing the diversity of the landscape and thereby improving its regulation capacity.

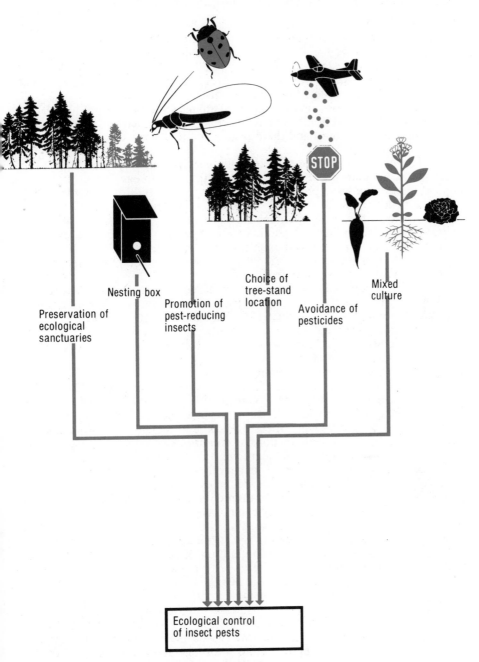

Nesting box

Preservation of
ecological
sanctuaries

Promotion of
pest-reducing
insects

Choice of
tree-stand
location

Avoidance of
pesticides

Mixed
culture

Ecological control
of insect pests

VARIOUS POSSIBILITIES FOR ECOLOGICAL PEST CONTROL

BIOLOGICAL PEST CONTROL BY BENEFICIAL INSECTS

An animal form is described as beneficial when it serves as the opponent of harmful insect life. The terms *beneficial* and *harmful* are relative in this context, as they are applied by man according to his concept of usefulness.

Creatures beneficial to man are classified as *predators,* whose prey is insect pests; *parasites,* which live on insect pests; and *morbific agents* (carriers of a disease), which communicate diseases to insect pests.

Typical predators among beneficial animals and insects are lizards, falcons, bats, wild and domestic cats, various insects such as ground beetles, ladybugs, assassin bugs and their larvae, and the larvae of syrphus flies and of certain gall gnats.

The parasites include the tachinids and ichneumons. The fully grown female of the plant-louse ichneumon will thus lay an egg in the full-fledged plant louse. The larva produced from the egg will feed for a couple of days on the inside of the plant louse. It will then pupate in the plant louse, and after a short time an ichneumon will slip from the empty shell of the plant louse and, after mating, will soon lay more eggs in other plant lice. Although only one plant louse is killed each time by the ichneumon larva, because of the high propagation rate a sizable plant louse population can be exterminated in a relatively short time.

In the group of morbific (pathogenic) agents are included viruses and microorganisms such as fungi, bacteria and protozoa which can communicate to the insect pests on which they prey an infectious disease that usually proves fatal. Once the diseases of the particular organisms are identified, the pathogenic agent can be isolated, cultivated intensively and applied to the biological destruction of insect pests.

In connection with the biological destruction of pests by animals and insects, a number of important factors have to be considered. In the first place, a particular animal species is regarded as a serious parasite only when the depredations for which it is responsible exceed a certain economic threshold. This occurs when measures taken to reduce mass propagation of the parasite are dropped. In normal conditions of ecological equilibrium, each species of organism is subject to certain limiting factors that are hardly discernible to the inexperienced observer, in the form in particular of the organism's natural enemies. This becomes increasingly obvious when the natural enemies of the parasite are unintentionally so incapacitated by spraying with toxic pesticides that they can no longer perform their role as limiting factors in the propagation of parasitic life. In certain circumstances one single spraying may be enough to upset the ecological equilibrium of a life community so severely that a proliferation of parasites will result. Everything possible should therefore be done to preserve the ecological equilibrium of nature or, insofar as it has been disrupted by agriculture, forestry and horticulture, to restore it to some extent.

An important ecological contribution can be made by the syrphus fly, for example. Its larvae suck out the insides of plant lice and so keep their population density down. The mature insect itself bears some resemblance to the wasp, in that its yellow, white or orange abdomen has black or dark brown stripes, according to the species to which it belongs. These extremely adept flying creatures can switch from zigzag dashes at lightning speed to remaining suspended, with wings still buzzing, at some point in the air. In contrast to their larvae, they are attracted to flowering plants and feed on

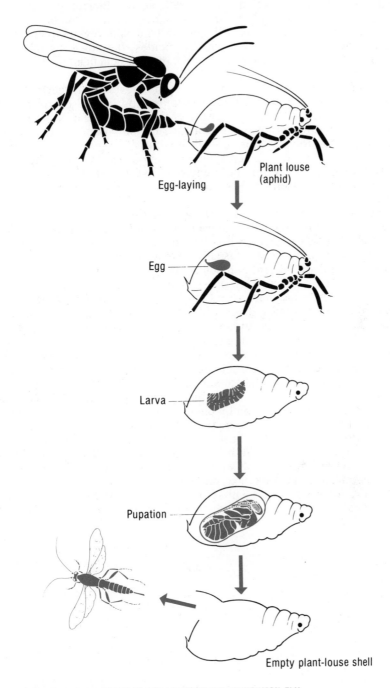

Egg-laying

Plant louse (aphid)

Egg

Larva

Pupation

Empty plant-louse shell

BIOLOGICAL EXTERMINATION OF THE PLANT LOUSE BY THE ICHNEUMON FLY

nectar. Thus if flowering plants are available in sufficient quantities, enough syrphus fly larvae should be present in a given area for the biological reduction of plant lice. In areas of intensive fruit and vegetable cultivation, in which every weed is treated with herbicides, the flowering plants are not present. It is not surprising, therefore, that no beneficial syrphus fly larvae are to be found here.

And strange though this may seem, the presence of a certain number of insect pests during the entire vegetation period may also prove beneficial, for only in this way can the presence of their predators be assured. The best guarantee that insect pests are available in small numbers (below the economic damage threshold) is ecological versatility, with as many varieties of plants as possible and numerous ecological niches. Provided there are sufficient weeds available for the numerous insect pests (who will not yet be endangering the useful plants), the survival of the beneficial insects is assured.

As beneficial insects are very sensitive to toxic chemical spraying, they are eliminated in most cases more rapidly and in greater numbers than the destructive pests for which it is intended. In addition, the pest insects recover more rapidly, as they usually have a shorter generation gap than their predators and are present in much greater profusion.

Creatures that can play a useful part in the biological elimination of parasites include ladybugs with their larvae, syrphus fly larvae, ichneumon flies, and assassin bugs; against fruit-tree parasites (especially caterpillars) many birds, such as the titmouse; earwigs are particularly partial to plant lice and the coddling moth; enemies of the mouse include the falcons and the weasel; and the widest varieties of ichneumons live in particular cases on a very specific type of insect pest. The viruses to which individual pests are prone have been investigated to only a very limited extent.

The great advantage of the biological destruction of insect pests, as opposed to their destruction by chemical means, lies in the fact that it does not impair the quality of foodstuffs. Viruses and parasites tend to attach themselves to a particular host, and so remain completely neutral with regard to other animals and to human beings. Another advantage of biological destruction of pests consists in the cheapness and simplicity of its methods. No complicated machinery is required for applying it and no great labor costs are incurred in frequent spraying. The biological destruction of pests leaves nature to do its work and makes full use of natural principles.

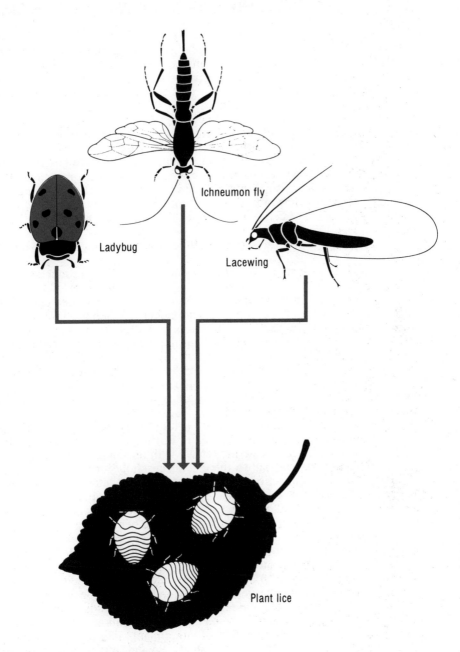

Ichneumon fly

Ladybug

Lacewing

Plant lice

BENEFICIAL PLANT-LOUSE EXTERMINATORS

USE OF ANIMAL AND PLANT ODOR COMPOUNDS IN BIOLOGICAL PEST CONTROL

Many animal species secrete particular stimulating substances, known as *pheromones*, which influence relations between individual members. They are most strongly developed in gregarious species such as ants, bees, mice, rats. But they also occur in nongregarious groups in the form of sexual lures which affect only the mating partner.

Thorough investigations have been made recently into pheromones for insects. These substances are effective for the most part in extremely low concentrations: the male of the American cockroach, for instance, reacts to a mere 30 molecules of the sexual lure emitted by the mating partner. Such substances can be perceived over areas many kilometers in extent. It has now been possible to isolate the sexual pheromones of the following pests, among others: coddling moths, Asiatic cotton worms, sugarcane bugs, night moths, various bark beetles and various kinds of moth that imperil the corn crop.

In principle there are two possibilities for controlling damage by pheromones:

1. The lure substance, extracted from the animal or produced synthetically, is inserted in traps or snares, into which the male of the species concerned is thus enticed. One example of this is the bark beetle, the pheromones of which can be reproduced synthetically. When this lure substance, which affects both sexes, is inserted in selected tree traps, the bark beetles in the vicinity are attracted. By felling these lure trees and removing the bark, the pupa of the beetle can be readily destroyed. The use of sexual pheromones for pest control by this method is likely to succeed, however, only when the population density of the pest in the locality concerned is low, so that the lure substance in the traps will not be masked by the lure substance of the particular insect.

2. By large-scale distribution of a lure substance during the nuptial flight of butterflies and moths, the males of the species can be so confused that they can no longer locate the female with its similar emission of pheromone. This process was put to the test successfully for the first time in the United States in connection with control of the vegetable owl (*Mamestra oleracea*) caterpillars. In this case a concentration of about 10^{-10} grams of pheromone per gram of air was used. In order to maintain this concentration, about 1.5 grams of substance were needed per hectare per night.

In contrast to the lure substances, certain odiferous agents given off by many plants have a repellent effect on various insects. Such repellents can be employed for plant protection in one of two ways: (1) The repellents from particular resistant plant forms can be isolated, or produced synthetically, and then sprayed over the field of cultivated plants in need of protection. From resistant species of potatoes, for instance, glucosides such as solanine and tomatine can be isolated, which act as deterrents to potato beetles. (2) Very much simpler is the method of siting plants that emit repellents in a mixed culture with selected useful plants, so that attacks by pests on the useful plants are avoided. If tomatoes and cabbages are grown in this way in mixed cultures, the repellents emitted by the tomatoes will prevent attacks on the cabbage plants by caterpillars of the cabbage butterfly.

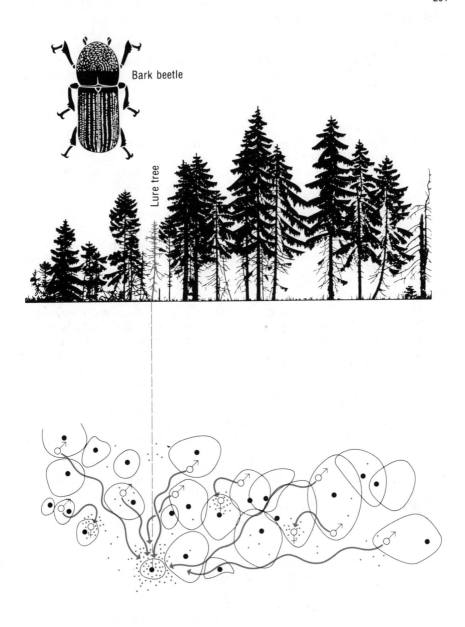

Bark beetle

Lure tree

APPLICATION OF SEXUAL LURE SUBSTANCES FOR THE BARK BEETLE IN A PINEWOOD

ECOLOGICAL WEED CONTROL

There are various methods for restricting the growth of weeds. Chemical weed-killers (herbicides) are used for the most part, especially in agriculture. They are sprayed on the weeds, which wither away under their effects. The herbicides can also have unfortunate incidental effects on other plants, however, and so on the quality of food crops.

For this reason a switch to ecological methods of weed control is to be recommended. Basically this can be done in three ways: by mechanical means, by the employment of animals that devour weeds, and by the use of plants that eradicate the weeds.

1. By working the soil (clearing it of weeds, plowing, etc.), the weeds can be exterminated or destroyed by mechanical means. This traditional method is very expensive and laborious, however.

2. Great success has been achieved by the employment of animals that consume weeds as fodder. Some imported weeds have been treated in this way. One example among many is the reduction of the prickly-pear cactus (*Opuntia*) in parts of Australia. About the year 1840 several *Opuntia* species were imported from Central America into the Australian states of Queensland and New South Wales, where they grew unexpectedly rapidly and by 1925 covered an area of some 24 million hectares. From 1913 attempts were made to check the spread of these cacti. Of some 160 animal species from North and South America known to prey on the prickly pear, 48 species were examined in a quarantine station for possibilities of damage to the ecological equilibrium of their new habitat. Of the 23 species ultimately released, 13 species (12 insect species and 1 mite) were able to propagate. Most successful was an Argentine small butterfly, the caterpillars of which ate seams out of the cacti, while putrefactive bacteria resulted in the death of the cacti. By 1936 a stretch of land in Queensland that had previously been overgrown by a dense cactus thicket was practically cleared of the weeds, and in New South Wales up to 10% more land was available for cultivation.

3. Eradication of weeds by other plants is based on the assumption that the plants that supersede are not in the nature of weeds themselves but have the effect, as far as possible, of improving the soil conditions. As the term *weed* is purely relative, many plants can have a harmful, neutral or beneficial effect on the cultivated plants and the soil according to their nature and conditions. For the most part a plant has a weed effect if it has a thick root structure which restricts the root growth of useful plants and deprives them of nutrients and trace elements. If a thick-rooted plant is replaced by one with light roots, which allow developing plants to germinate, and if by symbiosis with root bacteria combining with atmospheric nitrogen (as in the case of papilionaceous, or leguminous, flowers) it contributes to improving the soil by enriching it with nitrogen compounds, in most cases the weed problem will be solved. Covering the ground with an intermediate fruit growth of this order will also help to prevent drying out of the soil. The growth of microorganisms and the living conditions of earth-worms that help to break up the soil are also promoted in this way. For these reasons the suppression of weeds by introducing other plants to the area is certainly the most presentable and ecologically most satisfactory method of weed control.

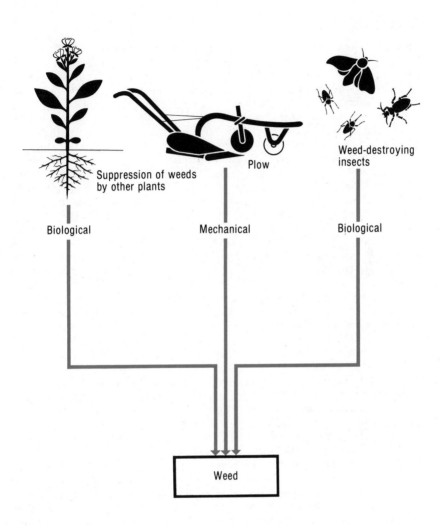

Suppression of weeds
by other plants

Plow

Weed-destroying
insects

Biological

Mechanical

Biological

Weed

VARIOUS FORMS OF ECOLOGICAL WEED CONTROL

Part Ten—Land Settlement and Configuration of the Landscape

URBANIZATION

The enormous growth in world population has been accompanied by considerable changes in its distribution. One of the most marked features of the population growth has been urbanization—migration by the rural population into big cities. These grow in consequence much more rapidly than the world population as a whole. Statistics regarding the growth of big cities in recent centuries illustrate the development. In the year 1700, no more than 40 cities in the world had populations of over 100,000, whereas the lists first published in 1870 of all the cities (of over 100,000) in the world put them at 164. By 1900 the number had risen to about 300, and by 1950 to 670. Since then the increase has been dramatic: to 1340 by 1960 and to 1872 by 1970.

Cities with a population of over a million inhabitants are a relatively recent development. In 1870 there were only 10 of these in the world; by 1900 the number had risen to 17, and by 1950 to as many as 65. By 1970 the number of cities with over a million inhabitants had more than doubled, to 152, most of the increase occurring in Asia. China has at least 17 of these giant cities, Japan and India 8 each, and Central and South America 15. In North America there are 8, in western Europe 13, in the Soviet Union 10, and in Africa 5.

In 1970, every tenth inhabitant of the earth lived in a big conurbation (continuous network of urban communities). Three percent of the inhabitants of the entire world reside in 14 major aggregations each exceeding the 5-million mark (Tokyo, Shanghai, Mexico City, Manila, Peking, New York, Sao Paulo (Brazil), London, Seoul (South Korea), Jakarta (Indonesia) to name 10). It is estimated that by 1990 more than half the population of the world is likely to be living in cities of more than 100,000 inhabitants.

Owing to heavy concentrations of people, industry and traffic, the physical and mental strains and stresses are generally greater in big cities than in small towns. As studies made in Great Britain and the United States show, in a big city there are on the average 15% less sunshine, 30% less ultraviolet radiation in winter and 10% more rain, hail or snow. There are 10% more cloudy days, 30% more mist in the summer and 100% more fog in winter. Temperatures are some 3°–8°C (37°–57°F) higher, and wind speeds are lower. In consequence of the high level of air pollution in big cities, many diseases occur on a large scale far more often. In cities of over 1 million inhabitants, lung cancer is twice as rife as in the country. Bronchitis and other lung ailments are also much more frequent. Apart from these physical effects, excessive urbanization also produces widespread suffering in the psychological and social spheres. The outcome of such developments is outlined under The Growth Catastrophe in New York, in Part Eighteen.

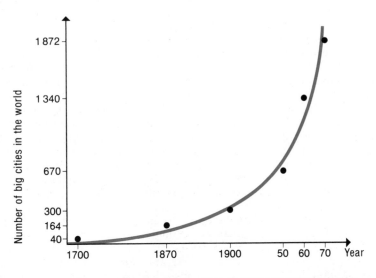

Diagram 1. DEVELOPMENT OF CITIES OF OVER 100,000 INHABITANTS

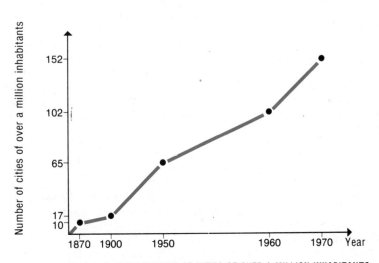

Diagram 2. DEVELOPMENT OF CITIES OF OVER A MILLION INHABITANTS

THE MICROCLIMATE IN CITIES

While it has not yet been possible to establish precisely the global changes in climate caused by industrial development, considerable variations in certain climatic elements have been found to occur in conurbations and big cities as compared with country districts (see diagram).

The lower wind velocity is due mainly to the presence of buildings, which weaken horizontal wind pressures by the irregularity they impart to the land surface. A big city usually has approach paths clear of buildings, such as watercourses, green belts and vacant plots, along which winds can penetrate to the city center and so supply fresh air to the populace. Since much waste heat is built up in the city by industrial processes, space heating, transport and accumulation from solar radiation, an upcurrent of warm air tends to form in the city center, by which air is drawn in along the approach paths from the surrounding district. This has a favorable influence on the foul city air and on the higher temperatures ruling in the city center, which in summer can often be oppressive. These advantageous climatic processes can be upset, however, if the fresh air channels are blocked, especially by tall buildings.

The concentration of chemical particles and dust suspended in the air in a big city is on the average 10 times as high as in the country. The vast quantity of finely distributed particles in the city atmosphere produces a haze canopy, which can blot out a considerable portion of sunlight. In cities the hours of sunlight can be 5%–15% less than in the country. Ultraviolet radiation in winter, which is a vital element for man in the formation of vitamin D, is thereby reduced by about 30%. At the same time the high dust content of the air impedes thermal radiation, which in consequence of the general increase in the released heat raises the temperature in the city to an undesirable degree.

A particularly striking climatic difference between town and country is the prevalence of fog, which rises in towns by an average of 100% in winter and 30% in summer. This is the result mainly of two processes: first, the emission of water vapor is greater in towns (the combustion of 1 liter of gasoline produces 1 cu m of water vapor); and second, the chemical agents suspended in the air are increased sharply. In this way the water vapor receives a large supply of condensation nuclei, and this results in turn in greater fog formation. These processes also affect the cloud canopy, which is 5%–19% greater in towns than in the country.

Another characteristic of the city climate is overheating. With their extensive asphalt, concrete and stone surfaces, cities can be compared to impervious rocks. Owing to the height of the buildings, the exposed surface of the city is multiplied several times. Stone and asphalt store much heat, the radiation of which accounts for the "baking oven" effects of summer nights. This temperature increase is intensified by the independent production of heat in homes, in industry and by transport. Then there is the lower release of heat induced by the restricted intracity vegetation. In the country about two-thirds of normal precipitation on woods and pastures evaporates or is absorbed by plants; and only about one-third drains away on the surface. In practically vegetation-free cities, on the other hand, all precipitation down to the last drop of surface moisture is drained away. As heat is expended in the process of evaporation (about 600 kcal per liter of water), this kind of heat elimination is almost totally missing in the town. In consequence, the temperature in a town is, on the average, some 0.5°–1.5°C (32.9°–34.7°F) above that ruling in the country.

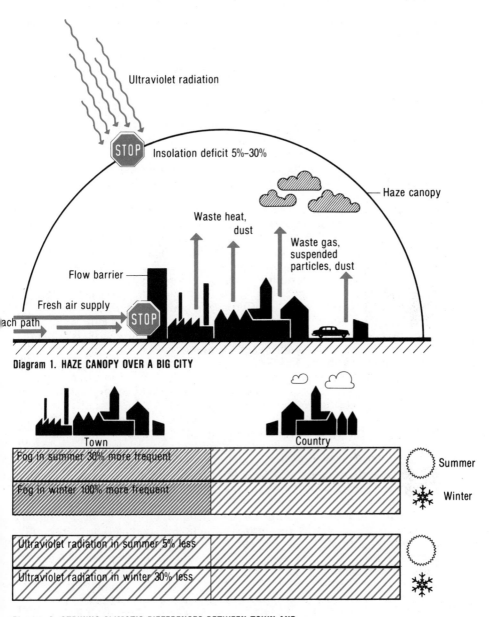

Diagram 1. HAZE CANOPY OVER A BIG CITY

Diagram 2. STRIKING CLIMATIC DIFFERENCES BETWEEN TOWN AND COUNTRY DISTRICTS

TREES AND GREEN BELTS AS MICROCLIMATE REGULATORS IN CITIES

Many of the unfavorable changes in the climatic factors in a city can be mitigated or reversed by growing plants, and by installing trees and green belts. Trees have a material effect on the dust content of the city's atmosphere. Comparative measurements taken in thoroughfares lined with trees and those free from trees show that with a comparable traffic flow the dust content in the road lined with trees is about 70% less. The reason for this is mainly that the dust adheres to the surface of the leaves and branches or settles more easily between the trees because of reduced wind pressure.

The reduction in the dust content of the air naturally has an influence on other climatic elements dependent on the dust. As dust is responsible both for the haze canopy (and the consequent reduction in hours of sunshine and of ultra-violet irradiation) and for the increase in fog (due to the condensation of water vapor), a reduction in dust by trees can have a favorable effect on the frequency and density of the haze canopy and fog.

A second important characteristic of trees in city precincts is the influence they exert on temperature and wind movement. Compared with country districts, the temperature in cities is higher. In the hot season of the year, in which the higher temperatures in cities can prove particularly unpleasant, trees can help to ameliorate the climate. In the summer, trees provide areas of shade, which because of the difference in temperature distribution sets up special air currents, which lead, in turn, to a pleasant, gentle wind movement. In the summer, too, a part of the irradiated solar energy is converted by plants (by the photosynthesis of the green leaves) into chemical energy, which moderates the rise in temperature. As plants draw water out of the ground through their roots and release it steadily by evaporation, a further part of the irradiated solar energy is converted into evaporation heat. The processes are the more effective the longer the sun shines and the higher the temperature rises. In this way an automatic control system comes into operation, which lowers the peak levels of solar radiation, temperature and aridity of the air and leads to a more acceptable city climate.

Apart from these physically measurable positive characteristics, trees and green belts in cities also have an esthetic and psychological function. They make a vital contribution to the beauty of a city and furnish identification points. A public opinion poll in big cities on the question ''What appeals to you most about this city?'' elicited the reply in most cases that verdure in the city was the prime attraction. Appreciation of this often unconscious attitude of city dwellers toward green belts accounts for the sharp reactions, from representative institutions, to the plans of municipal authorities to cut down fine trees to make way for new buildings or to widen streets. As the city dweller is usually able to visit country districts for recreational purposes only on holidays and weekends, trees and parks represent a vital opportunity to install at least a tiny fragment of nature in the city.

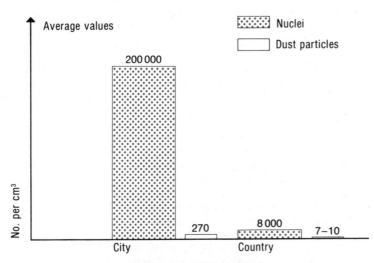

Diagram 1. AIR MIXTURES OF A PERMANENT NATURE
(nuclei: diameter 10–200 nm, dust: diameter >200 nm)

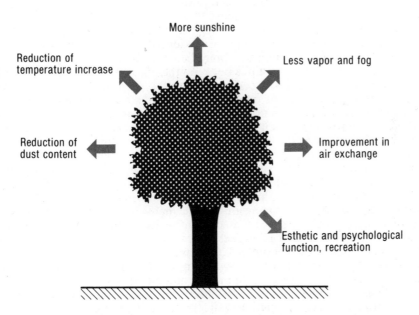

Diagram 2. VARIOUS POSITIVE EFFECTS OF TREES AND GREEN BELTS IN CITIES

Part Eleven—Transport and the Environment

One of the most serious pressures on the environment comes from motor transport. Its damage to the environment as air pollution is most severe in urban areas, in which much of the U.S. population is concentrated today.

The automobile illustrates how the free market principle, in this case the principle of freedom to select one's method of transportation, may conflict with the aim of maintaining an environment congenial to people. For a long time the growth of the automobile was regarded as an indication of prosperity and a good standard of living. The expansion in individual transport was promoted materially and psychologically from both a political and commercial point of view, and this led to the present situation.

Vehicle ownership in the United States has been increasing steadily. Between 1967 and 1977 the average number of motor vehicles in the country rose from 500 to 690 per 1000 inhabitants. The total miles annually traveled in motor vehicles increased from 665 billion miles to 1535 billion miles. In that 10-year period, the average number of automobiles rose from 407 to 535 per 1000 inhabitants. The proportion of automobiles, however, dropped from 81% to 76% of the total number of motor vehicles in the country.

In the 20 years from 1958 to 1978, about 973,000 people died in road traffic accidents in the United States. The fatality rate dropped sharply in 1974 and 1975 after highway speeds were limited to 55 miles per hour in response to the fuel shortage. Since 1976 an upward trend in the fatality rate has resumed.

Unless countermeasures are taken, it must be expected that both the number of automobiles and the deleterious effects of motor transport on the environment will continue to increase.

In the development of motor transport, several consequent effects have come into operation. These effects are essential factors in the sharp expansion in private transportation to a point beyond ecologically acceptable limits. One important relationship is between the automobile and the quality of life: deleterious effects produced by cars on the environment are one factor that lowered the quality of city life. An immediate consequence was that residents were driven from urban centers into the suburbs. Commuter travel between suburbs and the city was increased accordingly, producing a drop in the quality of life in the suburbs also. People were consequently driven to live farther and farther from the town, so consequentially motor transport went on increasing. Many people who did not use a car before came to depend on it as distances between home and business or shopping increased.

For years it appeared that these mechanisms, in their combined effects, would lead to constant extension of the highway systems, which would become increasingly independent of control by municipal authorities and planners. However, increasing fuel prices and concern over fuel shortages subsequently changed that outlook. In many cities, housing prices have gone up as people choose to live in downtown areas or other places where jobs and stores are accessible without private automobiles.

Along with fluctuations in the predicted availability of gasoline, the future promises technological advances in making automobiles more efficient and able to use alternative sources of fuel. Both factors make future trends in the automotive industry uncertain.

(in millions of gallons)

(in millions of miles)

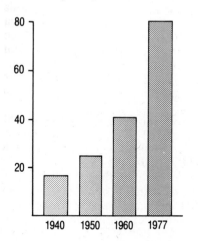

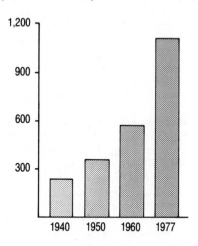

Diagram 1. U.S. FUEL CONSUMPTION

Diagram 2. TOTAL YEARLY MILEAGE OF U.S. PASSENGER CARS

Diagram 3. SALES OF PASSENGER CARS MANUFACTURED IN U.S.A.

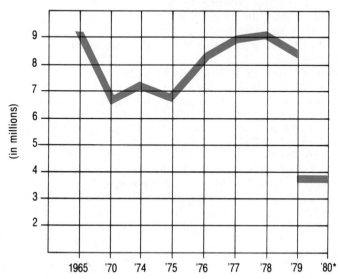

*between January 1 and June 1

GASOLINE—METHANOL IN PLACE OF LEAD

The four-, six- and eight-cylinder engines used in motor vehicles make certain demands on gasoline which are mostly determined by the engine construction. In the first place, the gas must form a highly homogeneous and highly flammable mixture with the air it needs for combustion. This mixture of fuel and air must also have a low chance of igniting spontaneously. That is, it must have a high *octane rating*. If the octane rating is low, the fuel and air mixture can ignite prematurely and disturb the smooth running of the engine and cause knocking. Until recently, the octane rating of gasoline was normally raised by the addition of lead in concentrations of between 0.3 and 0.6 grams per liter, despite the unfavorable effects it had on the environment.

Exhaustive scientific investigations have shown, however, that to obtain higher octane ratings methanol could be used as a fuel instead of leaded gasoline. This liquid (chemical formula CH_3OH) is to be distinguished from the normal fuels at present mainly in the following respects: The octane rating of methanol is substantially higher, at 130–140, than that of standard or premium fuel. The vaporization heat of methanol is about three times as great as that of gasoline. This means that methanol does not volatilize so easily as gasoline. The fusing temperature of methanol is also lower than that of gasoline. In fact it amounts to −98°C (−208.4°F), compared with a fusing temperature for gas on the order of −30° to −50°C (−86° to −122°F). Nevertheless, the calorific value of methanol is only some half that of gas (gas having about 10,000 kcal per kg, compared with about 5000 kcal per kg for methanol). This means that for a given radius of action the tank of a motor vehicle fueled by pure methanol must be about twice as large as one driven by gasoline. The lower calorific value of methanol has no serious effects on the size of the engine, however, since (owing to the reduced calorific value) the volume of air needed for combustion, compared with that for standard gasoline, is also only half as great. In order to convert an engine to run on methanol, only the carburetor needs to be converted so that for a given quantity of air for combustion, double the quantity of fuel is provided.

Owing to the considerably higher octane rating of methanol, a higher engine performance and a better energy output are consequently available. Because a high octane fuel will not ignite spontaneously, it can be compressed more than can a low octane fuel (which *will* ignite spontaneously). A higher compression ratio can be used in an engine driven by methanol, because despite the higher pressure and temperature no spontaneous ignition will occur in the fuel and air mixture. By increasing the compression ratio the performance coefficient of the engine can be raised.

The great advantage of using methanol as motor fuel, however, is its relatively favorable effects on the environment: the emission of toxic lead in the exhaust fumes is avoided. But for this purpose it is not necessary to replace the whole of the gas with methanol. Mixtures of lead-free gasoline and methanol can attain the octane ratings of standard commercial gasoline. It has been established by experiment that a normal lead-free gas with an octane rating of 90–92 can be raised to the standard octane rating of 98–100 for premium lead gas by the addition of 20% of methanol. Furthermore, a methanol engine emits considerably less carbon monoxide than a gasoline engine.

A problem concerning the use of methanol as fuel arises from possible damage to health from inhaling methanol fumes. This danger is also present, however, in the case of standard lead gas (volatilization of lead tetraethyl).

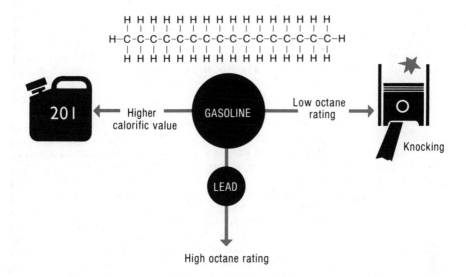

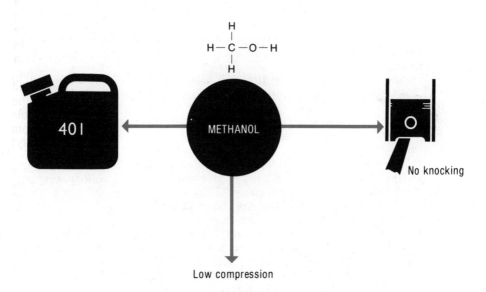

COMPARISON OF THE PROPERTIES OF GASOLINE AND METHANOL

Part Twelve—Atmospheric Pollution and Its Prevention

AEROSOLS

Combustion products from cars, industry and home heating represent by far the biggest source of air pollution caused by man's activities. Of the substances released into the atmosphere in this way, well over 100 have been identified as contaminants. The solid matter included in them contains over 20 metallic elements. The proportion of organic compounds is much higher, and includes numerous aliphatic (mostly saturated, mainly straight chain) and aromatic (unsaturated, annular) hydrocarbons, and also phenols, acids, bases, and many other compounds. By reactions between contaminants upon their arrival in the air, new compounds can also be formed; such reactions include photochemical ones (see also Photochemical Smog, later).

Among the atmospheric pollutants, substances in suspension consisting of solid and/or liquid particles are known as aerosols. These emanate either from condensation processes, by which molecular masses combine to form bigger particles (e.g., cloud formation from liquid particles), or from dispersion processes, by which coarse material is split into finer particles (e.g., flue dust from coal dust combustion). An essential feature of aerosols is the size of their particles. Coarse dust and soot, flue dust and the like, whose particles are over 10 μm in size, settle very quickly from the atmosphere under the force of gravity. Finer particles, on the other hand, with a diameter of less than 5 μm, remain suspended in the atmosphere. In this case the force of gravity is outweighed by the Brownian molecular movement in the atmosphere. For particles this small, the force of gravity is overruled by Brownian molecular movement, or the random motion of particles caused by their collision with molecules in the surrounding air. The velocity of aerosol particles due to Brownian movement is greater than their rate of vertical descent. Consequently, aerosols can be distributed by air currents almost like gases.

Owing to their low concentrations, natural particles such as fog (1–40 μm), bacteria (1–15 μm), plant spores (10–30 μm) and pollen (20–60 μm) do not usually cause atmospheric pollution; and from a medical point of view, furthermore, they are generally harmless (except for possible allergic reactions such as hay fever). Particles released by artificial processes, such as cement powder (10–150 μm), flue dust (3–80 μm), quartz and asbestos powder (0.5–10 μm), oil smoke (0.03–1 μm), tobacco smoke (0.01–0.15 μm) and radioactive aerosols (0.1–20 μm), can give rise to serious atmospheric pollution according to their concentration. They can also cause damage to living organisms. Particularly insidious are those aerosols that, owing to their diminutive size, can penetrate into the lungs.

On an extended area, aerosols can display considerable surface powers. This enables them to accumulate gas molecules, which facilitates chemical reactions of aerosols with the surrounding gases. Many substances which in the compact state combine very slowly with oxygen, oxidize in this way immediately when they enter the atmosphere as fine powder.

Finally, the effects of energy radiation from the sun can be severely modified by solid or liquid particles dispersed in the air. Such particles absorb the radiation and pass on the heat rapidly to surrounding gas molecules, which for their part can be fully pervious to radiant energy, so that without the aerosols no heating would occur. Owing to their effect as condensation nuclei, on which water vapor can be deposited, they also affect the formation of mist or fog.

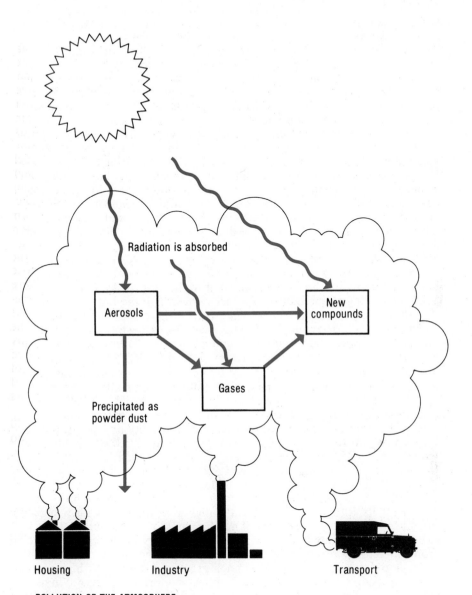

Radiation is absorbed

Aerosols

New compounds

Gases

Precipitated as powder dust

Housing

Industry

Transport

POLLUTION OF THE ATMOSPHERE

DAMAGE TO HEALTH BY DUST PARTICLES

Dust is generated by combustion processes (in power stations, by motor vehicles and in homes), and in various forms of industrial undertakings (cement works, for example). From a medical point of view, dust can be classified under two heads: coarse dust and fine dust. In recent times the emission of coarse dust has been cut down considerably by the installation of dust filters in new industrial plants, which can have an efficiency rating as high as 99% (electric dust filters). In the steel producing industry, for example, dust ejection has been reduced in the past ten years or so to about one quarter. But this reduction relates primarily to coarse dust.

In a medical context, coarse dust is less dangerous, as the dust particles are so large that they cannot penetrate the lung vesicles (alveoli). The real medical problem stems from fine dust (particles measuring 5–10 μm), which is only partially arrested by the filter mechanism in the human respiratory system. It gets into the lung vesicles and can lodge there for some time. A complicating factor is that fine dust often contains poisons, such as 3,4-benzopyrene which causes cancer, and heavy metal oxides, such as vanadium compounds, which act as catalyzers. These toxic substances can then develop their effects in the sensitive lung vesicles directly. By the catalyzing effects of various metallic oxides, moreover, gaseous sulfur dioxide can be converted into the even more dangerous sulfur trioxide, which for its part, in conjunction with the moisture present in the lung vesicles, forms sulfuric acid. According to the industrial process by which the fine dust is formed, the following poisons have been identified in it so far: arsenic, beryllium, cadmium, lead, selenium, thallium, uranium, asbestos, chromium compounds and mercury compounds, among others. Particular mention may also be made of fine dust composed of lead particles from automobile exhaust fumes and of fine dust emitted by refineries. To keep their distillation processes going, the latter consume the tailings from crude oil refineries.

An extensive American research program carried out in 1958 and 1959 (the Nashville Study Program) established a direct connection between the fine dust content of the atmosphere and the mortality and sickness rates of the population. In the course of the investigations, 375,000 individuals were examined and 25,000 deaths that had occurred between 1949 and 1958 were looked into. The findings established a direct connection between the floating dust content in the atmosphere and mortality from cancer in the digestive tract, the prostate gland and the bladder. Furthermore, mortality from cancer in all its forms was significantly higher in districts with a high dust content compared with districts of medium and low air pollution. It was also established that deaths from all diseases of the respiratory organs (especially from influenza and inflammation of the lungs) and the number of asthma cases and deaths of infants were much greater in districts of high air pollution. Altogether it emerged that an increase in mortality occurred in districts which had a floating dust content in the atmosphere of over 80–100 μg per cubic meter of air (24-hour average). Nevertheless, the legal limit for dust suspended in the atmosphere stands at 100 μg per cu m (long term) and 200 μg per cu m (short term).

Further investigations into the current trend of fine dust concentrations in the atmosphere have been carried out in recent years in the Ruhr district by the Medical Institute for Air Hygiene and Silicosis Research at the University of Düsseldorf. From this it emerges that the coarse dust content of the air has declined sharply, but the fine dust concentration in ventilating air has remained fairly constant (see diagram).

Diagram 1. AVERAGE ANNUAL MORTALITY FROM CHRONIC DISEASES OF THE
RESPIRATORY ORGANS ACCORDING TO THE DUST CONTENT OF THE ATMOSPHERE
(FOR MEN BETWEEN 50 AND 69 YEARS OF AGE IN BUFFALO AND ITS ENVIRONS)

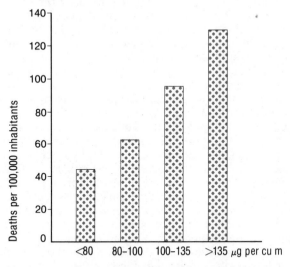

Floating dust content of the air per 24 hours

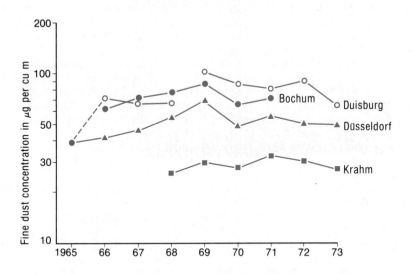

Diagram 2. ANNUAL AVERAGE RATIO OF FINE DUST CONCENTRATIONS AT FOUR
CONTROL POINTS (ASSESSMENT PERIOD: 1965 to 1973)

CHEMICAL INDUSTRY

Chemical reactions do not always continue to completion, so that in addition to the desired product, by-products occur, which on cost grounds are often released by the chemical industry into the atmosphere or discharged into the drainage system. The spectrum of products manufactured by the chemical industry is extraordinarily wide-ranging: inorganic substances such as sulfuric, nitric, hydrochloric, hydrofluoric and phosphoric acid and their salts; organic substances such as hydrocarbons, fertilizers, plant protection and pest destruction agents, plastics, man-made fibers, paints and lacquers, pharmaceutical products, adhesives, detergents, cosmetic products, polishing powders, and leather and textile accessories.

The principal emissions given off by the chemical industry are gases and vapors of organic chemical compounds such as hydrocarbons and their halogen derivatives, aldehydes, ketones, carboxylic acids, and nitrogen and sulfur compounds (amines, mercaptans, disulfides); gases and vapors of inorganic chemical compounds such as hydrogen sulfide, hydrochloric acid, fluorine compounds, sulfur dioxide, and hydrogen phosphides; and finally toxic powders such as fluorides and carbides, and powders from iron alloys, arsenic and asbestos. Extensive control is necessary, partly because the human sense of smell is very sensitive to substances emitted by chemical industries (such as hydrogen sulfide and mercaptans), even when they are highly rarefied. Thiophenol, for instance, is still perceptible to the human sense of smell in concentrations as low as 1:10 billion. To eliminate these substances, purification plants of a very high degree of efficiency are required. Furthermore, the chemical reactions take place in many cases under very heavy pressure. For safety reasons the reaction apparatuses and accessories must therefore be equipped with pressure-relief facilities (safety valves). In the event of breakdowns, which can be fairly frequent in a chemical works, the noxious substances are released in relatively large quantities. Through the safety valve and connecting attachments of the pipelines, pumps and storage tanks, etc., a multiplicity of small potential outlets are created, the sealing of which in the face of all contingencies cannot be guaranteed. Owing to the large number of noxious chemical substances in existence and the rapid changes that occur in chemical production, the overall technical development of specific filter appliances to meet all requirements is very hard to achieve.

Altogether the state of air purification technology in the chemical industry is thoroughly unsatisfactory. This is the more serious in that by 1985 the chemical industry reckons on an increase in turnover to about 3.2 times the level in 1970. A particularly sharp rise in production is planned for the sectors that affect the environment most seriously. These sectors, with figures in parentheses showing the average annual production increase planned by 1985, are crop protection and pest destruction agents (3.9%), plastics (4.1%), mineral and coal-tar dyes (3.4%), man-made fibers (4.8%), pharmaceuticals (3.6%), etc.

So far, improvements in the discharge of chemicals have been achieved mainly in the field of inorganic production. By the adoption of a new process for sulfuric acid production, the discharge of sulfur dioxide has been reduced by about 80% in relation to conventional production methods. This new technology was introduced not least because it has commercial advantages from the point of view of sulfur recovery.

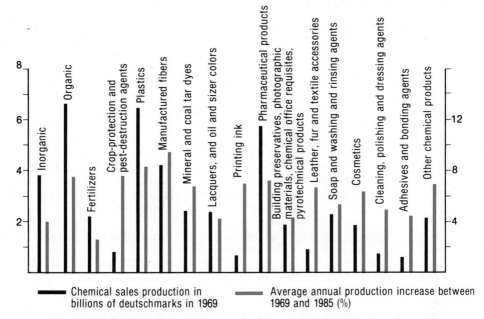

Chemical sales production in billions of deutschmarks in 1969

Average annual production increase between 1969 and 1985 (%)

Diagram 1. DEVELOPMENT OF THE CHEMICAL INDUSTRY IN WEST GERMANY BY PRODUCTION SECTORS

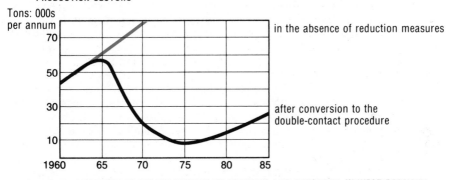

Tons: 000s per annum

in the absence of reduction measures

after conversion to the double-contact procedure

Diagram 2. DISCHARGE OF SULFUR DIOXIDE BY SULFURIC ACID FACTORIES IN WEST GERMANY

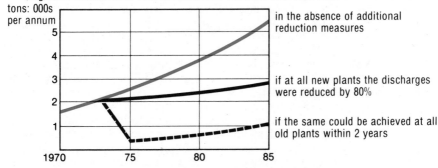

tons: 000s per annum

in the absence of additional reduction measures

if at all new plants the discharges were reduced by 80%

if the same could be achieved at all old plants within 2 years

Diagram 3. DISCHARGES OF MAINLY ORGANIC CHEMICAL GASES AND VAPORS IN THE PRODUCTION OF CROP-PROTECTION AND PEST-DESTRUCTION AGENTS IN WEST GERMANY

PETROLEUM INDUSTRY

The petroleum industry is characterized by the regular discharge of hydrocarbons and other organic compounds and of sulfur dioxide and fine dust. Crude oil imported from the oil-producing countries is processed in refineries into various petroleum products, in particular heating oil and gasoline. In the refining process, the crude oil is heated and vaporized and then condensed again at various temperatures. In this way the varying fractions, from highly volatile gasoline to heavy heating oil, are separated. In the process, tarlike bitumen is left behind for further processing in its turn.

In order to produce the energy needed to vaporize the crude oil, the distillation residues are used in the refineries as the main fuel. These residues contain large quantities of sulfur, which, after combustion, is given off into the atmosphere in the form of sulfur dioxide (see Part Fourteen). In addition, according to where it comes from, the material consumed can contain larger or smaller quantities of fine dust, which is also given off with the flue gas.

The second group of components in air pollution by refineries are organic substances such as hydrocarbons. These are discharged in the main from various sources, at ground level, spread over the entire area of the works, such as storage tanks, flanges, safety valves, vents, seals, settling tanks and torch flares. These organic gases and fumes are in some cases very pungent, and so can cause serious nuisance in the vicinity of the refinery. Between 0.4% and 1% of the crude oil put through a refinery is given off in the form of organic vapors into the environment. Assuming it to have been no more than 0.4%, direct discharges of organic gases and vapors from leaky pipelines and valves come to about 0.08%, the process gases of the torch flares to about 0.23%, and the heating gases of the torch flares and the discharges from the waste water treatment to 0.02% each. On the average the torch has a combustion efficiency rate of no more than 50%–70%. This gives an average discharge rate of organic gases and vapors of 4.3 tons per day per million tons annual average crude oil throughput for the refinery. It is assumed at present that one-third of production losses by the petroleum industry pass into the atmosphere as hydrocarbons.

An important source of losses is the storage tank. This is best shown by an example: At a temperature of 20°C (68°F) benzene has a vapor pressure of 75 millibars. This represents a saturation density of 320 g per cu m. When a benzene tank with a capacity of 100,000 cu m is filled at this temperature, with a fixed-top tank, and assuming that only half the saturation density is achieved, about 1.6 tons of benzene will be discharged in the process. When instead of the fixed-top tank a floating-top tank or a fixed-top tank with a floating cover is used, the discharge will drop to about 300 kg of benzene.

Discharges into the environment also occur when finished products are loaded into vehicles and vessels for distribution. Each time gasoline is loaded into a container or tanker for transport by land or sea, gas vapor will be discharged into the atmosphere with the expelled air to the amount of about 1.3% of the gasoline transported. The situation is very similar in the case of petrochemistry. Petrochemical production plants are usually situated in close proximity to refineries, and in them the end products from the refineries are processed further. The petrochemical plants also contain extensive pipeline systems and numerous valves and flanges through which hydrocarbons and other organic compounds are discharged. It is estimated that on the average some 1% of the substances processed in petrochemistry escape in the production process.

in millions of tons per annum

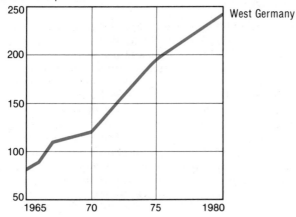

West Germany

Diagram 1. GROWTH OF REFINERY CAPACITY

in tons: 000s per annum

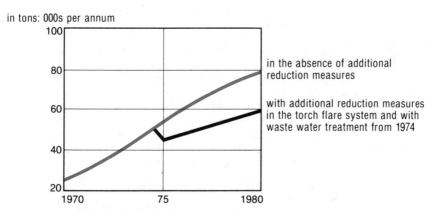

in the absence of additional
reduction measures

with additional reduction measures
in the torch flare system and with
waste water treatment from 1974

Diagram 2. DISCHARGE OF ORGANIC GASES AND VAPORS FROM ETHYLENE
PRODUCTION IN WEST GERMANY

in tons: 000s per annum

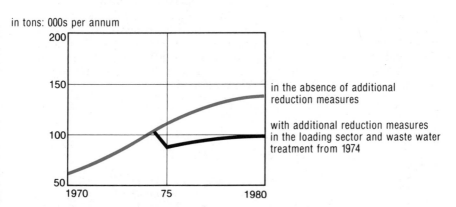

in the absence of additional
reduction measures

with additional reduction measures
in the loading sector and waste water
treatment from 1974

Diagram 3. DISCHARGE OF ORGANIC GASES AND VAPORS FROM REFINERIES
IN NORTH-RHINE WESTPHALIA

POLLUTION FROM SPRAYING

A good example of serious irreversible damage to the environment caused by an industrial product which was previously regarded as neutral in its effects is the spray gun, which is in increasing use today for a variety of purposes. As a propellant, the spray gun contains chlorofluorocarbons (CF_2Cl_2 and $CFCl_3$). When the spray gun is used, the propellants are released into the atmosphere. Until recently it was believed that the compounds were so stable that they would not be absorbed or reduced by either plants, soil or water. They were consequently regarded as harmless. In 1974, however, American scientists at the University of Michigan discovered that chlorofluorocarbons could cause serious disturbances in the environment. The gas rises into the stratosphere and damages the ozone belt surrounding the earth; the ozone belt intercepts a large part of the ionizing radiation coming in from outside and so reduces damage to the earth by this radiation.

The process goes as follows. The chlorofluorocarbon molecules are broken down by the strong ultraviolet radiation in the stratosphere. In this way chlorine atoms are released, which break down ozone molecules by a catalytic process (see diagram). The chlorine atom itself is not affected by the process, and in course of time it can split any number of ozone molecules. It is assumed that some 10^{31} ozone molecules per second are broken down in this way today.

The diagram indicates three results of these investigations. In Case 1 it is assumed that the use of spray guns and the consequent release of chlorofluorocarbons will go on increasing in the future at the same rate as today. The disintegration rate of the ozone belt, which has been fairly low hitherto, will then increase sharply after 1980, and this can result in considerable damage on the earth's surface (increase in cancer rate). For Case 2 it is assumed that use of spray guns will increase until 1975 and will remain constant thereafter at the level for 1975. In this case, too, the ozone belt is likely to be seriously upset, though at a slower rate.

A crucial problem in this process is illustrated by Case 3: that of ecological time-lag. Even if the release of chlorofluorocarbons can be checked completely today, the decomposition of ozone by the waste gases released previously will still rise until 1990, and only then will it decline slowly over the years.

The results indicated are based on the most optimistic assumptions. The American scientists point out that the reality could be considerably worse, since in their calculations for the chlorofluorocarbon molecule (CF_2Cl_2 and $CFCl_3$) they have taken account of the release and catalytic effect of only one chlorine atom in each case. It is highly probable, nonetheless, that all four halogen atoms (and therefore the fluorine atoms as well) per molecule will display the effects described.

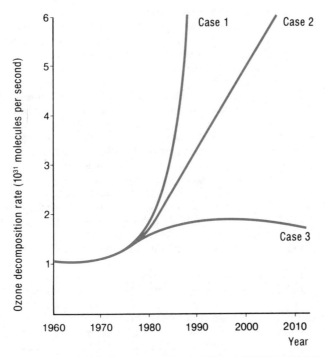

Diagram 1. NATURAL DECOMPOSITION OF OZONE IN EQUILIBRIUM WITH THE FORMATION OF OZONE

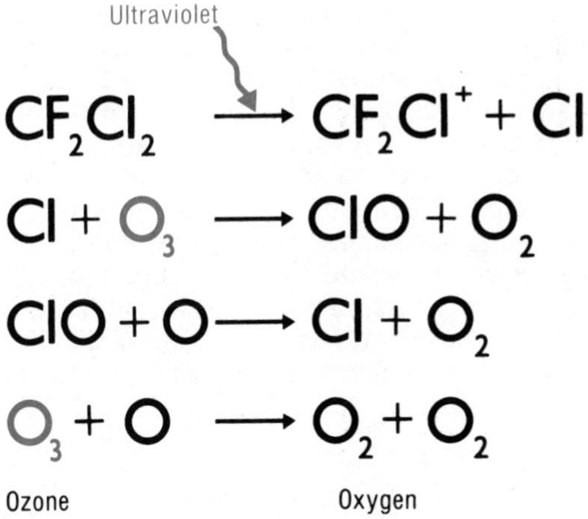

$$CF_2Cl_2 \xrightarrow{\text{Ultraviolet}} CF_2Cl^+ + Cl$$

$$Cl + O_3 \longrightarrow ClO + O_2$$

$$ClO + O \longrightarrow Cl + O_2$$

$$O_3 + O \longrightarrow O_2 + O_2$$

Ozone   Oxygen

Diagram 2. CHEMICAL REACTION OF OZONE DESTRUCTION

PHOTOCHEMICAL SMOG

Photochemical smog is formed from atmospheric pollutants that are generated under the influence of solar radiation.

The first effects of photochemical smog were established three decades ago in Los Angeles, where a sharply rising concentration of exhaust fumes from motor vehicles coincided with the unfavorable meteorological situation of frequent inversion weather conditions. At present there are over 7.5 million people living in Los Angeles in a residential area of some 4000 square kilometers (1500 square miles). From the Pacific Ocean a cool breeze is constantly blowing, which gives rise to a sharp atmospheric inversion at an altitude of 500–1000 meters (1640–3280 feet). Above this mass of cool air blown in from the ocean, layers of warm air build up at the altitude of the surrounding mountains. In this way a vertical exchange of air is held in check, and a meteorological "cover" is formed. All waste gases that form in Los Angeles are retained below this canopy layer and are concentrated there. This is one of the essential prerequisites for the formation of photochemical smog. On top of this, on many days in the year in sunny California, the sun shines through the cover of the inversion layer. In the enclosed air space the various pollutants are then transformed under the effects of sunlight.

Although it was long thought that this form of smog was peculiar to Los Angeles (for London smog, see next section), it is now known that photochemical smog occurs also in many other industrial agglomerations whenever certain chemical pollutants are exposed to sunlight in an enclosed air space. Photochemical smog has been identified in recent years in congested areas on the East Coast of the United States, in South America, in Japan, in Europe and elsewhere.

Photochemical smog manifests itself in the form of a more or less dense haze covering the town, which restricts visibility by the blurring of contrasts due to dissipation of light. The dissipation of light is caused by aerosols generated by chemical reactions occasioned by smog.

These chemical reactions are highly complicated, and have not been fully analyzed to this day. Initial products include various hydrocarbons, sulfur dioxide and nitrogen oxide. Thus unburned standard gasoline alone contains over 200 different hydrocarbons in the categories of aliphatics, olefins and aromatics. Greater still is the number of hydrocarbons that, because of incomplete combustion, are emitted in exhaust fumes.

The first reaction stage is the formation of oxidizing substances under the influence of photodissociation. The most important reaction is probably the formation of ozone (see Part Fourteen). Another important factor is the oxidation of sulfur dioxide to sulfuric acid in sunlight. In the process ozone is produced as a by-product. This reaction occurs in the following stages:

$$SO_2 + sunlight \rightarrow (SO_2)^+$$
$$(SO_2)^+ + O_2 \rightarrow (SO_4)^+$$
$$(SO_4)^+ + O_2 \rightarrow SO_3 + O_3$$
$$H_2O + SO_3 \rightarrow H_2SO_4 \text{ (sulfuric acid)}$$

In the second phase of the reaction, the ozone combines as an oxidizing agent with many initial products of atmospheric pollution, whereby new, often highly corrosive pollutants are formed. In the following processes certain important reactions and initial products are represented.

By the reaction of excess ozone with nitrogen dioxide, nitric acid is formed under the following formula:

$$2NO_2 + O_3 \rightarrow N_2O_5 + O_2$$
$$N_2O_5 + H_2O \rightarrow 2HNO_3 \text{ (nitric acid)}$$

The corrosive nitric acid occurs in the same way as sulfuric acid in the form of aerosols.

Owing to the effects of ozone and other oxidizing agents on hydrocarbons, chemical radicals are formed. These include alkyl, alcohol oxide, peroxide, acyl group, formic and peroxyacyl radicals. These radicals are chemically highly corrosive. They can either exert their noxious effects on human beings directly or produce further chemical reactions in conjunction with other substances, as a result of which new noxious substances will be formed. Overall, the number of possible photochemical primary and secondary reactions in this smog is estimated at several hundred.

The medical effects of photochemical smog are hard to pinpoint. Certainly no direct cases of death have been established (as in the case of London smog). It is not disputed, however, that various lung ailments, especially bronchitis, are caused and aggravated by smog. An increase in allergic complaints such as hay fever has also been found to result from exposure to photochemical smog. The corrosive substances in photochemical smog have a highly irritant effect on the mucous membranes in man, especially in the eye. Altogether the physical and mental well-being and the vitality of man can be seriously impaired thereby.

Photochemical smog can cause severe damage to organic materials such as rubber, leather, textiles and paintwork. Ozone and other oxidizing agents have a bleaching effect on coloring matter and render vehicle tires brittle. Cracks in automobile tires were one of the first effects of damage by smog to be noted in Los Angeles.

Damage to crops by photochemical smog is a much more serious matter. Characteristic mold and discoloration are to be noted on crops such as tobacco, spinach, tomatoes and lettuce exposed to concentrations of no more than a few parts per billion of certain oxidizing agents and chemical radicals. This severely reduces absorption of water by the plants and photosynthesis in them. Harvest yields, especially in the case of grapes and citrus fruits, suffer accordingly. In areas affected by smog, grape harvests are reduced on the average by 60%. An estimate made in the United States in 1966 put the total damage caused by photochemical smog in the region of $500 million.

LONDON SMOG

That there is a fundamental connection between air pollution and damage to health has been recognized for many years. Doctors, scientists and public health centers were alerted to the problem when serious smog disasters occurred in the valley of the River Maas in Belgium in 1930 and in the city center of Donora in the United States in 1948. Many people died as a result, and the coincidence in time of the atmospheric pollution and the resulting health damage highlighted the causes of the maladies and deaths.

Considerably more action for the reduction of atmospheric pollution was prompted by the occurrence of fog in London. From December 5 to 9, 1952, many regions in Great Britain were cloaked in fog. Particularly affected was the wide valley of the river Thames with London in its midst. Within about 12 hours of the appearance of the heavy fog (which owing to a sharp inversion of weather conditions entrapped all the waste gases from the city), an extremely large number of people in London were smitten with breathing difficulties. This was soon followed by an unusually high number of deaths. The symptoms of the malady were severe coughing and expectoration, increased nasal secretions, sore throats and sudden vomiting. Generally speaking the troubles began without warning. Many of the most serious cases, mainly people already suffering from chronic bronchitis, asthma or pulmonary fibrosis, occurred on the third or fourth day of fog. The symptoms of patients seriously affected were shortness of breath, cyanosis, fever, rattling in the throat and bronchospasms.

A subsequent assessment of the mortality figures revealed that in 14 days of the smog disaster 4000 more people died altogether than was normal in the period. From the very first day of the catastrophe, the number of deaths increased significantly; and the increase was greater in the center of London than in the outer ring of the city. A further 4000 people died in the following weeks and months. All age groups were affected, but those over 45 years of age and babies of up to 1 year most severely. In the age group from 1 to 14 years the death rate during the smog catastrophe was 1.3 times the previous rate, for over 45 year olds 2.8 times, and for babies 2.2 times.

During the smog disaster the concentration of sulfur dioxide in the atmosphere amounted on the average to 0.7 ppm, or about 6 times the normal level. The smoke concentration was about 5 times the normal. At that time it was still assumed that such a level was medically harmless.

Subsequently a number of other cases of smog occurred in London: January 3 to 6, 1956 (1000 deaths); December 2 to 5, 1957 (800); December 5 to 10, 1962 (700); and January 7 to 22, 1963 (700). It was only after these further catastrophes, in which thousands more victims perished, that atmospheric pollution over London was severely cut back by intensive countermeasures, so that the danger of serious smog disasters in London now seems to have been averted. By a change in heating techniques and by insisting on the use of smokeless fuels, the hours of sunshine in winter have been raised in London by 70%.

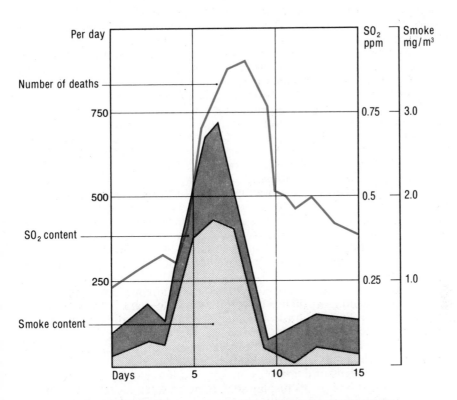

Per day

Number of deaths

750

SO₂ content

500

250

Smoke content

Days   5   10   15

SO₂ ppm   Smoke mg/m³

0.75   3.0

0.5   2.0

0.25   1.0

Diagram 1. THE DEATH RATE OF THE POPULATION IN CONSEQUENCE OF THE SMOKE AND SULFUR DIOXIDE CONTENT OF THE AIR OVER LONDON DURING THE SMOG DISASTER OF DECEMBER 1952

Inversion barrier

SMOG

City

Settles in bronchi and alveoli of lungs

Diagram 2. SMOG IN A CITY

CROP DAMAGE CAUSED BY ATMOSPHERIC POLLUTION

Among the destructive agents that cause damage to plants, and so to agriculture and forestry in general, sulfur dioxide and fluoride compounds play a leading role.

The substance that has been most thoroughly investigated so far is sulfur dioxide (see also Part Fourteen). This gas, which is released mainly by combustion processes, penetrates into the pores in the leaves of plants, combines there with water to form sulfurous acids, and so results in local poisoning. Individual kinds of plant react very differently to a particular maximum concentration of sulfur dioxide, which leads in all cases to the death of the plant cells. This probably depends in the first place on the different speeds at which the sulfur dioxide is absorbed by the leaves. Plants with sappy leaves and high physiological activity, such as corn, alfalfa, cotton and grapevines, are in general more sensitive, as in their case the sulfur dioxide is transmitted more rapidly and its poisonous effects develop faster as a result. Plants with pithy leaves or needles, on the other hand, are more or less resistant. Yet even for these, considerable damage has been reported. At many points in the Ruhr Valley in Germany, coniferous trees have been killed by the effects of sulfur dioxide. Plant growths that can keep their pores closed longer, such as corn and oak trees, are less sensitive to sulfur dioxide.

In lower concentrations, sulfur dioxide will affect photosynthesis and respiration in plants. At higher concentrations the plant cells die off. The rate of photosynthesis can also be affected when sulfur dioxide concentrations that would normally damage the leaves are operative for only a few hours. In these cases, however, after a temporary drop in assimilation performance the plants are able to recover.

The visible signs of damage by sulfur dioxide are different for different plants. One-seed-leaf plants display something between a slight speckling on the tips of the leaves and a complete bleaching of the leaves. In the case of two-seed-leaf plants, clearly defined speckles appear, which can be red, brown or yellowish. The leaves then dry up, curl and fall off. Under a microscope, disturbance of the plasma flow can be noted, often accompanied by plasmolysis. Through disturbance of the chlorophyll and tannin, color variations can arise.

The concentration at which sulfur dioxide has a toxic effect on plants depends very much on the presence of the toxic agent hydrogen fluoride. Concentrations of 0.3–0.5 mg of sulfur dioxide per cubic meter of air, which can normally be sustained by plants under optimum environmental conditions for a long time without damage, give rise to irreversible damage to the crops as soon as the merest trace of hydrogen fluoride gas occurs in the atmosphere.

Among the gaseous fluoride compounds that are highly injurious to plant life, hydrogen fluoride and silicon tetrafluoride are toxic in concentrations of only 0.0001 ppm. Furthermore, fluorides can build up on the inside and outside of the leaves and so attain concentrations of over 30–50 ppm. In short reaction periods of about one hour, high concentrations of fluoride can cause damage equivalent to that produced by sulfur dioxide. Lower concentrations operating for periods of weeks or months can lead to the death of the points and edges of the leaves and to the formation of smaller leaves and shoots. In contrast to the speckles produced by sulfur dioxide, which are usually gray or bleached, the dead parts of leaves affected by fluoride gases are brown.

AIR PURIFICATION—THE ELECTROSTATIC PRECIPITATOR

Air purification and the recovery of valuable raw materials, especially from fine powder, is often possible only by means of an electrostatic precipitator. The construction, size and performance of such a dust extractor depend to a large extent on the working conditions existing; and they will also be geared to the volume of gas, in particular to its temperature, condensation point, and dust content and to the physical and chemical properties of the dust and the supporting gas. Electrostatic precipitators are available for the separation of dust particles in whatever quantity and of whatever size. They are used in almost all dust-producing plants in industrial sectors such as mining, the chemical industry, blast furnaces, foundries, power stations and garbage disposal.

According to the method of dust extraction (scaling or rinsing), a dis-

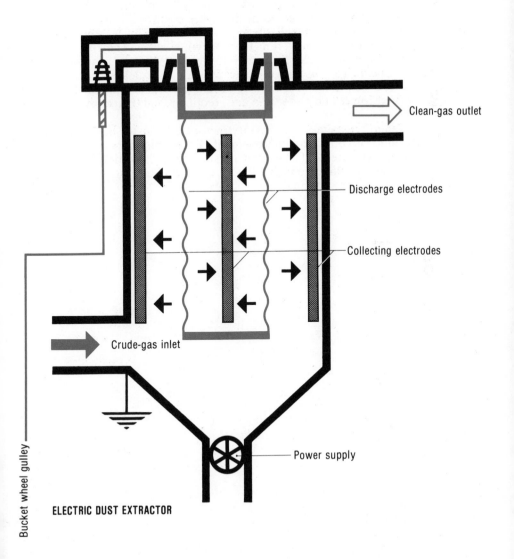

Clean-gas outlet

Discharge electrodes

Collecting electrodes

Crude-gas inlet

Bucket wheel gulley

Power supply

ELECTRIC DUST EXTRACTOR

tinction is made between dry and wet electric precipitators, though in their construction and method of operation they do not differ greatly from one another.

The air to be cleared of dust is passed between electrodes with a large potential difference (50 kilovolts). The negative electrode (the discharge or exit electrode) with a small radius of curvature can be made of wire, whereas the positive electrode (the collecting electrode) consists of a plate or tube made of sheet metal and having a large radius of curvature. In the vicinity of the negative electrode a discharge field will form. Electrons travel from there to the collecting electrode, which operates as an anode. In this way the electrons strike the gas atoms, which each emit an electron. This process goes on developing rapidly, owing to the newly released atoms, in the form of a chain reaction. On the basis of this chain reaction an avalanche of electrons travels constantly toward the collecting electrode. Thus both the negative electrons and the positive gas ions accumulate on the individual dust particles and charge them. The negatively charged particles travel under the influence of the electric field to the collecting electrode, while the positively charged particles go to the discharge electrode. Dust accumulates on both electrodes, from which it has to be removed. This is done by scaling or rinsing the layer of dust from the collecting plate. The removed dust drops in the form of cakes or clouds into the dust chamber situated below the electric field. The discharge electrodes are also cleared by scaling or rinsing. The high voltages required to ensure good separation are provided by an electric-powered high-tension unit, rectified, and then conveyed to the electrodes.

The general installation of dust extractors in industry has made a considerable contribution to the improvement of the emission situation. It may be assumed, therefore, that despite increasing industrialization, the emission of dust would decline considerably if all old plant installations were equipped with dust extractors.

Part Thirteen—Water Pollution (and Its Prevention) and Water Supplies

POLLUTION OF THE NORTH SEA

The North Sea is one of the most severely polluted seas in the world. Poisonous and waste matter is deposited into the North Sea by the rivers, by drainpipes and sewers, by the discharge of refuse from ships, and by contaminants washed out of the atmosphere. The rivers flowing into the

Severe pollution
Moderate pollution
Mild pollution
Regular discharge of waste from ships

Sapropel

Cinders and residues
from power stations

Waste water from
plastics production

Digested sludge

Sapropel from London

Acids.
salts

Iron sulphate. sulphuric acid

EXTENT OF WATER POLLUTION IN VARIOUS PARTS OF THE NORTH SEA

North Sea carry waste water into it from Great Britain, eastern France, Belgium, Netherlands, Luxembourg, West Germany, Switzerland, Denmark and Norway, because these waters have been quite inadequately purified by the responsible local authorities or by the industries concerned. Substances that are not reducible—such as salts from potash mines, heavy-metal waste from industrial undertakings, pesticides from agriculture, and phosphates from cleaning fluids and agricultural processes and from other sources—pass almost unchanged into the sea.

At many points on the North Sea coast, sewage from municipal districts and industrial estates is discharged directly into the coastal waters. In West Germany there are direct sewage discharge pipes at Wilhelmshaven, Bremerhaven, Cuxhaven and from the Frisian Islands. Although the volume discharged in this way is less than the waste water discharged by the rivers, it is still a serious hazard, since biologically irreducible pollutants are discharged unchanged into the North Sea. The discharge of domestic sewage water also has unpleasant esthetic and hygienic effects along the bathing beaches.

It is estimated that some 5000 tons of refuse from plastics manufacture, 1.6 million tons of waste from titanium oxide production (27% sulfuric acid and 6% iron sulfate), 18,000 tons of refuse from enzyme production (two-thirds of it organic), 60,000 tons from synthetic fabric manufacture, 4.5 million tons of sapropel, 40,000 tons of inorganic and organic acids and salts and a variety of other refuse are "disposed" of each year in the sea. By the discharge of sapropel from the city of London alone, each year the North Sea receives some 800 tons of zinc, 200 tons of copper, 100 tons of chromium, 50 tons of nickel and 20 tons of cadmium.

It has been realized only in recent years that a considerable amount of sea pollution is caused by noxious substances being washed out of the atmosphere. It is now known that about 3 million tons of sulfur dioxide, 1 million tons of solid matter, 300 tons of DDT, 30 tons of mercury and 1000 tons of lead are fed into the North Sea in this way every year.

A further source of pollution is shipping. Ships discharge almost all their refuse and waste water into the sea unpurified. The main items concerned are oils, sewage, packaging, bottles, kitchen refuse and tailings from chemical tankers. It has been estimated that about 100,000 tons of mineral oil find their way into the North Sea in this way every year, and not only seawater is contaminated thereby (1 liter of oil contaminates 1 million liters of water), but also adjoining bathing beaches.

Considerable further pollution of the North Sea is likely to result from the exploitation of the large reserves of natural gas and petroleum that have been located on the seabed.

OIL SLICKS—DISPERSAL BY MEANS OF A FLOATING SUCTION PUMP

Spills of oil from containers and appliances in which it is stored or utilized are among the most insidious forms of water pollution, as they spread very rapidly over wide stretches of water and seriously impair the exchange of gas and the other life functions of the biotope. For the most part, dispersal of the oil film is left to the self-purifying properties of the sea itself. The lighter constituents in the oil evaporate within one to two weeks. The less volatile components combine with the seawater to form a dark viscous slick, which after a few weeks either sinks to the seabed, drifts up onto beaches as lumps of tar, or collects in eddy currents.

Chemical processes to get the oil to sink by the application of dispersion agents or emulsifiers encounter strong opposition. Their use is particularly questionable in shallow coastal waters, as they are very capable of poisoning the creatures living on the seabed and in the water above it.

The best solution seems to be to confine the oil spills to the sea's surface by appropriate means and there to destroy them or pump them off. For dispersal of localized oil slicks of limited extent a suction appliance (floating suction pump) has been developed. It consists of a funnel-shaped pan, the outer rim of which is kept by means of floats a few millimeters below the surface of the sea. This outer rim is capped by a floating hollow rim. In the pan, the water level is lowered by continuous suction of the water by means of a rotary pump. In this way the hollow rim is made to sink and the floating oil film runs into the pan. When sufficient oil has collected, an oil pump sucks the oil away through suction funnels, the immersion level of which is controlled by another float. If no more oil is present in the hollow, the oil pump switches off automatically. The water pump, on the other hand, runs continually. Appliances of this sort are built with performances of up to 40 cubic meters per hour. In addition to this system and similar substantially stationary systems which absorb oil from one spot, mobile oil collectors are being developed with performances of up to 60 cubic meters per hour.

Appliances of this size are of use, however, only for limited oil mishaps on restricted water surfaces, as in harbors and bays. For major oil catastrophes an oil induction ship has been developed with a conventional bow and a twin hull. The 17,000-ton ship has a length of 90 meters (295 feet) and a beam of 30 meters (98 feet). The tapering interval between the tail hulls terminates in an induction port in the bow. The ship travels backward into the oil slick, which rises higher and higher in the tapering channel and is finally sucked up into the bow channel. The oil is pumped into tanks, and the water is discharged overboard.

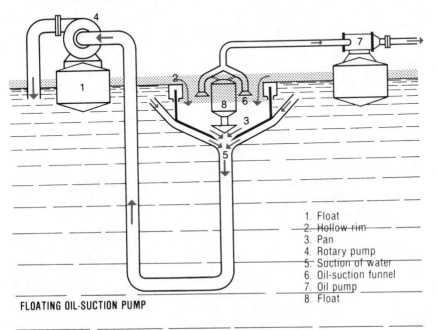

1. Float
2. Hollow rim
3. Pan
4. Rotary pump
5. Suction of water
6. Oil-suction funnel
7. Oil pump
8. Float

FLOATING OIL-SUCTION PUMP

HEATING OF RIVERS

Most power stations use river water for cooling purposes. This can give rise to far-reaching adverse ecological changes. The main problems are a reduction in the self-purification capacity of the river and the danger to river fauna caused by the heating of the river water, the extermination of water organisms in the condenser in the power station, and the climatic effects of heating of the waters.

By the heating of river waters, the dissolving power for the oxygen that is vital to the needs of water organisms is lowered, and at the same time the metabolic processes of the water organisms are accelerated. A higher consumption of oxygen is thus accompanied by a reduction in the supply. This can result in an impairment of self-purification capacity, in the disappearance of oxygen (with the consequent extinction of water organisms and the possible extermination of fish life) and, in extreme cases, in the complete disruption of the water biology. The heating of river waters leads to a sharp increase in bacteria. One result of this is that in addition to the physical reduction in the oxygen content of the water already caused by the rise in temperature, the remaining oxygen is consumed more quickly. The water acquires a musty smell and taste, which can seriously complicate the purification of drinking water from the river concerned. The bacterial cultures that develop can settle in quiet spots in the river, such as backwaters beside weirs, and putrefy there.

As this problem was recognized fairly early on, authorities imposed limits on the extent to which river water might be heated. These limits have been set too high, however, as they only take account of the physical factors present in clean rivers. The limits laid down stipulate that water temperatures may not be raised by more than 5°C (41°F), so that the upper limit of 28°C (82°F) is never exceeded. This threshold value takes no account of the fact that this range of temperature can give rise, in polluted rivers, to extensive disturbances in ecological processes to the point of complete disruption. Detailed investigations have been made into the matter on the river Main in West Germany, from which it emerges that once the level of 23°–24°C (73°–75°F) is overstepped, organisms die from lack of oxygen caused by pollution and heating of the water.

A further problem consists in the sharp increase in temperature of the water drawn into the condenser at a power station, possibly to 40°C (104°F). This is precisely the optimum temperature for pathogenic bacteria such as typhus and enterococci (intestinal bacteria). In clean cold water these disease germs do not multiply, but in polluted warm water well supplied with nutrients they do so freely. Another serious factor is that when the water heats to 40°C in the condenser, the animals that prey on bacteria—rotifers (wheel animalcules) and ciliates (slipper animalcules, etc.)—die off. An increase in pathogenic bacteria is thus matched by the extermination of the creatures that prey on them. In a 1000-megawatt power station, about 40,000 liters of water per second are absorbed and heated, which seriously impairs the self-purification capacity of polluted rivers.

A third problem arises from the influence on the climate of heating the river. Scientists at the Nuclear Research Center in Karlsruhe, Germany, have investigated this thoroughly as regards the Rhine. They reached the conclusion that with a rise in temperature of no more than 3°C (37.4°F) the quantity of additional water evaporated from the Rhine would be of the same order of magnitude as the total natural evaporation from the Rhine. In the foggy winter months of the year, the increase in evaporation is at its

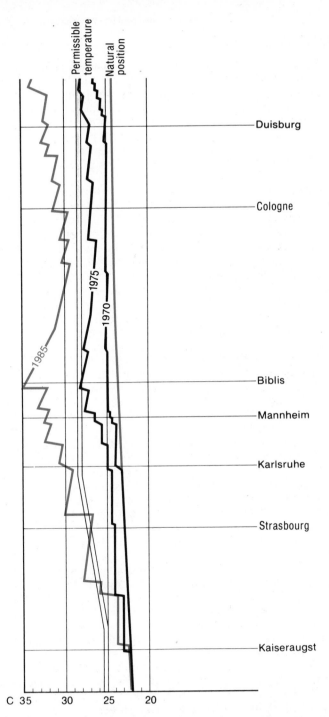

TEMPERATURE FORECASTS FOR THE RHINE UNDER THE SUMMER-HEAT LOAD PLAN

maximum. The study thus comes to the conclusion that a sharp increase in fog formation in consequence of heating of the river cannot be excluded, at least in the proximity of the river.

SELF-PURIFICATION OF WATERS

In the various zones of receiving streams (surface waters such as streams, rivers and lakes into which unpurified or purified waste waters are channeled and by which they are carried away), living creatures are to be found which are able to utilize any nutrients that are available. Natural self-purification of the waters by the decomposition of putrefactive substances, after a given period and distance of flow of the receiving streams, is due to these creatures. Under favorable conditions the pollution of the waters is substantially corrected in this way, so that the original pure state is at least approximately restored.

The self-purification processes depend mainly on biological processes (self-purification by organisms) or chemical processes (primarily oxidation and reduction processes), the effectiveness of which is determined by physical factors such as velocity of flow, state of the water bed, ratio of foul to clean water, temperature and depth of water, intensity and duration of solar radiation and fineness of waste substances. The main burden of self-purification falls on the biological processes.

The organisms contributing to the process of self-purification include fungi, algae, bacteria, protozoa, crustaceans, shellfish, worms, insect larvae, snails, fish, big predatory animals and waterfowl. The last two are the terminal members of the biological self-purification chain in the water.

In water and sewage, the bacteria, algae and fungi absorb dissolved and dispersed organic and inorganic constituents. In the metabolism of the organisms these substances are incorporated into the body matter or ultimately broken down into water and carbon dioxide for the purpose of providing energy. In order to sustain these processes, dissolved oxygen is absorbed from the water. Owing to their autotrophic manner of feeding, the algae containing chlorophyll are in a position by day to return the oxygen so absorbed. If the water is overrich in nutrients, i.e., overloaded with plant nutrients such as nitrogen or phosphorus, there can well be an explosive proliferation of algae. This will result in a shortage of oxygen as, owing to the limited absorptive capacity of the water, once saturation point is reached the oxygen produced by day will be given off in the form of gas. The absorptive capacity depends largely on the water temperature. At higher temperatures, the saturation point is reached more rapidly. If algae are present in the water in overabundance, the oxygen requirements at night will lead to a severe oxygen deficiency.

The protozoa, which absorb bacteria and algae as nutrients, are also able to utilize dissolved organic substances to some extent. Crustaceans, snails and worms feed on undissolved, deposited or suspended matter. They also ingest protozoa. Bigger crustaceans and insect larvae, for their part, feed on small crustaceans, worms and also on protozoa. Fish and waterfowl, which are also liable to fall victims to predatory animals in their turn, often prey on crustaceans and worms.

The intensity of self-purification is determined not only by optimum functioning of the living communities but also by the conformation of the riverbed. In naturally formed riverbeds, that is to say, in waters with large surfaces and strong turbulence (irregular strong water currents of high turbulence), the higher input of oxygen makes for more favorable living conditions for the organisms than are found in corrected or dammed river courses.

Even minor changes in one or another of the determining biological, chemical or physical factors can completely upset the self-purification capacity of the waters.

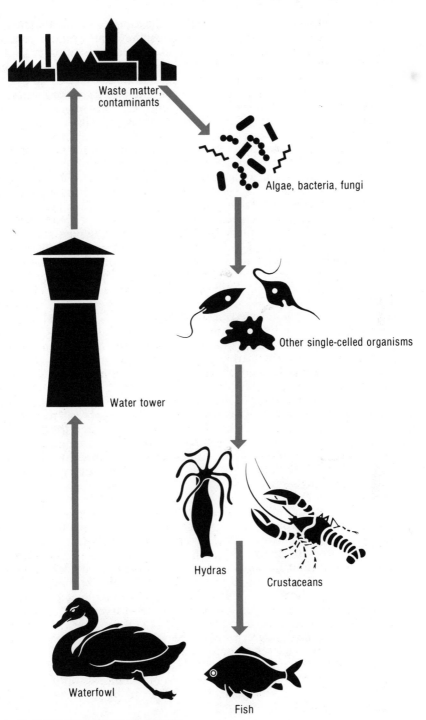

Waste matter, contaminants

Algae, bacteria, fungi

Other single-celled organisms

Water tower

Hydras

Crustaceans

Waterfowl

Fish

REDUCTION OF CONTAMINANTS IN WATERWAYS

SEWAGE PURIFICATION

Until relatively recent times, the self-purification capacity of static and running waters was still sufficient to reduce the contaminants contained in them. Loading the waters with waste and sewage from different sources has proliferated, however; and owing to the accretion of these contaminants, the reduction processes in the waterways have either come to a standstill by the extermination of microorganisms or been intensified by the increase in nutrients. With the multiplication of organisms, more oxygen has been extracted from the waters. The self-purification capacity of the waters has been overloaded, and the regenerative powers of the waters have been disrupted. The immediate consequences of such pollution have been the extermination of fish life, deposition of mud, and putrefaction processes.

The most serious loading of the waters stems from domestic and industrial waste disposal. The sewage is conducted through the drainage system to a purification plant, which as a rule operates in two stages: mechanical and biological treatment stages. The mechanical system comprises a grid, a sand trap and the preliminary settler. The coarser elements in the sewage are separated and retained by the grid. As the flow speed of the water slows, smaller mineral elements settle in the sand trap; the other removable matter is deposited in the preliminary settler, and the floating elements are removed by means of a scoop. The purification performance at the mechanical stage stands at about 20%–30%.

The water thus purified passes finally to the biological stage, which comprises a restoration basin (percolating filter) and a second filter, or final sedimentation tank. In the restoration basin, bacteria and other microorganisms convert the suspended and dissolved matter into removable sludge by absorbing the particles and dissolved matter as a nutritive substratum and by forming cell lumps as they proliferate, which, owing to their increase in weight, sink to the bottom. The whole process is facilitated and intensified by artificial induction of air by means of bellows, rotors and cylinder pumps.

In order to ensure that the microorganisms required for decomposition are present in sufficient quantities, parts of the microorganism sludge deposited on the floor of the secondary filter tank are returned to the restoration basin. The purified water on the surface of the secondary filter tank is fed into the receiving stream.

The sludge from the primary and secondary settlers is digested in septic towers with the aid of anaerobic bacteria. By this process, methane gas is formed which can be used to provide energy for the plant. Previously the digested sludge was usually dried out in beds to compact it. In new plants the preference is for mechanical dehydration plants, such as centrifuges and presses, because of the smaller space they take up. The dehydrated sludge can then be further processed together with household refuse.

Under optimum conditions the mechanical-biological sludge drying plant can achieve a purification performance of over 90%. For future purposes, however, this performance level is still too low, so that a further stage, the chemical stage, needs to be added. The chemical precipitation process employed serves to eliminate phosphates and other (especially industrial) pollution. With the aid of microsieves and similar technical appliances, organic residues can be further reduced. In addition, a hygienic improvement in the sewage may be achieved by means of chlorination, radiation, heating or ozonizing.

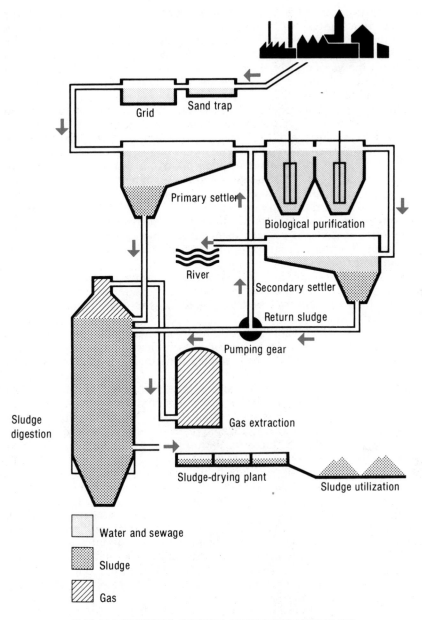

Grid · **Sand trap**

Primary settler

Biological purification

River

Secondary settler

Return sludge

Pumping gear

Sludge digestion

Gas extraction

Sludge-drying plant

Sludge utilization

☐ Water and sewage

▨ Sludge

▨ Gas

PLAN OF A MECHANICAL-BIOLOGICAL SEWAGE TREATMENT PLANT

THE CORRUGATED PLATE FILTER

For the purification of contaminated waste waters, a plant with corrugated-plate-filter muck piles can be installed wherever the water is charged with floating or deposited matter. The oil filters can be installed at any point in the petrochemical or mineral oil processing industry, in tanker depots, at airports, in big garages, etc. Plant for the removal of solids is installed for the purification of filter return water and for sludge filtration (e.g., in the foodstuff and textile industries).

The corrugated plate filter depends for its operation on the force of gravity. In the filter the particles of contaminants do not need to rise the whole way to the surface of the basin, nor to sink to its floor, since the filter contains a number of corrugated plates, one above the other, representing in effect a series of surfaces and of floors. Any one particle needs to cover only the distance between two plates and is then effectively deposited. The corrugations on the plates make for closer pooling of the contaminants from the water for onward transmission to the filter channels. Additional collecting channels on the inlet and outlet sides of the corrugated plate will ensure that the filtered matter is collected and carried away without being diverted (by the inlet or outlet currents) into the sewage water again or contaminating the clean water.

According to the specific gravity of the contaminants to be eliminated, the filter will be fed from above downward (for matter that is lighter than water, such as oil) or from below upward (in the case of matter that is heavier than water).

The way in which the filter plant and the filter itself function is illustrated in the following example, relating to oil filtering. The inlet tank produces an even distribution of the incoming contaminated water between the individual parallel cells of the filter tank, so that all the plate packs are equally loaded. In front of each pack a flow filter spreads the water flow evenly over the whole field. The oil and water mixture makes its way from above into the pack, which is set at an angle of 45° to the vertical. It flows down diagonally between the corrugated plates set one above the other. The flow between the plates is laminar; the oil droplets rise unhindered to the underside of the plate above, collect in the crests of the plate, and flow back upward to the entrance of the plate pack. There the oil is caught up in the mainstream and carried away from the flow of water coming in to the surface of the basin. The sludge present in the water collects in the troughs of the undulations, sinks down with the current flow of the water to the outlet of the pack, where it is similarly taken up by the collecting channel, and is carried in the mainstream to the floor of the basin or into an elutriating funnel. The cleansed water passes into the outlet tank, and from there over an overflow dam into the outlet channel. The separated oil collects as a slick on the surface of the water in the filter tank and flows over an oil scoop or skin pipe into the sump. The filter tank is covered with floating plates of plastic foam in order to reduce evaporation and offensive fumes.

For the separation of solid matter the direction of flow is reversed, but the way in which the entire plant works is, in other respects, the same.

The average performance of a set of plates, with a distance between the plates of 19 mm, is 30 cubic meters per hour. In special cases this average performance is reduced, however, to enable particles with lower rates of rise or fall to be thoroughly separated.

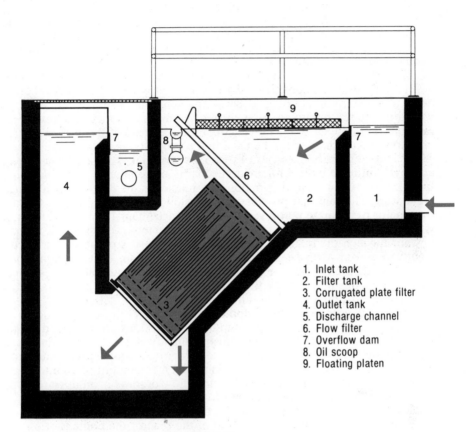

1. Inlet tank
2. Filter tank
3. Corrugated plate filter
4. Outlet tank
5. Discharge channel
6. Flow filter
7. Overflow dam
8. Oil scoop
9. Floating platen

CORRUGATED PLATE FILTER FOR OIL SEPARATION

COMPOSTING OF SEWAGE SLUDGE: THE COUNTERFLOW PROCESS

The counterflow process, which was developed for the composting of raw sludge from local sewage plants, is suitable for use in all sewage plant systems. The reactors are available in sizes of 25 cu m, 50 cu m, 100 cu m, and up to 500 cu m. Anaerobic or aerobic sludge stabilization (digestion tower) is superfluous. What is necessary, however, is drainage of the sewage sludge by mechanical means. For composting the sludge, owing to its high nitrogen and water content, an organic carbon carrier, such as peat, sawdust, chopped straw or lignite, is also required.

The sludge, fed into the sewage plant with a water content of about 98%, is dehydrated mechanically by means of presses and centrifugal driers down to a water content of 75%–80%. The dehydrated sludge can be mixed with the required organic carbon carrier by means of a mixing screw in the ratio of 1:1. In the case of a moving operation, instead of the carbon carrier, backflow (reflux) matter can be used in the proportions of 50% sludge, 40% reflux and 10% carbon carrier. The mixed material is raised by a sloping conveyor into the bioreactor, which consists of combined metal elements. In order to prevent heat dissipation, the reactor is insulated over its entire outer wall. The material provided passes slowly and continuously through the reactor from top to bottom (period of passage about 10 days). Ventilation is effected at the base of the reactor. The air injected through nozzles passes upward through the material. Control of the airflow is possible. Air is constantly removed at three points in the material store (reactor filling) and its carbon dioxide content examined with analysis equipment. Resistance pyrometers constantly check the temperature at six different points, which is then recorded on a six-point inkwriter.

The rapid group system is adopted for utilizing clean sewage sludge. By a regular supply of oxygen, optimum living conditions are provided for the reducing and converting microorganisms already present in the sludge. In this way they are stimulated to exercise higher metabolic activity and faster germination. The air injected has an initial oxygen content of about 21%. It penetrates the material slowly by a counterflow process in an upward direction. This promotes the respiration of oxygen by the organisms. Oxidation processes thus get under way and the oxygen content of the air is reduced from below upward. In the upper field of the reactor the content of oxygen in the air falls to 7%–10%. In accordance with the airflow the temperature rises from below upward. In the upper region immediately below the condenser water zone the temperature builds up to levels of 75°–82°C (167°–180°F). The material, which is slowly and continually traversed by the reactor from top to bottom, must necessarily therefore pass through this heat accumulation zone so that hygienic treatment of the sewage sludge is assured. The end product, considerably reduced in volume and weight compared with the original material, is a hygienically flawless, friable material.

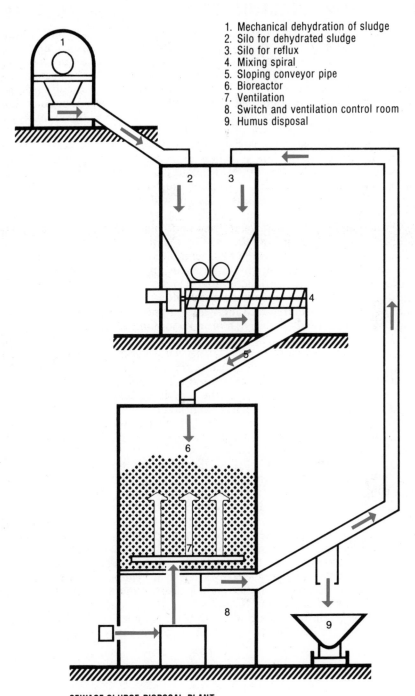

1. Mechanical dehydration of sludge
2. Silo for dehydrated sludge
3. Silo for reflux
4. Mixing spiral
5. Sloping conveyor pipe
6. Bioreactor
7. Ventilation
8. Switch and ventilation control room
9. Humus disposal

SEWAGE-SLUDGE DISPOSAL PLANT

WATER SUPPLY: PREPARATION OF SURFACE WATER

Water consumption in big cities amounts to some 200–300 liters (210–315 quarts) per person per day, rising in peak periods to as high as 450 liters (472 quarts). On top of this come industrial water requirements. To produce 1 kg (2.2 lb) of plastics, up to 500 liters (525 quarts) of water may be needed, and to produce 1 kg of paper up to 3000 liters (3150 quarts). Of the total supply of drinking water today about half comes from groundwater, about one-third from springwater, and about 15% or 16% from surface water in lakes and rivers.

In thickly populated industrial centers, groundwater supplies are now utilized practically to the limits of their capacity. Increasing recourse must consequently be had in the future to the surface water in lakes and rivers. But because of the high cost of treating surface water for drinking, the supply of drinking water from this source to wider sectors of the population will raise the price of water considerably.

An example of a river water treatment plant will be described: The untreated water is drawn from the river by means of a suitable suction plant and conveyed to the waterworks by a remote-control pumping plant. There the river water is sterilized with chlorine in premixers and treated with a flocculation agent. This produces heavy sludge flakes which sink to the bottom. The clear water remaining above flows on to the ozonizing plant. There ozone gas is emitted into the water in fine bubbles, by which means (much more intensively than by chlorine) additional sterilization and oxidation of dissolved organic matter are achieved. The ozone gas needed for this purpose is generated from oxygen at the waterworks by means of electric energy, and it reverts to oxygen again afterward, leaving no trace. In the adjoining rapid filter plant all the other still-dissolved foreign bodies are removed from the water, first of all the remaining suspended particles with the aid of a 2–3 meter thick quartz sand layer and then all the other still-dissolved foreign bodies by means of the active carbon filter inserted below it. The treated water is retained until its introduction into the filtrate reservoir.

A further possibility is to allow the treated water to seep away into suitable gravel deposits in the river valleys, to lower its temperature and assimilate it in other respects to natural groundwater, and after a specified period to remove it in the same way as groundwater together with natural groundwater. A pure water reservoir is needed to retain the water removed, from which the drinking water is conveyed by pumps to the final consumer.

Consumption of drinking water has risen in the past 50 years about 40-fold. This is explained, for the most part, by the enormous expansion in industrial production, by increased awareness of hygienic requirements, and by changes in man's consumption habits. Furthermore the population has practically doubled in the period.

The proportion of surface water in total supplies of drinking water is likely to expand in line with the constant development of industry.

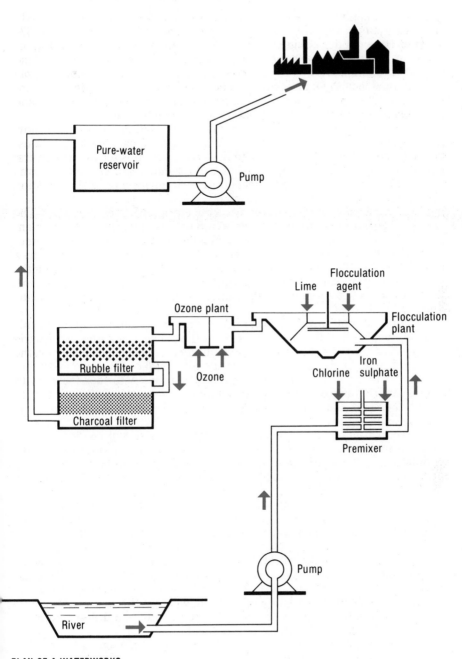

PLAN OF A WATERWORKS

FLUORINE AND THE FLUORIDATION OF DRINKING WATER

Fluorine, a member of the halogen family of elements, is the most corrosive chemical element that is known. It is a greenish-yellow gas, which, like the fluorine compounds, is highly toxic. The addition of fluorides to drinking water to prevent dental caries (tooth decay) had been opposed by some doctors and toxicologists but now has been endorsed by all major U.S. and international health organizations. The application of fluorides in toothpastes or for internal consumption hardens the enamel on teeth and so provides protection against destruction of the teeth by caries.

Against the fluoridation of drinking water, various toxicological and legal arguments have been adduced. Water is necessary for life, whereas fluorine and its compounds can be toxic substances. It is for the waterworks to provide drinking water that satisfies the hygienic requirements of comestibles (food). Fluoride at high concentration produces a corrosive effect on glass, steel and a number of other metals. Drinking water is treated with 1 mg of fluoride per liter of water. At concentrations over 2 mg per liter, people begin to react gradually with symptoms of mild dental fluorosis, as part of the daily intake of fluorine accumulates in the body. The fluorosis manifests itself as white flecks in the dental enamel. Pitting of the enamel can result from fluorine concentrations of 3–4 mg per liter. Only in a few places in the United States is the concentration above 4 mg per liter. In those areas the Environmental Protection Agency is working to reduce the fluorine level.

People do not absorb fluorine into their system only as an additive in drinking water, but fluorine is present in their diet in natural and artificial forms. This supply of fluorine in the daily diet varies in different countries and for different types of food, so that the total intake of fluorine in drinking water and foodstuffs cannot be assessed precisely. A further factor is the loading of the atmosphere with the fluorine waste gases from aluminum works and similar industrial plants, which can also result in an uncontrollable intake of fluorine.

Although fluorine has been shown active in a dental context only for children under 15 years of age, the entire water supply system is treated with fluorides. It is estimated that about 1000 liters of water would have to be treated with fluoride to enable a child whose teeth are still developing to drink 1 liter of treated water.

A difficult legal problem now arises from the fact that the consumer can in no way avoid being supplied with fluoridated drinking water. The situation amounts to enforced medication. However, the legal validity of fluoridation has been upheld in courts in the United States and in several other countries.

In many cities in the world, however, the fluoridation of drinking water introduced in the past on a trial basis has been abandoned. In 1971 the model project introduced in 1952 in Kassel-Wahlershausen, Germany, was suspended. In 1972 the fluoridation of drinking water in Sweden was discontinued. In the United States more than half the population drinks fluoridated water and that proportion is increasing slowly.

Caries is not a disease caused by fluorine deficiency but is the result of bacterial action exacerbated by general nutrient deficiencies and lack of dental care. Fluorine medication can, at best, influence the symptom of caries, but not the disease itself.

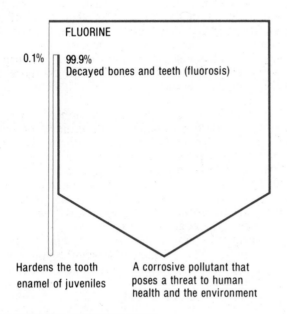

0.1%

FLUORINE

99.9%
Decayed bones and teeth (fluorosis)

Hardens the tooth
enamel of juveniles

A corrosive pollutant that
poses a threat to human
health and the environment

EFFECTS OF FLUORIDATION OF DRINKING WATER

Part Fourteen—Noxious Substances in the Environment

DAMAGE TO HEALTH BY CARBON MONOXIDE

Carbon monoxide (CO) is a colorless, odorless, inflammable, toxic gas which is present in large quantities in the waste from burned gases, especially in exhaust fumes from motor vehicles. The toxic effect of carbon monoxide arises from the fact that it combines with the red blood cell pigment hemoglobin and so impedes the combination that normally occurs in the lungs of oxygen with hemoglobin. It thus arrests the transport of oxygen through the blood and leads to symptoms similar to those that occur in suffocation. Carbon monoxide has a 200 to 300 times greater affinity with hemoglobin than oxygen.

A measure of the degree of acute carbon monoxide poisoning can be established from the proportion of hemoglobin in the blood that has reacted with carbon monoxide molecules (carboxyhemoglobin). With as little as 2% carboxyhemoglobin (corresponding to 10 ppm of carbon monoxide in the air inhaled), sensitive tests have disclosed the first effects on the central nervous system in the form of impairment of time judgment. At 3% carboxyhemoglobin (corresponding to 20 ppm of carbon monoxide in the air inhaled), disturbances are observed in light sensitivity and clarity of vision. At 4.5% to 5% carboxyhemoglobin (corresponding to 30 ppm of carbon monoxide in the air inhaled) impairment of vision and psychomotor disturbances can be established. These effects of low carbon monoxide concentrations have been recognized only recently. Previously it was assumed that at below a 10% and up to 20% carboxyhemoglobin level no distinguishable symptoms of poisoning would occur. Only at 30% carboxyhemoglobin does the individual affected himself perceive the damage occurring in the form of headaches, lassitude and vertigo. Carboxyhemoglobin concentrations of 45% to 50% normally result in collapse and loss of consciousness, and higher saturations result rapidly in death. From the results of more recent investigations, it is concluded that lower carbon monoxide concentrations produce chronic toxic effects.

Carbon monoxide exerts a special influence on the performance of vehicle drivers. An investigation in the United States disclosed that drivers involved in road accidents showed particularly high carboxyhemoglobin values. With an increase of 10% in the carboxyhemoglobin level, drivers of vehicles on the motorway at night reacted more slowly to stoplights and changes in speed limits. In order not to exceed the probably quite harmless carboxyhemoglobin value of 2%, carbon monoxide concentrations in big cities should not rise above 9 to 10 ppm. In some big cities, however, hourly values of 30 and even as high as 50 ppm are recorded at present, and peak values of 100 to 300 ppm are by no means rare.

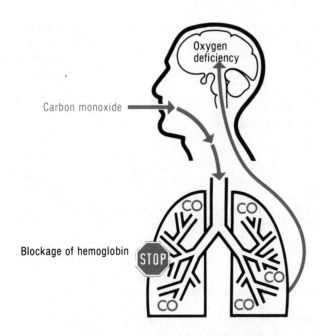

Carbon monoxide

Oxygen deficiency

Blockage of hemoglobin

STOP

Diagram 1. DAMAGING EFFECT OF CARBON MONOXIDE IN THE ORGANISM

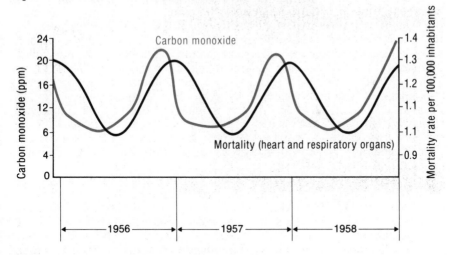

Carbon monoxide

Mortality (heart and respiratory organs)

1956 — 1957 — 1958

Carbon monoxide (ppm)

Mortality rate per 100,000 inhabitants

Diagram 2. MORTALITY (owing to diseases of the respiratory organs and the heart) AND CARBON MONOXIDE CONTENT OF THE ATMOSPHERE IN THE DISTRICT OF LOS ANGELES

DAMAGE TO HEALTH BY NITRIC OXIDES

Nitric oxides are released whenever combustion occurs at high temperatures, as in conventional power stations, boiler plants, vehicle and aircraft engines, the chemical industry and to a lesser extent domestic heating systems. Nitric oxides are toxic gases, including in particular nitrogen monoxide (NO) and nitrogen dioxide (NO_2), which attack the mucous membranes of the respiratory organs and encourage catarrhal and other infections. Together with the organic constituents of exhaust fumes, they are prime producers in sunlight of photochemical smog (see Part Twelve).

It has been established that as little as 0.1 ppm of nitrogen dioxide in the air can result, over a period of one to three years, in an increase in the incidence of bronchitis and have an adverse effect on the lung performance of children. For persons already suffering from chronic bronchitis, breathing is made more difficult by a rise in the nitrogen dioxide content of the atmosphere. In tests with animals, 0.25 ppm of nitrogen was found to produce changes in the pulmonary tissues, and 0.5 ppm to cause slight inflammatory reactions and cell changes.

A systematic investigation into the effects of nitrogen dioxide was carried out in Tennessee in 1968/69. In this Chattanooga study, four separate districts were examined: one with a high nitrogen dioxide concentration (0.06–0.11 ppm) and a low suspended dust content, one with a low nitrogen dioxide concentration (0.05 ppm) and a high suspended dust content, and two districts with generally low air pollution. In each of these districts, three schools with altogether 987 pupils and members of their families totaling 4043 adults were examined. A statistical analysis was compiled of their social and economic status, their ages, smoking habits, sex and other material factors. The most important results of this Chattanooga study were that the children in the district with high nitrogen dioxide values (0.06–0.11 ppm) recorded significantly lower values in a lung function test (maximum volume of air inhaled in 0.75 second) than those in the other districts. The influence of the nitrogen dioxide concentration on the children's breathing capacity was thus clearly demonstrated. In the case of children and adults alike, the frequency of acute disorders in the respiratory organs was significantly higher in the district with a high nitrogen dioxide content than in the two areas of low pollution. A higher sickness frequency was also regularly recorded when the 24-hour average value of the nitrogen dioxide concentration exceeded 0.06 ppm.

In another American investigation, the frequency of diseases of the inner respiratory organs (pneumonia, bronchitis and asthma) was examined in relation to the nitric oxide concentration. The investigations extended over a period of three years, and embraced 1800 schoolchildren and 1100 smaller children. The result was that in the districts with average to high nitrogen dioxide concentrations the frequency of acute bronchitis was found to be significantly higher for all children than in areas of low concentrations. Again a higher frequency was established when the nitrogen dioxide values exceeded 0.06 ppm.

Until 1974, the permitted limit for nitrogen dioxide was 0.5 ppm (long-term) or 1 ppm (short-term). Today the limit for nitrogen dioxide stands at 0.1 mg of nitrogen dioxide per cubic meter of air long-term (corresponding to 0.085 ppm) and 0.3 mg of nitrogen dioxide per cubic meter of air short-term (corresponding to 0.25 ppm). Motor transport in big cities today, however, often causes short-term values of 0.2 to 0.5 ppm of nitrogen dioxide.

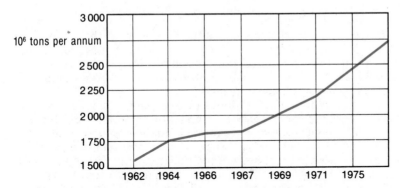

Diagram 1. EMISSION OF NITROGEN DIOXIDE IN WEST GERMANY

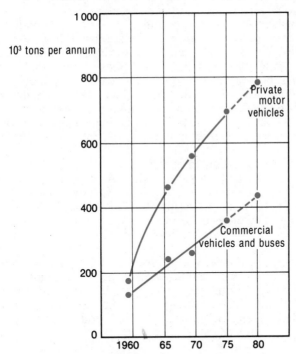

Diagram 2. EMISSION OF NITRIC OXIDE BY ROAD TRANSPORT VEHICLES IN WEST GERMANY

OZONE—FORMATION AND EFFECTS ON THE ORGANISM

Ozone develops as a result of photochemical processes at altitudes of over 30 km (19 miles). Molecular oxygen (O_2) separates into two oxygen atoms under the effects of ultraviolet sunlight (with a wavelength of 240 nanometers). An oxygen atom formed in this way can combine with an oxygen molecule (O_2) to form a triatomic oxygen molecule (O_3 or ozone). The O_3 molecule, for its part, rapidly absorbs ultraviolet light in the region of a wavelength of 300 nm and again separates into O_2 molecules and oxygen atoms. Some of the oxygen atoms combine again with O_2 molecules. In this way a photochemical balance is established. Other gases also participate in these processes by purely chemical reactions.

The ozone that is formed at altitudes of over 30 km finds its way into lower levels of the atmosphere only as a result of air turbulence. For this reason, the high O_3 concentrations are found in the atmosphere at altitudes of between 20 and 30 km (12 and 19 miles), while in the layer of air close to the earth only very low proportions are recorded. Enrichment of the ozone in lower air layers is not possible, since on coming into contact with the organic substances of firm ground, or with the sharply articulated upper surfaces of woodlands, ozone gives off the third oxygen atom to the organic substances and so returns to the state of molecular oxygen.

In the atmosphere of big cities polluted by nitric oxide and other noxious gases, a reaction between ultraviolet radiation and these noxious gases can result in the formation of ozone. The nitrogen dioxide contained in vehicle exhaust fumes, for instance, decomposes under solar radiation through photodissociation into nitrogen monoxide and atomic oxygen. Atomic oxygen combines with molecular oxygen, as already described, to form ozone. This explains why, in a smog situation in the daytime, the O_3 concentration in the air layer close to the ground in big cities can rise to five times the normal content and in extreme cases to a thousand times the normal content.

Ozone can cause irritation of the respiratory passages. It penetrates much deeper into the lungs than sulfur oxide. At very high concentrations the surfaces of the respiratory tract are so seriously affected that lethal pulmonary edema may result. Experiments with animals have shown, however, that repeated inhalations of ozone at low concentrations can promote a certain resistance to its irritant effects. Animals that were exposed for a long time to low concentrations of ozone did not die when exposed to higher (generally fatal) concentrations. It was also found that in animals that were exposed for months to near-lethal doses of ozone a thickening of the bronchiole walls occurred, as in the early stages of chronic bronchitis in human beings. Whether ultimately there is any connection between the ozone concentration in industrial agglomerations and the frequency of chronic bronchial complaints has not been established.

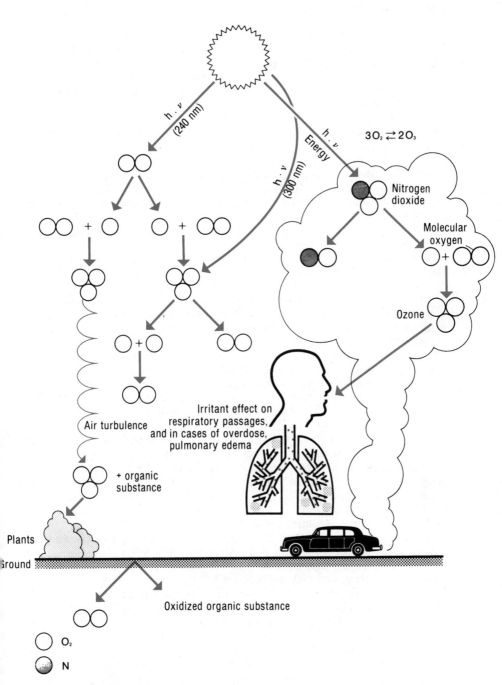

**FORMATION AND DECOMPOSITION OF OZONE AND ITS HARMFUL EFFECTS
ON THE ORGANISM**

SULFUR DIOXIDE

Sulfur dioxide is formed by the combustion of fossil raw materials which, because of their organic origin, contain sulfur, and by various processes in the chemical industry. Sulfur dioxide is a colorless, toxic gas, heavier than air, and in high concentrations it has a pungent odor. The dangerous nature of sulfur dioxide is due to the fact that it penetrates the respiratory tract and damages the numerous small delicate cilia of the bronchial mucous membrane, whose task it is to expel dust and aerosol particles. Owing to the effects of sulfur dioxide, inhaled dust and soot particles remain in the lungs and pursue their toxic activities there.

In small children, sulfur dioxide causes the Krupp syndrome, a sinister violent affliction which is characterised by a raucous hacking cough, fever and increasing and sometimes fatal breathlessness. The mucous membrane in the larynx and the vocal cords is swollen and inflamed and the windpipe becomes seriously obstructed by phlegm. The Krupp syndrome is particularly serious in the evening and at night and is especially prevalent in the winter months.

An interesting investigation into this problem has been carried out in recent years in the children's clinic at the University of Frankfurt, Germany. From 1967 to 1971, altogether 576 children suffering from the Krupp syndrome were admitted for treatment there. Most of the cases occurred in winter months in which high dust and sulfur dioxide concentrations were also recorded. Electronic data-processing methods were used to correlate air pollution levels with the onset of the disease. They showed that a significant increase in the number of cases occurred whenever the daily and maximum 3-hour average values of sulfur dioxide rose above 60 to 80 ppm (corresponding to 0.16 mg of sulfur dioxide per cu m of air). As regards the dust content, the critical limit above which cases of the Krupp syndrome rose sharply stood at 0.17 mg of dust per cu m of air.

Another very carefully conducted study was carried out in the United States in 1964. This was the Nashville Study, in which altogether 9313 patients were examined. As soon as the sulfur dioxide concentration in the atmosphere rose above 5 ppm, the sickness rate in the population increased. The increase was particularly marked for coronary and circulatory ailments.

Apart from its damaging effects on health, sulfur dioxide also exercises an influence on vegetation. It is highly probable that a synergism with fluorine waste gases plays some part in the damage to plants by sulfur dioxide. The damage manifests itself in discoloration of the tips of the leaves to complete bleaching of the leaves. The patches may be red, brown or yellow. The leaves then dry up, curl and fall off. Coniferous trees are particularly seriously affected, and may die off altogether.

Finally, sulfur dioxide is known to have a destructive effect on other inorganic materials. Many edifices from the Middle Ages, which had survived undamaged for centuries, have suddenly begun to disintegrate in recent decades. Extensive damage is thus evident, for instance, at the old picture-gallery in Munich and at Cologne Cathedral, attributable in both cases to the action of sulfur dioxide. Sulfur dioxide waste gases are particularly prone to attack limestone, since sulfur dioxide combines with water to form sulfurous acid, which renders calcium carbonate (lime, marble) soluble in water.

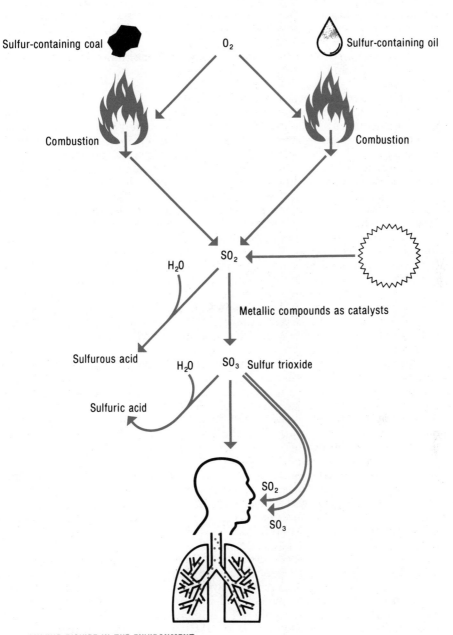

SULFUR DIOXIDE IN THE ENVIRONMENT

CHLORINATED HYDROCARBONS

The group of chlorinated hydrocarbons includes a large number of organic compounds of varying structure, in which one or more hydrogen atoms are replaced by chlorine atoms. A feature common to almost all these compounds is that they are insoluble in water, but they dissolve readily in fats, oils and organic solvents. Chlorinated hydrocarbons are used as pesticides (see Part Nine), solvents (e.g., chloroform, ethylene tetrachloride), and industrial agents and technical products (particularly PCB: polychlorinated biphenyl).

Chlorinated hydrocarbons, in particular pesticides (including DDT: dichlorodiphenyltrichloroethane) and the PCBs, represent a serious threat to the environment. When DDT and other chlorinated hydrocarbons enter into the diet of man, which is the final link in various food chains, they tend to concentrate, because of their fatlike character, mainly in the nerve tissues (including the brain), the liver, the gonads and the cardiac muscular system. A considerable concentration occurs in mothers' milk. In 1970, DDT was found to be present in mothers' milk in Sweden and the United States in quantities that exceeded the permitted maximum limits for foodstuffs by 70%. Once these results became known, a start was made on extensive investigations into the connection between DDT and disorders in man. In the United States it was established that patients who died from cirrhosis of the liver, high blood pressure, cerebral hemorrhage, brain tumors and various forms of cancer had a distinctly higher DDT concentration in their fat tissues than people dying from other causes.

In many countries DDT is already forbidden or its use limited to particular situations. In the United States DDT was banned in 1972, although millions of pounds of DDT are exported, mainly to underdeveloped countries with major insect control problems.

Considered more dangerous now than DDT are the chlorinated hydrocarbons called PCBs. Although they possess similar properties to DDT, the problem they present was recognized considerably later than that of DDT. PCBs in various forms are used in industry mainly as electric insulating fluids, fireproofing agents, hydraulic fluids, varnish additives and heat conducters. PCB was synthesized for the first time over 100 years ago, and for the past 40 years it has been manufactured by industrial processes in thousands of tons per annum. PCB was not identified in nature until 1966, because it had previously been confused with DDT. Detailed scientific investigations into the dangers of PCB were inaugurated as a result of an incident of poisoning, with about 1000 fatalities, that occurred in Japan in 1968. In addition to immediate effects on the skin and nervous system, the PCB contamination appeared to cause a delayed, but significant, increase in liver cancer.

Since 1968 PCB has been identified in human fat tissues and in mothers' milk. Detailed research established that PCB is present, in addition, in plants, birds, fish, waterways, the ground and the air. Today the PCB content in fish stands at between 0.03 and 1.5 ppm of the live weight. Animals' livers even contain up to 11 ppm of PCB in the North Sea and up to 9.5 ppm in the Baltic, compared with values of DDT of 3 and 1.8 ppm, respectively. There is concern that PCB-containing Baltic seals are unable to reproduce and that the species will become extinct.

In 1973, the Organization for Economic Cooperation and Development (OECD) passed a resolution demanding that PCB be permitted only in closed systems, such as insulation fluid in electrical equipment. Many countries have since acceded to this requirement. The United States has banned

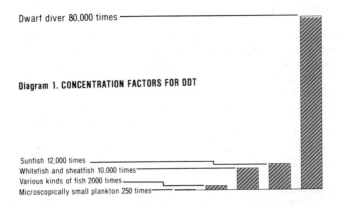

Dwarf diver 80,000 times ─────────────────

Diagram 1. CONCENTRATION FACTORS FOR DDT

Sunfish 12,000 times ─────────────
Whitefish and sheatfish 10,000 times─────
Various kinds of fish 2000 times ─────
Microscopically small plankton 250 times───

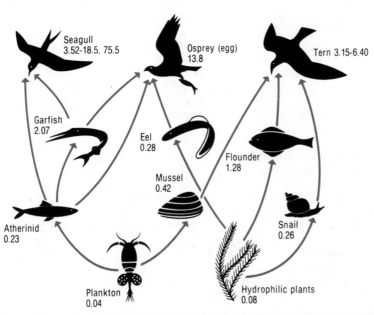

Seagull
3.52-18.5, 75.5

Osprey (egg)
13.8

Tern 3.15-6.40

Garfish
2.07

Eel
0.28

Flounder
1.28

Mussel
0.42

Atherinid
0.23

Snail
0.26

Plankton
0.04

Hydrophilic plants
0.08

Diagram 2. CONCENTRATION OF DDT IN A FOOD CHAIN FROM PLANKTON TO WATERFOWL (IN PPM)

manufacture of PCB but allows its continued use in electrical equipment.

An incident in 1979 dramatically illustrates how rapidly and widely PCB contamination can spread in the food industry, from a leak in a closed system. A chemical that escaped from a spare electrical transformer at a Montana packing company was incorporated into animal feed made with recovered solids from waste water. The feed was shipped to many farms, including the poultry farm where the first contaminated chicken was discovered in a routine Department of Agriculture check. Eggs, poultry, pork, grease and processed foods in 19 states and Canada and Japan were suspected of contamination.

As of 1979, almost 300 million pounds of PCB were still in use in the United States in large transformers. Replacing the PCB would be expensive and its destruction would have to be handled with care. PCBs can be destroyed by incineration at more than 1000°C (1832°F), but the process must be carefully controlled to avoid formation of even more toxic by-products.

LEAD DAMAGE TO HEALTH

Lead is the best known of the heavy metals. Lead dust is emitted by different industrial plants (through flues into the air) in the form of oxides and various salts. The most dangerous source for the contamination of the environment with lead, however, is motor transport. Lead is added to gasoline as an organic compound (tetraethyl or tetramethyl lead). Upon combustion of the gasoline the lead is converted into lead oxide, which is discharged from exhaust pipes in the form of fine dust particles capable of penetrating the lungs. Throughout the world, the total annual emission of lead by motor vehicles and industrial plants amounts to something like half a million tons.

Human beings, plants and animals absorb lead from the most diverse sources. From sewage water it gets into ground and river water; from waste gases it gets into the atmosphere, and from there into foodstuffs and beverages. By far the greatest volume is inhaled with the air we breathe, however. While some 5%–15% of the lead contained in the food we consume is absorbed by the intestines, the absorption by the lungs of lead from exhaust fumes in the air we inhale amounts to almost 100%.

The damage done by elemental lead released into the atmosphere is extremely difficult to eliminate. Particularly worrying, therefore, is the long-term buildup of lead in the environment. The ground on both sides of busy streets and highways is seriously contaminated with lead to a distance of 0.5 to 1 km (0.3 to 0.6 mile). The oceans of the world today have a lead content something like 50 times above the natural level.

Soluble lead salts, and insoluble lead compounds which can be rendered soluble by metabolic processes, are toxic. At the outset the symptoms of lead poisoning are uncertain: general upset, loss of appetite, loss of energy, etc. Later on the persons affected lose weight and suffer from anemia. In women the menstrual cycle is disturbed. Characteristic changes in the blood count set in; and the red blood cells appear granulated. In every case a blue line appears around the gums, and there is a slate-gray discoloration produced by a buildup of the metal in the oral cavity. The blue line, which is frequently the first specific sign of lead poisoning, may last a long time, well after the cause of the poisoning has been removed. At a later stage, more serious symptoms of lead poisoning, sometimes verging on the fatal, will manifest themselves in such forms as lead colic, feeble pulse and high blood pressure, cirrhosis of the kidney (nephritis), acute or nagging pains in the muscles, and finally brain fever (encephalopathy) accompanied by severe headaches, epileptic-type fits and psychosis. Also established are nervous ailments displaying symptoms of paralysis, arthritis, allergies and other skin reactions, anemia and various metabolic disorders. In cases of chronic lead poisoning severe damage can also be done to the chromosomes, which transmit hereditary factors.

Typical lead poisoning with clearly diagnosable symptoms mainly affects persons working in the lead industry, who in the course of their activity have absorbed large quantities of the heavy metal. Less prominent but probably more problematic is the gradual poisoning of the environment by smaller quantities of lead and the chronic lead poisoning of people, who from childhood onward, are exposed to higher accretions of lead throughout their lifetime. It must also be noted that lead concentrations well below the levels that give rise to physical symptoms can still touch off marked behavioral disturbances.

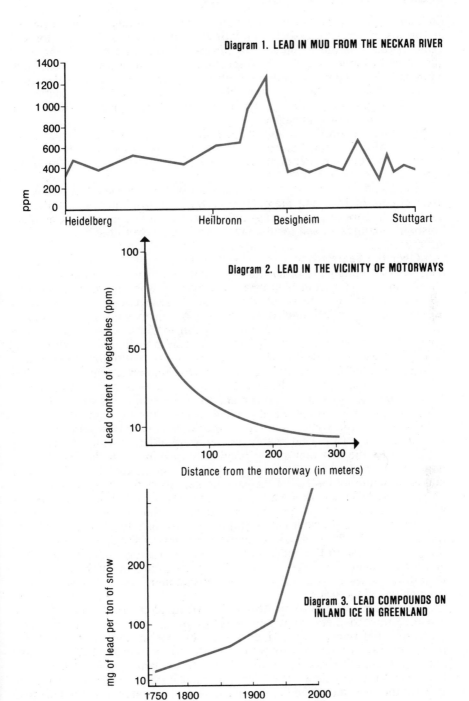

Diagram 1. LEAD IN MUD FROM THE NECKAR RIVER

Diagram 2. LEAD IN THE VICINITY OF MOTORWAYS

Diagram 3. LEAD COMPOUNDS ON INLAND ICE IN GREENLAND

CADMIUM DAMAGE TO HEALTH

Cadmium is a silvery white metal with similar properties to zinc. It occurs in various minerals in association with zinc. It is used in industry for galvanic plating to protect iron and steel from corrosion, for low-melting-point alloys, and to moderate the chain reaction in nuclear power stations. Cadmium sulfide (yellow) and cadmium selenide (deep red) are basic substances for dyes, which are used in ceramic glazing, porcelain dying and plastics. In the agricultural field, cadmium occurs in artificial phosphate fertilizers and in certain plant protection agents.

Cadmium is produced and utilized almost exclusively in the industrial countries of the world. Between 1925 and 1950 world use of cadmium rose from 457 to 5,800 tons per annum. By 1969 cadmium use had risen to 17,000 tons.

Like lead and mercury, cadmium is a toxic heavy metal. Whereas the toxic effects of lead and mercury have been known for a long time, the dangerous nature of cadmium has only recently been recognized. Cadmium poisoning manifests itself for the most part in damage to the bone and joint structures.

Over the years 1940–1958 in the Tojama district in Japan, 130 people died from an undiagnosed disease ("itai-itai" disease). The victims died in paroxysms of pain from neuralgia. The disease was regarded in the first years as something to be ashamed of, so that cases were concealed as far as possible from public knowledge. At postmortem examinations, cadmium was found in the kidneys, liver and skeleton in the amount of 4000–6000 ppm. The first symptoms of "itai-itai" disease are albumin in the urine, kidney trouble, and a decline in the phosphorus content of the blood serum. The patients suffer excruciating pains in the lumbar region and in other joints. The cause of this is disintegration and demineralization of the bones in consequence of cadmium poisoning. As these symptoms were found for the most part in older, physically ailing women, the cadmium catastrophe did not attract the same attention as the Minamata catastrophe (see next section, on mercury). That mainly women were afflicted with this disease is explained by the fact that during pregnancy a woman's body absorbs cadmium like a sponge, and if the diet is poor in vitamins and calcium, the body builds cadmium up instead of the calcium necessary for the bone substance of the fetus. As far as is known at present, the pregnancies took a completely normal course. But 10 to 30 years later the "itai-itai" disease developed in the aging mothers. Further manifestations of this malady are fatigue, kidney trouble, pains in the ribs, loss of teeth, and pains in the spinal column and the pelvis. Owing to the buildup of cadmium in the bones, they turn brittle and break under the slightest strain. The victims in Tojama had drawn all their drinking water from a river into which cadmium was fed in waste water from chemical factories.

A similar cadmium catastrophe occurred along the Tama River in Japan. Some 20 metal alloy undertakings discharged cadmium in waste water into the river. As the river water was used in the irrigation of rice fields, several hundred hectares of land under cultivation were contaminated with cadmium. The rice fields were found to contain 90 ppm of cadmium, the irrigation channels 35–220 ppm, and mud in the Tama River 380 ppm. Even at the river mouth 40 km (25 miles) away, the water contained 0.8 ppm of cadmium.

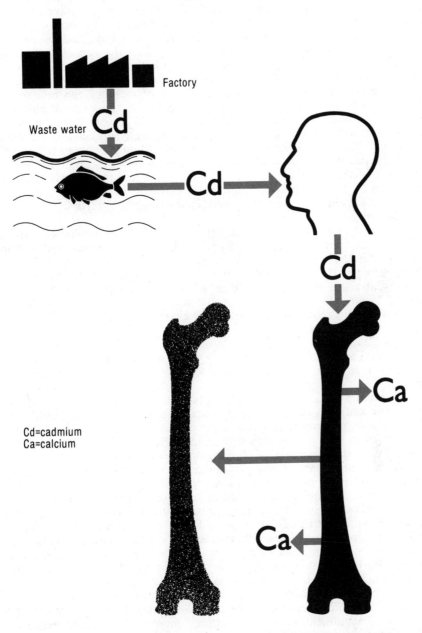

Factory

Waste water Cd

Cd

Cd

Ca

Ca

Cd=cadmium
Ca=calcium

CADMIUM WORKS ITS WAY INTO THE BONE STRUCTURE AND MAKES THE BONES BRITTLE

DAMAGE TO HEALTH FROM MERCURY

Mercury is a fluid heavy-metal, the toxicity of which has been known for a long time. Major environmental catastrophes from mercury have occurred so far mainly in Japan. Several industrial chemical concerns, especially those situated in the neighborhood of the Minamata Bay, had for decades discharged sewage water containing mercury into the sea. The mercury enriched itself in the food chain and ended up in the bodies of edible fish. It was present in the form of organic compounds and caused irreparable damage to the nervous system. A certain amount of mercury can be expelled from the body, but damaged brain and nerve cells cannot be replaced or repaired. According to the official figures, about 46 persons have died so far in Japan from the Minamata disease; 73 have been permanently disabled; and 19 children have serious mental disorders, although many of their mothers displayed no symptoms. But these figures only represent the poison cases established on the basis of court orders. According to investigations carried out by independent Japanese scientists, it is reckoned that about 15,000 persons in Minamata have sustained damage from fish contaminated with mercury.

The first symptoms of mercury poisoning occur in the sensory organs and manifest themselves in itching and numbness in the hands and feet and numbness in the region around the mouth. At roughly the same time, damage develops in the visual center, especially in limitation of the visual angle. The visual angle can decline within a week to a point at which vision is limited to straight ahead, as through binoculars. Damage to the hearing center leads to a reduction in hearing and eventually to deafness. Damage to the cerebellum results in physical movements not being adequately coordinated, culminating in disturbances of equilibrium and serious impediments in speech. The brain shrinks (by up to 35%), the intelligence quotient falls, growth is restricted, and the arms and legs are often deformed by muscular spasms.

Concentrations of mercury in foodstuffs of the order of several milligrams per kilogram can produce teratogenic effects in man (as established also in the case of mice) and mutagenic effects in various plants. In human lymphocyte cultures of persons with an increased blood-mercury concentration, a rise in the frequency of chromosome breaks was established.

As a contaminant in the environment, mercury is to be considered primarily in the form of methyl mercury. It can be assumed that metallic, ionic and also organically combined mercury (e.g., phenyl mercury) is converted relatively rapidly by microorganisms into methyl mercury. Very little is yet known about the distribution of heavy metal compounds in the biosphere and atmosphere, about their precipitation, about metabolic behavior in different organisms, including man, and about the precise toxicological properties. It is certain, nevertheless, that in food chains, from the lower water organisms up to the seal or to man, an accumulation of the methyl mercury concentration to several powers of ten will result.

The world consumption of mercury is estimated by UNO at 9200 tons per annum. Its utilization in West Germany amounted in 1969 to 760 tons, of which 27 tons was applied to plant protection in agriculture. Large quantities

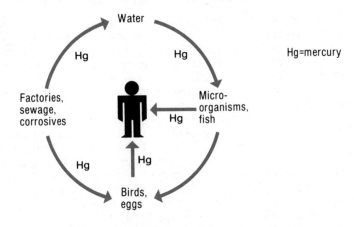

Hg=mercury

Diagram 1. TRANSMISSION OF TOXIC
MERCURY COMPOUNDS

Diagram 2. BRAIN DAMAGE BY
ORGANIC MERCURY COMPOUNDS

of metallic mercury were utilized for chlorine alkaline electrolysis. For every ton of chlorine produced, 200 to 300 grams of mercury are lost—carried away for the most part in sewage water. Large quantities of mercury are also used in the electrical and other industries. Every year some 10,000 tons of mercury pass into the ocean.

CIGARETTES AND TOBACCO—ACTIVE SMOKING

The deleterious consequences of smoking were first set out in broad outline in the Terry Report in 1964. This report by Dr. Luther Terry, then the surgeon general of the United States, touched off intensive research into the connection between diseases and cigarette smoking. As a result the following statistics were established: lung cancer is some 11 times more frequent among smokers than nonsmokers; and smokers die on the average 8.3 years earlier than nonsmokers. Connections exist in particular between smoking and cancer of the lungs, the lips, the oral cavity, the tongue, the throat, the larynx, the esophagus, the bladder, the kidneys and the pancreas.

So far over a thousand different chemical substances have been identified in cigarette smoke. A large number of them take the form of fine dust particles which, laden with cancer-forming hydrocarbons, penetrate the inner recesses of the lungs, the alveoli. One of the best-known poisons is the paralyzant nicotine. This can cause spasms and paralyze the breathing center in the brain. If present in a quantity of 50 mg it can prove fatal. One-hundredth part of this quantity (which corresponds to the amount absorbed from tobacco smoke) is enough to change the metabolism of the nerve cells perceptibly. Nicotine infiltrates from the inhaled air, contaminated with cigarette smoke, into the bloodstream and irritates the autonomic nervous system. This in turn affects the heart, the stomach, and other autonomic reactions of the body. In addition to the coronary vascular system, the other arteries in the body are also damaged by nicotine. On the average the arteries of a man who has smoked 20 cigarettes a day for 30 years can be as stiff and fragile by the time he is 50 as those of a nonsmoker fully 15 years older. As a result, circulatory disturbances and heart infarctions, strokes and other consequences of insufficient blood supply are similarly more frequent. The likelihood of death from a heart infarction is 3 to 5 times greater for smokers than for nonsmokers.

The injury potential of tobacco tar in cigarette smoke has so far been researched the least. Just a few puffs from a cigarette are sufficient to arrest the self-purification mechanism of the lungs, the minute filter hairs on the mucous membranes of the respiratory tract. The result of this for the regular smoker is a racking smoker's cough and chronic bronchitis. The tar contains a large number of poisons, which in some cases have not yet been closely analyzed. The fine dividing walls between the alveoli in the lungs can be broken down and demolished by such poisons, and this will result in under-functioning of the lungs (emphysema), with shortage of breath and increased susceptibility to disease.

In recent years the cigarette industry has turned its attention to brands containing less nicotine and tar. To judge by the results of tests conducted on animals, these milder brands of cigarettes are likely to reduce the danger of contracting bronchial cancer from cigarette smoking. On the other hand, according to medical authorities on smoking and health, there is also a fear that additional substances contained in the milder cigarettes, such as sodium nitrate, could form new cancer-inducing substances such as nitrosamines, which are capable in certain circumstances of causing cancerous affection in other parts of the human body.

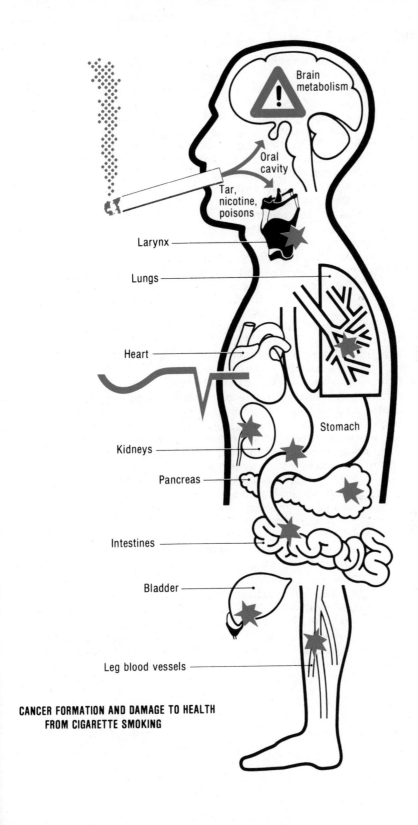

Brain
metabolism

Oral
cavity

Tar,
nicotine,
poisons

Larynx

Lungs

Heart

Kidneys

Pancreas

Stomach

Intestines

Bladder

Leg blood vessels

**CANCER FORMATION AND DAMAGE TO HEALTH
FROM CIGARETTE SMOKING**

PASSIVE SMOKING

Apart from the smoker himself, the problem of the absorption of contaminants from tobacco smoke also concerns the nonsmoking "co-smoker". It is now suspected that the additional smoke from a cigarette (that which is not inhaled by the smoker), to which the co-smoker is mainly exposed, contains as many cancer-producing and other dangerous substances (nicotine, pyridine, phenols and ammonia) as the mainstream of smoke inhaled by the smoker himself. The incidental flow of smoke contains, for example, three times more cancer-producing 3,4-benzopyrene than the mainstream. In the interval between puffs, all the poisonous constituents pass into the secondary flow. Members of the catering trade, such as waiters, even when they are nonsmokers, are affected more often by bronchial cancer than the rest of the population. Investigations show that cancer-producing 3,4-benzopyrene is present in smoke-filled catering establishments in concentrations of 2.8 to 14.4 mg per cu m (compared with an average in big city atmospheres of from 0.28 to 0.48 mg per cu m).

A special danger in the matter of passive smoking occurs for the embryo of a mother who smokes during pregnancy, for there is no possibility open to the embryo of escaping from the danger zone. The number of premature and stillbirths is higher for expectant mothers who smoke than for those who do not. The weight of the baby at birth is also lower, and its subsequent mental development may be impaired.

A clinical handicap caused by co-smoking that is difficult to assess is reduction in mental capacity. Cigarette smoke contains the poison gas carbon monoxide, which has a 250-times-higher capacity to combine with the red blood cell pigment hemoglobin than has atmospheric oxygen. The hemoglobin is obstructed thereby, is unable to absorb more oxygen, and is handicapped in performing the vital function of transmitting oxygen. A lack of oxygen has serious consequences for the brain and the nervous system in particular. Although the brain accounts for only about 2% of the entire body weight, it requires some 20% of the oxygen intake of the body as a whole. Under these circumstances it is understandable that the finer brain functions, such as powers of concentration, decision-making, discernment and responsiveness, should be affected adversely by reduced supplies of oxygen.

From a broad-based series of investigations it has emerged that nonsmokers who are obliged to smoke passively are subject to the following complaints: conjunctivitis, headaches, nausea, vertigo, reduced powers of concentration, etc.

Medical authorities on smoking and health and other organizations are accordingly demanding that the right of the nonsmoker to physical protection should be given priority over the smoker's right to indulge his addiction. A prohibition on smoking is called for wherever nonsmokers are obliged to congregate with smokers. In certain countries, notably Bulgaria and Romania, this protection for the nonsmoker is already embodied in legislation.

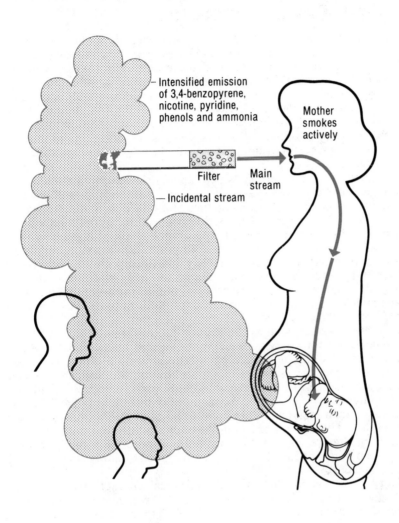

Intensified emission
of 3,4-benzopyrene,
nicotine, pyridine,
phenols and ammonia

Mother
smokes
actively

Filter

Main
stream

Incidental stream

HARMFUL EFFECTS OF CIGARETTE SMOKE ON DEVELOPING FETUS AND ON PASSIVE INHALERS

ENVIRONMENTAL POISONS AND CANCER

Although the precise biochemical process of cancer formation is not yet known, the following scientific information is available: the growth of cancer is an irreversible process, that is, the damage done by a cancer-producing (carcinogenic) poison cannot be repaired by the organism affected; cancer proceeds by cell division and is transmitted from cell to cell. It is assumed that the heritable substance deoxyribonucleic acid (DNA) suffers modification by mutation owing to ionizing radiation (radioactivity) or to cancer-producing chemical poisons, so that the cell concerned begins to multiply rapidly and, in each cell division, passes on to the new cells the modification leading to cancer.

Substances are known today which, upon a single administration, produce a cancerlike deterioration in the tissues. As a rule, however, most cancer-inducing substances take some time to produce their effects. In most cancer cases the latent period (the period between the initial reaction to a cancer-producing substance and the appearance of the malignant growth) can normally be put at between 10 and 40 years. By reason of this latent period it is very difficult to attribute any individual case of cancer to a particular initial reaction. In the body of a person suffering from cancer, it is thus possible to identify the malignant tumor but not the agent that produced it. In scientific experiments, this also makes it difficult to be 100% sure that a substance is carcinogenic.

Another important point in the field of cancer research is that there is no tolerance dose for cancer-producing substances below which the substance concerned would not touch off a cancer reaction. There is a direct proportional connection between the concentration of a cancer-producing substance and the number of carcinomas developed. The effects of the very smallest individual doses have to be included without loss—that is to say, the effects of each individual dose have to be aggregated, even if the substance has long been eliminated from the body. In the lower concentrations that are normally present in environmental pollution, the number of tumor agents is also fairly independent of the temporal distribution and the size of the individual doses.

Every year several thousand new chemical products are put on the market and transmitted into the environment without its being known whether they are cancer-producing or not. Of groups of active agents that have been sprayed into the environment in large quantities for a long time, only a small proportion have been subjected to carcinogenic tests. Of the pesticides utilized in agriculture for the destruction of insect pests, only about 15% have been tested in this way.

Research for such a carcinogenic test encounters considerable difficulty. Two major points involved are (a) consideration of any combination effects and (b) the transposition of the results achieved with animals to human beings. Researchers can certainly examine a particular substance very thoroughly as regards its cancer-producing effects; but they still cannot establish how this substance will react in combination with one or more of the thousand and one substances released into the environment. Many cancer-producing substances attain their true effects only in combination with other carcinogenic substances. An example is provided by the nitrosamines, which are among the strongest cancer-producing poisons known to man. They are formed from a combination of nitrates (e.g., nitrate concentration in foodstuffs from easily soluble fertilizers) or nitrous waste gases (e.g., in the chemical industry) with amines (intermediate products in the human digestive metabolism). Neither nitrous gases nor amines exert any influence on their own in cancer formation. Only when they react chemically with one another do they become carcinogenic.

Another problem is the application of tests on animals to human beings. In principle, suspected substances can only be tested by experiments on animals. To some extent, however, animals have a different biochemical metabolism from man. This can have the result either that poisons that produce cancer in man are broken down by a particular metabolic product of animal metabolism and so rendered harmless, or that a chemical substance is only converted into a cancer-producing substance in combination with a specific human metabolic product, which does not turn up in the animal test and so cannot be tested. For arsenic oxide, for instance, no carcinogenicity is identifiable in the animal test. As regards people, on the other hand, its long-term effects are severely cancer-productive. In animal tests the carcinogenicity of arsenic oxide cannot be identified for the following reasons: if the dose administered is too high, the animals under test will die (because arsenic oxide, in addition to its cancer-producing effects, is also highly toxic). If the dose is reduced with a view to lowering the poisonous effect, the latent period of the cancer will be so extended that it exceeds the life expectancy of the animal.

Among the substances proved to be carcinogenic, the polycyclic hydrocarbons (such as 1,2-benzanthracene, 1,2-benzopyrene and 3,4-benzopyrene) occupy a leading position. Best known is 3,4-benzopyrene. Together with other polycyclic hydrocarbons, it is produced mainly as a result of incomplete combustion of petroleum products in furnaces and motor vehicles. Whereas air in country districts contains on the average 0.01 μg of benzopyrene per 1000 cu m of air, the corresponding concentration in air in city areas averages 6.5 μg per 1000 cu m of air. By way of comparison, exhaust fumes from private motor vehicles contain between 1600 and 20,000 μg per 1000 cu m of air. Benzopyrene on its own has only a small cancer-producing effect, but this proliferates in the presence of iron oxide, sulfur oxide, ozone and certain other substances. Benzopyrene combines in particular with dust particles, and fine dust is likely to contain 10 to 100 times as much benzopyrene as coarse dust. As fine dust penetrates the lungs and settles in the alveoli, the benzopyrene contained in it can develop its cancer-producing effects in the lungs directly. It is for this reason, among others, that people who live on main traffic thoroughfares and are thus directly exposed to vehicle exhaust fumes are about four times as likely to contract and die of lung cancer as the rest of the population. Investigations at the University of Bochum, Germany, show that people earning a living in big cities in the open air (such as city gardeners and park keepers) contract lung cancer on the average three times as often as, say, electricians, bank employees or retailers. On the other hand, on the city outskirts, which are only mildly exposed to exhaust fumes, only half as many people (as those in the city) die of bronchial cancer.

Among the substances whose carcinogenic properties have been proved are chromic, beryllium, silver and mercury salts, nickel carbonyl, lead phosphate, benzol, asbestos, the herbicide amitrole, the fungicide thiocarbamide, and the pesticides aldrin, dieldrin and DDT.

RADIOACTIVE CONTAMINATION: THE EFFECT OF RADIOACTIVE RAYS ON LIVING CREATURES

The radiation released upon the disintegration of radioactive atomic nuclei takes the form of particulate or wave radiation of very high energy. When this radiation impinges on living cells, various interactions can result. The most important of these is the ionization of atoms. In the electron sheath of an atom, a certain number of negatively charged electrons are present which correspond to a like number of positively charged protons in the atomic nucleus. Consequently an atom is normally electrically neutral in its outward effects. If radioactivity, such as a negatively charged electron of beta particle radiation, bombards a neutral atom, it may be that owing to the high energy of the radiation one or more electrons will be ejected from the electron sheath of the atom. The atom then becomes an ion, a positively charged (electrically) atomic residue. Owing to their electrical attractive power, newly formed ions have a capacity for strong chemical reaction. If this takes place in dead matter, in the air for instance, it is of no importance. An ionized nitrogen atom, for example, can combine with ionized oxygen atoms; and ionized oxygen atoms can combine three at a time to form one ozone molecule. But if this process of ionization of atoms takes place in living tissue, in certain circumstances a variety of damage may result.

It is now known that the plan for the constitution of a living organism is contained in a long filamentary structure, in which, on the basis of a precise arrangement of small molecules, information regarding heritable characteristics is contained. This is deoxyribonucleic acid (DNA) and it consists of a basic structure of sugar and phosphate molecules to which four different basic molecules are attached in a particular sequence. This sequence is what is known as the genetic code, which represents the heritable information. In the case of each cell division the DNA is also divided and restructured on identical lines, so that the heritable information is fully retained in each cell in the case both of the formation of new organisms and of the decomposition and restructuring of body cells. If radioactive rays now impinge on a DNA molecule, there is a danger that, with the ionization of atoms and the chemical reaction ensuing therefrom, a variation may occur in the basic arrangement and so in the heritable information. Such a variation in the heritable information is known as a mutation. Almost all the mutations are negative; it is estimated that over 99.99% of the mutations change the organism's characteristics negatively. If the mutation occurs in germ cells—that is, in male sperm cells or in female egg cells—this can result, when a new organism is formed, in severe damage, such as deformities, stillbirths, enzyme defects and other metabolic disorders. In body cells, otherwise known as somatic cells, a mutation can cause cancerous degeneration.

It has to be assumed that no tolerance limits exist as regards this type of damage—that is to say, that the very smallest quantity of radioactivity is capable of causing such damage. High radiation exposure can touch off a chain reaction via ionization of atoms, chemical reactions, toxic molecule reaction and poisoning of the entire organism, leading to immediate danger in the form of fever, nausea, vomiting, loss of hair and death from radiation.

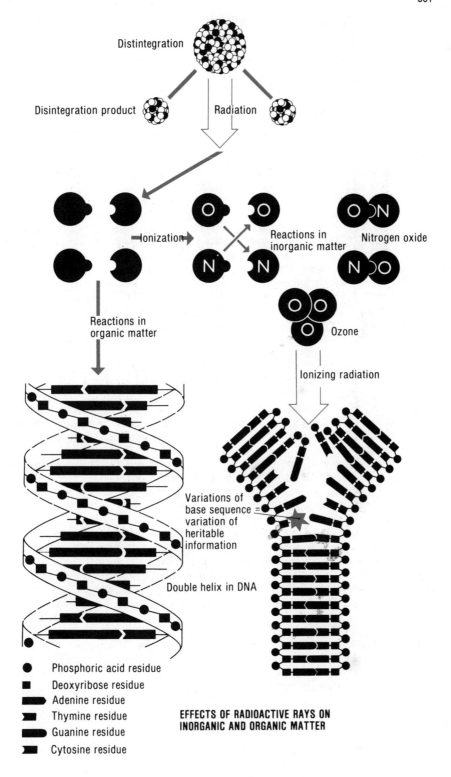

Distintegration

Disintegration product

Radiation

Ionization

Reactions in inorganic matter

Nitrogen oxide

Reactions in organic matter

Ozone

Ionizing radiation

Variations of base sequence = variation of heritable information

Double helix in DNA

● Phosphoric acid residue
■ Deoxyribose residue
▬ Adenine residue
▬ Thymine residue
▬ Guanine residue
▬ Cytosine residue

EFFECTS OF RADIOACTIVE RAYS ON INORGANIC AND ORGANIC MATTER

THE ENRICHMENT OF RADIOACTIVE SUBSTANCES

Like other environmental poisons, radioactive substances can build up strong concentrations in the food chain. The concentration factor varies enormously from one radioactive substance to another. It depends on the chemical element character of the radioactive substance and on the presence of other substances in the environment. Concentration factors of up to a million are now quite frequent.

The processes involved in such a concentration can be illustrated by an example. The element strontium occurs in nature in only very limited quantities. It is related chemically to calcium. Like the latter, it is an alkaline-earth metal, and so has similar chemical properties. When nuclear fission occurs, the radioactive isotope strontium-90 is one of the products. To build up their bodies (especially their bones) organisms need plenty of calcium, and they obtain this from their environment. The small quantities of calcium present in their food are preferentially extracted in the digestive processes and enriched in the body by metabolic processes. Owing to its similarity to calcium, strontium is also taken up and enriched. It is then absorbed with calcium into the bone structure of the body. If radioactive strontium is present in the environment (as a result, for instance, of nuclear weapons tests or troubles at a nuclear power station), this will be enriched in precisely the same way and absorbed in the bones. In this manner an internal source of radiation is formed in human beings, which in the case of strontium-90 tends to concentrate in the blood-forming bone marrow and can cause leukemia.

Here lies the real danger of radioactive contamination of the environment. When the radiation comes from an external source (such as a tank containing radioactive material), people can protect themselves by leaving the danger zone. But when they have absorbed and enriched radioactive substances out of the environment, an internal source of radiation builds up in them from which there is no escape as long as the substances remain in their bodies.

In the vicinity of several nuclear power stations that have been in operation in the United States for some time, higher rates of cancer and infant mortality have been established: in the neighborhood of the Shippingport, Pennsylvania, nuclear power station (90 megawatts), with a population of 200,000, the number of fatal cancer cases rose from 148 per 100,000 in 1958 to 205 per 100,000 in 1968. That is an increase of 39%, whereas the increase for the state as a whole averaged no more than 9%. A particularly sharp increase of 180% occurred in cancer deaths in the town of Midland, Pennsylvania, which is a mile and a quarter upriver from Shippingport on the Ohio. The town of Midland draws its drinking water from the Ohio, into which the nuclear power station discharges its radioactive sewage. Another example is the boiling water reactor (75 megawatts) at Big Rock Point on Lake Michigan. In the vicinity of the reactor there, infant mortality is some 50% higher, leukemia some 400% higher, and the frequency of deformed births about 230% higher than the overall averages for Michigan. These rises in the mortality and sickness rates occurred despite the fact that according to official statistics the permitted limits for radioactivity had not been exceeded.

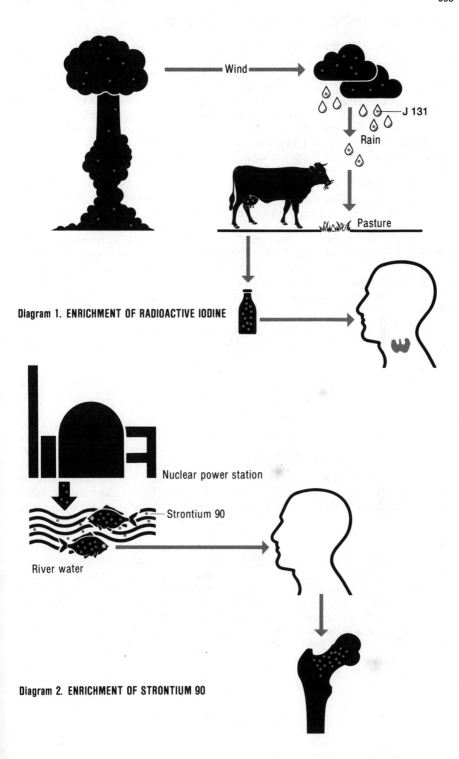

363

Wind

J 131

Rain

Pasture

Diagram 1. ENRICHMENT OF RADIOACTIVE IODINE

Nuclear power station

Strontium 90

River water

Diagram 2. ENRICHMENT OF STRONTIUM 90

RADIATION EXPOSURE AND RADIATION DAMAGE

The quantity of a radioactive substance is specified in curies (abbreviated Ci, named after Mme. Curie who discovered radium). A radioactive substance thus contains 1 Ci when 37 billion radioactive disintegrations occur in it per second, so 1 Ci is a very large quantity. The natural radioactivity of the earth per gram is of the order of 1 pCi or picocurie, which equals 1 trillionth of a curie. To measure radioactivity one uses the units roentgen (abbreviated r, or more recently R), rad (or rd), and rem. The unit roentgen (named after William G. Röntgen, the discoverer of x-rays) is a measure of the number of ionizations produced in air by radioactivity: in dry air of 0°C and 760 mm Hg, 1 r produces 2 billion ions per cc.

The unit rad indicates how much energy is given off by ionizing radiation to the corpuscles irradiated: 1 rad is the radiation dosage given off by 100 ergs of energy in one gram of any substance. In water and soft tissues 1 r = 1 rad.

For the assessment of biological effects of ionizing radiation, the unit rem has been created. The rem consists of the energy dosage (rad) plus a characteristic number (RBE factor) for the form of radiation concerned (alpha, beta, gamma, neutron and proton radiation, etc.). This RBE factor (relative biological effectiveness) has the following values for the various forms of radiation:

Alpha radiation	10
Beta radiation	1
Gamma radiation	1
Roentgen (x-ray) radiation	1
Slow neutron radiation	4
Fast neutron radiation	5–20
Proton radiation	10

In discussions on the environment the rem unit is used for the most part, as it is in this unit that the various effects of radiation forms have already been considered. The limit imposed by legislation in West Germany on radiation loads arising from the release of radioactive substances by nuclear power stations amounts to 30 mrem (millirems) per annum by radioactive waste gases and 30 mrem per annum by radioactive sewage. These legislative limits were adopted on the assumption that there is a tolerance dose for radioactivity below which no further damage is to be expected. Recent biological radiation research has shown, however, that this assumption must be abandoned. If recent investigations by American scientists are applied to conditions ruling in West Germany, it emerges that ionizing radiation at these permitted limits would result annually, in Germany alone, in from 1000 to 3000 additional deaths from cancer and leukemia and from 2000 to 20,000 additional cases of hereditary damage (stillbirths, deformed babies and hereditary diseases). These conclusions, which are unchallenged, have since been confirmed by the American authorities for protection of the environment.

Diagram 1. INCREASE IN CANCER RISKS FOR CHILDREN UNDER 10 YEARS OF AGE AS A RESULT OF EXPOSURE TO X-RAYS AT THE PRENATAL STAGE

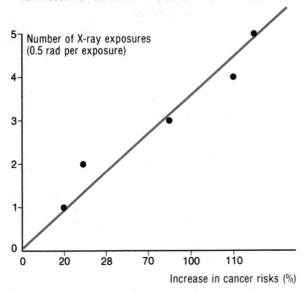

Diagram 2. CONNECTION BETWEEN THE EMISSION OF RADIOACTIVE GASES FROM THE DRESDEN REACTOR AND THE INCREASE IN INFANT MORTALITY (ILLINOIS) COMPARED WITH A RELATIVE DISTRICT (OHIO)

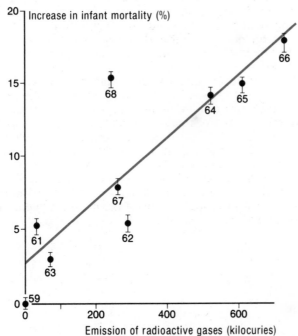

PLUTONIUM

Plutonium, chemical symbol Pu, is an artificially produced, radioactive, chemically and radiologically highly toxic metallic element in the actinide series, which also occurs in minute quantities as a result of natural disintegration processes in nature. It is formed in nuclear reactors from uranium (U) by the following process: U-238 + neutron → U-239; U-239 disintegrates by the emission of beta radiation into neptunium-239 (Np-239), and this decomposes in the same way into Pu-239. Plutonium has the atomic number 94; and from it the isotopes Pu-232 to Pu-246 are known, of which Pu-244, with 8.2×10^7 years, has the longest half-life. The other isotopes also have a very long life. The technically most important of them, Pu-239, has a half-life of 24,400 years.

As it is highly fissionable by slow neutrons, Pu-239 is used as nuclear fuel and to make atomic bombs (the atomic bomb that was dropped on the Japanese city of Nagasaki on August 9, 1945, was a plutonium bomb). It is easier to extract than uranium (U-235), and its critical mass amounts to no more than 8–16 kg, compared with a critical mass for uranium of 50 kg. Pu-239 is now obtained in large quantities from nuclear reactors, especially from fast breeder reactors. A fast breeder contains 1 ton of plutonium in its fuel rods.

Radiologically, plutonium, which burns in the air to form aerosols capable of penetrating into the lungs, is one of the strongest poisons known. When they get into the human organism, quantities of as little as one ten-millionth part of a gram are sufficient to cause cancer, for plutonium emits alpha rays of limited range which are capable of very high radiation doses locally. Investigations by Tamplin and Cochran in 1974 serve to demonstrate that the margins for plutonium hitherto considered tolerable, and the legal limits prescribed by law for plutonium contamination, are in fact too high by a factor of 300,000.

Plutonium is given off into the environment in limited quantities by reprocessing of nuclear fuels. There is likely to be in the future a substantial increase in the transport of plutonium to reprocessing centers by road and rail, so that the possibility of releases of plutonium by leakage or owing to terrorist activities cannot be ruled out. If a transport vehicle containing 25 kg were to overturn in an accident, the plutonium so released could cause up to 250 billion cases of lung cancer. From the same quantity of plutonium, given sufficient technical knowledge, an atomic bomb could be manufactured. The dangerous nature of plutonium, having regard in particular for the long life-span of its isotopes, is one of the main arguments against using nuclear fission as a source of energy.

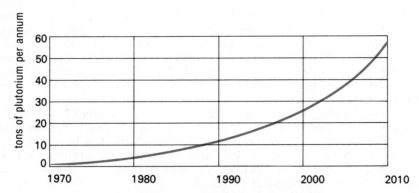

Diagram 1. ANNUAL PLUTONIUM PRODUCTION AT NUCLEAR POWER STATIONS

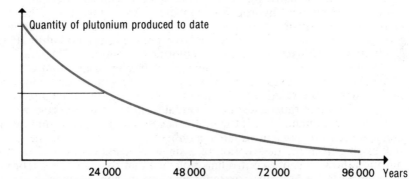

Quantity of plutonium produced to date

Diagram 2. DISINTEGRATION CURVE FOR PLUTONIUM (half-life, 24,000 years)

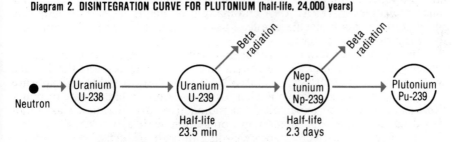

Diagram 3. TRANSFORMATION OF URANIUM-238 INTO PLUTONIUM-239

TRITIUM

Tritium is a radioactive hydrogen with a half-life of 12 years. It arises in nuclear power stations in large quantities. Its distribution in the environment is very difficult to check simply because its weak beta rays cannot be measured with normal actinometers. When it is present uncombined as a form of elementary hydrogen it can penetrate steel, concrete and other protective screens. Present-day nuclear power stations (1000 megawatts) discharge between 100 and 1000 Ci of tritium into the environment in waste water every year. Still larger quantities of tritium are discharged from reprocessing plants. These range from 10,000 to 20,000 Ci for the fuel of a nuclear power station of 1000 megawatts.

Because of the weakness of its beta rays, tritium produces only a low radiation charge, and until recently it has consequently been regarded as a relatively harmless radioisotope. Its radiotoxic significance has been seriously underestimated, however. It is now recognized that tritium can also affect living tissue by processes known as transmutations. *Transmutation* is the conversion of one chemical element into another during the radioactive decay of an isotope. In the radioactive decay process the tritium atom emits an electron and is converted into stable helium. Through radioactive decay the chemical element hydrogen is converted into a rare gas. Other biologically relevant transmutations are the conversion of radioactive carbon into nitrogen (C-14 into N-14), of radioactive phosphorus into sulfur (P-32 into S-32), and of radioactive sulfur into chlorine (S-35 into Cl-35).

Such transformation of the element character of an atom changes the chemical properties and consequently the biochemical and physiological importance of the relative molecule in which the transmuted atom is incorporated. There is thus a sort of "suicidal" effect on a molecule when such an atom is contained in it. If the molecules in which the transmuting atom is incorporated are present in large numbers in the organism, the biological risk arising from the destruction of a single molecule is negligible. If it is a question, however, of a controlling molecule that has biochemical or informative importance in a single number or in a few copies, as is the case with macromolecules of DNA, RNA and many proteins, then the transmutation of an atom of this molecule can lead to significant damage to the complete organism or one of its parts.

In the case of tritium, transmutative damage of the chromosomal structure was observed, inter alia, in cell cultures of the hamster, and the damage was intensified as these cell cultures were subjected to radiation exposure corresponding to the relative nuclear disintegration. A higher rate of mutations than was to be expected from radioactive disintegration was established several times in bacteria in connection with a buildup of tritium. Similar observations were made regarding the rate of recessive sex-related lethal mutations in the fruit fly *Drosophila*. In the case of tritium embedded in thymidine (a component of DNA), damage was caused by transmutations 50,000 times greater than was to be expected by radiation exposure to the tritium itself. In laying down legal limits for tritium, this problem of transmutations has not been considered. Tritium occurs in water from natural sources in a concentration of 40 pCi per liter. The limit for tritium in water was nevertheless set at 3,000,000 pCi per liter.

pCi per cu. m.

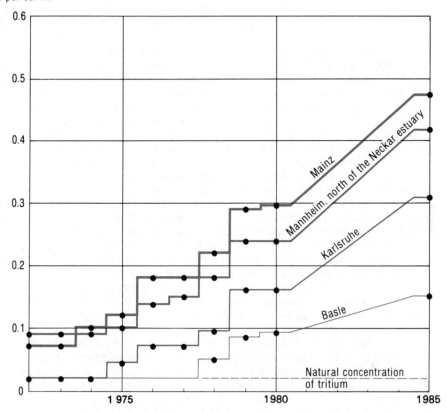

PROJECTED INCREASE IN THE AMOUNT OF TRITIUM RELEASED FROM
NUCLEAR PLANTS IN THE REGION OF THE UPPER RHINE UP TO 1985.

Part Fifteen—Sound and Noise

Sound is the result of any oscillation of air molecules that is perceptible to the organs of hearing. It is measured by reference to the pulsating load pressure generated in the air. To facilitate comparison of readings on a standard basis over the whole field, the sonic pressures are set out in a logarithmic scale. While the sonic pressure that a sound wave exerts on the eardrum can be measured objectively, there is no unit of measurement that can be applied to the physiological effects of sound or noise on the human organism.

The unit of measurement used to record the acoustic pressure level is the decibel (db). High audio frequencies are more clearly perceptible than lower frequencies. To allow for this circumstance in appraising a sound, evaluation curves have been prepared depending on the audio frequency. In general, the evaluation is made according to a curve bearing the letter A, and the results of sound-level measurements are recorded accordingly in terms of db(A). The evaluation curve is so devised that an increase in the sonic pressure level that seems to the individual to amount to a doubling of the sound volume is expressed in the scale as a rise of 10 db(A).

Apart from the intensity of sound, its duration is also a factor in determining the noise effect, so it is evaluated according to the duration of the average sound level over a period (average level, equivalent duration sound level). To enable consideration to be given to further factors such as the height and number of peak levels (for assessing sleep disturbance), their impact, whether they are customary in the district, and the nature and commercial background of the noise, an assessment level is established based on the average level. This should provide a measure by which to judge the physiological effect of a noise level. At present several divergent bases are in use for measurement and assessment purposes (DIN 45,633). The "phon" unit, which was frequently used previously, corresponds in general terms to the decibel unit in regular use today.

The term *noise* is difficult to define precisely, as in addition to measurable factors various subjective elements, such as the personal attitude and the general physical and mental makeup of the party concerned, also play a part. A good definition of the term has been produced by Klosterkötter: by *noise* is understood such sounds as influence the physiological functions of the organism unfavorably, and such as exert a psychic influence on people, and disturb, annoy, anger or frighten them, and damage their hearing.

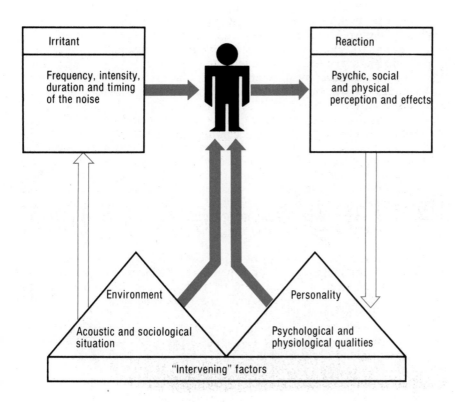

EFFECTS OF NOISE

NOISE AND HUMAN WELL-BEING

The noise problem assumes a somewhat different guise from the global environmental problems that are highlighted in literature and the mass media as exponential growth catastrophes. Consequently, attention should no longer be concentrated on the question of damage to health by noise but should be extended to take in the more general requirement that human well-being should not be burdened any longer by environmental circumstances imposed or influenced by man—in this case by noise.

Nuisance by noise depends on the physical factors of sound (intensity, frequency, recurrence of peak loads, etc.) and on the psychic condition of people. Sound irritation leads to measurable impulse responses in the central and autonomic nervous systems and in the glandular system. These variations can be identified by different means: the electroencephalograph records changes in electric currents in the brain, and the electromyograph the increases in muscle action potential, which characterize the general state of stress of a muscle group. The electrical skin resistance declines. The blood pressure can rise only marginally. The skin temperature drops slightly. The pupils expand. Stomach juice and saliva production are reduced. The breathing and pulse rates react with moderate changes; and the cardiac output declines somewhat. Maximum variations arise from alarm or shock reactions produced by short-term increases in the noise level (by an explosion, for instance). Very low thresholds of sensation are shown by changes (declines) in skin resistance. Significant reactions are to be distinguished once the noise threshold exceeds the general basic noise level by 3 to 6 db(A).

Undisturbed sleep is an essential prerequisite for the recuperation and consequently for maintenance of a person's working capacity. Frequent interruptions of sleep or curtailment of a night's rest are irksome to the individual and can lead to overexcitation of the psyche and eventually of the autonomic nervous system.

Less disturbing of sleep for most people are certain regular background noises to which one can grow accustomed, especially when they have their origin in nature and are thus inclined to be less sharp (e.g., running water, wind and rain). Unexpected and unaccustomed noises and sounds resulting from mechanical operations, on the other hand, are very prone to disturb sleep. Noises also affect the depth of a person's slumber. The deep sleep that promotes regeneration is transmuted by acoustic environmental irritants into a less recuperative twilight sleep. Further minor acoustic disturbances can awaken the deep sleeper altogether. Three minutes of acoustic radiation at 30 decibels—which is little more than whispered speech near the ear—correlates to a 10% awakening threshold for adults. A 50% awakening threshold is attained for adults with a noise effect of 45 decibels lasting for three minutes.

Although it is possible to grow accustomed to sounds of natural origin, adaptation to noises in respect to autonomic effects is not possible.

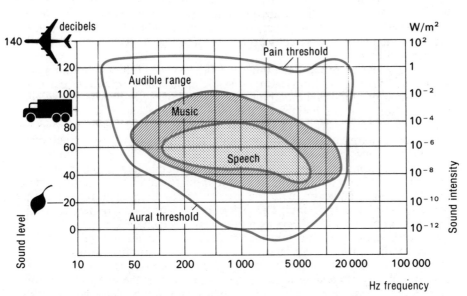

Diagram 1. SOUND PERCEPTION BY THE HUMAN EAR (AUDITORY SENSATION AREAS, THRESHOLDS AND FREQUENCY AREAS)

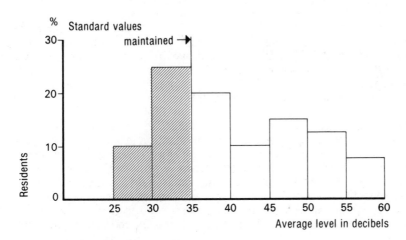

Diagram 2. NOISE NUISANCE FOR RESIDENTS (%) FROM STREET TRAFFIC (IN A BIG CITY, AT NIGHT WITH OPEN WINDOWS)

DEAFNESS CAUSED BY NOISE

Impairment of hearing caused by noise reflects metabolic exhaustion of the hearing cells in the inner ear accompanied by degenerative changes. Metabolic exhaustion under the effects of noise occurs when the oxygen requirements of the hearing sense cells exceed the amount of oxygen supplied from the bloodstream.

In the hearing process the inner ear functions as follows: Sound waves are carried via the eardrum and the ossicle apparatus to the inner ear fluid. In the inner ear fluid is a membrane composed of many hearing sense cells which absorb the oscillations of the inner ear fluid and pass them on for transmission to the brain. In this way the hearing sense cells receive the mechanical energy of the sound and their task is to convert the mechanical energy into nerve impulses.

The performance capacity of the sensory metabolism extends to sound intensities encountered in animate and inanimate nature. The metabolism is unable to cope, however, with the effects of severe industrial clamor that has developed over the years. The lack of oxygen occasioned thereby results in a drop in bioelectrical nerve potential. The oxygen deficiency is followed by disturbances in the protein metabolism and the related enzymes. The nuclei of the sensory cells assume swollen and shrunken forms, and the structure of the mitochondria changes. These consequences of acoustic overloading are reversible in the early stages. But if the exposure to noise continues, the sensory cells will swell up or become deformed and will eventually collapse.

It is now known that this noise damage arises from the persistent effects of noise during the greater part of a work shift at a level of 90 decibels (A). The damage to hearing only occurs first for only part of the frequency range. The individual concerned may have the impression that his hearing capacity is unaffected. In the case of particularly sensitive persons, however, the hearing may be affected at a sound level even below 85 decibels (A).

At the outset deafness develops in only a strictly limited hearing range. Above and below this level the aural threshold is normal. Subjective hearing troubles are still largely absent. Many of those affected complain, however, even at this stage, of annoying ear troubles, such as whistling and hissing noises in the ear. As the loss of hearing becomes more extensive, it finally rises to the upper hearing limit; that is, the victim has difficulty in hearing frequencies above a specific level. At this point difficulty will be experienced in understanding speech. The person affected can certainly still converse freely with another in a quiet room; but conversation in a noisier setting may present difficulties of comprehension. At the third stage the loss of hearing zone extends farther, to the middle frequencies, while in the upper frequencies the loss of hearing will increase only marginally. Difficulty in understanding speech in a normal noisy setting will further increase. The distance at which whispered speech can be heard is reduced from 0.1 to 0.5 meters (0.3 to 1.6 feet). In the final phase deafness will extend also to the lower frequencies.

General deafness cannot be relieved to any extent by medical treatment or by other means. This makes its prevention the more important. There are three ways of approaching this: by checking noise creation (e.g., by introducing less noisy production and manufacturing methods), by reducing noise diffusion (e.g., by screening off the noise producer and by architectural acoustic measures, such as the installation of sound-absorbent materials), and by personal soundproofing (e.g., the use of earplugs and ear covers).

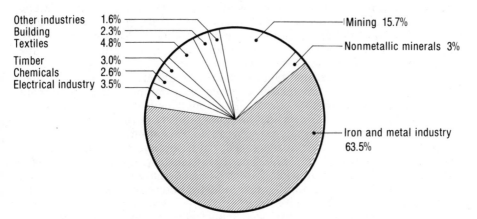

Diagram 1. **INCIDENCE OF DEAFNESS IN VARIOUS BRANCHES OF INDUSTRY (1971)**

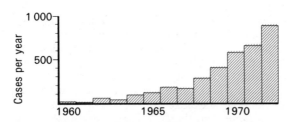

Diagram 2. **INCREASE IN DEAFNESS CAUSED BY NOISE**

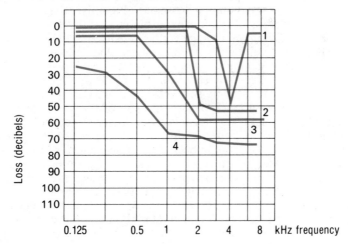

Diagram 3. **THRESHOLD AUDIOGRAM FOR THE VARIOUS PHASES OF DEAFNESS CAUSED BY NOISE**

SOUNDPROOFING

There are various methods of soundproofing. The first to be considered is the soundproof wall, which can be installed on building sites, at noisy industrial plants, on railways and motorways, and at airports. The individual elements of the soundproof wall are manufactured for the most part by an injection-molding process from ultraviolet-stabilized polyethylene of some thickness. Manufacturing it from plastic material ensures a measure of freedom from maintenance, durability with no loss of performance, and a high self-cleaning capacity. On the side exposed to the source of the sound there are numerous sound entry portals. The sound penetrates these openings onto an absorption material inside the soundproof wall, by which it is largely absorbed. As absorption material, a weather-resistant mineral fiberboard is used, and this is held by a spacing piece, at an optimum acoustic distance, as facing for the soundproof wall. The reverse surface of the wall is smooth. With a normal soundproof wall of about 51 kg per square meter, a reduction in the level of sound from traffic and industrial noises of about 12–13 decibels (A) can be achieved.

Soundproof walls are produced industrially in individual elements to dimensions of $100 \times 25 \times 15$ cm. These can be erected to any height and length required. Owing to the high wind forces encountered by free-standing soundproof walls (80 to 150 kg per sq m), the elements must be installed on a solid foundation.

Besides the fixed type of soundproof walls, mobile walls have recently been devised, which are of particular use in connection with noise of temporary provenance, as on building sites, and the possibility of using them again elsewhere has considerable cost advantages.

For the soundproofing of residential buildings, sound-deadening windows are employed. In extreme cases these can reduce the sound level by up to 50 decibels (A). As these are very costly to install, however, and as they cannot be opened, so that ventilation by means of an air-conditioning plant is required, in practice they do not fill a very important role.

As regards the damping down of traffic noise, the following factors need to be considered. On a four-lane highway on a level with the adjoining terrain and having an average traffic density of 2500 automobiles per hour, the noise level will be about 73 decibels (A) in the immediate vicinity, and around 65 to 66 decibels (A) in a multistory building (increasing with height) situated 50 meters (164 feet) from the roadway. As the distance from the roadway increases, the noise level rises more slowly at greater heights compared with ground level. This is a result of the sound-absorbent effects of the ground surface. The noise level on a city street with a traffic density of 1000 private cars an hour amounts to 70 decibels (A) at street level, 68 in the middle stories, and 66 decibels in the upper stories. In narrow streets between tall buildings, the noise level can rise by up to 10 decibels (A).

In city centers with pedestrian precincts not open to traffic, a substantial abatement of noise is achieved. On fast throughways some reduction in the noise load can be achieved by the installation of a belt of plants between the roadway and the housing zone (minimum breadth 30 meters, or 98 feet). A drop in the road level will also produce some reduction in noise, as far as the lower stories of the dwellings are concerned at any rate. A visible and perceptible improvement can also be achieved by installing a wall decorated with plants. In this way the noise load from a fast roadway 50 meters (164 feet) away can be reduced for the residents in a multistory building to 45 decibels.

AIRCRAFT NOISE AND ITS ABATEMENT

As far as relatively slow-flying piston-engined airliners are concerned, most of the noise comes from the engine and the propellers. The maximum sound radiation emanates from the turning circle of the propeller blades.

In the case of jet-propelled aircraft, the air sucked into the turbojet engine is compressed and then carried into a combustion chamber. Here fuel is injected and ignited. The hot gas-air mixture flows through the turbine, which drives the compressor, and leaves the turbojet through the outlet nozzle at high speed, thus propelling the aircraft. Behind the nozzle a turbulent zone is formed in which the thrust stream mixes with the air in the environment. It is the fluctuations in pressure caused in this way that pro-

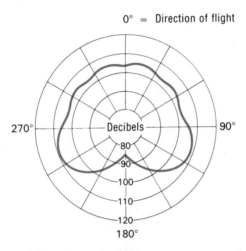

Diagram 1. DIRECTIONAL PATTERN OF THE OVERALL SOUND LEVEL PRODUCED BY A PROPELLER-DRIVEN AIRCRAFT (APPLICABLE TO AIRCRAFT BOTH AT REST AND IN FLIGHT)

duce the characteristic noise of the turbojet aircraft. As the maximum sound projection falls at an angle behind the aircraft, the jet-propelled aircraft emits the greatest sound intensity for those affected after it has passed overhead.

Turboprop aircraft occupy an intermediate position. In this case the turbine drives not only the compressor but also a propeller, which provides the bulk of the thrust, while the thrust element produced by the released gases is relatively low. The sound comes first from the propeller, and second from the compressor and the gases emitted by the turbine.

The highest sound intensity is produced by the aircraft taking off. In the case of a DC8 with a takeoff weight of 85 tons, for instance, a sound level of 85 decibels will be encountered for a distance of 12 km (7.4 miles) from the starting point in the direction of flight. The sound level then continues at 80 decibels for a distance of some 20 km (12.4 miles). Recordings show that particular localities in the vicinity of airfields face sound levels (on various days in the week and often for several hours at a time) of up to 100 decibels,

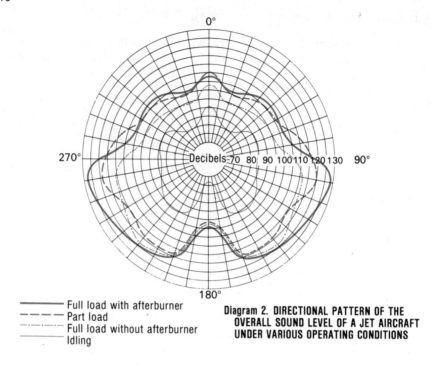

0°

270° Decibels 70 80 90 100 110 120 130   90°

180°

——————— Full load with afterburner
— — — — Part load
—·—·—·— Full load without afterburner
——————— Idling

**Diagram 2. DIRECTIONAL PATTERN OF THE
OVERALL SOUND LEVEL OF A JET AIRCRAFT
UNDER VARIOUS OPERATING CONDITIONS**

and where there are regular practice flights, especially with military planes, of over 110 decibels. At these levels permanent damage can be done to the hearing.

The first step in the battle against aircraft noise is the installation of sound-measuring equipment at individual recording points as widely dispersed as possible. With the aid of the measurement data obtained, zones subject to different levels of noise stress can be mapped out. By this means it is possible for air-traffic control to lay down departure routes by which only thinly populated areas in the vicinity of the airfield have to be traversed. In the case of landings, however, for technical flying reasons the range of choices of the terrain to be traversed is limited, making it harder to check noise nuisance in this way.

A sustained improvement in the aircraft noise situation can be achieved in the long run only by the adoption of aircraft with quieter power units, such as are already in use for some planes on shorter routes.

The measures adopted to combat the effects of aircraft noise on takeoff and landing must be accompanied by efforts to reduce ground noise. This can be done by erecting sound barriers around repair shops and soundproof walls at airports to shield local residents.

Part Sixteen—Waste Disposal and Utilization

DISPOSAL OF DOMESTIC AND INDUSTRIAL REFUSE IN INDUSTRIAL AGGLOMERATIONS

Social changes in the past twenty years have resulted in the inhabitants of big cities moving out to surrounding areas. Population centers have consequently been extended, and the cost of waste removal has risen accordingly, owing to the greater transport distances involved.

Local authorities responsible for refuse disposal have three main procedures to choose from. The cheapest of these is to deposit the refuse in a dump. As dumps may no longer be opened up at random and left unattended because of the threats they pose to the environment, big centralized dumps are now provided to take over the duties previously shared by a number of smaller ones. The refuse consequently has to be transported over long distances, which not only entails heavy expenses but has other disadvantages connected with increases in traffic. It is not uncommon for a city to have to handle well over a hundred truckloads of rubbish a day, for which the distance has to be covered twice (there and back). The burden could be eased only by installing a number of smaller dumps around the area, but this comes up against the difficulty that sufficient sites are not usually to be found that comply with the legal requirements. Furthermore the technical and mechanical equipment required costs as much to run and maintain on a small dump as on a large one. Staffing expenses are also disproportionately high on a small dump compared with a large one. If waste disposal has to be decentralized, the dump is thus not a favorable solution.

By decentralizing waste disposal, the long distances to be covered from the point of origin to the treatment point can be avoided and the costs of

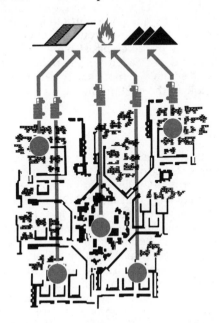

Diagram 1. CENTRALIZED REFUSE TREATMENT

Diagram 2. DECENTRALIZED UTILIZATION OF REFUSE

transport and staffing can be reduced. Two other methods of waste disposal merit consideration. Disposal of the refuse by burning (see later) is a practical solution provided the sites are well removed from residential dwellings and all necessary safety measures are complied with. Composting the refuse (see also later) meets the requirements of decentralization almost ideally. To judge by experience so far, compost plants operate to the best advantage in communities on the order of 60,000–80,000 inhabitants (the smaller handicraft and manufacturing undertakings in the area being assessed, as regards their refuse output, as equivalent to a particular number of inhabitants). In addition to refuse, sewage sludge (see also later) can also be treated by the composting process, thereby solving a particular problem facing every city authority. The compost, which is the end product of the process, is best disposed of in the vicinity of the compost plant. In the case of a decentralized plant (provided it is not faced with too heavy transport costs), the compost may be disposed of even more easily because of the extensive areas that should be available in the neighborhood.

REFUSE SUCTION PLANT

Refuse disposal by large-scale industry in densely populated districts presents special problems. On grounds of hygiene and practicality, the refuse should be transported from its point of origin to a central collecting point as far as possible automatically, that is, without contact with human beings. Various supply lines for water, electricity, gas, heating and the telephone are, like the sewage system, laid under ground. The removal of solid domestic and industrial refuse can be arranged underground in the same way by means of a fully automated refuse suction plant, by which the refuse is carried through a closed system directly to a central separator. There the refuse is fed into a compressor plant and is eventually taken away. Clearance of the feed shafts occurs at fixed intervals automatically and without noise nuisance by means of a programmed control mechanism. The capacity of the plant can be raised at any time without additional expense and can be adapted to new requirements if more frequent clearance is called for.

The route traversed by the refuse from its point of origin to the collecting point is as follows: The refuse is fed through inlet openings into one of the vertical feed shafts. Here it accumulates for a short time in a storage space pending onward transmission through the valves at the base of the shafts. These are the links between the feed shafts and the horizontal conveyor tubes below them. The main element in the valves is a horizontal

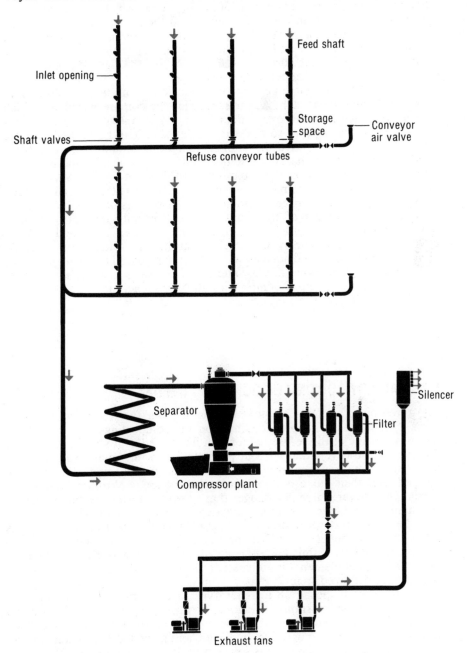

Inlet opening

Feed shaft

Storage space

Conveyor air valve

Shaft valves

Refuse conveyor tubes

Silencer

Separator

Filter

Compressor plant

Exhaust fans

PLAN OF A REFUSE SUCTION PLANT

movable steel disk at the base of the feed shaft which serves to retain the refuse. The conveyor system proper consists of steel tubes of an internal diameter of 500 mm (20 in.). They are placed horizontally in the ground and can, if necessary, be left at an angle or curved. At the start of the tube conveyor system is an air inlet valve, the purpose of which is to admit air when the clearance process commences. At the end of the horizontal tube system is a separator, in which the refuse and the air in which it is carried are separated. From there the waste passes into the compressor plant below. Owing to the dust load and possible smell nuisance, the conveyor air is purified in a filter. After purification the air passes through an exhaust system, equipped with a silencer, into the open air.

To assist the discharge process the exhaust fans produce a reduction in pressure in the tube system. At the same time the compressor plant, which had not been working up to that point, comes into operation. The air conversion inlet valve opens, so that the conveyor air can be sucked into the tubes. The first of the valves in the feed shafts opens, and the refuse drops from the vertical feed shaft into the horizontal conveyor tube and is carried by the air stream as far as the separator. At this point the first valve in the feed shafts closes. The remainder then open in succession until all the feed pipes are cleared. The process is then repeated in all its phases.

All the operations of the plant are electronically controlled from a power station, and recorded and supervised. In a self-contained suction, collection and conveyor system, large quantities of refuse can easily be conveyed considerable distances at a low labor cost. The plant performs well from a hygienic point of view and has no smell or noise effects. Driveways and extensive refuse dumps with all their unpleasant side effects are avoided completely in this process.

PRELIMINARY SORTING OF DOMESTIC REFUSE

The three main methods employed at present for the treatment of refuse from settled areas—dumping, combustion and composting—call for no preliminary sorting of the refuse, which can be treated as it stands. It must be recognized, however, that without preliminary sorting, many valuable raw materials such as paper, iron and nonferrous metals, and glass are destroyed, and their value is thus lost to the economy. Without preliminary sorting, moreover, there is a danger that noxious substances may be left in the dumps or in compost plants and cause considerable damage.

The elimination of particular refuse elements in the treatment process is also not without its difficulties and calls for heavy expenditure on machinery and labor. It thus has to be considered whether separate treatment of the individual elements in domestic refuse is of advantage in relation to the practice followed so far.

A separate disposal bin for each type of domestic refuse would, as a rule, be out of the question, as it would be far too difficult to supervise and would be uneconomic. If the constituents of domestic refuse are assembled in a few well-defined subgroups, however, and provided reasonable control and discipline are exercised, this solution should present no difficulties.

The most important subgroups for waste from settled areas would in-

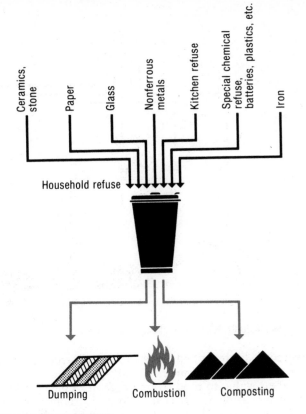

Ceramics, stone Paper Glass Nonferrous metals Kitchen refuse Special chemical refuse, batteries, plastics, etc. Iron

Household refuse

Dumping   Combustion   Composting

Diagram 1. MODERN WASTE DISPOSAL

clude organic kitchen refuse; paper and board; glass; stone, ceramic, ash and other noncombustible material groups; plastics; and iron and nonferrous metals. Altogether there are six subgroups, the separate assembly of which is of some economic importance. First, organic kitchen refuse, because of its susceptibility to putrefaction and the nuisance it can cause for the population through smell, should be collected more often and if possible converted into compost. All other waste is, for the most part, chemically and biologically noncorrosive and consequently need be collected less frequently. Second, paper can be reused as a raw material in paper production or, if it is not required for that purpose, can be used for energy production. Third, glass is similarly reused as a raw material in the manufacture of low-quality glassware (glass bottles). Fourth, iron and nonferrous metals can be handled together, as their magnetic separation presents no technical difficulties. These, too, represent a valuable raw material which can be used again in engineering processes. Materials in the ceramic, stone and ash group can be left in dumps without hesitation, as no chemical or biological reactions are to be expected in this case. Finally, plastics that cannot be reutilized for technical production purposes can be used for energy production.

The separate assortment of refuse in groups certainly entails difficulties in the home and for collecting and disposal organizations, but these can be

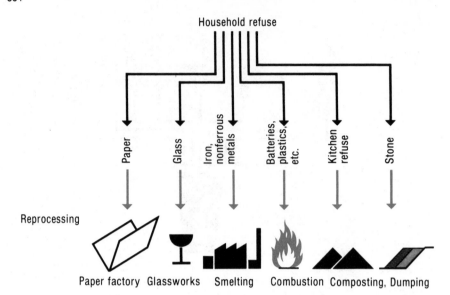

Household refuse

Paper — Glass — Iron, nonferrous metals — Batteries, plastics, etc. — Kitchen refuse — Stone

Reprocessing

Paper factory   Glassworks   Smelting   Combustion   Composting, Dumping

Diagram 2. PRELIMINARY SORTING OF HOUSEHOLD REFUSE

largely overcome by recent advances in the construction of suitable collecting bins. In any case, this form of refuse disposal and the related reallocation of parts of the residue to production processes considerably eases the load carried by disposal plants. It is therefore desirable that the steps already taken for the separate collection of old papers and aluminum cans should be continued and extended to other groups of materials.

ORGANIZED DUMPS

The predominant part of household and industrial waste will continue to be disposed of in organized dumps. This is mainly due to the fact that depositing it in this way is the cheapest method. Investment, labor and incidental costs together amount to roughly one-tenth of the costs incurred in other disposal processes. Organized dumps have the further advantage that problematic refuse (special waste) can also be disposed of in this way.

When refuse is disposed of by this method it is important to ensure that the body of the deposit does not come into contact with groundwater, that heavy metals and organic pollutants do not get washed away. Provided this requirement is satisfied, a start can be made on spreading the refuse in layers. The refuse is spread out in a layer of 20–50 cm (8–20 in.) and is then tamped down with a compressor. In this way the most intensive use is made of the space available, and the refuse cannot become a breeding ground for insect pests and rats. The danger of spontaneous combustion is also eliminated.

Upon completion of the depositing operation each day, a layer of impervious material is spread over the compressed refuse to reduce nuisance from smell and to prevent scraps of paper and plastic from being blown about. This layer consists mainly of rubble and other excavated material. If the application of this material presents any difficulties, a covering of foam can also be applied by spraying over the deposit in the evening, and its

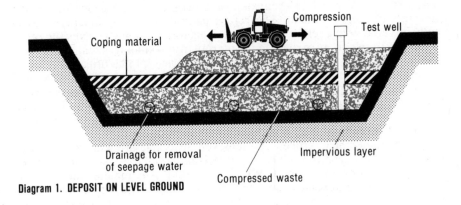

Diagram 1. DEPOSIT ON LEVEL GROUND

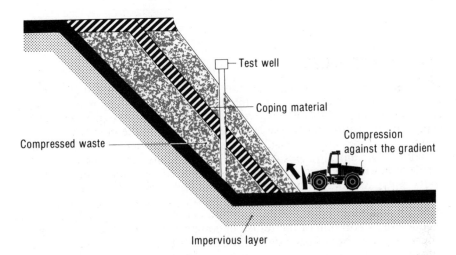

Diagram 2. DEPOSIT ON SLOPING GROUND

shielding effect will then last until the following day. This procedure also has the advantage that the space ordinarily taken up by the impervious material can be saved to a large extent so that more room is left for the deposition of layers of refuse.

In the case of surface deposits, which are normally applied on level terrain, the refuse coming in each day is laid out in strips, and is finally compressed and covered over. Once the whole surface has been treated in this way, a second layer is applied above it and treated in the same manner. The dump so produced can attain a height of 30–50 m (98–164 ft). The deposit is then sealed off and the land is cultivated again.

A variation is the trench method, which plays an important role in the

United States. A trench is excavated on level ground into which the refuse truck tips its load of waste. The refuse is compressed by machine and is finally covered with excavated material. This form of deposit saves the often expensive transport of excavated material from building sites, but it still requires extensive surface areas. The surface areas can be utilized to better advantage when an additional surface deposit is spread over the trenches.

In hill country waste matter is deposited on slopes. The refuse truck deposits its load at the top of the slope and the compressor operates from the bottom against the slope. In this way a uniform consistency is attained. The covering material is applied from the bottom upward.

A relatively neat process is achieved by what are known as "rot" deposits. In this case the refuse is pulverized in suitable machines and left to rot in stacks on the ground. When the rotting is complete, the waste is leveled off and compressed as previously described. The rotted deposit has the advantage that hardly any further decomposition will occur, so that subsidence is largely avoided. Owing to the settling by rotting, furthermore, considerable dumping space is saved.

THE DUMP COMPRESSOR

For many small and medium-sized municipal authorities that are responsible for disposing of the refuse, combustion and composting may prove too costly on account of the heavy investment and incidental expenses involved, especially if insufficient refuse is available to justify the costs of large-scale plants. It is not always feasible for adjoining districts to combine in the erection of a central disposal plant, if only because transport costs are increased sharply as road distances are extended. For many municipal districts this leaves the deposit method as the only viable alternative.

Straightforward dumping of domestic refuse presents serious dangers of both air and water contamination, which can be avoided only by the workmanlike incorporation of the refuse in compact deposits. For this purpose a refuse compressor has been developed to distribute, crush and compress the refuse spread over the dump. The refuse compressor is provided with an earth-moving blade, which in some models takes the form of a loading scoop, which serves to produce an even distribution of the refuse. The earth-moving blade is wider than the compressor, and so keeps the machine free from loose refuse. The second functional feature of the compressor is the tamper or lacerating wheel. By means of the tampers high pressures are exerted on small surfaces, whereby the refuse is crushed. Tamper wheels compress the refuse better than lacerating wheels, but they have by no means as good a reduction performance. If large quantities of long-fiber special refuse are deposited—plastic sheets, for instance—it is better to fit the compressor with lacerating wheels than with tamper wheels, as the latter get tangled up more easily. To provide a solution for special problems, combinations of tamper wheels and lacerating wheels are also possible. The compressor also has a high climbing performance, so it is unimportant whether the organized dump is sited on a slope or in a hollow.

By the constant application, crushing and compression of the refuse, better use can be made of the dump site. The smoldering which can be

Earth-moving blade

Tamping cylinder or lacerating wheel
for crushing and/or compressing

DUMP COMPRESSOR

caused by the formation of methane gas in loosely packed refuse is obviated by the compression. Plagues of rats and the growth of weeds are kept in check, because the rats cannot build breeding grounds and weeds cannot germinate. Settlements that occur in deposits (owing to the rotting of organic substances when the refuse is not compressed) are not completely eliminated by compression with tamper and lacerating wheels, but the uniform consistency of the material keeps them at a controllable level. Dumps treated in this way can be planted to woodland once the operations are complete and used as parkland or for leisure purposes, without any disadvantageous effects being likely on the plant stands.

The refuse compressor has a very high output performance in relation to the manpower required for its use. One man with one machine can distribute and compress between 300 and 500 cubic meters of refuse per hour, according to engine performance. As a rule the same worker can also handle without difficulty the other aspects of the operation, such as supervision and bookkeeping. It is unusual today for a modern organized dump to be run without mechanical equipment. With its aid all the tasks of distribution, clearance, crushing, homogenization, loading and recultivation can be carried out at relatively low investment and incidental costs.

DISPOSAL IN "REFUSE BLOCKS"

For many years a procedure has been in use by which the refuse is tamped with special wheels or some similar heavy deposit device. A machine has recently been developed in Japan whereby the tamping is effected much more efficiently.

Under the new system the refuse is fed into a bunker and, by means of a hopper, to a press. On arrival the waste is compressed from all sides by a tamping machine exerting a pressure of 200 kg per square meter. A cube of about 1 cubic meter is formed, and from the upper plate of the press smaller cylinders effect further compression inside the cube, with the result that the whole block forms a solid mass that will not disintegrate of its own accord. By this means any "spring return" effect is obviated, and the compressed material retains its existing condition free from any subsequent expansion. After removal of the pressure plates the cube is so firm that it can be removed by a crane.

In order to bind the smaller, loose external parts in the block, the whole is enclosed in a wire mesh and subsequently immersed in an asphalt mastic. After pressing, a block of 1 cubic meter should have a weight of about 1.2 tons. This represents a compression ratio of between 1:6 and 1:10, assuming an initial density of 150–200 kg per cubic meter.

According to a report from Japan, as this block continues to season, a gradual conversion should occur into a peatlike substance. Provided this happens it is to be regarded as an environmentally acceptable method of waste disposal. The procedure also offers considerable possibilities for the transmission of large quantities of refuse from densely populated congested areas to outlying dumps. The blocks can be loaded by cranes without difficulty onto standard open trucks or railway cars. They can thus be carried long distances to refuse dumps without causing nuisance from smell, dust and the like in transit. At the dump the blocks can be stacked on the ground without the need for installing expensive large-scale handling machinery and providing covering material, which is often difficult to secure and can take up a lot of space.

A further advantage of this deposit method is that no substances from the virtually gas- and water-proof refuse blocks can come into contact with the environment. There will consequently be no pollution of groundwater by seepage from the deposit, nor any spontaneous combustion of the material by heat and gas generation from bacterial decomposition processes. In this way the recultivation of the enclosed deposits and/or their employment in stacks is considerably eased. Furthermore, as is normally the case with an organized deposit, no settlement will occur. The refuse is excluded for long periods from the biosphere and from circulation in it.

For regions in which depositing as a process of refuse disposal is standard, this method developed in Japan is deserving of closer attention.

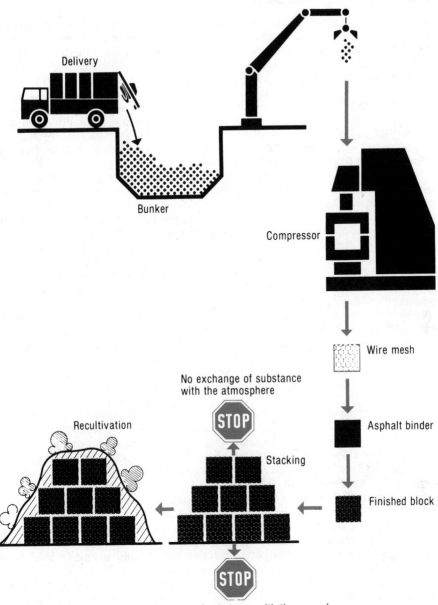

Delivery

Bunker

Compressor

Wire mesh

Asphalt binder

Finished block

No exchange of substance with the atmosphere

STOP

Recultivation

Stacking

No exchange of substance with the ground

STOP

DEPOSIT OF REFUSE BLOCKS

THE RANDOM REFUSE DUMP

Many local authorities have no regular refuse disposal outlets and depend on natural areas in which refuse is deposited untreated and uncontrolled. Refuse dumps of this type are to be found also on the outskirts of large urban aggregates, frequently in nearby leisure areas. Sites selected for random refuse dumps include deserted quarries, small valley rifts, and drained dredging ponds. The refuse is normally tipped into the hollow over a ledge at the top and left to roll down the length of the slope. As it makes its way down the refuse is "sorted," according to the size and specific gravity of the components: light objects and ones with rough surfaces tend to remain on the upper slope, while those of medium size stay in the middle and heavy objects come to rest lower down or at the foot.

The sorting is better defined the longer the slope. In the course of the sorting process a zone is formed in the middle and on the upper slope in which material heats up of its own accord as a result of bacterial decomposition and/or in which, according to the amount of oxygen present, methane gas can develop. In this sector temperatures of up to 55°C (131°F) and above have been recorded.

As a result of the self-heating process and the presence of methane gas, fires can break out, which, owing to the shortage of oxygen, mostly take the form of low-temperature smoldering accompanied by heavy smoke. This can ignite other articles in the refuse and produce noxious fumes. Fires in rubbish dumps, especially those occurring at the heart of them (core fires), are difficult to control. If water is sprayed on them, the activity of the anaerobic bacteria (forming methane in the absence of air) is heightened, giving rise to further danger of spontaneous combustion in the course of weeks or days. Core fires can be controlled with any certainty only when the deposit is broken up with heavy earth-moving equipment.

Next to the fire hazard, the most serious damage to the environment from uncontrolled refuse dumps is disturbance of the ground and surface water. Quite frequently small streams are found at badly sited dumps after rainfall which are severely contaminated by organic and mineral waste. If the ground below the dumps is pervious to water, pollution of a bacterial and chemical nature can infect the groundwater and be disseminated with it over areas several miles in extent.

Uncontrolled dumps provide almost ideal breeding grounds and living conditions for rats. If the food supplies are adequate, the self-heating of the dump provides the rats, even in periods of severe frost, with well-tempered habitats for breeding and rearing their offspring. As a result, deaths from freezing are rare even in severe winter, which would normally lead to a drastic reduction in the population.

Uncontrolled refuse dumps also provide fertile breeding grounds for insect pests and weeds, which spread out from there into adjoining cultivated areas.

Appreciation of the dangers entailed in these uncontrolled dumps should result in a general reform and in the introduction of organized refuse disposal.

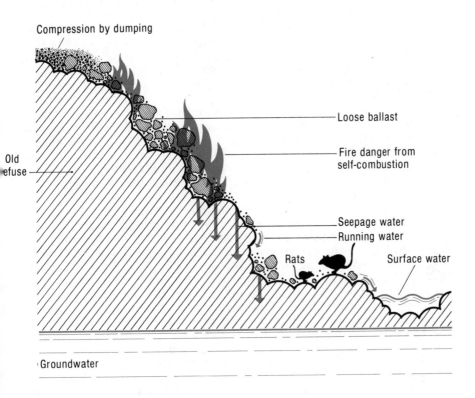

Compression by dumping

Loose ballast

Fire danger from
self-combustion

Old
refuse

Seepage water
Running water

Rats

Surface water

Groundwater

THE UNCONTROLLED DEPOSIT IN OUTLINE

PLASTICS IN REFUSE

Owing to changes in life-styles, the composition of domestic waste is subject to constant alteration. The supersession of coal fires by central and oil heating was responsible for a sharp upturn in the refuse of such materials as paper, board, wood and plastics, which previously were burned. The overall proportion of plastics of 2%–4% in refuse from settled areas is relatively limited, however, although far more plastics are produced than are to be found in domestic refuse. This is due to the fact that the bulk of plastic materials are employed in the manufacture of varnishes, glues and wood coatings. In terms of volume, plastic materials represent a small proportion of domestic waste.

Nevertheless, the plastic element in communal waste raises various problems in relation to the three most commonly used methods of waste disposal. With uncontrolled refuse dumps, which are likely to be abolished in the near future, scraps of plastic material, mainly from carrier bags blown about by the wind, are a constant nuisance to local residents. And if they start smoldering, such plastic materials can cause serious air pollution by the fumes they give off.

In supervised deposits, in which the bulk of household refuse will be disposed of in future, quite different conditions prevail. In this case the refuse is crushed, compressed and covered with rubble or other inert material so that there is no danger of plastic scrap being blown away. Owing to their compressed state the plastics themselves raise no sort of difficulties in the deposit. They give off no harmful substances into the atmosphere or into groundwater, either immediately or in the longer run. They are also easy to compress and crush and do not interfere with the decomposition processes. Long-fiber plastic waste can get tangled up in the cylinders of the compressor, however, and if large quantities of such waste have to be dealt with, this should be taken into account in selecting the compressor.

In the composting of refuse from settled areas, plastic material, owing to its high resistance to corrosion, represents a ballast element, which has to be extracted or burned. Difficulties still arise, however, in the case of long-fiber waste, such as women's nylon stockings, which get wound around the axles of the crushing and conveyor appliances and so reduce their performance or bring them to a standstill. During the actual composting process the plastics suffer hardly any change. At the most, some phosphorus-containing softeners may be released from them, so that the plastic parts become brittle. Provided they are pulverized sufficiently, plastics cause no problems either in compost or in the soil. But for the sake of appearance, the compost is usually sifted.

The possibility of developing and producing plastics that are reducible biologically or physically (by ultraviolet rays) has long been under consideration. These plastics are not suitable for use in a number of sectors, e.g., for durable goods, however, and could best be used for packaging purposes.

When refuse is burned, the bulk plastics polyethylene, polystyrene and polypropylene are reduced to innocuous carbon dioxide and water. Less favorable are the combustion products of polyvinyl chloride (PVC), which in addition contain hydrochloric acid. This gaseous hydrochloric acid, on the one hand, produces corrosion in the combustion plant and, on the other, has harmful effects on the environment. Both these dangers can be overcome with present technology, however, so that unless it is worthwhile from an economic point of view to restore them to the industrial cycle, plastics can be burned without hesitation.

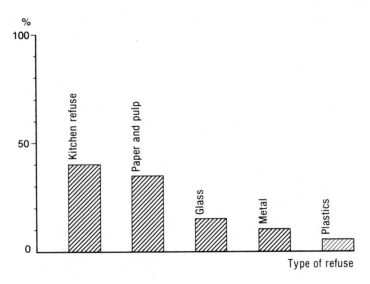

Diagram 1. COMPOSITION OF DOMESTIC REFUSE

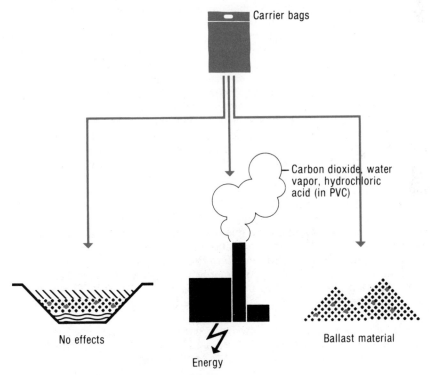

Diagram 2. EFFECTS OF PLASTICS IN REFUSE IN VARIOUS
MANUFACTURING PROCESSES

DISPOSAL BY BURNING

Refuse combustion plants should be kept running without interruption over long periods, as otherwise erosion of constantly reheated and cooled-down parts by thermal expansion and contraction is too great. To ensure continuous operation, combustible material must be constantly available. This is achieved by means of a refuse bunker, into which the refuse vehicles empty their loads directly. The capacious refuse bunker also helps to ensure that when refuse comes in in large quantities the plant will not be overloaded.

The refuse is transferred from the refuse bunker to the feed hopper of the furnace by means of a grab crane, without previous sorting, sifting or crushing. The removal from the bunker can be effected automatically or by hand control. The grab operator sits in a glass turret and does not come into contact with the refuse. Air to assist combustion is drawn from the refuse bunker, which lowers the air-pressure there and prevents dust or fumes from being driven out into the open.

The refuse is then loaded by a mechanical charger onto a grating, where it is burned into sterile slag. Throughout the burning process the refuse is turned over and raked about so that variations in its composition and fluctuations in water content and calorific value are evened out. The mechanical charger and the rake mechanism are driven by a pressure oil unit or an electric motor. Air is injected into the burning refuse from below to ensure that enough oxygen is present. A secondary airstream is provided at high pressure above the grating to make sure that any gases that form will burn off completely.

When the noncombustible elements leave the grating as slag, they are cooled in the water bath of the slag-removing plant at about 80°C (176°F). They are then ejected with a low residue of water in a sterile condition, free from dust and fumes. The slag can then be dumped or can be utilized on roadworks. If the operation has been carried out correctly, the slag will assume no more than 10% of the volume of the original refuse. Reduction of the refuse by combustion thus saves considerable deposit space.

Although the fluctuations in calorific value are considerable, combustion takes place normally at temperatures in excess of 800°C (1472°F). All the organic components of the combustion gases are burned at this level, and the gases are virtually odorless. A combustion problem arises, however, from the ever-increasing proportion of plastics in the refuse, especially in the form of PVC. Upon combustion of PVC, chlorine is released, which combines with water vapor in the outer air to form hydrochloric acid. This can only be counteracted by the installation of a gas purification plant. After leaving the furnace, the fumes are cooled, cleared of dust (up to 80%–90%) and discharged through a chimney into the atmosphere.

To recover some of the cost of the operation, the heat generated by combustion can be utilized to produce steam or hot water. Steam turbines can be used to generate electricity, and the hot water or steam can be used for heating.

By burning the refuse, waste from settlement areas is decontaminated, the volume of dumped material is reduced, and the energy contained in the refuse is exploited in the interests of the community.

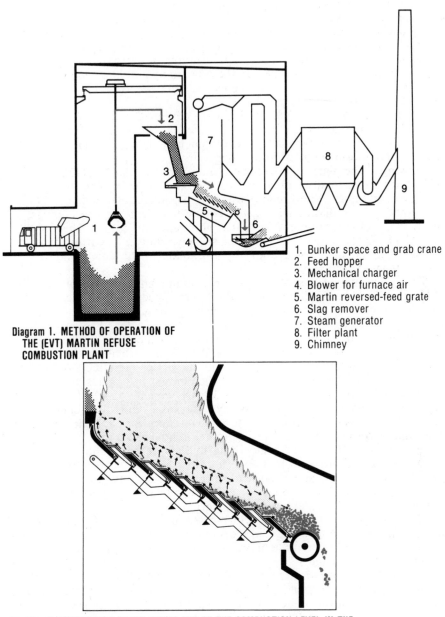

1. Bunker space and grab crane
2. Feed hopper
3. Mechanical charger
4. Blower for furnace air
5. Martin reversed-feed grate
6. Slag remover
7. Steam generator
8. Filter plant
9. Chimney

Diagram 1. METHOD OF OPERATION OF
THE (EVT) MARTIN REFUSE
COMBUSTION PLANT

Diagram 2. MOVEMENTS IN THE GRATE AND AT THE COMBUSTION LEVEL IN THE
REVERSED-FEED GRATE

EMISSIONS FROM REFUSE COMBUSTION PLANTS

In local-authority refuse combustion plants, in which household refuse is the main element consumed at present—but in which rubble, business waste of the household variety and suitable types of industrial waste will be consumed to an ever-increasing extent in future—the waste products should be reduced to a sterile condition no longer capable of putrefaction and, as far as possible, impervious to water. In the process both volume and weight are substantially reduced. During combustion, atmospheric contaminants are emitted in the form of dust and gases.

Almost all local combustion plants are equipped with electric filters to effect dust separation, the efficiency of which is over 95%. The emission of dust in this way from even large-scale municipal plants, compared with the total amount of dust emitted from other sources, is very low.

Owing to the high firebox temperatures of at least 800°C (1472°F), combined with the normally high air surplus and the length of time the combustion gases remain in the firebox (whereby organic compounds are largely consumed), the emission of organic compounds from refuse combustion plants is not of great importance, either now or for the future. The emission of fumes from the refuse bunker can be sharply reduced by cutting down the retention period of the waste and by extraction of the combustion air by suction from the bunker.

The emission of gaseous inorganic contaminants, on the other hand, will present increasing difficulties in the future. Special importance attaches to chloride compounds, which are formed by the combustion of chlorous organic substances and by the disintegration of chlorides. The most important chloride carrier in refuse is polyvinyl chloride (PVC). The chlorine content of pure PVC, amounting to about 57%, is normally reduced, however, by the addition of softeners and fillers. Under the effects of heating, PVC decomposes to release chloride. The amount of plastics contained in refuse usually averages about 2% to 3% by weight, of which PVC may account for about one quarter. As PVC possesses suitable chemical and physical properties, it is employed to a great extent for packaging material. The bulk of the plastic material to be found in household refuse consists, in fact, of packaging material. According to the present trend of technical development, the proportion of PVC in refuse is likely to quadruple in the next 10 years. As slag and airborne dust retain hardly any gaseous contaminants, a quadrupling of the emission of hydrogen chloride by refuse combustion plants is also likely to occur in the period.

The specific emission from refuse of sulfur oxides, particularly sulfur dioxide, has not changed much in recent years, so that an increase in sulfur emissions is expected to arise only from the constant expansion in the volume of refuse deposited.

Fluoride compounds are also expected to occur to an increasing extent in the emissions from refuse combustion. These arise essentially from plastics containing fluorides and from fluoride motive fluids in sprays. As the use both of plastics and of spray guns is on the increase, a substantial expansion in the emission of fluoride can be expected here too.

In order to separate chloride, sulfur and fluoride compounds from refuse combustion plants, two methods have been tried: (1) The dry waste-gas purification process, by which alkaline reagents are added to the acid contaminants. The degree of separation is very low, however, and bears no relation to the cost. (2) The wet waste-gas purification process, by which

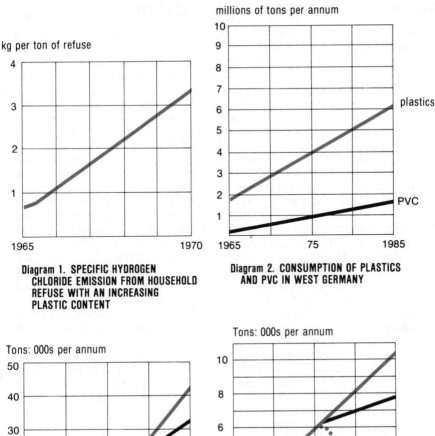

millions of tons per annum

kg per ton of refuse

Diagram 1. SPECIFIC HYDROGEN
CHLORIDE EMISSION FROM HOUSEHOLD
REFUSE WITH AN INCREASING
PLASTIC CONTENT

Diagram 2. CONSUMPTION OF PLASTICS
AND PVC IN WEST GERMANY

Tons: 000s per annum

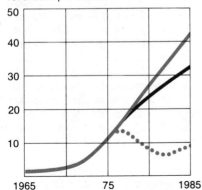

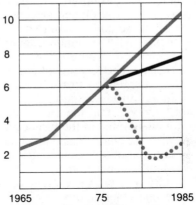

Diagram 3. EMISSIONS OF HYDROGEN
CHLORIDE FROM REFUSE COMBUSTION,
WITH AND WITHOUT WASTE-GAS
PURIFICATION

Diagram 4. EMISSIONS OF SULFUR
DIOXIDE FROM REFUSE COMBUSTION,
WITH AND WITHOUT WASTE-GAS
PURIFICATION

——— Without waste-gas purification
——— With waste-gas purification of all new plants
••••• With additional waste-gas purification of all old plants

dust and contaminants are washed away. The degree of separation is good,
but a solution still has to be found for the problem set by the washing
solution itself which is now being produced in ever greater quantities.

REFUSE SMELTING IN AN ELECTRIC ARC FURNACE

Refuse smelting in an electric arc furnace is a process that contains the chemical cycle within more narrow limits than other types of refuse combustion. With this process the slag left behind by the refuse can also be utilized, whereas otherwise it usually has to be discarded.

Refuse that is to be smelted is treated in an electric arc furnace at temperatures of 1500°–1700°C (2732°–3192°F), while directly beneath the electric arc, temperatures of 3000°–3500°C (5432°–6332°F) prevail. A metallurgical reduction is effected in the same way as in a blast furnace, so that it is fair to describe it as a smelting process.

The products resulting from the process are waste gas, ferrometals and slag, all of which are utilizable for industrial purposes. The waste gas is purified and is used to generate electric power and domestic heating, so that a flow of material and energy results. The ferrometal obtained from the runoff can be cast into pigs (laminated metal blocks). These consist of about 40% iron and 60% silicon, aluminum and calcium. This ferrometal can be cast either in an oxygen converter or in an electric arc furnace. In either case it can be used in concrete production. The slag from the refuse can be used as aggregate for building purposes (or road-building), since all the organic substances are destroyed completely under the high temperature.

The proceeds from the sale of the ferrometal, electric energy and slag will cover the costs of the plant and will leave a profit. But it must not be overlooked in principle that the refuse has to be destroyed in any case, so that commercial considerations are of secondary importance.

As regards environmental considerations, compared with traditional methods of refuse combustion, smelting in an electric arc furnace presents few problems. All the organic compounds and agents of disease are destroyed completely. There are no solid residues to be deposited at considerable expense. The ferrometal and the slag are made use of. Dust, fumes and acid are eliminated from the waste gas. The clean gas can be used for electric energy production. In the refuse smelting process, hydrogen chloride and hydrogen fluoride pass into the waste gas, and at the same time alkalis are evaporated in the furnace and neutralize the acids by washing. In this way alkaline chloride and alkaline fluoride pass into the waste water, so that the salt load of the settlement in waste water will be greater, though the increase should be marginal.

The large-scale employment of this process is to be recommended, despite certain reservations (such as the marginal waste-water contamination), as refuse disposal difficulties are reduced and the unmethodical processing of raw materials (iron ores, etc.) could be reduced.

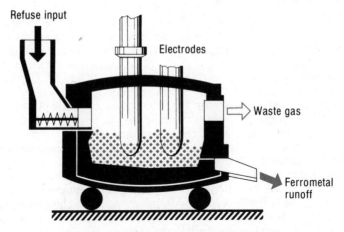

Diagram 1. ELECTRIC ARC FURNACE FOR REFUSE SMELTING

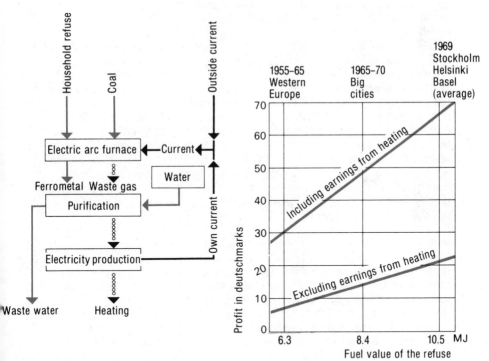

Diagram 2. SUBSTANCE AND ENERGY FLOW
IN REFUSE SMELTING

Diagram 3. POSSIBLE PROFIT FROM
1 TON OF RAW REFUSE

REMOVAL OF REFUSE FROM INTENSIVE STOCK FARMING—
THE LICOM SYSTEM

The removal of solid and liquid manure from large-scale stock farms is a serious problem. Collection and removal must be so arranged that groundwater and waterways (streams, rivers, etc.) are not contaminated.

Animal excrement contains plant nutrients and humic substances which contribute to humus and the fertilization of the soil. If manure is supplied in excessive quantities or at the wrong time there is a danger that the nutrients will be washed away or that there will be eutrophication (oversupply of nutrients leading to overabundant growth of plants) in the waterways.

Manure contains a series of strong-smelling compounds such as hydrogen sulfide, mercaptan and ammonia, which can cause serious nuisance to the community. Viruses and weed seeds are also contained in manure. If these germs and seeds are not killed off, weed growth will be encouraged and there will be a danger of soil and plant contamination.

In most intensive-stock-farming concerns the manure is in liquid form. In a liquid-manure silo, anaerobic conditions (poor in oxygen) prevail. One result of prevalent anaerobic conditions is the formation of ammonia, hydrogen sulfide and other strong-smelling substances. If oxygen is added, these compounds are converted by oxidation into odorless nitrates and sulfates, carbon dioxide and water. This is the process of aerobic decomposition into compost.

With the aid of the Licom system, aerobic composting can be applied to the liquid manure. The oxygen required is introduced into the manure by means of a device known as a Centri-Rator. The air is applied through a pipe at the lower end of a propeller that sucks in air and mixes it thoroughly with the manure. Owing to the high oxygen content, a population of aerobic microorganisms is created, which in the course of the composting process reduces the bulk of the organic substance to inorganic. In the reduction process energy is released whereby, after a short initial period, the temperature of the manure rises to 40°–60°C (104°–140°F). In this temperature range, thermophilic (heat-loving) microorganisms develop which are extraordinarily aggressive and which display a high level of decomposition performance. Pathogenic agents (viruses) and weed seeds are rapidly destroyed at these temperatures.

The Licom system can be installed as a continuous operating process with two, or if necessary more, interlinked reactors. The reduction process is inaugurated in the first reactor, and the decomposition proper takes place in the second. Because of the special circulation system in the reactors it is impossible for untreated or only briefly treated manure from the first reactor to pass directly through the connecting pipe into the second. This continuous operating system has some substantial economic advantages, such as optimum decomposition conditions stemming from a constant even temperature, reliable disinfection, low manpower requirements and a short operating period (about 15 days).

Diagram 1. THE CENTRI-RATOR

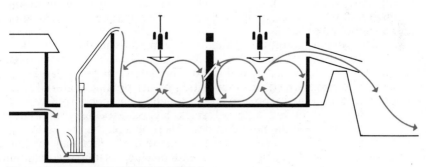

Diagram 2. LICOM II

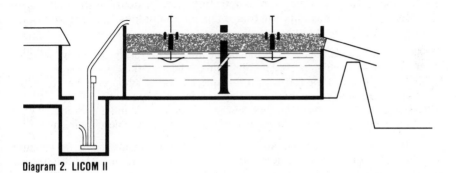

Diagram 3. CIRCULATION SYSTEM IN LICOM II

Diagrams 1–3. THE LICOM SYSTEM FOR THE COMPOSTING OF MANURE

THE BRIKOLLARE PROCESS FOR COMPOSTING OF SEWAGE SLUDGE

Household refuse loaded into collecting vehicles is deposited in concrete bunkers in the same way as industrial waste. From there the refuse is transferred by means of a grab crane to an impact pulverizer. After crushing of the refuse, iron is extracted by means of a belt magnet, and the refuse is then deposited into a giant sieve, in which plastics, textiles and other substances are sorted into groups. Stone, nonferrous metals and other hard substances such as glass, sand and ash are then removed from the litter by ballistic means with the aid of a sieve worm. The residue, on the one hand, and drained sewage sludge from communal sewage plants, on the other, are then deposited in a bunker to ensure that supplies are always available for feeding into the mixer and a Brikollare press.

The automatically palletized briquettes with a moisture content of 50%–55% are carried in a forklift truck to be stacked in a rotting shed. In a few hours' time intensive decomposition sets in (in the briquettes) free from unpleasant smells, and this is reflected in a rise in the temperature to 70°C (158°F) and in fungal infestation penetrating into the heart of the briquettes. The prerequisite conditions for this intensive decomposition are generated in the process. They include

Capillary formation in the compression of the fibrous refuse-sewage-sludge mixture, and the air supply ensured thereby into the heart of the briquettes

Unhindered growth of the fungi, as it is a question of a "static process" by which the fungal hyphae are not permanently mechanically taxed

A possibility of the accretion of high sewage sludge quotas and a consequent good nitrogen supply and the formation of a proliferation of microorganism flora

After two to three weeks of storage in the rotting shed, a residual moisture of about 20% is achieved by exothermic drying out, and the decomposition process comes to a halt from shortage of water. The decomposed briquettes are, in any case, completely sterilized by spore-forming microorganisms and in practice preserved. They can remain stacked in the open for a long time, where eventually the upper layer will mineralize and so help to preserve the lower layers.

The decaying of the refuse-sewage-sludge mixture need not necessarily be confined to a shed. It can also occur in the open, and in that case, like all decomposition processes, it will depend completely on the weather. The processes of sterilization, of decomposition of the organic material and of drying out to the point of preservation, which occur concurrently in the shed, are disrupted in the external stack layers, especially in extreme weather conditions, and the period of decay is prolonged.

The advantages of the Brikollare process lie in the fact that, owing to the pressure and final drying out, the end product assumes a minimum volume and weight, and is consequently cheap to transport. Furthermore, owing to the ease with which the briquettes can be stored, the fine preparation of the material (fine crushing and sifting) and consequently their distribution can be effected largely irrespective of time. The compost obtained in this way can be used as ground-improvement material without further exposure to moisture. It is characterized by a favorable carbon to nitrogen ratio and, in view of the shortness of the decaying period, by an extremely high decomposition rate for organic material.

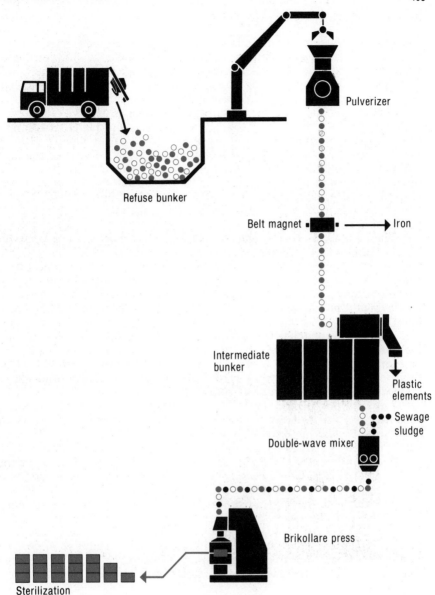

Refuse bunker

Pulverizer

Belt magnet ■—■ ——→ Iron

Intermediate bunker

Plastic elements

Sewage sludge

Double-wave mixer

Brikollare press

Sterilization

PLAN OF THE BRIKOLLARE PROCESS

The plants are so devised that a standard line in the single-layer installation can serve the requirements, as regards refuse disposal, of about 100,000 inhabitants. Higher performances are possible either with several-layer installations for one line or by the parallel connection of several lines.

THE JETZER COMPOST PLATE PROCESS

Processes for the composting and utilization of refuse can be regarded as commercially and ecologically viable only if they take account, on the one hand, of the rapid increase in environmental pollution through the buildup of refuse in urban aggregates and, on the other hand, of the increasing shortages of raw materials. What is known as the Jetzer process answers these requirements. It has the advantage that it makes use in its three stages of broadly known technologies—namely, composting, plate extrusion and clamping plate production.

The compost plant delivers compost obtained from mechanically fermented household refuse. In the process, which lasts from one to three days, complete decomposition of the easily reducible substances is achieved. Besides 35% to 50% of water and the fiber substratum, the compost contains a large number of small metal, glass, stone and plastic particles.

The compost is now subjected to the actual Jetzer process. The fiber base is fed into a horizontally rotating rotary drier, on one side of which hot air is injected at an input temperature of about 800°C (1472°F) to heat up the damp fibrous raw material. The refuse is stirred thoroughly while exposed to the hot-air current for two to seven minutes, the temperature on leaving the drying drum falling to about 100°–140°C (212°–284°F). The high temperature and the steam together serve to kill the protozoa, fungi, bacteria and viruses completely. The complete elimination of water as a result of high temperatures and the decomposition into individual fiber particles in constant movement result not only in coagulation of proteins but also in destruction of the cell wall or of the cytoplasmic membranes of the microorganisms.

The resulting fresh compost material has now been converted into an absolutely sterile, inert, stable fiber material. This fiber material is separated from air and steam in a cyclone and split up by sifting into five fractions, each of which is submitted to special air separation. The material is thus grouped in different sizes, and heavy items like glass, metals and ceramics are segregated. The fibers are subsequently collected in intermediate bunkers.

From the intermediate bunker the fibers are metered and mixed, according to need and the desired plate quality, with wood chips and shavings. Plates can also be made of 100% compost fibers. The fibers are treated with glue, combined in briquettes and finally compressed. The type of compression corresponds by and large to methods of plate pressing in general use. Then follows the final treatment of trimming, polishing and cutting to size of the plates.

The fiber plates so produced are used primarily for building walls, as wood and wood-chip plate substitutes and as insulating material. By large-scale technical adoption of this process, however, a multipurpose range of application is likely to emerge in the future.

Raw material treatment plant (compost works)

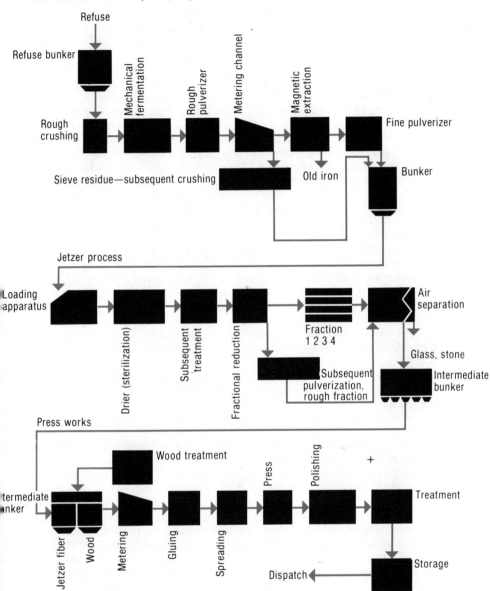

THE JETZER COMPOST PLATE PROCESS

APPLICATION OF COMPOST

The practical application of composts of different qualities for various purposes is a problem that has not yet been solved satisfactorily in all fields of use. This is one of the factors limiting sales of composts of one sort and another, in particular of sewage-sludge composts.

The application of compost by hand is feasible only in very small quantities, as in gardening as a pastime and in other small-scale areas. In vegetable and fruit plantations of any size, manure spreaders are used to spread the compost in thin layers over the cultivated area. According to its degree of maturity and the purpose for which it is required, compost spread in this way is worked into the soil immediately or left to rot on the surface in the form of mulch. Working compost into the soil is best done with a motor cultivator, rotary hoes or a combine crumbler. Plowing or deep digging is not to be recommended, as there is a danger, especially in the case of fresh compost, that biologically active material will get into lower layers in the soil (below 15 cm, or 6 in.), and since the amount of oxygen present at these levels is limited, anaerobic conditions will develop and result in damage to the plant growths.

In open country the compost is, as a rule, left lying on the surface, where it serves as a seedbed for grass or other verdure. In this case, two processes are employed. The compost either is applied in liquid form with the manure spreader, or is suspended in water, with the addition of seeds and a binding agent, in a pumping appliance and sprayed from a tank truck with a suitable pneumatic discharge appliance with a range of 20–50 meters (66–164 feet). In the latest application process, however, composts can be used only if the seed size is in the 10 mm range or below, as there is a danger that if coarser material is used nozzles and hosepipes may get choked. One disadvantage of this process is that, in addition to the compost, four to five times its volume of water must be carried. This raises the cost of the operation so much that it is economically viable only during road construction, for sowing grass on steep slopes, in cuttings and similarly inaccessible terrain.

The predominant part of large-scale technically prepared refuse-sewage sludge is used at present in vineyards. On level ground the compost is applied from tractors with loading platforms. Provided the rows of vines are planted more than 1.50 meters (5 feet) apart, specially constructed manure spreaders can be used. In small vineyards on sloping ground with a gradient of up to 60%, cables with sledges attached can be used. Like horse-drawn sledges and men carrying panniers, however, these provide a practical solution in only exceptional circumstances. With the aid of a Bühler appliance (see diagram), liquid composts can be applied by pneumatic pressure through a hosepipe on almost any kind of slope. The advantage of this appliance is that no additional water has to be provided. Damage to the vines by vehicles is also avoided. Hitherto the appliance has been used only from a stationary position, however, so that the compost has had to be shifted a number of times.

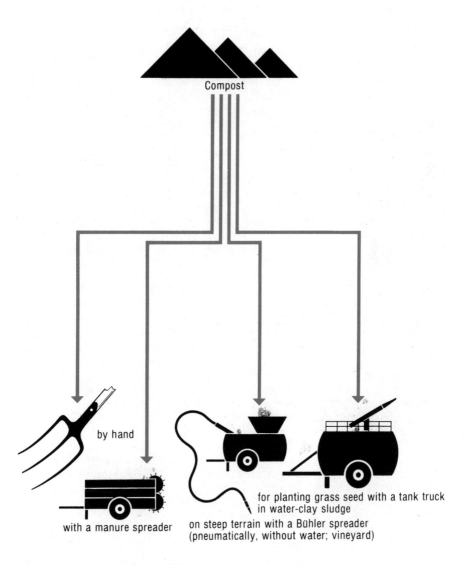

Compost

by hand

with a manure spreader

on steep terrain with a Bühler spreader
(pneumatically, without water; vineyard)

for planting grass seed with a tank truck
in water-clay sludge

METHODS OF COMPOST APPLICATION

AGRICULTURAL USE OF COMPOST FROM REFUSE AND FROM SEWAGE SLUDGE

In municipalities adjoining areas of specialized crop cultivation, composting is quite the best method of refuse disposal. One of the most important specialized crops, from the point of view of both size and economic return, is the grapevine, so the use of sewage sludge compost in viticulture will be adopted as an example.

A vineyard is a standing plantation normally designed to occupy a plot for thirty years or more. The soil surrounding the grapevines is normally kept clear of weeds, as the undergrowth competes with the vines for nutrient and water. Microorganisms in the soil, on the one hand, and the poor return from the grapevines, on the other, draw on the organic substances in the soil. Furthermore, when a new vineyard is planted, the soil is trench-plowed to a depth of about 1 meter (including the mineral undersoil). Owing to loss of humus in the upper soil, this situation is very liable to erosion. If the soil is washed away by rain, the trench walls, which cannot be rebuilt by machine, have to be restored at a high cost in labor.

It is known from experience that erosion of steep trenches in vineyards can be arrested by the application of refuse and sewage-sludge compost—or at least it can be limited to a large extent. The compost is distributed either by hand (the compost being carried into the vineyard and applied there) or mechanically by means of a manure spreader designed especially for use in vineyards, or by means of a spraying process by which the compost is pumped into the vineyard through a system of pipelines by air pressure, either in a water solution or dry.

Important factors regarding the correct use of compost are the volume employed and the maturity of the compost. By maturity of compost is understood the stage the composting has reached. A distinction is made between fresh and mature compost. Fresh compost is a material hygienized by rapid decay (48 hours) which still contains organic material fairly easily reducible by microorganisms. Fresh compost cannot be used for new plantations, as it is not yet tolerable to plants. Mature compost has been subject to a longer decomposition process (6–8 weeks), in which the predominant part of easily reducible organic material is decomposed or converted into resistant material. It is in a hygienically acceptable condition and is tolerable to plants.

In a vineyard both these forms of compost can be used. When fresh compost is used, care must be taken that it does not work into the soil, as it then gets into the roots and causes putrefaction. With mature compost there is little danger of this. The quantity applied in either case to any crops, not just grapevines, should not exceed roughly 1 cubic meter per 100 square meters of land. If larger quantities are used, not only is the nutrient balance of the soil-plant system likely to be seriously disturbed, but also the water and air balance of the soil.

The decomposition of the organic substance by microorganisms in the soil consumes oxygen and produces carbon dioxide. The plant roots also need oxygen and give off carbon dioxide. If most of the oxygen is consumed by microorganisms, and if in addition the gas exchange between soil and atmosphere is obstructed by a thick layer of compost, the plants will soon suffer from an oxygen deficiency in the root zone, leading to yellowing of the leaves and eventually to death of the plants. Sewage-sludge compost should be used only on the surface of the soil and in measured, not excessive, quantities, if damage is to be avoided.

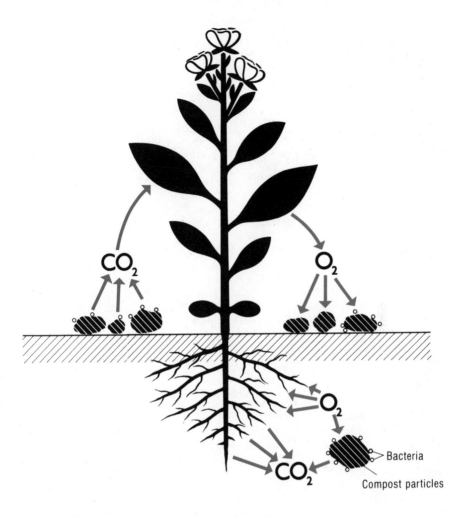

Bacteria
Compost particles

**SEWAGE-SLUDGE COMPOST SHOULD NOT BE WORKED INTO THE GROUND,
AS IT DEPRIVES THE ROOTS OF OXYGEN**

DEEP SINKING OF LIQUID WASTE

Owing to their toxic quality or radioactive nature, many liquid wastes from industrial production would be very expensive to reprocess and would be dangerous to dispose of in regular deposits. Nor can waste of this nature ordinarily be disposed of by combustion or composting. In the past, waste of this nature has been deposited in the sea where, owing to heavy dilution, it could do little damage. As a result of excessive use, however, this outlet has been overloaded and considerable restrictions have had to be imposed on its use.

Radioactive waste has for some time now been deposited in abandoned coal mines, where the material is largely shut off from the biosphere. Toxic sludge is also disposed of in this way on occasion, but the storage capacity here is strictly limited. Discussions are taking place on sinking liquid waste in underground cavities hollowed out by small atomic explosions. Also the formation of artificial caverns in salt mines by injecting fresh water to dissolve the salt and then pumping out the brine should help to solve this waste disposal problem.

A process increasingly used in the United States is connected with oil recovery. To provide more storage space, salt water is injected into the water zone adjoining an oil field. This raises the pressure in the oil pool and the deposit is more completely drained of oil. The salt water can now be replaced by selected liquid waste. Petroleum deposits occur only in storage areas whose contents have not participated for a long time in the hydraulic and biological cycles. It is fairly certain, therefore, that the liquid waste will not make an appearance in the hydrosphere or the biosphere for periods of significant geological dimension. This is an essential prerequisite for the storage of toxic or nuclear liquid waste.

In European countries this method of waste disposal is of particular interest for two reasons. Owing to the population density and the growing need for uncontaminated drinking water, toxic or radioactive liquids can be run off or disposed of only if the strictest precautionary measures are taken. Special care must be exercised to ensure that drinking water reserves are not affected. Before any such disposal project is embarked on, geological and hydrogeological investigations are therefore needed. If favorable underground geological structures are located, the sinking operation can forge ahead virtually without risk. As the area has been closely surveyed geologically, its delineation presents little difficulty. Storage of the liquid waste will take place in the pores of rocks that are sealed off from the biosphere by impermeable substances such as argillaceous rock. This can be effected in depressions (synclines), in horizontal sandstone beds, and best of all in folds (anticlines). Numerous structures of this kind of no economic significance (no petroleum, gas, etc.) are to be found.

Deep sinking of liquid toxic waste substances from industry provides a solution to the problem of acute damage to the environment for periods of great geological duration. Nonetheless, this method of waste disposal should be adopted only in the case of truly problematic waste, for storage capacities are by no means unlimited.

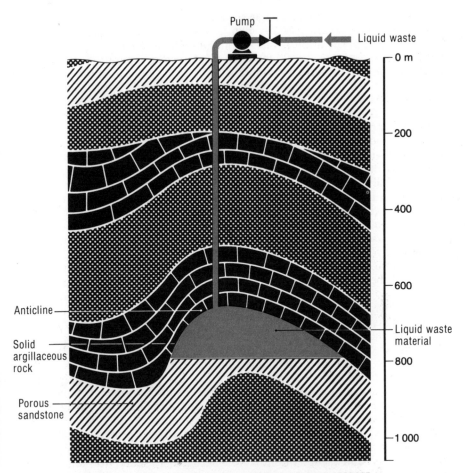

Pump

Liquid waste

0 m

200

400

600

Anticline

Solid
argillaceous
rock

Liquid waste
material

800

Porous
sandstone

1 000

UNDERGROUND SINKING OF SPECIAL LIQUID WASTE; NATURALLY SECURE STORAGE
CAVITIES IN SALINE AND ARGILLACEOUS ROCK SEAL OFF THE LIQUID WASTE
FROM THE BIOSPHERE

ATOMIC WASTE DISPOSAL PROBLEMS

In the operation of nuclear power stations, radioactive waste presents ever more pressing problems. *Mildly active* atomic waste consists of residues from filter and purification plants, from contaminated laboratory equipment and gloves and of sewage sludge from waste water separation. Its disposal has been effected hitherto by dumping in the sea, by burial in the ground, by depositing in salt mines, or in certain cases by discarding it irresponsibly in refuse dumps.

Moderately active atomic waste consists of component parts of nuclear power stations rendered radioactive by neutron radiation, radioactive residues from purification processes (such as ion-exchange resins) and waste from nuclear research. Moderately active atomic waste was formerly dumped in the sea and deposited in salt mines. As recently as 1972, 3800 tons of mildly to moderately radioactive waste packed in 7600 containers was sunk in the Atlantic by the European Atomic Energy Authority. As no containers will stand up to exposure to seawater for centuries, it must be expected that this and other radioactive waste deposited in the sea in large quantities will one day be released, be enriched in the food chain in the ocean, and sooner or later crop up in the foodstuffs of people.

The real problem, however, concerns *highly radioactive* atomic waste. This is left behind as a liquid upon the separation of uranium and plutonium from burned fuel in reprocessing plants. The quantity of long-life highly active atomic waste is estimated for the year 2000 at about one trillion curies. No satisfactory solution for the disposal of highly active atomic waste has yet been found. Atomic waste cannot be destroyed. In contrast to chemical waste, which can be transmuted and deprived of poison by chemical reaction, radioactive substances disintegrate according to a time scale (which cannot be varied) related to their half-life value. The principal problem thus concerns the disposal of the fission products which have a long half-life value, such as strontium-90 (with a half-life of 26 years), cesium-137 (30 years), samarium-151 (100 years), plutonium-239 (24,400 years), and iodine-129 (17,200,000 years). The atomic waste being produced today must therefore be stored away so securely, for periods hardly conceivable to man, that none of it can escape into the biosphere and so seep into the food chain of any living creature.

Some countries are exploring the possibility of sinking radioactive waste through the ice in the Antarctic. Existing international agreements concerning the Antarctic provide for special amendments if all the signatories agree. The heat released by radiation would make the atomic waste containers sink gradually into the ice and melt their way through. In America it is proposed to ship the containers and transport them overland into the Eastern Antarctic, where the ice is particularly thick.

In view of the long-term nature of the problem of disposing of atomic waste on the earth, the National Aeronautics and Space Administration (NASA) has carried out a study on behalf of the Nuclear Regulatory Commission (NRC) into the possibilities of extraplanetary atomic waste disposal. Using the universe as a depository for atomic waste had already been put forward by various representatives of the Nuclear Regulatory Commission as the only safe method of atomic waste disposal. Two obstacles stand in the way, however. The cost per kg of atomic waste is in the neighborhood of $200,000. The cost of disposing of 100 tons of highly active waste would

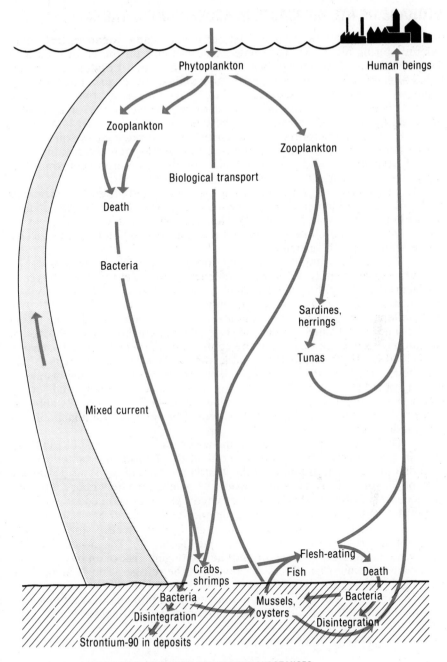

Phytoplankton

Human beings

Zooplankton

Zooplankton

Biological transport

Death

Bacteria

Sardines,
herrings

Tunas

Mixed current

Flesh-eating

Crabs,
shrimps

Fish

Death

Bacteria

Mussels,
oysters

Bacteria

Disintegration

Disintegration

Strontium-90 in deposits

BIOLOGICAL CONSEQUENCES OF SINKING RADIOACTIVE SUBSTANCES

work out, on this basis, to about $20 billion. Apart from this prohibitive
cost, there is a danger that a rocket loaded with atomic waste could make a
false start and disintegrate in the earth's atmosphere.

STORAGE OF ATOMIC WASTE IN ABOVEGROUND TANKS

As a "solution" to the atomic waste problem, many countries have considered storing highly active atomic waste in tanks on the earth's surface. This method of disposal has been in use in the United States for over 20 years already. Each of more than 200 steel and concrete tanks contains over 3 million liters of highly radioactive liquid. As the radioactive waste constantly generates heat, the tanks have to be cooled all the time. This is achieved by piping the steam from the tanks into a condenser and mixing the contents with compressed air to ensure that no radioactive solids settle on the floor of the tank, which could result in serious local overheating.

The danger of radioactive contamination of the environment from storage tanks on the earth's surface takes several forms:

1. In conjunction with the strong radioactive radiation, the chemicals in the waste solution can cause corrosion of the tank container. An accident of this kind occurred in Hanford, Washington, which is the main deposit for atomic waste in the United States. As a result, 490,000 liters of radioactive waste seeped into the ground.

2. The tanks containing fuming atomic waste must be constantly cooled. Approximately 9 kilowatts of energy are released by radioactive disintegration per cubic meter of highly active atomic waste, or about 31 megawatts of energy per tank. Although each tank is equipped with two quite independent refrigeration systems, there is still a danger that the refrigeration may fail through power shortage, floods, earthquakes, sabotage or human negligence. In that event the contents of the tanks would heat up to over 1000°C (1832°F). All the volatile radioactive fission products would then be released into the atmosphere. The results of such a mishap would be nothing short of catastrophic, both for the immediate vicinity and for remoter areas. According to a study carried out at the University of California an area double the size of Switzerland would be rendered uninhabitable for several decades.

3. Owing to radioactive radiation, water molecules are split radiolytically into hydrogen and oxygen. The rate of this hydrogen production is so high that in the event of failure of the ventilation system the lower explosion limit of 4% for hydrogen in the air would be reached in a few hours. Through spontaneous heating in this way, an oxyhydrogen explosion could result, by which the tank would be destroyed together with the refrigeration system. Attempts have recently been made to provide more secure storage conditions for the radioactive residues in liquid form. But the problem of the radiolytic disintegration of water and the contingent risk of an oxyhydrogen explosion remains. The effects of a failure of the refrigeration system would be roughly the same.

The storage of atomic waste in aboveground tanks is thus attended by substantial risks, the effects of which cannot be finally assessed.

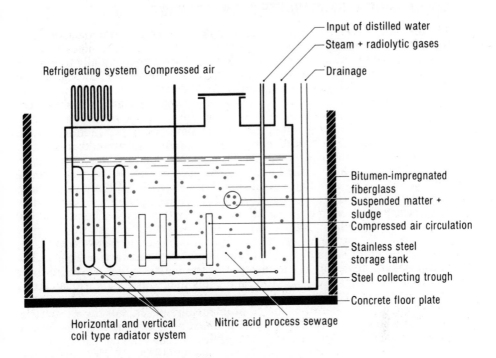

Diagram 1. **TANK FOR ABOVEGROUND STORAGE OF ATOMIC WASTE**

Year of accident	Amount of radioactive liquid released (in liters)	Release of cesium-137 (kCi)
1960	130 000	4
1965	190 000	40
1969	260 000	51
1973	440 000	40

Diagram 2. **ACCIDENTS RECORDED IN CONNECTION WITH THE STORAGE OF ATOMIC WASTE**

STORAGE OF ATOMIC WASTE IN SALT MINES

The idea was developed in West Germany of storing away radioactive waste material in salt mines. This was based on the fact that salt mines have no connection with groundwater (a fact that must have been equally true in the past, as otherwise the salt deposits would have been washed away), so that they provide a high degree of security for the storage of atomic waste. In the selection of salt mines for this purpose in West Germany, the choice fell on the abandoned Asse II mine at Wolfenbüttel. Many large and small caverns were prepared in the mine, filled with atomic waste and then sealed off. For a time, this method of disposal was regarded both by industry and by the authorities as the safest solution. It has since been discovered, however, that neighboring shafts Asse I and III have been permeated by water. Since 1967 about 10,000 containers loaded with mildly active atomic waste have been stacked in Asse II, and a further 500 containers loaded with moderately active waste were stored in special caverns. By the year 2000 up to 250,000 cubic meters of radioactive waste is likely to be stored in Asse II.

Despite the problems of salt disposal, it is currently believed to be the best solution for disposing of mildly and moderately radioactive wastes. The real problem, however, is the disposal of the highly active waste from the fuel rods. Attempts are made to seal off this fluid waste by various glazing and calcination processes and so make them fit for storage. These techniques entail a number of unsolved problems, however. For the waste to be sealed in glass the radioactive solutions must be neutralized and denitrated before being mixed with the glass material, dried and melted. The heating to 200°C (392°F) for drying and to 1000°–1300°C (1832°–2372°F) for melting causes loss of volatile radionuclides. About 20% of cesium, for instance, is released, and nearly 100% of ruthenium in the form of ruthenium oxide. The value of the process is reduced by the release of these nuclides; they play an important part in the biologically relevant fission product activity, but their separation and long-term storage pose additional problems.

The frequently discussed and varied methods of moving-bed calcination —by which fission products interstratified for a long time are converted into oxide form at burning temperatures of 600° to 1000°C (1112° to 1832°F)— also present a number of unsolved problems. The volatile fission products must further be given special treatment. A not inconsiderable portion of the fission products can be washed out of the oxide substance itself, in the course of time, according to the level of the burning temperature.

As regards the storage of such calcined waste in salt mines, the problem of heat development arises in connection with humidity of the air penetrating the shafts or percolation of water. In the case of storage of atomic waste in steel tanks, the separation of condensation water in consequence of thermoconvection in the deposits can result in the formation of corrosive salt solutions which, in conjunction with radiation corrosion, can disintegrate the container materials. A further possibility of damage can come from earthquakes, whereby a large part of the radioactive waste stored away in salt mines over the years could be released. This problem is increased by the fact that the highly active waste previously stored could work its way into the salt as a result of the heat developed and could not be retrieved.

In Canada, where storage in salt mines was also projected, the Atomic Energy Control Authority vetoed this form of atomic waste disposal and recommended storage aboveground.

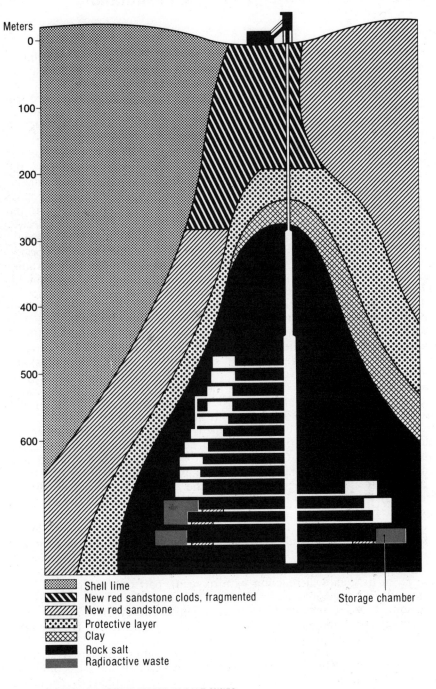

Meters

Shell lime
New red sandstone clods, fragmented
New red sandstone
Protective layer
Clay
Rock salt
Radioactive waste

Storage chamber

STORAGE OF ATOMIC WASTE IN SALT MINES

Part Seventeen—Energy and the Environment

WHAT IS ENERGY?

Like space, time and information, energy is one of the fundamental quantities in the world. It is present in a number of forms which differ basically from one another and together constitute the physical reality of our universe. All physical processes can be construed as a transition from one form of energy to another. The most important forms of energy are the following:

1. *Mechanical energy:* In order to raise a body of mass m by height h on the earth (acceleration due to gravity $g = 9.8m$ per sec²), work (= energy) $E = mgh$ must be expended. This energy expended in raising the body is then imparted in the form of potential energy (energy of position) to the body. If the body drops the same distance, the energy can be released again. In order to raise the speed of a body of mass m to the level v, energy must be imparted to the body so that $E = \frac{1}{2}mv^2$. If this energy is imparted to the moving body and the body makes impact with an obstacle, it can be released again (kinetic energy, energy of movement).

2. *Thermal energy:* In order to heat a body of mass m and of a specific heat c, which depends on the material of the body, by a fixed temperature gradient ΔT (in °C), a particular amount of energy $E = mc\ \Delta T$ is required. This thermal energy can be given off again by the body into the atmosphere in the form of heat radiation, for example. The supply of thermal energy need not necessarily result in a raising of the temperature of a body; but as the melting or boiling point of the body is approached, it can be used for a change in form from "solid" to "liquid" or from "liquid" to "vaporous."

3. *Electric energy:* If a current of strength I (measured in amperes) and of force V (measured in volts) flows for a time t, the amount of energy E produced by the current $= VIt$. With the aid of this energy from a flowing electric current, thermal energy can be released (for electric heating) or a machine can be driven. In order to create an electric field (or to separate two electric charges), energy is needed which will be released again when the field collapses (energy from the electric field). The energy of a charged condenser with capacity C and force V between the plates of the condenser $= \frac{1}{2}CV^2$. If the condenser is short-circuited, this field energy stored in a condenser can be reconverted into the energy of an electric current. Energy can also be stored in a magnetic field corresponding to the energy of an electric field.

4. *Chemical energy:* In chemical compounds, energy is stored in the linkage of atoms to molecules. This can vary greatly in amount. Compounds are accordingly described as "poor in energy" or "rich in energy." An energy-rich compound is fuel oil, for example, in the combustion of which (that is, in its chemical reaction with oxygen), part of the chemical bond energy is converted into and released as thermal energy. In the reverse direction, there are chemical reactions in which energy must be stored so that energy-rich compounds are created. One example of this is the photosynthesis that occurs in plants.

5. *Energy in matter:* Finally the whole of matter consists of concentrated energy, for which the connection between energy and mass of matter is given in the formula $E = mc^2$ (in which c = velocity of light). If, for example, a negatively and a positively charged electron collide, they convert their mass completely into radiant energy. Part of this energy can be released by nuclear fission or nuclear fusion (atomic energy).

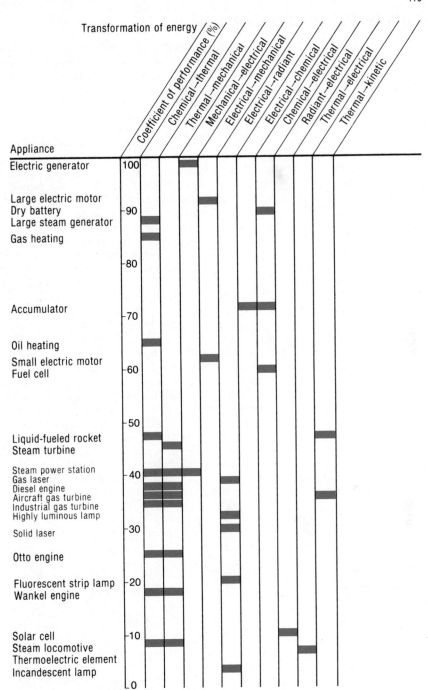

COEFFICIENTS OF PERFORMANCE OF ENERGY TRANSFORMATIONS
Based on: <u>Conservation of Energy</u>, Committee on Interior and Insular Affairs,
United States Senate, 1972

WHAT IS ENERGY USED FOR?

All living organisms have to transform energy to enable them to maintain their vital processes. They obtain this biological energy from their food intake, in which the solar energy obtained from the photosynthesis of plants is converted into chemical bond energy and stored.

For hundreds of thousands of years, every human being has been using up about 2000 calories of energy a day, as biological energy to maintain their metabolism. Today the inhabitants of highly industrialized countries consume some 200,000 calories per person each day, which (besides the biological energy they need) includes the energy required for heating, transport, television, refrigeration, industrial production, consumption and luxuries. For each calorie of energy needed to sustain life biologically, we thus consume over 100 calories for other purposes. It is now estimated that if energy growth continues at the present rate, in 10 years' time about 400,000 calories, and in 20 years' time about 800,000 calories, will be produced and consumed in the industrial countries per capita of the population every day. By way of contrast, many residents of developing countries do not obtain even the 2000 calories a day needed to sustain their metabolism.

Energy in the form of oil, coal, gas and electricity is used predominantly in three sectors: industry, households and transport. In the transport sector, some 92% of the energy is used in the form of gasoline and diesel oil, and the remainder in the form of electrical energy for public transport. Household consumption consists 60% of oil, 22% of coal and gas, and 18% of electricity. Industry, on the other hand, uses about 70% oil, 10% solid fuels and gas, and 20% electric power. In transport, the energy is used almost exclusively as the motive power for vehicles: and a small portion is used for heating the interior of vehicles. In the domestic sector, about 80% of the energy is used for space heating and the rest for household appliances, television, lighting, etc. In the industrial sector, the breakdown is more difficult. A large part of the energy consumed is swallowed up by the metal-producing industry (coal for blast furnaces and electric power for aluminum production) and the chemical industry. The energy is used primarily to provide heat to sustain chemical reactions. A large part of the energy consumed in the chemical industry goes into artificial fertilizer production.

Such energy consumption makes possible the increase in automation and mechanization of industrial production. In our economic structure there is a systematic compulsion to produce as economically and profitably as possible so that each individual can conduct his affairs in accordance with his own particular standard of living. What it previously took ten workmen a week to produce can today be produced with ease by one worker with a machine that only needs fuel to run it. Human energy and labor are being increasingly replaced by technical energy and machinery.

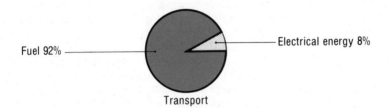

Fuel 92% ——— Electrical energy 8%

Transport

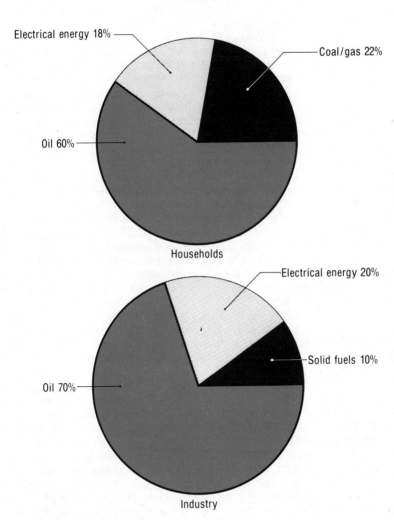

Electrical energy 18% ———

Coal/gas 22%

Oil 60% ———

Households

Electrical energy 20%

Solid fuels 10%

Oil 70% ———

Industry

CONSUMPTION OF TECHNICAL ENERGY

ENERGY RESERVES

There are two fundamentally different forms of energy reserves: *energy raw materials,* which are available in only limited quantities on the earth and are consumed in power stations for energy production (oil, coal and natural gas) or are split for the same purpose (uranium and thorium), and *regenerative natural forces* which can be used by man for energy production (sun, wind, tides, the heat of the earth, differences in temperature in the oceans, etc.). These latter sources of energy have the great advantage that they are never exhausted, as no raw materials are consumed. Whereas when energy raw materials are consumed waste materials are produced that contaminate the environment (atomic waste, carbon dioxide, sulfur dioxide), when recourse is had to regenerative natural forces no waste substances are produced.

Despite these enormous advantages, energy research and energy consumption have been concentrated in the past almost entirely on the utilization of fossil and nuclear fuels. This one-sidedness is a primary cause of the existing worldwide shortage of energy. One essential cause of this myopia in energy research is to be found in the economic field: when fuelstuffs are utilized, a profit-earning industrial apparatus has to be set up at various points. A profit can be earned on extraction of the raw material, on processing operations (e.g., refining petroleum), on marketing (by multinational mineral oil companies, for instance), on utilization in power stations, and on disposal of the residues (atomic waste disposal and filters for power stations). In the exploitation of regenerative natural forces, however, nothing is to be earned on fuel input nor on waste disposal.

Of fossil fuel reserves 89% take the form of coal. With the constant rise in consumption, oil reserves should last another 30 years and natural gas reserves for 20 to 25 years. By far the largest proportion of available fuel reserves is in the form of coal. The established and estimated reserves of pit coal and brown coal on the earth together amount to some 8.8 trillion tons. On the assumption that world energy requirements will remain at 10 billion tons of pit-coal units, which corresponds to the established world energy requirement for 1975, coal alone, disregarding all other sources of energy, should be able to satisfy world energy requirements for the next 880 years. In the EEC countries alone, established coal reserves amount to 147 billion tons, 132 billion tons of it in West Germany. The coal reserves of the United States are 1.5 trillion tons.

Supplies of uranium for light water reactors throughout the world correspond, in established reserves, to 37.4 billion tons of pit-coal units and to 81 billion tons in estimated supplies (at an extraction cost of $30 per pound). This represents about one eighth of the supplies of coal. If it were decided to use uranium in breeder reactors (and so to go over to the plutonium system), uranium supplies would rise to 2200 billion tons of pit-coal units (established reserves) and to 4320 billion tons of the estimated reserves. The uranium supplies thus stand at about three quarters of the level of the coal reserves. This transition to the plutonium system, however, entails serious risks that may prove insuperable in the military and ecological fields.

A final answer to the question of how long the energy reserves of man are likely to last can only be given in conjunction with the question of the future growth of energy consumption (see "Dissipation of Energy" and "Energy Planning" later).

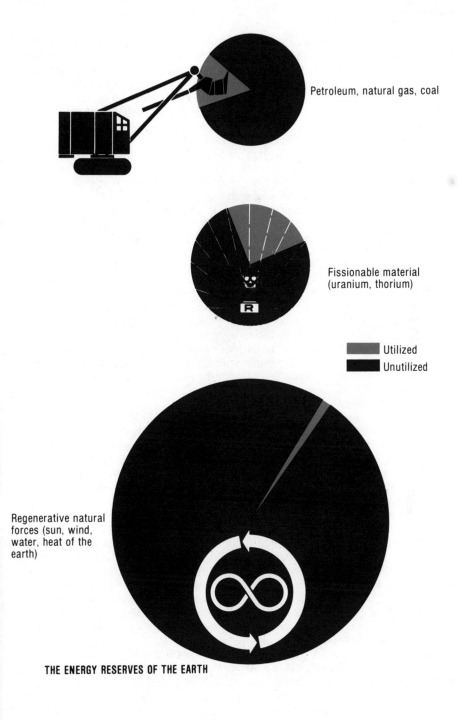

Petroleum, natural gas, coal

Fissionable material
(uranium, thorium)

Utilized
Unutilized

Regenerative natural
forces (sun, wind,
water, heat of the
earth)

THE ENERGY RESERVES OF THE EARTH

DISSIPATION OF ENERGY

In discussing the future development of energy, the wasteful ways in which energy is used must be considered. Since the oil crisis of 1973–1974, if not before, it has been generally acknowledged throughout the industrial countries of the world that a large part of the energy produced is not used at all or is used for unnecessary purposes. In any examination of the present-day energy situation, two factors must be investigated separately: *dissipation of energy* by misuse of energy transformation, and *waste of energy* by its application for luxury and trivial purposes.

A large proportion of the energy produced today is lost before it can be used, as a result of dispersion into the atmosphere. In the industrial sector the amount of energy lost in this way amounts to about 45%, in the domestic sector to some 55%, and in transport to perhaps 85%. The enormous amounts of energy so lost reflect the low coefficients of efficiency achieved in the transformation of energy. The automobile, for instance, has an efficiency factor of under 15%, which means that of every 100 calories consumed in the form of gasoline, only 15 calories are utilized for propelling the vehicle, and the remaining 85 calories are dissipated in the form of unburned hydrocarbons (unburned gasoline) and hot waste gases emitted through the exhaust system. Of the total energy production, only 35% is utilized effectively, and the remaining 65% is lost. The losses that occur in final consumption are thus much higher than the losses arising during production of the energy, including direct consumption by power plants.

Today there are a series of techniques by which these energy losses can be reduced. In the case of aluminum production, for instance, for every ton of aluminum produced, about 24,000 kwh of energy are needed. But if aluminum is recovered from scrap by recycling, for every ton of aluminum produced only about 750 kwh are consumed. The consumption of energy in the recycling process, which can also be justified by reference to the shortage of raw material and pollution of the atmosphere, thus amounts to no more than 3% of the energy consumed in normal aluminum production. To take another example, in the production of steel in blast furnaces, for every ton of steel produced, some 5400 kwh of energy are consumed. If the steel is recovered from scrap in electric melting furnaces, on the other hand, the energy consumption per ton drops to 780 kwh, a mere 15% of the normal consumption. In the case of transport by private automobile, some 500 watt-hours are expended per passenger-kilometer. For a journey by public transport, which is also to be recommended on pollution grounds, the specific energy requirement per passenger-kilometer in a streetcar, for instance, works out to about 50 watt-hours, or only about a tenth of the consumption by a private automobile. These and many other techniques for energy saving are little used today because the external incidental costs of energy production are not included in the cost-benefit analysis of the project. In many branches of production it is consequently cheaper to waste energy than to adopt technical methods for saving energy.

The second sector in which energy is wasted is the production of superfluous goods, which is often done on purely commercial grounds. Examples of this are to be found in the packaging industry (high energy consumption for nonreturnable bottles, aluminum packaging, etc.), in the textile industry (high energy consumption for synthetics), and in many other branches.

In view of the shortage of raw materials in the world, of pollution of the

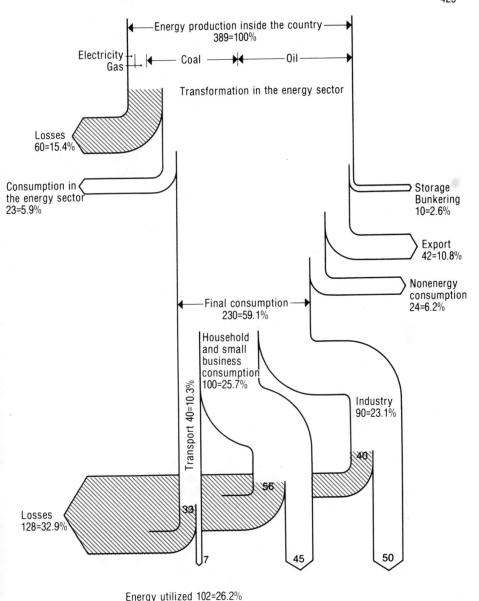

Energy production inside the country
389=100%

Electricity
Gas

Coal — Oil

Transformation in the energy sector

Losses
60=15.4%

Consumption in
the energy sector
23=5.9%

Storage
Bunkering
10=2.6%

Export
42=10.8%

Nonenergy
consumption
24=6.2%

Final consumption
230=59.1%

Household
and small
business
consumption
100=25.7%

Industry
90=23.1%

Transport 40=10.3%

Losses
128=32.9%

33

56

40

7

45

50

Energy utilized 102=26.2%

ENERGY BALANCE IN WEST GERMANY, 1970 (IN MILLIONS OF TONS OF PIT-COAL UNITS)

environment by industrial production, and of the limited sources of energy available, such wastage of energy can only reduce the chances of survival of succeeding generations.

ENERGY PLANNING—ECONOMIC AND SCIENTIFIC PROGNOSES

In the past, forecasts by the fuel and electricity industries indicated that energy requirements in industrial countries would continue to increase sharply in the future. In the United States a simple extension of the trend in energy use between 1950 and 1970 suggested the demand for energy would grow 3.4% per year. Since the perceived fuel shortage of 1973, however, there has been a steady decrease in the energy demand predictions and also in the actual increase in energy demand. Energy demand in the United States grew only 0.5% per year between 1973 and 1977. Prior to 1973, forecasters expected the United States to be consuming more than 90 quadrillion (quads) BTUs of energy by 1980 and 130 to 175 quads by the year 2000. But now they predict 1980 energy consumption to be about 80 quads and only 90 to 120 quads in 2000. Most of the difference is due to increased expectations for energy conservation.

It is more difficult to predict energy demands for the world. As other countries assume a larger share of world economic activity, their energy demand is expected to increase. But increased prices will probably slow the growth of that demand. The most serious problem arises in connection with the countries of the Third World. These nations, with their current low living standards and low levels of energy consumption, must in the future have much higher energy requirements to enable them to raise their living standards in line with their economic potential. In view of the limited energy resources available in the world, developing countries' growing demand for energy is another argument against further expansion in energy consumption in the industrial countries.

Ecological consequences must be taken into account in energy planning. Many energy-related activities threaten to damage the natural environment. Some of the environmental effects are so difficult to control that they may ultimately limit the use of some energy sources. Problems in this category include climatic effect of carbon dioxide from fossil fuel burning and perhaps radioactive waste disposal. Other problems are technically controllable, but not now managed satisfactorily, such as air pollution. Complexity and uncertainty make these problems difficult to resolve.

Federal agencies in the United States are required to consider the environmental impact of all their major activities—and courts have ruled that consideration applies to licensing of nuclear power plants. Some environmental problems, however, are indirect. The fission power plants, for example, are considered to be pollution-free in the sense that there are no toxic combustion products. But their ecological costs include the plants in Oak Ridge, Tennessee, that prepare uranium for nuclear fuel. These plants do produce polluting effluents and also consume large amounts of electrical power from coal-burning plants. The coal-burning plants, in turn, also pollute the air and have a major environmental impact in Kentucky where their coal is strip-mined.

The energy industries still have to depend to a large extent on forecasts of future energy requirements arrived at by extrapolation of consumption trends established in the past, but in recent times improved studies have been made on future energy requirements. The most comprehensive study so far available in this field was done by the National Science Foundation in the United States. It appears from this that electricity consumption by the three main consumer groups (households, small businesses, and industry) is most strongly influenced by the price of electric power, followed by these further factors: population growth, incomes, and the cost of other sources of energy. Whereas in the past a steady growth in population was evident,

Kwh millions

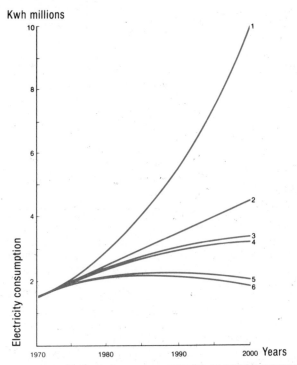

Electricity consumption

1970   1980   1990   2000 Years

ELECTRICITY CONSUMPTION BY THE YEAR 2000, BASED ON VARIOUS ASSUMPTIONS

even in industrial countries, the growth trend of the population is now beginning to level out. At the end of 1972 the number of children per family in the United States stood at 2.08, which is not enough to keep the overall population level constant.

The study by the National Science Foundation comes to the conclusion that an increase in the price of electricity and a decline in the population growth will result in electricity consumption being nearly five times lower than is assumed by the energy authorities. Constant electricity prices over the next 30 years would certainly raise consumption, but a 50% cut in the price might result in a doubling of consumption over 10-year stretches. Another investigation conducted by the Rand Corporation in California comes to similar conclusions.

The accompanying diagram shows the probable development of electricity consumption based on various assumptions made in the study by the National Science Foundation. Curve 1 indicates the forecast made by the energy industry by extrapolating past trends into the future. Curve 2 represents a National Science Foundation forecast based on the assumption that 1970 electricity prices will neither fall nor rise in future. Curve 3 adopts the same assumption regarding electricity prices and makes the further assumption that the population growth will decline. Curve 4 assumes that the population growth will decline by the year 2035 to the level at which the population remains constant. Curve 5 is based on a drop in population growth and a rise in electricity prices by 3.33% per annum, representing a doubling of electricity prices by the year 2000. Finally, Curve 6 makes the same assumption regarding a doubling of the cost of electricity by the year 2000 and a further assumption that by the year 2035 the population figure will have stabilized.

On the basis of these last two highly realistic assumptions, for the year

2000 only about one-fifth of the current consumption forecast by the energy authorities would be required. In this study no allowance is made for further important consumption-reducing factors such as the curtailment of energy waste, new techniques for the better utilization of primary energy, and a reduction in energy production or in economic growth on ecological grounds. Although no precise quantitative investigations are yet available on this score, it is estimated that considering these (likewise highly realistic) factors the energy consumption in highly industrialized countries will also fall in the future to an ecologically justifiable level.

MAGNETOHYDRODYNAMIC GENERATORS

In many countries work is going ahead on the development of magnetohydrodynamic generators (MHD generators) for electric power production. The first big American plants were already in operation in the 1960s. Two of the plants had a power output of over 10 megawatts. The Lorrho Generator in Tennessee produced almost 18 megawatts, and the Mark V Generator in Boston as much as 33 megawatts.

The operating principle on which the magnetohydrodynamic generator is based is very simple and has been used in practice in the conventional dynamo since the last century: if an electric conductor (such as a copper wire) is at right angles to a magnetic field, an electric field is set up in the conductor. In a closed conductor system a current then flows. In the dynamo on a motorcycle it is the copper wires of the armature that rotate in a magnetic field. A magnet is also used, of course, in a magnetohydrodynamic generator, but there are no rotating mechanical parts. In place of a mechanical conductor, hot gases are driven through the generator channel and are ionized (they carry a charge and conduct electricity). In such a medium (gas plasma), an electric charge is built up in the same way as in a dynamo across the magnetic field, and so across the direction of the current, and can be drawn off.

In combustion MHD power stations, a fuel (oil, coal, gas, etc.) is consumed in a rocketlike combustion chamber at over 2500°C. The combustion gas leaves the chamber at high speed. It is channeled into the MHD stage of the power plant and there forms the working medium. The hot combustion gases, in the form of a plasma, consist of electrically charged negative electrons and electrically charged positive ions. In passing through the magnetic field, the ions are deflected to one side and the electrons to the other, and are collected on electrodes. Between the electrodes, an electric field thus builds up. In the MHD section of the power plant, 20% to 25% of the energy delivered is thus converted into electrical energy. When it leaves the MHD section, the gas is still so hot that it produces steam by means of heat exchangers in the same way as in a normal high-temperature power plant, and the steam is used to drive turbines and generators. In the conventional second section of the power plant a further 30% or so of the energy delivered is converted into electric current. The coefficient of efficiency of a combustion MHD power plant is about 50%–55%, or more than 10% above that of a normal power station. This is the outstanding advantage of an MHD generator, for higher efficiency goes hand in hand with less strain on the environment from waste heat, better utilization of fossil fuels and less pollution of the environment.

For MHD generators to be installed economically, a series of technical

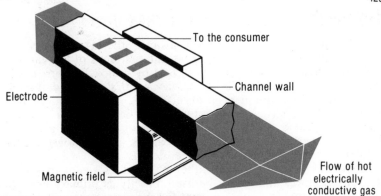

To the consumer

Channel wall

Electrode

Flow of hot electrically conductive gas

Magnetic field

Diagram 1. PRINCIPLE OF THE MHD GENERATOR: A TENSION IS BUILT UP IN THE FLOWING GAS BY THE MAGNETIC FIELD

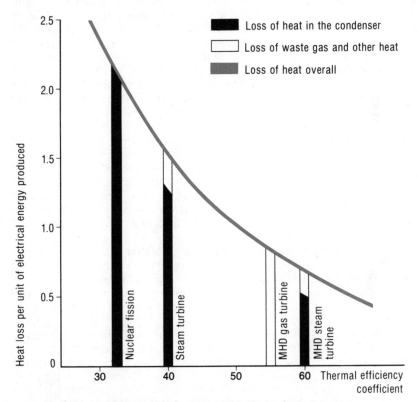

Loss of heat in the condenser

Loss of waste gas and other heat

Loss of heat overall

Heat loss per unit of electrical energy produced

Nuclear fission

Steam turbine

MHD gas turbine

MHD steam turbine

Thermal efficiency coefficient

Diagram 2. TOTAL THERMAL EFFICIENCY COEFFICIENTS OF VARIOUS ELECTRIC GENERATING SYSTEMS. WASTE HEAT INCREASES RAPIDLY AS THE COEFFICIENT OF EFFICIENCY DECLINES

problems remain to be solved (strong magnetic fields, high velocity of flow and high conductivity of the plasma). In the Soviet Union over 1500 scientists and engineers are currently engaged in MHD research work. And in the next few years Japan will be investing some $70 million in the field. In 1974 alone the United States invested $15 million in MHD research.

ENERGY FROM THE INTERIOR OF THE EARTH

Vast quantities of heat are stored away in the lower layers of the earth's crust. Some of the layers stem from the first days of the earth's existence, but they have also been formed in part by radioactive processes. The temperature of the earth's interior increases with depth, and at most sites temperatures suitable for use on an economic basis are to be found only at considerable depths. A temperature of 300°C (572°F), for instance, normally occurs only at a depth of about 10 km (6 miles). In geologically recent volcanic zones and in fissures in the earth's surface, however, temperatures of 300°C are not uncommon at lesser depths.

Geothermal energy can either be used as steam to produce electric current in power stations or be used directly as primary heat. Scientists in Germany are working on a project for the harnessing of geothermal energy on the Upper Rhine near Landau. There at a depth of 1000 meters (3280 feet) the prevailing temperature stands at 90°C (194°F). The process is simple: cold water is pumped down to a given depth, where it is heated up by the thermal flow and piped up again to the surface. There it is used for domestic heating, to provide heat for industry and for similar purposes.

In many countries a series of geothermal power plants have been in use for some time already. The geyser power stations in northern California, which are driven by geothermal steam power, have an electric energy output of 180 megawatts. This they produce at a much lower price than comparable power stations driven by fossil or nuclear fuel. In view of the good results obtained, it is planned to raise output to 400 megawatts. A geothermal power plant has been in operation at Larderello in Italy since 1904. Its output amounts at present to 370 Mw. The steam, which is emitted from boreholes under terrific pressure, comes from water that has seeped down from the earth's surface, probably mixed with seawater which flows in through newly formed fissures in the earth's crust. The steam is piped into big turbogenerators and, after serving its purpose, is condensed in large cooling towers. From there it is run into chemical plants in which boric acid, ammonia and other chemicals are extracted from it.

Most of the geothermal power plants are relatively small, having an output of between 1 and 20 Mw. The heat reservoirs below ground have been too little explored so far, and the exploration techniques are still at an early developmental stage. For these energy sources to be utilized on a large scale, various problems have still to be solved, such as corrosion of the turbines by water with a high salt content.

Geothermal power stations also face various potential environmental problems, such as pollution of air and water (by dissolved salts and gases from the interior of the earth), and ground subsidence and seismic disturbances caused by the removal of water from below ground. But these problems are capable of solution provided funds are available. In some places in the United States the salt content of geothermal waters is as high as 20%, compared with a standard salt content of 3.3% for seawater. The salts, which consist of various elements, can either be extracted chemically as a source of raw material or be returned to the boreholes. Returning the water in this way also helps to prevent the ground subsidence which often occurs when large quantities of water are removed from underground reservoirs.

On a conservative estimate, electric power production with the aid of geothermal energy could rise by the end of the century to some 100,000 megawatts, which would represent a substantial energy reserve.

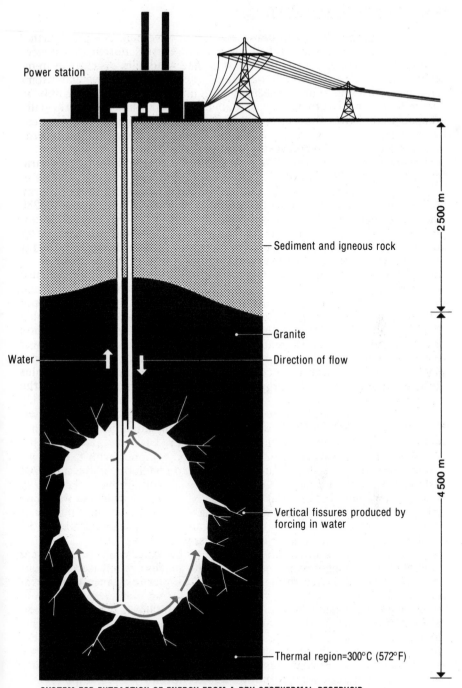

Power station

Sediment and igneous rock

Granite

Water — Direction of flow

Vertical fissures produced by forcing in water

2 500 m

4 500 m

Thermal region=300°C (572°F)

SYSTEM FOR EXTRACTION OF ENERGY FROM A DRY GEOTHERMAL RESERVOIR

WIND-DRIVEN POWER STATIONS

Wind is one of the oldest sources of energy used by man, but even today it is still one of the least-researched suppliers of energy. Formerly wind was used as a source of energy mainly for ships and windmills. As early as in the seventh century A.D. windmills were used in Persia for pumping and distributing water. At the start of the present century there were some 100,000 windmills on the North Sea coast between Holland and Denmark. They pumped water, ground corn, and drove sawmills, oil presses, paper mills, hammer mills, etc. As early as 1890 windmills were used in Denmark to generate electricity. The biggest wind-driven machine of this nature to date was installed in Vermont in 1941 with a rotor 58 meters (190 feet) in diameter. It had a power output of 1000 kilowatts.

Since the energy crisis of 1973–1974, interest in wind power has increased throughout the world. In West Germany the Solingen firm of SG-Energie Anlagen-Bau has aroused great interest in connection with its experimental wind-driven power station at Sylt. The average annual wind speed at Sylt amounts to 6 meters (20 feet) per second. The rotor blades of the wind-power plant resemble the wings of aircraft. Without gears, two rotors 11 meters (36 feet) in diameter working in opposite directions operate on a specially constructed generator. The plant cost about $70,000 and in the wind conditions prevailing in Sylt has an output of 150,000 kwh a year, which is utilized mainly in a block storage heater for five one-family houses. Thanks to the storage unit, lulls in the wind can be bridged for up to three days at a time. With an estimated life of 20 years and annual maintenance expenditure of $1100, the cost per kwh works out at some 3 cents. The wind machine does not make the occupants of the five houses completely self-sufficient in the matter of energy, but it at least replaces fuel oil for heating purposes.

A second wind-driven power station was in use at Stötten in the Swabian Alps from 1959 to 1968. Electrical output amounted to 100 kw from a two-bladed rotor 34 meters (111 feet) in diameter.

Whether wind-power appliances should be equipped with fixed or adjustable propellers depends mainly on the wind conditions in the area. Adjustable propellers are more expensive to install and are more liable to go wrong. They adapt better to all wind speeds, however, while the fixed propeller is only suited to particular working conditions. At one time, wind speeds of 3 meters (10 feet) per second were the lowest that could be utilized, but today, with adjustable propellers, winds of as little as 1.5 meters per second can be used. At the upper end of the scale, winds of 20 m/s can be exploited. At higher wind speeds the rotor blades are released automatically by a special device so that they cease to offer resistance to the wind currents.

The great advantage of wind-driven power stations is their environmental harmony. A wind-driven power station consumes no raw materials nor does it give off waste gases or other waste materials. Contrary to general misgivings on the subject, wind-power appliances produce little noise. As they reach full performance capacity at the relatively low rotation speed of 30 to 40 revolutions a minute, the sound they develop is only of the order of that produced by a glider, for example.

Wind-driven power stations would be particularly suitable for use in developing countries as a cheap source of energy, technologically simple to manage and presenting no problems for the environment. But in industrial countries, too, they can bring welcome relief to the energy market, espe-

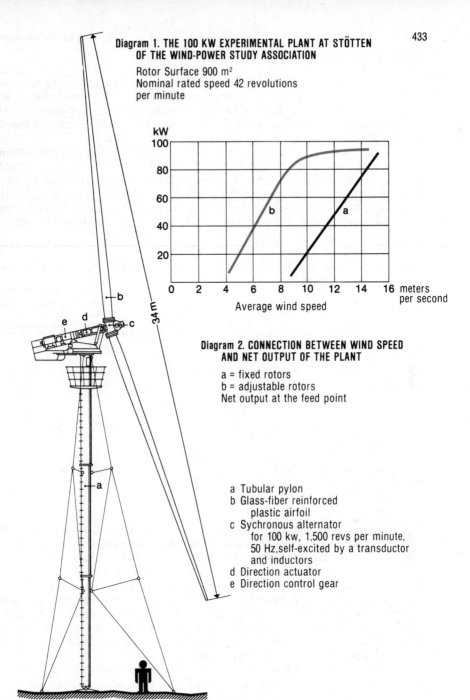

Diagram 1. THE 100 KW EXPERIMENTAL PLANT AT STÖTTEN OF THE WIND-POWER STUDY ASSOCIATION

Rotor Surface 900 m²
Nominal rated speed 42 revolutions
per minute

kW

Average wind speed

meters per second

Diagram 2. CONNECTION BETWEEN WIND SPEED AND NET OUTPUT OF THE PLANT

a = fixed rotors
b = adjustable rotors
Net output at the feed point

a Tubular pylon
b Glass-fiber reinforced
   plastic airfoil
c Sychronous alternator
   for 100 kw, 1,500 revs per minute,
   50 Hz,self-excited by a transductor
   and inductors
d Direction actuator
e Direction control gear

cially in areas of high winds—on the coastline and in hill and mountain country. According to estimates made by the International Meteorological Organization, at selected points in the world up to 20 million megawatts of electric power could be produced by means of wind-driven power stations.

WATER ENERGY

Water energy is converted solar energy. Water on the earth's surface evaporates under solar radiation, forms clouds in the earth's atmosphere, and returns to the earth's surface in the form of rain. Then when it runs down in a stream or river (owing to a difference in elevation) into a valley, it can be used as a form of energy.

Water energy has been known to man for thousands of years (waterwheels for grinding corn, hammer mills, etc.); but its use for electricity production is relatively recent. Electricity production by the use of water power has many advantages, such as cleanliness, no raw material consumption, low production costs, and a fully developed technique. Nevertheless, this source of energy is used relatively little, as the following table shows:

WATER ENERGY: POTENTIAL PERFORMANCE AND AMOUNT UTILIZED

Territory	Potential performance (10^3mega-watts)	Proportion available (%)	Amount utilized (10^3 Mw)	Proportion of amount utilized to possible performance (%)
North America	313	11	76	23.
South America	577	20	10	1.7
Western Europe	158	6	90	57.
Africa	780	27	5	0.6
Middle East	21	1	1	4.8
Southeast Asia	455	16	6	1.3
Far East	42	1	20	48.
Australia	45	2	5	11.
USSR, China and satellite countries	466	16	30	6.4
World as a whole	2857	100	243	8.5

The total potential output of water power available on the earth is thus estimated at about 2.9 million megawatts. This corresponds to about half the output of all the power plants installed in the world by the end of 1969. Of the potential output available, only about 8.5% is actually utilized at present. The continents having the biggest water power reserves are Africa with 780,000 Mw and South America with 577,000 Mw. The performance output obtainable at any point is related both to the water flow and volume and to the height of drop. The most suitable places for installing water-driven power stations are therefore in districts with high precipitation and pronounced differences of altitude in the terrain.

Since the beginning of the present century the industrialized countries have used the most suitable locations to erect a large number of water-driven power stations, so that remaining locations suitable for the installation of water-driven power stations are rare. Furthermore they are mainly to be found in hill country in attractive settings. Countries that have already sacrificed much of their territory for industrial purposes are accordingly inclined to protect these regions and place them under preservation orders. For developing countries, however, the further construction of water-driven power stations represents a cheap, clean, safe and inexhaustible means of

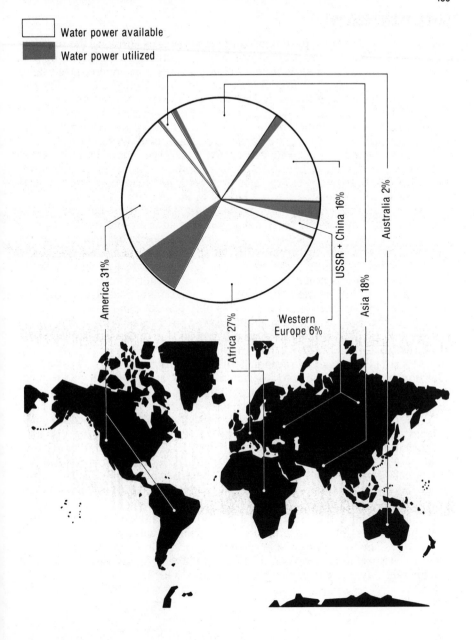

Water power available

Water power utilized

America 31%

Africa 27%

Western Europe 6%

USSR + China 16%

Asia 18%

Australia 2%

WATER POWER AVAILABLE AND UTILIZED IN VARIOUS CONTINENTS

covering their energy requirements. Storage lakes are often constructed for the provision of water power, and this offers good opportunities at the same time for watering agricultural crops.

TIDAL POWER PLANTS

Tidal power plants are a particularly attractive way of utilizing the regenerative forces of nature for purposes of power production. Solar energy and lunar energy can be converted into electric power by this means in the same way as in a waterworks. The process extends over a period of 12 hours and 24 minutes, that is, half the period it takes the moon to circle the earth. As the moon is the nearest of all the heavenly bodies to the earth, the force of gravity exerted by the moon has a measurable influence on the earth. In the big water-zones of the earth (the oceans) the result is that where the moon is directly overhead, owing to its attractive power, the water level is raised somewhat (flood tide), whereas in other regions it will be below the norm (ebb tide). These two phases are particularly sharply delineated on the coastlines of seas and oceans (see also "Tides" in Part Two).

At specially favorable points on the coast, tidal differences can be distinguished of 10 meters (32 feet) and more. If at such a point on the coast, a bay or a river mouth is shut off by a sluice or floodgate, energy can be obtained with the aid of turbines driven by water currents set up by the alternate filling and emptying of the bay. The maximum power produced by a tidal power plant is determined by the potential energy of the water mass stored in a basin during the flood tide and by the tidal period. The coefficient of efficiency of this energy utilization lies between 20% and 25%.

The pioneer in the erection of tidal power plants was West Germany. In the First World War a small tidal power station was in operation in Husum, using the flow and ebb of the current, in a former oyster-culture basin, in order to supply houses in the neighborhood with electricity. The first big tidal power station came into operation in 1966 at the mouth of the river Rance in France. Today its output amounts to 240 megawatts, and should be raised eventually to 320 Mw. Altogether 10 turbines are set in a dam 750 meters long, and they work in both directions, using both the incoming and outgoing tides. The tidal range (the difference between high and low tide) averages about 10 meters, with a maximum of 13 meters. In 1968 a small plant of 400 kilowatts was started up in the USSR at the mouth of the Kislaya, 80 km northeast of Murmansk. A larger plant of 320 Mw is projected for the Lombowska River on the northeast coast of the Kola Peninsula.

The following table shows part of the power available on the earth from tidal energy. Possible performance in the various locations ranges from 2 to 20,000 Mw. The total potential performance for all these locations amounts, according to preliminary estimates, to 64,000 Mw (compared with the output of a present-day nuclear power plant of 1200 Mw).

Place or region	Average potential output (Mw)	Possible annual power production (Mwh millions)
North America		
Bay of Fundy (9 locations)	29,000	255
South America		
Argentina (San Jose)	6,000	52
Europe		
England (R. Severn)	2,000	15
France (9 locations)	11,000	98
USSR (4 locations)	16,000	140

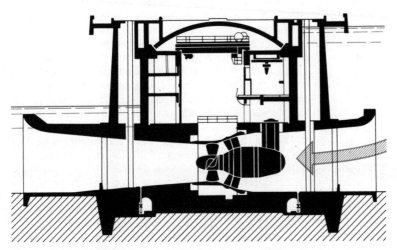

Diagram 1. OPERATION OF A TIDAL POWER PLANT ON A RISING TIDE

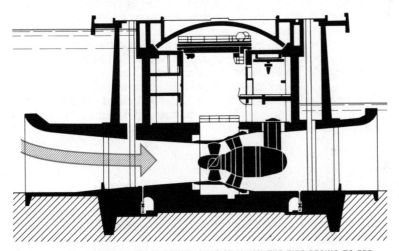

Diagram 2. OPERATION OF A TIDAL POWER STATION WHEN THE TIDE BEGINS TO EBB

ENERGY FROM THE SEA

If it were possible to utilize a mere 0.5% of the heat stored in the form of temperature differentials in the oceans of the world, man's energy problems would all be solved. This concept, however utopian it may sound, is not in fact utterly unrealistic. Sea-heat power plants fall within the field of technical possibility. The idea of utilizing the energy stored in the ocean is not new. It was first suggested in 1881 by the French physicist Jacques d'Arsonval. His fellow countryman George Claude erected the first sea-heat power plant in Cuba in 1929. Its power output then amounted to 22 kilowatts. Its performance was satisfactory, but it was uneconomical, as Claude's technical resources were inadequate. American environmental engineers have now developed the idea. Design work has begun at the University of Massachusetts for a sea-heat power plant to be erected in the Gulf Stream off the coast of south Florida.

The theory of a sea-heat power plant is as follows: between various water depths there is normally a temperature differential which can be utilized for energy production. In the tropics, that is, between the celestial spheres of Cancer and Capricorn, the surface waters of the oceans have an almost unvarying temperature of 25°C (77°F) over the whole year. At a depth of 1000 meters (3200 feet) or so, on the other hand, the prevailing temperature is only 5°C (41°F). This temperature differential can be utilized as in conventional power plants by letting the liquid on the "warm side" evaporate or simmer. The steam drives a turbine and is condensed on the "cold side." As the heat differentials are in a narrow range, water is not suitable as a medium. First calculations indicate that propane gas would be a very suitable gas for circulation in seawater power plants. It boils at temperatures of under 25°C, and can return to liquid form at 5°C. The power plant could be installed on a floating island in the open sea.

Power plants of this kind could provide a realistic technical solution for the utilization of solar energy, for the water is heated by the sun, and the oceans serve as energy stores. The temperature differentials arise as a result of circulation between the poles and the tropics (see "Sea Currents" in Part Two).

Sea-heat power plants could also acquire much greater importance. The cold water pumped up from the depths of the sea could serve to do more than just cool the turbines. It still remains cool enough to condense water vapor drawn off from seawater into a vacuum chamber. In this way the power plant can extract drinking water from the sea. It is estimated that a plant with an output of 100 Mw of electric power could provide some 200 million liters of drinking water a day.

In contrast to the development of nuclear energy, especially by fast breeder reactors, no serious new technical problems are posed by this form of utilization of solar energy.

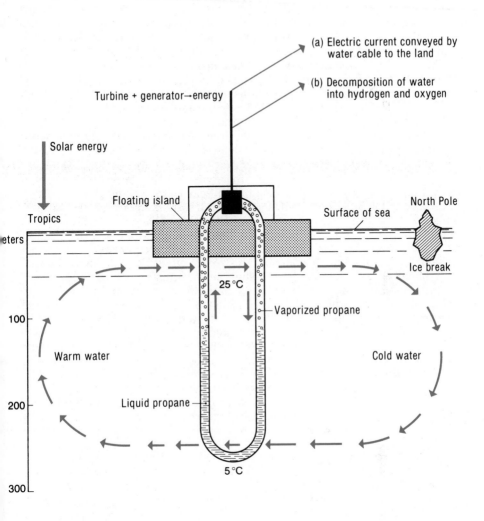

ENERGY FROM THE SEA

GLACIER POWER PLANTS

After many years' research work in Arctic stations, where he was conversant with the structure and dynamics of the Greenland ice sheet, a Swiss hydrobiologist came up a short time ago with an unusual project for energy production. Enormous quantities of ice melt in Greenland every summer and run down into the sea from land 2000–3000 m (6500–9800 feet) high. If normal power stations were built on the coast in Greenland, enormous quantities of electric power could be produced by this means. The technology of the necessary hydraulic power stations would be standard, but the construction material for the dams and the supply and pressure ducts would be something quite new, namely rock-hard glacier ice.

As the biggest island in the world, Greenland has a surface area of about 2 million sq km (760,000 sq mi). On a conservative estimate something like 500,000 sq km (190,000 sq mi) would be available for the installation of storage basins. With the sun shining for about 2000 hours per annum, some 8 kwh of energy could be produced each year from 1 sq m of storage lake area. From the estimated 500,000 sq km of storage lake area, about 4000 billion kwh of useful energy should be obtainable each year. This represents an electric power output of about 200,000 Mw, approximating the output of 200 large atomic power stations. During the summer an extensive canal system, corresponding to a network of streams, would have to be built inside Greenland. The ice melted by the sun's heat would run along these canals into big storage lakes. In the course of the flow of the melted ice water, which would be warm compared with the ice it came into contact with, the streams would expand of their own accord, so that relatively little technical energy would be required for the construction of the canal system. Owing to the differences in elevation from 2000 to 3000 m, the melted ice water would shoot through ducts from the storage lake down to normal, big hydraulic power stations installed on the coast. The storage lakes are required mainly to ensure that energy production will be available also in winter. In the winter a layer of ice 1 to 2 meters thick forms on the surface of the storage lakes and protects the water below from further freezing. The water below the layer of surface ice could thus be drawn off for energy production as required.

The necessary barrages, and the supply and pressure ducts, can be modeled by suitable techniques with the aid of the ice. Tested procedures already exist for the construction of ice channels in glaciers. By means of a circular cutting guide (a steel tube with an interfacing rotating sawtooth rim), cylinders can be cut out of the glacier ice having a diameter of about 10 m (33 feet). With a subsidiary circular saw appliance the ice cylinder cut out lengthways can be split up into semicircular portions and lifted out onto the canal bank by means of a rotating table turned at an angle of 180°. These segments can be stacked together quite easily to form dams, whereupon they rapidly freeze up again.

By means of such glacier power plants, cheap energy could be produced in large quantities without causing any pollution of the environment and without the consumption of raw materials. For transmission of the energy

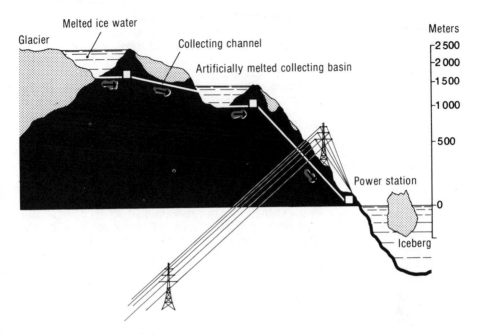

Meters
-2 500
-2 000
-1 500
-1 000
-500
-0

Glacier
Melted ice water
Collecting channel
Artificially melted collecting basin
Power station
Iceberg

GLACIER POWER PLANT

there are two possibilities: (1) The electric current produced can be conveyed directly by submarine cable to North America and Europe or (2), and this is probably the better solution, with the aid of the electric energy produced in the hydraulic power station the water can be split up into hydrogen and oxygen, and the hydrogen can be liquefied and conveyed by tanker to the country of consumption. It could then be used for heating, for driving advanced motor vehicles, or in fuel cells for electricity production.

USE OF SOLAR ENERGY FOR ELECTRICITY PRODUCTION

Until a few years ago any proposals regarding the use of solar energy for electricity production were received with the utmost skepticism. This attitude is now beginning to change, however. Of all forms of energy, solar radiation is the one available to man in the greatest abundance. The total energy needs of the United States could be covered by the amount of solar energy imparted to as little as 0.15% of the land surface of the country. In European latitudes the amount of energy radiated by the sun amounts to about 1200 kwh per sq m per year.

In the United States and certain other countries such as Japan and Australia, the first steps have already been taken to develop big central solar power plants. For modern steam turbines temperatures are required of between 300° and 600°C (572° and 1112°F), which complicates both the accumulation of solar radiation and the storage of the thermal energy. In order to attain these high temperatures, sunlight must be concentrated by means of mirrors or lenses. A promising plan has been developed by A. Meinel and his associates at the University of Arizona. Under this plan the sunlight would be intensified tenfold by means of lenses mounted on tubes of stainless steel. The tube is encased in a special black plastic coating which releases only a very small proportion of the thermal energy received. This appliance is also enclosed in a vacuum glass chamber, whereby the loss of heat by conduction and convection is reduced. Nitrogen is passed through the tubing at a speed of about 4 meters (13 feet) per second so as to carry the heat from the collectors to a central storage plant. For the heat storage medium a latent energy storer with dissolved salts is used. If required, steam can then be produced to drive a turbogenerator.

Owing to the large area of land required and the increase in efficiency derived from solar radiation, such solar power stations should be installed in hot desert or semidesert areas. In the proximity of Europe, installation of plants in North Africa (Sahara) and in southern Europe (Spain, southern Italy and Sicily) would be suitable. For a solar power station with a capacity of 1000 Mw, a land surface of about 12 sq km (5 sq mi) is required. By this means, electric current could be produced at a price of 1 to 3 cents per kwh.

Another uncomplicated and dependable method of converting solar radiation into electric current has been employed successfully for a number of years in the supply of energy in spaceships: *solar cells*, or semiconductor chips, which convert the impinging solar radiation directly into electric current. The special advantage of this method is that no mechanical movement of parts is needed whatsoever in order to produce electricity. The current flows directly out of the relatively simply constructed semiconductor chips. The reliability of the operation is extraordinarily high. Even under severe space conditions a maintenance-free life-span of 10 or more years was achieved. The performance coefficient of solar cells stands at present between 10% and 16%; and in theory 22% to 25% is possible. The one disadvantage of solar cells is their high price.

Possible environmental problems from solar power plants can certainly not be excluded, but at least they are considerably less than in the case of other sources of energy such as oil, coal, gas and nuclear energy. Changes in the local heat balance must be contemplated in particular, since the surfaces of the collectors absorb more sunlight than the earth's surface.

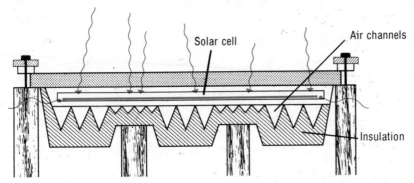

Diagram 1. "SOLAR TILES" FOR COVERING ROOFS IN PLACE OF THE USUAL TILES

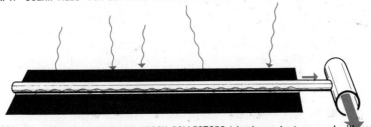

Diagram 2. IN SCHÖLL'S PILOT PLANT, BLACK COLLECTORS (aluminum sheets covered with asphalt) ARE USED. THE THERMAL TRANSPORT MEDIUM FLOWS IN STEEL TUBES.

PERFORMANCE COEFFICIENT OF A SOLAR ENERGY PLANT

	Present plant values	Attainable plant values
Average incident solar energy	700 w/m^2	700 w/m^2
Proportion fed into the process	64%=450 w/m^2	85%=600w/m^2
Extraction capacity of the collector from the collector to the heat carrier	80%	90%
Transmitted energy flow	360 w/m^2	540 w/m^2
Theoretical quality factor	100	200
Technical quality factor	52	124
Heat-carrier heating temperature	450°C	600°C
Process performance coefficient	37%	48%
Turbine performance coefficient	75%	75%
Total thermodynamic performance coefficient	28%	36%
Average total performance coefficient of the entire solar energy power plant	14%	25%

Calculation based on a daily solar energy radiation of
8 hours with a midday intensity of 930 w/m^2

SOLAR ENERGY FOR HEATING AND COOLING

Ideally, solar energy could be trapped on the unutilized surfaces of countless numbers of house roofs. According to one estimate, in which the developing countries are not included, roof surfaces on buildings of all types throughout the world represent about 20 sq m of space per person. Solar energy imparted to this area amounts to about 24,000 kwh per person per year. This corresponds to the sum raised to the power of ten of all the energy consumed per person in the world today in the form of oil and nuclear energy. The same roof area could give off into the atmosphere at night between 3.5 and 8.5 million kcal of heat per year without warming up the air in outer space.

Solar heating has rapidly gained popularity in the United States. In 1979 there were 40,000 solar installations, compared with 24 in 1970. Such growth suggests that as much as 10% of the population by 1985 may live in homes with solar space or water heating.

Solar-heated buildings vary widely in size and cost, and they are found in all kinds of climate. Some use passive systems, in which sunlight commonly is admitted by south-facing glazing, stored in walls and floors and distributed by convective airflow. Other buildings use active systems in which mechanical means move the heat from sunlight collectors to storage and from storage to the rooms of the house. The most practical strategy for a house in Boston can be quite different from that for a house in Arizona.

Many houses use both active and passive collectors to take best advantage of the sun. The first solar-heated home in Maine, for instance, built in 1974, uses 190 square feet of double-glazed windows for passive heat collection and a 520 square foot "trickle collector" for the active collection. The trickle collector is one of the simplest heat-transfer devices. Water trickles down the valleys of corrugated aluminum that is heated by the sun. In the Maine house, the heated water flows into a 1600 gallon tank surrounded by 20 tons of small rocks. A fan blows air across the heated rocks, and the warm air rises into the living areas of the house. The solar system meets about 70% of the house's heating needs. The rest of the heat is supplied by a fireplace and wood furnace. The house's owners estimate their solar system saves them $600 a year in heating expenses.

As the periods of energy production and energy consumption do not usually coincide, storage of the energy is essential in solar-heated buildings. Owing to the high temperature differentials between storage containers and the environment, normal heat storage suffers from the disadvantage that, even when well insulated, the heat slowly escapes in course of time. But by the use of what are known as *latent energy storers,* this can be avoided. Here the heat energy applied is used only to a minor extent for raising the temperature, and is used in the main for changing the storage medium in the aggregate. The storage medium consists of specific salt mixtures which are transformed by heating from a solid phase to a liquid condition. In the liquefaction process, a large part of the thermal energy is established in the form of fusion heat, and can be recovered later in the form of useful heat. Such latent energy storers can take in up to 20 times more energy than heat accumulators of like weight.

Another scheme for the utilization of solar energy for heating and air conditioning uses, as roof plates, adjustable systems with a heat rectifying effect. In this case solar energy taken in is passed onto a thin latent storage layer which can be composed so that its constantly maintained temperature corresponds to the room temperature. In this way the solar energy absorbed

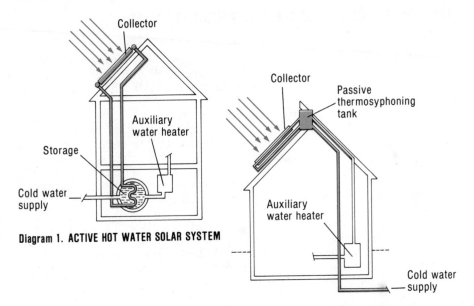

Diagram 1. **ACTIVE HOT WATER SOLAR SYSTEM**

Diagram 2. **PASSIVE HOT WATER SOLAR SYSTEM**

Diagram 3. **SOLAR HEATING AND COOLING**

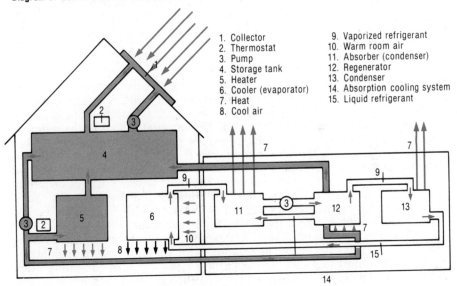

1. Collector
2. Thermostat
3. Pump
4. Storage tank
5. Heater
6. Cooler (evaporator)
7. Heat
8. Cool air

9. Vaporized refrigerant
10. Warm room air
11. Absorber (condenser)
12. Regenerator
13. Condenser
14. Absorption cooling system
15. Liquid refrigerant

by day is stored in the latent storer, and is given off again into the space of the room at night. If during the summer the room temperature rises too much, the rectifier effect of the roof plates can be reversed for cooling purposes. The overheated room air now imparts energy to the latent storer, which gives off energy into the atmosphere at night in the form of infrared radiation.

SPECIAL PROBLEMS CONCERNING NUCLEAR ENERGY: NATURAL RADIOACTIVITY

The natural radiation to which man is exposed emanates from three sources: cosmic radiation from outer space, terrestrial radiation from the earth's crust (natural radionuclides), and radiation from radionuclides formed as a result of cosmic radiation.

The cosmic radiation that impinges on the earth's surface with great intensity from outer space is to a large extent blocked off by the earth's atmosphere. According to altitude it amounts, on the earth's surface, to between 35 millirems per annum at sea level and 100 mrem per annum at a height of 2000 meters (6500 feet). The primary radiation from outer space is a corpuscular radiation consisting mainly of energy-rich protons (hydrogen atoms). By their interaction with atomic nuclei in the upper layers of the atmosphere, new radioactive isotopes and mesons are formed, which for their part can again become active on the earth's surface. The "hard" component of the cosmic rays is very full of energy, has a high penetrative capacity, and can be traced at considerable depths below the earth's surface, in mines for example (mesonic components). The "soft" component consists of electrons, positrons and gamma rays, which have less penetrative power.

Terrestrial radiation derives from radioactive materials in the earth's crust. The main source for human exposure stems from the concentration of such materials in the human environment, i.e., in the earth and in building materials. In regions of normal radiation it amounts to between 80 and 120 mrem per annum, and in uranium deposits or other regions with a high concentration of natural radionuclides it can attain a level of several thousand mrem per annum. Investigations carried out on 1.2 million live births in the state of New York suggest that an increase in natural radiation will result in an increased number of genetic defects.

When the earth was formed, a large number of radioactive substances came into being. On emitting rays, radioactive substances undergo fission, so that today we still find radioactive substances whose half-life is of the order of the geological age of the earth. The most important of the radionuclides in the earth's crust (radioisotopes) are potassium-40 (half-life 1.3 billion years), uranium-238 (4.5 billion years) and thorium-232 (14 billion years). Upon fission of uranium-238 and thorium-232 a series of intermediate unstable isotopes are formed, which for the most part are also radioactive. One speaks of "radioactive families" of uranium and thorium or of radioactive disintegration series. Within this radioactive disintegration series, natural radionuclides with a shorter half-life also occur.

A further source of natural radioactive nuclides is represented by cosmic rays, from which by interaction with the atmosphere radioactive hydrogen (tritium) and radioactive carbon (^{14}C) are formed among other substances. The natural radionuclides absorbed by man with his food give rise to a radiation load of between 20 and 30 mrem per annum.

Since life began it has been exposed to a persistent natural radiation load. It is now known that this is an important factor in the evolution of organisms. In relation to the mostly negative mutations (changes in heritable substances) caused by radiation load, owing to the hard conditions present in the environment the positive mutations were given preference and passed on in the selection process. It can safely be assumed that this process is continuing today.

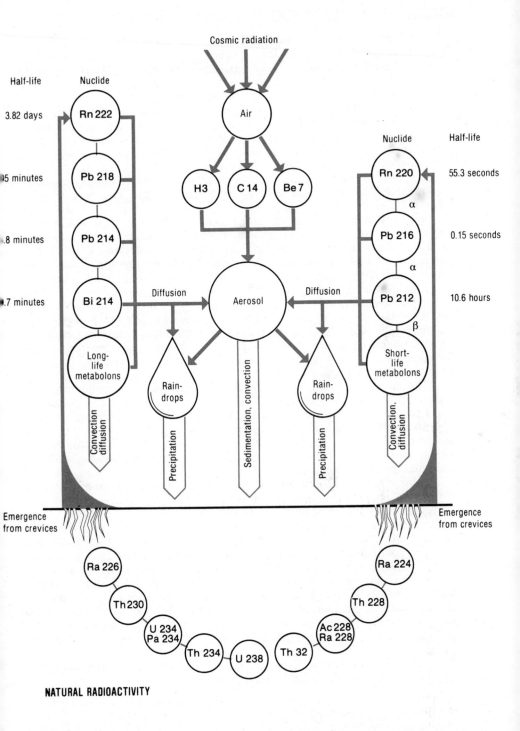

NATURAL RADIOACTIVITY

NUCLEAR FISSION AND RADIOACTIVITY

All atoms consist of an atomic nucleus and an electronic sheath, in which electrons rotate about the nucleus. When energy is imparted as a result of chemical reactions (as by the combustion of oil or coal), decisive energy processes take place in the electronic sheath. In contrast to this, the energy obtained by nuclear fission comes from the atomic nucleus.

The atomic nucleus is composed of a specific number of protons and neutrons for each type of isotope. Protons have positive electrical charges, while neutrons possess no electrical charge. For nuclear fission in a nuclear power station the isotope uranium-235 is used. The number 235 indicates that the atomic nucleus of the uranium isotope consists of 235 nucleons (protons and neutrons together). This particular uranium isotope possesses the property that it can be split by releasing energy. The process is as follows:

When a neutron (emanating, for instance, from cosmic radiation in outer space) impinges on the atomic nucleus of a uranium-235 atom, the atomic nucleus splits. This produces two smaller atomic nuclei and 2 to 3 free neutrons, which are able for their part to split new uranium atom nuclei. As for each neutron injected 2 to 3 new neutrons are formed which can touch off further nuclear fission, this is known as a *chain reaction*. If the process is uncontrolled (as in an atomic bomb, for instance) this can result in a split second in the release of an enormous quantity of energy. In an atomic power plant the reaction process is kept under control by capturing so many neutrons (by the use of various suitable absorbent materials) that for each injected neutron only one more neutron is formed that is able to produce further nuclear fission.

The energy released by nuclear fission consists of thermal energy and radioactive radiation. The thermal energy is generated by the fact that the two new atomic nuclei formed by the fission of the uranium atom fly off at high speed (that is, at a high level of kinetic energy), collide with other atoms and so cause thermal agitation of the atoms and molecules. With this thermal energy water can be heated, which can be used to drive turbines and produce electricity from generators.

A large part of the new atomic nuclei produced in the form of fragments is not stable. This instability, which is known as *radioactivity,* arises from a particular relationship of neutrons to protons in the atomic nucleus. Radioactive atoms possess the property of disintegrating after a certain time span so that radioactive radiation is released. This time span, which is different for each particular type of radioactive atom, indicates how long it takes for half of the radioactive atoms to disintegrate. This period is known as the *half-life.* To take an example: of 1,000,000 atoms of a radioactive isotope with a half-life of one year, after one year 500,000 radioactive atoms will consequently be present, after 2 years 250,000, after 3 years 125,000, and so on. After 10 half-lives, in this case after 10 years, one-thousandth of the original radioactive atoms will still be present, or in this case about 1000 atoms.

Upon the radioactive disintegration of an atom, radioactive radiation is released. There are three kinds of radioactive radiation:

Alpha radiation is a corpuscular radiation, which consists of helium nuclei, that is, each of 2 protons and 2 neutrons.

Beta radiation is also a corpuscular radiation, consisting of electrons of very high velocity.

Gamma radiation is an electromagnetic wave radiation of very high energy.

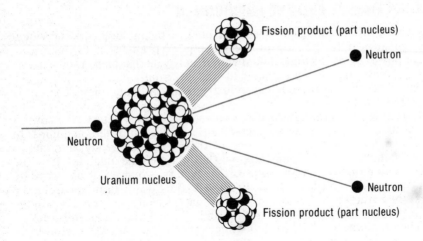

Fission product (part nucleus)

Neutron

Neutron

Uranium nucleus

Fission product (part nucleus)

Diagram 1. NUCLEAR FISSION

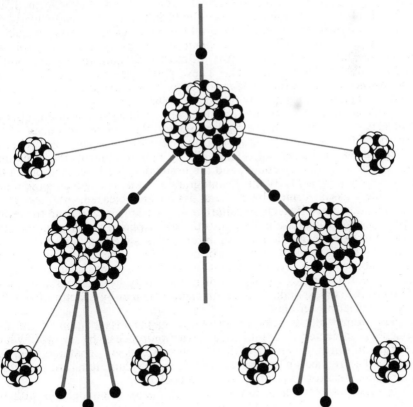

Diagram 2. CHAIN REACTION

NUCLEAR ENERGY AND THE ENVIRONMENT

In assessing the radiological effects of nuclear technology, the individual power plant is only "the tip of the iceberg." To enable it to operate, a nuclear power plant has to be linked with a fuel cycle that emits radioactivity at many points and so contaminates the environment.

The first stage in the nuclear industry is the uranium mine. The ore is pulverized and subjected to a leaching process to separate the uranium. The waste from this separating process, known as tailings, contains the subsidiary products of the natural radioactive series and is deposited on dumps. In the United States alone, the volume of these tailings already amounts to some 100 million tons. Rainwater washes the soluble nuclides into the ground, into groundwater and into surface waters, whence it is absorbed by organisms in the soil and water. By the extraction of uranium from the mines, the natural radioactive substances that normally lie deep down in the earth's crust are brought to the surface and released into the biosphere.

The uranium extracted from the mines then passes into the factories for preparing fuel elements, where the fissionable uranium-235 isotope recovered from nature in small quantities is enriched. In this highly energy-consuming enrichment process further radioactive waste is formed and given off into the environment. Once the uranium has been sufficiently enriched it is fed, in the form of small tablets, into fuel elements for nuclear power plants. In the nuclear power plant the real process of nuclear fission takes place, whereby a large number of mostly radioactive fission products are formed from the uranium-235. These partly gaseous radioisotopes escape to some extent in the nuclear power plant and are given off into the air and water below the legally permitted limits for radioactivity.

After about a year the fuel elements are exchanged and, after a period of intermediate storage in the nuclear power plant to permit decay of the short-period isotopes, are transported to a reprocessing plant. For reconditioning purposes the fuel cells are split by remote control, the individual rods are cut into short sections, and the uranium oxide is washed out of the sheaths with nitric acid. By this disintegration of the fuel elements the radioactive inert gases formed by nuclear fission are released. As inert gases cannot be combined by a chemical process, they are emitted from the reprocessing plant through a chimney into the atmosphere. Other radionuclides released in gaseous and liquid form in this process are kept out of the waste air and water of the plant by means of filters. But as these filters are not 100 percent absorbent, a certain amount of the radioisotopes escapes into the environment. Overall the emission of radioactivity by reprocessing plants, related to the corresponding fuel equivalent, is higher by a factor of 100–200 than in nuclear power plants.

The uranyl nitrate solution produced in the dissociation of the fuel elements is subjected to a multistage extraction process, by means of which the uranium, the plutonium and the fission products are separated from one another. The refined end-products, uranium and plutonium, are processed again by manufacturers to provide new fuel elements.

Special problems arise in reprocessing plants in connection with the production of tritium and plutonium (see Part Fourteen).

The fission product solutions remaining after the separation of uranium and plutonium cannot be reutilized and must be disposed of as atomic waste (see Part Sixteen).

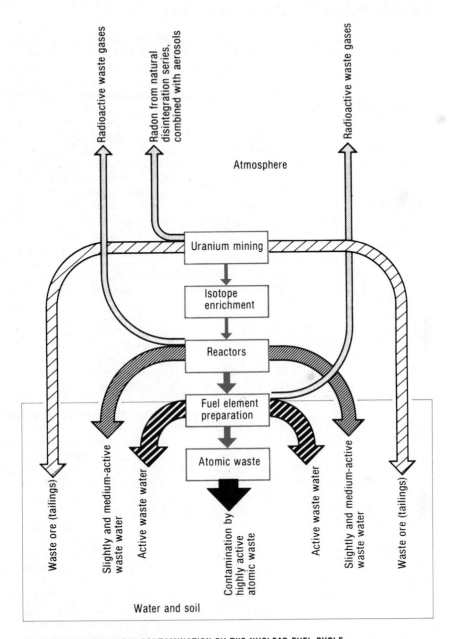

PLAN OF ENVIRONMENTAL CONTAMINATION BY THE NUCLEAR FUEL CYCLE

NUCLEAR POWER PLANT CONSTRUCTION

The essential difference between a nuclear power station and a conventional power station consists in the way in which energy is provided. In both cases energy is used to heat water to produce steam to drive a generator by means of a turbine. This produces electrical energy which is fed into the public supply system. In a nuclear power plant the energy is obtained by fission of uranium nuclei. The uranium is piled up in fuel rods in the form of uranium dioxide tablets. Some tens of thousands of these fuel rods hang in the core of the reactor. The nuclear fission takes place inside the fuel rods. The thermal energy released spreads outward and is absorbed on the surface of the fuel rods by the cooling water which is propelled through the core by pumps. The water in the primary cooling circuit gives off its energy through a heat exchanger to a secondary circuit. It is the steam from the secondary circuit that drives the turbines. The secondary circuit is a safeguard to ensure that any radioactive contamination caused by a defect in the primary circuit cannot reach the turbines.

Besides the fuel rods, control rods are installed in the core. These consist of neutron-absorbent material, by means of which the chain reaction can be controlled. If the reactor has to be shut off suddenly, the control rods are injected into the core where they absorb a large amount of the neutrons and reduce the rate of nuclear fission.

The reactor pressure vessel that surrounds the core is enclosed in a shell, a concrete casing with walls about 2 meters (6.5 feet) thick. The entire primary cooling circuit is enclosed in a spherical safety casing made of steel about 50 meters (164 feet) in diameter. The safety tank also contains a fuel element storage basin, a loading and unloading device for fuel elements, a waste water tank, and various safety appliances such as an emergency cooling system and a pressure reservoir.

As small leakages occur regularly in the large number of fuel rods, the water in the primary cooling circuit is always subject to mild radioactive contamination. This radioactivity is partly removed by purification of the primary cooling agent, and the rest escapes by leakage of steam from the primary cooling circuit into the safety tank. In order to prevent leakage of this radioactively contaminated air into the environment, a partial vacuum is maintained in the safety tank. Part of the air is removed by constant suction, fed into various filter systems and, due regard being had to the legally prescribed limits for radioactivity, discharged into the air through a chimney. The radioactive waste water resulting from the decontamination of the primary cooling water is retained for some time and then, after being decontaminated down to the prescribed limits, is mixed with the cooling water and allowed to run away.

Owing to the strong neutron radiation, in time the components inside the reactor become radioactive. A nuclear power plant can be expected to last for 20 to 40 years. At the expiration of that period, the nuclear plant must be either demolished or bricked up.

Apart from the type of light water-cooled, pressurized-water reactor described here, there are a number of other types of nuclear power plant. The boiling-water reactor operates with only one cooling circuit. The pressure inside the reactor is relatively low. The steam produced inside the core is fed into turbines directly. High-temperature reactors are gas-cooled. Their fuel elements are contained in globes cased in graphite. High-temperature reactors have a high operating temperature and consequently a high efficiency coefficient.

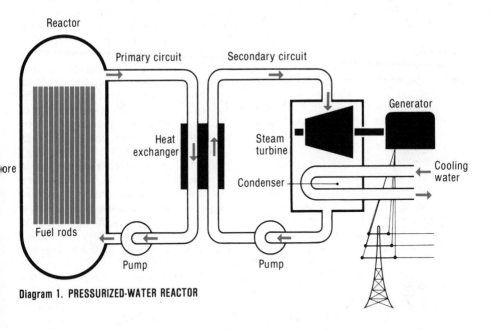

Diagram 1. PRESSURIZED-WATER REACTOR

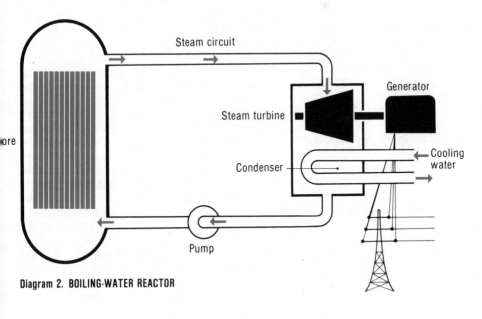

Diagram 2. BOILING-WATER REACTOR

FAST BREEDER REACTORS

As supplies of fissionable uranium-235 are limited, *breeder reactor* nuclear power plants will be constructed in the future to "breed" fissionable plutonium-239 out of nonfissionable uranium-238, which is available in large quantities, with the aid of fast neutrons (hence the name "fast breeders"). So that nuclear power plants now being built can continue to operate in the future, the nuclear power industry is now aimed at the installation of these fast breeders. The technology of the fast breeder entails grave risks, however.

In nuclear fission, "fast" neutrons with a force of 100,000 to 10 million electron volts are released. The usual "thermal" reactors "moderate" these neutrons—that is, they slow them down to thermal energies (0.1 of an electron volt). Fast breeders, however, have no "moderator." In a medium-cooled fast breeder, about 0.5 megawatt of heat is released per liter of reactor core volume. That is 5 to 10 times the power density of a light water reactor and 50,000 times the power density of a reactor with natural uranium metal fuel elements and gas cooling. The reactor core of a sodium breeder is only 1 to 3 cubic meters in size. Inside the core hang tens of thousands of fuel elements, no thicker than the lead in a pencil, containing highly enriched uranium oxide. The fuel elements are cooled by means of liquid metallic sodium. Every second several tons of sodium flow past the fuel elements at a speed of about 6 meters per second and are heated up to about 560°C thereby. Two thermal circuits carry the heat away to a steam generator, the steam from which drives a normal turbogenerator.

The reactor core of the sodium breeder is subject to mechanical stress, vibration, turbulence in the liquid sodium (high velocity of flow), high temperatures from the steel casing of the fuel elements (up to 700°C), extremely fast neutrons (which make the steel swell), and sharp differences in the heat and neutron flow. Nonetheless the measurements and structure of the 6-mm-thick fuel rods must be kept within very narrow limits. A reduction in their volume by only 2% will set off an explosive power delivery by the reactor. A slight expansion of the fuel elements, on the other hand, will bring the chain reaction to a standstill.

There are a number of ways in which a reactor catastrophe could occur in a fast breeder. If one or more of the cooling channels were to be blocked (as happened in an accident to a small Fermi reactor in the United States in 1969, for instance), overheating of the nuclear fuel would result, as the heat could no longer be carried away by the cooling agent. The result would be that the sodium comes to a boil and the reactivity (rate of nuclear fission) and consequently the amount of energy released would rise sharply. This could result in the bursting of the casing. Nuclear fuel and fission products react explosively in such a case with the hot sodium. If fuel elements in the lower half of the reactor core are destroyed in this way, the fission products and the sodium steam bubbles will be swamped by the sodium stream in the center of the reactor core, and this will also sharply increase the reactivity of the reactor. The remains of defective fuel rods may be flung, as a result of the explosion, against other fuel rods, and a chemical chain reaction may be touched off.

Attempts have sometimes been made to simulate such accidents with a reactor. One result is that for each megawatt of electric power, a maximum

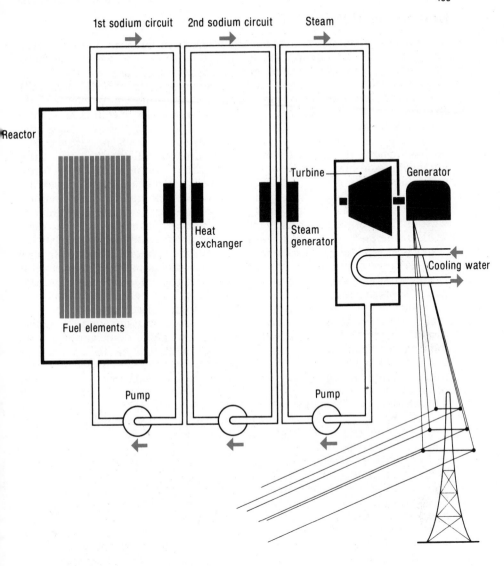

1st sodium circuit   2nd sodium circuit   Steam

Reactor

Turbine   Generator

Heat
exchanger

Steam
generator

Cooling water

Fuel elements

Pump   Pump

FAST BREEDER

energy of 1 Mw (which corresponds to the explosive force of 250 g TNT) should be produced for rupturing the safety casing. In a 1000 Mw reactor this would correspond to an explosive force of 250 kg TNT. An accident of this order could thus blow up parts of the reactor core or the entire core together with the safety casing.

NUCLEAR FUSION

Right from the start of the atomic age it has been recognized that the basic reaction of nuclear fusion occurring in the sun and also in hydrogen bomb explosions would constitute an enormous source of energy if the process could be conducted on a controlled basis in a nuclear reactor. Since the first experiments were carried out over 20 years ago in the United States, Great Britain and the Soviet Union, nuclear fusion has passed into the sphere of major research.

The process of nuclear fusion contrasts with that of nuclear fission. In nuclear fusion, atomic nuclei of heavy hydrogen isotopes (deuterium with one proton and one neutron, and tritium with one proton and two neutrons in the nucleus) are fused at a high temperature and under high pressure, whereby nuclear binding energy is transformed into kinetic energy and can thus be utilized as thermal energy. In theory, fusions are possible with various types of nuclei, but in practice a nuclear fusion power plant should work in the main on the basis of a deuterium-tritium fusion. Materials that result from this fusion include helium, tritium, and protons and neutrons of various powers. A chain reaction such as is used in nuclear fission reactors is not possible, because no particles are left behind which could promote new fusions at rising reaction rates.

Nuclear fusions in reactors follow the same lines as chemical combustion reactions; but in quantitative terms they are very different. In nuclear fusion the energy gain per reaction is about one million times as great as in the case of chemical combustion. Although deuterium and tritium are present in only very limited proportions in natural water, if nuclear fusion were successful the energy requirements of man would be covered for thousands of years ahead.

Despite these tempting figures, it has not yet been possible to construct a fully operative nuclear fusion power plant. This is mainly because the deuterium and tritium nuclei that are to be fused possess similarly electrified charges. Their approximation, which is necessary for purposes of nuclear fusion, consequently has to overcome the repelling electrical force. To overcome this repelling effect the nuclei must come together violently with very high kinetic energy. The temperature in a fusion reactor must consequently be of the order of 100 million degrees. At these high temperatures extremely high pressures develop in the plasmas. The hot fuel mixture must be contained at a given volume until such time as more usable energy is released by a sufficient number of nuclear fusion reactions, as required for heating the mixture and covering radiation losses. At such high temperatures the plasma can be held together long enough at high pressure only with the aid of a magnetic field.

A nuclear fusion power plant will probably affect the environment far less than a nuclear fission power plant. Owing to the high operating temperature, high thermal efficiency can be achieved, probably in the region of 55%–60% compared with 35% for normal nuclear power stations.

One problem that arises is the disposal of the radioactive tritium which occurs as an end product of the fusion in addition to the nonradioactive helium. Account must also be taken of the fact that in a nuclear fusion power plant a considerably stronger neutron radiation would occur which, owing to neutron capture, would produce new radioactive substances in the structure of the reactor. It is not yet known whether this problem can be kept under control by suitable selection of the building materials used.

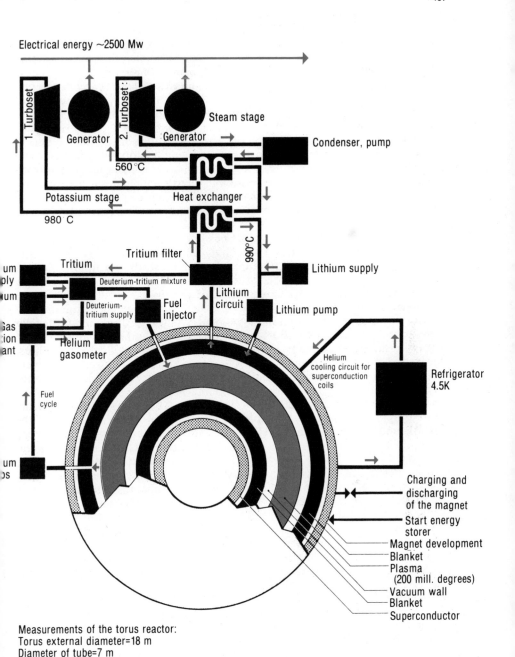

Electrical energy ~2500 Mw

1. Turboset

Generator

2. Turboset

Generator

Steam stage

Condenser, pump

560 °C

Potassium stage

Heat exchanger

980 C

990°C

Tritium filter

Tritium

Lithium supply

um
ply

Deuterium-tritium mixture

um

Deuterium-
tritium supply

Fuel
injector

Lithium
circuit

Lithium pump

Gas
tion
ant

Helium
gasometer

Helium
cooling circuit for
superconduction
coils

Refrigerator
4.5K

Fuel
cycle

um
os

Charging and
discharging
of the magnet

Start energy
storer

Magnet development

Blanket

Plasma
(200 mill. degrees)

Vacuum wall

Blanket

Superconductor

Measurements of the torus reactor:
Torus external diameter=18 m
Diameter of tube=7 m

NUCLEAR FUSION REACTOR

SAFETY OF NUCLEAR POWER PLANTS

Heightened concern about the risks of operating nuclear power plants followed a reactor accident in 1979 at the Three Mile Island power plant near Harrisburg, Pennsylvania. A series of equipment failures, misleading instrument readings and human error resulted in an overheated reactor core and prevented routine emergency systems from operating properly. Small amounts of radioactive gases were released from the plant during that crisis. Estimates varied of the health risks associated with that escaped radiation; the Department of Health, Education and Welfare predicted only 1 excess cancer death among the 2 million people living within 50 miles of the plant.

The crisis reversed earlier confidence that major reactor accidents are unlikely. The overheated reactor core might have led to further overheating and to a *meltdown,* the term for an uncontrolled nuclear reaction that causes the core to melt through the containment vessel into the earth and release radioactive gases.

Sabotage or an earthquake, as well as human error or equipment failure, could cause nuclear plant crises—such as an accident in which a main pipe in the primary cooling circuit fractures. In that event, the control rods would switch off the reactor, immediately eliminating the nuclear fission process. However, the radioactive disintegration of the fission products cannot be arrested. In a nuclear power plant of 650 megawatts, the heat formation by radioactive disintegration amounts to about 200 Mw three seconds after the reactor is switched off, to 30 Mw after one hour, and to 12 Mw after 24 hours. In fact, the radioactive disintegration continues at a substantial level for several months.

Under normal operating conditions for the reactor, the external surface of the fuel casing has a temperature of about 350°C (660°F), while the interior of the fuel rods is very much hotter, as a rule 2200°C (4000°F). This temperature is approaching the melting point of the material. If the cooling liquid is lost, the outer surface of the rods would begin to heat up rapidly, owing both to the high temperatures inside and to continuous heating from the fission products. Within 10 to 15 seconds the fuel casing would begin to break down; and within a minute the casing would melt and the fuel rods themselves would begin to melt. Unless the emergency cooling of the core comes into operation in these first few minutes, the whole of the reactor core, the fuel (about 100 tons of it) and the supporting structure would all begin to melt away and to collapse on the floor of the innermost fuel tank.

To meet an accident such as this (loss of the cooling agent), the nuclear power plant is equipped with several emergency cooling systems quite independent of one another. These are based on purely theoretical calculations. The first experimental test made on them in the United States proved a complete failure: the emergency coolant could not cool the reactor core down sufficiently because it was able to escape through the leak in the cooling circuit, and owing to a layer of steam forming between the hot surface of the fuel rods and the emergency coolant, the rest of the emergency coolant was not able to carry away the heat imparted by the fuel rods. In 1978, a successful loss-of-coolant test was conducted at the Department of Energy's experimental facility. In that test loss of pressure in the coolant system triggered the reactor to shut down and the emergency system to flood the reactor core. The temperature rose to only 488°C (910°F)—meltdown would begin at 1650°C (3000°F)—and the test was over in two minutes. However, just a few months later at Three Mile Island, the emergency systems did not operate properly.

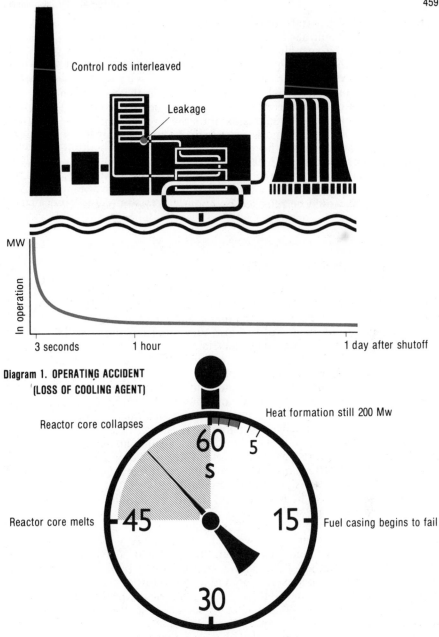

Control rods interleaved

Leakage

MW

In operation

3 seconds   1 hour   1 day after shutoff

Diagram 1. OPERATING ACCIDENT (LOSS OF COOLING AGENT)

Heat formation still 200 Mw

Reactor core collapses

Reactor core melts

Fuel casing begins to fail

Boiling layer of emergency coolant

Diagram 2. THE CRUCIAL MINUTE FOLLOWING THE REACTOR CUTOFF

If upon the failure of the cooling system the reactor core melts, emergency coolant added at this point would only make the situation worse. The melted metals in the fuel would react violently with the emergency cooling water to produce a great volume of heat; steam and hydrogen would be released in such quantities and at such pressure that the pressure tank would be brought to bursting point. If the containing tanks did not explode, the melted mass of fuel and concomitant mounting would get melted down further under the extra heat produced by the radioactivity of the fission products. At this point there would be no other technical measure whereby the melting process could be arrested. It would be beyond control. How deep the molten reactor core would sink into the ground and what form the material would finally assume is not precisely known. But it is reasonably certain that practically all the gaseous fission products and some of the volatile and nonvolatile products would be given off into the atmosphere. Inside a nuclear reactor of the present-day size (1000 Mw), the long-life radioactive fission products accumulated after one year would approximate the amount that would be released by about 1000 atom bombs of the Hiroshima variety.

COOLING OF POWER STATIONS

All power plants that release energy to generate electricity by the combustion of fossil fuels or the fission of uranium have to be cooled. The physical reason for this is to be found in the manner in which energy is transformed from heat energy by means of turbines into mechanical energy in order to drive a generator which produces electricity.

Inside every power plant is a combustion chamber in which thermal energy is released by burning coal, oil, gas, etc., or by uranium fission. The heat so produced is used to bring a medium, mostly water, to a boil. Liquid water is thus converted into steam and conveyed through pipes under high pressure to a turbine, which it drives. After passing through the turbine, the steam is fed into a condenser in which it is turned back into water. This water is then heated and converted into steam again, and again used to drive the turbine. To convert steam back into water in the condenser the steam must be cooled down again; that is, thermal energy must be removed from the steam. As this heat is at a lower temperature level, technically it cannot be used again. It has to be released into the atmosphere in the form of waste heat. In the case of fossil-fuel power plants, some 55%–60% of the energy released by combustion is given off as waste heat.

As regards disposal of the waste heat, there are various possibilities. Hitherto most power plants have been provided with a river water cooling system. By this method cold river water is drawn into the power plant, passed through the condenser, heated in it, and returned to the river or other channel in its heated condition. A power plant of the present-day capacity (1000 Mw) uses between 40 and 50 cubic meters of water per second, which it returns to the river heated up by about 10°C (18°F).

As this method of waste heat disposal comes up increasingly against statutory ecological limits, big power stations recently constructed are furnished with cooling towers, through which the waste heat is emitted into the atmosphere. In the case of wet cooling towers, heated water from the condensers is pumped up and sprayed into the atmosphere in tiny drops. In this way part of the water evaporates and the total water heat is dissipated. The rest of the water falls to the ground, where it is collected and returned to the condenser as cold water for reuse for cooling purposes. The evaporated portion is released into the atmosphere as water vapor.

In dry cooling towers, which outwardly differ very little from wet cool-

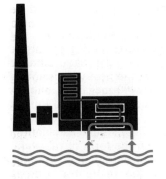

Diagram 1. RIVER WATER COOLING

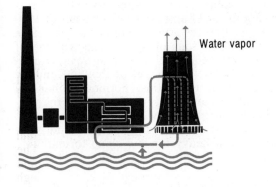

Water vapor

Diagram 2. WET COOLING TOWER

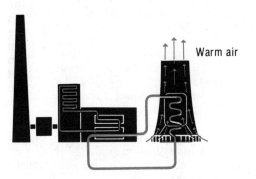

Warm air

Diagram 3. DRY COOLING TOWER

ing towers, the water circulates in a closed circuit. The water heated in the condenser flows through a series of small pipes with broad surfaces and so gives off a substantial quantity of its heat into the atmosphere. To assist the exchange of heat, ventilation can be installed in big dry cooling towers. Dry cooling towers suffer from the disadvantages, however, that they are the most expensive type of cooling process and that they lower the performance of the power plant. As regards the ecological and climatological effects of dry cooling towers, no reliable information is yet available.

CLIMATIC EFFECTS OF BIG COOLING TOWERS

Owing to the adverse effects of direct river-water heating in the operation of power plants, the tendency today is increasingly toward cooling by means of wet cooling towers. Of course, wet cooling towers also have adverse effects on the environment. The main problem lies in the heavy emission of water vapor into the atmosphere. In the case of a 2400 megawatt nuclear power station with a light water reactor, for instance, at least 5000 tons of water vapor are emitted through the cooling tower every hour. Some idea of what this amounts to can be obtained from the following simple calculation: If this quantity of water vapor were evenly spread in the form of rainwater over a surface of 100 sq km (38 sq mi), it would represent an annual rainfall of about 300 mm (12 inches). Natural precipitation in central Europe amounts to 600–700 mm per sq km per year. This example demonstrates clearly that such an emission of water vapor is bound to have considerable consequences for the climate in the locality. Another comparison brings this out even more clearly. The cooling tower of a nuclear power plant of 1500 Mw emits about 1 ton of water vapor into the atmosphere per second. In a full year this represents about 30 million tons of water. This volume of evaporated water corresponds to about one-sixth of the average evaporation from Lake Tahoe. But whereas Lake Tahoe has an area of about 500 million square meters, in the case of the cooling tower this enormous volume of water is concentrated in a very small area and is given off mostly in the very unfavorable (meteorologically) situation of river valleys, often subject to temperature inversions. Such an amount of water vapor can do enormous harm to the local climate in the form of heavy fog and cloud formation, a decline in solar radiation, more frequent precipitation, and more frequent and more severe thunderstorms.

A particular problem is caused by the release of water vapor into the atmosphere when the moisture content of the atmosphere is already high, as in the autumn, for instance. If the air is dry, the water vapor emitted remains in the atmosphere in gaseous form without causing mist or obstructing the sun's rays. But if the moisture content in the atmosphere is already high, possibly approaching the absolute moisture limit for the air, a small quantity of water vapor will be enough to saturate the air completely. The consequence of this will be that any further addition of water vapor will be suspended in the form of tiny particles of water, or mist.

As no experience of large-scale wet cooling towers is yet available anywhere in the world, it is very difficult to form an estimate of the precise quantitative operating results. Preliminary investigations indicate, however, that the climate is likely to be adversely affected by a cooling tower, especially in the autumn, on at least 1–3 days in the month.

A further effect to which sufficient attention has not yet been paid arises from the emission of droplets from the cooling tower. As part of the water circulating between the cooling tower and the condenser is constantly evaporating, the water lost to the cooling circuit has to be replaced. Owing to the large quantities involved, river water is mostly used for the purpose. In view of the strong upward current of air inside the cooling tower, part of the water is carried away in the form of small drops of water and aerosols. In a 1000 megawatt nuclear power station, about 36 liters (9 gallons) of water a second issues from the cooling tower in the form of tiny droplets. In this way bacteria, viruses and toxic agents pass from the contaminated river water into the air, are carried away by the wind and are deposited on agricultural crops or inhaled into people's lungs.

**ONE OF THE FOUR COOLING TOWERS PLANNED FOR WYHL
ON THE KAISERSTUHL IN THE BLACK FOREST**

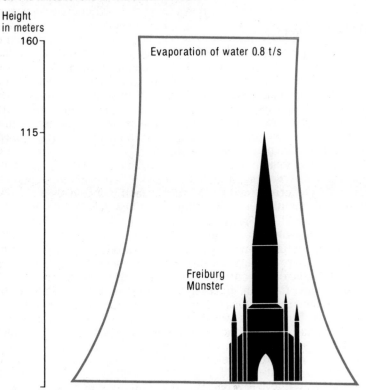

Height
in meters

160 — Evaporation of water 0.8 t/s

115 —

Freiburg
Münster

Data relating to wet cooling towers with a natural draft

		Fossil-fuel power station	Nuclear power station
Electrical output of power station	M/We	1000	1000
Performance coefficient	%	40	32
Performance of cooling tower	MJ	1400	2000
Dimensions of cooling tower			
height	m	110	130
Diameter base	m	90	110
shank	m	55	65
opening	m	60	75
Operating data			
Water circulation	m³/s	24	36
Evaporation loss	m³/s	0.4	0.6
Emission of water	1/s	≤ 24	≤ 36
Rate of air flow	m³/s	20 000	20 000

Part Eighteen—Growth and the General Economic Aspects of Growth

EXPONENTIAL GROWTH

Growth is classified in three categories: linear, exponential and superexponential. Normally growth is understood to mean linear growth. This occurs when a magnitude increases by a uniform amount at regular intervals. A tree displays linear growth when it increases in height by 50 cm per annum. If a man puts ten dollars in a piggy bank every month, his savings grow at a linear rate. The increase in savings is independent of the amount already saved: the savings grow by ten dollars a month irrespective of the amount already deposited in the bank.

In the case of exponential growth, the growth depends on the level already achieved. Here the magnitude increases by a constant percentage at regular intervals. A bacterial culture in which each cell divides every ten minutes shows exponential growth. Within a given ten-minute period a growth of 100% occurs. The growth is the greater in absolute terms the longer the process of growth continues.

Although exponential growth is standard, it is always likely to have surprises in store. There is the fairy tale about the servant who presented the king with a valuable chessboard and asked in return for one grain of corn for the first square and for each successive square twice the number for the previous one: for the second square 2 grains, for the third square 4, for the fourth 8, and so on. This represents an exponential increase with a growth rate of 100% per square on the chessboard. On the tenth square 512 grains were due, and on the twenty-first over 1 million grains. There are hardly as many grains of corn on the entire earth as the king was called on to pay for the sixty-fourth square.

Exponential growth is deceptive, because with only relatively low rates of growth astronomically high figures are attained in a very short time. The process becomes especially problematical when the growth is directed at a fixed growth target. There is a French story about a pond in which a water lily was growing. The plant had such vital strength that it doubled in size every day. In 30 days it would cover the whole pond. Observing this, the owner of the pond decided to stop the growth as soon as the water lily covered half the surface of the pond. To do this the water lily required 29 days. But once this point was reached it needed only one more night to cover the entire pond.

In many respects humankind is today in a similar situation. The overall political economy has developed over the centuries to its present size. The population of the world has been growing for several thousands of years. The general impression is that the population growth could easily continue for a similar period in the future. But as the following discussions show, this is just not possible.

Superexponential growth denotes the process when not only does a magnitude grow at an ever faster rate but when at the same time the doubling period constantly shortens. This form of growth occurs, for instance, at times of severe monetary inflation or upon the massive intervention of man in sensitive ecosystems in which several factors fluctuate wildly up and down (on the basis of superexponential growth) and so precipitate the collapse of the ecosystem.

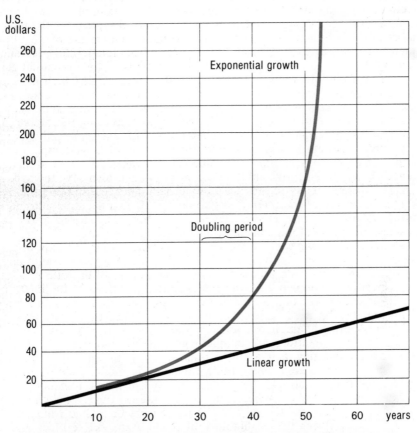

EXPONENTIAL GROWTH ILLUSTRATED BY THE EXAMPLE OF A SAVINGS ACCOUNT BALANCE.
(ONE DOLLAR SAVED ANNUALLY GROWS ON A LINEAR BASIS TO $10 OVER 10 YEARS;
BUT IF INTEREST IS ADDED AT A FIXED RATE OF 7%, THIS AMOUNT IS DOUBLED
EVERY 10 YEARS)

Doubling period

Growth rate (in percent per annum) ich)	Doubling period (in years)
0.1	700
0.5	140
1.0	70
2.0	35
4.0	18
5.0	14
7.0	10
10.0	7

WHAT IS FEEDBACK?

A distinction has to be made between negative and positive reactions (the adjective indicating the direction of the reaction). One example of a *negative feedback automatic control system* is the biochemical system for the maintenance of the body temperature of man. The body temperature of a healthy human being remains constant at 37°C (98.6°F). This temperature is maintained by the heat released by biochemical processes. If the individual gets into cold surroundings, this is recorded by the sense cells, which pass an order through the nervous system to produce more heat. Conversely, in warmer surroundings measures are promoted through the same channels for reduction in temperature by giving off sweat and increasing the blood circulation in the external body parts. The criterion for such a negative automatic control system is a critical level (in this case of body temperature) which is maintained at a standard value (in this case 37°C) by a dynamic balance of factors. Negative automatic control systems also have the task of keeping a system steady in the face of external influences. In both animate and inanimate nature there are a large number of such negative automatic control systems (e.g., blood sugar level, the vestibular apparatus of the ear and sense of balance, food consumption and feelings of hunger).

Positive automatic control systems are characterized by the exponential growth of the fundamental quantities. One example of a positive automatic control system is the increase of bacteria. The number of bacteria in a test tube is positively coupled with the fundamental quantities of the bacterial growth, or with itself; that is, the growth of the bacteria is the more rapid and the greater, the more bacteria there are, or the longer the growth process continues. Another example of a positive automatic control system in which the fundamental quantities are coupled, not directly but only via several intermediate quantities in relation to themselves, is the growth of private motor vehicles compared with public transport in modern cities. Let us consider the two quantities, "passengers carried in public transport" and "private vehicle owners." When some public transport users switch to private vehicle ownership, the number of passengers on public transport is reduced. This reduces the profitability of public transport services and is reflected eventually in an increase in the time schedule between vehicles. This makes public transport less attractive and prompts more users to switch to private vehicles. If these and similar feedbacks continue, the scope of public transport services will become so uneconomic and consequently so unattractive that it will be increasingly difficult to reverse the process.

Positive feedbacks always lead in nature to growth catastrophes when the exponential expansion in magnitudes comes up against growth thresholds. Almost all the automatic control systems in nature consequently display negative feedbacks. The positive feedbacks disappear, if they occur at all, in consequence of growth catastrophes in the shortest possible time.

One of the causes of the present environmental crisis arises from the fact that man has broken down some of the natural, negative feedback automatic control systems in the course of civilization and has converted them into a process of positive feedback exponential growth, which, if the growth process is sustained, must sooner or later lead inevitably to catastrophe.

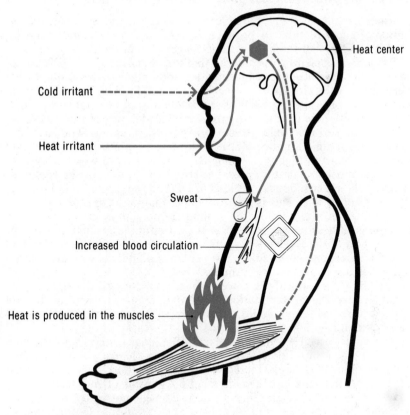

Heat center

Cold irritant

Heat irritant

Sweat

Increased blood circulation

Heat is produced in the muscles

Diagram 1. NEGATIVE FEEDBACK

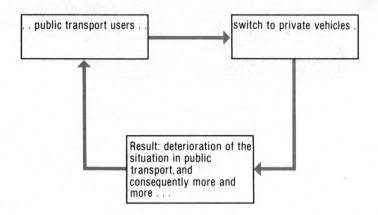

. . public transport users . .

switch to private vehicles .

Result: deterioration of the situation in public transport, and consequently more and more . . .

Diagram 2. EXAMPLE OF A POSITIVE FEEDBACK

DELAYING FACTORS IN ECOLOGICAL PROCESSES—DDT

An important aspect of many ecological processes is the time that many interventions in nature take to produce results, sometimes amounting to years or decades, so that the harm can no longer be rectified.

In 1940 a Swiss scientist discovered that the chemical agent DDT could be used very successfully as an insecticide. Soon afterward it came to be produced on a large scale. Its use in agriculture and forestry and to combat malaria rose sharply, and by 1970 about 160,000 tons were absorbed per annum. In the 1960s scientific investigations revealed that the hitherto highly prized DDT had serious toxic effects on the environment. The first announcements went almost unheeded. It took ten years, in fact, for the realization to dawn that the highly resistant DDT, which there was hardly any means of decomposing in nature, posed a serious threat to many ecosystems in the world. The highest concentrations of DDT in the ground build up one to two years after its use. This is due to the fact that in the spraying process much of the DDT does not fall to the ground at once but is carried away by the wind and is only later washed out of the air onto the ground by rain. A considerable part of the DDT is swept by wind or river currents into the sea. There the DDT gets caught up in the food chain and finds its way eventually into fish, which are consumed by humans.

Even if the utilization of DDT were severely restricted throughout the world immediately, the contamination of fish by DDT would continue to rise for about 11 more years and would only return to the present level some 11 years later, which is a time span of 22 years.

Similar dangers are presented by many other long-lived poisons that are released by humans into the environment: mercury, lead, cadmium, insecticides other than DDT, chlorinated hydrocarbons, and radioactive substances. Cancer and leukemia can develop as a result of radioactive rays after a latent period of 15 to 20 years. Genetic damage caused by radioactive radiation sometimes manifests itself only after generations. Unfortunately, delays of this order between cause and effect, which are somewhat outside the normal range of reflection by man, are not sufficiently considered in discussions of the environment, especially in relation to more complex problems.

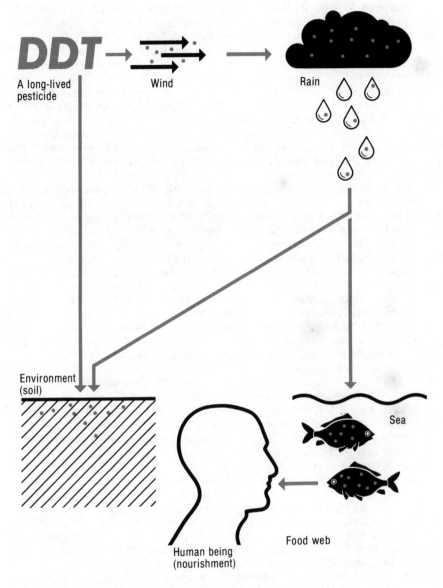

DDT →
A long-lived pesticide

Wind

Rain

Environment (soil)

Sea

Food web

Human being (nourishment)

THE PATH OF DDT IN THE ECOSYSTEM: THE INFLUENCE OF DELAYING FACTORS

LIMITS ON GROWTH

The planet earth with its limited land surface cannot face the prospect of unlimited growth with equanimity. In the context of ecological equilibrium there is an optimum growth level for any population, which is determined by its type of food and space needs, on the one hand, and the availability of these life factors, on the other. Only in the case of humankind has this principle seemed not to apply hitherto: he has always been able to overcome limitations of space. The acquisition of new living space was still being discussed as a serious population policy at the beginning of the current century. With the help of industrial production, all natural limiting factors seemed capable of solution. Food shortages, sickness and death were not viewed as biological barriers, but as problems that could be overcome. The population of humans was governed in contrast to all others by the law of irresistible progress.

It is essential to recognize that for humankind, too, there exist growth thresholds that cannot be overcome, the forcible supersession of which is bound to result in a global catastrophe. Insofar as this is viewed in relation to an explosive increase in the world population, it is easy enough to grasp. But the fact that industrial production, too, is up against impregnable barriers is far from being accepted by those responsible for our future. The existence of such limits on industrial production is, in fact, frequently contested.

It is commonly argued that the raw material reserves of the earth, though certainly limited and not replaceable, have so far been prospected and exploited to only a limited extent, and no predictions can be made regarding the undiscovered treasures of the earth: that raw materials in short supply might be replaced at any time by new materials about which nothing is yet known. By recourse to nuclear energy, moreover, the energy supplies of the earth are potentially inexhaustible. Valuable chemical energy sources such as petroleum and coal could be replaced by nuclear energy and so released as raw materials for chemical production. Limits on growth of all kinds are in any case technically surmountable, and there is no cause for concern or for expectations that the world might succumb in the near future.

These questions are gone into in detail later in the discussion of the Meadows study and the criticisms of it.

In principle, individual problems have individual solutions. But as the various high-level calculations made in the Meadows study show, the key points are only shifted thereby and potentially catastrophic developments are deferred temporarily (and magnified in extent). Even if it is assumed that the raw material resources are many times greater than the latest estimates indicate, and if the additional problem of the presumably more difficult and more expensive application of alternative materials (compared with those in current use) is left out of account, an acute shortage of raw material is merely being deferred to a much later date. The exponential growth in environmental pollution—economically valuable raw materials in the vast majority of cases contaminate the environment in proportion to their consumption (e.g., coal and petroleum after combustion)—would simply advance the time of the catastrophic overpollution in the world. The acute

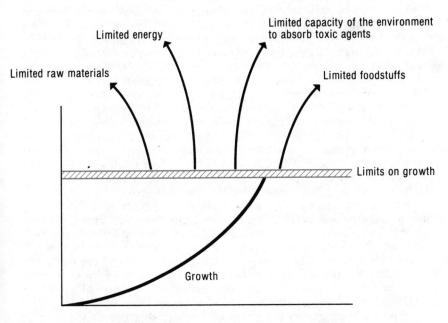

Limited energy

Limited capacity of the environment to absorb toxic agents

Limited raw materials

Limited foodstuffs

Limits on growth

Growth

Diagram 1. NATURAL LIMITS ON GROWTH

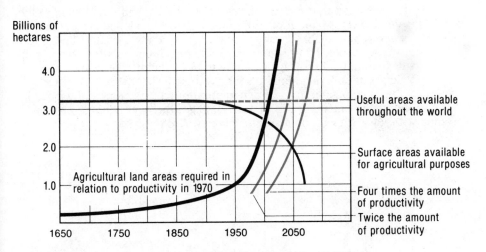

Billions of hectares

4.0

3.0

2.0

1.0

Agricultural land areas required in relation to productivity in 1970

Useful areas available throughout the world

Surface areas available for agricultural purposes

Four times the amount of productivity

Twice the amount of productivity

1650   1750   1850   1950   2050

Diagram 2. AGRICULTURAL LAND AREAS IN RELATION TO POPULATION GROWTH

threat this poses thus arises not merely from shortages of raw materials but from the prevailing pollution of the environment.

The growth tendencies have reached ominous culmination points everywhere, in fact, but mainly in industrial and socioeconomic sectors, where they tend to refute the ideology of the potentially unlimited advance of humankind and to imply the presence of limits on growth which should serve as a warning regarding our continued existence. Where growth gets out of control, it will undoubtedly overstep a natural boundary.

The classical symptoms of this can be recognized at all points in the economy and the community, however: a decline in the principles of market economy to monopoly structures, chronic poisoning with long-lived pesticides and radioactive fission products, surplus and reject production, escalating delinquency, increasing social disintegration, etc., are apparently only structurally distinguishable from the principle of a free market economy and the dependence of prosperity on the growth rate mechanism. In every sector in which growth exceeds its natural limits, defective growth takes over.

A modest stocktaking of the raw materials available today in no way testifies to a surplus situation. If the consumption (or dissipation) of resources by the industrial countries remains at the present level, supplies of lead will last for 21 years, tin for 15 years, and mercury and silver for 13 years, until alternatives (substitute materials) or reprocessing are taken into account. Although tin and copper can perhaps be replaced by substitutes (which is by no means certain), the photographic and film industries, by which 25% of world silver consumption is absorbed, are utterly dependent on silver production, and in the event of a silver shortage their existence would be seriously threatened. The recovery of silver from used fixing baths is still insufficiently resorted to, however.

If it is assumed that at least 0.4 hectare of farmland per person in the world is needed to provide foodstuffs, and a further 0.08 hectare per person is required for uncultivable living space (housing, roads, airfields, and industrial and waste-disposal purposes), and if the present population trends continue, a desperate land shortage is bound to occur before the year 2000, even if every scrap of cultivable land on the earth's surface were turned to agricultural use. The peculiarities of exponential processes come out especially clearly here: the emergence of sudden change, the overstepping of a limit, come without warning, and a surplus gives way overnight to a severe shortage.

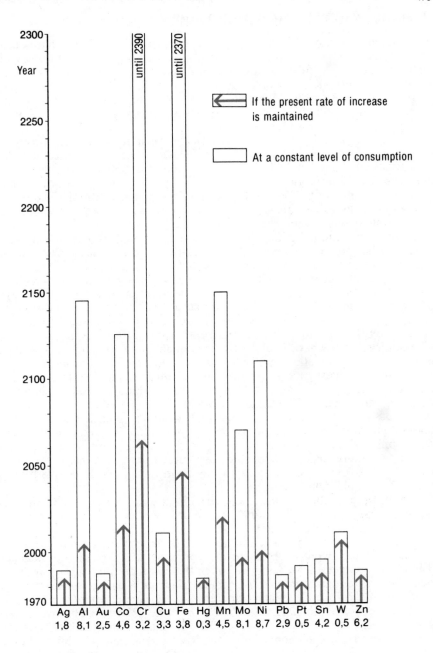

METAL SUPPLIES IN THE WORLD

MEADOWS STUDY OF LIMITS ON GROWTH

In the scientific study "Limits on Growth" published in 1972, which touched off lively discussion throughout the world, for the first time in the history of industrial development the main aims of civilization—growth and progress —were gone into seriously on a scientific basis. The study was carried out by a team of international scientists at the Massachusetts Institute of Technology under the direction of D. Meadows at the instigation of the Club of Rome.

The study was based on a comprehensive world model in which consideration was given to the various factors related to natural science and the survival of man, and in which their interrelations are represented. The model contains five basic variables, in particular: population figures, economic growth, raw materials, foodstuffs, and environmental pollution. The overriding questions to be considered can be set out as follows: How will the world system react when the growth of the population and the economy approaches maximum limits? How long can the growth be maintained, and what will be the consequences of the growth aimed at today? What image will the world present when growth is halted?

To provide answers to these questions, various possibilities were examined by computer which differ from one another in the matter of hypotheses relating to the growth and the structural requirements of growth, such as raw materials supplies and environmental pollution. The period covered by the investigations ranged from 1900 to 2100. The first aspect to be examined was what the consequences might be if the current levels of growth of the population and industry were to continue unchecked. The results of this investigation showed that the trend was undoubtedly toward an overstepping of the limits on the part of the system, followed by complete collapse (see diagram). The collapse would be precipitated by the exhaustion of limited supplies of raw material, which would be whittled away by the enormous growth in the economy by the year 2020. The resulting growth catastrophe in the economic sector would drag agriculture, which by then would be totally dependent on industry, down with it. Finally a growth catastrophe for the population, with the death of billions of people by the year 2100, would be unavoidable.

Another hypothetical case to be examined was whether economic collapse could be prevented by an improvement in raw material supplies. It was assumed for this purpose that the raw material supplies available in the world were actually twice as great as those known to exist today, while all the other factors were adopted for the computer analysis without change. The result was very depressing: although the raw material supplies are now being drawn on much more slowly, industrialization can go on expanding. The outcome will be an immense increase in contamination of the environment. The growth threshold will thus no longer be determined by the limited raw material situation and shrinkage of the economy, but by pollution of the environment by the economy with long-lived contaminants. This pollution of the environment is likely to result in a growth catastrophe for the population at about the same time as could be expected in the ordinary course, though the number of deaths could be somewhat greater than in the ordinary course.

Worse still was the result of a study based on the hypothesis that raw material supplies would be unlimited. In this case it was assumed that with the aid of nuclear energy the available supplies of raw materials could be

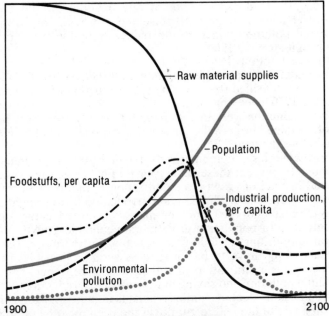

Diagram 1. **NORMAL COURSE OF THE WORLD MODEL**

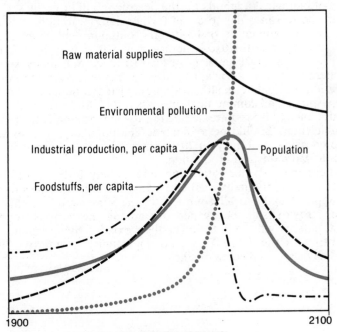

Diagram 2. **"UNLIMITED" RAW MATERIAL SUPPLIES**
According to Meadows

utilized twice as effectively and that, also with the aid of nuclear energy, further utilization and replacement of raw materials would be possible. Here, too, the computer analysis presented a growth catastrophe due to environmental pollution which would reduce the population to below the level at which it stood in 1900.

On the assumption that all these computer simulations are correct— even if raw material supplies were unlimited, if the control of environmental pollution were intensified (by reducing the production of contaminants to a quarter of the 1970 level while industrial production continued to expand), if agricultural production were increased and if birth control were perfect—in the face of sustained growth the growth catastrophe could be deferred only to shortly before the year 2100.

In a further series of computer runs, the question was examined of what could be done to prevent these catastrophes. For these, the hypothesis was adopted that instead of growth, a stabilization in the fields of raw material consumption, industrial production, and population figures might occur. According to the results of the computer analysis, a growth catastrophe can be averted only if both population growth and economic growth move into a position of equilibrium as rapidly as possible. Furthermore, the following requirements would have to be satisfied as soon as possible: recycling of waste, that is, the reutilization of refuse with a consequent reduction in environmental pollution and saving of raw materials; reduction in the release of long-lived poisons; technical improvements in industrial goods in order to increase their useful life and to cut down the need for repairs; utilization of solar energy and other regenerative natural forces as sources of energy; adoption of biological methods for the destruction of insect pests, and fertilization of the soil in order to avoid further deterioration and disruption of the soil and contamination of foodstuffs; optimum employment of contraceptives; reduction in the use of natural raw materials from 1975 onward to one quarter of the 1970 level in order to reduce deficiency symptoms in nonregenerative raw materials; and improvements and growth in fields such as education and public health, training and recreational activities, and in the social sphere and communications. According to the results of the Meadows study, once these requirements are satisfied, growth catastrophes in the foreseeable future should be avoidable. The population figures would certainly go on rising until the year 2030, but would settle down thereafter. The same applies to industrial production.

As neither goods nor total economic activity in the world are evenly distributed among the individual countries, the consequences of this study do not apply equally to all countries in the same way. To this extent, if economic growth is to be evened out among the various countries, the industrial nations will have to lower their existing living standards to give the countries of the Third World an opportunity to improve their living standards by sustained economic growth.

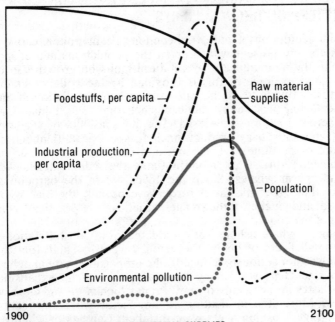

Diagram 1. "UNLIMITED" RAW MATERIAL SUPPLIES, INCREASED INDUSTRIAL AND AGRICULTURAL PRODUCTIVITY

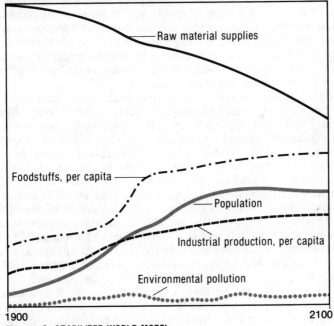

Diagram 2. STABILIZED WORLD MODEL
According to Meadows

EXTINCTION OF THE WHALE—EXAMPLE OF THE CONSEQUENCES OF OVERSTEPPING GROWTH LIMITS

In particular sectors of the industrial economy, catastrophic economic consequences already present will threaten the populations and economies of the world in the near future unless natural limits on growth can be maintained. A good example of this is provided by the collapse of the whale fishing industry owing to the decline in the whale population in the world.

Whale fishing has been practiced since the earliest historical times, certainly before 1000 B.C. in Alaska. The main product of whale fishing is whale oil, and subsidiary products include spermaceti (ambergris for the manufacture of perfume), whalebone, and more recently whale meat (for human consumption). Until modern times the main catches were right whales and sperm whales. Since the 1860s, when the harpoon gun was introduced, the bigger and faster rorquals, especially the blue whale, have been hunted, and catches of the smaller varieties were practically suspended at the turn of the century.

As long as whale fishing was conducted from coastal stations and by relatively small fleets of boats, the catches were so small that the whale population was not seriously reduced. The propagation rate matched annual catches in size. This was changed, however, with the expansion of the whaling industry in the twentieth century, in which more and more countries participated. More efficient floating whaling factories were brought into operation and bigger fishing fleets were installed. Catches of whales rose accordingly from year to year. The ecological limits set by the natural breeding capacity of the whale were thus overstepped. Stocks of the blue whale in the oceans of the world declined rapidly, and the quota of catches per ship suffered accordingly. By extending the technological facilities and improving tracking and catching techniques, some success was achieved in increasing catches in the short run. But at medium and long term these improved exploitation methods led to near extinction of the whale and to a drop in the return from whale fishing to virtually nil.

This development, which is illustrated in the accompanying diagrams, reached a peak in the years following the Second World War. While in the 1930s some 30,000 blue whales were still being caught each year, by 1970 catches had fallen off almost completely. The blue whale, the biggest mammal in the world, was practically extinct. Thereupon the whaling industry turned its attention to the second biggest whale, the fin whale. Between 1945 and 1955 catches of fin whales rose from 2000 to 30,000 a year. This high catch rate was maintained for six years or so, but by 1970 was down to a few thousand. The fin whale had come to share the fate of the blue whale. By 1960 the whaling industry was turning to the third biggest species, the sperm whale. By 1965 catches of the sperm whale had reached 25,000 in the year, but from then on catches were on the decline from year to year.

Today, as in the Middle Ages, attention is being paid to small whales, which had been ignored for some time because of the relatively poor return on them. To offset the poor return, expenditure on fishing technology has been increased, which only means that the extinction of the species will be quicker and more complete. Thus the fate of this branch of industry is sealed. In the 1971–1972 whale fishing season, only Japan and the Soviet Union were active in this field, other countries having given it up as uneconomic.

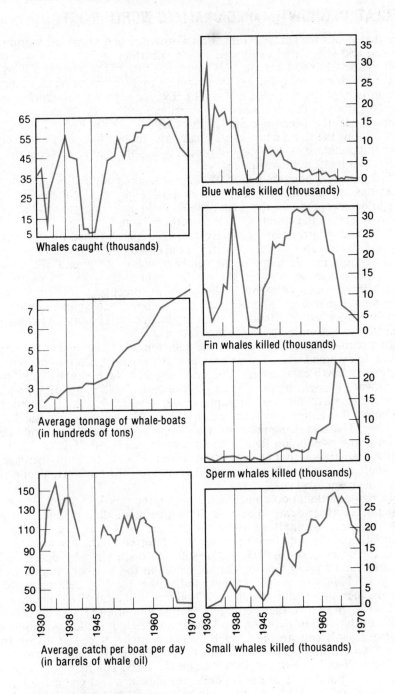

Whales caught (thousands)

Average tonnage of whale-boats
(in hundreds of tons)

Average catch per boat per day
(in barrels of whale oil)

Blue whales killed (thousands)

Fin whales killed (thousands)

Sperm whales killed (thousands)

Small whales killed (thousands)

WHALE CATCHES BETWEEN 1930 and 1970
(modified according to Meadows)

POPULATION GROWTH—REGIONALIZED WORLD MODEL

After the Meadows study, "Limits on Growth," had attracted worldwide attention and stimulated lively discussion, a further world model was published by the Club of Rome in 1974 under the title "Humanity at a Turning Point," which was compiled as a contribution to the recognition and solution of the growth problem by some 50 well-known scientists from various countries. This study is also described as a "regionalized world model," because, in contrast to the Meadows study, the earth is not treated as a uniform structure, but the five factors—raw materials, foodstuffs, population, environmental pollution, and industrial production—are examined separately in relation to ten different world regions.

For purposes of examination of the problems of population growth, the ten regions are split into the two sectors north and south of the equator, as it has to be accepted that the main problems of population growth are likely to crop up first in the countries in the southern latitudes.

First a standard computer analysis was prepared based on the current birth and death rates in the countries concerned. This showed that there would be more people living in the southern region at the end of the twentieth century than are alive in the whole world today—and 25 years later perhaps three times as many. A longer-term forecast produced so much higher figures that it must be assumed that such a development would automatically be prevented either by voluntary birth control or by an increase in the death rate promoted by ecological factors.

In a second computer analysis the question was examined of the development that would follow if countermeasures were duly taken to prevent the threatened growth catastrophe. This was based on the hypothesis that from 1975 onward it might be possible, by adopting suitable population policies, to lower the birth rate to the replacement level (2 children per couple) throughout the entire southern region within 35 years and to stabilize it thereafter. The surprising result of this computer assessment was that equilibrium in the population figures could only be achieved 75 years after the effective population policy had been adopted, i.e., that an increase in the population could only be halted 40 years after the birth rate dropped to the replacement level.

In two additional computer assessments the possible effects were examined of a further delay in adopting effective population policies. On precisely the same assumptions as for the two previous runs, the deadline for the adoption of the population policies was deferred, in the one case to 1985 and in the other case to 1995. The result was disturbing: by deferring the measures for 10 years the population figures in the southern region would rise by 1.7 billion to some 8 billion, and in the event of deferment for 20 years the increase would amount to 3.7 billion for a total of 10 billion.

Finally, in two further computer analyses an attempt was made to establish a relationship between the last-mentioned population situation and possible growth catastrophes (such as the number of people dying from hunger). In the first of these the drastic population measures were set to come into effect in 1990, and in the second in 1995. The final calculation of the probable number of deaths (of children) indicates that given a delay of 5 years (from 1990 to 1995), by the year 2025 some 170 million children up to 15 years of age would die of hunger.

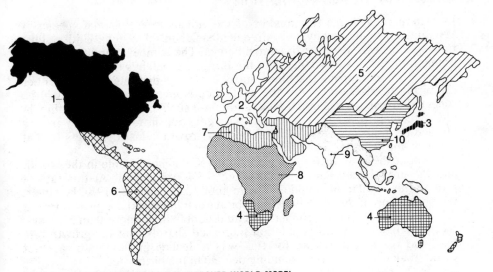

Diagram 1. THE TEN REGIONS OF THE IMPROVED WORLD MODEL

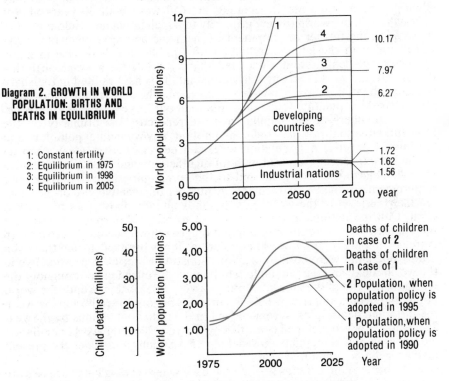

Diagram 2. GROWTH IN WORLD POPULATION: BIRTHS AND DEATHS IN EQUILIBRIUM

1: Constant fertility
2: Equilibrium in 1975
3: Equilibrium in 1998
4: Equilibrium in 2005

World population (billions)

Developing countries

Industrial nations

10.17
7.97
6.27

1.72
1.62
1.56

1950   2000   2050   2100   year

Child deaths (millions)

World population (billions)

Deaths of children in case of **2**
Deaths of children in case of **1**
2 Population, when population policy is adopted in 1995
1 Population, when population policy is adopted in 1990

1975   2000   2025   Year

Diagram 3. CONSEQUENCES OF A DELAYED POPULATION POLICY IN SOUTHERN ASIA

GROWTH OF WORLD POPULATION

In natural ecosystems the number of individuals in any animal species is kept at a constant level by a negative feedback control system. Until a short time ago this was also true of human beings. The number of individuals in a population remains constant when the birth rate matches the death rate. In nature it often happens that this control system is disrupted, in that either the birth rate rises sharply or the death rate is unusually low. This will be reflected in a sharp rise in the population until such time as a growth threshold is reached, owing for instance to a reduction in foodstuffs or ground surface or to social stress. At that point a growth catastrophe sets in that reverses the process.

About the year 1650 there were some 500 million people in the world, and the growth rate amounted to about 0.3% per annum. At this rate of growth the population would double in about 250 years. By 1970, however, the population of the world stood at about 3.6 billion, and the growth rate at 2.1%, at which level the population could double in no more than 33 years. Not only had the world population increased sharply, but the growth rate had also risen. The reason for this was a decline in the death rate not counterbalanced by a corresponding decline in the birth rate.

In the past, humans had both a high birth rate and a high death rate, so that for long periods the population figures remained constant or rose only slightly. The average life expectancy in 1650 was about 30 years almost everywhere in the world (owing primarily to a high infant and child mortality rate). With the further development of medicine and improvements in hygiene, and with the later introduction of a public health service in many countries, the death rate has declined sharply, while the average birth rate throughout the world remains fairly constant. This has resulted in the sharp superexponential growth shown in the diagram. The average life expectancy for the world population today amounts to about 53 years and is still rising.

The numbers of the population have repercussions primarily on the foodstuff situation, raw material consumption, environmental pollution, and the human psyche. A population level can be regarded as ideal when its continued existence is assured without qualification and when opportunities are available to the individual and to the community alike to satisfy their requirements to the best advantage. A number of scientists are of the opinion that the level of the world population is already above that figure. But even if all the nations in the world were to adopt a purposeful birth-rate policy, the dynamic strength of population growth would still lead to a sharp increase in the size of the world population. It has been calculated that even if only one child were born by way of "substitute" for each person alive in the world today and the two-child family could be introduced throughout the world by the end of the present century (a very improbable event), the world population would still rise by 60% to some 5.8 billion. If equilibrium between the birth and death rates were achieved in the industrial nations by the year 2000 and in underdeveloped countries by the year 2040, the world population would remain at something approaching 15.5 billion, four times the present level, for the next hundred years.

We are dealing here (as is often the case where ecological processes are concerned) with important delaying factors, which are not allowed for in the normal notions of mankind. In this case the delaying factors will result, owing to the sharp growth in the population, in a preponderance of young over older people. But a proliferation of young persons today means that there will be many older people and many children in the future.

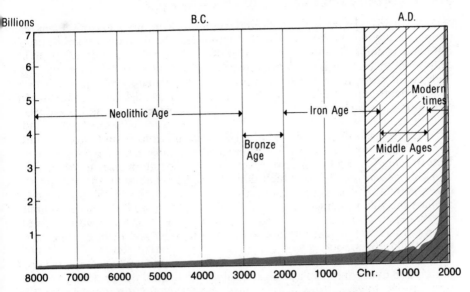

Diagram 1. GROWTH OF THE WORLD POPULATION OVER TEN THOUSAND YEARS

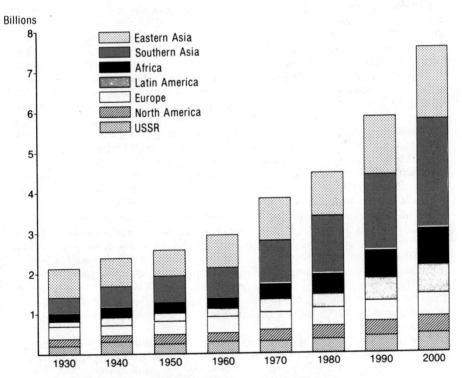

Diagram 2. GROWTH IN THE WORLD POPULATION FROM 1930 TO YEAR 2000, ACCORDING TO UNITED NATIONS STATISTICS

POPULATION PROBLEMS IN THE THIRD WORLD

Since roughly the end of the Middle Ages, the population trend among peoples enjoying the benefits of the technical advances of civilization has followed a definite pattern: after a period of relative stability or a slight preponderance of births, in which high birth rates were roughly matched by high death rates, improvements in medical and hygienic conditions led to a drop in death rates, which was reflected in turn in a surplus of live births. In due course the birth rates came to exceed the death rates as these continued to decline.

At relatively high civilization levels an equilibrium again tends to set in, at which the population level stagnates in the long run or even declines. Determining factors for this are economic and social change, urbanization, and changes in life-styles, which demand higher expenditure to maintain a given standard of living for the individual, and which, on the other hand, replace the social security of the big family and ties of kinship with community benefits (social insurance and care for the aged), and so favor the small family. In recent times, additional family planning and birth control have made their appearance.

Whereas the Western industrial countries have almost completed this population cycle and display substantially stabilized if not declining population figures, the countries of the Third World are for the most part in the initial phase of the process. The effects of technological improvements are only beginning to make themselves felt and are reflected in a substantial expansion in the population, but stabilizing factors have not yet developed. These population changes often assume very different dimensions from those in the industrialized nations. Technological development cannot keep pace. Hunger is unavoidable. It is estimated that in the "colonies" of the Western nations, which were so rich in resources only a few decades ago, 4 million people now die of hunger every year. As technological development is not indigenous, but was exported from the Western countries primarily in their own interests, the individual stages are not integrated and have a disruptive effect on the social structures. The Western work and production methods which are geared to the third growth stage of the population cycle —that is, to stagnating population figures and manpower shortages, and so are capital-intensive, labor-saving, rationalized and automated—when transferred to the Third World consequently come up against the second phase of the cycle, which is marked by a superfluity of manpower upon which it is economically dependent.

The negative economic and social consequences are clear enough: industrial plant in the Western mold (as provided under development aid) in a short time undermines the existence of all the local production plant and appliances of a related kind because of more efficient operation. The newer methods provide far fewer employment opportunities, however, than the majority of the smaller old production methods. While, on the one hand, they thus contribute to economic growth, on the other hand they promote unemployment, social disintegration and slum formation in industrial agglomerations.

In agriculture, too, the utilization of modern technologies (mechanization, fertilization and chemical herbicides) makes for a highly necessary

Food supplies

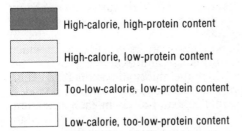

High-calorie, high-protein content

High-calorie, low-protein content

Too-low-calorie, low-protein content

Low-calorie, too-low-protein content

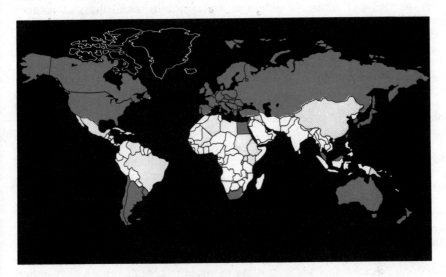

THE COUNTRIES OF THE THIRD WORLD DIFFERENTIATED ACCORDING TO THEIR FOOD SITUATION

increase in the production of foodstuffs; but at the same time manpower is released on a large scale. As a result of the abandonment of the community production system in favor of capital-intensive industrial production, the social framework is also disrupted. A gap develops between haves and have-nots, the former often only stepping into the shoes of the former "white bosses" and the dependency of the mass of the population being maintained.

In the social sphere the disintegration of family groupings and ties of kinship stemming from the adoption of Western work and production methods is significant, but the family groupings are not superseded by new organic social forms, as has happened in Western industrial countries since the last century. The big family grouping is a social unit with a mainly rural background which provides its members with economic security and a measure of local status: in the event of unemployment, sickness or old age every member of the family is cared for by the others, and in case of death the widow and children are provided for.

The big family grades its members in an order of precedence in which each is aware of his standing based on his age and experience of life, his personality and working capacity, in which the ability of each is matched as economically as possible to the appropriate locality, and in which no one is superfluous. Each one can expect unqualified support from each of the others.

The modern technological company had to break down the economic unit of the big family (which naturally is set against economic change of any sort) into smaller, more flexible and more mobile social units of smaller families of parents and children. The larger number of economic units promotes consumption. The small family is, for practical purposes, more adaptable and economically productive than a like number of people in a large family group, and this also leads to the "release" of those members who are not or are no longer suitable for industrial production, e.g., the old and the sick.

The economic and social protection of these groups of persons is no longer effected by members of the family but by means of impersonal structures (social insurance, old age pensions, sickness insurance), just as authority and dependency relationships are becoming increasingly impersonal (legislation, replacement of family connections and personal trust and feudal obligations by work contracts, wage agreements and bureaucratic relationships).

We have described these sociological changes as population stabilizing factors. With the disintegration of the big family groupings, the number of births declines as the number of children ceases to have the same importance as regards care of the aged.

Western communities have also implemented similar changes. Here they took place earlier and according to circumstances over a longer period and within observable limits, whereas in the Third World they have occurred suddenly, precipitately and at unscheduled development points. As a result it was the negative aspects of the production system—such as performance pressure, disruption of communication between people, and cooperation—that came out more clearly. As the development aid provided by the industrial countries supports and expands the present economic and social tendencies from both a material and an ideological point of view, the effects of overpopulation in the near future are more likely to be heightened than reduced.

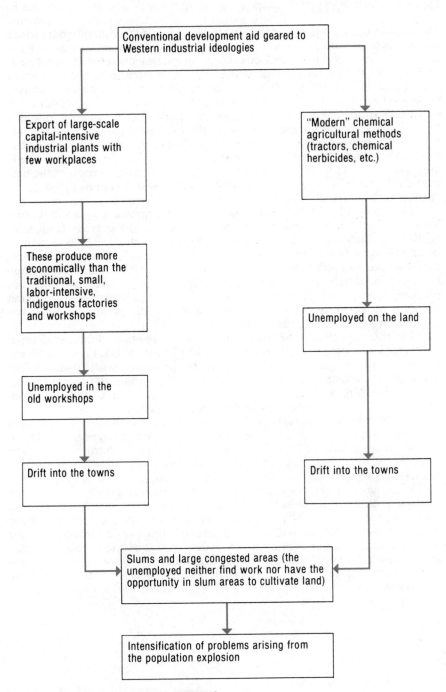

POPULATION GROWTH AND SOCIAL PROBLEMS

THE GROWTH CATASTROPHE IN NEW YORK

Although major growth catastrophes are likely to afflict humanity only in the future, there are already possibilities today for studying limited growth catastrophes in their causes and effects. A staggering case for study of self-destructive growth, the original causes of which stem in part from former decades, is offered by the millions-strong city of New York. By uncontrolled expansion and its side effects in the past, some vital growth thresholds of an ecological and social nature have been overstepped in New York, and this has led directly, or after some delays, to the present situation.

Owing to the massive concentration of people and the cleavage between the operations of "living" and "working," a practically insoluble traffic problem arose. At least twice a day (as indeed in other big cities throughout the world) the entire road transport system collapses: first thing in the morning and at the close of business.

The second problem is the pollution of the atmosphere around New York, which is conditioned by the high traffic ratio, the great number of heating installations and the excessive interchange of air. The pollution of the atmosphere has led to an above-average death rate occasioned by particular diseases and to smog disasters. Many inhabitants escape from the polluted city precincts to the suburbs and only return in order to work. It is precisely this reaction, however, that causes the high traffic congestion and is indirectly responsible for the severe atmospheric pollution—a vicious circle from which no one can escape.

The third problem is the total anonymity that prevails in the city. People no longer know one another, and they no longer care about their neighbors. Instead of the social links that exist in villages and small towns, social disintegration reigns there: no one cares any longer about the commonweal. The relationship between fellowmen is lost. The spirit of humanity has shriveled up and is striving for extreme forms of experience.

The first extreme passive response is a resort to drugs, and the other is an aggressiveness that degenerates into criminal activities. There are at least 100,000 drug addicts in New York, who seek refuge in heroin, one of the strongest of the drugs. Both the number of drug addicts and the number of crimes continue to rise from year to year.

What now are the basic underlying causes of this growth catastrophe? It is not a question, presumably, of individual source factors distinguishable from one another, but of polycausal relationships. In the course of their development the people have split into small distinctive communities. Their biological and social capacities are extended in the direction of such distinctive linkups. If the concentration of a population rises beyond a certain point, there is a tendency for social relationships among its members to break down.

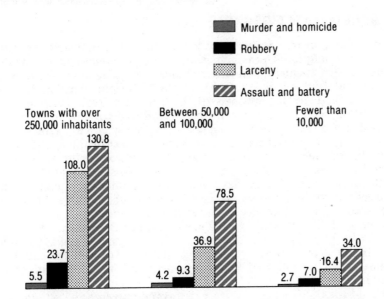

Diagram 1. INCREASE IN THE CRIME RATE IN THE UNITED STATES: INCIDENCE OF MAJOR OFFENSES PER 100,000 INHABITANTS

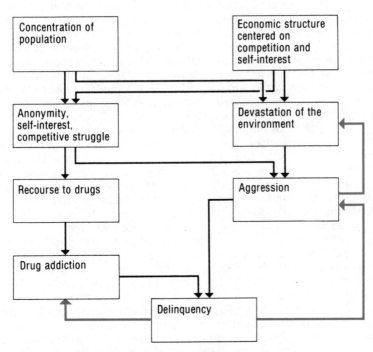

Diagram 2. DISASTROUS REGULAR CYCLE IN BIG CITIES

THE INFORMATION AVALANCHE

The production of information is growing today far faster than the population or industrial production. This is demonstrated, inter alia, by the development of the manual "Numerical Values and Functions from Natural Sciences and Technology," which was started by the chemist H. Landolt (1831–1910) and the meteorologist R. L. Börnstein (1852–1913) and which sets forth (in six editions to date) the overall numerical basis of physical, chemical, astronomical and geological data (see diagram). While the first edition published in 1883 gave all the essential data at that time on 250 pages, the number of pages increased over the years to the enormous figure of some 20,000 by 1964. As the curve corresponds closely to an exponential growth curve, and the further development of scientific knowledge will probably continue in the future at the same rate as hitherto, an attempt can be made to extrapolate the curve as regards the future. From this it appears that a new edition in the year 2050 would require the astronomical number of about 1 million pages. At 500 pages to the volume, some 2000 volumes would be needed, enough to fill a large library. The volumes would then contain the whole range of knowledge acquired in the field of scientific research.

Could this knowledge still be put to productive use? Does the use to which information can be put increase in proportion to its amount, or is there an optimum level above which the amount of information is so great that it cannot be validly assessed and utilized? A possible answer might be derived from a comparison between technical and biological stores of information.

All the technical data supplied from scientific sources are recorded, classified and stored away. As scientific knowledge gets more and more comprehensive in range and produces more and more rapid results, this leads to an exponential growth in the amount of information stored. Already the volume of scientific information stored exceeds the human capacity to absorb it. The amount of information and of scientific research is so enormous that even highly specialized scientists can no longer scrutinize all the new technical literature being produced in their fields. Most scientific information is thus of no value to the community at large.

The results of biological information storage are quite different. One of the most important qualities of the human brain as an information storage center is its capacity to examine the information absorbed by the senses for its meaning and utility and then to single out the information that is important to life. In this process over 99.9% of the information is discarded, either upon receipt or after a longer or shorter storage period. The result is that the brain only retains the information that is necessary to life. Only in this way can the brain direct the processes of life effectively.

In the current situation of the information explosion there is thus a deep cleavage between those who produce the information (scientists) and those who have to use the information for directing and controlling the social processes. A way out of this dilemma is possible only when scientists are found who can break out of the trap in the direction of specialization and who pursue scientific inquiry in the sense of a wide-ranging human ecology. In this way it is for the scientists themselves to sift and assemble the scientific knowledge that is essential to the survival of mankind and that must be made available for the processes of political control.

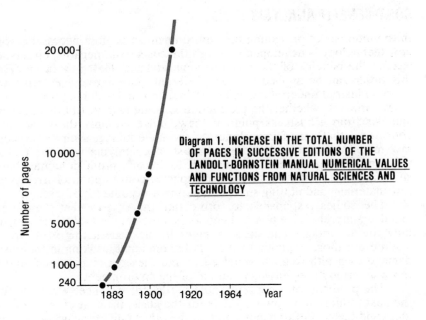

Diagram 1. INCREASE IN THE TOTAL NUMBER OF PAGES IN SUCCESSIVE EDITIONS OF THE LANDOLT-BORNSTEIN MANUAL <u>NUMERICAL VALUES AND FUNCTIONS FROM NATURAL SCIENCES AND TECHNOLOGY</u>

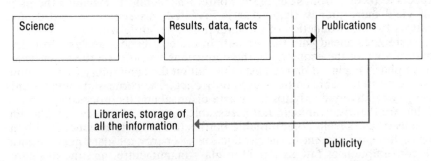

Diagram 2. STORAGE OF TECHNICAL INFORMATION

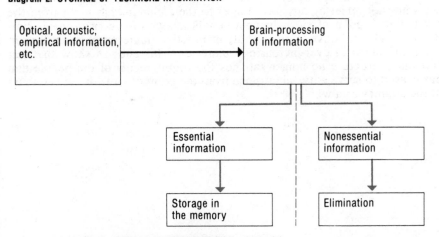

Diagram 3. BIOLOGICAL STORAGE OF INFORMATION (in the brain)

COST-BENEFIT ANALYSIS

In the interests of protecting the environment, it is often necessary when a new technology is developed to weigh the costs (risk, negative effects, etc.) against the benefits of the technological advance. Cost-benefit analysis of this order can be applied on very different planes. Every enterprise and every industrial undertaking will examine, before developing and producing a new product, whether the production is going to pay. In this cost-benefit analysis from a business point of view, however, only those factors are considered that are of importance to the undertaking, such as the cost of raw materials, cost of labor input, cost of complying with the technical environmental protection measures in force, and profit potential, but not such factors as pollution of the atmosphere, consumption of irreplaceable raw materials, and putting small competing firms out of business.

The bodies responsible for protecting the environment therefore demand a comprehensive political-economic cost-benefit analysis in which not only the advantages and disadvantages to the undertaking itself are considered but those applying to the whole community, taking in the costs of damage to health (e.g., hospital costs and the cost of pensions) and also those incurred in remedying pollution of the environment.

The producer of a nonreturnable bottle, for instance, would work out the cost to himself of raw materials for the glass, the cost of processing the glass and the cost of transport, and on the other side of the account what he expects to receive from sales of the nonreturnable bottle. Provided the sales will yield more money than what is invested, his economic cost-benefit analysis for the production of the nonreturnable bottle will be positive. He therefore goes ahead with the project. In the cost-benefit analysis from the point of view of the economy of the country as a whole, on the other hand, the emphasis is placed on the costs that fall on the community from the fact that the nonreturnable bottle is used only once. The community must in this case pay relatively dearly for the waste disposal and its processing. On top of this are the disadvantages not assessable in terms of money, such as the remains of glass from nonreturnable bottles in the waste residue, the pollution of the environment in the production of energy for glass manufacture, the consumption of raw materials in glass manufacture, and the disfigurement of the landscape by discarded nonreturnable bottles. These disadvantages are not offset by any advantages to the community, so that from the community's point of view the cost-benefit analysis for nonreturnable bottles is wholly negative. For all that, in practice nonreturnable bottles are being produced in ever-increasing quantities. This goes to show that our economic structure no longer satisfies the requirements of the people and has ceased to serve a useful purpose from the point of view of the economy of the country as a whole.

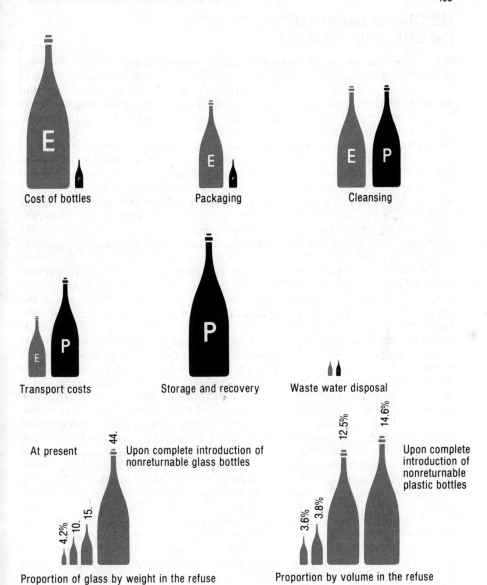

Cost of bottles

Packaging

Cleansing

Transport costs

Storage and recovery

Waste water disposal

At present

Upon complete introduction of nonreturnable glass bottles

4.2% 10. 15. 44.

Proportion of glass by weight in the refuse

3.6% 3.8% 12.5% 14.6%

Upon complete introduction of nonreturnable plastic bottles

Proportion by volume in the refuse

THE NONRETURNABLE BOTTLE IN COST-BENEFIT ANALYSIS

N=Nonreturnable
D=Deposit charged on bottle

THE COST OF ENVIRONMENTAL BURDENS—
THE CAUSATION PRINCIPLE

It is a principle of the free-market economy that basically all costs must be charged to the products and services that give rise to the individual costs. The basis of cost allocation is the causation principle. On the same grounds, the costs of environmental burdens and of their removal should be borne by the persons responsible for their occurrence. It does not follow, however, that the party involved in environmental pollution during or at the end of a production or consumption process was necessarily responsible for its emergence. The pollution may well have been caused by someone using a particular product who lays the foundation for future pollution of the environment.

In apportioning the costs of environmental pollution the causation principle is frequently breached, since the costs attributable to a product or process may be charged to the public purse. The profits accrue to private enterprise while the costs are borne by the public. Today the public not only has to put up with the damage done by environmental pollution but also has to find the resources for its removal.

A valid cost apportionment on the causation principle could be arrived at by levying charges on products that do harm to the environment, graduated according to the nature and amount of the damage. This entails the danger, however, that the charges would be passed on to the consumer in higher prices. If the same effect is now produced in the case of corresponding competitive products, in the long run nothing will have changed as regards the production and consumption of products that pollute the environment. For particular products that are produced and consumed only on grounds of convenience, the strict application of the causation principle can have surprising consequences. One example of this is the nonreturnable bottle, which in many cases (e.g., beer and fruit juices) only leads to the unnecessary consumption of raw materials and an unnecessary increase in refuse disposal. The extra burden is borne by the consumer, in that he has to pay a higher price for the nonreturnable bottle. As furthermore the "glass problem" cannot be solved satisfactorily from the point of view of the refuse dump or of combustion or composting of the refuse, a pointless product is retained, and is only "tolerated" by the application of the causation principle.

A second problem stemming from the causation principle is the impossibility of repairing intangible damage (dereliction of the landscape, elimination of animal and plant life, esthetic damage and injury to health) by financial expenditure. Preventive measures aimed at avoiding the production of particular products that are harmful to the environment when no real need for such products exists are consequently more sensible than imposing restitution payments under the causation principle after the event.

STRESS AND THE ENVIRONMENT

By *stress* is understood physical and mental overloading of the individual to the limits of his capacity. The stress caused by mental conflict arising from a sense of hopelessness and inability to see the end of the road in the modern technical world can easily lead to damage to health.

It is assumed that many diseases have no physical causes but are brought on by mental stress. Among the stress factors, first of all, modern work styles (such as assembly-line production) may be mentioned, but there are also the monotony and desolation of life in big cities, lack of natural organic relationships, the turmoil of traffic, and the noise. A large number of ailments could be checked by measures for the improvement of the environmental situation of people in relation to social and psychological factors.

From a medical point of view, a stress situation raises the catecholamine level (primarily norepinephrine and epinephrine, hormones that are emitted by the adrenal glands). As a result free fatty acids are mobilized in abundance, which owing to a sedentary life-style a person is unable to utilize. The surplus fatty acids are incorporated directly into the walls of the vascular system, which raises dangers of arteriosclerosis. Driving a car in city traffic is alone enough to raise the catecholamine level in the blood by 80%–100%, and high-speed motoring can raise it by as much as 1000%. Further consequences of stress are hormone-related injuries to the autonomic nervous system which can result in metabolic disturbances, circulatory disturbances, and disturbances to the immune defense system. The principal manifestations are heart disease, proneness to infection, inability to concentrate, aggressiveness and neuroses.

Mental stress arises primarily from the confrontation of a person's consciousness (as limited by biological interrelationships) with the multiplicity of scientific and technical information and impressions. An aggravating factor in this case may be a performance drive that exceeds the receptive capacity or the will to absorb new information. This performance drive may have to come to grips with a technical or industrial process that is becoming increasingly meaningless. As the technical and industrial development of the community advances, the individual gets more and more heavily involved in the technical process. With each advance in technology, the conflict situations and the negative repercussions of the process on people and on the environment increase, and the stress problem will inevitably rise.

Is there any way in which stress can be reduced or held in check? One way would certainly be to relax on holiday in natural surroundings and to resort to organic systems. But four weeks' holiday a year will not sort out the stress problems built up over twelve months. What is needed to reduce stress consequences of this order is the complete removal of the stress factors exerted on the individual in one's profession, in one's home, in the town and in one's leisure activities. This calls for more humane working conditions, in which purposeful application is possible without pressure; a drastic reduction of traffic and noise nuisance and of pollution in towns, together with an increase in leisure zones, parks and greenbelts; and finally the provision of leisure areas which can be reached on foot and without disturbance from motor traffic after work and on weekends.

THE HUMAN MIND AND TECHNICAL PROGRESS

One of the basic requirements for the rational implementation of the modern life-style—namely, the mastery and direction of technology, and consequently the long-term exploitation of technical data—is for extensive sectors of technology no longer fulfilled. Frequently it happens that technology does not serve people so much as people serve technology or, to be more precise, serve the technical, economic and industrial complex. One of the principal reasons for this is that the technical-industrial complex is expanding steadily, whereas owing to biological interrelationships the powers of endurance of the human mind are limited. For structures that exceed human capacities and possibilities, the concept of the *superstructure* has been developed.

Let us take an example. People are so made that the death of someone close goes to their heart. They can also take an interest in the deaths of several, possibly one or two dozen people known to them. Above this figure it will not matter to them whether the deaths number 80 to 90, or 2000 to 3000. Technical developments that have become so powerful and draconian that they could inflict death on thousands or even hundreds of thousands of people thus have no direct effect on an individual's mind. A technical development that can involve so many deaths as to be too much for a person's capacity to bear is thus no longer conceivable. And this is precisely the situation in which we find ourselves today. Motor vehicles claim 40,000–50,000 victims a year in the United States. A person's mental capacity is simply not able to grasp the extent of the disaster. One has little feeling regarding such deaths, unless a member of one's own family or a friend happens to be involved.

What consequences can be drawn from these considerations? If the gap between the constantly expanding technical-industrial complex and the individual's mental capacity is not to remain unbridgeable, either people must adapt to the technical-industrial complex or the complex must be reduced to a level at which it can be controlled and directed by people. The first of these alternatives is, for all practical purposes, out of the question. Over hundreds of thousands of years humankind has developed in small readily grasped technical and social systems. This development has left its imprint on the heritage that we enjoy today. Only recently, in the final tiny fraction of this development, have humans been confronted by structures that they themselves have created and are now to become superstructures. It is not biologically possible to assimilate the heritage of humankind to this superstructure in a few generations. Thus there remains only the other possibility, of readapting the technical and industrial complex to man. People must reestablish a relationship to what they produce. They must be able to assess the consequences of their activities personally to enable them to accept the responsibility themselves.

STRAINS IMPOSED ON THE HUMAN MIND BY THE
TECHNOLOGICAL SUPERSTRUCTURE OF THE WORLD

INDEX

Page numbers in **boldface** type indicate main references.